OPERATIONS MANAGEMENT
Decision Making in the Operations Function

McGraw-Hill Series in Management

Fred Luthans and Keith Davis, Consulting Editors

OPERATIONS

MANAGEMENT
Decision Making in the Operations Function

THIRD EDITION

Roger G. Schroeder
Curtis L. Carlson School of Management
University of Minnesota

McGraw-Hill Publishing Company

New York   St. Louis   San Francisco   Auckland   Bogotá
Caracas   Hamburg   Lisbon   London   Madrid   Mexico   Milan
Montreal   New Delhi   Oklahoma City   Paris   San Juan
São Paulo   Singapore   Sydney   Tokyo   Toronto

OPERATIONS MANAGEMENT
Decision Making in the Operations Function

34567890 HDHD 99876543210

ISBN 0-07-055618-0

This book was set in Palatino by Black Dot, Inc.
The editors were Kathleen L. Loy and Ira C. Roberts;
the production supervisor was Janelle S. Travers.
New drawings were done by Fine Line Illustrations, Inc.
Arcata Graphics/Halliday was printer and binder.

Library of Congress Cataloging-in-Publication Data

Schroeder, Roger G.
    Operations management.

    (McGraw-Hill series in management)
    Includes index.
    1. Production management. 2. Decision making.
I. Title. II. Series.
TS155.M335 1989   658.5′036   88-13477
ISBN 0-07-055618-0

About the Author

ROGER G. SCHROEDER is Chairman and Professor of Operations and Management Science at the Curtis L. Carlson School of Management, University of Minnesota. He received his B.S. degree in industrial engineering with high distinction from the University of Minnesota, MSIE University of Minnesota, and his Ph.D. from Northwestern University. Prior to joining the faculty at the University of Minnesota, he was a member of the faculty of the U.S. Naval Postgraduate School, Monterey, California, and an analyst for the office of the Assistant Secretary of Defense. Professor Schroeder has conducted research for the Ford Foundation, the Exxon Education Foundation, and the American Production and Inventory Control Society, and he has published numerous research articles. His current research interests include operations strategy, management of technology, quality improvement, and materials requirements planning systems. Professor Schroeder is a recipient of the Morse-Amoco Award for outstanding teaching at the University of Minnesota. He is on the faculty of the Minnesota Executive Program and has been a consultant for many public and private organizations. Professor Schroeder is currently a member of the Editorial Board of the *Journal of Operations Management*, and he is a past President of the Operations Management Association.

To:
Marlene, Kristen, and Bethany

Contents

Inventory Management

Work Force Management

Quality Management

Integration of Operations

Appendixes

Preface

This book is intended for the introductory course in production and operations management offered by most schools of business administration and some schools of engineering. It may be used at either the undergraduate or introductory graduate level, and it addresses the "production" accreditation requirement of the AACSB for both manufacturing and service industries.

This book has several features which set it apart from others in the field.

1. **Functional emphasis.** In this text, operations is treated as a major functional area of business along with the marketing and finance functions. While other books recognize operations as a functional area of business, they do not always stress the management of the operations function—rather, they tend to emphasize quantitative analysis or a planning and control approach to operations. As a result, students can become confused about the organizational importance of operations and the role of the operations function in a business enterprise.

2. **Decisions in operations.** In this text, the important decision responsibilities in operations are organized into five major decision categories—process, capacity, inventory, work force, and quality—each of which is the theme of a major part of the text. Each chapter within a part is devoted to one or more critical decisions topics, while management concepts and quantitative analysis are treated as underlying disciplines supporting decision making. This is the first text to use this decision-making framework.

3. **The general business student.** This text is written primarily for the general business student. For this audience, it is important to stress management decision making, responsibilities, and the relationship of operations to other business functions. The main chapters do not require prior preparation in quantitative analysis, the behavior sciences, economics, or other underlying disciplines. For courses in which quantitative disciplines are taught, chapter supplements are provided. The chapter supplements generally treat more advanced quantitative methods, while the basic methods are included in the chapters themselves.

4. **Manufacturing and service industries.** The manufacturing and service industries are presented together in a common conceptual framework. For each decision topic, the book provides a framework which is independent of any particular industry. The examples are then balanced between manufacturing and service industries. In other texts, material on service industries has often been "tacked on" and not properly integrated with manufacturing topics.

5. **Case studies.** Cases are included in the text to improve the student's skills in the

identification and formulation of problems. These are substantive cases derived from real companies and not just "enlarged problems." Twenty-one case studies are included in the last part of the book under major section headings. This permits the use of cases which are somewhat more integrative than the short case sketches typically included at the end of each chapter.

6. **New material.** Since it is based on a great deal of research, this book provides an up-to-date treatment of the field. About one-third of the material is new or revised over that found in other operations management textbooks. Important chapters with new material are those on operations strategy, choice of technology, service operations design, just-in-time manufacturing, managing quality, international operations, and productivity.

The book's educational objectives can be summarized as follows:

• To provide an understanding of operations as a major functional area of business, including its five management decision areas in operations.
• To show how operations decision making can be improved by utilizing all the underlying disciplines: behavioral, quantitative, economic, and systems.
• To present manufacturing and service industries within a common conceptual framework.

Since a wide variety of courses are taught in operations management, a modular approach is used in organizing this text. Various chapters and supplements can be selected or omitted without interrupting the flow of material. Past adopters have also found that they can choose to either emphasize or deemphasize the quantitative material, depending on their own particular orientation to operations management.

The third edition has incorporated decision examples near the beginning of each chapter. Some of these examples include: forecasting at Rubbermaid, operations strategy at IDS Life Insurance, service improvement at SAS Airlines, CIM at Allen-Bradley, inventory control at Blue Bell, JIT at IBM, Total Quality Control at Ford Motor, and Statistical Quality Control at Hewlett-Packard. Numerous other examples are included throughout the text to help students grasp operations management concepts.

The third edition has been thoroughly updated. New chapters were added on Service Operations Design and International Operations. Major revisions were made to chapters on Operations Strategy, Choice of Technology, Managing Quality, and Productivity to bring them up-to-date. Several new case studies were added and others were improved. The problems at the end of each chapter were revised and expanded by 50 percent to provide greater variety. The objective of the third edition is to maintain the most current and best organized textbook in the operations management field.

The third edition comes with or without software. The text can be ordered with a computer disc which will run on an IBM PC or compatible computer. The disc contains thirty Lotus 1-2-3® templates and three basic programs which can be used to aid in the solution of the problems at the end of the chapters. Lotus templates are available for many types of problems including: forecasting, queuing, financial analysis, aggregate planning, inventory models, MRP, quality control, and some of the case studies. Basic programs are provided for linear programming, transportation, and project scheduling. These programs are specifically written for this edition of the text which eliminates the usual confusion of a separate software manual or package. Those problems which are supported by a program on the disc are noted by the special computer symbol in the text.

Many people have helped to prepare this book. I want to express my appreciation to the following reviewers who read the third edition manuscript and helped to refine and improve the material presented: R. Balachandra, Northeastern University; Thomas Billesbach, University of Nebraska; Peter Billington, Northeastern University; Sudhakar Deshmukh, Northwestern University; Sidney Siegel, Drexel University; R. Daniel Reid, University of New Hampshire; and Om C. Sharma, St. John's University.

I also want to acknowledge the contributions of my colleagues on the faculty at the University of Minnesota. In addition there are many graduate students who have helped with the text over the years and I am grateful for their support along with the efforts of the office staff in my department. In particular, I appreciate the invaluable contributions of Karen Goodner and Susan Misterek who helped with this third edition. I also want to thank my editors at McGraw-Hill, Kathy Loy and Ira Roberts, for their helpful advice and assistance. The IBM Grant for the Management of Information Systems to the University of Minnesota provided assistance in developing the computer disc for the text. I am very grateful to Doug Chard for preparing the index to the book.

Finally, I wish to thank my family for their patience and perseverance during the many years of text development and editing. Without their continued support and encouragement this textbook would not be possible.

Roger G. Schroeder

OPERATIONS MANAGEMENT
Decision Making in the Operations Function

PART ONE

INTRODUCTION

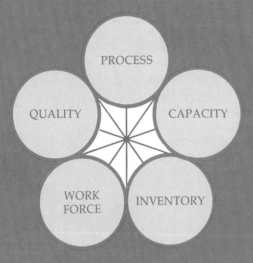

- **THE OPERATIONS FUNCTION**
- **OPERATIONS STRATEGY**
- **FORECASTING**
- **PRODUCT DESIGN**

The introductory part of this book will provide an overview of the operations management field and a survey of some of the underlying disciplines required for further study. In Chapter 1, a decision-making framework is developed which is the basis for organizing the remainder of the text. This framework identifies five major decision responsibilities of the operations function in all organizations: process, capacity, inventory, work force, and quality. Each subsequent section of the book is devoted to one of these decision types.

Chapter 2 deals with operations policy and strategy. It is intended to show how the five decision-making areas in operations can be integrated within an overall policy framework and how operations can be guided by a strategic orientation. Operations objectives are defined, tradeoffs among objectives are discussed, and the focused factory concept is presented. It is also shown how operations strategy can be used to integrate operations with the external environment.

Forecasting, discussed in Chapter 3, is a major input to operations decision making. Chapter 3 describes the types of forecasting methods available and the interaction between forecasting and operations decisions. Some of the important organizational considerations for the use of forecasting in operations are also discussed, along with the requirements for a successful forecasting system.

Another important input for all operations decisions is the design of the product or service, as discussed in Chapter 4. Product design, however, should not precede the design of the productive process; rather, product and process should be designed together. Product design is viewed as interfunctional in nature, requiring close cooperation between the product designers and the operations function.

After studying this section, the reader should be able to define the operations management field, describe operations strategy, and discuss the relationship of forecasting and product design to operations. The reader should also have gained some basic skills related to these subjects. This section will provide background for studying the five major decision responsibilities of operations in the remainder of the text.

CHAPTER 1
The Operations Function

In the broadest sense, operations management is concerned with the production of goods and services. Everyday we come in contact with an abundant array of goods or services, all of which are produced under the supervision of operations managers.

One example of an operations manager is the plant manager who is in charge of a factory. All other managers who work in the factory—including production and inventory control managers, quality managers, and line supervisors—are also operations managers. Collectively, this group of factory managers is responsible for producing the supply of products in a manufacturing business. Carrying this example one step further, we should also include in the group of operations managers all manufacturing managers at the corporate or divisional level. These managers might include a corporate vice president of operations (or manufacturing) and a group of corporate staff operations managers concerned with quality, production and inventory control, facilities, and equipment.

But operations managers are not employed only in manufacturing companies; they work in service industries as well. In the government, for example, there are operations managers in the post office, welfare department, and housing department, to name only a few. In private service industries, operations managers are employed in hotels, restaurants, airlines, banks, and retail stores. In each of these organizations, operations managers—much like their counterparts in manufacturing who produce the supply of goods—are responsible for providing the supply of services.

On the surface, it may appear that service operations have very little in common with manufacturing operations. However, a unifying feature of these operations is that both can be viewed as transformation processes. In manufacturing, inputs of raw materials, energy, labor, and capital are transformed into finished goods. In service operations, these same types of inputs are transformed into service outputs. Managing the transformation process in an efficient and effective manner is the task of the operations manager in any type of organization.

There has been a tremendous shift in our economy from the production of goods to the production of services. It comes as a surprise to many people that today more than 80 percent of the American work force is employed in service industries.[1] Even though the predominance of employment is in the service sector, manufacturing remains important to provide the basic goods needed for export and internal consumption. Because of the importance of both service and manufacturing operations, they will be treated on an equal basis in this text.

For many years, when the field was related primarily to manufacturing, operations management was called "production management." Later, the name was expanded to "production and operations management" or, more simply, "operations management" to include the service industries as well. The term "operations management" as used in this text refers to both manufacturing and service industries.

DEFINITION OF OPERATIONS MANAGEMENT

The above ideas can be summarized by the following definition:

Operations managers are responsible for producing the supply of goods or services in organizations. Operations managers make decisions regarding the operations function and the transformation systems used. Operations management is the study of decision making in the operations function.

There are three points in this definition which deserve emphasis:

1. *Function.* As we have indicated, operations managers are responsible for managing those departments or functions in organizations that produce goods and services. These departments, however, often have different names in different

---

[1]U.S. Bureau of the Census, *Statistical Abstract of the United States*, Washington, D.C., 1986, p. 404.

industries. In manufacturing companies, the operations function may be called the manufacturing, production, or operations department. In service organizations, the operations function might be called the operations department, or it may be given some other name peculiar to the particular industry. In general, the generic term "operations" is used to refer to the function which produces goods or services in any organization. Treating operations management in this manner, as an organizational function, puts it on a similar footing with other business functions such as marketing and finance.

2. *System.* The above definition refers to transformation systems which produce goods and services. The systems view provides not only a common ground for defining service and manufacturing operations as transformation systems but also a powerful basis for design and analysis of operations. Using the systems view, to be described later, we consider operations managers as managers of the conversion process in the firm.

The systems view of operations also provides insights for the design and management of productive systems in functional areas outside the operations function. For example, a sales office within a marketing function may be viewed as a productive system with inputs, transformation, and outputs. The same is true for an accounts payable office and for data entry operations within a data processing center. In terms of the systems view, operations management concepts have applicability beyond the functional area of operations.

3. *Decisions.* Finally, the above definition refers to decision making as an important element of operations management. Since all managers make decisions, it is natural to focus on decision making as a central theme in operations. This decision focus provides a basis for dividing operations into parts based on major decision types. In this text, we identify the five major decision responsibilities of operations management as process, capacity, inventory, work force, and quality. These decisions provide the framework for organizing the text and describing what operations managers do.

Since the operations management field can be defined by function, systems, and decisions, we will expand on these three elements in detail in this chapter. Before doing so, however, a brief historical survey of operations management is given, followed by a review of the current status of the field.

1.2 HISTORY OF OPERATIONS MANAGEMENT

Operations management has existed for as long as people have produced goods and services. Although the origins of operations can be traced to early civilizations, most of our attention in this section will be focused on the last 200 years.

In the following discussion, the history of operations management is organized according to major contributions or thrusts rather than in strict chronological terms. On this basis, there are seven major areas of contribution to the operations management field.

Division of labor. The division of labor is based on a very simple concept. Specialization of labor to a single task can result in greater productivity and efficiency than the assignment of many tasks to a single worker. This concept was recognized in 400 B.C. by Plato in *The Republic* when he said, "A man whose work is confined to such a limited task [e.g., shoe stitching] must necessarily excel at it." [See George (1968).] The ancient Greeks also recognized the concept of the division of labor when they assigned some workers to do nothing but sharpen stone chisels.

The first economist to discuss the division of labor was Adam Smith, author of the classic *Wealth of Nations* (1776). Smith noted that specialization of labor increases output because of three factors: (1) increased dexterity on the part of workers, (2) avoidance of lost time due to changing jobs, and (3) the addition of tools and machines. Later, in 1832, Charles Babbage expanded on these ideas with his study of pin manufacturing. [See Babbage (1832).] He noted that specialization of labor not only increases productivity but also makes it possible to pay wages for only the specific skills required. Although division of labor has been widely applied, it is now being reevaluated because of its effect on worker morale, turnover, job boredom, and job performance. We shall discuss this issue at length later.

Standardization of parts. Parts are standardized so that they can be interchanged. According to Chase and Aquilano, standardization was practiced in early Venice, where rudders on warships were made to be interchangeable. [See Chase and Aquilano (1977), p. 5.] This provided a great advantage when rudders were damaged in battle. Eli Whitney used interchangeable parts in musket production. Prior to this time, musket parts and even ammunition were tailored to each individual musket. When Henry Ford introduced the moving automobile assembly line in 1913, his concept required standardized parts as well as specialization of labor. The idea of standardized parts is by now so ingrained in our society that we rarely stop to think of it. For example, it is difficult to imagine light bulbs which are not interchangeable.

Industrial revolution. The industrial revolution was in essence the substitution of machine power for human power. Great impetus was given to this revolution in 1764 by James Watt's steam engine, which was a major source of mobile machine power for agriculture and factories. The industrial revolution was further accelerated in the late 1800s with the development of the gasoline engine and electricity. Early in this century, mass-production concepts were developed, but they did not gain widespread use until World War I, when heavy demands for production were placed on American industry. The age of mass marketing has continued this pressure for automation and high-volume production. However, our society has now entered a postindustrial period, characterized by a shift to a service economy and greater concern for the natural and social environment.

Scientific study of work. The scientific study of work is based on the notion that the scientific method can be used to study work as well as physical and natural systems. This school of thought aims to discover the best method of work by using the following scientific approach: (1) observation of the present work methods, (2) development of an improved method through scientific measurement and analysis, (3) training of the workers in the new method, and (4) continuing feedback and management of the work process. These ideas were first advanced by

Frederick Taylor in 1911 and later refined by Frank and Lillian Gilbreth throughout the early 1900s. [See Taylor (1911).] The scientific study of work has come under attack by labor unions, workers, and academics. In some cases, these attacks have been justified because the approach was misapplied or used as a "speedup" campaign by management. Nevertheless, the principles of scientific management can still be applied in today's world by recognizing the interaction between the social and technical work environments.

Human relations. The human relations movement highlighted the central importance of motivation and the human element in work design. Elton Mayo and others developed this line of thought in the 1930s at Western Electric, where the now famous Hawthorne studies were conducted. [See Wren (1972).] These studies indicated that worker motivation—along with the physical and technical work environment—is a crucial element in improving productivity. This led to a moderation of the scientific management school, which had emphasized the more technical aspects of work design. The human relations school of thinking has also led to job enrichment, now recognized as a method with a great deal of potential for "humanizing the work place" as well as improving productivity.

Decision models. Decision models can be used to represent a productive system in mathematical terms. A decision model is expressed in terms of performance measures, constraints, and decision variables. The purpose of such a model is to find optimal or satisfactory values of decision variables which improve systems performance within the applicable constraints. These models can then help guide management decision making. One of the first uses of this approach occurred in 1915, when F. W. Harris developed an economic order-quantity formula for inventory management. In 1931, Shewhart developed quantitative decision models for use in statistical quality control work. In 1947, George Dantzig developed the simplex method of linear programming, which made possible the solution of a whole class of mathematical models. In the 1950s, the development of computer simulation models contributed much to the study and analysis of operations. Since the 1950s, the use of various decision models in operations has been greatly expanded, and detailed discussions of models are provided throughout this text.

Computers. The use of computers has dramatically changed the field of operations management since computers were introduced into business in the 1950s. Most manufacturing operations now employ computers for inventory management, production scheduling, quality control, computer-aided manufacturing, and costing systems. In addition, computers are used extensively in office automation, and they are used in virtually all types of service operations. Today the effective use of computers is an essential part of the operations management field.

Each of these seven areas of contribution has advanced the operations management field in a major way. Furthermore, the contributions are still applicable to the management of modern operations, although sometimes in modified form. At later points in the text, these basic developments will be amplified and discussed in more detail.

RESURGENCE OF INTEREST IN OPERATIONS MANAGEMENT

While the history of operations management is rich, there has recently been a resurgence of interest in operations management, as indicated in Box 1.1. This is happening not only in business, but in universities as well.

The current interest in operations is being fueled by the lackluster performance of U.S. industry. Foreign competition is invading many of our basic industries, including automobiles, steel, TV, and electronics. The competition is coming not only from Japan but also from Germany, France, and others. In addition, productivity growth in U.S. manufacturing and service industries has been lagging behind that of other countries. The low level of productivity growth is one of the reasons that our economy is in trouble. Many see the key to solving these problems as falling directly within the purview of operations managers.

Much has been written about how to solve our economic ills. Many economists advocate more investment; technologists argue for more R&D; human resource people say we should alter our approach to managing people. In the end, all these solutions impinge on operations. Operations managers will have to take the best of these ideas and put them into action.

The next decade promises a return to the basics. As stated by John Young, the president and chief executive officer of Hewlett-Packard: "It's a 'back to blocking and tackling' mood that is moving into the chief executive's view. So I see the operations area as a place where giant strides are not only possible, but are absolutely essential to the international competitive stance of American business."[2] Some businesses have been concentrating on slick advertising, product gimmicks, and financial maneuvering, but have failed to emphasize the basics in operations.

Along with these critical needs in business has come an awakening of interest by American business schools. Many are adding courses in operations management, and there is greater student interest in line jobs and operations careers. According to *Business Week*, "U.S. companies are beginning to demand that business schools supply them with graduates who have specialized in operations and people—not just numbers. In the past the focus was on numbers and marketing, says James C. McGee, director of pharmaceuticals production planning at Pfizer, Inc. Now, he adds, the emphasis is on working with new technologies, improving productivity, and managing people."

This resurgence of interest in operations management in both business and universities is taking several forms. First, there is a return to emphasizing quality. We are recognizing that it does not necessarily cost more to produce a higher-quality product; rather, it costs less when errors are reduced. Higher quality is being seen as the key to competitive advantage in many industries.

---

[2]John A. Young, "Production and Operations Management," a speech delivered at the POM Workshop, American Institute of Decision Sciences, November 5, 1980.

BOX 1.1
TAKE A HIKE: MANUFACTURING REBOUNDS

World fairs and even Epcot Center offer pale views of the future compared with what you can see if you hike through some of today's modern manufacturing plants. Any doubts you may have about the future of American manufacturing can be eased if you look at companies that are developing the "right stuff" for becoming worldclass competitors.

You'll see some exciting glimpses of the future in the fireworks of a massive, multiple-welding station. Or maybe the magic of a CAD system that leaps from sketch to finished model. More likely, you'll find it in the people working together to solve production problems or launch a new product. The industrial sector is pulsing with new production techniques, new communications and trasportation arrangements, and countless business services and financial instruments.

Despite all the talk of American manufacturing's demise, her industrial core steadily pumps out more and more goods year after year. It continues to account for 21% of our growing economy in the face of competition from all over the world.

A trillion dollars! That's the size of the bet that U.S. manufacturers will lay on their future for purchases of new facilities over the next half dozen years. And they'll spend billions more for the software and services to lubricate this machine for 21st century production.

Manufacturing can also be an exciting place to work. Despite the downsizing that has caused turn-offs and layoffs, some manufacturers are creating organizations that turn people on.

The last two manufacturing plants I hiked through have something in common. Teams of workers in production areas are made up of high-school grads, people with a year or two of college, former school teachers, and graduate engineers. Supervisors wear no neckties, so they, too, blend in with the others. Who is bluecollar? And who is management? What's really confusing—and exciting—is the fact that anybody can contribute to improving quality and productivity.

As a manager in one of these plants put it: "People *can* make a contribution in manufacturing." Skilled and professional people are finding exciting jobs there. Even some of the highfliers from graduate schools of business are gravitating toward manufacturing companies.

It was, after all, the manufacturing sector that introduced quality of work life and quality circle concepts to the U.S. It's where productivity first became a management priority. It's where the attack on poor quality was launched first.

Hiking around U.S. manufacturing companies today you can see why people would be attracted to manage there. Some managers are riding high, proud of their drive to become worldclass organizations. Some can already boast of repatriating their business to the U.S.

The next time someone tells you there's no future in manufacturing, tell him to take a hike.

Source: Perry Pascarella, Editor, *Industry Week,* June 29, 1987, Reprinted by permission.

There is also a greater awareness of the role that people must play in operations. This has caused more emphasis to be placed on teamwork, participation, innovative compensation plans, and so on. People, rather than technology or control systems, are being seen as the most important resource in operations.

Greater focus on operations has brought attention to production and inventory systems. New approaches, including computerized inventory systems and just-in-time inventory principles, are being developed to reduce inventories and to improve adherence to schedules. These approaches are integrated into the very fabric of successful operations.

Operations managers are also paying more attention to new technologies. Radical changes are occurring in robotics, computer-aided design, automated offices, and so on. Operations managers are at the forefront of integrating these technologies into their businesses.

Finally, senior operations managers are beginning to see the need for strategy in operations in order to provide a competitive focus. Operations cannot be "all things to all people" but must have a mission and task that are focused by the overall business strategy. How conflicting pressures in operations can be resolved to develop an effective operations strategy is the subject of the next chapter.

Operations management is a key factor in the success of all firms. There is a great opportunity here for students because of the shortage of managers who can effectively manage operations. However, only those who can cope with the changes needed and the challenge will be successful.

1.4 THE OPERATIONS FUNCTION

In this section, we will expand the idea that operations management is a functional area of business. Figure 1.1 helps describe this idea by showing four types of business administration fields: functional areas, methodology areas, industry areas, and integrating areas.

Functional areas are concerned with a particular focus of responsibility or decision making in an organization. The marketing function is typically responsible for creating demand and generating sales revenue, the operations function is responsible for the production of goods or services (generating supply), and finance is responsible for the acquisition and allocation of capital. Functional areas tend to be closely associated with organizational departments because businesses typically are organized on a functional basis.

Figure 1.1 also shows methodology areas, which are characterized by a particular methodology or discipline base. For example, the quantitative analysis area deals with the use of mathematical models for decision support, the systems area deals with the study of organizations as systems, and organizational behavior deals with the study of human behavior in organizations. Methodology areas develop methods or tools which can be applied to problems in any of the functional areas.

Industry areas involve the study of a particular industry such as banking, insurance, transportation, and manufacturing. Industry areas may draw on ideas from both methodology and functional fields.

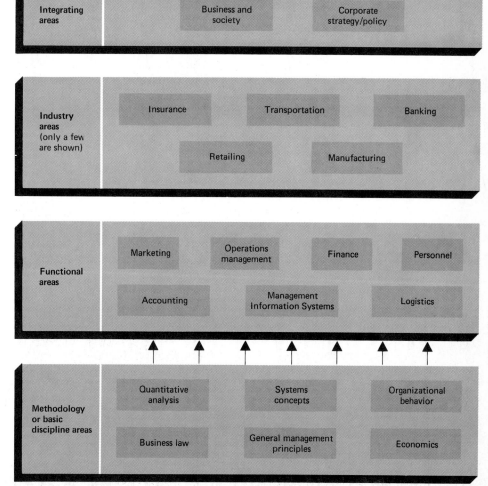

FIGURE 1.1
Fields of study in
business
administration.

Finally, there are two integrating areas. The business and society area is concerned with the relationship of business to its societal, governmental, and economic environment. Corporate strategy is concerned with top management, the integration of the functional areas within business, and the formulation and implementation of strategy.

This view of business administration clearly illustrates the relationship between methodology areas and functional areas. In general, each of the functional areas utilizes a blend of the appropriate methodology areas to address its specific problems and decisions. This textbook follows the blended approach throughout; certain chapters draw heavily on quantitative analysis, while others draw on systems concepts, organizational behavior, economics, general management principles, or a combination of these areas.

Managers in operations functions practice operations management. They do not practice behavioral science, quantitative methods, or systems analysis, although they utilize these underlying disciplines. Likewise, doctors do not practice biology although they know how to use biological methods. While methodologies are certainly important, they are not the essence of operations management.

Figure 1.1 also indicates the distinction between operations management and the manufacturing industry. Operations functions occur in every industry, such as manufacturing, banking, and retailing. As we discussed earlier, operations management is not industry-specific.

1.5 OPERATIONS AS A PRODUCTIVE SYSTEM

We have also defined operations management as the management of transformation systems which convert inputs into goods and services. The inputs to the system are energy, materials, labor, capital, and information as shown in Figure 1.2. These inputs are converted into goods and/or services by the process technology, which is the particular method used to make the transformation. Changing the technology alters the way one input is used in relation to another, and it may also change the outputs produced.

The types of inputs used will vary from one industry to another. If the operation is automobile manufacturing, inputs of capital and energy for machines, facilities, and tools will be necessary. Labor will be required to operate and maintain the equipment, and materials inputs will form the basis for the conversion process from raw materials to finished goods.

Operations in the service industries use a somewhat different mix of inputs from those used in manufacturing. For example, an airline operation requires inputs of capital for aircraft and facilities, highly skilled labor (pilots, mainte-

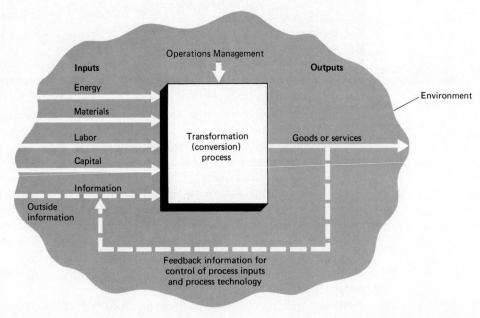

FIGURE 1.2
An operation as a
productive
system.

nance), low-skilled labor, and a great deal of energy. Very little raw material input is used in comparison with the requirements of a manufacturing company. The primary service provided by the airline is transportation, although other services such as hotel reservations and air freight may also be provided.

Figure 1.2 also shows feedback information used to control the process technology or inputs. It is essential in operations that feedback be used for control purposes to produce the desired outputs. It is the operations manager's responsibility to use feedback information to continually adjust the mix of inputs and technology needed to achieve desired outputs. These mix decisions are complex and require constant attention to the tradeoffs available.

The operations transformation system is in constant interaction with its environment. There are two types of environments to consider. First, other business functions or upper management, inside the firm but outside of operations, may change policies, resources, forecasts, assumptions, goals, or constraints. As a result, the transformation system in operations must adapt to fit the new internal environment. Second, the environment outside the firm may change in terms of legal, political, social, or economic conditions, thereby causing a corresponding change in the operations inputs, outputs, or transformation system. Constant change in the environment of operations appears to be the rule rather than the exception.

Managing the transformation system involves continual monitoring of the system and environment. A change in the environment may cause management to alter inputs, outputs, the control system, or the transformation system itself. For example, a change in economic conditions may cause operations managers to revise their demand forecast and as a result hire more people and expand capacity. Likewise, a reduction in output quality levels may cause operations managers to review their quality assurance procedures in order to bring the transformation system back into line. The role of the operations manager is to constantly monitor the transformation system and its environment in order to plan, control, and improve the system.

Table 1.1 provides some additional examples of productive systems in society. By studying operations as transformation systems, a great deal can be learned about how to improve operations design and decision making.

1.6 OPERATIONS DECISIONS—A FRAMEWORK

Since operations management is concerned with decision making for the transformation system and the operations function, a framework which categorizes and defines decisions in operations is needed. Although many different frameworks are possible, the primary one used here is a functional scheme for grouping decisions. In this framework, similar decision responsibilities concerning facilities or inventories, for example, are grouped together. This is the first textbook to use such a decision framework.

The decision framework conforms quite closely to the assignment of management responsibilities within an operations organization. However, management assignments will vary from one operation to another on the basis of local

TABLE 1.1
EXAMPLES OF PRODUCTIVE SYSTEMS

Operation	Inputs	Outputs
Bank	Tellers, staff, computer equipment, facilities, and energy	Financial services (loans, deposits, safekeeping, etc.)
Restaurant	Cooks, waitresses, food, equipment, facilities, and energy	Meals, entertainment, and satisfied customers
Hospital	Doctors, nurses, staff, equipment, facilities, and energy	Health services and healthy patients
University	Faculty, staff, equipment, facilities, energy, and knowledge	Educated students, research, and public service
Manufacturing plant	Equipment, facilities, labor, energy, and raw materials	Finished goods
Airline	Planes, facilities, pilots, flight attendants, maintenance people, labor, and energy	Transportation from one location to another

organizational preferences. What is proposed here is a theoretical framework of decision responsibility for operations which classifies decisions according to function or purpose.

In the proposed framework, operations has responsibility for five major decision areas: process, capacity, inventory, work force, and quality. These decision areas are found in most, if not all, operations.

1. *Process.* Decisions in this category determine the physical process or facility used to produce the product or service. The decisions include the type of equipment and technology, process flows, layout of the facility, and all other aspects of the physical plant or service facility. Many of these process decisions are long-range in nature and cannot be easily reversed, particularly when heavy capital investment is needed. It is, therefore, important that the physical process be designed in relation to the long-term strategic posture of the business.
2. *Capacity.* Capacity decisions are aimed at providing the right amount of capacity at the right place at the right time. Long-range capacity is determined by the size of the physical facilities which are built. In the short run, capacity can sometimes be augmented by subcontracting, extra shifts, or rental of space. Capacity planning, however, determines not only the size of facilities but also the proper number of people in operations. Staffing levels are set to meet the needs of market demand and the desire to maintain a stable work force. In the short run, available capacity must be allocated to specific tasks and jobs in operations by scheduling people, equipment, and facilities.
3. *Inventory.* Inventory decisions in operations determine what to order, how much to order, and when to order. Inventory control systems are used to manage materials from purchasing through raw materials, work in process, and finished goods inventories. Inventory managers decide how much to spend on inventory,

where to locate the materials, and a host of related decisions. They manage the flow of materials within the firm.

4. *Work force.* Managing people is the most important decision area in operations because nothing is done without the people who make the product or service. Work force decisions include selection, hiring, firing, training, supervision, and compensation. These decisions are made by the line managers in operations, often with the assistance of the personnel or human resources office. Managing the work force in a productive and humane way is a key task for operations today.

5. *Quality.* The operations function is typically responsible for the quality of goods and services produced. Quality is an important operations responsibility which requires total organizational support. Quality decisions must ensure that quality is built into the product in all stages of operations: standards must be set, equipment designed, people trained, and the product or service inspected for quality to result.

Careful attention to the five decision areas is the key to management of successful operations. Indeed, the well-managed operations function can be defined in terms of the decision framework. If each of the five decision areas is functioning properly and well integrated with the other areas, the operations function can be considered well managed.

In some cases, students feel that operations management is a hodge podge of techniques and methods—that there is no central theme. The decision framework was specifically designed to overcome this problem. Each major section of this text is devoted to one of the five decision categories.[3] The framework thus provides an integrating mechanism for the text.

1.7 DECISION FRAMEWORK—EXAMPLE

To illustrate the use of the decision framework, a company will be described in terms of the five decision categories. The example is a simplified description of Pizza U.S.A., Inc., a company which produces and markets pizza pies on a national basis. It consists of 100 company-owned and franchised outlets (each called a store) in the United States. The operations management function in this company exists at two levels: the corporate level and the level of the individual store.

The major operations decisions made by Pizza U.S.A. can be described as follows:

Process. Since uniformity across different stores is desired, most of the process decisions are made by the corporate staff. They have developed a standard facility which is simply sized to fit a particular location. The standard facility incorporates a limited menu with high-volume equipment. As pizzas are made, customers can watch the process through a glass window; this provides entertainment for both children and adults as they wait for their order to be filled. Because this is a service

---

[3]Students have developed a memory aid for these five categories, "PICWQ," pronounced "pick wick."

facility, special care is taken to make the layout attractive and convenient for the customers. The location of facilities is based on a mathematical model which is used to project revenues and costs for particular sites. Each potential site must have an adequate projected return on investment before construction can begin.

Capacity. Pizza U.S.A. faces a series of decisions related to the maximum level of output. First, when the initial location and process decisions are made, the corporate staff fixes the physical capacity of each facility. Individual store managers then plan for annual, monthly, and daily fluctuations in service capacity within the available physical facility. During peak periods, they employ part-time help, and advertising is used in an attempt to raise demand during slack periods. In the short run, individual personnel must be scheduled in shifts to meet demand around the clock.

Inventory. The individual store managers buy the ingredients required to prepare the recipes provided by corporate staff. They select their own suppliers and decide how much flour, tomato paste, sausage, etc., to order and when to place orders. Store operators must carefully integrate purchasing and inventory decisions to control the flow of materials in relation to capacity.

Work force. Store managers are responsible for hiring, training, supervising, and, if necessary, firing workers. They must decide on exact job responsibilities and on the number of people needed to operate the store. They also advertise job openings, screen applications, interview candidates, and make the hiring decisions. They must measure the amount of work required in relation to production and also evaluate the performance of each individual. Management of the work force is one of the most important daily responsibilities of the store manager.

Quality. Finally, the corporate staff has set certain standards for quality which all stores must follow. These standards include procedures to maintain service quality and to ensure the quality of the pizzas served. While service quality is difficult to measure, the quality of the pizzas can be more easily specified by using criteria such as temperature at serving time, the amount of raw materials used in relation to standards, and so on. In Pizza U.S.A., each store manager must carefully monitor quality to make sure that it meets company standards.

The five decision categories provide a framework to describe the important operations decisions made by Pizza U.S.A. It should be recognized, however, that these five types of decisions cannot be made separately; they must be carefully integrated with one another and with decisions made in other parts of the business. Toward this end, the integration of decision making is emphasized throughout this text.

Because Pizza U.S.A. is only one example of an operation, students often ask, "What do operations managers do in more general terms?" Box 1.2 provides examples of nine typical operations management positions and describes the associated decision-making responsibilities. The descriptions have been greatly simplified, perhaps oversimplified, for illustration purposes.

BOX 1.2
MANAGEMENT POSITIONS IN OPERATIONS

Operations Manager. In manufacturing organizations, titles include plant manager, director of manufacturing, and vice president of manufacturing. In service industries, titles include store manager, office manager, and vice president of operations. These positions are concerned with overall coordination and direction of the operations function. Specific responsibilities include strategic planning, policy setting, budgeting, management of other managers, and control of operations.

Materials Manager. This position is concerned with managing and integrating the flow of materials from raw materials to finished products. The materials manager will typically have subordinate managers in purchasing, inventory control, and production control.

Purchasing Manager. The purchasing manager is concerned with assuring an adequate flow of raw materials. Purchasing managers work closely with vendors. They negotiate prices, perform vendor selection, and evaluate vendor performance.

Inventory Manager. The inventory manager is concerned with ordering the proper amount of material at the right time. Inventory managers often utilize computerized systems to help them provide the best customer service at the lowest possible inventory cost.

Production Control and Scheduling Manager. The production control manager is responsible for developing a production plan and ensuring the best use of resources in meeting that plan. Production control responsibilities include planning schedules, balancing workloads, and making sure that the product is delivered on time. In the service industry, this function is often called scheduling.

Quality Manager. The quality manager is concerned with planning and controlling product quality. Responsibilities include setting quality standards, developing quality control standards, developing quality control systems, and assisting workers in producing quality. The quality manager monitors the quality of the product or service at every stage.

Facility Manager. The facility manager is concerned with the design and control of operations facilities and processes. Responsibilities include work-flow analysis, technology management, facilities choice, facilities location, and equipment planning.

Line Manager. The line manager is concerned with the management of the work force and of operations units. Job titles include first-line supervisor, production superintendent, and unit manager. The line manager is concerned with proper performance of work, personnel development, work organization, and reward systems.

Operations Planning Analyst. An operations planning analyst deals with the overall planning, budgeting, and control of an operation. A planning analyst serves as staff to the operations manager and may develop models and information systems to support planning and decision making.

As Box 1.2 indicates, there are a great variety of management positions in operations. These range from first-level supervisory positions to middle- and top-management positions of considerable responsibility. These positions also cut across all the functions of operations and apply to both manufacturing and service operations.

Operations managers must have both behavioral and quantitative skills. While the line supervisory positions require more behavioral skill, the supporting staff positions often require a greater degree of quantitative skill.

Furthermore, some positions are more concerned with day-to-day operations, while others are more concerned with policy and planning. Typically, the staff and higher-level management positions are more concerned with policy and planning than with day-to-day operations. Lower- and middle-line managers are more concerned with daily operations.

1.8　DECISIONS IN OPERATIONS—ANOTHER VIEW

Another way of classifying operations decisions is as (1) decisions affecting the design of the operations function and (2) decisions related to utilization of an existing operation. While the design decisions tend to be strategic, long range, and irreversible for long periods of time, the utilization decisions are tactical, short range, and implementation-oriented. In Pizza U.S.A., there was a tendency for corporate staff to handle design decisions and for store managers to be responsible for utilization decisions.

Table 1.2 is a matrix which shows how the five decision categories are related to design and utilization decisions. Each decision category contains some decisions of both types. For example, some decisions in the inventory area involve long-range design considerations, while others are concerned with utilizing an

TABLE 1.2
DESIGN AND UTILIZATION DECISIONS IN OPERATIONS

Decision category	Design decisions (strategic)	Utilization decisions (tactical)
Process	Select process type Choose equipment	Analyze process flows Provide for maintenance of equipment
Capacity	Determine facilities size Determine facilities location Set work force levels	Decide overtime Arrange for subcontracting Determine scheduling
Inventory	Set overall inventory size Design inventory control system Decide where inventory is held	Decide when to order and how much to order
Work force	Design jobs Select compensation system Design work rules	Provide supervision Set work standards
Quality	Set quality standards Decide on quality organization	Decide on amount of inspection Control quality to meet standards

existing inventory system. The functional decision categories, therefore, do not correspond to either long- or short-range decisions; rather, both types of decisions are included in each category.

In making decisions in operations, no particular sequence is followed in practice. There is, however, a tendency for many of the process and physical capacity decisions to precede other decisions in the inventory, work force, and quality areas. Because of this tendency, process and capacity decisions are treated first in the text. The reader should be cautioned, however, that decisions are often intertwined; therefore, no strict, logical sequence can be constructed, particularly for ongoing operations. This phenomenon makes it difficult to organize the operations management field by using a sequential decision approach. This book, therefore, groups decisions into functional categories and discusses interrelationships rather than sequence.

1.9   PRODUCERS OF SERVICES AND GOODS

Throughout the text we will be describing decisions in both service and manufacturing operations. It is therefore important to compare these two types of operations as a prelude to further discussion. Before going further into the distinction between goods and services, however, some definitions will be helpful. A good is a tangible entity. Since goods are physical in nature, they can be stored, transformed, and transported. A service is intangible in nature. A service can be defined as something which is produced and consumed more or less simultaneously. Because it is intangible, a service cannot be stored or transported.

Because services are intangible, service producers differ from goods producers in important aspects of their operations. Several of the more interesting differences are described below. [For excellent treatments of services, see Sasser, Olsen, and Wyckoff (1978) and Fitzsimmons (1982).]

Capacity and inventory. A service can be viewed as an extremely perishable product; it cannot be stored as inventory for future use. Thus, the delivery of services presents a special problem for inventory and capacity planning. The service producer needs to build capacity in advance of demand as workers are hired, facilities are built, and equipment is installed. If the demand does not materialize, the capacity is wasted and high costs result. On the other hand, a goods producer can use current capacity to produce an inventory of goods for consumption in future periods.

Quality. Since a service is intangible, quality cannot be readily assessed by potential customers before the service is delivered. In service organizations, reputation is crucial because much of the quality image for services is passed on by word of mouth. The future customer cannot look at the product or test it to form an impression of quality.

Dispersion. Service organizations are often dispersed geographically. Since a service cannot be stored and shipped, it must be produced at the point of consumption or the customer must be brought to the service. This leads to a dispersion of service outlets. Examples are retail stores, barbershops, car-rental agencies, banks, and hospitals. On the other hand, goods producers can centralize their operations because their goods can be shipped to the final destination.

Marketing and operations. In service organizations, the operations and marketing (and sales) functions tend to be closely related. This is because services are consumed at the same time and place that they are produced. Service organizations are both marketing and operations entities. In goods-producing organizations, the opposite is true. Marketing and operations are organized as separate functions because goods are produced and sold separately. The integration of marketing and operations then becomes a difficult problem for goods producers.

The distinction between goods producers and service producers can be made even more precise by referring to Box 1.3, which is a detailed classification of industries in terms of firms that primarily produce goods and those that mainly provide services.

Many organizations produce a mixture of goods and services. Thus a classification of industries on a continuous scale between pure goods and pure service is

BOX 1.3
PRODUCERS OF GOODS AND SERVICES

Primarily goods producers	Primarily service producers
Agriculture, forestry, and fishing Crops, livestock, agriculture services, forestry, fishing, hunting, and trapping	**Transportation and public utilities** Railroads, local passenger transit, trucking, warehousing, U.S. Postal Service, water transportation, airlines, pipelines, communication, electricity, gas, and sanitation
Mining Metal mining, coal mining, oil and gas extraction, and nonmetallic minerals	
Construction General building contractors, heavy-construction contractors, and special trade contractors	**Wholesale trade** Durable goods and nondurable goods
	Retail trade Building materials, general merchandise stores, food stores, automotive dealers and service stations, apparel and accessory stores, furniture and home furnishing stores, and eating and drinking places
Manufacturing Food, tobacco, textile mills, apparel, lumber, furniture, paper, printing, chemicals, petroleum, coal products, rubber, plastic, leather, stone, clay, glass, primary metal, fabricated metal products, machinery, electric and electronic equipment, transportation equipment, instruments, and miscellaneous manufacturing industries	**Finance, insurance, and real estate** Banking, credit agencies, security brokers, insurance carriers, and real estate
	Services Hotels, personal services, business services, auto repair, motion pictures, amusement, health, legal, education, social services, museums, zoological gardens, and membership organizations
	Public administration

Industries listed are based on the U.S. Department of Commerce Standard Industrial Classification System.

FIGURE 1.3
Continuum of
goods and
services.

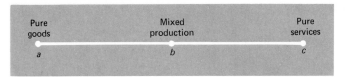

appropriate. In Figure 1.3, point *a* represents the pure goods producers. These producers might include factories, farms, mines, and other organizations that typically produce goods only. Pure goods operations have little or no customer contact, and they do not offer services as part of their marketing package.

Point *b* in Figure 1.3 represents an organization which produces both goods and services. Many companies manufacturing consumer goods are in this category. For example, automobile manufacturers provide many services in addition to the automobiles they sell. These services include financing, insurance, warranty, repair, and so on. Another example of a producer of both goods and services is the fast-food outlet.

Point *c* represents the pure service producer. Any tangible good delivered in connection with the service is incidental. For example, dentists provide fillings for teeth, but these materials are incidental to the main service provided. Other examples of pure service producers are consulting firms, government agencies, hospitals, banks, education, and personal services.

Richard Chase (1978) has suggested that service organizations be classified by the percentage of time during which the producer is in direct contact with the customer while the product is being produced. Pure goods producers would have zero percent contact, and pure service producers would have 100 percent contact. This proposal provides a precise method of classification for all types of operations.

Chase goes on to point out that operations with low customer contact can be made more efficient, since the customer is not involved as much in the process of production. On the other hand, systems with a high degree of customer contact must respond to customers' time and quality demands, and they suffer a corresponding loss in efficiency of operations. This explains why service firms are standardizing outputs and limiting customer interaction in order to reduce costs.

As will be noted at many points in the text, the service industries present a substantial challenge to operations management. Most operations management concepts can be applied in service organizations, but they have not been widely used in these areas to date.

KEY POINTS

The purpose of this book is to provide a broad overview and survey of the field of operations management for a first course. Decision making, responsibilities, and the relationship of operations to other business functions are stressed. The functional orientation and the five decision categories are used as major organizing principles.

The following key points are stressed in the chapter:

- Operations management is defined as decision making for the operations function and systems which produce goods or services.
- The history of operations management includes seven major contributions: division of labor, standardization of parts, industrial revolution, scientific study of work, human relations, decision models, and computers.
- There is a great resurgence of interest in operations management in both business and the universities. This interest is being fueled by foreign competition and the lack of productivity growth. The challenge will be met only by integrating new ideas into operations practice.
- Operations management, like marketing and finance, is a functional area of business. As a functional area, the focus is primarily on decision-making responsibility and secondarily on methodology.
- Managers in operations manage the transformation process which supplies goods and services. The transformation process converts inputs (materials, energy, labor, capital, and information) into outputs (goods or services). Changes in the environment frequently require corresponding changes in operations.
- Operations management is defined by five key types of decision responsibilities: process, capacity, inventory, work force, and quality. These five decision categories are useful for describing an existing operation or identifying the decisions required to establish a new operation.
- A service is produced and consumed more or less simultaneously. Service-producing and goods-producing organizations differ on the following characteristics: capacity, quality, dispersion of operations, and the relationship of marketing and operations. Service and goods producers may be described on a continuous scale from pure goods producers to pure service producers.

QUESTIONS

1. Why study operations management?
2. What is the difference between the terms "production management" and "operations management"?
3. How does the function of an operations manager differ from the function of a marketing manager or a finance manager? How are these functions similar?
4. How is the operations management field related to the fields of quantitative analysis, computer systems analysis, economics, and organizational behavior?
5. Describe how the concept of division of labor applies to the following situations:
   a. College teaching
   b. Accounting
   c. The construction trades
   d. A fast-food restaurant
6. Using the history of operations management, what approaches have been used to improve productivity over the last century? Can these same approaches be used to improve productivity in today's world and in the future?
7. Discuss the impact of mathematical models and computers on the field of operations management.
8. Describe the nature of operations management in the following organizations. In doing

this, first identify the purpose and products of the organization; then use the five decision types to identify important operations decisions and responsibilities.

a. A college library

b. A hotel

c. A small manufacturing firm

9. For the organizations listed in question 8, describe the inputs, transformation process, and outputs of the productive system.

10. Describe the decision-making view and the transformation system view of operations management. Why are both these views useful in studying the field of operations management?

11. Contrast and compare a service organization to a goods-producing organization. Use the decision framework to identify important points of similarity and difference.

12. Write a short paper on some of the challenges facing operations management in the future. Use newspapers and business magazines from the library as your primary sources.

13. Review the want ads in the *Wall Street Journal* and look for the management positions that would be available for operations management graduates.

14. How do changes in the environment, such as demand changes, new pollution control laws, the changing value of the dollar, and price changes, affect operations? Name specific impacts on operations for each change.

15. What are the major factors leading to a resurgence of interest in operations management in both business and universities?

SELECTED BIBLIOGRAPHY

ADAM, EVERETT E., JR., and RONALD J. EBERT: *Production and Operations Management: Concepts, Models, and Behavior*, 3d ed., Englewood Cliffs, N.J.: Prentice-Hall, 1986.

BABBAGE, CHARLES: *On the Economy of Machinery and Manufacturers*, London: Charles Knight, 1832.

BUFFA, ELWOOD S., *Modern Production/Operations Management*, 7th ed., New York: Wiley, 1983.

Business Week: "Hard Times Push B-Schools into Basics," Aug. 30, 1982, pp. 23–24.

CHASE, RICHARD B.: "Where Does the Customer Fit in a Service Operation?" *Harvard Business Review*, November-December 1978.

—— and NICHOLAS J. AQUILANO: *Production and Operations Management: A Life Cycle Approach*, 2d ed., Homewood, Ill: Irwin, 1977.

DILWORTH, JAMES B.: *Production and Operations Management: Manufacturing and Non-Manufacturing*, 2d ed., New York: Random House, 1983.

FITZSIMMONS, JAMES A., and ROBERT S. SULLIVAN: *Service Operations Management*, New York: McGraw-Hill, 1982.

GAITHER, NORMAN: *Production and Operations Management*, 3d ed., Chicago: Dryden Press, 1987.

GEORGE, CLAUDE S., JR.: *The History of Management Thought*, Englewood Cliffs, N.J.: Prentice-Hall, 1968.

SASSER, W. EARL, R. PAUL OLSEN, and DARYL WYCKOFF: *Management of Service Operations: Text, Cases and Readings*, Boston: Allyn & Bacon, 1978.

SCHMENNER, ROBERT W.: *Production/Operations Management: Concepts and Situations*, 3d ed., Chicago: SRA, 1987.

SMITH, ADAM: *An Inquiry into the Nature and Causes of the Wealth of Nations*, London: A. Strahn & T. Cadell, 1776.

STEVENSON, WILLIAM J.: *Production/Operations Management*, 2d ed., Homewood, Ill.: Irwin, 1986.

TAYLOR, FREDERICK W.: *The Principles of Scientific Management*, New York: Harper, 1911.

WREN, DANIEL A.: *The Evolution of Management Thought*, New York: Ronald Press, 1972.

CHAPTER 2
Operations Strategy

There is an increasing recognition that operations must help the firm achieve a competitive position in the marketplace. Operations should not be only a place to make the organizations' products and services but should lend some competitive strength to the business as well. As noted in the last chapter, this realization is being fostered by increasing foreign competition, the need for improved produc-

24

tivity, and increasing customer demands for quality. Gaining a competitive advantage through improved operations performance requires a strategic response on the part of the operations function. See Box 2.1 for an excellent example of operations strategy in the life insurance business.

Wickham Skinner (1969) stated that operations is seldom neutral: "It is either a competitive weapon or a corporate millstone." In his now classic article he goes on

BOX 2.1
THE DRIVE TO COMPETE: IDS LIFE INSURANCE CO.

When a policyholder writes to the operations center of IDS Life Insurance in downtown Minneapolis, the computer knows.

The computer knows which of 250 clerks is qualified to handle the letter. The computer decides whose workload is lightest that day. And the computer tracks how long before an answer is in the mail.

The operations center, a carpeted 12th-floor office humming with activity, is an assembly line for information. And like many of the nation's assembly lines, it has begun to run faster and more accurately in the last two years.

Without inflation to swell their profits and cover their costs, many of the nation's businesses have had to tighten their belts and become more competitive. To accomplish this, they have adopted any number of competitive strategies—computerization, quality control, acquisitions, divestitures, consolidations, layoffs, incentive pay, robots and other measures. Many of the strategies can be seen in factories and offices around the U.S.A.

IDS, for example, faced the same dilemmas facing many service companies: how to define its product and how to measure its productivity. Any one of 769,150 policyholders might want to add a beneficiary to an insurance policy. Any one of IDS's 5,300 financial planners might call to check the status of a client's account. Its product, executives finally decided, is service.

"Historically, the customer-service strategy here was to keep costs down," said Earlon Milbrath, executive vice president for operations. "In the late 1970s we started to realize we needed to be more market-driven and that quality was an important part of our product."

Milbrath's operations department installed a computer to track the flow of mail. Then it set a series of standards for accuracy, speed and responsiveness for the clerks who answer letters and phone calls. Clerks can earn productivity bonuses of up to $1,200 a year for meeting or exceeding the standards. Managers, too, are eligible for incentive bonuses.

The result? A 25 percent increase in productivity, a 27 percent improvement in timeliness and 98 percent accuracy performance over the last two years.

IDS LIfe Insurance's example is unusual, because productivity can be hard to measure in service industries and because productivity issues are found more frequently in manufacturing companies. But the drive to become more competitive can be found in industries across the board, whether they are manufacturers, retailer-wholesalers or service companies.

Source: David Hage and Neal St. Anthony, *Minneapolis Star and Tribune,* Jan. 4, 1987. Reprinted by permission.

to argue that operations decisions must be consistent with business strategy. Operations should be focused on the "primary task," as Skinner calls it, and should not be all things to all people. By linking operations decisions and corporate strategy, operations can help the business achieve a competitive advantage.

In the United States we have tended to emphasize finance and marketing, often at the expense of operations. This emphasis has taken the form of new products which have created little value (e.g., Pet Rocks) and a "wheeling and dealing" mentality concerning mergers and acquisitions. Meanwhile, fundamental creation of value for the customer has taken the back seat. The remedy for this is new leadership and the development of a strategic role for operations in the business.

On the other hand, the Japanese are well known for their use of manufacturing operations to help them compete in world markets. By designing and producing goods with better quality, and sometimes lower costs, the Japanese have captured a large share of the world markets in automobiles, electronics, and motorcycles, to name just a few. The success of this strategy is not due to their national culture, but their determination to excel at operations.

All too often, operations is a stepchild of the strategic planning process. Operations is brought in after the fact to implement strategic plans which are made by marketing, finance, and general management. As a result the capability of operations is not used as a competitive force in the business. This situation can be corrected by developing an operations strategy as an integral part of the business strategy and by including operations as an equal partner in developing and implementing the business stragegy. How this can be done will be addressed in this chapter.

2.1 DEFINITION OF OPERATIONS STRATEGY

A working definition of operations strategy is as follows:

Operations strategy is a vision for the operations function that sets an overall direction or thrust for decision making. This vision should be integrated with the business strategy, and is often, but not always, reflected in a formal plan. The operations strategy should result in a consistent pattern of decision making in operations and a competitive advantage for the company.

Several definitions of operations strategy have been given in the literature which help to amplify and expand on the above definition. Schroeder, Anderson, and Cleveland (1986) have defined operations strategy as consisting of four components: mission, objectives, distinctive competence, and policies. These four components help define what goals operations should accomplish and how it should achieve those goals. The resulting strategy should help guide decision making in all phases of operations.

Another definition has been given by Hayes and Wheelwright (1984), who define operations strategy as a consistent pattern in operations decisions. The more consistent those decisions are and the greater the degree to which they support the business strategy, the better. They go on to define how major decisions in operations should be made and integrated with each other. While Hayes and Wheelwright emphasize the result of operations strategy, a consistent pattern in decision making, Schroeder et al. emphasize operations strategy as an antecedent to decision making. But both agree that a consistent pattern of decision making must be the result.

Wickham Skinner (1985) defines operations strategy in terms of the linkage between decisions in operations and the corporate strategy. He notes that when operations is out of step with the corporate strategy, operations decisions are often inconsistent and short range in nature. As a result operations is divorced from the business, and the linkage with corporate strategy is weak. The remedy, according to Skinner, is to develop an operations strategy, derived from the corporate strategy, which defines a primary task (what operations must do well for the business to succeed) and a consistent set of operations policies to guide decision making.

All these approaches lend important insight into what operations strategy is and how the strategy can be developed or improved. In the next section we will expand on these definitions with a specific model for the formulation and implementation of operations strategy.

OPERATIONS STRATEGY MODEL

Most authors agree that operations strategy is a functional strategy, that it should be guided by business strategy, and that it should result in a consistent pattern in decisions. These relationships are described by Figure 2.1. The four elements inside of the dashed box: mission, distinctive competence, objectives, and policies, are the heart of operations strategy. The other elements in the figure are inputs or outputs from the process of developing operations strategy.

Corporate and Business Strategy

At the top of Figure 2.1 is corporate and business strategy. The corporate strategy defines what businesses the company is in. For example, Walt Disney Productions considers itself in the business of "making people happy." The Disney Corporation includes not only the theme parks, but production of cartoons, movie production, and a variety of entertainment-related businesses.

The business strategy defines how a particular business will compete. Most corporations consist of a group of related businesses, each of which is identified as a strategic business unit or division. Each business needs to find its own basis of competition depending on the particular market segments and products that it decides to pursue. Michael Porter (1980) has identified three generic business strategies: low-cost producer, product differentiation, and market segmentation. Each of these business strategies will have a related operations strategy, as we shall see later. Therefore, it is extremely important that the business strategy be defined before operations strategy is formulated.

In an ongoing business, however, a particular operations capability may make a certain business strategy a clear choice. Thus operations strategy can also

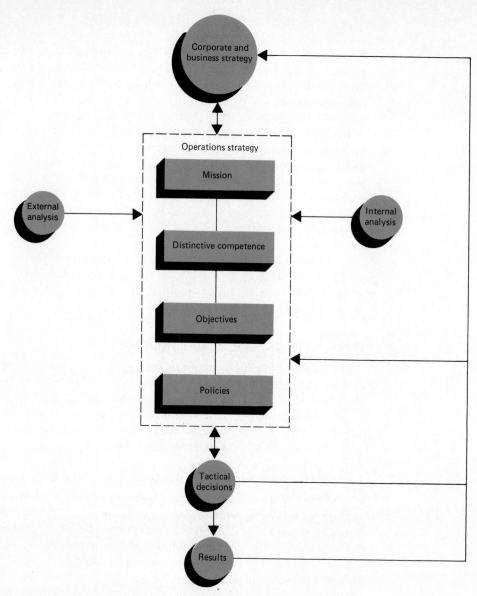

FIGURE 2.1
Operations
strategy model.

influence business strategy in a reverse fashion. Robert Hayes (1985) has made
this clear in his article "Strategic Planning—Forward in Reverse?" where he
argues that operations capabilities can be used to generate viable business
strategies.

External/Internal Analysis

In formulating an operations strategy, and a business strategy too for that matter,
an analysis should be made of the external and internal environment. The external

environment usually includes competition, customers, economics, technology, and social conditions. The external environment can have a dramatic influence on operations and should shape the operations strategy in addition to corporate and business strategies. Some examples of external influences which have had dramatic effects on operations in the past are increased foreign competition, the changing price of oil, inflation, fluctuating currency rates, and the changing demands of the work force.

In a similar way, the internal environment can affect the operations strategy through the availability of resources, the existing organization culture, the skills and abilities of the work force, the location and age of existing facilities, the types of control systems in place, and so on. An analysis of the internal environment usually leads to the identification of strengths and weaknesses of the existing operation. Operations strategy attempts to overcome weaknesses and build on existing strengths.

Operations Mission

The mission of operations, which is the first of the four elements of operations strategy, defines the purpose of the operations function in relation to the business and corporate strategies. The mission should state the priority among the operations objectives of cost, quality, delivery, and flexibility. A typical statement of operations mission for an insurance company is as follows:

> The mission of our insurance operations is to provide the services needed to meet market demand in becoming the share and quality leader in insurance and personal financial planning. This will be accomplished by providing superior service through new-product innovation at a reasonable cost.

This particular mission statement would be appropriate for a company which is emphasizing a business strategy of differentiation through new-product introduction and financial planning, but not for a company which is emphasizing cost as its business strategy. Note that reasonable cost is stated in the operations mission, not lowest cost. The operations mission will often be a restatement of the business strategy in operations terms and is derived directly from the business strategy.

Distinctive Competence

The distinctive competence of operations is what operations must excel at relative to the competition. The distinctive competence should match the mission of operations. For example, if the mission calls for operations to excel at new-product introduction, then operations should develop a distinctive competence in this particular area. Distinctive competence leads to competitive advantage and is thus at the heart of operations strategy. Most successful businesses are able to identify a distinctive competence, and they work hard to protect that competence.

A distinctive competence can take on a variety of forms. Operations can be distinctive in terms of operations objectives: lowest cost, highest quality, best delivery, or greatest flexibility. Operations can also be distinctive by use of its resources: it may be the most people-oriented, it may have the only source of raw materials, or it may have the best technology compared with competition, to name just a few. A distinctive competence in resources, however, should translate into results that the customer values and that meet the firm's strategy. In other words, it does no good to have an advantage as the low-cost producer when the firm is stressing quality or new-product introduction. Distinctive competence requires operations to concentrate on what it must do best, since it is frequently not possible to excel on all dimensions at once.

Operations Objectives

The third element of operations strategy is objectives. As we have noted above, four general operations objectives are possible: cost, quality, delivery, and flexibility. Objectives in operations should be stated in specific quantitative and measurable terms. They are the results that operations is expected to achieve in the short and long run. Objectives should be thought of as a refinement of the mission in quantitative and measurable terms. Examples of operations objectives are shown in Table 2.1 for a typical manufacturing company.

The cost of operations includes the cost of labor, materials, and overhead. In a manufacturing company this represents the cost of goods sold. Normally these costs are expressed as a percentage of sales or as a unit cost for particular products. Costs should not only be viewed in terms of annual changes, but should be compared with the competition's costs. For example, if the company is pursuing a low-cost producer strategy, costs should be lower than those of the competition.

TABLE 2.1

TYPICAL OPERATIONS OBJECTIVES

	Current Year	Objective: 5 years in the Future	Current: World-Class Competitor
COST			
Manufacturing cost as a percentage of sales	55%	48%	50%
Inventory turnover	4.1	5.2	5.0
QUALITY			
Customer satisfaction (percentage satisfied with products)	75%	85%	75%
Percentage of scrap and rework	15%	5%	10%
Warranty cost as a percentage of sales	1%	0.5%	1%
DELIVERY			
Percentage of orders filled from stock	90%	95%	95%
Lead time to fill stock	3 wk	1 wk	3 wk
FLEXIBILITY			
Number of months to introduce new products	10 mo	6 mo	8 mo
Number of months to change capacity by +20%	3 mo	3 mo	3 mo

Costs are defined to include the costs of production, costs of carrying inventory, and any other costs incurred in using resources.

Quality as an objective means the quality of the product or service as perceived by the customer. Quality is the value of the product, its prestige, and its perceived usefulness. This definition includes not only conformance to specifications, but the design of the product as well. Typical quality measures include customer satisfaction as measured by surveys or consumer tests, the amount of rework or scrap created as part of the production process, and measures of warranty or return of the product. Quality, of course, should also be measured relative to the competition and can be an important point of differentiation.

Delivery refers to the ability of operations to deliver the product or service when and where the customer needs it. Delivery can be measured in a variety of ways. When the product is made to stock, delivery can refer to the percentage of orders filled from inventory and the amount of time (lead time) required to refill stock. In the case of make-to-order products, delivery may refer to the length of time that it takes to deliver the order from start to finish and the percentage of orders delivered by the promised due date. Delivery frequently is measured by the ability to quickly process and make a product when it is needed (throughput time).

The fourth measure of operations objectives is flexibility either in the ability to make new products or in the time that it takes to change volume. If an operation is flexible, new products can be introduced quickly and volume changes can be made rapidly. For example, automobile manufacturers typically take 3 or 4 years to introduce a new automobile design, and volume is difficult to change because of rigid production systems. In the future this may not be adequate as product life cycles become shorter and competition develops faster ways to introduce new products. Flexibility can provide a competitive advantage when the firm chooses to compete on the basis of new-product innovation or quick response to customer demands. In some cases, however, it may cost more to design and operate a flexible operation. Then the value of flexibility must be weighed against the added cost.

Operations Policies

Operations policies define how the objectives of operations will be achieved. Operations policies should be developed for each of the five decision categories: process, capacity, inventory, work force, and quality. For example, one policy is to emphasize new process technology; another is to develop a superior inventory control system; a third is to develop a highly skilled work force.

There are a wide variety of policies to consider, and the choice typically involves tradeoffs or conflicting choices. For example, a highly skilled work force may be costly but provides the flexibility needed to make a large variety of different products. The choice of policies ultimately hinges on the objectives that have been set.

Some of the major operations policy choices are shown in Table 2.2. These choices should be made by senior management and will involve strategic considerations. Later in this book many of these major policies will be dealt with

TABLE 2.2

EXAMPLES OF IMPORTANT POLICIES IN OPERATIONS

Policy Type	Policy Area	Strategic Choice
Process	Span of process	Make or buy
	Automation	Handmade or machine-made
		Flexible or hard automation
	Process flow	Project, batch, line, or continuous
Capacity	Facility size	One large or several small facilities
	Location	Near markets, low cost, or foreign
	Investment	Permanent or temporary
Inventory	Amount	High levels or low levels of inventory
	Distribution	Centralized or decentralized warehouse
	Control systems	Control in great detail or less detail
Work force	Job specialization	High or low specialization
	Supervision	Highly decentralized or centralized
	Wage system	Type of pay incentives used
		Good paying or low paying
	Staffing	Many or few staff
Quality	Approach	Prevention or inspection
	Training	Technical or managerial training
	Suppliers	Selected on quality or cost

at length. The important point to understand here is that these policy choices are ultimately related to the objectives of operations and to the business strategies in effect.

Tactics and Results

Tactics should follow the development of strategy. Tactical decisions typically fall within a short time frame (1 or 2 years) and are developed to implement the operations strategy. Tactical decisions are usually made by middle management and lower management in order to carry out strategies developed by upper management. Examples of tactical decisions are selecting a particular supplier from among several suppliers, deciding on how much inventory to carry of a particular part, deciding on whom to hire, setting budget levels, and deciding on intermediate objectives.

Results are, of course, usually measured in the same terms as objectives and are used to determine if the strategy and tactics are working. In this case operations results would be measured in terms of cost, quality, delivery, or flexibility. If the results are not satisfactory, management could change any of the tactics or strategies as may be needed. The measurement of results closes the loop and provides feedback on the usefulness of the strategies selected.

It should be noted that even though we have represented operations strategy as a formal logical process, strategy can often be incremental and disjointed. Strategy is developed not only through formal planning, but through the series of decisions as they are actually made. Strategy can sometimes start with decisions and work backward toward objectives. Thus a very fluid, and even irrational, process might be used. Regardless of the process, however, a strategy should arrive at the same end result, a consistent pattern in decision making.

2.3 TYPES OF OPERATIONS STRATEGIES

One of the most important considerations is that operations strategy be linked to business strategies, and to marketing and financial strategies as well. Table 2.3 illustrates this linkage by showing two diametrically opposite business strategies that can be selected and the resulting functional strategies. First, there is the low-cost-producer business strategy which would be typical of a mature, price-sensitive market, with a standardized product. In this case the operations mission would emphasize cost as the dominant objective, and operations could strive to reduce costs through such policies as superior process technology, low personnel costs, low inventory levels, a high degree of vertical integration, and quality assurance aimed at saving cost. Marketing and finance would also pursue and support the low-cost business strategy as shown in Table 2.3.

TABLE 2.3
STRATEGIC ALTERNATIVES

Businesss Strategy	Strategy A Low-Cost Producer	Strategy B Product Innovator
Market conditions	Price-sensitive Mature market High volume Standardization	Product-features-sensitive Emerging market Low volume Customized products
Operations mission	Emphasize low cost while maintaining acceptable quality and delivery	Emphasize flexibility while maintaining reasonable cost, quality, and delivery
Distinctive competence operations	Low cost through superior process technology and vertical integration	Fast and reliable new- product introduction through product teams and flexible automation
Operations policies	Superior processes Statistical process control Central location Economy of scale Tight inventory control Low-skill work force Highly automated	Superior products Flexible automation Fast reaction to changes Economies of scope Use of product teams Skilled workers Low automation
Marketing strategies	Mass distribution Repeat sales Maximizing of sales opportunities National sales force Low-cost advertising	Selective distribution New-market development Product design Sales made through agents High-cost advertising
Finance strategies	High capital needed Low risk Low profit margins	Low capital needed Higher risks Higher profit margins

The second business strategy shown in the table is one of product innovation and new-product introduction. This strategy would typically be used in an emerging and possibly growing market where advantage can be gained by bringing out superior products in a short amount of time. Price would not be the dominant form of competition, and higher prices could be charged, thereby putting lower emphasis on costs. In this case operations would emphasize flexibility to rapidly and effectively introduce new products as the dominant objective in its mission. Operations policies could include the use of new-product introduction teams, flexible automation which could be adapted to new products, a highly skilled work force with flexible skills, and possibly purchase of some of the key services and materials from outside to retain flexibility. Costs would not be emphasized to the same degree as in the first strategy. Once again, finance and marketing also need to support the business strategy to achieve an integrated whole.

What this table indicates is that drastically different types of operations are needed to support different business strategies. There is no such thing as an all-purpose operation which is best for all circumstances. Thus when asked to evaluate operations, one must immediately consider the business strategy as well as the mission and objectives of operations. Table 2.3 also suggests that all functions must support the business strategy in order for the strategy to be effective.

In addition to the business strategies shown in the Table 2.3, there are several other possibilities, including a high-quality emphasis, a service strategy, product variety, high growth or low growth, and so on. Any single objective in operations can be used as a point of differentiation. Obviously, these additional business strategies would also require other kinds of operations, marketing, and financial strategies.

2.4   RESPONSE TO EXTERNAL FACTORS

One of the most important issues in developing operations strategy is adapting to external factors in the environment. Operations is sometimes internally focused and as a result is noncompetitive. The central theme in operations strategy is developing a strategy which is externally focused relative to the competition, the economy, social conditions, and the customers' needs.

In the past there has probably been too much attention in operations to internal efficiency. Operations has been asked to concentrate on internal improvements and leave the external concerns to others. As a result, operations finds itself unable to compete in a changing world.

In today's worldwide competitive markets, external factors need to be considered more than ever before. The following external forces seem to be particularly important for the future: customer needs, new technologies, raw materials, legal factors, changing work forces, and competition.

Customer need, as reflected by demand level or product type, is one of the most visible external factors which affects operations. Demand level can be partly managed and controlled by the firm through pricing, promotion, and other market strategies. Nevertheless, some demand changes cannot be controlled or easily foreseen—for example, those changes caused by economic downturns and upturns, changes in customer preferences, and new competitors. Customers also require new products or different products from time to time. As a result, operations not only must plan for current customer needs but future needs, too.

Available technology is another external factor which has a major impact on operations. As product and process technologies change, operations technologies must change too. The firm can choose to be a technological leader or follower, or it may pursue other technological strategies. The role of the operations strategy is to forecast technological conditions and then to develop an appropriate response. In these times, with rapidly changing technologies in robotics, computer-aided design (CAD), computer-integrated manufacturing (CIM), and automated offices, to name just a few, the future survivability of the firm may depend on the strategic posture taken toward technology.

The availability of raw materials should also be considered in formulating operations strategy. For example, in the case of the iron ore depletion in northern Minnesota, the response was to develop an entirely new taconite industry. Another example was the oil crisis which caused major dislocations in many operations. Specific policies should be developed to deal with vulnerable sources of raw materials.

Legal factors should be considered in formulating operations strategy. For example, deregulation is causing major changes in some industries today. In banking, operations must be more concerned than ever with productivity and quality as new competition develops. Examples of other legal changes which have major effects on operations are environmental pollution standards, safety regulations, and equal opportunity legislation.

Changing social attitudes and values affect the work force and managers in operations. The operations strategy should recognize such changes in society and develop responses in the form of work force policy. This promises to be one of the most important areas of future change as operations are being positioned to emphasize teamwork and participative approaches and to assimilate workers more fully into operations.

Finally, competition is an external factor of overriding concern to operations. Competition may be reflected in new products, more pressure to control costs, quality differences, and changes in the level of demand. In many of the basic industries of the United States (e.g., steel, textiles, electronics, and autos) foreign competition is a major concern because the competition is producing better products at lower costs. For example, in the early 1980s Japan could produce a small automobile for $2200 less than we could in the United States [Cook (1982)]. The reasons for this cost difference were mainly found in operations. The Japanese didn't have better automation, but they did have lower wage rates, which accounted for about $550 of the difference. The remaining difference of $1650 was due to better productivity of labor, less investment with smaller inventories, and smaller factories for the same output. The Japanese achieved this by a highly coordinated system oriented toward quality, very low inventories, and teamwork in production.

How should U.S. companies respond to this kind of competitive disadvantage? It is the function of operations strategy not only to meet the competition but also to regain our position through superior strategies. As the nature of competition changes, the business strategy and the operations strategy must be modified to provide a defensible competitive stance for the company. The most important function of any strategy is to be prepared to handle competition and other external factors while meeting customer needs.

INTERNATIONAL OPERATIONS

Markets are becoming global in nature. Due to expanding worldwide communications systems and global travel, consumer demand is more homogenized on an international basis. Many products are global in nature, including soft drinks, VCRs, TVs, automobiles, motorcycles, farm equipment, machine tools, and a wide variety of other products. To be sure, there are still market niches which are national in character, but the trend is toward more global markets and products.

As a result of these changes, business and operations are becoming more internationalized. Traditionally businesses have operated on a multinational basis rather than a global basis. In a multinational company, decisions are handled differently in each country around the world. The business sees itself as selling to local markets, there is mostly local competition, and there is limited export and import. Also, each country has its own quality, process technology, and cost structure. Sources of supply are handled locally, or regionally, and export is subject to currency fluctuations. A multinational company is also organized with a separate division or subsidiary for each country in which the company operates.

A multinational company is at a competitive disadvantage when operating in global markets. The scale of operations is wrong, products may be inadequate, and the company is organized the wrong way to produce and market its products. As a result, the global corporation has emerged with the following characteristics.

Plants and facilities are located on a worldwide basis, not country by country. Products and services can be shifted back and forth between countries. This is being done in the automobile industry today.

Components, parts, and services are sourced on a global basis. The best worldwide source of supply is found, regardless of its national origin.

Worldwide product design and process technology are used. A basic product or service is designed, whenever possible, to fit global tastes. When local variations are needed, they are handled as options rather than as a separate product. Process technology is also standardized globally. For example, Black and Decker has recently designed worldwide hand tools. Even fast food is becoming a global product.

Demand is considered on a worldwide, not a local, basis. Therefore, the economies of scale are greatly magnified, and costs can be lower. The VCR came out as a worldwide product and was never marketed locally. Its demand and cost were scaled for a global market right from the start. Local competitors were kept out of the market.

Logistics and inventory control systems are global in nature. This makes it possible to coordinate shipments of products and components on a worldwide basis. For services operations, facilities are interconnected through a worldwide communications system, e.g., consulting firms, fast food, banks, and travel services.

A global corporation is organized with divisions which have global responsibility for the marketing, R&D, and operations functions. These functions are not fragmented in several domestic and international divisions.

The implications for operations management of this change toward global business are profound. Operations strategy must be conceived of as global in nature. A global distinctive competence should be developed for operations, along with a global mission, objectives, and policies. Product design, process design, facility location, work force policies, and virtually all decisions in operations are affected. To achieve an international perspective in this text, we will provide a global orientation to decisions throughout, as well as a separate chapter on international operations at the end of the text.

FOCUSED OPERATIONS

The primary advantage of a strategic approach to operations decision making is that it helps focus operations to achieve a coordinated set of policies. Wickham Skinner (1974), who developed this approach for manufacturing companies, has called this a "focused factory." He tells the story of an electronic instrument company that made fuel gauges and automatic-pilot instruments in the same plant. After years of failure to make a profit on fuel gauges, the company was ready to sell off that portion of the business. As a last resort, the plant manager decided to build a wall around the fuel-gauge production facilities and manage them separately. As a result, the equipment and the process technology was segregated, production and inventory control was handled separately, the fuel-gauge operation had its own quality control function, and work force policies were separated to some extent. After 4 months, the fuel-gauge business had become profitable, apparently due to the development of a plant within a plant (PWP).

The explanation for this result is that the autopilot production requirements had been imposing more stringent quality control policies, a different type of production and inventory control system, and work force policies which were not appropriate to both types of production. As a result, the production of the fuel gauges was excessively costly. This story indicates how incompatible product lines within the same plant can reduce effectiveness.

The rationale for production has traditionally been economies of scale. Through the addition of more products, it is supposedly possible to spread fixed costs over more units and to achieve production efficiencies. While this strategy works in some cases, it does not work in others because additional products increase complexity and may unfocus operations to the point where economies are lost.

Traditional economies of scale do not occur when management adds staff to coordinate the additional complexity imposed by more products in the same facility. The economies in direct labor are then more than offset by the diseconomies in indirect labor. Skinner argues that some plants have been made too large and complex under the banner of economies of scale. In these cases, the plant should be divided and focused on a specific product or product group which demands a consistent set of manufacturing tasks. Each smaller plant or PWP could then concentrate on the particular set of cost, quality, delivery, and flexibility objectives which are most appropriate to it. Thus the plants would once again become weapons of business strategy rather than attempting to be "all things to all people."

Marketing managers clearly understand the problem of focus. Market segmentation is aimed at finding that part of the market in which the business can compete. In a similar way, operations should find that set of policies which implement the business strategy and focus the efforts of operations on a particular set of tasks which can be well done. This set of tasks has been called the "distinctive competence" of operations. As we have noted above, it defines those operations activities which give the business a unique competitive advantage.

For years the distinctive competence of the Harvard Business School has been the case study method. This distinctive competence influenced all parts of operations: staffing, facilities, student admissions, etc. Faculty who were good at teaching and developing cases were selected and promoted. Special classrooms were developed to teach cases, and the curriculum was developed to help students analyze them. The Harvard Business School is a good example of the "focused factory" concept.

In general there is an astounding lack of focused operations in practice. The principal reasons for this appear to be:

1. The rise of professional staffs (quality, accounting, engineering, production, inventory control, etc.) pursuing their own set of internal standards. Professionals need to be guided by general management toward a consistent set of operations objectives.
2. The addition of more and more products to existing facilities in the name of economies of scale. This futile attempt to reduce costs had unfocused operations and made the operations less competitive.
3. Failure to define the distinctive competence of the operations. As a result, various elements of operations develop in an uncoordinated way over time and the inconsistencies are often never recognized.
4. A change of objectives in operations while most staff and service departments continue to serve prior goals.

To avoid these problems, focused operations can be developed as part of the strategy process described above. If it is determined that two or more different missions are being served by the same facility, this is the signal for the need to have separate focused facilities or a plant within a plant. Generally speaking, a single facility can only support one operations mission.

Several types of focus dimensions need to be considered. These include the following:

1. Product focus
2. Process type: project, batch, line or continuous
3. Technology
4. Volume of sales
5. Make-to-stock and make-to-order
6. New products and mature products

Several of these dimensions may be combined when focusing operations. For example, a recent case study of focus in a refrigeration company included separating compressor production for high-volume, standardized, and mature products from compressor production for low-volume and customized products. In this case one factory was divided into two separate focused factories, with consequent improvements in all measures of operations performance. [See Ruwe and Skinner (1987).]

EXPERIENCE CURVE

One of the principles underlying operations strategy and business strategy is the experience curve, or the learning curve. The experience curve describes how costs behave as a function of volume. It is based on the notion that learning occurs as the firm gains more experience producing a product or service. When learning is present, each successive unit takes less time to complete than the preceding unit because the work force becomes more proficient at the production task. The cost of materials can also be reduced through experience gained in producing the product.

Examples of learning occur in everyday life. A grade school student learns, with practice, to read and to do arithmetic faster. When aircraft are produced, each unit takes less direct labor hours than the previous unit. A second identical house can be constructed for less cost than the first one. Due to learning, the cost of each succeeding unit will be less than the cost of the previous one by the amount of learning or experience which occurs. This happens for any number of reasons: the process is changed, people become faster at doing their jobs, the product is redesigned to be more efficient, cheaper sources of materials are found, or better methods are developed.

The experience curve is used to express the relationship between cost and the cumulative number of units produced. The experience curve percentage rate indicates the reduction in unit cost for each doubling of volume. For example, with an 80 percent experience rate, the unit cost will be reduced by a factor of 80 percent whenever output is doubled. In this case if the first unit costs $100 to produce, the second unit will cost $80 (.8 × $80), the fourth unit will cost $64 (.8 × $80), the eighth unit will cost $51.20 (.8 × $64), and so on. In practice experience curves typically have rates between 60 and 90 percent. The higher experience rates (e.g., 90 percent) occur because the process is more difficult to improve or human learning is not as pronounced as in the lower experience rates.

The experience curve can be expressed mathematically as follows:

$$y(x) = kx^n$$

where $y(x)$ = cost to produce the xth unit
k = cost of the first unit
x = total number of units produced
n = log ϕ/log 2
ϕ = experience rate
1 − ϕ = progress ratio

An example, using this formula, is shown in Box 2.2.

BOX 2.2
EXPERIENCE CURVE CALCULATION

Problem: If the first unit of a certain product costs $100 to produce, what will be the cost of the second, fifth, and one-hundredth unit using a 70 percent experience curve.

Solution: Since the first unit costs $100, k = 100.

We can solve for the values in the experience curve formula with the following very simple computer program written in Basic. The values could also be computed by using logarithm tables or by using a pocket calculator with log functions.

```
10 Input x
20 Print 100*x^(log(.7)/log(2))
```

Run this program and input successive values of x = 2, 5, and 100. The results printed on the screen are:

x	$y(x)$
2	70.00
5	43.68
100	9.35

Note: This problem illustrates the tremendous effects on costs of the experience curve.

Experience curves for different experience rates have been plotted in Figure 2.2. As may be noted, the lower the experience rate, the steeper the curve. Each of these curves, however, approaches zero as the value of x increases.

When the experience curve is plotted on log-log paper, a straight line is obtained.[1] Use of log-log paper is thus helpful for plotting values of the experience curve and for fitting learning curves to actual production data. One such curve is shown in Figure 2.3 for a certain type of computer memory device.

Experience curves are useful for estimating costs and for measuring the progress that operations is making in reducing its costs. In addition, experience

---

[1] Log-log graph paper can be purchased with a logarithmic scale on each axis.

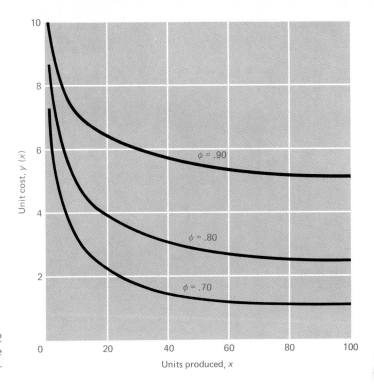

FIGURE 2.2
Experience
curves.

curves are very useful for developing strategies. A company which takes advantage of the experience curve can make its products at a lower cost than its competitors who do not. When experience effects are present, one strategy is to be the low-cost producer by moving down the experience curve ahead of your competitors. The steeper the experience curve, the more effective this strategy becomes. Competitors are kept out of the market unless they can match your volume, rate of learning, and costs.

Ghemawat (1985) has made an extensive review of experience curves and their use in strategic planning. He describes some famous cases of the use of the experience curve, including production of Ford Model T automobiles, aircraft, hand-held calculators, and contact lenses. He notes that the experience curve is more significant in the introductory phase of the product life cycle, since costs decline faster for the first units of cumulative production than for later units. He also notes that the experience curve is valuable when prices are dropping very rapidly and there is a great deal of competitive pressure. In this case, reducing costs become a matter of survival.

However, blind adherence to the experience curve can be disastrous, as Ford Motor learned with the Model T. Between 1909 and 1924 the price of a Model T was reduced from $950 to $290 by modernizing plants, integrating vertically to reduce the cost of purchased inputs, increasing the division of labor, and eliminating model changes. Market share soared from 10 to 55 percent, and Ford was enormously profitable. But by its single-minded emphasis on cost reduction,

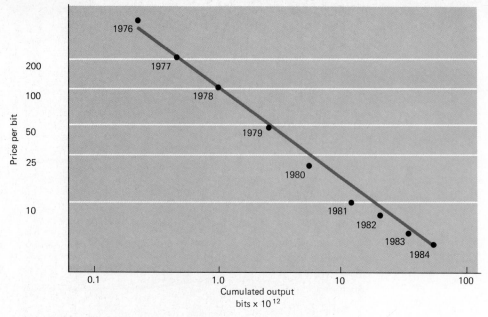

Data: Integrated Circuit Engineering Corporation.

FIGURE 2.3   Seventy percent experience curve for dynamic RAMs.
Source: Pankaj Ghemawat, "Building Strategy on the Experience Curve," Harvard Business Review, *March–April 1985, p. 145.*

Ford had sown the seeds of its own downfall. As the market developed, Ford did not introduce new models soon enough and eventually lost market share to General Motors and a great deal of money.

Thus, an experience curve strategy can be very useful, provided a company continues to meet customer needs and does not become preoccupied with costs alone. A niche strategy or product differentiation strategy can sometimes be used to avoid competitors who are aggressively pursuing an experience-curve-based strategy. This was done by Hewlett-Packard in the hand-held calculator business in which the company adopted a high-quality and new-product innovation strategy. The experience curve is only one of many possibilities that must be considered in setting strategy.

STAGES OF OPERATIONS EFFECTIVENESS

In an insightful article Wheelwright and Hayes (1985) have proposed four stages of operations effectiveness. They observe that operations can progress from a very ineffective stage 1 posture to an effective stage 4 position through the use of operations strategy principles discussed in this chapter. These stages help illustrate how operations can be dynamically positioned to be more competitive over time.

Stage 1 (Internally Neutral)

The first stage represents an "internally neutral" operation aimed at minimizing any negative impact that operations may have on the business. Top management wants operations to maintain things under control and not to "rock the boat." This is done by operations executing the strategies which others have formulated and by meeting short-range goals.

In stage 1, operations is kept flexible and reactive. Management uses detailed control systems to monitor performance, and outside experts are called in to make decisions about strategic issues. Most of top management's attention is focused on structural decisions (equipment and facilities) and associated capital expenditures. Little attention by top management is directed to infrastructure decisions (people, quality, systems, and organization). Top management attempts to minimize its involvement in operations.

The aim of stage 1 is to guard against any damaging problems caused by competition, not to make use of operations competitive potential. As a result, operations managers are divorced from business strategy; they are simply expected to run operations. Under these circumstances, operations managers become experts at fire fighting on day-to-day decisions.

Operations in stage 1 often does not attempt to develop new process technology. Production equipment is bought from outside vendors. Little risk is assumed, and "safe" technologies are employed. Operations is viewed as the embodiment of a series of once-and-for-all decisions. Managers are uncomfortable with the notion that continuous learning can be a basis for creating and extending operations capability. A self-limiting view of what operations can do prevails.

Stage 2 (Externally Neutral)

Stage 2 also represents a form of neutrality, but in this case operations is neutral with respect to external factors in addition to being internally neutral. Operations tends to be as good as any of the competitors in the industry. In stage 2, operations generally follows industry practice, including the use of industrywide wage rates and technology which is available to the industry as a whole.

Top managers of stage 2 companies regard resource allocation as the basis for managing operations. They tend to make investment decisions only when necessary and usually reluctantly in order to keep up with the industry. Technology comes from outside operations; either from the company's R&D laboratories, or from outside vendors.

A stage 2 company at least recognizes the industry dynamics in which the company must compete. However, operations is not seen as a source of competitive strength. The company focuses on new products or promotional efforts to gain competitive advantage. Many companies in consumer goods and mature industries tend to have stage 2 operations. Nevertheless, some companies in these industries are now recognizing the necessity of developing stage 3 and stage 4 operations to become more competitive.

Stage 3 (Internally Supportive)

Stage 3 is characterized by operations becoming internally supportive of the business strategy. In this case, operations decisions are made to be in concert with the business strategy, and operations seeks to actively support and enhance the company's competitive strength.

In stage 3 top management takes an active role in directing operations through the business and operations strategy. An operations strategy must be formulated and implemented, as we have discussed in this chapter, to claim stage 3 status. In this case operations will have a clear mission, long-range objectives, strategic policies, and a distinctive competence. Investment decisions will be screened for their consistency with the business and operations strategy.

Companies often arrive at stage 3 as a result of operations strategic planning. Operations is expected to take a long-range view of itself and to be supportive of the business strategy. Stage 3 companies view technological progress as a natural response to changes in business strategy and may develop different technologies than the rest of the industry.

Stage 4 (Externally Supportive)

This most progressive stage of operations effectiveness is based on the idea that operations should be a competitive force in the business. This does not mean that operations necessarily takes the major role in the business; other functions also contribute to a coordinated and integrated whole.

In stage 4, operations anticipates new practices and develops unique ways of managing operations, as well as new process technologies leading to competitive advantage. These new capabilities can often become the basis for the business strategy. One example of such a capability is the moving assembly line developed by the Ford Motor Company in the early 1900s. Another is the methods of quality improvement instituted by the Japanese companies. These capabilities revolutionized industry practices and became the basis for competitive advantage.

Stage 4 companies have well-integrated functional management. All functions in the company: marketing, finance, operations, and R&D, work together to develop and implement the business strategy. Not only is the operations role supporting the business strategy, but operations becomes part of formulating business strategy and makes new business strategies possible. Also, operations is involved up front in major marketing, finance, and R&D decisions, and vice versa.

In stage 4 companies, operations frequently develops proprietary processes and its own equipment. While some equipment may be bought from outside, the company also develops its own equipment and systems in order to be at the leading edge of technology. The key to this is organizational learning, which a stage 4 company values. For example, a number of banks have developed their own proprietary computer systems in order to be able to offer unique banking services and continually lead their competitors.

In a stage 4 company, top management is involved in not only capital decisions but other decisions, as well. Top management understands the need to develop superior operations capability as a basis for business strategy in addition to looking at market opportunities and needs. Top management's role is to integrate the various functions into a smoothly operating team.

Over time companies can manage the transition from stage 1 to stage 4 operations. It is difficult to skip any of these stages since each stage depends on the mastery of the previous one. Companies will, however, find certain aspects of operations in different stages. A company may be very advanced in one area but not in another. However, it is the dominant mode of thinking about operations which tends to determine the stage at any particular time.

Most of the excellent companies described by Peters and Waterman (1982) have a significant number of stage 3 or 4 operations. These companies gain strength from their operations capability and are considered to be world-class competitors. Examples of companies with significant stage 3 or 4 operations are Hewlett-Packard, General Electric, 3M, IBM, Delta Airlines, McDonald's, Mars (candy), and Blue Bell.

2.9 KEY POINTS

This chapter discusses gaining competitive advantage through operations strategy. The key points discussed in the chapter are as follows:

- Operations strategy is a vision for the operations function that sets an overall thrust or direction for decision making. The purpose of operations strategy is to connect business strategy to decision making in operations. A consistent pattern of decision making should be the result.
- Operations strategy consists of mission, distinctive competence, objectives, and policies. The mission defines the purpose of operations. Objectives are cost, quality, delivery, and flexibility. Distinctive competence is what you do better than the competition. Policies are the strategic decisions which guide more detailed decision making (tactics) in the areas of process, capacity, inventory, work force, and quality.
- Three inputs to operations strategy are business strategy, external analysis, and internal analysis. Operations strategy should help the firm adapt to external factors, including customer needs, technology, raw materials, legal or social conditions, and competitors.
- Operations strategies and decisions differ depending on whether the company is pursuing a low-cost or differentiation business strategy. There is no one best operation for all circumstances.
- The emergence of the global corporation is changing operations strategy by requiring a worldwide perspective toward facility location, sourcing, product design, process technology, logistics, and organization.
- Focused operations are more competitive than unfocused operations. Operations can be focused by specifying only one mission for each plant or facility. Focused operations generally utilize one or more of the following dimensions: product, process, technology, volume, make-to-order or make-to-stock, and mature or new products.
- The experience curve specifies the relationship between unit cost and cumulative

volume produced. Each doubling of volume reduces cost by the amount of the experience rate. Competitive advantage can be gained, in some cases, by following the experience curve.

- Operations effectiveness can be described by the following four stages: internally neutral, externally neutral, internally supportive, or externally supportive. An operations strategy is required for a business to achieve stage 3 or 4 status.

QUESTIONS

1. What are the reasons for formulating and implementing an operations strategy?
2. Describe a possible mission for operations and some associated strategies that would fit the following business situations.
   a. Ambulance service
   b. Production of standard automobile batteries
   c. Production of electronics products that have a short product life cycle.
3. An operations manager was heard to be complaining, "The boss never listens to me—all the boss wants from me is to avoid making waves. I rarely get any capital to improve operations."
   a. What stage is operations probably in?
   b. What should be done about the situation?
4. Define the following terms: experience curve, focused operations, mission of operations, and distinctive competence.
5. How would you determine whether a company had an operations strategy or not? What specific questions would you ask, and what information would you gather?
6. What are some of the classic signs of an unfocused operation?
7. Describe the differences between a stage 1 and a stage 4 operation.
8. Evaluate your local hospital in terms of its emphasis on the four objectives of operations: cost, quality, delivery, and flexibility. Are all departments focused on the same objectives?
9. Define some of the strategic decisions that might be required in grocery store operations depending on whether the mission was emphasizing cost or quality.
10. What are the pros and cons of organizing a plant within a plant?
11. What kinds of external factors might affect the following types of operations:
    a. Airline
    b. Bank
    c. Semiconductor manufacturing
12. Using newspapers and magazines, find examples of operations strategies. Write a few paragraphs describing the situation and the strategies which are being pursued.
13. Suppose that you are producing calculators on an 85 percent experience curve and the eighth unit costs $100 to produce.
    a. How much did the first unit cost?
    b. How much will unit number 500 cost?
14. A 90 percent experience curve can be used for the production of aircraft. The first unit costs $100,000.
    a. How much will the tenth unit cost?
    b. How much will the hundredth unit cost?
15. Company A follows an 85 percent experience curve, and a competitor (Company B) follows an 80 percent experience curve in producing a similar product. Both companies start with a unit cost of $200 for the first unit.

a. How much of a cost advantage does company B have by the time that each company produces 1000 units?

b. What would you suggest that company A do about this situation?

c. What if company A produces 1000 units by the time that company B produces 500 units. Which company has the advantage in this case?

16. The Piper Cub aircraft company produced a new line of aircraft which costs $500,000 for the first unit produced and $300,000 for the eighth unit.

a. What is the company's experience curve rate?

b. What will the twentieth unit cost at the present rate of experience?

SELECTED BIBLIOGRAPHY

ANDERSON, JOHN C., GARY CLEVELAND and ROGER G. SCHROEDER: "Operations Strategy: A Literature Review," Working Paper, Operations Management Center, Carlson School of Management, University of Minnesota, April 1986.

BHIDE, AMAR: "Hustle as Strategy," *Harvard Business Review,* September–October 1986, pp. 59–65.

BUFFA, ELWOOD S.: *Meeting the Competitive Challenge.* Homewood, Ill.: Irwin, 1984.

COOK, DAVID T.: "Why GM's Small Car Experts Threw in the Wrench," *Christian Science Monitor,* June 2, 1982.

GHEMAWAT, PANKAJ: "Building Strategy on the Experience Curve," *Harvard Business Review,* March–April 1985, pp. 143–149.

HAAS, ELIZABETH A.: "Breakthrough Manufacturing," *Harvard Business Review,* March–April 1987, pp. 75–81.

HAYES, ROBERT H.: "Strategic Planning—Forward in Reverse?" *Harvard Business Review,* November–December 1985, pp. 111–119.

———— and STEVEN C. WHEELWRIGHT: *Restoring Our Competitive Edge: Competing through Manufacturing,* New York: Wiley, 1984.

HILL, TERRY: *Manufacturing Strategy—The Strategic Management of the Manufacturing Function,* New York: Macmillan, 1985.

PETERS, THOMAS J., and ROBERT WATERMAN, JR.: *In Search of Excellence,* New York: Harper & Row, 1982.

PORTER, MICHAEL E.: *Competitive Strategy: Techniques for Analyzing Industries and Competitors,* New York: Free Press, 1980.

RUWE, DEAN M., and WICKHAM SKINNER: "Reviving a Rust Belt Factory", *Harvard Business Review,* May–June 1987, pp. 70–76.

SCHROEDER, ROGER G., JOHN C. ANDERSON, and GARY CLEVELAND: "The Content of Manufacturing Strategy: An Empirical Study," *Journal of Operations Management,* vol. 6, no. 4, August 1986, pp. 405–416.

SKINNER, WICKHAM: "Manufacturing—Missing Link in Corporate Strategy," *Harvard Business Review,* May–June 1969, pp. 136–145.

————: "The Focused Factory," *Harvard Business Review,* May–June 1974, pp. 113–121.

————: *Manufacturing: The Formidable Competitive Weapon,* New York: Wiley, 1985.

WHEELWRIGHT, STEVEN C.: "Japan—Where Operations Really Are Strategic," *Harvard Business Review,* July–August 1981, pp. 67–74.

———— and ROBERT H. HAYES: "Competing through Manufacturing," *Harvard Business Review,* January–February 1985, pp. 99–109.

CHAPTER 3
Forecasting

Forecasting is the art and science of predicting future events. Until the last decade, forecasting was largely an art, but it has now become a science as well. While managerial judgment is still required for forecasting, the manager is aided today by sophisticated mathematical tools and methods. Forecasting has indeed come a long way from the black art of fortune-telling by use of the stars, tea leaves, or crystal balls.

Many different methods of forecasting and their uses are described in this chapter. One of the main points in the chapter is that a forecasting method must be carefully selected for the particular use it is intended to serve. There is no universal forecasting method for all situations.

Forecasts will almost always be wrong. It is rare for sales to equal the exact amount forecasted. A little variation from the forecast can often be absorbed by extra capacity, inventory, or rescheduling of orders. But large variations from forecast can wreck havoc in operations. For example, suppose 100,000 cases of a product are forecast to be sold in a particular year, and only 80,000 cases are actually sold. The extra 20,000 cases can end up in inventory, or perhaps employment might be cut to reduce production levels. It is also equally painful if the forecast is too low. Then capacity is strained, extra people may be added in a rush, or sales may be lost owing to stockouts.

There are three ways to accommodate forecasting errors. One is to try to reduce the error through better forecasting. The second is to build more flexibility into operations. And the third is to reduce the lead time over which forecasts are required. Even good forecasts will have some error, but the lowest possible error is the goal consistent with reasonable forecasting costs.

In recognition of inherent forecasting error, all forecasts should have at least two numbers: one for the best estimate of demand (e.g., mean, median, or mode) and the other for forecasting error (e.g., standard deviation, absolute deviation, or range). To produce forecasts with only one number is to ignore error, but this is a common occurrence in practice.

Forecasting problems are often very complex and difficult. One example is forecasting 10,000 different varieties of thread used in a textile factory. Each different color, spool size, and thickness of thread requires a forecast for procurement. Lack of the proper thread can cause the line to shut down or require an expensive change over to another product. In large retail stores, as many as a million different forecasts may be required for different items, styles, sizes, and colors. A stockout here may result in a lost sale or even a loss of future business if the customer is dissatisfied. Thus, forecasting occupies a central role in operations because of its complexity and its impact on all operations decisions. Forecasting is an input to many of the operations decisions treated in the remainder of the text.

In the first part of this chapter, a descriptive framework of forecasting is presented. Several methods and their potential applications are then discussed at length. Following this, the uses of forecasting in organizations are described.

3.1 A FORECASTING FRAMEWORK

Although there are many types of forecasting, this chapter will focus on the forecasting of demand for output from the operations function. Demand and sales, however, are not always the same thing. Whenever the demand is not constrained by capacity or other management policies, the forecasting of demand will be the same as the forecasting of sales. Otherwise, sales may be somewhat below real customer demand.

We should also clarify at the outset the difference between forecasting and planning. Forecasting deals with what we think *will* happen in the future. Planning deals with what we think *should* happen in the future. Thus, through planning, we consciously attempt to alter future events, while we use forecasting only to predict them. Good planning utilizes a forecast as an input. If the forecast is not acceptable, a plan can sometimes be devised to change the course of events.

Forecasting is one input to all types of business planning and control, both inside and outside the operations function. Marketing uses forecasts to plan products, promotion, and pricing. Finance uses forecasting as an input to financial planning. The main focus in this chapter, however, will be on forecasting for the operations function, where it serves as an input for decisions on process design, capacity planning, and inventory. A typical forecasting system is described in Box 3.1.

BOX 3.1
FORECASTING AT RUBBERMAID

Forecasting at Rubbermaid Home Products Division is a routinized but flexible system that incorporates several major advantages. Forecasting is not confined to a single individual working feverishly behind a PC. The Group Product Managers have final authority over all numbers, but personnel from all functional areas participate. Thus, responsibility for input is widely distributed horizontally and vertically. State-of-the-art statistical modelling and practical business knowledge and experience are synthesized in the process. Constant monitoring of forecast accuracies serves as an impetus for reducing error. Most important of all, the forecasts are not just 'show' numbers; they are incorporated into the short-term and long-term business plans to which people willingly react.

All products are presently partitioned into ten distinct product lines which are in turn subdivided into various product groups. Because items are often marketed in several different packaging schemes to facilitate customer preferences, the 30, 60, and 90-day and annual forecasts are performed on approximately 600 item packs. Forecasts are initially done in units, but forecasted average selling prices subsequently translate unit quantities into total dollars for each item, group, and line. The computer system then distributes each item-pack forecast between colors and raw material requirements in three manufacturing sites.

In the first week of each month a forecast analyst applies a battery of statistical forecast methods to the demand history of each item-pack. These methods range from the most sophisticated such as state-space models and Box-Jenkins to the simplest such as exponential smoothing. A number of statistical criteria are employed to select the "best" forecast for each 30, 60, and 90-day period. The Product Manager then constructs his or her own forecast adding judgment to the statistical data.

As we move past each month during the current year, the open order numbers become actual demand history. Error percentages for the Product Managers and the statistical forecasts are calculated and displayed. This becomes the basis for monitoring the accuracy of the forecasts.

Several mechanisms ensure a weekly reevaluation of the 30, 60, and 90-day forecasts. Every Monday morning, the Vice Presidents of Marketing, Sales, and Manufacturing meet to discuss month-to-date order entry, shipments, backlog, and inventory. These statistics are compared with the forecasted monthly totals and the current business plans, and adjustments are made as needed. Every Friday morning, a new forecast/demand history report is printed and distributed to all Product Managers. This report serves as the basis for updating the forecast.

Extracted from an article by Richard B. Barrett and David J. Kistka, "Forecasting System at Rubbermaid," *The Journal of Business Forecasting*, Spring 1987, pp. 7–9.

For process design purposes, forecasting is needed to decide on the type of process and the degree of automation to be used. For example, a low forecast of future sales might indicate that little automation is needed and the process should be kept as simple as possible. If greater volume is forecast, more automation and a more elaborate process including line flow might be justified. Since process decisions are long range in nature, they can require forecasts for many years into the future.

Capacity decisions utilize forecasts at several different levels of aggregation and precision. For planning the total capacity of facilities, a long-range forecast several years into the future is needed. For medium-range-capacity decisions extending through the next year or so, a more detailed forecast by product line will be needed to determine hiring plans, subcontracting, and equipment decisions. Besides being more detailed, the medium-range forecast should be more accurate, if possible, than the long-range forecast. Short-range-capacity decisions, including assignment of available people and machines to jobs or activities in the near future, should be detailed in terms of individual products, and they should be highly accurate.

Inventory decisions resulting in purchasing actions tend to be short range in nature and deal with specific products. The forecasts that lead to these decisions must meet the same requirements as short-range scheduling forecasts: they must have a high degree of accuracy and individual product specificity. For inventory and scheduling decisions, because of the many items usually involved, it will also be necessary to produce a large number of forecasts. Thus a computerized forecasting system will often be used for these decisions.

In summary, there are different types of decisions in operations and different associated forecasting requirements, as shown in Table 3.1. The table also indicates the three types of forecasting methods to be described in this chapter: qualitative, time series, and causal.

In general terms, qualitative forecasting methods rely on managerial judgment; they do not use specific models. Thus different individuals can use the same qualitative method and arrive at widely different forecasts. Qualitative methods

TABLE 3.1
FORECASTING USES AND METHODS

Uses of forecasting for operations decisions	Time horizon	Accuracy required	Number of products	Management level	Forecasting methods
Process design	Long	Medium	Single or few	Top	Qualitative and causal
Capacity planning facilities	Long	Medium	Single or few	Top	Qualitative and causal
Aggregate planning	Medium	High	Few	Middle	Causal and time series
Scheduling	Short	Highest	Many	Lower	Time series
Inventory management	Short	Highest	Many	Lower	Time series

are useful, however, when there is a lack of data or when past data are not reliable predictors of the future. In this case, the human decision maker can utilize the best available data and a qualitative approach to arrive at a forecast.

There are two types of quantitative forecasting methods: time-series and causal forecasting. In general, quantitative methods utilize an underlying model to arrive at a forecast. The basic assumption for all quantitative forecasting methods is that past data and data patterns are reliable predictors of the future. Past data are then processed by a time-series or causal model to arrive at a forecast.

The relationship between the methods and uses of forecasting is summarized in Table 3.1. As may be noted, each method has certain uses for which it is particularly well suited.

In the remainder of this chapter we will be referring to long, medium, and short time range. "Long range" will mean 2 years or more into the future, which is a common horizon for the planning of facilities and processes. "Medium range" is defined as from 6 months to 2 years, which is the normal time frame for aggregate planning decisions, budgeting, and other resource acquisition and allocation decisions. "Short range" will refer to less than 6 months, where the decisions involve procurement of materials and scheduling of particular jobs and activities. For short-range decisions, forecasts that extend through procurement or production lead times are sufficient.

QUALITATIVE FORECASTING METHODS

As we have indicated, qualitative forecasting methods utilize managerial judgment, experience, relevant data, and an *implicit* mathematical model. Because the model is implicit, two different managers both using qualitative methods often arrive at widely different forecasts.

Some people think that qualitative forecasts should be used only as a last resort. This is not strictly true. Qualitative forecasts should be used when past data are not reliable indicators of future conditions. When this happens, past data must be tempered by judgment before a forecast can be developed. Qualitative forecasting must also be used for new-product introductions, where a historical data base is not available. In this case, qualitative methods can be used to develop a forecast by analogy or by the selective use of market research data. As we shall see, a systematic approach is possible even though an explicit mathematical model is not formulated.

Table 3.2 describes four of the best-known qualitative methods and some of the characteristics of each. As can be seen, qualitative methods are typically used for medium- and long-range forecasting involving process design or capacity of facilities. For these decisions, past data are not usually available or, if they are, may show an unstable pattern.

One of the qualitative forecasting methods, the so-called Delphi method, is used to obtain a forecast from a panel of experts or managers. A feature of this method is that all estimates from the panel are treated anonymously. This tends to eliminate the influence of the supposed greatest authority as well as the bandwagon effect which is so common when face-to-face panels are used.

TABLE 3.2
QUALITATIVE FORECASTING METHODS

Qualitative methods	Description of method	Uses	Accuracy			Identification of turning point	Relative cost	References
			Short term	Medium term	Long term			
1. Delphi	Forecast developed by a panel of experts answering a series of questions on successive rounds. Anonymous responses of the panel are fed back on each round to all participants. Three to six rounds may be used to obtain convergence of the forecast.	Long-range sales forecasts for capacity or facility planning. Technological forecasting to assess when technological changes might occur.	Fair to very good	Fair to very good	Fair to very good	Fair to good	Medium to high	North and Pyke; Basu and Schroeder
2. Market surveys	Panels, questionnaires, test markets, or surveys used to gather data on market conditions.	Forecasts of total company sales, major product groups, or individual products.	Very good	Good	Fair	Fair to good	High	Bass, King, and Pessemeier
3. Life-cycles analogy	Prediction based on the introduction, growth, and saturation phases of similar products. Uses the S-shaped sales growth curve.	Forecasts of long-range sales for capacity or facility planning.	Poor	Fair to good	Fair to good	Poor to fair	Medium	Spencer, Clark, and Hoguet
4. Informed judgment	Forecast may be made by a group or an individual on the basis of experience, hunches, or facts about the situation. No rigorous method is used.	Forecasts for total sales and individual products.	Poor to fair	Poor to fair	Poor to fair	Poor to fair	Low	

Source: Reprinted by permission of the *Harvard Business Review.* Exhibit adapted from John C. Chambers, Satinder K. Mullick, and Donald D. Smith, "How to Choose the Right Forecasting Technique," July–August 1971, p. 55; and David M. Georgoff and Robert Murdick, "Manager's Guide to Forecasting," *Harvard Business Review,* January–February 1986, pp. 110–120.

The Delphi method, named after the famous Greek oracle of Delphi, proceeds through a series of rounds. On the first round, each person on the panel provides a written response to the questions asked. After these responses are tabulated, they are fed back to the panel along with statistics on the mean, median, interquartile range, and standard deviation. Each member of the panel is then asked to reconsider his or her previous answers and to respond once again to the questions. The responses from the second round are again summarized and fed back to the panel for a third round, and so on. This procedure is often repeated for four to six rounds (a minimum of three) until sufficient convergence is achieved. The estimates from the last round are then used as the forecasts.

The Delphi method has sometimes been referred to as "pooled ignorance." This criticism is derived from the tendency of the feedback process to force convergence toward the group center. Nevertheless, the method can be used to obtain reasonable forecasts in the face of a great deal of uncertainty and a lack of data.

An example of the use of the Delphi method to obtain a 5-year forecast of sales for facility-planning purposes was reported by Basu and Schroeder (1977). In this case, sales at American Hoist and Derrick had been constrained by insufficient capacity and sales were therefore not a reliable predictor of future demand. Furthermore, economic conditions were changing rapidly, making past data unreliable. Therefore, the Delphi method was used to bring managerial judgment to bear on the available past data and to reflect expected future conditions.

In this case, a panel of 23 managers, who had knowledge of the overall market and sales picture, was selected from different functional parts of the corporation. This panel was given a questionnaire which requested three estimates—the GNP, industry sales, and company sales—for each of the next 5 years. These three estimates were requested in order to encourage panel members to think about the interrelationships between the economy, industry, and the company and to allow validity and correlation checks on the results. The managers were given the past 5 years of data on these three scales and asked simply to fill in their best estimates for each of the next 5 years.

Both the anonymous estimates of all the managers and summary statistics were fed back on the second round. The data indicated a fairly wide spread of estimates. For example, the industry sales estimates in one year ranged from a low of 0 percent increase to a high of 35 percent increase with a mean of 9.5 percent and a standard deviation of 8 percent.

In addition to a revised estimate, the panel members were asked to give their reasons for their estimates on the second round; this resulted in an outpouring of views on future conditions. These reasons were then fed back, along with the revised estimates and statistics for the third round.

The result of the three successive rounds was a striking convergence of the managers' forecasts. For GNP in one year, the first-round forecast ranged from 0 to 12 percent increase, while the third-round estimate had converged to a 5 to 8.5 percent increase. In addition to providing a forecast, the convergence produced a common outlook among the managers, which had been lacking before the use of the Delphi procedure.

Top management at American Hoist and Derrick was presented with three forecasts: the Delphi forecast, another developed using regression, and a third using exponential smoothing. The Delphi forecast was considered most credible by top management because it incorporated the judgment of 23 knowledgeable corporate managers. This confidence was subsequently justified when corporate sales for the first year were within one-third of 1 percent of the forecast and the second-year sales were within 4 percent of the forecast. In the past, forecasting errors of + 20 percent had been common.

Three additional qualitative forecasting methods are described in Table 3.2. Notice that all these qualitative methods are best suited to long-range forecasting problems, where judgment is required to deal with inherent variability. Also notice that the Delphi and market-survey methods are fairly expensive and therefore must be used sparingly for only the most important decisions.

TIME-SERIES FORECASTING

Time-series methods are used to make detailed analyses of past demand patterns over time and to project these patterns forward into the future. One of the basic assumptions of all time-series methods is that demand can be divided into components such as average level, trend, seasonality, cycle, and error. A sample of these components for a representative time series is shown in Figure 3.1. When the components are added together (or in some cases multiplied), they will equal the original time series.

The basic strategy used in time-series forecasting is to identify the magnitude and form of each component based on available past data. These components (except the random component) are then projected forward into the future. If only a small random component is left over and the pattern persists into the future, a reliable forecast will be obtained.

One example of the decomposition of a time series is as follows:

$$y(t) = (a + bt)[f(t)] + e \tag{3.1}$$

where $y(t)$ = demand during period t
    a = level
    b = trend
    $f(t)$ = seasonal factor (multiplicative)
    e = random error

As can be seen, this time-series model has a level, trend, seasonal factor, and random-error term. Each of these terms would be estimated from past data to develop an equation which is then used to forecast future demand. See the chapter supplement for an example of this method.

In discussing time-series forecasting, the following symbols and terminology are used:

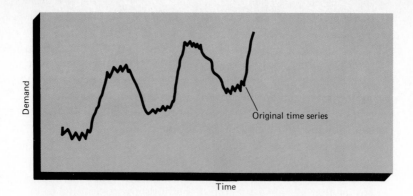

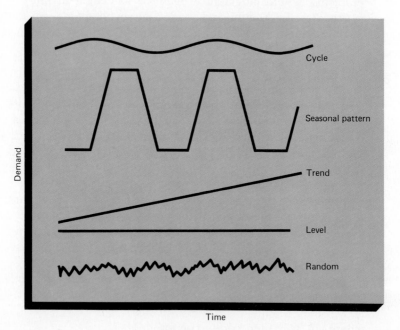

FIGURE 3.1
Decomposition of
time-series data.

	Observed demands					Forecasts at time t			
Data	D_1	D_2		D_{t-2}	D_{t-1}	D_t	F_{t+1}	F_{t+2}	F_{t+3}
Period	1	2	⋯	$t-2$	$t-1$	t	$t+1$	$t+2$	$t+3$	⋯

Present time

D_t = demand during period t

F_{t+1} = forecast demand for period $t + 1$

$e_t = D_t - F_t$ = forecast error in period t

A_t = average computed through period t

The general picture is that we are at the end of period t, just having observed the value of D_t, and are making a forecast for periods $t + 1$, $t + 2$, $t + 3$, etc.

Moving Average

The simplest method of time-series forecasting is the moving-average method. For this method, it is assumed that the time series has only a level component plus a random component. No seasonal pattern, trend, or cycle components are assumed to be present in the demand data. More advanced versions of the moving average can, however, include all the various components; see, for example, Wheelwright and Makridakis (1985).

When the moving average is used, a given number of periods N is selected for the computations. Then the average demand A_t for the past N periods at time t is computed as follows:

$$A_t = \frac{D_1 + D_{t-1} + \ldots + D_{t-N+1}}{N} \tag{3.2}$$

Since we are assuming that the time series is flat (or horizontal), the best forecast for period $t + 1$ is simply a continuation of the average demand observed through period t. Thus we have

$$F_{t+1} = A_t$$

Each time F_{t+1} is computed, the most recent demand is included in the average and the oldest demand observation is dropped. This procedure maintains N periods of demand in the forecast and lets the average *move* along as new demand data are observed.

In Box 3.2, a three-period moving average is used for forecasting purposes. Notice how the moving *average* is offset by one period to obtain the moving *forecast*. The forecast error is also shown in the box as the difference between actual and forecast demand. Always use the forecast for period t, F_t, in computing forecast errors, not the average for period t, A_t.

BOX 3.2
MOVING-AVERAGE FORECASTS

Period	D_t (demand)	A_t (three-period moving average)	F_t (three-period forecast)	$D_t - F_t$ (error)
1	10			
2	18			
3	29	19.0		
4	15	20.7	19.0	−4.0
5	30	24.7	20.7	+9.3
6	12	19.0	24.7	−12.7

7	16	19.3	19.0	−3.0
8	8	12.0	19.3	−11.3
9	22	15.3	12.0	10.0
10	14	14.7	15.3	−1.3
11	15	17.0	14.7	0.3
12	27	18.7	17.0	10.0
13	30	24.0	18.7	11.3
14	23	26.7	24.0	−1.0
15	15	22.7	26.7	−11.7

The graph in Figure 3.2 shows the demand data from the example, the three-period moving average, and a six-period moving average. It is a good idea to always plot the data and forecasts before making comparisons. Notice how the six-period moving average responds more slowly to demand changes than the three-period moving average. As a general rule, the longer the averaging period, the slower the response to demand changes. A longer period thus has the advantage of providing stability in the forecast but the disadvantage of responding more slowly to real changes in the demand level. The forecasting analyst must select the appropriate tradeoff between stability and response by selecting the averaging length N.

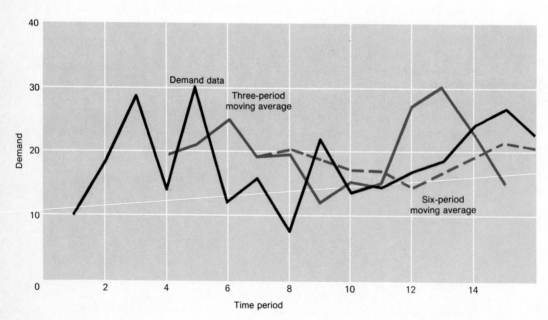

FIGURE 3.2 Time-series data.

One way to make the moving average respond more rapidly to changes in demand is to place relatively more weight on recent demands than on earlier ones. This is called a weighted moving average, which is computed as follows:

$$F_{t+1} = A_t = W_1 D_t + W_2 D_{t-1} + \ldots + W_N D_{t-N+1} \tag{3.3}$$

with the condition

$$\sum_{i=1}^{N} W_i = 1$$

With the weighted moving average, any desired weights can be specified so long as they add up to 1. For example, if we have the three demands $D_1 = 10$, $D_2 = 18$, and $D_3 = 29$, the ordinary three-period moving average is 19.0. With weights of .5, .3, and .2, the three-period weighted moving average is 21.9. In this case the weight of .5 was applied to the third period, .3 to the second period, and .2 to the first period. Notice, for this example, how the weighted moving average has responded more rapidly than the ordinary moving average to the increased demand of 29 in the third period. Notice also that the simple moving average is just a special case of the weighted moving average with all weights equal ($W_i = 1/N$).

One of the disadvantages of a weighted moving average is that the entire demand history for N periods must be carried along with the computation. Furthermore, the response of a weighted moving average cannot be easily changed without changing each of the weights. To overcome these difficulties, the method of exponential smoothing has been developed.

Exponential Smoothing

Exponential smoothing is based on the very simple idea that a new average can be computed from an old average and the most recent observed demand. Suppose, for example, we have an old average of 20 and we have just observed a demand of 24. It stands to reason that the new average will lie between 20 and 24, depending on how much weight we want to put on the demand just observed versus the weight on the old average.

To formalize the above logic, we can write:

$$A_t = \alpha D_t + (1 - \alpha) A_{t-1} \tag{3.4}$$

In this case, A_{t-1} is the old average (20), D_t the demand just observed (24), and α the proportion of weight placed on the new demand versus the old average ($0 \leq \alpha \leq 1$).

To illustrate, suppose we use the values $\alpha = .1$, $D_t = 24$, and $A_{t-1} = 20$. Then, from Equation (3.4), we have $A_t = 20.4$. If $\alpha = .5$, we have $A_t = 22$, and if $\alpha = .9$, we have $A_t = 23.6$. Thus A_t can vary between the old average of 20 and the demand of 24, depending on the value of α used.

If we want A_t to be very responsive to recent demand, we should choose a large value of α. If we want A_t to respond more slowly, then α should be smaller. In most forecasting work, α is given a value between .1 and .3 to maintain reasonable stability.

In simple exponential smoothing, just as in the case of moving averages, we assume that the time series is flat with no cycles and that there are no seasonal or trend components. Then the exponentially smoothed forecast for the next period is simply the average obtained through the current period. That is,

$$F_{t+1} = A_t$$

In this case the forecast is also offset one period from the smoothed average.

We can substitute the preceding relationship into Equation (3.4) to obtain the following equation:

$$F_{t+1} = \alpha D_t + (1 - \alpha)F_t \tag{3.5}$$

Sometimes this alternate form of simple (or first-order) exponential smoothing is more convenient to use than Equation (3.4) because it uses forecasts instead of averages.

Another way to view exponential smoothing is to rearrange the terms on the right-hand side of Equation (3.5) to yield:

$$F_{t+1} = F_t + \alpha(D_t - F_t)$$

This form indicates that the new forecast is the old forecast plus a proportion of the error between the observed demand and the old forecast. The proportion of error used can be controlled by the choice of α.

Students often wonder why the name "exponential smoothing" has been given to this method. This can be explained by writing Equation (3.5) in terms of all the previous demands. By substitution for F_t into Equation (3.5), we have

$$F_{t+1} = \alpha D_t + (1 - \alpha)[\alpha D_{t-1} + (1 - \alpha)F_{t-1}]$$

Then, substituting for F_{t-1} in the above equation, we have

$$F_{t+1} = \alpha D_t + (1 - \alpha)\alpha D_{t-1} + (1 - \alpha)(1 - \alpha)[\alpha D_{t-2} + (1 - \alpha)F_{t-2}]$$

If this substitution is continued, we will arrive at the expression

$$F_{t+1} = \alpha D_t + (1 - \alpha)\alpha D_{t-1} + (1 - \alpha)^2 \alpha D_{t-2} \\ + \cdots + (1 - \alpha)^{t-1}\alpha D_1 + (1 - \alpha)^t F_1$$

This expression indicates that the weights on each preceding demand decrease exponentially, by a factor of $(1 - \alpha)$, until the demand from the first period and the initial forecast F_1 is reached.

If $\alpha = .3$ and $t = 3$, for example, we will have

$$F_4 = .3D_3 + .21 D_2 + .147 D_1 + .343 F_1$$

Notice that the weights on the demands decrease exponentially over time and all the weights add up to 1. Therefore, exponential smoothing is just a special form of the weighted average, with the weights decreasing exponentially over time.

In Box 3.3, two exponentially smoothed forecasts are computed for $\alpha = .1$ and $\alpha = .3$ using the same demand data as in Box 3.2. As can be seen, the $\alpha = .3$ forecast responds more rapidly to demand changes but is less stable than $\alpha = .1$. Which of these forecasts is then the best?

To answer this question, two measures of forecast errors are computed in Box 3.3. One measure is simply the arithmetic sum of all errors, which reflects the bias in the forecasting method. Ideally this sum should be 0. In Box 3.3, both methods have a positive bias, with $\alpha = .1$ producing more bias than $\alpha = .3$.

The second measure of forecast error is the absolute deviation. In this case the absolute value of the errors is added, so that negative errors do not cancel positive errors. The result is a measure of variance in the forecasting method. The total absolute deviation for $\alpha = .1$ is less than for $\alpha = .3$.

Thus, we have the interesting result that the $\alpha = .1$ forecast has more bias but less absolute deviation than the $\alpha = .3$ forecast. In this case there is no clear choice between the two methods; it just depends on one's preference between bias and deviation. However, if a forecast has both lower deviation and lower bias, then it is clearly preferred.

BOX 3.3
EXPONENTIAL SMOOTHING*

Period	D_t (demand)	F_t $\alpha = .1$ (forecast)	$D_t - F_t$ (error)	F_t $\alpha = .3$ (forecast)	$D_t - F_t$ (error)	MAD_t ($\alpha = .3$)	T (tracking signal)
1	10	15	−5.0	15	−5.0	6.4	−.8
2	18	14.5	3.5	13.5	4.5	5.8	−.1
3	29	14.85	14.15	14.85	14.15	8.3	1.6
4	15	16.26	−1.26	19.09	−4.09	7.1	1.3
5	30	16.14	13.86	17.86	12.14	8.6	2.5
6	12	17.52	−5.52	21.50	−9.50	8.8	1.4
7	16	16.97	−.97	18.65	−2.65	7.0	1.4
8	8	16.87	−8.87	17.85	−9.85	7.9	−.1
9	22	15.98	6.02	14.90	7.10	7.6	.9
10	14	16.58	−2.58	17.03	−3.03	6.2	.6
11	15	16.33	−1.33	16.12	−1.12	4.7	.6
12	27	16.19	10.81	15.78	11.22	6.7	2.1
13	30	17.27	12.73	19.15	10.85	7.9	3.1
14	23	18.54	4.46	22.40	0.60	5.7	4.4
15	15	18.99	−3.99	22.58	−7.58	6.4	2.8

$\Sigma(D_t - F_t)$ Bias   36.01   17.74
$\Sigma|D_t - F_t|$ Absolute Deviation   95.05   103.38

*Assume $F_1 = 15$, as an arbitrary starting point. Also assume $MAD_0 = 7$. See pages 62–63 for definitions of MAD and tracking signal.

The procedure for choosing a value of α is now clear. A forecast should be computed for several values of α. If one value of α produces a forecast with less bias and less deviation than the others, then this value of α is preferred. If no clear choice exists, then a tradeoff between bias and deviation must be made in choosing the preferred value of α.

Unfortunately, simple exponential smoothing cannot always be used in practice because of trends or seasonal effects in the data. When these effects are present, second-order smoothing, third-order smoothing, trend-corrected smoothing, or seasonal smoothing might be used. Some of these more advanced methods are presented in the chapter supplement. [Also see Brown (1963) and Wheelwright and Makridakis (1985).]

Forecast Errors

When exponential smoothing is used, whether it is simple smoothing or more advanced smoothing, an estimate of forecast error should be computed along with the smoothed average. This error estimate might be used for several purposes:

1. To set safety stocks or safety capacity and thereby ensure a desired level of protection against stockout
2. To monitor erratic demand observations or outliers which should be carefully evaluated and perhaps rejected from the data
3. To determine when the forecasting method is no longer tracking actual demand and needs to be reset

The first use will be covered later in the text, but the last two uses are described more completely below.

In forecasting work, a commonly used measure of forecasting error is mean absolute deviation, or MAD. The MAD is mathematically defined as follows:

$$\text{MAD} = \frac{\Sigma |D_t - F_t|}{n}$$

where $|D_t - F_t|$ is the absolute value of the error in time period t
$\qquad n$ is the number of periods used in the summation

The above expression is just the average error observed, without regard to sign, over all the past periods of forecasting. The MAD is similar to the standard deviation, except we have not squared the errors for each period and then taken the square root of the sum. Instead, the absolute deviations have been added and the average taken.

When exponential smoothing is used, it is common to calculate the smoothed mean absolute deviation, which is defined as follows:

$$\text{MAD}_t = \alpha |D_t - F_t| + (1 - \alpha)\text{MAD}_{t-1}$$

In this case the new MAD, or MAD_t, is simply a fraction α of the current absolute deviation plus $(1 - \alpha)$ times the old MAD. This is analogous to Equation (3.4), since the MAD is being smoothed in the same way as the average.

The current MAD$_t$ should be computed each period along with the forecast average. The MAD can then be used to detect an outlier in demand by comparing the observed deviation with the MAD. If the observed deviation is greater than 3.75 MAD, we have reason to suspect that the demand may be an extreme value. This is comparable to determining whether an observed demand value lies outside three standard deviations σ for the normal distribution. This is true because $\sigma = 1.25$ MAD for the normal distribution. In Box 3.3 MAD was computed for $\alpha = .3$. As can be seen, none of the demand errors fall outside 3.75 MAD, so no outliers are suspected in the data.

The second use of MAD is to determine whether the forecast is tracking with the actual time-series values. To determine this, a tracking signal is computed, as follows:

$$\text{Tracking signal} = T = \frac{\text{cumulative sum of forecast deviation}}{\text{MAD}}$$

The tracking signal is thus a computation of bias in the numerator divided by the most recent estimate of MAD. If demand variations are assumed to be random, then control limits of ± 6 on the tracking signal should ensure only a 3 percent probability that the limits will be exceeded by chance.[1] Thus, when the tracking signal exceeds ± 6, the forecasting method should be stopped and reset to more nearly equal observed demand. In Box 3.3, the tracking signal does not exceed ± 6 in any period. Therefore the forecast is considered to be tracking sufficiently close to actual demand.

In computerized forecasting systems it is extremely important to incorporate error controls of the type discussed above. This will ensure that the system does not run out of control. Instead, the user is notified when outliers in demand are detected or when the tracking signal becomes too large.

Advanced Time-Series Forecasting

A variation of exponential smoothing which has received considerable recent attention is *adaptive* exponential smoothing. In one form of this approach, Chow (1965) used first-order smoothing but varied the smoothing coefficient at each forecast by $\pm .05$ to determine which of the three forecasts had the lowest forecast error. The resulting value of α was used for the next period forecast. The smoothing coefficient was allowed to increase to a maximum of .95 and to decrease to a minimum of .05.

Another type of adaptive smoothing is used by IBM in its MAPICS inventory software package. For this method, α is adjusted for the value of the smoothed forecasting error. If there is a large forecasting error, α will be large until the forecast comes back on track. When the error is smaller, α will also be small and a stable forecast will result. This method appears to work quite well for inventory forecasting situations. [See IBM (1985).] For other references on adaptive smoothing, see Whybark (1972), Trigg and Leach (1967), and Raine (1971).

---

[1]These numerical limits and probabilities are based on the normal probability distribution and a value of $\alpha = .1$. [See Thomopoulos (1980), p. 306.]

Table 3.3 summarizes four time-series forecasting methods. We have already discussed two of them, moving average and exponential smoothing, at some length. The remaining two are described briefly below.

Any desired mathematical model can be fitted to a time series such as the one shown in Equation (3.1), with level, trend, and seasonal components. For example, a model can be fitted by the methods of linear regression or the use of nonlinear methods. In some cases the resulting model may provide a more accurate forecast than exponential smoothing. However, a custom-fitted model is more expensive, so the tradeoff between accuracy and model cost must be made.

Within the past few years, the sophisticated Box-Jenkins method has been developed for time-series forecasting. This technique has a special phase for model identification, and it permits more precise analysis of proposed models than is possible with the other methods. The Box-Jenkins method, however, requires about 60 periods of past data and is too expensive to use for routine forecasting of many items. For a special forecast of sales involving a costly decision, however, the use of Box-Jenkins may be warranted.

In summary, time-series methods are useful for short- or medium-range forecasts when the demand pattern is expected to remain stable. Time-series forecasts are often inputs to decisions concerning aggregate output planning, budgeting, resource allocation, inventory, and scheduling. Time-series forecasts are not typically useful for decisions on facility planning or process selection because of the long time spans involved.

 3.4 CAUSAL FORECASTING METHODS

In general, causal forecasting methods develop a cause-and-effect model between demand and other variables. For example, the demand for ice cream may be related to population, the average summer temperature, and time. Data can be collected on these variables and an analysis conducted to determine the validity of the proposed model. One of the best-known causal methods is regression, which will be described next, followed by very brief descriptions of additional causal methods.

For regression methods, a model must be specified before the data are collected and the analysis is conducted. The simplest case is the following single-variable linear model:

$$\hat{y} = a + bx$$

where $\hat{y}$ = estimated demand
x = independent variable (hypothesized to cause $\hat{y}$)
a = y intercept
b = slope

For this model, we assume that n pairs of x and y values have been observed. We denote these pairs (x_1, y_1), (x_2, y_2), . . . ,(x_n, y_n). Notice that the symbol y denotes observed values of y and that the symbol $\hat{y}$ denotes points on the line expressed by the equation $\hat{y} = a + bx$.

TABLE 3.3
TIME-SERIES FORECASTING METHODS

Time-series methods	Description of method	Uses	Accuracy			Identification of turning point	Relative cost	References
			Short term	Medium term	Long term			
1. Moving averages	Forecast is based on arithmetic average or weighted average of a given number of past data points.	Short- to medium-range planning for inventories, production levels, and scheduling. Good for many products.	Poor to good	Poor	Very poor	Poor	Low	Neter, Wasserman, and Whitmore
2. Exponential smoothing	Similar to moving average, with exponentially more weight placed on recent data. Well adapted to computer use and large number of items to be forecast.	Same as moving average.	Fair to very good	Poor to good	Very poor	Poor	Low	Brown, Adam, Wheelwright, and Makridakis
3. Mathematical models	A linear or nonlinear model fitted to time-series data, usually by regression methods. Includes trend lines, polynomials, log-linear, Fourier series, etc.	Same as moving average but limited, due to expense, to a few products.	Very good	Fair to good	Very poor	Poor	Low to medium	
4. Box-Jenkins	Autocorrelation methods are used to identify underlying time series and to fit the "best" model. Requires about 60 past data points.	Limited, due to expense, to products requiring very accurate short-range forecasts.	Very good to excellent	Fair to good	Very poor	Poor	Medium to high	Box and Jenkins; Nelson

Source: Reprinted by permission of the *Harvard Business Review.* Exhibit adapted from John C. Chambers, Satinder K. Mullick, and Donald D. Smith, "How to Choose the Right Forecasting Technique," July–August 1971, pp. 55–56; and David M. Georgoff and Robert Murdick, "Manager's Guide to Forecasting," *Harvard Business Review,* January–February 1986, pp. 110–120.

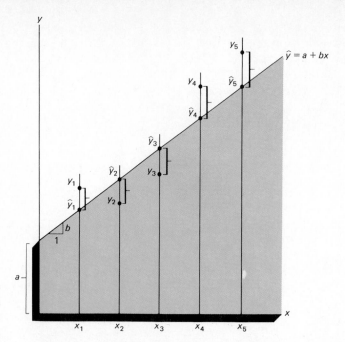

FIGURE 3.3
Regression
forecasting.

The situation is shown in Figure 3.3. The y values which have been observed do not fall exactly on the line because of random errors in the data. For each observed point, the error can be expressed as $\hat{y}_i - y_i$, and the total variance or squared error due to all the points is then

$$\Sigma(\hat{y}_i - y_i)^2 = \Sigma(a + bx_i - y_i)^2$$

In regression analysis, the objective is to minimize the error equation shown above by choosing values of a and b. The minimum error can be found by using calculus, which results in the following set of equations:

$$a = \frac{\Sigma y_i}{n} - b\frac{\Sigma x_i}{n} \tag{3.6}$$

$$b = \frac{n\Sigma x_i y_i - [(\Sigma x_i)(\Sigma y_i)]}{n\Sigma x_i^2 - (\Sigma x_i)^2} \tag{3.7}$$

For a given set of n data pairs $(x_1, y_1), (x_2, y_2), \ldots, (x_n, y_n)$, the values of a and b can be found from Equations (3.6) and (3.7). These values describe the straight line which is the best (least squares) predictor of demand y based on the independent variable x.

We can also calculate the strength of the relationship between y and x by means of r^2, the coefficient of determination.[2] The value of r^2 represents the proportion of

---

[2]The correlation coefficient r is the square root of the coefficient of determination. However, r^2 has a direct physical meaning, which r does not have.

variation in y which is explained by the relationship with x, the remainder of the variation $1 - r^2$ being due to chance or factors other than x. It is therefore desirable to have the value of r^2 as close to 1 as possible.

A value of $r^2 = .8$ indicates that 80 percent of the variation in y is predicted or explained by the regression line with x; only 20 percent is due to chance. In this case, a quite reliable forecast for y can be obtained when the value of x is known.

The quantity r^2 can be computed as follows:

$$r^2 = \frac{[n\Sigma x_i y_i - (\Sigma x_i)(\Sigma y_i)]^2}{[n\Sigma x_i^2 - (\Sigma x_i)^2][n\Sigma y_i^2 - (\Sigma y_i)^2]}$$

We will illustrate linear regression forecasting with a simple example. Suppose we are interested in estimating the demand for newspapers on the basis of the local population. The demand for newspapers over the past 8 years and the corresponding population in a small town are shown in Table 3.4. Using the available data, the first step is to compute the values of a and b for the line. This is done by computing the cross product of xy and the values of x^2 as shown in the table. If the totals of all columns are obtained, the data are then available to plug into Equations (3.6) and (3.7). The result in this case is $a = -1.34$, $b = 2.01$. The best (least squares) equation for predicting demand for newspapers is thus $y = -1.34 + 2.01x$.

In a similar way, the value of r^2 was computed from Table 3.4, resulting in $r^2 = .97$. This indicates that the straight-line regression equation shown above explains 97 percent of the variation in newspaper demand; only 3 percent of the variation is unexplained or due to chance. As shown by the high value of r^2, population is a very good predictor of newspaper demand. If population can be projected accurately for the future, we can also accurately forecast newspaper demand through the regression equation.

Simple linear regression illustrates the principles of causal forecasting. The forecast for demand is related to one or more variables which are hypothesized to be independent in nature. It is the user's responsibility to determine the appropri-

TABLE 3.4
REGRESSION EXAMPLE*

i	y_i	x_i	$x_i y_i$	x_i^2	y_i^2
1	3.0	2.0	6.0	4.0	9.0
2	3.5	2.4	8.4	5.8	12.3
3	4.1	2.8	11.5	7.8	16.8
4	4.4	3.0	13.2	9.0	19.4
5	5.0	3.2	16.0	10.2	25.0
6	5.7	3.6	20.5	13.0	32.5
7	6.4	3.8	24.3	14.4	41.0
8	7.0	4.0	28.0	16.0	49.0
	39.1	24.8	127.9	80.2	205.0

*The demand for newspapers y_i is expressed in thousands of copies. The population x_i is expressed in ten thousands of people.

ate causal variables and whether the relationships are linear, nonlinear, additive, or multiplicative. The form of the forecasting model must ultimately be specified by the user.

Single-variable regression can be extended to multiple regression, which utilizes more than one x variable. Because of the additional variables, multiple regression is often more useful than simple regression in practice. For the newspaper example, we might hypothesize that demand for newspapers is related not only to population but also to family income and educational level. These additional variables might help explain more of the variation in newspapers sales, although the single-variable model is already very good in this case.

One example of the use of multiple regression for demand forecasting has been given by Armstrong and Grohman (1972). They developed the following model for predicting U.S. air travel:

$$M_{t+f} = (1.12)^f \, M_t \left(\frac{P_{t+f}}{P_t}\right)^{-1.2} \left(\frac{S_{t+f}}{S_t}\right)^{0.2} \left(\frac{I_{t+f}}{I_t}\right)^{0.5} \left(\frac{N_{t+f}}{N_t}\right)^{1.0} \left(\frac{D_{t+f}}{D_t}\right)^{-.05}$$

where t = current year
   f = number of years in the future
   M = U.S. domestic revenue passenger miles
   P = price of air travel (cents per passenger mile in constant dollars)
   S = average airborne speed (miles per hour)
   I = measure of income (GNP per capita in constant dollars)
   N = U.S. population
   D = death rate per 100 million revenue passenger miles

In their study, Armstrong and Grohman compared the forecast obtained from the above model with qualitative forecasts and time-series forecasts. The above causal model was found to provide superior forecasts in this case.

Other forms of causal forecasting—econometric models, input-output models, and simulation models—are described in Table 3.5. In general, these models are more complex and more costly to develop than regression models. However, in situations where it is necessary to model a segment of the economy in detail, the econometric or input-output models may be appropriate.

Simulation models are especially useful when a distribution or logistics system is modeled for forecasting purposes. Chambers, Mullick, and Smith (1971) describe such a simulation model for forecasting the demand for TV picture tubes. In this case a simulation model was built representing the distribution pipeline from the glass tube manufacturer to the TV tube manufacturer to the TV set manufacturer and finally to wholesale and retail distribution chains; all imports, inventories, and exports from the system were included. Through the use of this model, a quite accurate forecast for glass TV tubes several years into the future was obtained.

One of the most important features of causal models is that they can be used to predict turning points in the demand function. In contrast, time-series models can be used only to predict the future demand pattern on the basis of the past; they cannot predict upturns and downturns in the demand level.

TABLE 3.5
CAUSAL FORECASTING METHODS

Causal methods	Description of method	Uses	Accuracy Short term	Accuracy Medium term	Accuracy Long term	Identification of turning point	Relative cost	References
1. Regression	This method relates demand to other external or internal variables which tend to cause demand changes. The method of regression uses least squares to obtain a best fit between the variables.	Short- to medium-range planning for aggregate production or inventory involving a few products. Useful where strong causal relationships exist.	Good to very good	Good to very good	Poor	Very good	Medium	Neter, Wasserman, and Whitmore
2. Econometric model	A system of interdependent regression equations that describes some sector of economic sales or profit activity.	Forecast of sales by product classes for short- to medium-range planning.	Very good to excellent	Very good	Good	Excellent	High	Huang
3. Input-output model	A method of forecasting which describes the flows from one sector of the economy to another. Predicts the inputs required to produce required outputs in another sector.	Forecasts of company- or countrywide sales by industrial sectors	Not available	Good to very good	Good to very good	Fair	Very high	Leontief
4. Simulation model	Simulation of the distribution system describing the changes in sales and flows of product over time. Reflects effects of the distribution pipeline.	Forecasts of companywide sales by major product groups.	Very good	Good to very good	Good	Good	High	Forrester, Chambers, et al.

Source: Reprinted by permission of the *Harvard Business Review*. Exhibit adapted from John C. Chambers, Satinder K. Mullick, and Donald D. Smith, "How to Choose the Right Forecasting Technique," July–August 1971, pp. 56–57; and David M. Georgoff and Robert Murdick, "Manager's Guide to Forecasting," *Harvard Business Review*, January–February 1986, pp. 110–120.

Because of this ability to predict turning points, causal models are usually more accurate than time-series models for medium- to long-range forecasts. Causal models are, therefore, more widely useful for facility and process planning in operations.

3.5 COMPUTERIZED FORECASTING SYSTEMS

Many computerized systems are available today to assist the manager and forecasting analyst. A few of these systems are briefly described below.

A program called CENSUS X-11 is available from the U.S. Census Bureau. It uses a moving-average method with trends and seasonal factors to decompose and forecast a time series. The CENSUS X-11 program has been found to be quite useful provided that a reasonable amount of historical data is available. See Shiskin, Young, and Musgrave (1967) for more details.

There is also a library of interactive computer forecasting programs called SIBYL/RUNNER; it contains over 20 of the most commonly used forecasting techniques. These programs are divided into those which assist in identifying the underlying patterns in the time series and those which forecast using a given pattern. A complete description is given by Makridakis and Wheelwright (1977).

The IBM MAPICS system for production and inventory control includes a forecasting module. [See IBM (1985).] This module utilizes an adaptive forecasting technique which adjusts for seasonality and trend. The module also computes the MAD and tracking signal as a basis for evaluating the forecasting error and resetting the forecasting method when needed. The forecasting methods were specifically designed to handle thousands of items typically encountered in a manufacturing environment.

The casual forecasting methods are quite well covered by standard statistical packages such a SPSS, SAS, and BMDP and many different microcomputer packages. These methods will, however, have to be substantially tailored to the individual situation.

3.6 SELECTING A FORECASTING METHOD

In this section we will present a framework for selecting from among qualitative, time-series, and causal methods. The framework is based in large part on the survey conducted by Wheelwright and Clarke (1976), who identified factors that companies consider important when they select a forecasting method. The most important of these factors are as follows:

1. *User and system sophistication.* How sophisticated are the managers who are expected to use the forecasting results? It has been found that the forecasting method must be matched to the knowledge and sophistication of the user. Generally speaking, managers are reluctant to use results from techniques they do not understand.

   Another, related factor is the status of forecasting systems currently in use.

Wheelwright and Clarke found that forecasting systems tend to evolve toward more mathematically sophisticated methods; they do not change in one grand step. So the method chosen must not be too advanced or sophisticated for its users or too far advanced beyond the current forecasting system. Furthermore, simpler models can sometimes perform better, so sophistication is not the ultimate goal. [See Makridakis, et. al. (1984).]

2. *Time and resources available.* The selection of a forecasting method will depend on the time available in which to collect the data and prepare the forecast. This may involve the time of users, forecasters, and data collectors. The preparation of a complicated forecast for which most of the data must be collected may take several months and cost thousands of dollars. For routine forecasts made by computerized systems, both the cost and the amount of time required may be very modest.

3. *Use or decision characteristics.* As was pointed out in the beginning of the chapter, the forecasting method must be related to the use or decisions required. The use, in turn, is closely related to such characteristics as accuracy required, time horizon of the forecast, and number of items to be forecast. For example, inventory and scheduling decisions require highly accurate short-range forecasts for a large number of items. Time-series methods are ideally suited to these requirements. On the other hand, decisions involving process and facility planning are long range in nature; they require less accuracy for, perhaps, a single estimate of total demand. Qualitative or causal methods tend to be more appropriate for those decisions. In the middle time range are aggregate planning and budgeting decisions which often utilize time-series or causal methods.

4. *Data availability.* The choice of forecasting method is often constrained by available data. An econometric model might require data which are simply not available in the short run; therefore another method must be selected. The Box-Jenkins time-series method requires about 60 data points (5 years of monthly data). The quality of the data available is also a concern. Poor data lead to poor forecasts. Data should be checked for extraneous factors or unusual points.

5. *Data pattern.* The pattern in the data will affect the type of forecasting method selected. If the time series is flat, as we have assumed in most of this chapter, a first-order method can be used. However, if the data show trends or seasonal patterns, more advanced methods will be needed. The pattern in the data will also determine whether a time-series method will suffice or whether causal models are needed. If the data pattern is unstable over time, a qualitative method may be selected. Thus the data pattern is one of the most important factors affecting the selection of a forecasting method. One way to detect the pattern is to plot the data on a graph. This should always be done as the first step in forecasting.

Another issue concerning the selection of forecasting methods is the difference between fit and prediction. When different models are tested, it is often thought that the model with the best fit to historical data (least error) is also the best predictive model. This is not true. For example, suppose demand observations are obtained over the last eight time periods and we want to fit the best time-series model to these data. A polynomial model of degree seven can be made to fit exactly through each of the past eight data points.[3] But this model is not necessarily the best predictor of the future.

The best predictive model is one which describes the underlying time series but is not "force fitted" to the data. The correct way to fit models based on past data is to separate model fit and model prediction. First, the data set is divided into two parts. Several models based on reasonable assumptions about seasonality, trend, and cycle are then fitted to the first data set. These models are used to predict values for the second data set, and the one with the lowest error on the second set is the best model. This approach utilizes fit on the first data set and prediction on the second as a basis for model selection.

Finally, an interesting question concerning model selection is the accuracy of qualitative human forecasting versus quantitative model-based forecasting. Ebert (1976) compared humans to models for a variety of underlying time-series demand patterns. He found that when the data included a great deal of random noise or nonlinear seasonal patterns, models did better than humans provided that care was taken in fitting the models. However, when simple (first-order) exponential models with an arbitrary value of α were used, the humans often performed better than the models. This research indicates that quantitative models do not always provide better forecasts than humans.

3.7 USING FORECASTS IN ORGANIZATIONS

Every forecasting method must be embedded in an organizational setting. However, some unusual things can happen to forecasts within their organizational contexts. First of all, forecasts are often passed from one manager or group to another through successive levels of the organization. In the process, these forecasts are sometimes modified or information is lost. This may stem from a lack of a clear distinction among goals, performance measures, and forecasts.

When sales forecasts are made by the marketing department, they are sometimes really goals rather than forecasts. These so-called sales forecasts are set on the high side in order to push salespeople on to greater achievement. Such "forecasts" cannot be used by operations as a basis for output or production planning because they are inspirational targets which will probably not be met.

On the other hand, sometimes performance measures are confused with forecasts. When performance measures are being set, it is customary for each manager up the line to reduce the so-called forecast slightly so that it can easily be met or even exceeded. The pessimistic forecasts that result will probably be exceeded at each level and are also not suitable for output planning by operations.

A forecast should be an unbiased projection of what we expect *will* happen. The forecast should not be confused with a plan, a goal, or a performance measure which indicates what we think *should* happen.

One way to avoid this problem is to ask that forecasts be based on probability. This can be done by producing a frequency distribution showing the likelihood of various forecast estimates. Another approach is to forecast pessimistic, most likely,

---

[3]The model would be $Y = a_1 + a_2t + a_3t^2 + \ldots + a_8t^7$, where t = time.

and optimistic demand values which can be defined in terms of percentiles: the pessimistic at the tenth percentile, the most likely at the fiftieth percentile, and the optimistic at the ninetieth percentile. When such a range of values is produced and transmitted through the organization, the confusion between what will happen and what should happen is greatly reduced.

Very few organizations routinely produce probability forecasts for demand. This stems from a failure to recognize uncertainty and to come to grips with the problem. If probability forecasts are produced, one can plan for contingencies and properly assess the risk inherent in a decision. Without such estimates, the plan cannot properly account for uncertainty or, worse yet, will be set at a medium or low level so that it can be exceeded.

A second issue in using forecasts in organizations is the question of who should make the forecasts. There are many possibilities—including marketing, operations, finance, a central corporate forecasting office, and various corporate or division levels depending on the size and type of organization.

Ideally, sales forecasts should be made by incorporating the best models and judgments available from all sources. All users should have an input to and knowledge of the assumptions behind the forecasts. The aggregate and individual forecasts should be additive, resulting in more coordinated planning by the various functions. The forecasting responsibility must also be carefully coordinated and monitored, because, otherwise, inflated inventories and missed delivery dates can result. When forecasting is really the driving force behind planning, it must be done by a coordinated organizational process. See Box 3.1 for an example of just such an approach.

3.8 KEY POINTS

Demand forecasts are crucial inputs to planning decisions within operations and other parts of business. In this chapter, we have highlighted several important uses and methods of forecasting. Some of the chapter's main points are the following:

- Different decisions require different forecasting methods, including the following decisions in operations: process design, capacity planning, and inventory management. The available methods may be classified as qualitative, time-series, and causal methods.
- Four of the most important qualitative methods are Delphi, market surveys, life cycle analogy, and informed judgment. These methods are most useful when historical data are not available or are not reliable in predicting the future. Qualitative methods are used primarily for long- or medium-range forecasting involving process design or facilities planning.
- Time-series forecasting is used to decompose demand data into their principal components and thereby to project the historical pattern forward in time. The primary uses are short- to medium-term forecasting for inventory and scheduling decisions. Some of the best-known time-series techniques are the moving average, exponential smoothing, mathematical models, and the Box-Jenkins method.

- Causal forecasting methods include regression, econometric models, input-output models, and simulation models. These methods attempt to establish a cause-and-effect relationship between demand and other variables. Causal methods can help in predicting turning points in time-series data and are therefore most useful for medium- to long-range forecasting.
- Two types of errors in forecasting are bias and deviation. Both these errors should be monitored routinely to control the accuracy of the forecasts obtained.
- A forecasting method should be selected on the basis of five factors: user and system sophistication, time and resources available, use or decision characteristics, data availability, and data pattern.
- In many organizations, different forecasts are made by different departments, and there is no coordinated planning. This may be caused by confusion about goals, plans, performance measures, and forecasts. To help overcome this confusion, probability forecasts can be used, and forecast errors should be monitored after the fact.

QUESTIONS

1. Is there a difference between forecasting demand and forecasting sales? Can demand be forecast from historical sales data?
2. What is the distinction between forecasting and planning? How can organizations become confused over forecasting when this distinction is not clear?
3. Define the terms "qualitative method," "time-series method," and "causal forecast."
4. It has been said that qualitative forecasting methods should be used only as a last resort. Comment.
5. Describe the uses of qualitative, time-series, and causal forecasts.
6. How could the Delphi method be used to predict, for 5 years into the future, the demand for hospital beds in a given community? Under what circumstances would you recommend use of the Delphi method?
7. It has been said that qualitative forecasts and causal forecasts are not particularly useful as inputs to inventory and scheduling decisions. Why is this statement true?
8. What type of time-series components would you expect for the following items?
   a. Monthly sales of a retail florist
   b. Monthly sales of milk in a supermarket
   c. Daily demand for telephone calls
   d. Monthly demand for newspapers
9. What are the advantages of exponential smoothing over the moving average and weighted moving average?
10. How should the choice of α be made for exponential smoothing?
11. Describe the difference between "fit" and "prediction" for forecasting models.
12. A request has gone out to all salespeople in a company to make forecasts for their sales territories for next year. These forecasts will be aggregated by product lines, districts, regions, and—finally—at the national level. Describe the problems in using this forecast for planning aggregate levels of operations for the next year and for specific inventory and scheduling decisions.
13. What are the advantages and disadvantages of preparing a probability forecast of demand?
14. In the Stokely Company, marketing makes a sales forecast each year by developing a

salesforce composite. Meanwhile, operations makes a forecast of sales based on past data, trends, and seasonal components. The operations forecast usually turns out to be an increase over last year but still 20 percent less than the forecast of the marketing department. How should forecasting in this company be done?

PROBLEMS

1. In the Atlanta area, the number of daily calls for repair of Speedy copy machines has been recorded as follows:

October	Calls
1	92
2	127
3	103
4	165
5	132
6	111
7	174
8	97

a. Prepare a three-period moving-average forecast for the data. What is the error on each day?
b. Prepare a three-period weighted-moving-average forecast using weights of $w_1 = .5$, $w_2 = .3$, $w_3 = .2$.
c. Which of these two forecasts is better?

2. The ABC Floral Shop sold the following number of geraniums during the last 2 weeks.

Day	Demand	Day	Demand
1	200	8	150
2	134	9	182
3	157	10	197
4	165	11	136
5	177	12	163
6	125	13	157
7	146	14	169

a. Calculate a forecast of the above demand using a three- and five-period moving average.
b. Plot these forecasts and the original data on graph paper.
c. Which of the above forecasts is the best? Why?

3. The Handy-Dandy Department Store had forecast sales of $110,000 for the last week. The actual sales turned out to be $125,000.
a. What is the forecast for this week, using exponential smoothing and $\alpha = .1$?
b. If sales this week turn out to be $120,000, what is the forecast for next week?

4. The Yummy Ice Cream Company projects the demand for ice cream using first-order exponential smoothing. Last week the forecast was 100,000 gallons of ice cream, and 80,000 gallons were actually sold.
a. Using $\alpha = .1$, prepare a forecast for next week.
b. Calculate the forecast using $\alpha = .2$ and $\alpha = .3$ for this problem. Which value of α gives the best forecast, assuming actual demand is 95,000 gallons?

5. Using the data in Problem 1, prepare exponentially smoothed forecasts for the following cases:
   a. $\alpha = .1$ and $F_1 = 90$
   b. $\alpha = .3$ and $F_1 = 90$
6. Compute the errors of bias and absolute deviation for the forecasts in Problem 5. Which of the forecasting models is the best?
7. At the ABC Floral Shop, an argument developed between two of the owners, Bob and Henry, over the accuracy of forecasting methods. Bob argued that first-order smoothing with $\alpha = .1$ would be the best method. Henry argued that the shop would get a better forecast with $\alpha = .3$.
   a. Using $F_1 = 100$ and the data from Problem 2, which of the two managers is right?
   b. Plot the two forecasts and the original data on graph paper.
   c. Maybe the forecast accuracy could be improved even more. Try additional values of $\alpha = .2, .4,$ and $.5$ to see if better accuracy is achieved.
8. A grocery store sells the following number of frozen turkeys over the 1-week period prior to Thanksgiving:

	Turkeys sold
Monday	80
Tuesday	55
Wednesday	65
Thursday	40
Friday	85
Saturday	105

   a. Prepare a forecast of sales for each day, starting with $F_1 = 85$ and $\alpha = .2$.
   b. Compute the MAD and the tracking signal for the data given above in each period. Use $MAD_0 = 0$.
   c. On the basis of the criteria given in the text, are the MAD and tracking signal within tolerances?
   d. Recompute parts a and b using $\alpha = .1, .3,$ and $.4$. Which value of α provides the best forecast?
9. The famous Widget Company uses simple exponential smoothing to forecast the demand for its best-selling widgets. The company is considering whether it should use $\alpha = .1$ or $\alpha = .4$ for forecasting purposes. Use the following data for daily sales to arrive at a recommendation.

Day	Demand	Day	Demand
1	35	8	39
2	47	9	24
3	46	10	26
4	39	11	36
5	26	12	43
6	33	13	46
7	24	14	29

a. For the first 7 days of data compare the absolute deviation for forecasts using $\alpha = .1$ and $\alpha = .4$. Start with $A_0 = 33$. Which method is best?

b. Use the second week of 7 days of data (days 8 to 14) to make the same comparison. Use $A_7 = 32$ for both methods. Which method is best now?

c. What does this example illustrate?

*10. Ace Hardware handles spare parts for lawn mowers. The following data were collected for one week in May when replacement lawn mower blades were in high demand.

Day	Demand
1	10
2	12
3	13
4	15
5	17
6	20
7	21

a. Simulate a forecast for the week, starting with $F_1 = 10$, $T_0 = 2$, $\alpha = .2$, and $\beta = .4$. Use the trend model given in the supplement.

b. Compute the MAD and tracking signal for the data. Use $MAD_0 = 0$.

c. Are the MAD and tracking signal within tolerances?

d. Simulate a forecast using simple smoothing for the week, starting with $F_1 = 10$ and $\alpha = .2$. Plot the forecast and the data on graph paper. Note how the forecast lags behind the data.

11. Ace Hardware also collected the following data on the total sales dollars generated by the store. The manager of the store would like to know if total sales are a good predictor of lawn-mower-blade sales.

Day	Total Sales
1	$10,000
2	13,000
3	14,000
4	16,000
5	19,000
6	20,000
7	22,000

a. Use regression to answer management's question. What percentage of the variance is explained by the equation? Is this a good fit?

b. Plot the forecast and the data on graph paper.

c. Compare the absolute deviation error from the regression equation to the error from Problem 10a. Which forecast is better?

12. The manager of Redline Trucking Company believes that the demand for tires used on his trucks is closely related to the number of miles driven. Accordingly, the following data covering the past 6 months have been collected.

---

*These problems require use of the supplement.

Month	Tires used	Thousands of miles driven
1	100	1500
2	150	2000
3	120	1700
4	80	1100
5	90	1200
6	180	2700

a. Calculate the coefficients a and b for the regression line.

b. What percentage of the variation in tire use can be explained by mileage driven?

c. Suppose we plan to drive 1,200,000 miles next month. What is the expected number of tires that will be used?

*13. The daily demand for chocolate donuts from the Donut-Hole Shop has been recorded for a 2-week period.

Day	Demand	Day	Demand
1	80	8	85
2	95	9	99
3	120	10	110
4	110	11	90
5	75	12	80
6	60	13	65
7	50	14	50

a. Simulate a forecast of the demand using trend-adjusted exponential smoothing. Use values of $A_0 = 90$, $T_0 = 25$, and $\alpha = \beta = .2$.

b. Plot the data and the forecast on a graph.

c. Does this appear to be a good model for the data?

*14. The SureGrip Tire Company produces tires of various sizes and shapes. The demand for tires tends to follow a quarterly seasonal pattern with a trend. For a particular type of tire the company's current estimates are as follows: $A_0 = 10,000$, $T_0 = 1,000$, $R_0 = .8$, $R_{-1} = 1.2$, $R_{-2} = 1.5$, and $R_{-3} = .75$.

a. The company has just observed the first quarter of demand $D_1 = 6000$ and would like to update its forecast for each of the next four quarters using $\alpha = \beta = \gamma = .4$.

b. When demand is observed for the second quarter, $D_2 = 15,000$. How much error was there in the forecast?

c. Update the forecasts again for the coming year, using the second-quarter demand data.

*15. Management feels there is a seasonal pattern in the above data for the Donut-Hole Shop, with the first 2 days of a week representing one level; the third and fourth days representing a second level; and the fifth, sixth, and seventh days a third level. Thus, three seasonal factors have been suggested: $R_0 = .9$, $R_{-1} = 1.3$, and $R_{-2} = .8$.

a. Simulate a forecast of demand for days 1 to 7 using $A_0 = 85$, $T_0 = 0$, and $\alpha = \beta = \gamma = .1$. Use Winters's method from the supplement to this chapter.

b. Comment on the appropriateness of the forecasts developed.

*These problems require use of the supplement.

*16. Management of the ABC Floral Shop feels that its sales are seasonal in nature with a monthly seasonal pattern and no trend. The demand data and seasonal ratios for the past 3 years are given below.

Month	Year 1 Demand	Year 2 Demand	Year 3 Demand	Seasonal Ratio
Jan.	$12,400	$11,800	$13,600	0.8
Feb.	23,000	24,111	21,800	1.8
Mar.	15,800	16,500	14,900	0.9
Apr.	20,500	21,000	19,400	1.6
May	25,100	24,300	26,000	2.0
June	16,200	15,800	16,500	1.0
July	12,000	11,500	12,400	0.7
Aug.	10,300	10,100	10,800	0.6
Sept.	11,800	11,000	12,500	0.7
Oct.	14,000	14,300	13,800	1.2
Nov.	10,700	10,900	10,600	0.9
Dec.	7,600	7,200	8,100	0.6

a. Calculate a forecast for the past year using $A_0 = 15,000$, $\alpha = \gamma = .3$, and the seasonal ratios shown above. For each period calculate the forecast and the updated seasonal ratio.

b. Plot the original data and the forecast on graph paper.

c. Calculate the tracking signal and $MAD_0 = 0$. Are they within tolerances?

d. Using the classical decomposition method described in the supplement, calculate the seasonal ratios from the data, and determine the trend and average levels. Use these ratios and estimates of trend and level to make a forecast for the next year.

SELECTED BIBLIOGRAPHY

ADAM, EVERETT E., JR.: "Individual Item Forecasting Model Evaluation," *Decision Sciences*, vol. 4, October 1973, pp. 458–470.

ARMSTRONG, J. SCOTT, and MICHAEL C. GROHMAN: "A Comparative Study of Methods for Long-Range Market Forecasting," *Management Science*, vol. 19, no. 2, October 1972, pp. 211–221.

BARRETT, RICHARD B., and DAVID J. KITSKA: "Forecasting System at Rubbermaid," *The Journal of Business Forecasting*, Spring 1987, pp. 7–9.

BASS, FRANK M., CHARLES W. KING, and EDGAR A. PESSEMEIER (eds.): *Applications of the Sciences in Marketing Management*, New York: Wiley, 1968.

BASU, SHANKAR, and ROGER G. SCHROEDER: "Incorporating Judgements in Sales Forecasts: Application of the Delphi Method at American Hoist & Derrick," *Interfaces*, vol. 7, no. 3, May 1977, pp. 18–27.

BOX, G. E. P., and G. M. JENKINS: *Time Series Analysis, Forecasting, and Control*, San Francisco: Holden-Day, 1970.

BROWN, R. G.: *Smoothing, Forecasting and Prediction*, Englewood Cliffs, N.J.: Prentice-Hall, 1963.

CHAMBERS, JOHN C., SATINDER K. MULLICK, and DONALD D. SMITH: "How to Choose the Right Forecasting Technique," *Harvard Business Review*, July–August 1971, pp. 45–74.

CHOW, W. M.: "Adaptive Control of the Exponential Smoothing Constant," *Journal of Industrial Engineering*, September–October 1965.

*These problems require use of the supplement.

EBERT, RONALD J.: "A Comparison of Human and Statistical Forecasting," *AIIE Transactions*, vol. 8, no. 1, March 1976, pp. 120–127.

FORRESTER, JAY W.: *Industrial Dynamics*, Cambridge, Mass.: M.I.T. Press, 1961.

GEORGOFF, DAVID M., and ROBERT MURDICK: "Manager's Guide to Forecasting," *Harvard Business Review*, January–February 1986, pp. 110–120.

HUANG, D.S.: *Regression and Econometric Methods*, New York: Wiley, 1970.

IBM: "Forecasting Reference Manual, IBM System/36 MAPICS Version 2," January 1985.

LEONTIEF, WASSILY W.: *Input-Output Statistics*, New York: Oxford University Press, 1966.

MAKRIDAKIS, SPYROS: *Handbook of Forecasting*, 2d ed., New York, Wiley, 1987.

———, ———, and STEVEN WHEELWRIGHT: *Interactive Forecasting*, San Francisco: Holden-Day, 1977.

———, ———, and VICTOR E. McGEE: *Forecasting: Methods and Applications*, 2d ed., New York: Wiley, 1983.

——— et al.: *The Forecasting Accuracy of Major Time Series Methods*, New York: Wiley, 1984.

NELSON, CHARLES L.: *Applied Time Series Analysis*, San Francisco: Holden-Day, 1973.

NETER, JOHN, WILLIAM WASSERMAN, and G. A. WHITMORE: *Fundamental Statistics for Business & Economics*, 4th ed., Boston: Allyn & Bacon, 1973.

NORTH, HARPER Q., and DONALD PYKE: "Probes of the Technological Future," *Harvard Business Review*, May–June 1969, pp. 68–82.

RAINE, J. E.: "Self-Adaptive Forecasting Reconsidered," *Decision Sciences*, vol. 2, no. 2, April 1971, pp. 181–191.

SHISKIN, JULIUS, ALLAN H. YOUNG, and JOHN MUSGRAVE: "The X-11 Variant of the Census Method II Seasonal Adjustment Program," Bureau of the Census, Technical Paper no. 15, February 1967.

SPENCER, MILTON H., COLIN G. CLARK, and PETER W. HOGUET: *Business & Economic Forecasting*, Homewood, Ill.: Irwin, 1961.

THOMOPOULOS, NICK T.: *Applied Forecasting Methods*, Englewood Cliffs, N.J.: Prentice-Hall, 1980.

TRIGG, D.W., and A. G. LEACH: "Exponential Smoothing with an Adaptive Response Rate," *Operational Research Quarterly*, vol. 18, no. 1, March 1967, pp. 53–59.

WHEELWRIGHT, STEVEN, and DARRAL G. CLARKE: "Corporate Forecasting: Promise and Reality," *Harvard Business Review*, November–December 1976, pp. 40–60.

——— and SPYROS MAKRIDAKIS: *Forecasting Methods for Management*, 4th ed., New York: Wiley, 1985.

WHYBARK, D. C.: "A Comparison of Adaptive Forecasting Techniques," *The Logistics and Transportation Review*, vol. 8, no. 3, 1972, pp. 13–26.

WILKINSON, GARY F.: "If Only We Could Get Accurate Forecasts," *The Journal of Business Forecasting*, Winter 1986–1987, pp. 2–4.

WINTERS, PETER R.: "Forecasting Sales by Exponentially Weighted Moving Averages," *Management Sciences*, April 1960, pp. 324–342.

SUPPLEMENT
Advanced Methods

This supplement describes three additional methods for time-series forecasting which have trend and seasonal components. These methods are extensions of the techniques described in Section 3.3.

When the time-series model has a trend component, an exponential smoothing model can be developed which is based on updating two variables in each time period, an average level and a trend. The average level is computed as an expanded version of the first-order equation to include trend, as follows:

$$A_t = \alpha D_t + (1 - \alpha)(A_{t-1} + T_{t-1})$$

This average is then, in turn, used to update the estimate of trend by taking the difference in averages and smoothing this difference with the old trend. The updated trend is thus

$$T_t = \beta(A_t - A_{t-1}) + (1 - \beta)T_{t-1}$$

In this case, the smoothing constant β, which can be the same as or different from the constant α used for level, is used for trend. The model requires initial estimates of A_0 and T_0 to get started. These estimates can be based either on judgment or on past data.

Using the above values, we can compute forecasts for the future. The procedure is now slightly different from the first-order case, because a constant trend is assumed in the time series. The

forecast for period $t + K$ in the future is therefore

$$F_{t+K} + A_t + KT_t \qquad K = 1, 2, 3, \ldots$$

One unit of trend is added for each period into the future. An example using these formulas is shown in Table S3.1.

Time series having both trend and seasonal components can be forecast by a method developed by Winters (1960). In this case three variables—average, trend, and a seasonal factor—are updated for each time period.

The average is computed for period t as follows:

$$A_t = \alpha\left(\frac{D_t}{R_{t-L}}\right) + (1 - \alpha)(A_{t-1} + T_{t-1})$$

In this case the demand is adjusted by the seasonal ratio and smoothed with the old average and old trend. The trend for period t is

$$T_t = \beta(A_t - A_{t-1}) + (1 - \beta)T_{t-1}$$

The seasonal ratio for period t is

$$R_t = \gamma\left(\frac{D_t}{A_t}\right) + (1 - \gamma)R_{t-L}$$

In this case we are assuming that the seasonal cycle is L periods. There are L seasonal ratios, one for each period. If the demand is monthly and the seasonal cycle repeats on an annual basis, then $L =$

TABLE S3.1
TREND-ADJUSTED EXPONENTIAL SMOOTHING*

t	D_t (demand)	A_t (average)	T_t (trend)	F_t (forecast)	$D_t - F_t$ (error)
1	85	85	15	85	0
2	105	100.5	15.05	100	5.00
3	112	115.2	15.01	115.55	−3.55
4	132	130.4	15.03	130.21	1.79
5	145	145.4	15.03	145.43	−.43

*Assume $A_0 = 70$, $T_0 = 15$, $\alpha = .1$, $\beta = .1$.

81

12. Each month, one of the seasonal ratios will be updated to a new value, along with the trend and average.

The model requires initial estimates of A_0, T_0, and R_0, R_{-1}, . . . , R_{-L+1}. These initial estimates can be based on judgment or data, if available.

Using the updated values, the forecast for future periods in period t is

$$F_{t+K} = (A_t + KT_t)(R_{t-L+K})$$

An example of this method is shown in Table S3.2.

If there is no trend, Winters's method can also be used with seasonal factors alone. In this case, the above trend equation and T_t values are simply dropped from the method.

One of the techniques used frequently in time-series forecasting is classical decomposition. This involves decomposing a time series into level, trend, seasonal, and possibly cyclic components. Decomposition will be illustrated by means of an example with 3 years of quarterly data from a store that sells children's toys. It is assumed that the seasonal pattern is quarterly in nature, and there may be trend and level components in the data as well. Since only 3 years of data are available, no cyclic component will be estimated.

The quarterly data on the sales of toys are shown in Table S3.3. The biggest sales of toys, by far, are in the fourth quarter, at Christmas time. Visual inspection of the data indicates an upward trend, but how can this trend be disentangled from the seasonality of the data? This is done by first computing a four-quarter moving average. Decomposition requires the same number of periods in the moving average as the seasonality of the data (i.e., four periods for quarterly seasonality, twelve periods for monthly seasonality). This is done to average out the high periods and the low periods of demand over the seasonal cycle. The four-period moving average is shown in the third column of Table S3.3. These moving averages are centered between periods, because a four-period average should represent a point with two periods on each side. From column 3, the upward trend is clear, because the seasonality has been removed from the data.

In order to calculate seasonal ratios, we need an average for each period. This is done in column 4 of Table S3.3 by constructing a two-period moving average of column 3. These new averages are then once again centered on the periods of data instead of in between periods. Column 4 then represents the best average of the data for estimating the trend. It is also used to calculate seasonal ratios directly by dividing sales by column 4 to produce the seasonal ratios in column 5. Interpretation of these ratios is as follows: demand in the third quarter is 95.8 percent of the annual average, demand in the fourth quarter is 170.9 percent of the yearly average, and so on. To obtain a best estimate of the seasonal ratios we simply average the ratios for corresponding quarters. This calculation is shown on the bottom of Table S3.3. Note that the seasonal ratios are quite stable in this example, but we have a minimal amount of data to work with. Ordinarily, at least 4 years of data should be used to establish seasonal ratios.

The original sales data and the deseasonalized moving average, from column 4, are plotted in Figure S3.1. The moving average indicates an upward trend line. Actually, the trend might be slightly nonlinear, but let us assume for this example a linear trend line. Then a regression line can be fitted through the eight moving-average points shown on the graph. The result is

TABLE S3.2

THE WINTERS SEASONAL EXPONENTIAL SMOOTHING METHOD*

t	D_t (demand)	A_t (average)	T_t (trend)	R_t (seasonal ratio)	F_t (forecast)	$D_t + F_t$ (error)
1	66	80.5	10.1	.804	64	2.0
2	106	90.1	10.0	1.195	108.7	+2.7
3	78	99.5	9.9	.799	80.4	+2.4
4	135	110.1	10.0	1.201	130.7	4.3

*Assume $A_0 = 70$, $T_0 = 10$, $L = 2$, $R_{-1} = .8$, $R_0 = 1.2$, $\alpha = .2$, $\beta = .2$, $\gamma = .2$.

TABLE S3.3
CLASSICAL DECOMPOSITION METHOD

Quarter	Sales*	Four-Period Moving Average	Two-Period Moving Average	Seasonal Ratio
1	30			
2	42	56.75	57.4	.958
3	55	58	58.5	1.709
4	100	59	59.5	.588
5	35	60	62.5	.736
6	46	65	66.0	.894
7	59	67	68.4	1.754
8	120	69.75	71.3	.603
9	43	72.75	75.5	.755
10	57	78.25		
11	71			
12	142			

Seasonal Ratios Quarter			
1	**2**	**3**	**4**
		.958	1.709
.588	.736	.894	1.754
.603	.755		
Av. .596	.746	.926	1.732

*Sales are in thousands of dollars.

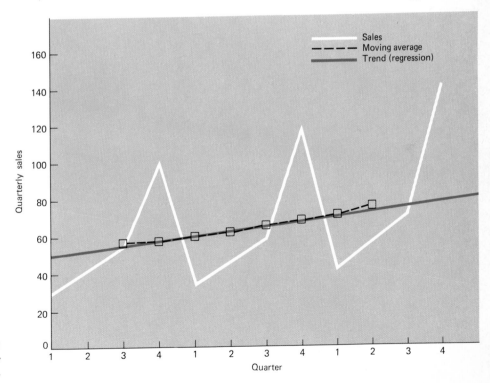

FIGURE S3.1
Seasonal toy
sales.

$$Y(t) = 47.8 + 2.63t$$

where $Y(t)$ = sales and t = time.

A trend line could also be fitted to the original sales data, but it is customary in classical decomposition to use moving averages before fitting the trend line. This seems to give a slightly more stable forecast.

In order to forecast sales for the coming year, the following method is used. First, use the trend-line equation to predict the average for quarters 13, 14, 15, and 16 by plugging these values of time into the above regression equation. This yields column 2 in Table S3.4. Then multiply the seasonal ratio for each quarter by the predicted average. The result is a forecast for each quarter of the next year, as shown in Table S3.4.

TABLE S3.4
SEASONAL FORECAST CALCULATIONS

Quarter	Predicted Average	×	Seasonal Factor	=	Forecast
13	82.0		.596		48.8
14	84.6		.746		63.1
15	87.2		.926		80.7
16	89.9		1.732		155.7

CHAPTER 4
Product Design

New-product design is crucial to the survival of most firms. While a few firms experience little product change, most firms must continually revise their products. In fast-changing industries, new-product introduction is a way of life, and highly sophisticated approaches have been developed to introduce new products.

Product design is seldom the sole responsibility of the operations function, but operations is greatly affected by new-product introduction and vice versa. Operations is on the "receiving end" of new-product introduction. At the same time, new products are constrained by existing operations and technology. Therefore, it is extremely important to understand the new-product design process and its interactions with operations.

In this chapter we will be concentrating primarily on the design of manufactured products. A product can be defined, however, as the output of the operations function—either a good or service. Service design issues will be discussed later, in Chapter 6.

Product decisions affect each of the five decision-making areas of operations. Therefore product decisions should be closely coordinated with operations—to

ensure that operations is integrated with product design. Through close cooperation between operations and marketing, the market and product strategy can be
integrated with decisions regarding process, capacity, inventory, work force, and
quality.

Product definition is the result of the development of a business strategy. For
example, the business strategy might call for a full product line to serve a
particular set of customers. As a result, new products are defined to fill out the
product line. These new-product definitions then become an input into the
operations strategy, and operations decisions are adjusted to fit the new-product
strategy. By taking an active role from the beginning, operations can assume an
externally supportive, stage IV, role in terms of its operations strategy and decision
making. Box 4.1 illustrates new-product introduction decisions which were faced
by the Dorsey Corporation.

Product design is a prerequisite for production, along with a forecast of
production volume. The result of the product design decision is transmitted to
operations as product specifications. These specifications state the desired characteristics of the product and allow production to proceed.

This chapter is divided into three major parts. First, there is a discussion of a
new-product design process. The view presented is that product design is
interfunctional in nature and requires a great deal of cooperation between
organizational functions. The second part of the chapter presents a model of
product-process interaction which stresses the important relationship of product
and process design. In the third part, product variety and the effect of multiple
products on operations are discussed.

STRATEGIES FOR NEW-PRODUCT INTRODUCTION

There are three fundamental ways to view the new-product introduction process:
it may be seen as market-pull, technology-push, or interfunctional in nature.

1. *Market-pull.* According to this view, "You should make what you can sell." In
   this case, new products are determined by the market with little regard to existing
   technology and operations processes. Customer needs are the primary (or only)
   basis for new-product introduction. One can determine the types of new products
   which are needed through market research or customer feedback. These products
   are then produced.

2. *Technology-push.* This approach would suggest that "You should sell what you
   can make." Accordingly, new products should be derived from production
   technology, with little regard for the market. It is marketing's job to create a
   market and to "sell" the products that are made. This view is dominated by
   vigorous use of technology and simplicity of operations changes. Through
   aggressive R&D and operations, superior products are created which have a
   "natural" advantage in the marketplace.

3. *Interfunctional.* In this view, new-product introduction is interfunctional in
   nature and requires cooperation among marketing, operations, engineering, and

BOX 4.1
DORSEY CORPORATION

Nathaniel C. Wyeth, one of Dupont's engineers, developed in 1968, a 2-liter bottle made of a resin known as PET, polyethylene terephthalate. This development was a major break for the consumers of 2-liter containers. The PET 2-liter container was 11 times lighter than its glass counterpart. This significantly reduced the materials handling costs along the entire distribution chain. It also increased customer satisfaction since it was easier for the customer to transport the bottle. A second major advantage was the product's shatterproof quality. It was estimated that more than 20,000 serious injuries had resulted each year from breaking or exploding glass. And, finally, the 2-liter PET bottle was cheaper than glass. The product's limitations were that it could not protect its contents on an indefinite basis and it did not have the aesthetic appeal of glass.

In 1977, Charles K. Sewell and John T. Pollock convinced the board at the Dorsey Corporation that they should back their Sewell Plastics Division in a venture to start producing the 2-liter PET bottle. By this time the bottle had received approval from the FDA, and a machine for mass-producing the product had been developed by Cincinnati Milacron. Charles Sewell decided to purchase the machines from Cincinnati Milacron even though the bottle produced by this machine did not produce a one-piece bottle. Instead, the bottle required a base cap to be attached for support. Sewell purchased the machines from Cincinnati Milacron because he felt that in a commodity-type market it was critical to move quickly in order to establish a competitive advantage against his company's formidable opponents.

Continental Group, one of Sewell's major competitors, decided to develop their own methods for creating a one-piece bottle rather than use the available technology that produced a two-piece bottle. The development process took 2 years, which was costly in terms of market share. Continental Group had 1.6 percent of the market while Dorsey had 28 percent of the market.

Dorsey's market share was not only a result of getting into the market early. It was also attributable to their efforts to modify the product design in a manner that would result in lower unit costs without forfeiting customer satisfaction. They were able to make advances in reducing the amount of raw materials used for each unit, thus reducing the cost of producing the unit. In addition, they were able to expand the number of industries using their container.

Dorsey was not as successful with their moves into the 1-liter and the half-liter markets. They jumped into the market with the purchase of $4 million worth of 1-liter machines and six half-liter machines before they had assessed the product's ability to be competitive in the container market. In the 1-liter market, the demand for containers was decreasing. In the half-liter market the characteristics of PET made the use of glass for the small beverage container financially desirable. It was 10 to 20 percent cheaper to make the half-liter container out of plastic encapsulated glass rather than PET.

Abstracted from Edward Boyer, "Turning Glass to Plastic to Gold," *Fortune*, April 4, 1983, pp. 172–176.

The factory designs a swing for the children.

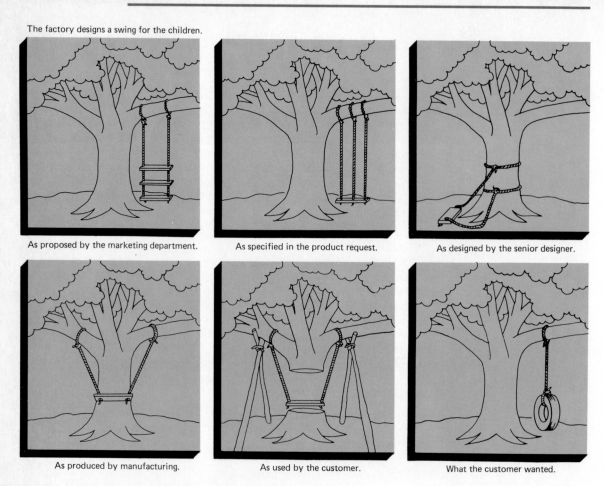

As proposed by the marketing department.   As specified in the product request.   As designed by the senior designer.

As produced by manufacturing.   As used by the customer.   What the customer wanted.

FIGURE 4.1   Lack of cooperation in designing a swing.

other functions. The new-product development process is neither market-pull nor technology-push but determined by a coordinated effort between functions. The result should be products which meet customer needs while utilizing technology to the best advantage.

The interfunctional view usually produces the best results. [See Souder (1977).] It is also the most difficult approach to implement because of interfunctional rivalry and friction. In many cases, special organizational mechanisms, such as matrix designs or task forces, are used to integrate diverse organizational elements. The result of a lack of interfunctional cooperation is shown in Figure 4.1.

NEW-PRODUCT DEVELOPMENT PROCESS

Regardless of the organizational approach used for new-product development, the steps followed in developing new products are usually the same. Figure 4.2 is an idealized model of the new-product development process, which consists of the six steps described below.

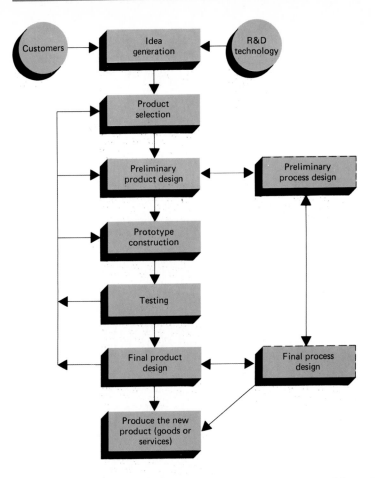

FIGURE 4.2
New-product
development
process.

1. *Idea generation.* As noted above, ideas can be generated from the market or from technology. Market ideas are derived from customer needs. For example, there might be a need for a new breakfast food which is nutritional and still good to eat or for a new type of house paint which does not peel. Identification of market needs can then lead to the development of new technologies and products to meet those needs.

   On the other hand, ideas can spring from available or new technology. When nylon was invented by Du Pont, a whole range of new products was made possible. Examples of other technologies which have spawned new products are involving plastics, semiconductors, integrated circuits, computers, and microwaves. Exploitation of technology is a rich source of ideas for new products.

2. *Product selection.* Not all new ideas should be developed into new products. New-product ideas need to meet at least three tests: (1) market potential, (2) financial feasibility, and (3) operations compatibility. Before a new-product idea is put into preliminary design, it should be subjected to analysis organized around these three tests.

   The purpose of product selection analysis is to identify the best ideas, not to reach a conclusive decision to market and produce the product. After initial development, more extensive analysis may be conducted through test markets and pilot operations before a final decision is made to introduce the product. Thus product selection analysis may be quite subjective in nature and based on somewhat limited information.

To assist in product analysis, several methods have been developed. One is a checklist scoring method that involves developing a list of factors along with a weight for each. Each factor is rated on a scale, and a total weighted score is computed. If the total score is above a certain minimum level, the new-product idea may be selected for further development. Alternatively, the method may be used to rank products in priority order for selection. An example of this type of scoring is given in Table 4.1.

A new-product idea may also be subjected to standard financial analysis by computing an approximate return on investment. To do this, cash flows must be estimated for investments, revenues, and costs for future product sales. In the early stages of product development, cash flows will be difficult, if not impossible, to estimate with any reasonable amount of accuracy because of the extreme uncertainty in market acceptance, volumes, revenues, and costs. Nevertheless, estimates should be made at the earliest possible time to get a feel for a product's financial prospects. These estimates can be updated as more information becomes available. Methods for calculating internal rates of return and present values from cash flows are covered in the supplement to Chapter 7.

3. *Preliminary product design.* This stage of product design process is concerned with developing the best design for the new-product idea. If the preliminary design is approved, a prototype or prototypes may be built for further testing and analysis. In preliminary design, a great number of tradeoffs between cost, quality, and product performances are considered. The result should be a product design which is competitive in the marketplace and producible by operations. These design goals are, of course, exceedingly difficult to meet.

As a result of product selection, only the bare bones of a product will be

TABLE 4.1
PRODUCT SELECTION BY CHECKLIST

Product characteristics	Poor	Fair	Good	Very good	Excellent	Weight
Selling price		✔				15%
Product quality				✔		10%
Sales volume			✔			20%
Operations compatability	✔					10%
Competitive advantage				✔		10%
Technical risk		✔				15%
Fit with corporate strategy				✔		20%
						100%

Each rating in the table is valued as follows: poor = 1, fair = 2, good = 3, very good = 4, and excellent = 5. The total weighted product score is computed as follows: total score = .15 (2) + .10 (4) + .20 (3) + .10 (1) + .10 (4) + .15 (2) + .20 (4) = 2.9. In this formula the weights have been multiplied by the product characteristic scores and added.

defined. Preliminary product design must then specify the product completely. For example, suppose that a new CB radio is to be designed because the product selection phase has identified a weakness in the existing products on the market. It is thought that a radio with top-of-the-line performance can be designed for a middle-of-the-line price by incorporating new advances in miniature electronics. If such a radio can be built, it will lend considerable strength to marketing efforts. This is the extent of the information available at the end of the product selection phase.

During preliminary design of the radio, a great number of tradeoff decisions will be made. The radio will contain many components, and each of them has cost-performance tradeoff features. Furthermore, size may be a problem assuming the radio must eventually fit into a small housing. During preliminary design, all tradeoff decisions should be based on the design objective: a medium-priced radio with top-of-the-line performance. As part of preliminary design, the radio will probably be built in a laboratory to test the integration and performance of the circuits. If these tests are successful, drawings of the preliminary design will be made.

4. *Prototype construction.* Prototype construction can take many different forms. First of all, several prototypes which closely resemble the final product may be made by hand. For example, the auto industry regularly makes clay models of new automobiles.

In the service industry, a prototype may be a single site where the service concept can be tested in actual use. Service can be modified, if necessary, to better meet customer needs. When the prototype has been tested successfully, the final design can be finished and the service franchised or developed on a large-scale basis.

Ray Kroc, the owner of McDonald's restaurants, started with a prototype restaurant in San Bernardino, California. It was characterized by a very clean appearance, the original red and white colors, the limited menu, low prices, and so on. Kroc closely duplicated this facility as the McDonald's franchise began to expand. The original restaurant was, in effect, a prototype service installation.

5. *Testing.* Testing of prototypes is aimed at verifying marketing and technical performance. One way to assess market performance is to build enough prototypes to support a test market for the new product. Test markets typically last from 6 months to 2 years and are limited to a small geographical region. The purpose of a test market is to gather quantitative data on customer acceptance of the product.

Prototypes are also tested for technical product performance. For example, all new military aircraft are tested by use of prototypes. Up to six prototype planes may be built and tested extensively before management approves the final production design. Engineering changes initiated as a result of prototype testing are then incorporated into the final design package.

6. *Final Product Design.* During the final design phase, drawings and specifications for the product are developed. As a result of prototype testing, certain changes may be incorporated into the final design. If changes are made, the product may be tested further to ensure final product performance. Attention will then focus on completing the design specifications so that production can proceed.

But R&D should not only develop design specifications for operations. An information package should be developed to ensure that the product is producible. This information package should contain details concerning process technology, quality control data, testing procedures for product performance, and the like. All too often, product design ends with a set of specs and nothing more.

4.3 DISCUSSION OF THE NEW-PRODUCT DEVELOPMENT PROCESS

The process of new-product development described thus far can be thought of as a funnel or filter. A great many ideas originate at the beginning, but only a few are successfully introduced to the market as products; see Figure 4.3.

David Uman has depicted this process of elimination graphically in Figure 4.4. His study of the mortality of new-product ideas in 51 companies indicates that only 1 out of 60 new-product ideas results in a successful product. The greatest reduction, however, takes place before preliminary product design begins. Thus, one must place great weight on the initial product selection phase and the associated analysis.

It should be noted that new-product design can result in a good deal of iteration between stages. For example, prototype testing may require a return to the preliminary design phase or to prototype construction. In actual practice, the new-product design process does not proceed sequentially from beginning to end; some steps may be skipped, and others may be repeated several times.

The production process should be designed in parallel with the new product. Figure 4.2 shows preliminary process design and a final process design which are developed simultaneously with the corresponding stages of product design. This implies that process design should not wait until product design is completed but that process design should be developed as part of the product design process.

Sometimes in practice, process design follows product design. When this

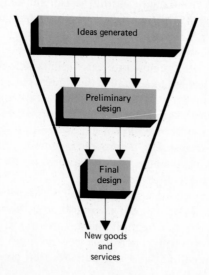

FIGURE 4.3
The new-product
filtering process.

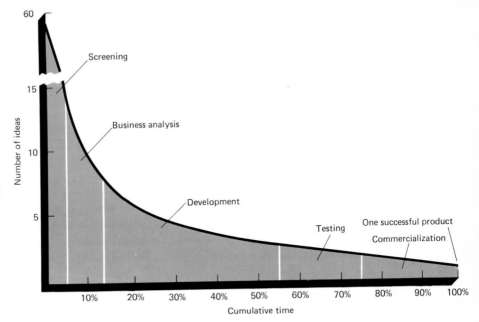

FIGURE 4.4
Mortality of
new-product
ideas.
Source: David B.
Uman, New-Product
Programs: Their
Planning and
Control, *New York:*
American
Management
Association, 1969,
p. 67.

happens, a product which is costly or impossible to produce may result. This is one reason why operations personnel should be involved in product design from the start. In this way, process design and product design can proceed together.

If communications between functions have been effective, a production process will be designed which is effective, efficient, and sufficiently flexible for future operations. Also, good communications should allow the product to be put into production faster than a design approach where process design follows product design.

New technology is radically affecting the new-product introduction process. Computer-aided design (CAD) and computer-aided manufacturing (CAM), as described in Chapter 7, will allow firms to dramatically speed up the design of products and to make them more producible from the start. The new technology will also provide a flexible production process, so that modifications can be more easily made. This will allow the firm to "make a little, sell a little," and then adjust the product before making a little more. Many more options and varieties of products can also be made through flexible technology, as customer needs change. This computerized technology, however, will not overcome the substantial organizational problems which must be solved. These organizational problems can only be handled by greater interfunctional cooperation or by changes in the organizational structure itself, as described below.

International competition is also affecting product design. Today, products must be designed for global markets from the start. In the past, products were designed for domestic markets and then modified later for export. Today's products, such as autos, electronics, and machine tools, are designed for global markets from the beginning. This means that different manufacturing plants around the world will be making the same product. Worldwide product design will be controlled from a single location.

4.4 TECHNOLOGY DEVELOPMENT PROCESS

Dorothy Leonard-Barton (1987) has identified the technology development process as one of frequent misalignment. No matter how excellent the advanced planning, or the technology, misalignment between the product design and operations is a common occurrence. On the basis of her study of 10 comprehensive cases, Leonard-Barton identifies three types of misalignments: misalignments in technology, infrastructure, and reward systems.

Technology misalignment occurs when the product designed by R&D cannot be made by operations. This occurs when technologies are new or unproven or not well understood. Operations can also have an infrastructure which is misaligned with the new product in terms of labor skills, control systems, quality assurance, and organization. Finally, reward systems might reinforce the use of current technology rather than the new processes needed.

To overcome these problems in technology development, a simultaneous R&D, production, and marketing approach has been suggested. The traditional approach proceeds in stages or steps as shown in part *a* of Figure 4.5. It is assumed that technology will be transferred in stages, as a handoff, between R&D, operations, and marketing. This is a sequential process, with each function completing its work before the next one starts.

Figure 4.5*b* illustrates a simultaneous development process. All functions are involved from the beginning, frequently by forming a new-product development team, as soon as development is started. In the first stage, R&D has the major effort, but other functions also have a role. After the product is designed, R&D reduces its effort, but not to zero, while operations has the major role. Finally, sales picks up the lead as the new product is launched into the market. The traditional approach is more like a relay race, while the simultaneous approach is like rugby. In a relay race, each runner picks up the baton for one portion of the race. In rugby the entire team runs down the field together, pushing and shoving in a group, to advance the ball toward the goal.

Peters and Waterman (1982) have noted that the excellent companies do not

FIGURE 4.5
Technology
transfer.

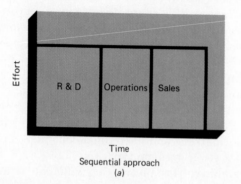

Time
Sequential approach
(*a*)

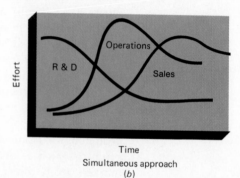

Time
Simultaneous approach
(*b*)

attempt to excessively plan and control innovation. They tend to establish autonomous teams that have significant latitude and authority to reach new-product goals established by management. These teams are allowed to take risks, they learn by doing, and there is much trial and error. This approach provides a high degree of tolerance for ambiguity.

Imai, Nonaka, and Takeuchi (1984) point out the important role that suppliers play in technology transfer. Suppliers should be included early and consulted regularly in problem solving for new designs. Suppliers can provide valuable knowledge that the firm does not have.

These authors also view technology transfer as a learning process. Learning should take place in all functions as the new product is introduced. Learning, rather than planning, is the dominant form of activity. In addition, the firm must unlearn its old ways so that the new product can be accepted. Operations is viewed not only as a production system, but as a social system and learning system as well.

Not all technologies should be developed by means of autonomous teams. Large, complex innovations require the use of elaborate project planning and control systems in addition to the use of teams. The single inventor and entrepreneur still has a role, especially in small companies where one person can call the shots. New-product introduction teams are best in medium-size and large bureaucratic companies where interfunctional cooperation is typically weak.

4.5 INTERACTION BETWEEN PRODUCT AND PROCESS DESIGN

We have been discussing the process of new-product development prior to initial production. But products are also developed or changed during their product life cycle; this might be called product redesign. This section focuses on the product innovation process after initial product introduction, with special emphasis on the nature of product and process interaction.

Products in use are continually being subjected to redesign and innovation. Good examples are automobiles, telephones, and appliances. William Abernathy has studied this phenomenon of product and process innovation. As a result of these studies, Abernathy and Townsend (1975) have suggested that product-process innovation typically follows three stages.

Stage I. The early life of products is characterized by constant change brought about by uncertain market conditions and technological advances. The production process is typically suited to low volume, and it is "uncoordinated" in nature. Typically, the product is made on general-purpose equipment which can be changed as the product changes. The situation for both product and process can best be described as fluid. The rates of product and process innovation are high, and there is great product diversity among competitors. The production process itself is largely uncoordinated between various operations. Bottlenecks and excess capacity result from the lack of a stable product flow. Decisions in operations are oriented toward the flexibility objective in this stage.

While we often think in terms of physical products, the situation is similar for services. For example, consider the high rate of initial innovation in health maintenance organizations, no-fault auto insurance, and fast-food chains. In these cases both the product and the process were initially in a highly fluid state.

Stage II. As development takes place, price competition becomes more intense. Operations managers respond by becoming more cost-conscious. The result is better integration of product flow, more specialized tasks, greater automation, and better production planning and control. The process is best characterized at this stage by the term "islands of mechanization." Some subprocesses may become highly automated with specific process equipment while others continue to rely on general-purpose equipment. Such automation cannot occur, however, until the product line is mature enough to have sufficient volume and at least a few stable product designs. This stage might best be described by the phrase "product and process standardization with increasing automation."

Stage III. As the product reaches maturity, competition becomes even more intense. Further standardization is required, and even more emphasis is placed on cost reduction, while acceptable delivery and quality standards are maintained. At this point the process becomes highly integrated and automated. A change in any part of it is likely to make an impact on the entire process as product and process become interdependent and hard to separate. Further changes in the product are exceedingly difficult and costly to make. Change comes more slowly but may be caused by sudden alterations in the inputs, in government regulations, or in the marketplace. Examples of processes in this stage of development are automobile assembly lines, chemical plants, food processors, and high-volume services such as social security, medicare, and the telephone company.

Figure 4.6 illustrates the nature of process-product interaction and development. While product innovation declines as the product matures, process innovations increase once the product becomes standardized. In the mature stage, both types of innovations drop off as the product and process become intertwined and difficult to change.

The traditional stages of product development require some modification to fit with the new flexible computerized automation. CAD/CAM, CIM, and robotics provide more latitude for product changes and automation in all three stages. Nevertheless, flexible automation has its limits and cannot be extended to every volume and degree of product standardization. Therefore, the three stages still occur, but the lines between stages may be blurred, the stages may occur more quickly, and automation may be used more extensively at each stage. Much more will be said about the use of flexible automation in Chapter 7.

VALUE ANALYSIS

There is a need to improve constantly the products and services we produce in order to stay competitive. Innovation is a basic necessity in all that we do. A

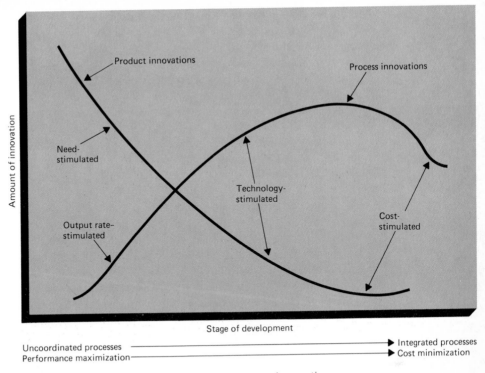

FIGURE 4.6   A dynamic model of product-process innovation.
Source: J. M. Utterback and W. J. Abernathy, "A Dynamic Model of Process and Product Innovation by Films," Omega, 1975.

convenient way of organizing innovation, aimed at improving the value of products and services, is called value analysis or value engineering.

Value analysis is a philosophy of eliminating anything which causes cost but does not contribute to the value or function of the product or service. It is aimed at meeting product performance requirements and customer needs at the lowest possible cost. Value analysis is also an organized approach for analyzing products and services in which several steps and techniques are routinely used.

There is a major difference between cost and value. Cost is an absolute term, expressed in dollars and cents, which measures the resources used to create a product or service. The cost frequently includes labor, material, and overhead. Value, on the other hand, is the customer's perception of the ratio of the usefulness of a product or service to its costs. Usefulness includes quality, reliability, and performance of a product for its intended use. Value is what the customer is looking for: meeting his or her needs at the lowest cost. Thus, the value of a product can be improved by increasing its usefulness to the customer for the same cost or lowering the cost for the same degree of usefulness. This is done by eliminating unnecessary or costly functions which do not contribute to value.

In value analysis the following terms or definitions are used:

- *Objective:* The purpose or reason that the product or service exists.
- *Basic function:* A basic function, if eliminated, would render the product useless in terms of its stated objective.
- *Secondary functions:* Secondary functions exist to support a basic function because of the way the particular product was designed.

For example, in opening a tin can, we might have the following:

- *Objective:* Remove contents.
- *Basic function:* Open can.
- *Secondary functions:* Cut lid.

In order to remove the contents of a can, we must open the can; thus "open can" is a basic function. There are other ways to seal a can, however, such as using a screw lid or a plastic top. In these cases, the secondary function would change because a different approach is used to accomplish the basic function. Identifying basic and secondary functions is at the heart of value analysis. As an exercise, try to identify the basic and secondary functions of a stapler and a cup.

Typically, value analysis is conducted in five steps: planning, information, creative design, evaluation, and implementation. The planning step begins by orienting the organization to the concept of value analysis. Senior and middle management are informed of the potential for value analysis and of the procedures involved so they can provide the needed support. Next, a value analysis team consisting of all those affected by the potential changes is formed. In a manufacturing organization, this might include design engineering, production engineering, purchasing, quality control, and accounting people. The team is then trained and given a scope of work to define what kinds of product changes will be considered and some expected result, such as 10 percent reduction in cost for the same product performance. The team is then ready to start the analysis itself.

The information phase of the study begins by identifying the product or service objective, the basic functions, and the secondary functions. The functions are usually described by two words; a verb-noun pair, as in the example above. This process of identifying basic and secondary functions is shown for the claims section of an insurance office in Table 4.2. Here the functions considered essential to production of the service provided by the office are receive claims, process claims, and pay claims. Secondary functions are also identified, but they can be changed or eliminated if improved value can be provided.

As a way to start the analysis, the cost of each primary and secondary function is also determined. The team then looks to see if any secondary functions can be consolidated, revised, or eliminated while improving the value ratio.

The third phase of value analysis is aimed at generating creative alternatives. For example, it may be possible to reorganize the claims office and reduce the need for sorting mail, or new equipment may be purchased to automate some of the processing stages. An open and innovative atmosphere should be maintained in the team during this phase so as to not stifle ideas.

In the evaluation step, ideas are evaluated for feasibility, cost, and contribution

TABLE 4.2
**VALUE ANALYSIS
EXAMPLE FOR
INSURANCE CLAIMS
OFFICE***

Functions	Annual cost
Receive claims	$110,000
Open letters	15,000
Read mail	45,000
Code letter	42,000
Sort letters	8,000
Process claims	160,000
Request files	30,000
Search files	80,000
Match letters	10,000
Evaluate claims	40,000
Pay claims	80,000
Authorize payment	20,000
Issue check	60,000

*In the table three basic functions are shown along with secondary functions for each one.

to value. The best ideas are consolidated into a plan for product or service improvement. The resulting plan is then put into effect by the team members and management. Usually, it is best to form the team initially with people who will have to carry out the results of the value analysis study. This provides enthusiasm and commitment to the implementation process.

Value analysis is an organized way for improving the usefulness of a product relative to its cost. Value analysis is like zero-based budgeting in that each product function is carefully examined for possible elimination or improvement. Nothing is taken for granted. The results can be quite dramatic: usually more than a 10 percent improvement in value and sometimes as much as 50 percent or more.

PRODUCT VARIETY

We have been dealing with the problems of designing and redesigning an individual product. This section will address product design decisions dealing with multiple products. The key question addressed is: How much product variety is enough?

The issue of product variety must be considered from both a marketing and an operations point of view. In each case, there are advantages and disadvantages in having a large number of products.

From a marketing point of view, the advantage of a large number of products is the ability to offer customers more choices. Marketing often argues that sales will drop if the firm does not offer as many products as its competitors. Marketing managers may also argue for a complete product line to meet nearly all conceivable customer needs.

But high product variety also makes the marketing function difficult. Too many products can confuse the customer, who may not differentiate between similar products. It is more difficult to train salespeople, and advertising is more costly and less focused with high product variety. Thus, it is likely that too much product variety will lead to a leveling off of sales increases and, possibly, even a decline in sales. Nevertheless, marketing managers often tend to prefer more product variety.

From an operations viewpoint, high product variety is seen as leading to higher costs, greater complexity, and more difficulty in specializing equipment and people. The ideal operations situation is often seen as a few high-volume products with stabilized production configurations. Operations managers often prefer less product variety.

On the basis of the foregoing discussion, it is possible to formulate an economic theory of product variety. We have argued that high product variety may lead to lower increases in sales. At the same time, higher product variety leads to higher unit production costs, as shown in Figure 4.7, along with the resultant effect on profits. We therefore theorize that there is an optimum amount of product variety which results in maximum profits. Both too little and too much product variety will lead to low profits.

In using this theory, one of the key problems is the analysis of a given product line to determine whether or not there are too many products. This analysis immediately raises the question of how to allocate fixed costs to product lines.

In the short run, the argument is made that as long as a product contributes to overhead and profits, it should be retained. In the short run, a product need only cover its variable expenses and none of the fixed expense. Although this reasoning is correct, it leads to the dangerous practice of retaining the products in the long run also, where the short-run reasoning does not apply. Therefore, except in special circumstances, it is best to retain only products which carry their full cost, including allocated overhead. This is difficult for managers to accept, because the immediate effect of trimming out a product which has a positive contribution

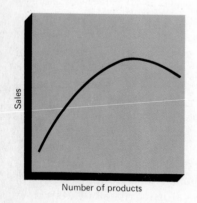
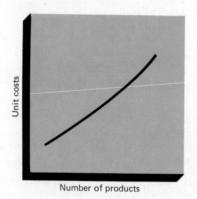
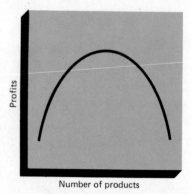

FIGURE 4.7   An economic theory of product variety.

margin is to reduce profits. However, as inventory is reduced, accounts receivable are collected, and overhead is cut, long-run profits will be improved. It is the desire on the part of managers for short-run profits which often leads to inflated product lines and, eventually, lower profits.

Herbert Woodward (1976) illustrates the problem with a story about product proliferation:

> A few years ago, one of our operating companies disposed of a line of portable positive-displacement pneumatic machines that had an annual sales volume of about $500,000. Although the line was a natural companion to a much larger and long-established line of fan-operated equipment and a prodigious effort had been devoted to get it going, it had not made money and the prospects of success were poor. We finally made the painful decision to sell the line for a nominal amount. The buyer was one of our employees, who set it up as a separate business that later proved modestly successful.

> The beneficial effects of that sale on the company's operation were substantial and almost instantaneous. Our balance sheet improved dramatically as we collected the remaining accounts receivable, worked off the inventory, and—by buying no more material—cut our accounts payable. Our earnings improved more than the elimination of this relatively minor line seemed to justify. Only then did top management realize how much this one activity had demanded in attention and effort from almost everyone in the parent company. The product line had had a disproportionately high overhead, but the figures didn't show it.

> The advantages of simplification are hard to quantify, but they are real. Despite all that the computer can do to make possible a wide span of control, there is no better road to efficiency than to eliminate complexity entirely, usually by shrinking the business to a smaller and more manageable size.

4.8   MODULAR DESIGN

The problem of product variety requires not only an analysis of product lines but also a way to limit and control the number of products. The concept of modular design is one approach to this problem. [See Starr (1965).]

Modular design makes it possible to have relatively high product variety and low component variety at the same time. The basic idea is to develop a series of basic product components (or modules) which can be assembled into a large number of different products. To the customer, it appears there are a great number of different products. To operations, there is only a limited number of basic components.

Controlling the number of different components which go into products is of great importance to operations, since this makes it possible to produce more efficiently for larger volumes while also allowing standardization of processes and equipment. A large number of product variations greatly increases the complexity and cost of operations.

Modular design offers a fundamental way to change product design thinking. Instead of designing each product separately, the company designs products around standard component modules. If this is done, the product line must be carefully analyzed and divided into basic modules. Common modules should be developed that can serve more than one product line, and unnecessary product frills should be eliminated. This approach will still allow for a great deal of product variety, but the number of unnecessary product variations will be reduced.

The usual way to develop products is to design each one separately without much attention to the other products in the line. Each product is optimized, but the product line as a whole is not. Modular design requires a broader view of product lines, and it may call for changes in individual products to optimize the product line in its entirety.

The modular design approach can best be illustrated by an example. A group of students at the University of Minnesota studied the operations of a large manufacturer of beds—a company that produces over 2000 different combinations of mattresses. The team discovered that 50 percent of these combinations accounted for only 3 percent of sales. Market surveys showed that this much product variety was not advantageous to marketing. At the same time, the amount of variety had increased costs. Therefore, modular production was suggested as a way to trim the product line.

On the basis of modular design ideas, a mattress product line would be produced in four basic sizes: regular, twin, queen, and king. The inside construction of the mattress would be limited to only a few different spring arrangements and thicknesses of foam padding. A moderate variety of mattress covers would be used to meet consumer preferences for color and type of design. The result would be a greatly reduced number of mattress components but still a substantial amount of variety for the customer. For example, if there were four bed sizes, three types of spring construction, three types of foam, and eight different covers, a total of 288 different mattresses would be possible.

$$4 \times 3 \times 3 \times 8 = 288 \text{ combinations}$$

Not all the mattresses would be produced because some might be unacceptable to the customer (e.g., the expensive springs with the thin foam pad). Although there are still many product combinations in the example, the number of components has been limited.

The team suggested that marketing, operations, and engineering get together to define the basic components that would be made and the product combinations desired. They also suggested that the company rigorously adhere to those components once the decision had been made, with a periodic revision perhaps once a year. The team not only dealt with the problem of product proliferation but, by using the concept of modular production, retained the advantages of product variety.

4.9 KEY POINTS

New-product development has a great impact on the operations function, because any new product which is designed must be produced by operations. Furthermore, existing operations may constrain the development of new products.

Product decisions are a prerequisite to production. Product specifications must be provided to operations before production can begin and before some major decisions in operations can be made. Other operations decisions such as process design, however, should not wait until the product specifications are completed. Rather, process design decisions should be made at the same time as the product is being designed.

This chapter deals with the nature of product design and its relationship to the operations function. Major points are:

- A product is the output of a productive system. The product may be either a good or a service or both.
- There are three ways to view the new-product introduction process: as market-pull, technology-push, or interfunctional. The market-pull view corresponds to "making what you can sell," while the technology-push view is "selling what you can make." The interfunctional view is a combination of these two, which requires cooperation between the functions in designing products. The interfunctional approach usually produces the best results. However, it requires an organizational approach which cuts across functional lines.
- The new-product development process consists of six steps: idea generation, product selection, preliminary design, prototype construction, testing, and final design. In practice, this process does not proceed sequentially from the beginning to end. Many iterations may be required.
- During the life cycle of a product, there are three stages of product-process interaction: the fluid stage, the semiautomated stage, and the fully automated stage. During these stages of product development, there is a great deal of interaction between product and process.
- The product design greatly affects the objectives of operations: cost, delivery, quality, and flexibility. When the product is first introduced, flexibility may be the most important objective. Later, when price competition develops, cost may be the most important objective.
- Value analysis is a method for improving the usefulness of a good or service relative to its cost. This is done by reviewing and improving the functionality of the product so as to increase its value.
- An economic theory of product variety was proposed where both too little variety and too much variety result in low profit. According to this theory, there is an optimum amount of product variety.
- Modular production is an approach used to produce a wide variety of products from a limited number of product components. This approach can be used to control product proliferation by limiting the number of components or modules available.

QUESTIONS

1. Why is interfunctional cooperation important for new-product design? What are the symptoms of a possible lack of interfunctional cooperation?
2. Under what circumstances might a market-pull approach or a technology-push approach to new-product design be the best approach?
3. Describe the steps which might be required in writing and producing a play. Compare these steps to the six steps for new-product development described in Section 4.2. Is there a correspondence?
4. Consider the development and production of a new course in a college setting. Describe how this course might proceed through the three stages of product-process interaction. How would the course be taught at each stage? How would the "product" develop?
5. Why has there been an increase in product variety in our economy?
6. Three new-product ideas have been suggested. These ideas have been rated as follows:
   a. Using an equal point spread for all five ratings (i.e., P = 1, F = 2, G = 3, VG = 4, E = 5), determine a weighted score for each product idea. What is the ranking of the three products?

	Product			
	A	B	C	Weight
Development cost	P	F	VG	15%
Sales' prospects	VG	E	G	10%
Producibility	P	F	G	20%
Competitive advantage	E	VG	F	15%
Technical risk	P	F	VG	10%
Patent protection	F	F	VG	20%
Compatibility with strategy	VG	F	F	10%
				100%

P = poor, F = fair, G = good, VG = very good, E = excellent.

   b. What are some of the advantages and disadvantages of this method of product selection?
7. How can the modular design concept control production variety and at the same time allow product variety?
8. What is the proper role of the operations function in product design?
9. What form does the product specification take for the following firms: a travel agency, a beer company, and a consulting firm?
10. Perform a value analysis on the following items:
    a. A stapler
    b. A hotel room
    c. An algebra class

SELECTED BIBLIOGRAPHY

ABERNATHY, W. J.: "Production Process Structure and Technological Change," *Decision Sciences*, vol. 7, no. 4, October 1976, pp. 607–619.

———, and P. L. TOWNSEND: "Technology, Productivity and Process Change," *Technological Forecasting and Social Change*, vol. 7, August 1975, pp. 377–396.

———, and JAMES UTTERBACK: "Innovations and the Evolving Structure of the Firm," Harvard Business School Working Paper 75–78, June 1975.

DECKER, ROBERT: "Computer Aided Design and Manufacturing at GM," *Datamation*, May 1978, pp. 159–165.

DiSYLVESTER, BEN: "Value Analysis Aids Managers in Search of Most Effective Office Procedures," *Industrial Engineering*, September 1981, pp. 72–77.

GALBRAITH, JAY R.: "Matrix Organization Design," *Business Horizons*, February 1971, pp. 29–40.

GEORGE, WILLIAM W.: "Task Teams for Rapid Growth," *Harvard Business Review*, March–April, 1977, pp. 71–121.

GLUCK, FREDERICK, and R. N. FOSTER: "Managing Technological Change: A Box of Cigars for Brad," *Harvard Business Review*, September-October 1975, pp. 139–150.

HISE, RICHARD, and M. A. McGINNIS: "Product Elimination: Practices, Policies and Ethics," *Business Horizons*, June 1975, pp. 25–32.

IMAI, KEN-ICHI, IKUJIRO NONAKA, and HIROTAKA TAKEUCHI: "Managing the New Product Development Process: How Japanese Companies Learn and Unlearn," Harvard Business School Colloquium on Productivity and Technology, March 1984.

LEONARD-BARTON, DOROTHY: "Implementing New Technology: The Transfer from Developers to Operations," Working Paper, Harvard Business School, June 1987.

PETERS, THOMAS J. and ROBERT H. WATERMANN, JR.: *In Search of Excellence*, New York: Harper & Row, 1982.

PUTNAM, ARNOLD D.: "A Redesign for Engineering," *Harvard Business Review*, May–June 1985, pp. 139–144.

SOUDER, WILLIAM, "An Exploratory Study of the Coordinating Mechanisms between R&D and Marketing as an Influence on the Innovation Process," Working Paper, Technology Management Studies Group, Department of Industrial Engineering, University of Pittsburgh, Pa., August 1977.

STARR, MARTIN K.: "Modular Production: A New Concept," *Harvard Business Review*, November-December 1965, pp. 131–142.

UTTERBACK, J. M., and W. J. ABERNATHY: "A Dynamic Model of Process and Product Innovation," *Omega*, vol. 3, no. 6, 1975, pp. 639–656.

WOODWARD, HERBERT H.: "Management Strategies for Small Companies," *Harvard Business Review*, January-February 1976, pp. 113–121.

PART TWO

PROCESS DESIGN

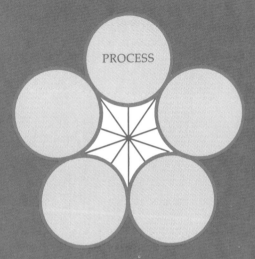

PROCESS

- **PROCESS SELECTION**
- **SERVICE OPERATIONS DESIGN**
- **CHOICE OF TECHNOLOGY**
- **PROCESS-FLOW ANALYSIS**
- **LAYOUT OF FACILITIES**

Among the most important decisions made by operations managers are those involving the design of the physical process for producing goods and services. This series of decisions encompasses process selection, service operations design, choice of technology, process-flow analysis, and layout of facilities. When these decisions have been made, the process type, degree of automation, physical layout, and design of jobs have largely been determined. Process design is not merely a technical matter but involves social, economic, and environmental choices as well.

The range of processes which can be selected is described in Part 2, along with the important factors in process selection decisions. As previously discussed, process selection is highly interactive with product design. To reflect this interaction, process choices and product choices constitute the two sides of a product-process matrix. A decision requires the selection of a cell in this matrix, thus fixing both the product and the process.

Service operations design is given special attention in this part because of the high level of customer contact required by most services. Several frameworks for thinking about services are presented, and a method is defined for service operations design. The method includes definition of service strategy, design of the service product, and design of service processes.

The choice of technology determines the degree of process automation. This choice is not merely a technical decision but also a social choice which determines jobs and other social factors. This leads to the idea of a decision-making process which considers the environmental, social, and economic implications of technological alternatives.

The design of processes also requires decisions on a micro level concerning process-flow analysis and facility layout. These decisions determine the physical flow of materials, customers, and information through the process. Process analysis methods describe the flow of the process through use of flowcharts and mathematical models. Layout decisions improve process flow by the arrangement of physical facilities.

There are two themes which underlie and unify Part 2: first, the idea of designing a process to enhance the flow of materials, customers, and information and, second, the idea of combining social and technical considerations in process design. These ideas can be used to design a process which is not only efficient but socially and environmentally acceptable as well.

In the first three chapters of Part 2, macro process design decisions are treated. These macro decisions have to do with process selection and the choice of technology. The macro decisions are long range in nature, require considerable resources, are irreversible for long periods of time, and involve top management. The last two chapters of this part treat micro decisions of process design. These micro decisions involve process-flow analysis and layout. The micro decisions are made at lower levels in the organization, they require less resources, and they can be changed more easily than the macro decisions.

Process design decisions interact with decisions in each of the other four decision areas of the operations function. Capacity decisions affect the type of process selected. The type of process design, in turn, affects the jobs available and the type of work force employed. The process also affects the quality of the product produced, because some processes are more easily controlled than others. Thus process decisions are intertwined with most other decisions in operations.

CHAPTER 5

Process Selection

Process selection decisions determine the type of productive process to be used and the appropriate span of that process. For example, the managers of a fast-food restaurant may decide whether to produce food strictly to customer order or to inventory. The managers must also decide whether to organize the process flow as a high-volume line flow or a low-volume batch-production process. Furthermore, they must decide whether to integrate forward toward the market and/or backward toward their suppliers. All these decisions help define the type of process which will be used to make the product.

Process selection is sometimes viewed as a layout problem or as a series of relatively low-level decisions, but this is a mistake, since process selection is, on the contrary, strategic in nature and of the greatest importance. Process decisions affect the costs, quality, delivery, and flexibility of operations. As Wickham Skinner (1969) points out, process selection decisions tend to bind the firm with equipment, facilities, and a particular type of labor force. This, in turn, tends to limit future strategic options.

This chapter addresses process selection decisions from a strategic management point of view. The main emphasis is on the description of different processes and the conditions which might lead to the selection of one process over another.

Before the process selection decision can be made, the planned volume of product output must be known. Thus a forecast of demand and a decision on the physical capacity of operations must precede process selection. We treat capacity decisions in the next part, however, in order to integrate long-, medium-, and short-range capacity decisions. For the purposes of this part, we will assume that the long-range capacity decision has already been made.

In this chapter, two main types of process classifications are examined. First, a process is classified by type of product flow: line, intermittent, or project. Second, a process is classified by type of customer order: make-to-stock or make-to-order. These dimensions of classifications greatly affect costs, volumes, flexibility, and virtually all aspects of operations. Since these classifications are so crucial to operations, they are described in some detail in the first part of the chapter.

After the static case is considered, process selection decisions are put into a dynamic context. Process selection is portrayed as a dynamic series of decisions over time, where the product and process evolve together. Finally, at the end of the chapter, the scope of process selection is expanded to include forward and backward integration. A typical decision problem of process selection is illustrated in Box 5.1.

BOX 5.1
TYPICAL DECISION PROBLEM

The microwave oven business has been expanding rapidly over the past 10 years. One of the leading American companies in this industry is Radarwave, Inc., which has captured a 30 percent market share and has rapidly expanded sales and profits over the past 5 years. In viewing this situation, Mary Lipton, the vice president of operations, wondered how long the sales growth would continue and at what point changes in market conditions might require a corresponding change in the manufacturing process.

At the present time, Radarwave has two plants, one in Boulder, Colorado, and the other in Rapid City, South Dakota. These plants have been using a partially connected assembly line, with some parts of the product also being made in a job-shop facility. Because of the rapid growth in sales as well as frequent product changes, the product flow was somewhat irregular; moreover, the assembly line was not engineered to achieve the most efficient process possible. It was highly labor-intensive, and many parts for the microwave ovens were purchased from outside suppliers.

Recently Japanese competition entered the market with a low-priced microwave oven. American manufacturers also standardized their ovens, and some of the large appliance manufacturers were considering adding microwave products to their appliance lines.

In view of this situation, Mary decided to analyze the possible effects of moving toward a more standard assembly line, with increased automation and more vertical integration. To conduct the analysis, she called in Roger Kirk, her assistant for operations planning. Mary asked Roger to lay out the various available options and to prepare an analysis of the impact of each of these options on operations. She cautioned Roger to consider not only the costs of the proposed alternatives but also the effect on operations quality, delivery, and flexibility.

5.1 PROCESS-FLOW CHARACTERISTICS

The first dimension of process classification is the product flow or sequence of operations. There are three types of flows: line, intermittent, and project. In manufacturing, product flow is the same as material flow, since materials are being converted into a product. In pure service industries, there is no physical product flow, but there is, nevertheless, a sequence of operations performed in delivering the service. This sequence of service operations is considered as the "product flow" for service industries.

Line flow. Line flow is characterized by a linear sequence of operations used to make the product or service. Examples are assembly lines and cafeterias. For line-flow operations, the product must be well standardized and must flow from one operation or work station to the next in a prescribed sequence. The individual work tasks are closely coupled and should be balanced so that one task does not delay the next. The pattern typical of line flows is shown in Figure 5.1. Notice that the good or service is created sequentially from one end of the line to the other. There may be side flows which impinge on this line, but they are integrated to achieve a smooth flow.

Line-flow operations are sometimes divided into two types of production: mass and continuous. "Mass production" generally refers to an assembly-line type of operation, such as that used in the automobile industry. "Continuous production" refers to the so-called process industries such as the chemical, paper, beer, steel, electricity, and telephone industries. Although both types of operations are characterized by linear flow, continuous processes tend to be more highly automated and they produce more highly standardized products.

Traditional line operations are extremely efficient but also extremely inflexible. The efficiency is due to substitution of capital for labor and standardization of the remaining labor into highly routine tasks. The high level of efficiency requires that a large volume be maintained in order to recover the cost of specialized equipment. This, in turn, requires a standard product line which is relatively stabilized over time. Because of this standardization and the sequential organiza-

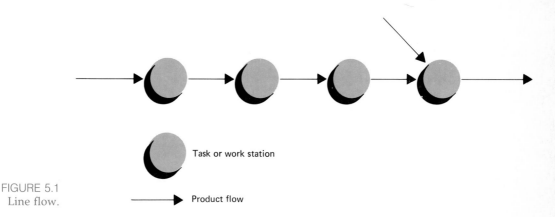

FIGURE 5.1
Line flow.

tion of work tasks, it is difficult and expensive to modify the product or volume in line-flow operations; therefore these operations are relatively inflexible.

Recently, new technology is making it possible for assembly lines to be more flexible. This is being done by use of computerized control of equipment and reduction of changeover times. By assigning a product family to a flexible line, it is possible to produce several hundred product types (different sizes and shapes) within the given product family in small or large lot sizes. As a result, substantial flexibility is gained in cases where the new technology can be used. More details will be made available in later chapters.

Of course, line operations can be justified in only a limited number of situations. The general requirements are for high volume and a standardized product or product family. If these conditions are present, competition will usually force the use of a line flow because of its great potential efficiency. Nevertheless, a firm must carefully analyze the decision to use line operations; this choice should not be based simply on efficiency. Other factors which should be considered are the risk of product obsolescence, possible labor dissatisfaction due to job boredom, and the risk of changing process technology.

Intermittent flow (job shop). An intermittent-flow process is characterized by production in batches at intermittent intervals. In this case, equipment and labor are organized into work centers by similar types of skill or equipment. A product or job will then flow only to those work centers that are required and will skip the rest. This results in a jumbled flow pattern, as shown in Figure 5.2.

Because they use general-purpose equipment and highly skilled labor, intermittent operations are extremely flexible in changing the product or volume; but they are also rather inefficient. The jumbled flow pattern and product variety leads to severe problems in controlling inventories, schedules, and quality.

If an intermittent operation is functioning near capacity, high in-process inventories will build up and throughput time for the batches will increase. This is due to job interference when different jobs require the same equipment or the

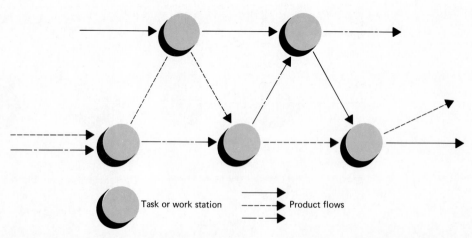

FIGURE 5.2
Intermittent flow.

same labor at the same time, leading to much lower utilization of equipment and labor than in a line type of operation.

Constable and New have suggested a way to measure this loss of efficiency by a ratio they call throughput efficiency, or TE:

$$TE = \frac{\text{total work involvement time for the job}}{\text{total time in operations}} \times 100\%$$

In the numerator, total work involvement time for the job is the machine hours or labor hours actually spent working on the job. This does not include the time the job waits because of job interference. The denominator is the total time it takes to complete the job in operations, including all waiting time. Intermittent operations typically have a TE of about 10 or 20 percent, rarely higher than 40 percent. In contrast, the TE of a line-flow operation approaches 90 to 100 percent.

One key characteristic of an intermittent process is that similar equipment and work skills are grouped together. This is also known as a process form of layout. In contrast, the line flow is called a product layout because the various processes, equipment, and labor skills are put into sequence according to the way the product is made.

To further complicate the terminology, intermittent operations are often called job shops. However, sometimes the term "job shop" is reserved for only those intermittent operations that make to customer order. Because of this confusion and the factory connotations of "job shop," we prefer the use of the term "intermittent operation."

Intermittent operations can be justified when the product lacks standardization or the volume is low. In this case, the intermittent operation is the most economical and involves the least risk. Such forms of operations are common in the early life cycles of all products, for products which are customized in nature, and for products with a low-volume market.

Project. The project form of operations is used to produce a unique product such as a work of art, a concert, a building, or a motion picture. Each unit of these products is produced as a single item. Strictly speaking, there is no product flow for a project, but there is still a sequence of operations. In this case, all individual operations or tasks should be sequenced to contribute to the final project objectives. A conceptual sequence of project tasks is shown in Figure 5.3, which indicates precedence among the various tasks required for project completion. A significant problem in project management is the planning, sequencing, and control of the individual tasks leading to completion of the entire project.

The project form of operations is used when there is a great need for creativity and uniqueness. It is difficult to automate projects because they are only done once; nevertheless, general-purpose equipment can sometimes be used to reduce labor requirements. Projects are characterized by high cost and difficulty in managerial planning and control. This is because a project is often hard to define initially, and it may be subject to a high degree of change and innovation.

The characteristics of the process we have been discussing are summarized in

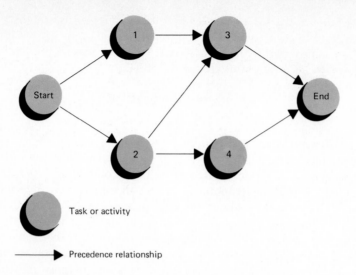

Task or activity

FIGURE 5.3
Project flow.

Precedence relationship

Box 5.2, which makes a direct comparison between process types for each characteristic. For an excellent and more detailed work on this subject, see Schmenner (1987).

BOX 5.2
PROCESS CHARACTERISTICS

Characteristics	Line	Intermittent	Project
Product			
Order type	Continuous or large batch	Batch	Single unit
Flow of product	Sequenced	Jumbled	None
Product variety	Low	High	Very high
Market type	Mass	Custom	Unique
Volume	High	Medium	Single unit
Labor			
Skills	Low	High	High
Task type	Repetitive	Nonroutine	Nonroutine
Pay	Low	High	High
Capital			
Investment	High	Medium	Low
Inventory	Low	High	Medium
Equipment	Special purpose	General purpose	General purpose
Objectives			
Flexibility	Low	Medium	High
Cost	Low	Medium	High
Quality	Consistent	More variable	More variable
Delivery	High	Medium	Low

Control and planning			
Production control	Easy	Difficult	Difficult
Quality control	Easy	Difficult	Difficult
Inventory control	Easy	Difficult	Difficult

At this point, examples from the housing industry may help to solidify some of the concepts. At the project end of the continuum is the custom-built house. A unique plan for it may be drawn up by an architect, or existing plans may be modified for each house built. Since the construction of the house is customized, planning, sequencing, and control of various construction activities often become major problems. The customer is highly involved in all stages of construction, and sometimes the plans are modified while the house is being built. The operation is labor-intensive, time-consuming, and costly.

The intermittent operation is characterized by the batch production of houses. In this case, the customer can select one of a few standard houses with only minor options on things like colors, fixtures, and carpets. The house is produced with little reference to blueprints, since identical or very similar houses have been produced elsewhere. The contractor may buy materials in large carload lots, and specialized equipment or jigs may be used to speed up construction. A crew which is very familiar with the type of house being built is brought in, and the entire structure—except for final touches—may be put up in only a few weeks. Such a house is usually less expensive per square foot than the custom-built project house.

The line method of house production is characterized by modular or factory operations. Standard houses are produced in sections, in a factory, by relatively cheap labor. The use of expensive plumbers, carpenters, and electricians is largely avoided by installing complete electrical and plumbing systems at the factory. Special-purpose machines are also used in the factory to cut costs still further. After being built on an assembly line, the house sections are brought to the site and erected in a day or so by a crane. These modular houses are typically the least expensive of all.

Obviously, a contractor faces a major strategic decision in choosing the type of process to use for the construction of houses. All three approaches may be used, but then care must be taken to separate these operations because of their different requirements for labor, management, and capital. If all three types of houses are to be offered, the contractor might form a separate division for each type of process as well as a separate operation for each.

5.2   CLASSIFICATIONS BY TYPE OF CUSTOMER ORDER

Another critical dimension affecting process choice is whether the product is made to stock or made to order. Each of these processes has its own advantages and disadvantages. While a make-to-stock process will provide fast service at low cost, it offers less flexibility in product choice than a make-to-order process.

A make-to-order process essentially responds to the customer's request for a product. At some point in the make-to-order production process, it must be possible to identify a particular customer order. However, in a make-to-stock process individual orders are not assigned to customers during production. One can then tell whether the process is make-to-order or make-to-stock by examining the work orders in the conversion process.

Even though the process is make-to-order, a wide range of order specifications may remain. In some cases, nothing is done until the order is received, and the product is then designed and produced entirely to customer specifications. In other cases, components are built up in advance, and the product is merely assembled at the last minute to meet the customer's choices. In this case, the finished product is standardized but not carried in stock.

In a make-to-order process, the processing activities are keyed to individual customer orders. The order cycle begins when the customer specifies the product that he or she wants. On the basis of the customer's request, the producer will quote a price and delivery time. This quotation may be offered immediately if the order is standard, or for custom orders, it may take a period of time. If the customer accepts the quotation, the product will be either assembled from components or designed and built completely to customer specifications. If the order is built to customer specifications and special materials are needed, they will be placed on order. When the materials arrive, they will be fabricated and assembled as capacity permits. Finally, the product will be delivered to the customer. This sequence of events is essentially the same whether the product is a good or a service.

The key operations performance measure for a make-to-order process is the delivery time. Before placing the order, the customer will want to know how long it will take for delivery. If the delivery time is accepted by the customer, then operations should control the order flow to meet the delivery date. This means, of course, that delivery times should be set realistically by operations and marketing working in cooperation. The measures of operations performance will be delivery parameters such as length of delivery time and percentage of orders delivered on time.

A make-to-stock firm has a completely different problem. First, the make-to-stock operation must have a standardized product line. The product availability objective then is to provide the customer with these standard products from inventory at some satisfactory service level, say, 95 percent of orders filled from stock. In meeting the service level, the company will build up inventory in advance of demand. The inventory will then be used to meet demand uncertainty and, possibly, to smooth out capacity requirements. Therefore forecasting, inventory management, and capacity planning become essential for a make-to-stock operation.

In a make-to-stock company, very little in operations is keyed to actual customer orders; rather, the focus is on replenishment of inventory. With the rare exception of back orders, it will not be possible to identify actual customer orders in the production process.

In a make-to-stock operation, the cycle begins with the producer, rather than the customer, specifying the product. The customer takes the product from stock if the price is acceptable and the product is on hand. Otherwise, a back order may be placed. Quite separately from the actual flow of orders, the production process seeks to replenish inventory. At any particular time, there may be little correlation between actual orders being received and what is being produced. The production system is building stock levels for future orders, not current ones. Current orders are being filled from available stock. This split between the order cycle and the replenishment cycle is illustrated in Figure 5.4. The figure also indicates that such a split does not occur in a make-to-order system, since the production process starts when the order is received.

In a make-to-stock situation, the key performance measures are utilization of production assets (inventory and capacity) and customer service. These measures might include inventory turnover, capacity utilization, use of overtime, and percentage of orders filled from stock. The objective of the operation is to meet the desired level of customer service at minimum cost.

In summary, a make-to-order process is keyed to delivery time and control of the order flow. The process must be flexible so as to meet customer orders. A make-to-stock process is keyed to replenishment of inventories and efficiency of operations. The process is streamlined to produce only standard products. The essential differences between these processes are summarized in Box 5.3.

BOX 5.3
MAKE-TO-STOCK VERSUS MAKE-TO-ORDER

Characteristics	Make-to-stock	Make to order
Product	Producer-specified Low variety Inexpensive	Customer-specified High variety Expensive
Objectives	Balance inventory, capacity, and service	Manage delivery lead times and capacity
Main operations problems	Forecasting Planning production Control of inventory	Delivery promises Delivery time

Source: Adapted from Constable and New (1976).

Classic examples of make-to-stock and make-to-order processes are the McDonald's and Burger King fast-food chains. The hamburgers at McDonald's are, in some cases, made-to-stock. When the demand is steady, McDonald's will build up inventory of various types of hamburgers. In this case, the operation attempts to forecast demand and replenish inventory.

At Burger King the slogan is "Have it your way." Customers can specify the ingredients they want in their hamburgers or those they don't want. In this case, the exact order cannot be kept in stock, and the measure of performance shifts to delivery time. Burger King is a make-to-order operation.

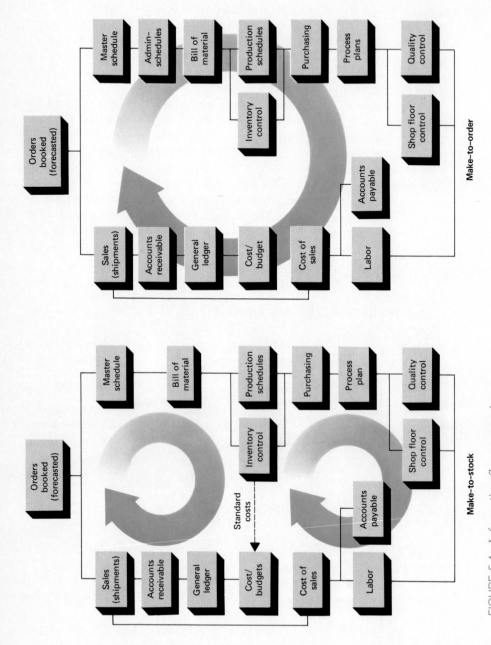

FIGURE 5.4 Information flow comparison.
Source: Daniel S. Appleton, "A Strategy for Manufacturing Automation," Datamation, October 1977, pp. 65–66.

5.3 PROCESS SELECTION DECISIONS

We have classified processes according to two dimensions: product flow and type of customer order. These dimensions are shown in Table 5.1 on a matrix with six different processes. In a firm, each particular product is produced by one of these six processes; however, a mixture of products often leads to a mixture of process types in the same firm. It is very common for organizations to have several different types of processes within the same physical facility. This can, however, become the basis for cells or a plant-within-a-plant as described in Chapter 2.

All six process combinations shown in Table 5.1 are used in practice. For line flows it is common to make to stock, but a line can also make to order. For example, automobile assembly lines put together specific combinations of options requested by customers. To be sure, the product is standardized, but it is nevertheless made to order. At the other extreme, projects usually make to order, but the project form of operations can make to stock too. For example, a builder who constructs a few speculation houses is making to stock while using a project type of process.

It should also be noted that all six processes apply to services as well as goods. A pure service operation can only produce to order. But most services are delivered along with some accompanying goods. These accompanying goods can be made to stock, as in the case of fast-food hamburgers.

The six-cell process classification system can be used for several purposes: first, it can be used to categorize different types of decision problems encountered in operations. For example, cost, quality, production, and inventory control decisions differ greatly among these process types. The second use of the classification matrix is for process selection, which is the main issue discussed in the rest of this section.

TABLE 5.1
PROCESS CHARACTERISTICS MATRIX

	Make-to-stock	Make-to-order
Line flow	I Oil refining Flour milling Cannery Cafeteria	II Automobile assembly line Telephone company Electric utility
Intermittent flow	III Machine shop Fast food Glassware factory Furniture	IV Machine shop Restaurant Hospital Custom jewelry
Project	V Speculation homes Commercial paintings	VI Buildings Movies Ships Portraits

In discussing the process selection decision, we shall begin with an example and generalize from there. Let us consider the contractor, mentioned in Section 5.1, who can choose to build houses using either the project, intermittent, or line process. With any of these processes, the contractor can also choose to make the houses to stock or to order. What, then, are the factors which should be considered in making this choice?

First of all, the contractor should consider market conditions. The line approach requires a mass market for inexpensive houses, the intermittent process requires a lower-volume market for medium-priced houses, and the project process requires a market for expensive houses.

But the market should also be considered from the standpoint of competition. Can the contractor enter the market at the right time and gain an advantageous position? This will depend on competitors' plans and how they react to the contractor's process choice. In the end, matching the process to the market will be a key strategic decision involving both product and process choices.

Second, the contractor should consider capital. The line-flow process will require a great deal more capital than the project or intermittent flow. The line flow requires capital to equip the factory assembly line and to finance the partially completed houses. If the houses are built to stock in advance of customer orders, more capital is required to finance finished goods inventories. By way of contrast, construction of custom project houses would require much less capital, since only one or a few houses are being built at any one time and no factory is needed.

The third factor which should be considered is the availability and cost of labor. The project and intermittent processes require costly skilled labor such as plumbers, electricians, and carpenters. The factory line approach requires relatively cheap low-skilled labor. Unionization may affect both the supply and cost of labor.

The fourth factor the contractor should consider is the management skills required for each process. The project approach can be managed on a small scale without a great deal of sophistication. However, even in this case, certain project planning and control techniques will be helpful, as will the principles of good supervision and quality control. For the intermittent process, the contractor will require operations management skills in forecasting, scheduling, and inventory control. The contractor must also become more concerned with standardization and cost control, since the houses are being made in batches. The line process requires the most sophisticated management skills of all. The contractor will need to manage and coordinate a factory, construction at the site, and a distribution network.

The fifth factor which will be important to the contractor is the availability and price of raw materials. The project form of process is very flexible and can adjust to different materials if necessary. The line approach is much less flexible and may require costly changes if the supply of raw materials is interrupted. For example, a change from copper to plastic plumbing pipes could be a big changeover problem for the line flow but pose little problem for the intermittent or project process.

Finally, the contractor should consider the state of technology for both process and product. Are innovations likely to come along which will make a process obsolete before costs are recovered? Assessment of these conditions is part of risk evaluation for the process. Generally speaking, the risk in order of highest to lowest is line, intermittent, and project.

In summary, six factors appear to influence process selection from among the processes shown in Table 5.1.

1. Market conditions
2. Capital requirements
3. Labor
4. Management skills
5. Raw materials
6. Technology

A convenient way to remember these factors is to use the systems view of operations and think in terms of the different types of inputs, transformation technologies, and outputs. All six factors will then be apparent.

A good process selection decision requires a careful analysis of each of the above factors through several types of studies. A market research study should be done to assess potential demand and other market conditions. Whenever possible, future sales should be projected not only as a single figure but also as a range of possible estimates. For example, three estimates—pessimistic, most likely, and optimistic—might be used, thereby allowing an analysis of risks involved in the decision.

Many of the other factors can be considered by an economic analysis of process alternatives. The key to this is to consider the cash flow for each alternative by determining the investments, revenues, and costs on a year-by-year basis. The net cash-flow streams for each can then be discounted to present values, or a return on invested capital can be computed. The alternative with the largest present value or largest rate of return is then preferred from an economic point of view. The details of these calculations are given in the supplement to Chapter 7.

In our discussion of the economics of process choice, it will also be helpful to consider fixed and variable costs. Generally speaking, if the choice were between a project, intermittent, or line process, the cost comparison would appear as in Figure 5.5. The figure shows that the project would have the least cost for a low volume, followed by the intermittent flow at medium volume and the line process at high volume. The project process has the lowest fixed cost and highest variable cost, which makes the project least costly in total for low volumes. The line has the highest fixed cost and the lowest variable cost, which makes the line least costly in total for high volumes.

When the marketing and economic studies have been completed, they should be synthesized into the decision process. In some cases, these studies will indicate a definite preference for one process alternative over another. If this is the case, subjective factors are liable to play only a small role in process selection. Usually, however, process selection will require considerable judgment because of the different cost and risk factors involved.

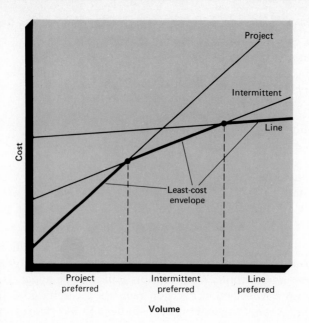

FIGURE 5.5
Cost curves for
process
alternatives.

PRODUCT-PROCESS STRATEGY

We have been treating process selection as a static decision. But it actually is dynamic in nature, since it continues as the process evolves from one stage to another over time. Furthermore, changes in the process are closely related to product changes.

Hayes and Wheelwright (1979) have suggested that process and product be viewed as two sides of a matrix, as in Figure 5.6. On the product side is the product life cycle of a firm whose output ranges from low-volume, one-of-a-kind products through high-volume, standard commodity products. As the product line matures, it moves from the left side of the matrix to the right side.

On the process side of the matrix is the type of process, ranging from a job shop (jumbled flow) through a continuous process. Abernathy and Townsend (1975) have observed that processes go through a "process life cycle" similar to the product life cycle. In this case, the process moves from a fluid and flexible process at the top of the matrix to an efficient and highly standardized process at the bottom of the matrix. See Chapter 4 for a complete discussion of this process life cycle.

Firms are often positioned along the diagonal of the matrix. In the upper left-hand corner is the printer who produces many jobs to customer order on general-purpose equipment in a job-shop environment. Further down the diagonal, there is the heavy-equipment manufacturer who makes products in batches. The product flow in this case is higher in volume and more connected, and the product line has been standardized. Still further down the diagonal is the automobile assembly line, which represents a line-flow process with a few major

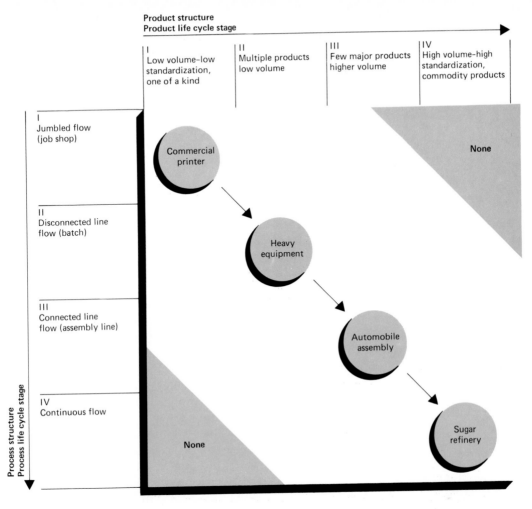

FIGURE 5.6 Process-product matrix.

Source: Exhibit adapted from Robert H. Hayes and Steven C. Wheelwright, "Line Manufacturing Process and Product Life Cycles," Harvard Business Review, *January–February 1979.*

product lines, specialized equipment, and highly structured jobs. Finally, in the lower right-hand corner, there is the sugar refiner, representing the continuous-process type of operation with a high-volume commodity product.

The process-product matrix helps describe the relationship between process and product strategy. In some cases, corporate strategy is developed only in light of products and markets. This limits the firm to a choice along only one dimension of the matrix. By recognizing the process dimension, the firm can also take advantage of competence in operations processes. This considerably expands the strategic options available and allows the use of operations as a "weapon" of corporate strategy.

Hayes and Wheelwright (1979) illustrate this interaction of product and process strategy with the following example from Litton, a manufacturer of microwave ovens.

As the market leader since the early 1960's, Litton has emphasized flexibility in its production facilities so as to be responsive to the frequent product changes required by a young, rapidly growing market. However, with the maturing market expected in the late seventies and the entry of more traditional appliance manufacturers, Litton recently has been forced to review how far it should move towards vertical integration and more efficient production processes.

Thus, Litton is being forced to consider changing both product and process strategies, thereby moving down the diagonal.

Abernathy (1976) has studied the matter of product and process evolution in great detail. He observes that product and process changes rarely occur simultaneously. Rather, these changes occur in alternating vertical or horizontal steps on the product-process matrix. A change in product strategy may move the firm to the right, off the diagonal, if the old process remains in effect. The competitors who are operating on the diagonal or below it can then produce at lower costs. This forces a change in process technology to move the firm back down to the diagonal or below it. If the firm moves below the diagonal, this could, in turn, force further product changes.

On the basis of the foregoing discussion, one might wonder whether the best strategy is to operate below the diagonal or simply to move down the diagonal ahead of the competition. Although the latter strategy has cost advantages, the firm adopting it can suffer from a lack of flexibility. If product standardization does not occur in line with expectations, changes to the process can be expensive, even forcing the firm back up to the diagonal. Thus, a firm should not venture too far from the diagonal unless this is part of a conscious business strategy.

All the members of an industry do not necessarily move down the diagonal together. For example, some producers might choose to be low-volume–intermittent-process companies which stress flexibility and quality products. Meanwhile, other companies might move down the diagonal and stress standard products at low cost. In the hand-calculator business, it appears that Hewlett-Packard has chosen to stay in the upper left-hand corner while Texas Intruments operates in the lower right-hand corner. Hayes and Wheelwright (1979) report that for a time, Hewlett-Packard attempted to move toward more standard high-volume products without automating the process further. This caused Hewlett-Packard to operate above the diagonal. Soon after, it retreated to its more traditional end of the matrix rather than competing directly with Texas Instruments.

This story indicates the interesting phenomenon of distinctive competence. As noted in Chapter 2, a firm defines its distinctive competence by that set of tasks which sets it apart from the competition. Choosing a distinctive competence amounts to choosing a patch on the matrix. If the distinctive competence is defined only in terms of market strategy without regard for process, the firm is missing an important dimension of strategy. Furthermore, a one-dimensional strategy may cause the firm to operate off the diagonal without recognizing the problem and thereby encounter competitive trouble. Wickham Skinner (1974) calls this problem a lack of operations focus. This occurs when the operations process is not properly matched to the marketing concept.

The new flexible automation makes possible some interesting alterations to the product-process matrix. A firm can now operate over a wider range of product choices with the same physical process. This computerized technology allows the business to produce standardized large-volume products and partially customized lower-volume products from the same process. As a result, the firm can operate on a horizontal line which cuts partly across the product-process matrix. However, flexible technology has limitations and is costly, so that the matrix still applies; but strict adherence to the diagonal may not be necessary when the new technology is used.

5.5 VERTICAL INTEGRATION

To this point we have been considering the process selection decision for one particular site or location. For a single site we have considered the inputs and outputs of the productive process as given. But there is a larger question: Should the inputs or outputs of the productive process also be brought under ownership of the same enterprise? This is the vertical integration decision.

There are two types of vertical integration: backward and forward. Backward integration is concerned with expanding ownership "backward," toward the souce of supply. Backward integration may apply to any of the inputs of a productive process, including raw materials, labor, and capital equipment. Backward integration occurs when, for example, a newspaper buys a pulp mill to control one of its critical inputs, newsprint; a steelmaker buys iron mines in northern Minnesota to control the supply of ore; a vegetable canner buys farms and starts raising its own vegetables; or General Motors opens a training institute for its managers and technical employees.

Forward integration is concerned with expanding ownership of the process "forward," toward the market. Forward integration then brings the distribution channels under the control of the same firm. Forward integration occurs when, for example, a farmers' cooperative buys a processing plant and begins processing the sugar beets grown by the farmers; a maker of solid-state components expands its operations and marketing into the computer-terminal market (after forward integration, it makes not only the components for the terminals but also the terminals themselves); or a maker of basic steel expands into the production of finished steel product as well as iron ingots.

When a vertical integration decision is made, the process of production becomes either larger or smaller, depending on whether the firm is expanding or contracting. In many cases, factories or offices are consolidated, or new facilities are built after a vertical integration decision. As a result, the physical process of production changes as more or less of the production-distribution chain comes under the ownership of the firm.

Since the vertical integration decision is made in relation to the production-distribution chain, one must first identify the particular inputs and outputs of a firm's process. Backward integration then occurs along the chain toward the firm's suppliers. Forward integration occurs along the chain toward the firm's markets. For any particular point in the chain, one can then easily identify the backward and forward integration paths. If a particular firm owns the entire chain, we say that the firm is completely integrated vertically. Some examples of production-distribution chains are shown in Figure 5.7.

The vertical integration decision varies depending on whether backward or forward integration is being considered. In the case of backward integration, the key decision factors are costs and reliability of supply. If a firm is a major user of certain inputs, it may be less costly for it to produce its own inputs than to procure them from another supplier. In this case, however, the capital required to purchase from an existing supplier or to start up a business must be considered. The analysis required here is the classic acquisition question involved in deciding on ownership of any business. But even if the economics are not entirely favorable in relation to other uses of capital, a firm may integrate backward to ensure reliability of supply. This might be especially important if the inputs are supplied by only a few firms or are otherwise subject to uncertainties of supply and price.

In the case of the forward integration decision, the focus shifts to issues of marketing and channels of distribution. In this case, acquisition economics must still be considered in the same way. However, reliability of demand, rather than reliability of supply, is the crucial factor. A firm may be able to improve its competitive position greatly by integrating forward and thereby controlling more of the distribution chain.

Vertical integration includes a number of subtle factors which can best be understood by example. Litton Microwave, Inc., is a large producer of microwave ovens and ranges. When Litton first started to produce microwave ovens, it only assembled the final product. Sheet-metal parts, controls, plastic parts, and the magneton (microwave) tube were all purchased from outside suppliers. Litton was simply in the assembly business. As volume expanded and the product line stabilized, management decided to make its own sheet-metal parts. This decision was made not only on the basis of acceptable return on investment but also because of Litton's desire to control quality carefully and to be in charge of its own destiny. It did not want to be too dependent on the suppliers. Eventually, Litton manufactured all parts for the oven except the magnetron tubes. It continued to buy those tubes at low cost from four different Japanese suppliers. With multiple suppliers, a low unit cost and a reliable source of supply could be maintained.

Bowmar Corporation represents quite a different case. Bowmar started as a manufacturer of instrumentation for aircraft and developed electronic display devices (liquid-emitting diodes) which could be used in aircraft instruments. It also turned out these same displays could be used in hand-held calculators. Bowmar integrated forward into the calculator business, starting from the dis-

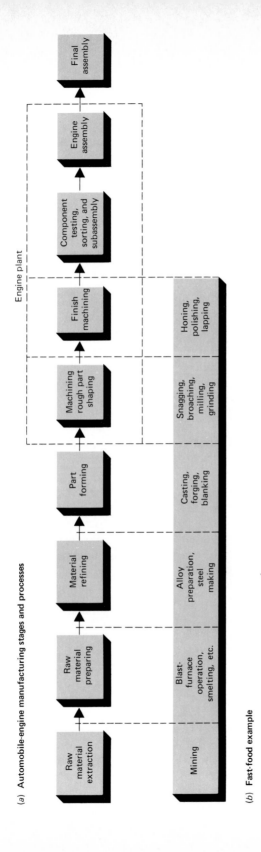

(a) Automobile-engine manufacturing stages and processes

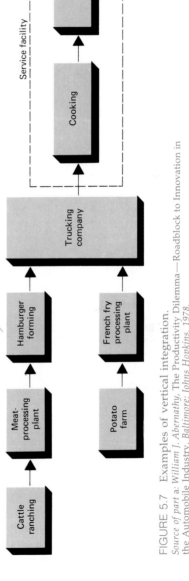

(b) Fast-food example

FIGURE 5.7 Examples of vertical integration.
Source of part a: William J. Abernathy, The Productivity Dilemma—Roadblock to Innovation in the Automobile Industry, Baltimore: Johns Hopkins, 1978.

plays. It bought calculator semiconductor chips and other parts from suppliers to use in the finished products. Eventually, Bowmar went bankrupt because it could not maintain control of its calculator business and because it lacked a reliable supply of chips. As a matter of fact, it was buying chips from its competitor, Texas Instruments, when bankruptcy was declared. Even though Bowmar made money on calculators for a short period of time, it decided on forward integration for the wrong reasons (to use the displays), and it was not a strong enough company to survive in the calculator business in the long run.

The important lesson to be learned is that vertical integration decisions should be viewed as strategic in nature. They are not simply investment decisions where return on investment is the overriding consideration. The decision should, of course, be financially sound, but it must also support the marketing and operations objectives of the firm. Because of this strategic importance, vertical integration decisions are often made by the chief executive officer with the involvement of all functions. Vertical integration decisions should support the corporate strategy and be a part of the operations strategy as well.

Today, vertical integration can occur on a global scale. Parts are bought in one country and assembled in another and the finished product sold in yet a third country. This is happening today along the border between the United States and Mexico, in Mexican "maquiladoras" factories. Parts are made in the United States, assembled in Mexico, and then brought back and sold in the United States and in world markets. There are also many examples of products manufactured around the world in health care, electronics, automobiles, and other industries. Vertical integration can thus cut across nations, as well as across companies. More on this issue is provided in Chapter 22 on International Operations.

5.6   KEY POINTS

This chapter has emphasized process selection decisions, including selection of process type and span of vertical integration. Process type was specified in terms of two key dimensions—product flow and type of customer order—leading to six major process types. The process-product matrix was introduced as a way of describing the dynamic nature of process selection and its relationship to market strategy. Specific points covered in the chapter are as follows:

- There are three types of process flow: line, intermittent, and project. Line flow is characterized by a linear sequence of operations and a product layout. Line processes utilize specialized equipment, are very efficient, and are usually inflexible in adapting to product or volume changes. Intermittent operations use a process layout with similar equipment or skills grouped together. The resulting flow pattern is jumbled, since the product is made in batches and flows through only the processes needed. Intermittent operations are highly flexible but much less efficient than line processes. The project is used to make a unique product. All tasks are sequenced to support the single product being made. Projects provide the most flexibility but are usually quite expensive.

- Operations processes can also be classified as make-to-order and make-to-stock. The make-to-order process is set in motion by customer orders and geared to delivery performance. The make-to-stock process is geared to the replenishment of inventory; it does not respond to specific customer orders. Make-to-stock operations are measured by use of capacity, inventory levels, and stockout performance.
- The combination of product flow with type of customer order yields six types of operations processes. Selection from among these processes is made by considering capital requirements, market conditions, labor, management skills, raw materials, and technology. These factors are evaluated by conducting marketing and economic studies, but the process selection decision is always strategic in nature.
- The process-product matrix describes stages in the life cycles of products and processes. A firm should define its distinctive competence in terms of both process and product by selecting a patch on the matrix. The matrix helps relate process selection decisions to product decisions and the market.
- Vertical integration defines the ownership question in process selection. Forward integration extends ownership of the process forward toward the market. Backward integration extends ownership of the process backward toward suppliers. Both types of integration involve economic considerations; however, backward integration is concerned with reliability of supply, while forward integration is concerned with reliability of demand. All vertical-integration decisions should be viewed in a strategic context.

QUESTIONS

1. Classify the following types of processes as line, intermittent, or project:
   a. Doctor's office
   b. Automatic car wash
   c. College curriculum
   d. Studying for an exam
   e. Registration for classes
   f. Electric utility
2. Why are line processes usually so much more efficient but less flexible than intermittent processes? Give three reasons.
3. The rate of productivity improvement in the service industries has been much lower than in manufacturing. Can this be attributed to process selection decisions? What problems would be involved in using more efficient processes in service industries?
4. The project process is typically used for skyscraper construction. Does this lead to higher costs? Could more efficient processes be used? If so, how?
5. Several industries—including those that produce furniture, houses, sailboats, and clothing—have never progressed down the diagonal of the process-product matrix to become highly standardized and efficient. Why do you think this is so? Is this a serious problem?
6. Compare the expensive restaurant, fast-food restaurant, and cafeteria in terms of process characteristics such as capital, product type, labor, planning, control systems, etc.

7. An entrepreneur is planning to go into the food business. How would he or she decide whether to open a cafeteria, fast-food restaurant, or fine restaurant? What factors should be considered in this decision?

8. A company is in the business of making souvenir spoons to customer order. The customers select the size of the spoons and may specify the design to be embossed on them. One or more spoons may be ordered. The company is considering going into the make-to-stock spoon business for souvenir spoons and everyday tableware as well. What will it have to do differently? How is the business likely to change?

9. What are the possible consequences of defining a marketing strategy independently of the process strategy?

10. What are the distinctive competencies of the following organizations? Is the distinctive competence defined in terms of product or process?
    a. McDonald's
    b. AT&T Telephone Co.
    c. General Motors
    d. Harvard Business School

11. Identify the following examples as using either forward or backward integration. Explain.
    a. A shoe company going into the leather business
    b. A food processor going into the restaurant business
    c. A paper mill buying a publishing house
    d. A restaurant chain buying a cattle ranch

12. The oil industry is heavily integrated vertically. What are the possible reasons for this? What would be the effects, pro and con, of breaking up the oil companies?

13. Suppose a firm integrates backward quite rapidly while its products are still in the early phase of their life cycles. What could be the possible adverse effects of this strategy?

SELECTED BIBLIOGRAPHY

ABERNATHY, WILLIAM, J.: "Production Process Structure and Technological Change," *Decision Sciences*, vol. 7, no. 4, October 1976, pp. 607–619.

—— and P. L. TOWNSEND: "Technology, Productivity, and Process Change," *Technological Forecasting and Social Change*, vol. 7, August 1975, pp. 377–396.

APPLETON, DANIEL S.: "A Strategy for Manufacturing Automation," *Datamation*, October 1977, pp. 64–70.

BOAS, MAX, and STEVE CHAN: *Big Mac*, New York: Mentor, 1976.

BUZZELL, ROBERT O.: "Is Vertical Integration Profitable?" *Harvard Business Review*, January–February 1983, pp. 92–102.

CHASE, RICHARD B., and NICHOLAS AQUILANO: *Production and Operations Management: A Life Cycle Approach*, rev. ed., Homewood, Ill.: Irwin, 1977.

CONSTABLE, C. J., and C. C. NEW: *Operations Management: A Systems Approach through Text and Cases*, New York: Wiley-Interscience, 1976.

HAYES, ROBERT H., and STEVEN C. WHEELWRIGHT: "Line Manufacturing Process and Product Life Cycles," *Harvard Business Review*, January–February 1979, pp. 133–140.

MARSHALL, PAUL W., et al.: *Operations Management: Text and Cases*, Homewood, Ill.: Irwin, 1975.

SCHMENNER, ROGER W.: *Production/Operations Management: Concepts and Situations*, 3d ed., Chicago: SRA, 1987.

SKINNER, WICKHAM: "Manufacturing—Missing Link in Corporate Strategy," *Harvard Business Review*, May–June 1969, pp. 136–145.

——: "The Focused Factory," *Harvard Business Review*, May–June 1974, pp. 113–121.

Service Operations Design

As noted in Chapter 1, the United States has become a service economy, with over 70 percent of the GNP and 80 percent of the work force in the service sector. This is also true of industrialized countries outside the United States; in Japan 75 percent of the work force is employed in services, and in Europe 72 percent of employment is in services. [See Heskett (1986), p. 184.] Thus, service is the dominant economic force in the industrialized world today, and growth projections indicate this trend will continue.

Everyone has a favorite story about poor service. Why can't you get your car fixed right the first time, or when was the last time that you were satisfied with the service on some airlines? Problems of poor service are becoming commonplace, and most of them can be directly related to the way that services are produced. Box 6.1 indicates how service operations at SAS Airlines were greatly improved by putting the customer first and by paying attention to the service delivery system.

This chapter deals with service operations and what can be done to remedy the problems of inefficient and poor-quality service delivery. The focus here is on the design of the strategy, the product, and the process for delivering service. Later parts of this text deal with capacity planning, scheduling, work force management, and quality control. As a matter of fact, services are addressed throughout the text, but special emphasis is given to service process design and related issues in this chapter.

BOX 6.1

SCANDINAVIAN AIRLINE SYSTEM

In 1981 the Scandinavian Airline System (SAS) lost $8 million. The Board of Directors decided to replace the SAS president with Jan Carlzon, who set out to turn the company around. Carlzon's strategy was to make SAS the most customer-oriented airline in Europe, and he succeeded—within 12 months SAS had earned a $71 million profit while the rest of the industry was still losing money.

SAS for too many years had concentrated on flying airplanes, not on improving the quality of the customer experience. Carlzon said, "We are really in the business of serving the traveling public." This meant shifting everyone's focus to the customer—20,000 employees in all. Frontline people tended to be preoccupied with their tasks. Managers seemed to focus on getting the work done. "Who," Carlzon asked, "is paying attention to the needs of the customer?"

Carlzon redesigned the services offered. SAS instituted Euroclass service to provide better *perceived* service for the business traveler. This service included special business-class seats in the aircraft and more in-flight attention.

SAS also decided that it would have the best on-time schedule in Europe within 6 months. At first, management estimated that this improvement would cost $1 million. The program was so enthusiastically received that it only cost $125,000 and only took 3 months to become the most punctual airline.

Carlzon communicated the vision of improved service to a wide range of employees and managers by hundreds of meetings and an extensive training program. A number of customer improvement projects were also instituted. The idea was to identify the cycle of service provided and to improve service at every point in the cycle. Carlzon said, "We have 50,000 moments of truth out there every day." A moment of truth, by Carlzon's definition, is anytime the company comes in contact with the customer who can form an impression of the company as a result of this contact.

Carlzon grasped all the important elements of service improvement: strategy, people, system, and customer. The strategy was focused on the customer, and the system and people were reoriented to serve the customer's needs.

Source: Karl Albrecht and Ron Zemke, *Service America,* Homewood, Ill.: Dow Jones-Irwin, 1985.

DEFINING SERVICE

Most definitions of service stress the intangibility of service as contrasted to the tangibility of goods. This is an unsatisfactory definition because it does not come to grips with the fundamental nature of services. A better definition is that service is something which is produced and consumed simultaneously. A service, therefore, never exists; only the result can be observed after the fact. When you get a haircut, the service is consumed as it is produced, but the effect or result, of the service is apparent and will last for some time.

From an operations point of view, simultaneous production and consumption is a very important distinction. It highlights the fact that the customer is brought into direct contact with operations. The customer is, therefore, an important source of uncertainty which is difficult to control. Also, the service must be brought to the customer or the customer brought to the service. The service cannot be produced in one place and shipped to another, as goods can, nor can it be stored. All these characteristics can be attributed to the simultaneity of production and consumption.

As Normann (1984) states, service consists of *acts* and *interactions* which are social contacts. Service is more than the production of something intangible; it is a social interaction between the producer and the customer. This highlights the importance, from a definition point of view, of the customer being intimately involved with the production process and the associated uncertainty which may be introduced into the production process.

Service, to some, implies servitude and personal service, such as that provided by maids, chauffeurs, and cleaning people. This is an inaccurate view of service today as a whole. There are professional services such as medicine, law, education, and architecture. There are highly capital-intensive services such as air travel, hospitals, and trucking. There are also mass services such as retailing, wholesale, and fast food. Only a small segment (less than 1 percent) of the service industry is related to personal service.

Another inaccurate perception is that service jobs are low-paying. To be sure, some service occupations earn less than manufacturing, but some service occupations also earn more, particularly in the service professions and in capital-intensive service industries. Perhaps, the perception of low pay is directly related to the perception of servitude, rather than the broader range of services produced today.

It has been said that services are the same as manufacturing with a few "odd characteristics." While there are certainly many similarities, some of the most important differences between manufacturing and services are shown in Table 6.1. The impact of these differences on operations are significant and have been discussed above.

6.2 FRAMEWORKS FOR SERVICES

In designing service processes it is important to have an underlying framework. The framework, shown in Figure 6.1, has been suggested by Albrecht and Zemke (1985) in *Service America*. This framework, the service triangle, assumes there are four elements which must be considered in producing services: the customer, people, strategy, and the system.

The customer, of course, is at the center of the triangle because service should always be customer-centered. People are the employees of the service firm. The strategy is the vision or philosophy which is used to guide all aspects of service delivery, and the system is the physical system and procedures which are used.

The lines connecting the elements in Figure 6.1 have some interesting interpretations. The line from the customer to the strategy indicates that the strategy should put the customer first, by meeting the true needs of the customer.

TABLE 6.1

DIFFERENCES BETWEEN MANUFACTURING AND SERVICE

Manufacturing	Service
The product is tangible	The service is intangible
Ownership is transferred at the time of purchase	Ownership is generally not transferred
The product can be resold	No resale is possible
The product can be demonstrated before purchase	The product does not exist before purchase
The product can be stored in inventory	The product cannot be stored
Production precedes consumption	Production and consumption are simultaneous
Production and consumption can be spatially separated	Production and consumption must occur at the same location.
The product can be transported	The product cannot be transported (though producers can be)
The seller produces	The buyer takes part directly in the production process and can indeed perform part of the production.
Indirect contact is possible between the company and the customer	In most cases direct contact is needed
The product can be exported	The service cannot normally be exported, but the service delivery system can be
Business is organized by functions, with sales and production separated	Sales and production cannot be separated functionally.

Source: Adapted from Richard Normann, *Service Management: Strategy and Leadership in the Service Businesses,* New York: Wiley, 1984.

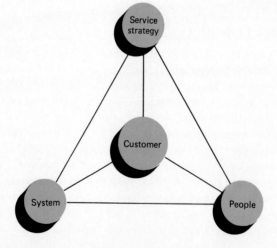

FIGURE 6.1
Service triangle.
Source: Karl Albrecht and Ron Zemke,
Service America,
Homewood, Ill.: Dow Jones–Irwin, 1985.

Management should ask what goes on in the customer's mind. How does the customer think? What does the customer really want? Also, the company must communicate the service strategy to the customer. What does the company provide that is unique? Why should the customer buy from this company?

The line from customer to system indicates that the system (procedures and equipment) should be designed with the customer in mind. Crowded seats in airplanes, forms that can't be understood, and uncomfortable restaurants don't lead to good customer service. Customer service is not an afterthought, but must be designed into the delivery system.

The customer-to-people line indicates that everyone should be customer-driven, not only the operations people who deliver the service, but all people in the organization. If people do not serve the customer directly, they should be serving someone who is; even the accountants, computer people, and engineers have "internal" customers inside the organization. People are the most important element in delivering superior service.

The outside lines in the triangle in Figure 6.1 also have a direct meaning. The people-to-system line indicates that people depend on the system to deliver good service. Most service problems have been attributed to poor systems rather than people. Is it too much to ask that the computer system work at the car-rental desk, and that the check-in procedure at the airline should be hassle-free? Service systems should be designed to be simple, fast, and foolproof to operate.

The strategy-to-system line indicates that the system should follow logically from the strategy, but it rarely does. Often the systems have grown up over time and have been designed in an incremental fashion. As a result, the systems do not really support the intended strategy, and furthermore they are not well integrated.

Finally, the strategy-to-people line indicates that everyone in the organization should be aware of the strategy. The frontline people who deliver the service are often divorced from the strategy. Management views them as a "cog in the wheel" and not in need of knowing the service strategy. As a result, poor service is delivered.

The concepts related to the service triangle provide an interesting way to think about service operations. These concepts are useful for designing service systems and for solving service problems. The service triangle can also be used to diagnose service problems and to determine what the causes of poor service might be.

Every service is delivered in a cycle of service. The cycle starts with the point at which the customer first contacts the service delivery system. It continues with each subsequent contact that the customer makes with anyone in the company. For example, if you contact an airline, the first point of contact may be a telephone inquiry about the departure and arrival times of various flights. Later, you may actually make the reservation. Then you receive your ticket and pay your bill. When you arrive at the airport, you are greeted by customer service personnel to take your ticket and check your baggage. Then you are ushered onto the plane, are served in flight, depart the plane, and retrieve your baggage. At each of these events, you as the customer form an impression, conscious or unconscious, of whether the airline meets your needs or not. A typical cycle of service for an airline is shown in Figure 6.2.

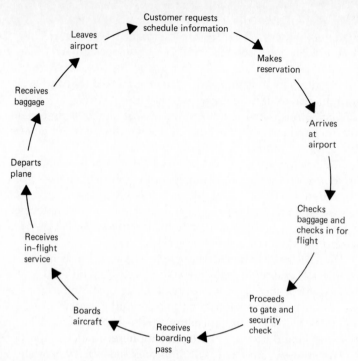

FIGURE 6.2
Cycle of service
for an airline.

Albrecht and Zemke stress the idea of "moments of truth." A moment of truth is anytime that the customer comes in contact with the service system during the cycle of service delivery. At that moment, the customer can receive either good or poor service and therefore forms an impression of the service received. It is the cumulative effect of these moments of truth that ultimately determines whether the customer will continue to buy from the company.

A bad moment of truth can delete many favorable moments, so it is important that each encounter in the service cycle be favorable, and some should be outstanding. All points in the service cycle should be managed. At SAS airlines it is said that there are 50,000 moments of truth each day. At Marriott Corporation there are an estimated 6 million moments of truth every day from a total of 140,000 employees.

The customer's perception of service is a function of all the previous moments of truth experienced.

Service $= f$(moments of truth)

Managing the moments of truth to create a positive service experience is the essence of service management.

Working from the above concepts we define the model for service, shown in Figure 6.3, that will be used to organize the remainder of this chapter. First the service strategy is discussed, next the service product is defined, then the service delivery system is defined, and finally service measurements are made. Each element of this model will be described in subsequent sections.

FIGURE 6.3
Service model.

 DEFINING THE STRATEGY AND SERVICE PRODUCTS

In Chapter 2 we discussed development of strategy in detail. Therefore, we will only briefly summarize service strategy here.

The service strategy defines what business you are in. It provides guidance for designing products, delivery systems, and measurements. The service strategy provides a vision for what kind and type of service the company should provide. It describes the way the business is perceived by the customers and the employees, or at least how it should be viewed by them.

An example of service strategy is the Deluxe Check Inc. strategy of providing fast and reliable delivery of printed checks to customers. [See Albrecht and Zemke (1985).] This strategy was further defined as delivery of checks within 2 days of receipt of the order with zero defects. This strategy helps differentiate Deluxe Check from its competitors, and it meets a need of the customer, which is to receive checks rapidly after opening an account or when placing a reorder. Deluxe Check has built its products, delivery system, and measurement systems to support this strategy.

Service strategy should consider the international scope of services offered. Many services, such as consulting, travel, telecommunications, banking, and shipping, are international in character. These services are standardized around the world, the basis of competition is international, and the scale of operations is global in nature. Many service firms can adopt a global strategy, just like manufacturing firms do.

The second step in the model is to define the service products. Most service products come "bundled" with goods as well. A ride in a taxi cab—transportation from one point to another—is a service. However, the taxi service is delivered by means of a facilitating good, the taxicab. Likewise, telephone companies use facilitating goods—telephones, wires, and equipment—and so do most other service operations.

Sasser, Olsen, and Wyckoff (1978) have defined a service product as consisting of the following bundle of goods and services:

1. The physical items or facilitating goods
2. The sensual benefits, or explicit services
3. The psychological benefits, or implicit services

In the case of a restaurant, the physical items consist of the facility, food, drinks, napkins, etc. The sensual benefits are taste, waiter service, the smell of food, and the sounds and sights of people. The psychological benefits include comfort, status, and a sense of well-being.

The key to the design of service products is to properly define the items in the service bundle. An appropriate mix of each of the three components should be delivered. But it is not enough to define the attributes of good service in general terms; one must also specify standards. These standards should cover each of the attributes in the goods-service bundle; they should be specifically defined and measurable. The standards can thus be used as a basis for training, quality control, and measurement of management performance.

In designing services, management should carefully read customer expectations. For example, the management of a restaurant may concentrate its efforts on presenting the very best food. But what the customer may want is a night out on the town. Management must, therefore, carefully design the service to meet the real expectations of the customers. Too much emphasis on the facilitating good may result in too little service, or vice versa.

Sasser, Olsen, and Wykoff (1978) have indicated three ways that consumers think about service attributes:

1. *One overpowering attribute.* One attribute receives overwhelming consideration; the others receive little or no weight.
2. *Single attribute with threshold minimums.* One attribute is considered primary, with the others meeting at least the minimums required. For example, in fast photo finishing, time is the primary attribute, with quality of printing and other services meeting thresholds.
3. *Weighted average of attributes.* Each attribute receives a certain weight, and the total of the weighted attributes is considered. In this case, less service on one attribute can be traded off for more service on other attributes. For example, good food at a restaurant can make up for the long wait.

Which of these models is used by the customer will, of course, determine how the various attributes of service are combined in order to arrive at the customer's buying decisions. It should also determine how management evaluates the importance of various attributes in the goods-service bundle. The typical mix of services and facilitating goods for some well-known services is shown in Figure 6.4.

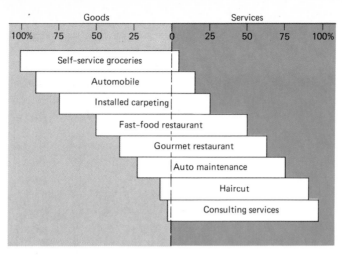

6.4 CUSTOMER CONTACT

The third step in service management is designing the service process. Chase (1978) has observed that a key element in choosing a process is the amount of customer contact. If the degree of contact is low, the process can be buffered from the customer and other external influences. In this case there is little potential for the customer to disrupt the process of production. Low contact corresponds to a manufacturing type of process, and efficiency can be high.

On the other hand, if customer contact is high, the customer can disrupt the production process by demanding certain types of services or special treatment. Therefore, high customer contact can lead to inefficient production processes. But the presence of the customer in the system is not all bad. Sometimes the customer can be a source of efficiency by using the customer to do part of the service task. For example, customers in self-serve situations do some of the work such as pumping their own gas or serving themselves in a cafeteria.

High contact may introduce a source of uncertainty into the production system, through the presence of the customer, which is not there in the low-contact situation. Chase and Tansik (1983), in their now famous article, propose that this can lead to a loss of potential efficiency, as stated in the following formula:

Potential efficiency = f(degree of customer contact)

The degree of customer contact is measured by the percentage of time that the customer is in the system as a fraction of the total time it takes to produce the service. For example, at McDonald's the degree of contact might be about 70 percent. Most of the time that the service is being produced, the customer is at the front counter in a high-contact situation. But some of the food can be cooked in the back in a low-contact environment, while the customer is not in the system or not waiting. Thus some efficiency is possible through low-contact, back-room operations.

McDonald's also illustrates the separation of high-contact and low-contact services by a front- and back-room type of layout. A small buffer of food is kept between the front and back room during busy hours. This not only improves efficiency, but reduces customer waiting time as well. Chase and Tansik advocate separating high-contact and low-contact services in order to improve operations. This is an application of the principle of focused operations, discussed in Chapter 2.

Characteristics of low-contact and high-contact systems are as follows:

1. Low-contact systems can be used when face-to-face contact is not required or desired by the customer, or when rapid exchange of information is not needed. For example, mail-order catalog sales and bank-by-mail plans utilize low-contact systems which respond to standard customer needs. High-contact systems are ideal for responding to a variety of changing or uncertain customer demands.
2. Low-contact systems generally require people with technical skills oriented toward efficient processing, well-defined procedures, and smooth flow. High-contact systems require people with good interpersonal skills, including versatility, personality, flexibility, and a customer orientation.
3. High-contact systems must respond to the demand as it occurs. Therefore, they must accommodate peak demand. Low-contact systems can work to average demand and can be more efficiently planned for smooth flow of work.
4. High-contact systems generally require higher prices and offer more customization and convenience. Low-contact systems provide lower costs and more standardization.

The degree of customer contact can be an important ingredient in designing processes or service delivery systems. However, customer contact, by itself, does not lead to inefficiency when the service can be standardized and the customer subsequently agrees not to intervene into the production process. It is the customer-introduced uncertainty, rather than customer contact, which is at the source of the inefficiency in operations. Therefore, customer contact, coupled with uncertainty, is an important consideration in designing service operations. While we have shown how the customer contact model can be used to separate, or focus, service operations, other factors which should also be considered will be described next.

 SERVICE MATRIX

There are many different ways to think about service processes. What really tends to differentiate fast food from a gourmet restaurant? What distinguishes the airlines from legal firms and consulting firms? Is it the labor intensity? The degree of customer contact? The customization of the service? Or some other characteristic?

In an attempt to answer these questions Schmenner (1986) has suggested that capital intensity is one of the dimensions which should be considered in differentiating services. The capital required for an airline or a hospital is certainly much greater than for a highly labor-intensive service such as a consulting

TABLE 6.2
LABOR INTENSITY OF SOME SERVICES

Low Labor-Intensive Services:	Capital-Labor Ratio
Electric utilities, gas, sanitation services	14.21
Communications	5.31
Amusement & recreation	2.49
Hospitals: —Teaching —For-profit —All other (e.g., community)	 1.59 1.63 1.75
Auto & other repair	1.60
Transportation	1.27
Banking	1.20
Hotels, etc	1.01

High Labor-Intensive Services:	Capital-Labor Ratio
Security, commodity brokers	0.15
Insurance agents & service	0.18
Business services (e.g., advertising, credit reporting, mailing & reproduction, building services, personnel supply, computer & data processing, management consulting & public relations)	0.42
Personal services (e.g., laundry, photo, beauty/barber shops, funeral services)	0.53
Wholesale trade	0.54
Retail trade	0.62

Source: Roger W. Schmenner, "How Can Service Businesses Survive and Prosper?" *Sloan Management Review,* Spring 1986, p. 22.

business or a travel agency. Table 6.2 shows the ratio of capital to labor for a range of services. This ratio is computed by dividing the total book value of buildings and equipment by the annual cost of labor (all forms of personnel). As Table 6.2 indicates, the ratio varies from a high of 14.2 for capital-intensive electric utilities to a low of .15 for labor-intensive security brokers.[1] Schmenner argues that this ratio will have an effect on efficiency, as well as on the managerial task.

Schmenner also suggests that customer interaction combined with customization should be considered as a second dimension of importance. For example, most doctors and lawyers tend to provide highly customized services, and interaction is high. They are open to feedback from the client and willing to modify the service in response to the client's needs. An exception to this is Joel Hyatt Legal Services, which handles only a limited set of legal services such as wills, divorces, and real estate contracts. Interaction is high when the customer can intervene in the process and requires special treatment. Customization is high when the firm will provide tailor-made services for the customer.

---

[1] For comparison purposes, the corresponding average ratio for manufacturing industries is 1.9.

Most fast-food services provide a low level of customization and interaction. The customer must select from a prescribed menu, and interaction is limited. Even though these services are high in customer contact, they are low in customer specification.

There are some services in the middle which have low interaction but high customization. For example, Lloyd's of London will insure almost anything, but much of the transaction can be handled by means of low interaction. On the other hand, the typical business traveler requires low customization but high interaction. The business traveler will select from a standardized list of airport departure times but requires frequent interaction to handle changes in the selected schedule.

Using these dimensions, Schmenner has proposed a service matrix which can be used to classify different types of services. This matrix is somewhat like the one we have used in the last chapter to classify manufacturing processes as line, intermittent, and project together with make-to-stock and make-to-order processes. The service matrix, shown in Figure 6.5, can be used to identify different types of processes and different operations management tasks.

In the matrix there are four types of service operations. The service factory is characterized by low interaction and customization together with low labor intensity. These services, such as airlines, trucking, and hotels, are produced in a factory–like setting with high efficiency. Another type of service operation shown in Figure 6.5 is the service shop, which provides highly automated services but with a high degree of customization. These services include hospitals, auto repair, and other repair. Although the service shop is highly automated, it is flexible enough to meet a variety of customer choices, something like the job shop in manufacturing.

The service matrix in Figure 6.5 also shows mass service and professional service. Mass service is highly labor-intensive and low in interaction and customization. These services utilize a highly standardized format such as retailing, schools, and retail banking, and they are produced on a mass basis.

Professional service, the last cell in the matrix, provides a high level of customization and very little automation. These services are characterized by the traditional professions such as accounting, law, and medicine. Services in this cell

FIGURE 6.5
Service matrix.
Source: Roger W. Schmenner, "How Can Service Businesses Survive and Prosper?" Sloan Management Review, Spring 1986, p. 25.

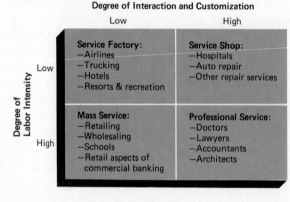

Degree of Interaction and Customization

Low   High

Degree of Labor Intensity — Low / High

Service Factory:
—Airlines
—Trucking
—Hotels
—Resorts & recreation

Service Shop:
—Hospitals
—Auto repair
—Other repair services

Mass Service:
—Retailing
—Wholesaling
—Schools
—Retail aspects of commercial banking

Professional Service:
—Doctors
—Lawyers
—Accountants
—Architects

tend to be quite inefficient because of both high labor costs and high interaction and customization.

The service matrix indicates how services can be positioned. For example, Joel Hyatt Legal Services has moved from the professional service cell to the mass service cell because the services are much more standardized, but still labor-intensive. This provides a basis for differentiation of the service to the customers, and different managerial tasks as well.

The service matrix can be used to illustrate how the operations management task varies with different types of services. The highly automated services require familiarity with technology, correct capital decisions, management of demand to avoid peaks, and careful scheduling to utilize expensive capacity. On the other hand, the highly labor-intensive services require more attention to managing the large work force associated with these services.

As Schmenner points out, the highly customized services provide challenges for management to hold down costs, maintain quality, control customer intervention, and reduce turnover of highly skilled people. The highly standardized services require operations management to present an image of service, to motivate employees doing routine work, and to maintain standard procedures.

The service matrix provides a concept of how a large variety of services differ in terms of their management needs. It also presents additional insights into the customer contact model discussed above. As we have previously noted, high customer contact, in itself, is not necessarily an impediment to efficiency when the service is standardized and the interaction is low. Chain hotels and airline service fall into this category; they are highly efficient and have high customer contact, but the form of contact is limited. On the other hand, low contact does not guarantee high efficiency, particularly if a high degree of variety in the service is permitted or if automation is low. Efficiency may have more to do with capital investment and low variety than with contact itself. As Wathen (1988) has pointed out, the degree of uncertainty introduced by the customer is, perhaps, of more consequence than the level of customer contact itself.

The service matrix also provides a basis for defining the critical management tasks that are required. Service operations managers can then focus their energies on the important decisions and issues.

6.6 SERVICE DELIVERY SYSTEM

The service delivery system consists of the physical elements and the work force which is used to produce the service. Normally the following five elements are considered as part of the service delivery system.

1. *Technology.* The degree of automation, the equipment, the degree of vertical integration
2. *Process flow.* The sequence of events used to produce the service
3. *Process type.* The amount of contact involved (high or low), the degree of customization and integration

4. *Location and size.* The place where the service process is located, the size of each service site
5. *Work force.* The skills, the type of organization, the reward systems, the degree of participation

Some guidance has been given above on how these elements should be chosen. All the five elements are a function of customer contact, the degree of customization and interaction. These elements in turn are directed by the service strategy and the service product design.

It is also extremely important to ensure that the service process is well integrated. Each of the elements should fit together with each other. How this can be done is illustrated by Jean-Claude Decaux, a successful French firm which specializes in the construction and maintenance of bus stops. [See Normann (1984) for more details.] These bus stops are made available to French cities free of charge, and the costs are paid for through advertising.

Before the development of this concept, bus stops were ugly, frequently vandalized, and generally in poor condition. When Mr. Decaux first suggested his concept, no one would hear of it. Finally, a few cities tried the idea, and it has spread from there.

Attractive, pleasing, and well-constructed bus stops were offered to cities in France. While the bus stops were designed to be rugged and to require little maintenance, vandalism and maintenance could not be totally eliminated. At first, maintenance was provided by the cities, which generally used low-paid and unmotivated public employees who had a high rate of absenteeism and turnover. Contract maintenance was also tried without much success.

Finally, Mr. Decaux decided to hire his own maintenance force. They were well paid and each given their own car, not one that had to be returned to the pool at the end of the day. Maintenance people were also equipped with special tools and given an assigned set of bus stops that were their own to maintain. Each bus stop is visited by the maintenance employee at least three times a week on a regular basis, with emergency maintenance also provided as needed. Anyone in the company who notices that a bus stop is in need of maintenance will call the emergency phone number. A maintenance worker is dispatched immediately to the scene.

The maintenance employees are highly motivated and do an excellent job. They have flexible working hours and take pride in their work. They also have access directly to Mr. Decaux if that should be needed. The organization stresses the key relationships among the maintenance people, advertisers, and the cities. These relationships are reinforced by the service delivery system which has been described above. Note how all elements of this system are integrated: the technology, the work force, and the service strategy.

This example illustrates how a service delivery system should be designed. The physical elements, the signs and bus stops themselves, are designed to be rugged and attractive. The maintenance work force is motivated and given the tools to maintain the bus stops in good condition at all times. A feedback system is developed to constantly monitor service and provide corrective action. All these elements are well integrated to support the service strategy, which is to provide attractive and useful bus stops at no cost to cities.

6.7 ANALYZING PROCESS FLOWS

Most processes, for manufacturing or service, can be improved by flowcharting them. The basic idea is to define each step in the process and to draw a flowchart of all the steps and their interrelationships. As a result of these diagrams, the process can be analyzed for efficiency and customer service improvement.

A flowchart for a typical car-rental service is shown in Figure 6.6. This flowchart indicates each step in checking out and checking in a car. It also shows all the steps required to get a car ready behind the scenes. Note that each customer interaction point is shown on the chart. Each of these points is basically a moment of truth, where the customer can be satisfied or disappointed depending on the level of service rendered.

Flowcharts can be used for several things. One is to study the layout and capacity of the facility for customer convenience or efficiency. For example, how long does the customer have to wait to check out a car? Can the process be simplified if the waiting time is too long? How long does it take to check in a car? Can the arrangement for check-in be laid out better?

Another use of flowcharts is to check the information required at each step and the information processing used. Is all the necessary information obtained? Can some unnecessary information be eliminated? Is the proper level of automated information processing used?

Flowcharts are also convenient for purposes of analyzing the way employees are utilized in the process. Are the type of people selected suited to the tasks at hand? Can better training methods be developed, and are people rewarded for the right things?

A flowchart will tend to precipitate the above questions, because managers can easily visualize the process. By thinking through the physical flows, the information flows, and the use of people, important questions become clear.

Shostack (1984) has advocated the use of flowcharting, "blueprinting" as she calls it, to analyze existing or new processes. She describes the blueprint for a discount brokerage, shown in Figure 6.7. In this figure most of the service is invisible to the customer since many of the activities take place behind the scenes. The figure also indicates possible service failure points where special attention should be given. Telephone contact, for example, has a very critical impact on customer perceptions but is difficult to control. To deal with this potential failure point, management decided to carefully script telephone calls, to define procedures, and to train people in proper telephone protocol.

Figure 6.7 also shows the time required for various steps. These times can be used to balance capacity and to ensure that the proper level of service is provided at each step. How this can be analyzed in a much more sophisticated way through the use of queuing analysis is given in the chapter supplement.

As mentioned earlier, most of the problems with service are due to the process used and not the people who deliver it. But most of management effort is on fire fighting and resolving people problems without attacking the root causes. There is

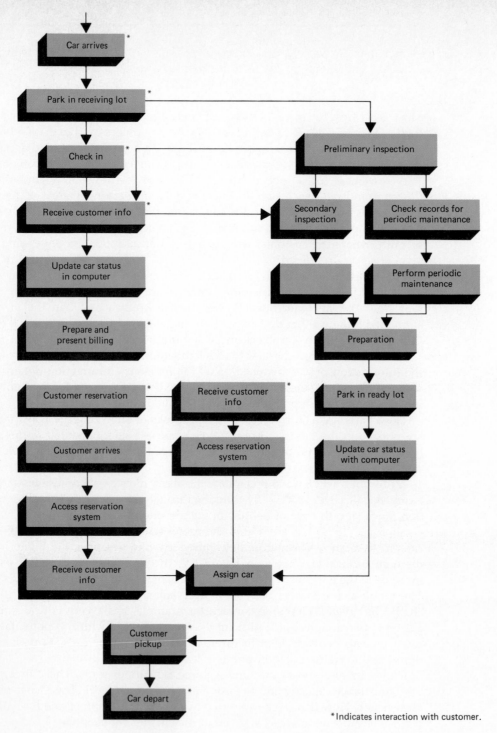

Car arrives *

Park in receiving lot *

Check in *

Preliminary inspection

Receive customer info *

Secondary inspection

Check records for periodic maintenance

Update car status in computer

Perform periodic maintenance

Prepare and present billing *

Preparation

Customer reservation *

Receive customer info *

Park in ready lot *

Customer arrives *

Access reservation system

Update car status with computer

Access reservation system

Receive customer info

Assign car

Customer pickup *

Car depart *

*Indicates interaction with customer.

FIGURE 6.6   Flowchart of car-rental check-in and check-out process.
Source: W. Earl Sasser, R. Paul Olsen, and D. Daryl Wyckoff, Management of Service Operations:
Text, Cases and Readings, *Boston: Allyn and Bacon, 1978.*

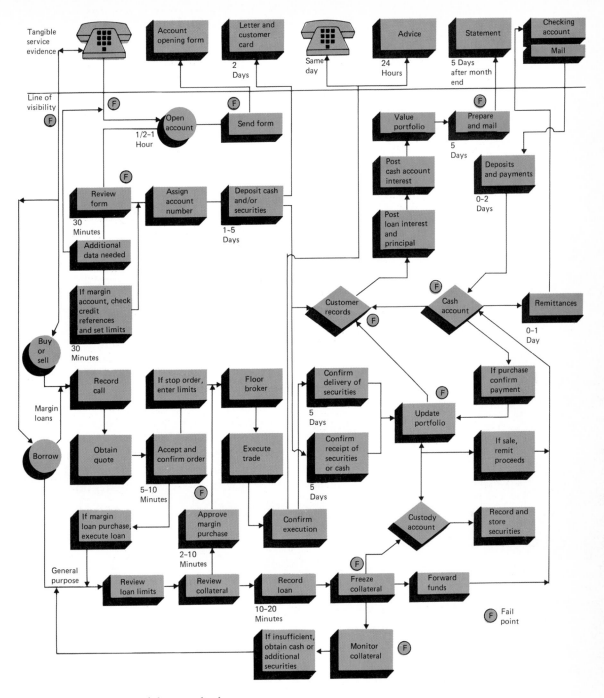

FIGURE 6.7   Blueprint of discount brokerage.
Source: G. Lynn Shostack, "Designing Services That Deliver," Harvard Business Review,
January–February 1984, pp. 133–139.

great room for process improvement by use of simple techniques such as process flowcharting.

 6.8 KEY POINTS

This chapter has emphasized the design of service products and processes. The key points are as follows:

- A service is a product which is produced and consumed simultaneously. The customer is frequently involved in the production of the service and influences the efficiency of operations. Services consist of acts and interactions which are social contacts. Thus services must be managed as human exchanges, not merely as programmed technical actions. The service cycle indicates the important contact points in delivering services.
- The service triangle demonstrates the interaction among the customer, people, the system, and strategy. These four elements are the important things for operations managers to focus on in managing services.
- Services are provided in a bundle of goods and services. This bundle consists of facilitating goods, sensual benefits, and psychological benefits. The customer seeks an appropriate mix of the items in this bundle.
- Services may be defined as high contact or low contact in nature. Generally speaking, low-contact services can be made more efficient than high-contact services when there is less involvement of the customer. Uncertainty introduced by customer demands is more important than the level of customer contact itself.
- The service matrix defines services by the degree of customization and interaction and the capital intensity of the service. On this basis four types of services are defined: service factory, service shop, mass service, and professional service. Each of these service types has its own operations management tasks.
- The service delivery system should be designed to integrate physical and human elements with the service strategy. A lack of integration often leads to poor performance.
- Each interaction between the customer and the service provider is a "moment of truth." The level of service delivered is the summation of these many moments of truth which occur each day.
- Service processes should be flowcharted. A flowchart (or blueprint) will indicate each step in the delivery of the service and each point of customer contact. Flowcharts can be analyzed to improve process flow, information, automation, and the use of service personnel.

QUESTIONS

1. Classify the following services by their degree of customer contact (high, medium, or low).
   a. Check clearing in a bank
   b. Bank teller
   c. Bank loan officer

2. Who is the customer in a school, a jail, and a personnel office in a firm? Identify some moments of truth experienced by these customers.
3. Locate each of the following services on the service matrix.
   a. Vending machine business
   b. Housecleaning service
   c. Appliance repair
4. How do the managerial tasks differ among the services described in Question 3?
5. Define the nature of the four elements of the service triangle, and their interactions, for the following services:
   a. Hospital
   b. Lawyer
   c. Trucking firm
6. Describe the goods-service bundle for each of the services listed in Question 5.
7. Critique the customer contact model.
8. Identify the front-room and back-room services for the following organizations. Could these services be improved by increasing or decreasing the degree of customer contact? By separating low- and high-contact services?
   a. Hospital
   b. Trucking firm
   c. Grocery store
   d. Appliance repair firm
9. Develop a flowchart for checking a book out of the library. Identify the approximate time required for each activity. Also, identify the points of customer contact in the flowchart. How could this process be improved?
10. Draw a flowchart for a routine annual physcial at the doctor's office. Identify some of the moments of truth. How could this process be improved from a customer-service point of view?

SELECTED BIBLIOGRAPHY

ALBRECHT, KARL, and RON ZEMKE: *Service America,* Homewood, Ill.: Dow Jones–Irwin, 1985.

CHASE RICHARD B.: "Where Does the Customer Fit in the Service Operation?" *Harvard Business Review,* vol. 56, 1978, pp. 137–142.

———: "Managing the Sales/Efficiency Trade-Off in Services," Working Paper, University of Southern California, March 1986.

——— and DAVID A. TANSIK: "The Customer Contact Model for Organization Design," *Management Science,* vol. 29, no. 9, September 1983, pp. 1037–1050.

COLLIER, DAVID, A.: *Service Management: The Automation of Services,* Reston Va.: Reston Publishing Co., 1985.

HESKETT, JAMES L.: *Managing in the Service Economy,* Boston: Harvard Business School Press, 1986.

KIRKLAND, RICHARD, I., JR.: "The Bright Future of Service Exports," *Fortune,* June 8, 1987.

LEVITT, THEODORE: "Production Line Approach to Service," *Harvard Business Review,* September–October 1972, pp. 41–52.

MAISTER, DAVID, H., and CHRISTOPHER H. LOVELOCK: "Managing Facilitator Services," *Sloan Management Review,* Summer 1982, pp. 19–31.

NORMANN, RICHARD: *Service Management: Strategy and Leadership in Service Businesses,* New York: Wiley, 1984.

SASSER, W. EARL, R. PAUL OLSEN, and D. DARYL WYCKOFF: *Management of Service Operations: Text, Cases and Readings,* Boston: Allyn and Bacon, 1978.

SCHMENNER, ROGER W.: "How Can Service Businesses Survive and Prosper?" *Sloan Management Review,* Spring 1986, pp. 21–32.

SHOSTACK, G. LYNN: "Designing Services That Deliver," *Harvard Business Review*, January–February 1984, pp. 133–139.

———: "Service Positioning through Structural Change," *Journal of Marketing*, vol. 51, January 1987, pp. 34–43.

WATHEN, SAM: "A Contingency Approach to the Design of Service Transformation Processes," Ph.D. thesis, University of Minnesota, 1988.

In many operations, waiting lines for service are formed, as when customers wait in a checkout lane at a grocery store, machines wait to be repaired in a factory, or airplanes wait to land at an airport. The common characteristic of these apparently diverse examples is that a number of physical entities (the arrivals) are attempting to receive service from limited facilities (the servers). As a consequence, the arrivals must sometimes wait in line for their turn to be served.

Waiting-line situations are also called queuing problems, after the British term "queue." A tremendous number of queuing problems occur in operations, including the design of facility layouts, staffing decisions, and physical capacity problems. Queuing theory is useful in analyzing many of the problems associated with process design.

A queuing problem may be solved by either analytic formulas or simulation methods. The usefulness of analytic formulas, however, is limited by the mathematical assumptions which must be made to derive the formulas. As a result, analytic queuing models sometimes do not closely match the real situation of interest, although they do have the advantage of being simpler and less costly than simulation methods. Analytic queuing models may be used to obtain a first approximation to a queuing problem or to make a low-cost analysis. The simulation method is used to solve queuing problems that are more complex and require a more precise solution.

In this supplement, general ideas about queuing problems and analytic solution methods are developed. Simulation methods for solving queuing problems are described in the supplement to Chapter 8.

QUEUING CHARACTERISTICS

Every queuing problem can be described in terms of three characteristics: the arrival, the queue, and the server.

1. The arrival. The arrivals are described by their statistical arrival distribution, which can be specified in two ways: by arrivals per unit of time or by the interarrival time distribution. If the arrival distribution is specified in the first way, the numbers of arrivals that can occur in any given period of time must be described. For example, one might describe the number of arrivals in 1 hour. When arrivals occur at random, the information of interest is the probability of n arrivals in a given time period, where $n = 0, 1, 2, \ldots$

If the arrivals are assumed to occur at a constant average rate and are independent of each other, then they occur according to the Poisson probability distribution. In this case the probability of n arrivals in time T is given by the formula:

$$P(n, T) = \frac{e^{-\lambda T} (\lambda T)^n}{n!} \qquad n = 0, 1, 2, \ldots$$

where λ = mean arrival rate per unit of time
T = time period
n = number of arrivals in time T
$P(n, T)$ = probability of n arrivals in time T

Three typical Poisson probability distributions are shown in Figure S6.1. Notice that for the value of $\lambda T = .5$, there is a high probability of zero arrivals in the time interval T, and that most of the probability is concentrated on 0, 1, 2 arrivals. As the value of λT increases, the shape of the distribution changes dramatically to a more symmetrical ("normal") form and the probability of a larger number of arrivals increases. It has been found that Poisson distributions can be used in practice to approximate many actual arrival patterns.

The second method of arrival specification is the time between arrivals. In this case one specifies the probability distribution of a continuous random variable which measures the time from one arrival to the next. If the arrivals follow a Poisson distribution, it can be shown mathematically that the

151

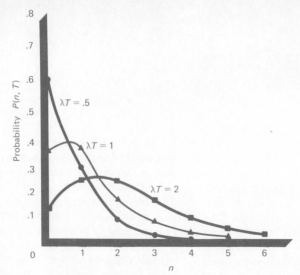

interarrival time will be distributed according to the exponential distribution.

$$P(T \le t) = 1 - e^{-\lambda t} \qquad 0 \le t < \infty$$

where $P(T \le t)$ = probability that the interarrival time T is $\le$ a given value t
λ = mean arrival rate per unit time
t = a given value of time

The exponential probability distribution is shown in Figure S6.2. Notice that as the time t increases, the probability that an arrival has occurred approaches 1.

The Poisson and exponential distributions are entirely equivalent in their underlying assumptions about arrivals. Therefore, either can be used to specify arrivals, depending on whether the time between arrivals or the number of arrivals in a given time is desired. Which of these specifications is used depends strongly on the form of arrival data available.

There are other distributions which can be used to specify arrivals. One of the most common is the Erlang distribution. The Erlang provides more flexibility than the Poisson distribution, but it is also more complicated. [See Saaty (1961) for details.]

A factor which affects the choice of arrival distribution is the size of the calling population.

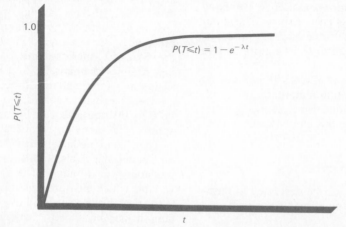

FIGURE S6.2
Exponential
distribution.

For example, if a repairer is tending six machines, the calling population is limited to the six machines. In this case it is unlikely that the arrival distribution will be Poisson in nature because the failure rate is not constant. If five machines have already failed, the arrival rate is lower than when all machines are operating.

2. The queue. The nature of the queue also affects the type of queuing model formulated. For example, a queue discipline must be specified to describe how the arrivals are served. One queue discipline is the well-known first-come–first-served rule. Another queue discipline is one where certain arrivals have a priority and move to the head of the line.

When the queue is described, the length of the line must also be specified. A common mathematical assumption is that the waiting line can reach an infinite length. In some cases this assumption causes no practical problems. In other cases, a definite line-length limit may cause arrivals to leave when the limit is reached. For example, when more than a certain number of aircraft are in the holding pattern at an airport, new arrivals are diverted to another field.

Finally, customer behavior in the queue must be defined. How long will the customers wait for service before they leave the line? Some customers may not even join the line if they observe a congested situation when they arrive. The customer behavior assumed in simple queuing models is that customers wait until they are served.

For analytic purposes, the most common queuing assumptions are that there is a first-come–first-served discipline, that the line length is infinite, and that all arrivals wait in line until served. These assumptions lead to mathematically tractable models. When the assumptions are changed, however, the mathematics of the queuing model quickly becomes complex.

3. The server. There are also several server characteristics which affect the queuing problem. One of these characteristics is the distribution of service time. Just like the arrival time, the service time may vary from one customer to the next. A common assumption for the distribution of service time is the exponential distribution. In this case, the service time will vary as shown in Figure S6.2. Other distributions of service times also used in queuing problems are a constant service time, normal service times, and uniform service times.

The second characteristic of the server which should be specified is the number of servers. There may be a single server or multiple servers, depending on the amount of capacity needed. Each server is sometimes called a channel.

The service may also be rendered in one phase or in multiple phases. A multiple-phase situation is one where the customer must go through two or more servers in sequence to complete the service. An example of multiphase service is where each patient sees a nurse and then a doctor before leaving a clinic.

The combination of multiple servers and multiple phases gives rise to the four queuing problems shown in Figure S6.3. In addition to these problems, the multiple-channel queues can also have more than one line. As a result, a great variety of queuing problems are possible.

FORMULATING QUEUING PROBLEMS

Given assumptions about arrivals, the queue, and the servers, we wish to predict the performance of a specific queuing system. The predicted performance of the system may be described, for example, by the average number of arrivals in the queue, the average waiting time of an arrival, and the percentage of idle time of the servers. These performance measures can be used to decide on the number of servers which should be provided, changes which might be made in the service rate, or other changes in the queuing system.

When queuing performance measures are being evaluated, total costs should be determined whenever possible. This is done by adding the cost of the arrival waiting time and the cost of the servers. In cases such as the repair of machines, the machine waiting time can be equated to the cost of lost production. In cases where the arrivals are customers, however, it is very difficult to estimate the cost of waiting time. As a result, total costs of queuing systems cannot always be determined, and surrogate objectives are used instead. One surrogate objective, for example, is that customers should not wait more than an average of 5 minutes to get service. With this service objective, a required number of servers can be determined without reference to the cost of waiting time.

Performance measures and parameters for

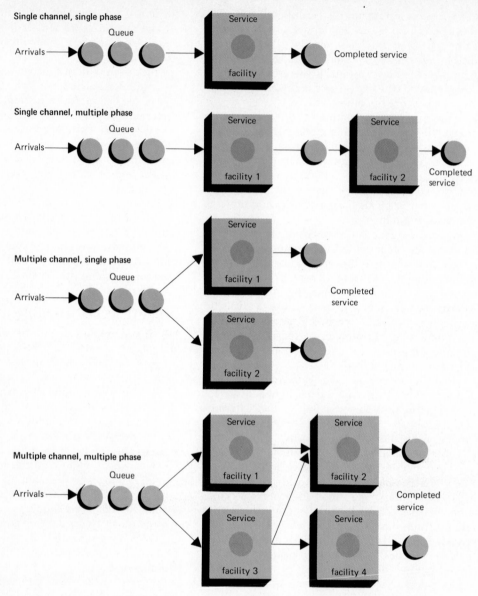

FIGURE S6.3
Different queuing
situations.

queuing models are specified by the following notation:

λ = mean arrival rate (the number of arrivals per unit time)

$1/\lambda$ = mean time between arrivals

μ = mean service rate (the number of units served per unit time when the server is busy)

$1/\mu$ = mean time required for service

ρ = server utilization factor (the proportion of the time the server is busy)

P_n = probability that n units (arrivals) are in the system

L_q = mean number of units in the queue (average length of the queue)

L_s = mean number of units in the system

W_q = mean waiting time in the queue

W_s = mean waiting time in the system

In the above notation, "in the system" refers to units that may be in the queue or in service. Thus W_q refers to waiting time of a unit in the queue before service starts and W_s refers to the total waiting time in the queue plus the time spent being served.

Queuing model formulas are derived for the last six variables specified above, given input values of λ and μ. These formulas are derived for steady-state conditions, which represent the long-run equilibrium state of the queuing system. In steady state, initial starting conditions do not affect the performance measures. The steady state will be achieved, however, only when $\mu > \lambda$; the service rate must be greater than the arrival rate for steady state to occur. Whenever $\mu \leq \lambda$, the queuing system is unstable and the line can potentially build up to an infinite length because the units are arriving faster than they can be served. We will thus assume that $\mu > \lambda$ for the remainder of this supplement.

Simple Queuing Model

The simplest queuing model which has been defined in the literature is based on the following assumptions:

1. Single server and single phase
2. Poisson arrival distribution with λ = mean arrival rate
3. Exponential service time with μ = mean service rate
4. First-come–first-served queue discipline, all arrivals wait in line until served, and infinite line length possible.

From these assumptions, the following performance statistics can be derived:

$$\rho = \lambda/\mu$$
$$P_0 = 1 - \lambda/\mu$$
$$P_n = P_0(\lambda/\mu)^n$$
$$L_q = \frac{\lambda^2}{\mu(\mu - \lambda)}$$
$$L_s = \lambda/(\mu - \lambda)$$

$$W_q = \frac{\lambda}{\mu(\mu - \lambda)}$$
$$W_s = 1/(\mu - \lambda)$$

Example. Suppose a bank teller can serve customers at an average rate of 10 customers per hour ($\mu = 10$). Also, assume that the customers arrive at the teller's window at an average rate of 7 per hour ($\lambda = 7$). Arrivals are believed to follow the Poisson distribution and service time follows the exponential distribution. In the steady state, the queuing system will have the following performance characteristics:

$\rho = 7/10$; the server will be busy 70 percent of the time.

$P_0 = 1 - 7/10 = .3$; 30 percent of the time there will be no customers in the system (in line or being served).

$P_n = .3 (7/10)^n$; a formula for finding the probability of n customers in the system at any time: $n = 1, 2, 3, \ldots$; $P_1 = .21$; $P_2 = .147$; $P_3 = .1029$; etc.

$L_q = \dfrac{7^2}{10(10 - 7)} = 1.63$; on average, 1.63 customers will be in the queue.

$L_s = 7/(10 - 7) = 2.33$; on average, 2.33 customers will be in the system (queue and server).

$W_q = \dfrac{7}{10(10 - 7)} = .233$; the customer spends an average of .233 hour waiting in the queue.

$W_s = 1/(10 - 7) = .333$; the customer spends an average of .333 hour in the system (queue and service).

If customers walk away from the teller whenever there are three or more customers ahead of them in the system, the proportion of customers lost is

$$1 - (P_0 + P_1 + P_2 + P_3)$$
$$= 1 - (.3 + .21 + .147 + .1029) = .2401$$

In this case, 24 percent of the customers will be lost because the wait is too long.

The performance of the queuing system can now be evaluated. The manager will have to consider the idle time of the server (30 percent), the time the customer waits (.233 hour), and the length of the line which forms (1.63 customers). If this performance is unacceptable, a second server might be added or other changes in arrival, queue, or server characteristics can be made.

Multiple Servers

The simple model with Poisson arrivals and exponential service times can be extended to multiple servers without too much difficulty. If we let s equal the number of servers, the performance measures of the multiple-server queuing system are

$$\rho = \frac{\lambda}{s\mu}$$

$$P_0 = \frac{1}{\left[\sum_{n=0}^{s-1}(\lambda/\mu)^n/n!\right] + \frac{(\lambda/\mu)^s}{s!}(1 - \lambda/s\mu)^{-1}}$$

$$P_n = P_0[(\lambda/\mu)^n/n!] \quad 1 \le n \le s$$

$$P_n = P_0\left[\frac{(\lambda/\mu)^n}{s!(s)^{n-s}}\right] \quad n \ge s$$

$$L_q = \frac{P_0(\lambda/\mu)^s\rho}{s!(1-\rho)^2}$$

$$L_s = L_q + \lambda/\mu$$

$$W_q = L_q/\lambda$$

$$W_s = W_q + 1/\mu$$

These formulas are for the steady-state conditions and assume Poisson arrivals, exponential service time, first-come–first-served queue discipline, all arrivals wait in line until served, and infinite line length.

Example. Suppose we add a second bank teller to the example described above. How much will service be improved? The performance calculations for $s = 2$ are as follows:

$$\rho = \frac{7}{2(10)} = .35 \text{ (the servers are utilized}$$
$$35 \text{ percent of the time)}$$

$$P_0 = 1/\{(1 + \lambda/\mu) + \frac{(\lambda/\mu)^2}{2!}(1 - \lambda/2\mu)^{-1}\}$$

$$= 1/\{(1 + 7/10) + \frac{(7/10)^2}{2}(1 - 7/20)^{-1}\}$$

$$= .4814 \text{ (the probability that no customers are in the system)}$$

$$P_1 = .3369 \text{ (the probability that one customer is in the system)}$$

$$P_2 = .1179 \text{ (the probability that two customers are in the system)}$$

$$P_3 = .0413 \text{ (the probability that three customers are in the system)}$$

$$P_4 = .0145 \text{ (the probability that four customers are in the system)}$$

etc.

$$L_q = \frac{.4814(7/10)^2(.35)}{2!(1 - .35)^2}$$

$$= .0977 \text{ (an average of .0977 customer will be in line)}$$

$$L_s = L_q + 7/10 + .7977 \text{ (an average of .7911 customer will be in the system)}$$

$$W_q = L_q/7 = .0139 \text{ (the customer spends an average of .0139 hour in the queue)}$$

$$W_s = W_q + 1/10 = .1139 \text{ (the customer spends an average of .1139 hour in the system)}$$

With two servers, the customer statistics have improved dramatically. Now an average of only .0977 customer is in line, and the average customer waits for only .0139 hour for service (less than a minute). The price for this good service is that the servers are busy only 35 percent of the time. Unless extraordinarily good service is desired, the bank would probably not want to incur the cost of the second teller. Other approaches, such as cutting the average service time or reducing services offered during peak hours, might be considered. In queuing terms, the distribution of service time might be changed by eliminating the long service times.

Comments on Queuing Models

One use of queuing models is to study the relationship between capacity and customer service. In Figure S6.4, for example, customer service is measured on the y axis by waiting time or length of the queue. On the x axis is ρ, the server-utilization factor. The value of ρ is a measure of relative capacity, since it is a ratio of average arrival rate to average service rate.

As Figure S6.4 indicates, waiting time increases rapidly as the service-utilization factor ρ approaches 1. For example, in Figure S6.4, utilization above 70 to 80 percent will have an adverse effect on waiting time and queue length. It is important to recognize the nonlinear effect of the service-utilization factor on customer service. As the facility becomes saturated (ρ approaches 1), customer service rapidly deteriorates. For good customer service, it is therefore prudent to operate at somewhat less than full capacity. If the cost of customer waiting time and the cost of servers can be estimat-

ed, an optimal decision can be made regarding the amount of capacity provided. If these costs are not available, the curve in Figure S6.4 can still be used to examine the tradeoff between customer service and capacity provided. From Figure S6.4, capacity utilization objectives which are related to customer service levels can also be established.

Although we have treated only the simplest cases of queuing models in this supplement, many more elaborate models are available in the literature. See, for example, Saaty (1961) or Hillier and Lieberman (1974) for additional models. More elaborate queuing situations will also be discussed in the supplement to Chapter 8 where simulation is covered.

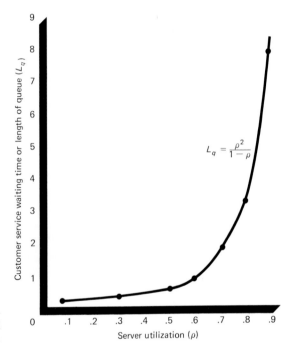

FIGURE S6.4
Capacity and customer service.

QUESTIONS

1. What are the two major costs in any queuing study?
2. What are the three basic elements of any queuing system?
3. What is meant by "steady-state conditions"?
4. What characteristics of the arrivals, the queue, and the server must be specified in a queuing problem?

5. Define the term "queue discipline."
6. What is the difference between waiting time in the system and waiting time in the queue?
7. How are the Poisson and exponential distributions related for arrivals?
8. Why must we have $\mu > \lambda$ for queuing problems?
9. Describe the queuing characteristics of a barbershop.
10. In which of the following situations would you expect service times to be exponentially distributed? Explain.
    a. Service by a teller at a bank
    b. A ride on the ferris wheel at a carnival
    c. Purchasing a hot dog from a service counter at a football game
    d. Riding the bus to work each day
11. In which of the cases in Question 10 would you expect the arrival times to be exponentially distributed? Explain.

PROBLEMS

1. A tugboat serves ships arriving in a harbor. The average time between ship arrivals is 3 hours. The average time required to tow a ship to its berth is 2 hours. Studies have shown that ship arrivals are nearly Poisson and service time is exponentially distributed.
    a. Calculate all the queuing performance statistics for this case.
    b. If ships call another tugboat service whenever there are more than two ships in the harbor, what percentage of the ship arrivals are lost?
    c. A faster tugboat is being considered which will tow a ship to its berth in 1 hour. What effect will this have on waiting time and total time?

2. At the jewelry counter in Macy's Department Store in New York, customers arrive at an average rate of 8 per hour during the day. One sales clerk is assigned to the department and can handle a customer in an average of 5 minutes each. Arrivals and service appear to be exponentially distributed.
    a. How many customers would you expect to see if you walked by the jewelry counter?
    b. How long would it take a customer to get served on the average? How long would the customer spend in total in the jewelry department?
    c. How busy is the sales clerk?
    d. Do you think arrivals and service would be exponentially distributed in this case? Explain.

3. At the Able Medical Clinic, elderly people line up for flu shots during the flu season each year. One nurse gives the shots to these people. The people average 2 minutes between arrivals (Poisson), and the nurse takes an average of 1 minute to give the shot (exponential).
    a. How long should people plan to be at the clinic?
    b. How many people would you expect to see waiting when you arrive at the clinic?
    c. What is the probability that there are more than two people in line waiting?
    d. Fewer patients are expected, which will increase average time between arrivals to 3 minutes. What effect will this have on the patients and the nurse?

4. At the annual family picnic, lemonade is available for self-service. People line up at the jug and help themselves to a cup of lemonade. Of course, the relatives use different sizes of cups and take different times for service. One of the family members observed that service times were exponentially distributed, with an average of 30 seconds to fill a

cup. The relatives were arriving at various times during the afternoon at a rate of 1 every minute (Poisson).

a. How many people would you expect to see on average at the lemonade jug?

b. How long would it take you on average to get a cup of lemonade (total time)?

c. What is the probability that you will find more than 2 people at the jug?

d. Do you expect arrival rates and service rates to be exponentially distributed in this case? Explain.

5. A gas station currently has two pumps and is considering adding a third. A vehicle arrives at the system on an average of once every 12 minutes. Each vehicle requires an average of 8 minutes for servicing. Assume that the vehicles arrive in a Poisson fashion and that service times are exponentially distributed.

a. What would be the effect on waiting time of adding the third pump?

b. How would you evaluate the costs in this situation?

6. Two accountants have an office, and each has a secretary. The accountants are considering pooling their secretaries to gain efficiency in office operations. Currently, a task is given to a secretary on the average of once every 20 minutes. It takes an average of 10 minutes to complete the task. On the basis of available data, the task arrival times are Poisson distributed and service times are exponentially distributed.

a. What effect will the pooling of secretaries have on task waiting time and secretary utilization?

b. What advantages or disadvantages, other than those in *a*, are to be gained from pooling secretaries?

7. A computer processes jobs on a first-come–first-served basis. The jobs have Poisson arrival times with an average of 6 minutes between arrivals. The objective in processing these jobs is that no job spend more than 8 minutes on average in the system being processed. How fast does the processor have to work to meet this objective?

8. A barbershop has three barbers to handle customers. At the present time, customers arrive at an average rate of 8 customers per hour. Each barber can cut hair at a rate of 4 customers per hour. Arrivals appear to follow the Poisson distribution, and service times follow the exponential distribution.

a. How long will the waiting line be on average?

b. How long does the average customer wait until service begins?

c. What is the utilization of the barbers?

d. Suppose customers arrive at a rate of 10 per hour. What effects will this have?

9. A clerk handles phone calls for an airline reservation system in an average of 4 minutes per call, with an exponential distribution of service time. The calls arrive on an average of 10 minutes apart with a Poisson distribution. Recently, some of the customers have complained that the line is busy when they call. Investigate this complaint by means of queuing theory.

10. At a toll booth on the Pennsylvania Turnpike, it takes an average of 30 seconds to collect the toll. There are 10 booths at this particular station, and an average of 12 vehicles arrive per minute. Both the arrival rates and the service rates can be assumed to be exponential in nature.

a. How long can a driver expect to spend in line waiting for service on average?

b. How busy are the toll collectors?

c. If only 8 of the booths are staffed, can they still handle the load? What does this do to the waiting time of drivers in part *a* of this question and the idle time of collectors in part *b?*

11. Management is considering adding one more sales clerk at the jewelry counter described in Problem 2.

a. What would this do to the average number of people you would expect to see if you walked by the counter?

b. By how much would the additional server reduce the time that the customer can expect to spend before being served and the time that the customer can expect to be in the department?

c. How busy would the two sales clerks be?

d. If it costs $50 per day to hire the additional sales clerk and the customer's time is evaluated at $10 per hour, what is the net cost or the savings from this change? Assume the counter is open 9 hours per day.

12. Aircraft wait for a refueling station at O'Hare field. It takes an average of 20 minutes to completely refuel an airplane, and aircraft arrive at the rate of 2 planes per hour. Crews have been complaining that it takes too long to get service, and the airport management is considering adding a second station. The station will cost $1000 per day to build and operate. It costs $10,000 an hour for a plane to wait in line. This is the cost of the plane and the crew being tied up during refueling.

a. Would it be a good idea to add the second station?

b. How many stations are needed to ensure that planes average 30 minutes to refuel in total?

SELECTED BIBLIOGRAPHY

COOPER, ROBERT B.: *Introduction to Queuing Theory*, New York: Macmillan, 1972.

GROSS, DONALD, and CARL M. HARRIS: *Fundamentals of Queuing Theory*, New York: Wiley, 1974.

HILLIER, FREDERICK S., and GERALD J. LIEBERMAN: *Operations Research*, 2d ed., San Francisco: Holden-Day, 1974.

MORSE, PHILLIP M.: *Queues, Inventories, and Maintenance*, New York: Wiley, 1958.

PANICO, J.A.: *Queueing Theory*, Englewood Cliffs, N.J.: Prentice-Hall, 1969.

SAATY, T. L.: *Elements of Queuing Theory*, New York: McGraw-Hill, 1961.

WAGNER, HARVEY: *Principles of Operations Research*, 2d ed., Englewood Cliffs, N.J.: Prentice-Hall, 1975.

CHAPTER 7
Choice of Technology

Technology has become a dominant factor in business and in our lives. The relentless advancement of technology has been termed "technological determinism," meaning that technology determines the course of society and seems to leave us no choice in the matter. But people have finally realized that they do have a choice of technologies. This was dramatically illustrated by the decision not to produce the supersonic transport (SST) aircraft.

Peter Drucker argues that we do have a choice and must learn to become aggressive managers of technology by choosing certain technologies and rejecting others. He points out that survival on this planet requires intelligent technological decisions; we should not adopt every new "technological advance" regardless of the negative side effects on humans and the environment. We therefore need to become "managers of technology," not only "users of technology."

In this chapter, two definitions of technology are offered. One is: *the application of knowledge to solve human problems.* This definition is extremely broad and includes almost all human activity. A narrower definition of technology, and one which is used for the remainder of the chapter is: *that set of processes, tools, methods, procedures, and equipment used to produce goods or services.* This definition is clearly one of process technology rather than product technology.

In the last two chapters, process selection was discussed, which, in the broadest sense, is a matter of technological choice. In a more narrow sense, there are also many possible choices of technology within a specific process. For example, a line flow does not require a highly automated machine conversion process, although a great deal of automation is often used. One could choose to use a labor-intensive line flow and still gain considerable efficiencies over intermittent flows. Similarly, an intermittent process can use a range of automation from very low to very high. Thus, the level of technology, or degree of automation, is a different decision from the type of process used.

Nevertheless, decisions about process selection and technology choice are closely related and intertwined. One decision does not necessarily precede the other because, in practice, the two decisions are often made together. These decisions have been divided into separate chapters simply for the sake of discussion.

The question of technological choice has a great impact on all parts of operations. In particular, job design is greatly affected by the choice of technology. In the past, it was assumed that job design followed choice of technology. In other words, the job is dictated by the technology; this is technological determinism. Job design and choice of technology are now seen by many as simultaneous decisions resulting in a sociotechnical design. In this view, the social and technical systems are jointly optimized, as shown in Figure 7.1. The result is not merely the most cost-efficient system but one which considers human and social values as well. A good deal more will be said about this in Chapter 18.

But in addition to jobs, choice of technology affects all aspects of operations, including productivity and product quality. Productivity is, of course, affected through the substitution of capital inputs for labor. Quality is affected, since

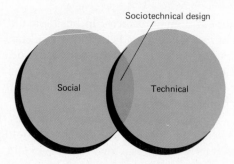

FIGURE 7.1
Sociotechnical
systems design.

high-technology systems often have more uniform output than lower-technology systems. The technology decision also affects the corporate strategy by binding it with processes, equipment, facilities, and procedures. Thus, choice of technology is not an isolated decision; it affects all parts of operations and business.

In the first part of this chapter, the role of managers and society in technological choice will be discussed. This part of the chapter essentially deals with the question of who influences a firm's choice of process technology. The second part of the chapter briefly describes some of the newly emerging technologies, with emphasis on the factory of the future, the automated office, and the service industries. The chapter concludes with a section on the technological decision itself and the problem of technological choice.

7.1 TECHNOLOGY AND THE MANAGER

What should the manager know about technology? After all, shouldn't the matter of technology choice be left to scientists and engineers? How can a manager be expected to master the intricacies of technology when technologists have spent their lifetimes studying the subject? These are important questions, and they reflect the fears that some managers have about technology.

All of us make technological choices in everyday life. We purchase color TVs, microwaves, and automobiles, all of which utilize complex technologies. In making these everyday choices, we concentrate on the performance characteristics of the technology, not the engineering or technical details. When we buy a color TV, we are interested in such performance characteristics as the clarity of the picture, the energy consumption, and the cost. We are not particularly interested in the number of radio frequency stages or the voltage of the picture tube. When we buy an automobile, we are interested in its handling qualities, gas consumption, and possible future repair bills. We are not very interested in the engine's revolutions per minute or the front-end differential ratio. In the same way, a manager should be concerned with the performance characteristics of a technology, not the technical details.

The decisions of technological choice are of extreme importance and require managerial attention. These decisions, in the end, are not really technical in nature. Technology is only one component of a decision which involves economics, strategy, products, and all aspects of management responsibility. Thus, managers should be willing to understand enough about technology to be able to integrate their technical knowledge with the management factors involved.

Researchers at the Harvard Business School have illustrated the problem of technology choice as follows:

Consider a simple example of equipment technology, a process for cutting grass, a lawn mower.

A lawn mower could be described to a prospective purchaser as follows: "It costs $128. It has a gasoline engine and cuts a 24-inch wide swath of grass and is well made by a well-known manufacturer."

A technology-aversive prospective buyer might say, "I'll take it," only to get home to the 8-inch grass and find that:

The cutting technology was based on a reel moving past a cutter bar. It could not handle grass much higher than one-half of the reel diameter. It simply pushed the 8-inch crop forward and down.

It was self-propelled but had no effective free-wheeling device, so that it was not possible to work close to and around a formal garden.

It took 30 minutes to change the cutting height so that the hillside grass could be cut longer (to cut down on erosion) than lawn grass.

It was not powerful enough to cut wet, thick grass going uphill.

It did not mulch leaves.

It had a two-cycle engine which meant that oil had to be mixed with the gasoline each time the little tank was filled.

This buyer should have purchased an extra-powerful, four-cycle, self-propelled rotary mower with easy handling for tight maneuvering and with a simple height-adjustment mechanism.

Understanding the equipment and process technology of lawn mowing in order to make a wise purchase of machinery would have required the owner-manager to develop an accurate mental concept or picture of the process of cutting grass with the machine operating on the hillside and on the level, under a variety of physical conditions, with consideration for the operator's time, money and skills. The most crucial mistake, of course, was in the choice of a reel mower rather than one with a rotary blade. But for a house with low, big glass windows and with close-by neighbors' houses which were similarly constructed, the buyer would have also needed to consider the danger from flying stones propelled by the rotary mower. In either case, a reasonably good conceptual approximation of the actual grass-cutting action would have suggested enough of the right questions to lead to other useful questions.

Choosing technology in manufacturing or service industry operations has many parallels to the lawn-mower problem. The lawn-mower example illustrates that managers should study the operations process in depth before choosing a technology. The manager should assess the performance characteristics of the technology along with its economic and managerial implications. How this should be done will be illustrated in detail later in the chapter.

TECHNOLOGY AND SOCIETY

The choice of technology is never neutral with respect to society and the work force. Technology makes implicit assumptions about human values for material outputs, for the quality of working life, and so on. Recently, as people have become more and more concerned about the effects of technology on society, some of these values have been questioned.

In the past few years some sociologists and economists have begun to consider "appropriate technology," "voluntary simplicity," or the notion that "small is beautiful." According to this thinking, modern technology has advanced too far in terms of efficiency and mechanization, to the point where human and environmental values have been sacrificed. These effects are reflected in low job satisfaction, loss of a sense of meaning in work, absenteeism, environmental pollution, and other social ills. According to this thinking, the way to solve many of these problems is to select a more appropriate technology—a lower form of technology which has fewer such social and environmental effects. Writers on appropriate technology do not suggest a return to cottage industry but rather the choice of an intermediate form of technology, between the highest and lowest forms. Some forms of mass production might even be retained, but technological decisions would always be made in light of their environmental and social consequences as well as their economic effects.

Perhaps the best-known proponent of this thinking is E. F. Schumacher, who writes in his book *Small Is Beautiful* (pp. 13–15):

One of the most fateful errors of our age is the belief that "the problem of production" has been solved. Not only is this belief firmly held by people remote from production and therefore professionally unacquainted with the facts—it is held by virtually all the experts, the captains of industry, the economic managers in the governments of the world, the academic and not-so-academic economists, not to mention the economic journalists. They may disagree on many things but they all agree that the problem of production has been solved; that mankind has at last come of age. For the rich countries, they say, the most important task now is "education for leisure" and, for the poor countries, the "transfer of technology." . . .

The illusion of unlimited power, nourished by astonishing scientific and technological achievements, has produced the concurrent illusion of having solved the problem of production. The latter illusion is based on the failure to distinguish between income and capital where this distinction matters most. Every economist and businessman is familiar with the distinction and applies it conscientiously and with considerable subtlety to all economic affairs—except where it really matters: namely, the irreplaceable capital which man has not made, but simply found, and without which he can do nothing.

A businessman would not consider a firm to have solved its problems of production and to have achieved viability if he saw that it was rapidly consuming its capital. How, then, could we overlook this vital fact when it comes to that very big firm, the economy of Spaceship Earth and, in particular, the economies of its rich passengers?

One reason for overlooking this vital fact is that we are estranged from reality and inclined to treat as valueless everything that we have not made ourselves. . . .

Schumacher points out that our economic system does not properly consider the cost of using up irreplaceable natural resources. These inputs are considered as free except for the cost of extracting them from the earth. Furthermore, the costs of pollution and human dissatisfaction with work are not accounted for in our economic systems. Schumacher believes the result is technologies which become larger and larger and rapidly consume our natural resources.

The solution to these problems which has been suggested by Schumacher and others is to adopt appropriate technologies. Wakefield and Stafford (1977) describe an appropriate technology as one which utilizes a mix of high, intermediate, and low technologies which are in harmony with the environmental and human needs of society.

It is clear that changes in technology will not come easily or quickly or without social and political effects. What is significant about appropriate technology thinking is the realization that managers do have a choice. We can be managers of technology. We should seriously question whether the highest form of technology is the best and whether traditional economics properly reflect today's value systems.

But one cannot choose a technology without understanding the various technologies available. A brief summary of technologies available for the factory will be covered in the next section followed by a description of technologies for offices and service industries.

FACTORY OF THE FUTURE

The "factory of the future" is a term that has recently received much notice by the press. The popular conception is that the factory of the future will be populated by robots, so-called steel-collar workers, and it will manufacture products without people. To be sure, some of these "peopleless" factories already exist, and more will be built in the future. But the essence of the factory of the future is not more automation and fewer people, but a different type of automation organized around the computer. The factory of the future will use computers for design of products, control of machines, handling of materials, and control of the production process in an *integrated* fashion. The computerization and integration of various separate processes and functions through a centralized computer data base is the key. This concept of the factory of the future is also called computer-integrated manufacturing (CIM).

Recently, IBM installed a CIM factory in Austin, Texas, to produce lap-top portable computers. This is the first computer to be entirely built by robots. Actually, the factory can be programmed to build any electronic product which can fit into a 2-foot by 2-foot by 14-inch cube [see Saporito (1986)]. Allen-Bradley has also built a CIM factory in Milwaukee, Wisconsin, as described in Box 7.1. But these factories are more the exception than the rule at the present time. It will take many years before CIM technology is widely adopted.

BOX 7.1
ALLEN-BRADLEY COMPUTER INTEGRATED MANUFACTURING

A computer-integrated manufacturing facility can be an impressive sight. The Allen-Bradley factory in Milwaukee, Wisconsin, is such a facility. This factory makes electric contactors which are used as motor starters in over 125 different varieties and produced at a rate of 600 contactors per hour.

The most impressive aspect of the Allen-Bradley factory is that it produces each day what was ordered the previous day. This requires the factory to make contactors in lot sizes as small as one and in whatever amount the customer orders. This feat is accomplished by an impressive array of computers and 26 automatic machines. There are no operators in the factory, and only a few maintenance people, a supervisor, and some support people. Material is put into one door of the factory and finished contactors are shipped out of the other door, in a more or less continuous flow.

Each morning the orders from 40 sales offices and 400 distributors around the world are down loaded into the Allen-Bradley main computer. Each order is then scheduled to be produced as the customer ordered it. Before the end of the day the order is produced, packaged, and shipped to the customer. This approach virtually eliminates inventory and allows the facility to turn its inventory in the range of 50 to 100 times a year.

An extensive array of quality checks is also built into the system. Each part is automatically inspected, and equipment is shut down for maintenance if statistical control limits are exceeded. Routine maintenance assures that a high level of system uptime is maintained.

This factory was designed by a team of people with input from all specialties including marketing, quality control, data processing, product development, manufacturing, packaging, and cost and finance. This integrated approach made it possible to design the product and the process for automatic assembly. Much of the machinery was specifically designed for this application, and suppliers were involved in the project from the beginning.

This is an example of a stage 4 operation (see Chapter 2) which has achieved world-class competitive status. The product and process were designed to meet specific strategic objectives, and all functions were well integrated from the beginning. The investment cost of $15 million is being paid off in inventory savings alone compared with a traditional assembly approach. Through use of CIM, Allen-Bradley has achieved its manufacturing and business objectives.

Source: Site visit by the author, and "Allen-Bradley Puts Its Automation Where Its Market Is," *Material Handling Engineering,* July 1985.

The factory of the future, or CIM, will have the following elements integrated through a computer data base: computer-assisted design, computer-aided manufacturing, robotics, and materials-requirements planning or MRP (see Figure 7.2). These elements are essential for designing the product and manufacturing it from its inception through its production and eventual distribution. Each of these elements is described below, except for MRP, which is discussed in Chapter 15.

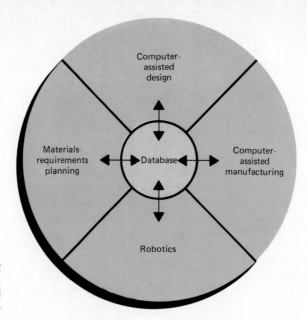

FIGURE 7.2
Computer-
integrated
manufacturing.

Computer-Assisted Design

"Computer-assisted design" (CAD) is a term used to describe computer support of the engineering design function. In the mid-1960s, General Motors and IBM set out to put engineering drawings (blueprints) into computer storage so that they could be easily updated and changed. The input of the initial drawings is done through a computer terminal or by use of a special drawing table which permits the engineer to draw the product design on a computer screen. The geometry of the part being designed is stored in the computer data base. If desired, a drawing can be printed out or the electronic design information can be accessed directly by manufacturing. Most CAD facilities today, however, do not have this link through the data base directly to manufacturing. Rather, they are stand-alone facilities used for automated drafting. Even so, CAD has greatly simplified engineering changes and allowed designers to update products rapidly.

But CAD goes further than mere automated drafting. Three additional features are needed for a full CAD system: design calculations, parts classification, and a link to manufacturing. Once the part geometry is stored in the computer, engineering design calculations can be made including stress analysis, strength of materials, thermal calculations, and so on. As a result, engineering is simplified, and design problems can be uncovered without building expensive prototypes for testing.

Parts classification is used to code and classify existing parts so that they can be easily identified by shape and function. When designing a new part, the designer may find a similar part which is already in production or one which can be easily modified to perform the new function. According to Gunn (1982), "analysis has shown that in many companies only 20 percent of the parts initially thought to require new designs actually need them; of the remaining parts 40 percent could be built from an existing design and the other 40 percent could be created by modifying an existing design."

In order to classify parts, however, it is necessary to devise a coding scheme so that existing parts can be identified by size, shape, type, and function. A simple coding scheme, for example, might be 14932. The first digit may indicate that the part is cylindrical in shape; the second digit, that the part weighs less than 4 pounds; the third digit, the maximum dimension of the part; the fourth, the type of material; and so on. When this scheme is used, parts can be easily found in the data base.

As part of the classification process, parts are grouped into families and assigned code numbers. This is a large task because a typical company may have 50,000 separate parts and many of them may have nonstandard part names. A bolt, for example, may be listed in the records as a bolt, screw, machine screw, cap screw, or threaded fastener. The company may use bolts in many similar sizes and thread configurations, each only slightly different. This happens when each product is designed separately without regard for other parts already in use. Parts classification should, therefore, result in the elimination of unnecessary parts and in a scheme for rapidly identifying those remaining parts.

The final element of CAD is a link to manufacturing. The first step in manufacturing a product, after its physical design, is to design the manufacturing process. This requires choosing the proper type of machines and designing the tooling which is used to facilitate production of the product. These design steps are simplified if the product geometry and specifications are already in the computer data base. The efficiency of different machine processes can be simulated, and tools can be matched to the product shape. As a matter of fact, it is advisable that various manufacturing steps be simulated before the design is completed as a coordinated effort between the engineering design department and manufacturing. In the factory of the future, this will be done by use of a common data base linking design and manufacturing.

CAD is already being heavily used in several industries, including aircraft, autos, shipbuilding, construction, and electronics. The application of CAD frequently reduces labor in the drafting room by a factor of 3 or 4, and it has brought striking benefits to manufacturers. For example, at General Motors, the redesign of a single automobile model was reduced from 24 months to 14 months. Another company reduced the time needed to design custom valves from 6 months to 1 month [see Gunn (1982)]. Many companies are now installing CAD to get these benefits and to remain competitive.

Computer-Aided Manufacturing

Computer-aided manufacturing (CAM) may well provide batch manufacturing companies with the efficiencies long enjoyed in the process and line-flow industries. Line production implies manufacturing at high volume in a predetermined sequence with resulting low costs. Batch (intermittent) production on the other hand, implies small volumes, high product variety, and a jumbled flow of materials. Through use of CAM it is now possible to streamline batch manufacturing, which constitutes about 35 percent of all U.S. manufacturing, according to Gerwin and Tarondeau (1982).

CAM utilizes the computer to design production processes, to control machine tools, and to control the flow of materials in batch manufacturing. By use of the computer it is possible to change over machines rapidly when producing small lot sizes. It is also possible to operate machines automatically following a prescribed set of instructions and to move materials from one machine to the next under computer control. In order to do so, however, it is necessary to organize the products to be produced by similar families or groups using an approach called group technology.

In the last section, we described classification and coding of similar parts for design purposes. This classification can be carried one step further by organizing the production machines by part families. This process of classifying parts by families and subsequently dedicating production equipment to a specific family or families of parts is called group technology (GT).

The typical intermittent (functional) layout is shown in Figure 7.3. In this layout, also described in Chapter 5, machines are grouped by similar type, and the product follows a jumbled flow pattern as it moves through the factory. At the bottom of Figure 7.3, this facility has been reorganized by group technology cells. In this case, all machines needed to produce a given part family are grouped together, and a straight line flow is achieved.

When a similar parts family is produced in a cell, some machines may be duplicated from one cell to the next and capacity utilization may be reduced over the jumbled flow alternative. Nevertheless, the overall benefits of GT are significant, provided that a large enough number of parts can be included in each cell. See Box 7.2 for one example at Northrop Aircraft Company.

BOX 7.2
NORTHROP AIRCRAFT MANUFACTURING CELL

Northrop Aircraft has established a group technology cell to manufacture all the small brackets, clips, spacers, fillets and gussets, etc., that make up more than 30% of the aluminum sheet metal parts used on the Northrop-made portion of the F/A-18 Hornet strike fighter. Northrop manufacturing technology engineers have developed a new system of manufacturing these parts with a manufacturing cell approach. This brings together, under one roof, and integrates, everything needed to fabricate the thousands of small sheet metal parts. Northrop anticipates a saving of $15 million over the life of the F/A-18 program.

It used to take an average of five to twelve weeks to produce a batch of small parts. Parts and production orders were brought together from different locations. Work-in-progress had to be moved from one work station to another. Parts used to travel through more than 16 work stations spread out over five miles. Actual fabrication time was only one day, the rest of the time consisted of waiting for large batches to be finished, handled and transported.

Now an 80 × 200-ft. area contains everything needed to complete the

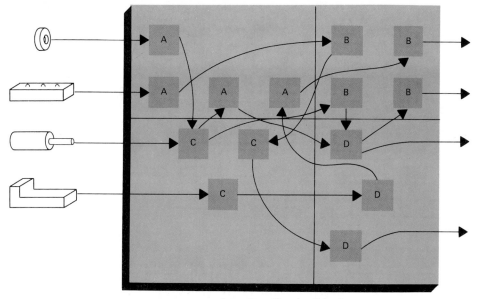

Intermittent (functional) layout

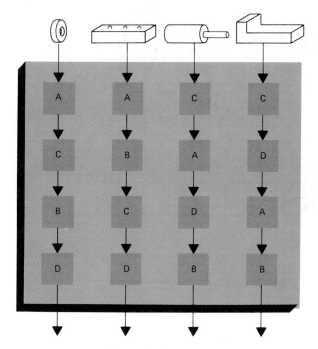

Group technology layout

FIGURE 7.3   Intermittent layout versus group technology layout.
Adapted from Hyer and Wemmerlov (1982).

manufacture of these parts, including raw materials, machinery, tooling, computer links and quality assurance. Twenty-five work stations are linked by conveyor belts, computer controlled. Parts are fabricated by family groups. Total fabrication flow time is reduced to less than one week. Overall, work-in-progress is cut 92%; transportation, labor are reduced; quality is improved; everything associated with fabrication is reduced. Northrop plans to implement many new cells under their flexible manufacturing program.

Source: National Productivity Report, 1987. Reprinted by permission.

The principal benefits of GT are to speed up the manufacturing process and to reduce in-process inventories. This is done by moving parts more quickly through the manufacturing process. In a typical intermittent facility, parts may spend as much as 95 percent of the time waiting in line for machines to become available. Given a GT layout, it is possible to speed up the flow of materials greatly and also to bring more of the materials handling functions between machines under computer control. The result is sometimes called a flexible manufacturing system (FMS).

A typical FMS is shown in Figure 7.4. It consists of a computer for routing parts and controlling machine operations, several computer-controlled machines, and load and unload stations. Raw materials are manually loaded onto a cart at the first work station. The cart is routed from one machine to the next by the computer, and successive machine operations are performed under computer control. These computer-controlled carts are typically towed by a cable in the floor, or they follow an electronic tape between machines. Parts are automatically

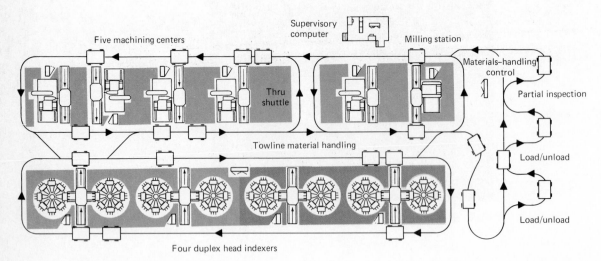

FIGURE 7.4
Typical flexible manufacturing system.

loaded and unloaded at each machine and then continue on to the next machine. This procedure is carried out simultaneously for several parts of different types with different routings.

Machines similar to an FMS, called automatic transfer machines, have been used for years in high-volume production. For example, the Ford Motor Company has an engine transfer line which performs 150 separate machining operations on an engine block. The raw block is fed in at one end of the line, and it is automatically transferred from one machine to the next as the machine automatically positions the block and adjusts for tool wear. This transfer line is called "hard" automation since a product change usually requires extensive changes in the transfer line. With an FMS, the so-called soft automation, it is now possible to link together general-purpose machines which can produce a variety of products in small-lot sizes. This is, of course, only possible by use of computerized machine controls and computerized material transfer.

The range of possible machine types as a function of product variety and volume is shown in Figure 7.5. Notice how FMS is intended for the mid-volume and mid-variety area. At the right side of the graph, less automation is warranted, and at the left side, more specialized (hard) automation is justified.

CAM also utilizes computer-aided process planning (CAPP) as one component of the CAM system. With CAPP each process in manufacturing is planned with assistance from the computer. After the parts design is downloaded from the CAD system, CAPP is then used to decide on routings, equipment, and tools for producing the part.

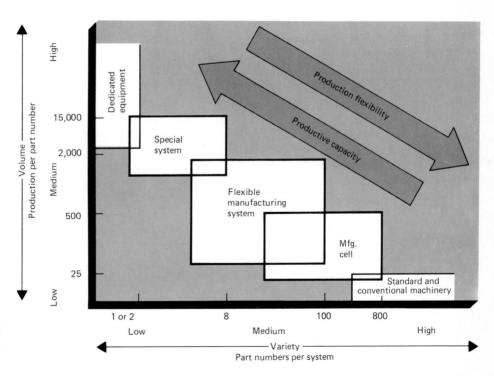

FIGURE 7.5
Types of
manufacturing
systems.

Computer-aided manufacturing thus involves designing the manufacturing process and tools through the data base and then control and movement of materials by the computer. This can be accomplished by organizing batch manufacturing according to group technology and by using flexible manufacturing systems. This speeds up the flow of the product and increases machine utilization in batch manufacturing environments.

Robotics

Robots have captured the minds of the public, science fiction writers, moviemakers, and the press. An industrial robot, however, is nothing more than a computer-controlled machine which can be programmed to perform various production tasks. The distinctive part of the robot is its "hand," or gripper, and the arm, which can make humanlike movements. The first applications of robots were for hot, dirty, or heavy work which was not well suited to humans. Use of robots has subsequently been expanded into a variety of production jobs, including welding, painting, fixed assembly work, and materials handling.

Robots are still limited in their ability to perform many production jobs. The most serious limitation is the ability to pick up a randomly positioned part. To do so, a robot would need to "see" and to position its "hand" accordingly. Most current applications are limited to parts which have a fixed and known location, but the technology is rapidly developing to provide more visual ability.

A related form of automation is the numerically controlled (NC) machine tool. While NC tools are not normally thought of as robots, they are controlled by a computer and can be programmed for a variety of metal cutting tasks. The NC machine, however, does not have the distinctive robot arm and is not, perhaps, as flexible as a robot. Nevertheless, the factory of the future is likely to consist of a mixture of NC machines, conventional machines, and robots.[1]

While robots can sometimes be justified by reduction of direct labor, they provide many more benefits, including flexibility to redesign parts, 24-hour operation, performance of hazardous tasks, and more uniform quality. The traditional return-on-investment justification tends to ignore these benefits and emphasize only cost reduction. As a result, the use of robots in the United States is lagging behind other countries and is not as extensive as some have predicted.

It seldom pays to introduce one robot into a production process because of the maintenance and software support needed. These costs should be spread over several robots. Also, a single robot operating 24 hours a day will simply pile up inventory waiting for other machines. A coordinated flow of material is needed to

---

[1]In addition to NC machines there are also computer numerically controlled (CNC) machines and direct numerically controlled (DNC) machines. NC machines are controlled by magnetic tape. CNC machines are on-line to a computer and can be controlled without the use of magnetic tape. DNC machines utilize a central computer to control several CNC machines at the same time. These machines have now evolved into flexible manufacturing systems that control not only a bank of machines but the associated materials-handling equipment as well.

achieve true economies. This requires a long-range plan of automation and not simply machine replacement by robots in an incremental fashion.

Whitney (1986) points out that robots should not be substituted for people on a one-for-one basis in existing processes. On the contrary, the production process, and possibly the product, should be redesigned to take maximum advantage of robots and other automation. After this redesign, certain steps may be eliminated or combined, thereby eliminating the need for a robot at that step. Processes should always be simplified before being automated. This can hardly be overemphasized. Robots are not mechanical people; they are part of an integrated production process.

Justification

It is clear that the factory of the future cannot be justified one machine at a time. The justification and the ultimate benefit come from the integration of the various elements from product design through manufacturing engineering, production, and materials handling. The factory of the future is, therefore, a strategic decision which affects all parts of operations and all objectives of operations: cost, quality, flexibility, and delivery.

If a strategy for computer-integrated manufacturing is adopted, then many steps must be taken to transform the factory. It is likely that "islands of automation" will be built up as certain machines are computerized and parts of the information system are put on the computer. If the ultimate goal is CIM, all this computerization should be linked through a common data base so that separate "islands of automation" can eventually be tied together. As this occurs, the benefits of CIM will become more apparent.

Since CIM is not just another type of automation effort where one machine type is replaced by another, this level of automation is more difficult to achieve and more expensive than past efforts. But CIM promises benefits beyond mere cost reduction. Those companies that can effectively implement CIM can reap the benefits of a competitive advantage through better delivery, better quality, or more flexibility. This is the promise and the hope of the factory of the future.

Voss (1985) illustrates that the higher the degree of integration achieved, the greater the benefits from CIM. In Table 7.1 note that each successive level of integration achieved more reduction in the lead time required to design and produce the product. These greater benefits, of course, also require greater interfunctional cooperation across departments. Such cooperation has been one of the most difficult things to achieve in actual CIM installations.

Writing in the *Harvard Business Review*, Goldhar and Jelinek (1983) argue that the factory of the future, particularly in batch manufacturing, should be justified on the basis of economies of scope rather than economies of scale. Economies of scope is defined as the ability to efficiently produce a wide variety of products rather than a large volume of standardized products. The new CIM technology reduces changeover costs and product modification costs. As a result, small batches of similar products can be economically produced. It is not necessary to standardize the product and to develop associated mass markets using an economies-of-scale rationale. As a result, companies can compete on the basis of economies of scope by offering more customized products, fast delivery, and smaller lots. This opens up a whole new realm of competition.

TABLE 7.1
EFFECT OF INTEGRATION

Degree of automation and integration	Lead time (weeks)	Saving (weeks)
No automation	52	
CAD alone	50	2
Integration with product and process design within CAD	44	8
Total system integration (CAD/CAM)	35	17
Integration with supplier	26	26

Source: Voss, C. A., "The Management of New Manufacturing Technology, Eight Propositions," *Systèmes de production*, vol. 19, no. 4, 1985.

7.4 FUTURE OFFICES AND SERVICES

As indicated in the last section, factory technologies are rapidly changing. However, office and service technologies are changing just as rapidly, as described next.

Office Technology

Until recently, office technology had not advanced much since the invention of the typewriter. To be sure, offices used electric typewriters, electronic copiers, and dictaphones, but most office work was still labor-intensive and largely fragmented. With the development of the personal computer and interconnected networks, an office revolution is now under way.

In offices, the transformation process consists of the following activities:

1. Handling messages
2. Typing and retyping paperwork
3. Copying printed materials
4. Filing
5. Keeping a calendar

How have these activities been changed by the automated office?

The automated office has a computer terminal for each secretary and each manager, connecting them together in a network fashion. When the manager arrives in the office, he or she uses the terminal to obtain all messages from the computer memory—an electronic in-basket. After each message is reviewed, it can be filed in the computer according to date, sender, subject, etc., and a response can be typed into the computer terminal if desired. The response is then routed electronically to whoever is selected. If some individuals do not have terminals, the computer can be used to type out paper copies for them. The manager can select from a file of standard responses if that is appropriate.

In handling the in-basket, the manager may have occasion to refer to previous messages or correspondence. These can be accessed through the electronic filing system of the computer.

In the automated office, all the office activities previously identified are performed through electronic media. Paperwork is drastically reduced. Repetitive tasks are simplified by electronic filing, on-line correction of errors, and the use of standard responses. This drastically reduces the cost of office functions and increases productivity. As the cost of technology is reduced, more and more offices will be able to afford this new technology.

The automated office can also have other impacts on society. For example, offices can be dispersed to outlying sites or even to homes. There is no need to have all office functions centralized in large skyscraper buildings with the attendant transportation and energy costs.

For certain types of businesses, such as life insurance companies, the automated office will provide a reprieve from an avalanche of paperwork. In this type of office of the future, each person will perform his or her task on a computer terminal and then pass the work electronically on to the next work station. With automated offices, managers can easily track the flow of transaction processing to manage and improve the process-flow characteristics. Such an application is very similar to the concept of control of work flow used in factories.

The largest impact of the office of the future will be on professional and managerial jobs, the so-called knowledge workers, and not on secretarial jobs. Today, about 80 percent of office compensation is paid to knowledge workers and only 20 percent to clerical workers. Therefore, improved productivity will need to focus on the knowledge workers. Fortunately, automated office systems can save a great deal of knowledge-worker time and improve the effectiveness of managers and professionals. However, proposed office automation projects must be directed toward knowledge workers and not merely toward clerical cost reduction.

The key concept in office automation is the same as it is in the factory, namely, integration of the functions. Previously separate departments and functions are linked together by means of the computer. As islands of automation become linked, the benefits of the integrated office become apparent: not only a reduction in costs, but faster throughput, better coordination, greater utilization of knowledge, and lower error rates.

Service Industries

Theodore Levitt (1972) has described an approach to the delivery of services which he calls the "production-line approach to service." With this approach, services are standardized and delivered in an efficient and cheerful manner. The service facility itself is designed so that mistakes are minimized. Various stages of service delivery are automated so that costs are reduced and standardization is achieved.

FIGURE 7.6
Production-line
approach to
service.

Levitt uses the McDonald's chain to illustrate these concepts. He points to the special wide-mouth scoop which has been developed to fill French-fry bags to the correct levels more efficiently. All the food inputs at McDonald's are carefully specified to ensure consistency. Procedures for cleaning the restaurants are prescribed. All this is done to standardize the service and to deliver it in a controlled and efficient manner.

In his classic article, Levitt indicates that service people tend to think their problems are different from those of people in manufacturing. Service is often thought of as something which is delivered "out there in the field" under highly variable conditions, while manufacturing is done in a factory under highly controlled and automated conditions. Levitt argues that until the delivery of services is thought of as a transformation process similar to that of manufacturing, little improvement in efficiency or quality will be possible.

Another factor in service thinking is the attitude of personal ministration or servitude. This goes back hundreds of years to when service was equated with obedience, subordination, and subjugation. According to this view, if the service delivered is low in quality or costly, the solution is to try harder. The solution to service problems is not seen as one of changing the procedures, the task, or the equipment available. Service managers think in humanistic terms, and this, according to Levitt, is at the heart of the problem. As long as they are managed in terms of humanistic thinking, services will be inefficient and lacking in quality control. The attitude of servitude distracts management from looking for solutions in the process technology itself.

In contrast, manufacturing problems are often seen in technocratic terms. If there is poor quality or high cost, an analysis is made of the tasks performed, the work flow, and the equipment used. A solution is sought in the technology of the process.

But automating services is not the solution to all service problems. As we have seen in the last chapter, there are four types of services in the service matrix. Automation simply moves a service into the "service factory" or "service shop" category. While the resulting service may be more efficient, automation can change the very nature of the service itself toward a more standardized service. The market will ultimately determine how much automation customers want, how standardized service should be, and what service will cost. At the present time, all four types of service seem to have market appeal.

7.5 TECHNOLOGY CHOICE

Considerable evidence is being accumulated that the United States is not investing enough in its technological base to remain competitive. Capital spending and R&D investment by the private sector, as a percentage of GNP, has remained roughly constant in real terms since the 1950s, but the capital invested per labor hour and the share of GNP devoted to new investment have both declined over the past decade. Why is this happening?

A very large number of reasons have been suggested for the decline in investment by U.S. industry. These range from high interest rates to government regulation to inflation. Until recently, however, not enough attention has been paid to management itself as one of the key reasons.

In a landmark article entitled "Managing Our Way to Economic Decline," Hayes and Abernathy (1980) argue that management has been diverted from the true task of technological innovation and investment for the future. Management has apparently forgotten that the key to any business over the long run is new products and new processes which hold existing customers or open up new markets. Rather than creating new products and services with fundamental value, many managers have been content with short-term efficiencies and current products and processes. As a result, business has been systematically disinvesting itself.

Hayes and Abernathy go on to argue that management has been content with products that imitate existing products rather than developing new product innovations. After all, it is less risky to develop a lemon cake mix than a synthetic steak. The lemon cake mix, because it imitates current products, can be thoroughly analyzed and will assure more short-term profit. Too much attention to current markets and customers, along with strict financial control policies, stifles investment in the future of the business.

Lack of investment in U.S. industry has also been related to the improper use of present value techniques. These techniques are based on the notion that a dollar today is worth more than a dollar tomorrow. For example, at 12 percent annnual interest, a dollar today will be worth $1.12 at the end of the year. Similarly, a dollar received in 1 year at 12 percent interest is worth only 89 cents today $\left(\frac{1}{1.12} = .89\right)$. If present value concepts are used, current investment can be compared with projected future earnings. The future earnings streams are converted to present value, and alternative investment projects are thereby evaluated. For more detail, see the supplement to this chapter.

There are several problems with present value techniques, and misuses have occurred in industry. One problem is that these techniques do not allow for interactions among alternative investment projects. Present value techniques are most useful for replacement of a single machine or a project that can be easily isolated. When one contemplates the factory of the future, for example, a whole host of machines must be replaced because the factory is evolving toward a new competitive concept. While some of the individual machine replacements may exceed the hurdle rate for investment, others may not. Yet what is being replaced is the entire factory system. A systems perspective is, therefore, needed rather than a series of machine replacement decisions.

Use of capital budgeting techniques has sometimes resulted in hurdle rates which are too high.[2] The problems caused by a low hurdle rate are well understood. It is not always clear that the reverse is equally damaging. A hurdle rate which is too high can lead to disinvestment of capital and loss of competitive position. Hayes and Garvin have observed, "Such (high) hurdle rates often bear little resemblance either to a company's real cost of capital or to the actual rate of return that the company can reasonably expect to earn from alternative investment. Again and again we have observed the use of pretax hurdle rates of 30 percent or more in companies whose actual pretax returns on investment were less than 20 percent." See Box 7.3 for more details.

A point of confusion arises over whether the discount rate should be used with inflated or real cash flows. Kaplan (1986) points out that the *real* historical cost of capital has been around 8 percent, before inflation.[3] This is the appropriate rate to use if future earnings and costs are held constant for inflation. However, if an inflated discount rate of 10 to 15 percent is used as the cost of capital, then future cash-flow streams should also be inflated to be consistent. This is frequently not done.

BOX 7.3
TOOLMAKER PRACTICES WHAT IT PREACHES

Machine tool and machinery builders may urge customers to buy the newest and latest, but in their own shops they frequently make do with older equipment. Not Ingersoll Milling Machine Company, Rockford, Illinois. There each production department must annually write a justification to *keep* any machine that's over 7 years old. The only generally accepted reason for not replacing equipment is that a new machine doesn't offer any significant improvements over older models. The average age of machines at Ingersoll is 6 years. In the tool industry as a whole, 76 percent of the machines are over 10 years old, and 40 percent are over 20 years old.

Source: Industry Week, September 1980, p. 11.

---

[2]The hurdle rate is the return on investment that must be earned to justify an investment.

[3]This surprisingly low figure is based on the average real return in the equity and fixed security markets over the last 60 years. Current market interest rates incorporate not only real returns but expected inflation rates.

Present value techniques tend to be biased toward expansion of existing facilities rather than construction of new facilities. This is true because it is usually less expensive to expand an existing facility with modified technology than start a new facility with new technology. A series of such incremental expansion decisions over the long run, however, may result in a large centralized facility which has older modified technologies rather than new innovative technologies.

Present value techniques should carefully consider what the alternative is to the investment proposal being considered. The "do-nothing" alternative, in a competitive market, can result in a loss of revenue and profits, especially if competitors are innovative in adopting technology and capturing market share. Such losses in cash flow should be appropriately credited to the proposal being considered, since they are the result of maintaining the status quo. These effects are sometimes overlooked in present value calculations.

Finally, revenue effects are a way of reflecting market share gains due to reduced lead times, better quality, and the like. These kinds of benefits are often omitted because they are "soft," or hard to estimate. Omitting revenue effects is a particularly serious problem when evaluating the new technologies because the benefits frequently go far beyond cost reduction.

It is important that the present value calculations be done correctly by using the proper discount rate, by handling the status quo correctly, and by incorporating all benefits as revenues, even if they are difficult to estimate. Management must ultimately assume responsibility for the technical strategy of the firm. Management needs to be long-term-oriented and willing to take risks. Strategies should facilitate more innovation and less imitation of existing technology. These steps, along with a healthy economic climate, should help the United States to regain its technological vigor in basic industries.

This chapter has indicated that technology choice is a complex decision which involves not only present value calculations, but strategic considerations and social impacts as well. Managers now have an exciting range of integrative computer technologies to choose from, but the choice must be informed and managers must become "masters of their own destiny" in the matter of technological choice.

KEY POINTS

In this chapter, we have considered the choice of process technology for operations.

The key points discussed are as follows:

- Technology is that set of processes, tools, methods, procedures, and equipment which is used to produce goods or services. This definition is broader than simply "equipment selection" and includes choice of procedure and methods as part of the technology.
- One of the most important points in the chapter is that technology choice, by fixing jobs and working conditions, also automatically includes social choice. It is, therefore, important to consider the joint social and technical consequences

through the concept of a sociotechnical design. Through the use of this concept, technologies are chosen to optimize both social and technical variables.

- Sociologists and economists have proposed the concept that "small is beautiful" and have advocated the adoption of both "appropriate technology" and "voluntary simplicity." According to this thinking, the effects of pollution, job dissatisfaction, and environmental depletion may render intermediate technologies more appropriate than the highest forms of technology for some types of production. In terms of this approach, our analysis must include traditionally noneconomic costs of environmental and social effects. The result could be a mix of high, intermediate, and lower technologies.

- Managers should have knowledge of the performance characteristics of technologies they manage. These performance characteristics include possible effects on inputs, outputs, process flow, and costs, which can be properly evaluated only by managers.

- The factory of the future implies movement toward computer integration of manufacturing functions. This can be done through a common data base which incorporates computer-assisted design, computer-aided manufacturing, robotics, and materials-requirements planning.

- With the introduction of computers and the interconnection of previously separate office components and offices, office technology is rapidly changing. This new office technology promises to reduce the volume of paperwork, to reduce clerical costs, and to enrich clerical jobs. In a similar way, the automation of service operations offers great potential. As services are viewed in technical rather than humanistic terms, automation and standardization become possible. This can result not only in lower costs but also in more uniform quality.

- The choice of technology should not be based solely on present value. The effects of technology on operations objectives, on the work force, and on the environment should also be considered. A strategy for technological change should be devised.

QUESTIONS

1. How is the problem of technology choice related to process selection and product design?
2. Schumacher says that a fateful error of our age is the belief that "the problem of production" has been solved. What are the consequences of this error?
3. How much detailed technical knowledge on the part of managers is required to make a decision regarding the selection of computer hardware?
4. Suppose you need to select a computer terminal to use in your office. What performance characteristics of the technology would you assess? How would you get the necessary information to make the selection?
5. Describe a sociotechnical approach to the selection of computer input devices from among alternatives including an on-line terminal and printed document reader.
6. How do the concepts of a sociotechnical approach and appropriate technology fit in with the profit-making objectives of a business?
7. What does it mean to choose an appropriate technology for the following processes?
   a. Electricity generation
   b. Production of automobiles

8. Do higher forms of technology necessarily result in more pollution, boring jobs, and other societal ills? Discuss.

9. Suppose your boss has asked you to evaluate the possibilities of office automation. How would you approach this problem? What information would you gather?

10. What is meant by a manufacturing or technocratic approach to the delivery of services?

11. Is the success of McDonald's chain attributable to a marketing concept or an operations concept? Discuss.

12. What is the main obstacle to using a manufacturing approach to the delivery of services?

13. It has been proposed that robots replace several people who do painting on an automobile assembly line. Explain why robots should not replace people on a one-for-one basis.

14. What are the common pitfalls encountered when justifying a CIM project?

15. What are the major benefits that one can expect from implementing CIM? How can these benefits be incorporated into present value calculations?

16. Explain what is meant by the terms CAD, CAM, CAPP, CIM, GT, and FMS?

17. Under what circumstances can the use of a group technology cell be expected to be economically justified over traditional batch manufacturing?

18. Explain the differences between economies of scale and economies of scope.

19. Find some newspaper or magazine articles which deal with technological choice issues or examples of automated factories, offices, or services. Summarize the key points in each article.

SELECTED BIBLIOGRAPHY

ABERNATHY, WILLIAM J.: "Production Process Structure and Technological Change," *Decision Sciences*, vol. 7, no. 4, October 1976, pp. 607–619.

BRIGHT, JAMES: "Does Automation Raise Skill Requirements?" *Harvard Business Review*, July–August 1958, pp. 85–98.

DASAI, DILIP T.: "How One Firm Put a Group Technology Parts Classification System into Operation," *Industrial Engineering*, November 1981, pp. 77–86.

DRUCKER, PETER: *The Age of Discontinuity*, New York: Harper & Row, 1969.

GERWIN, DONALD: "Do's and Don't of Computerized Manufacturing," *Harvard Business Review*, March–April, 1982, pp. 107–116.

GERWIN, DONALD, and JEAN CLAUDE TARONDEAU: "Case Studies of Computer Integrated Manufacturing Systems: A View of Uncertainty and Innovation Processes," *Journal of Operations Management*, vol. 2, no. 2, February 1982, pp. 87–99.

GOLD, BELA: "CAM Sets New Rules for Production," *Harvard Business Review*, November–December 1982, pp. 88–94.

GOLDHAR, J. D., and MARIANN JELINEK: "Plan for Economies of Scope," *Harvard Business Review*, November–December 1983, pp. 141–148.

———: "Computer Integrated Flexible Manufacturing: Organizational, Economic, and Strategic Implications," *Interfaces*, vol. 15, no. 3, May–June 1985, pp. 94–105.

GUNN, THOMAS G.: "The Mechanization of Design and Manufacturing," *Scientific America*, vol. 247, no. 3, September 1982.

HARVARD BUSINESS SCHOOL: "Technology and the Manager," Working Paper 9-671-060, Boston: Intercollegiate Case Clearing House, rev. March 1977.

HAYES, ROBERT H., and WILLIAM J. ABERNATHY: "Managing Our Way to Economic Decline," *Harvard Business Review*, July–August 1980, pp. 67–77.

———: and DAVID A. GARVIN: "Mananging As If Tomorrow Mattered," *Harvard Business Review*, May–June 1982, pp. 70–79.

HYER, NANCY LEA, and URBAN WEMMERLÖV: "MRP/GT: A Framework for Production Planning and Control of Cellular Manufacturing," *Decision Sciences*, vol. 13, 1982, pp. 681–695.

JAIKUMAR, RAMCHANDRAN: "Postindustrial Manufacturing," *Harvard Business Review*, November–December 1986, pp. 69–76.

KANTROW, ALAN M.: "The Strategy Technology Connection," *Harvard Business Review*, July–August 1980, pp. 6–21.

KAPLAN, ROBERT S.: "Must CIM Be Justified by Faith Alone?" *Harvard Business Review*, March–April 1986, pp. 87–95.

LEVITT, THEODORE: "Production-Line Approach to Service," *Harvard Business Review*, September–October 1972, pp. 41–52.

MAIN, JEREMY: "Toward Service without a Snarl," *Fortune*, Mar. 23, 1981, pp. 54–66.

MERTES, LOUIS H: "Doing Your Office Over—Electronically," *Harvard Business Review*, March–April 1981, pp. 127–135.

POPPEL, HARVEY L.: "Who Needs the Office of the Future?" *Harvard Business Review*, November–December 1982, pp. 146–155.

SAPORITO, BILL: "IBM's No-Hands Assembly Line," *Fortune*, Sept. 15, 1986.

SCHOEN, DONALD: "Managing Technological Innovation," *Harvard Business Review*, May–June 1969, pp. 156–162.

SCHUMACHER, E. F.: *Small Is Beautiful*, New York: Harper & Row, 1973.

VOSS, C. A.: "The Management of New Manufacturing Technology, Eight Propositions," *Systèmes de Production*, vol. 19, no. 4, 1985, pp. 311–330.

WAKEFIELD, ROWAN, and PATRICIA STAFFORD: "Appropriate Technology: What Is It and Where Is It Going?" *The Futurist*, April 1977, pp. 72–77.

WHITE, JOHN A.: "Factory of Future Need Bridges between Its Islands of Automation," *Industrial Engineering*, Apr. 19, 1982, pp. 61–68.

WHITE, ROBERT B.: "A Prototype of the Automated Office," *Datamation*, April 1977, pp. 83–90.

WHITNEY, DANIEL E.: "Real Robots Do Need Jigs," *Harvard Business Review*, May–June 1986, pp. 110–116.

SUPPLEMENT
Financial Analysis

Decisions regarding the choice of technology or process design require investment of capital. Therefore, these decisions utilize financial analysis of discounted cash flows or present values to determine the economic worth. In this supplement, several methods of financial analysis will be described, particularly as they relate to decisions in operations.

Typical operations decisions which require detailed financial analysis are:

1. The purchase of new equipment or facilities
2. The replacement of existing equipment or facilities

An example of each of these decisions will be described later in the supplement.

TIME VALUE OF MONEY

In evaluating investments, we should consider the time value of money. We would rather have a dollar now than a dollar a year from now because we could invest the current dollar and earn a return on it for a year. Therefore, any future cash flows have less value to us than current cash flows. As a result, future cash flows must be discounted or reduced in value to their present values in order for future dollars to be comparable to present dollars.

Discounting of future cash flows is based on the idea of compound interest. If we have P dollars at the present time and invest it at an interest rate of i, the future value in 1 year will be

$$F_1 = P + iP = P(1 + i)$$

In n years, at compound interest, the value of our P dollars will be

$$F_n = P(1 + i)^n$$

This assumes that the interest is reinvested each year as it is earned.

If we divide the above equation by $(1 + i)^n$, we will have

$$P = \frac{F_n}{(1 + i)^n}$$

By turning the compound interest equation around, we see that the present value of an amount F_n paid in n years is simply P. We can, therefore, discount F_n to its present value by multiplying by the quantity $\frac{1}{(1 + i)^n}$. This quantity is known as the discount factor of the present value of $1 in year n. Values of the discount factor are tabulated in Appendix C. These factors can be used to convert any future cash flow to a present value amount.

For example, suppose an investment has an annual cash flow of $1000 after taxes for 5 years. The present value of this cash stream at 10 percent interest is $3790.

n Year	Return	$\frac{1}{(1 + .1)^n}$	Present value
1	$1000	.909	$ 909
2	1000	.826	826
3	1000	.751	751
4	1000	.683	683
5	1000	.621	621
			$3790

In this case, each future cash amount was converted to a present value and the present values were then added. As a result, if we want to earn 10 percent on our money, we would be willing to invest $3790, the present value, now so as to get the future earnings of $1000 a year for 5 years.

In discounting future cash flows, it is also convenient to know the present value of a $1 annuity each year for n years. The annuity's present value is

185

$$P = \frac{1}{1 + i} + \frac{1}{(1 + i)^2} + \cdots + \frac{1}{(1 + i)^n}$$

Here we have discounted $1 each year back to the present time and added. The resulting values of P are tabulated in Appendix D for various interest rates and numbers of years.

We can solve the above problem directly by using the annuity's present values. For example, the present value of $1 a year for 5 years at 10 percent interest, from Appendix D, is 3.791. If $1000 is earned each year for 5 years, the present value is

$$P = \$1000\ (3.791) = \$3791$$

This is the same figure we arrived at above by adding the present values for each year.[4] The annuity table, therefore, saves time when uniform annual payments are present. The modern calculator, however, may be even more convenient than the table.

In some investment problems, it is necessary to calculate an internal rate of return (IROR). The IROR is the interest rate which will just make the present investment equal to the future stream of earnings. In mathematical notation, suppose that an investment I has after-tax cash flows C_1 in year 1, C_2 in year 2, . . . , C_n in year n. The IROR is obtained by solving the following equation for i:

$$I = \frac{C_1}{1 + i} + \frac{C_2}{(1 + i)^2} + \cdots + \frac{C_n}{(1 + i)^n}$$

In general, the value of i is obtained by trial and error or iteration using the above equation. Suppose, for example, that we invest $5000 and earn $3000 in the first year, $2000 in the second year, and $2500 in the third year. Arbitrarily, assume $i = 20$ percent and solve the equation

$$I = \frac{\$3000}{1 + .20} + \frac{\$2000}{(1 + .20)^2} + \frac{\$2500}{(1 + .20)^3}$$
$$= \$5335$$

Since $5335 is larger than the $5000 investment, we need a larger value of i to reduce the right-hand side. Assuming $i = .30$, we have

---

[4]With the exception of roundoff error in the last digit.

$$I = \frac{\$3000}{1 + .30} + \frac{\$2000}{(1 + .30)^2} + \frac{\$2500}{(1 + .30)^3}$$
$$= \$4629$$

Since $I = \$4629$ is smaller than the investment of $5000, the true value of i lies between 20 and 30 percent. Using linear interpolation, we can estimate that

$$i = .30 - .10 \left(\frac{\$5000 - \$4629}{\$5335 - \$4629} \right) = .2475$$

Using $i = .2475$ in the equation to check the result, we have

$$I = \frac{\$3000}{1 + .2475} + \frac{\$2000}{(1 + .2475)^2} + \frac{\$2500}{(1 + .2475)^3}$$
$$= \$4977$$

Since this result, $I = \$4977$, is slightly below $5000, we should reduce the interest rate at little more, perhaps to .24. By successive approximation, we will finally arrive at the interest rate to any desired degree of approximation.

In cases where the annual payments are equal, we can use the annuity tables (Appendix D) to find the IROR directly. For example, if the $5000 investment earns $2500 each year for 3 years, the following equation must be solved:

$$\$5000 = \$2500 \left[\frac{1}{1 + i} + \frac{1}{(1 + i)^2} + \frac{1}{(1 + i)^3} \right]$$

The annuity factor is therefore $5000/2500 = 2.0$. From Appendix D, the interest rate for 3 years will be between 22 and 24 percent. The estimated figure, by interpolation, is 23.4 percent.

CHOOSING INVESTMENT PROJECTS

Now that we know how to calculate present values and internal rates of return, we can apply these ideas to choosing investment projects. Suppose there is a portfolio of investment alternatives. How should we choose among these alternatives or rank them in order of preference?

In general, there are three ways to make the choice; payback, present value, and IROR.

Payback. According to the payback method, a

payback period for each investment is calculated as follows:

$$N = \frac{I - S}{A}$$

where N = payback period in years
I = investment
S = salvage value
A = annual cash flow after tax

The investments in the portfolio are then ranked in order of their payback periods.

For example, suppose a $10,000 investment will earn $2000 a year after taxes, and there is no salvage value. The payback period for this investment is then 5 years.

The payback method has several shortcomings. First, the length of the earning period of the investment is not taken into account. Two investments could have the same payback period but drastically different lifetimes. The second problem with the payback method is that it does not consider the time value of money. Thus different earnings streams are not evaluated differently. Finally, the above formula requires a constant annual cash flow. This assumption could easily be relaxed, however, by determining the time required for earnings to equal the investment.

Although the payback method has serious weaknesses, it is still quite popular because it gives a sense of time to recover the investment. Nevertheless, it is being replaced by the next two methods as ways to rank investment alternatives.

Net present value. Whenever a hurdle rate or cost of capital is specified for investment comparisons, the investments can be compared through the use of present values. The given hurdle rate is used as the "interest" rate, and all future cash flows are discounted to the present time. The net present value (NPV) is then computed as follows:

$$\text{NPV} = -I + \sum_{j=1}^{N} P_j$$

where I = investment required
P_j = present value of cash flow for year j

Whenever the net present value exceeds zero, the investment is worthwhile at the specified hurdle rate. If capital is limited, the investments can be ranked in terms of NPV from largest to smallest and funded in order of priority until capital is exhausted.

Internal rate of return. The IROR can also be used to rank investments and select those for funding from the portfolio. Figure S7.1 shows several investments ranked by IROR and the cost of capital as a function of the amount invested. Notice how the cost of capital increases when large amounts of investment are required. As a result, the IROR falls below the cost of capital for alternatives E and F. In this case, alternatives A, B, C, and D should be funded because their IROR exceeds the cost of capital, and alternatives E and F should not be funded.

The NPV and IROR methods are the opposite of each other. With NPV, the "interest" rate or cost of capital is used to compute NPVs; a positive NPV indicates a worthwhile investment. For IROR, the "interest" rate is not given but is computed and compared with the cost of capital. An IROR greater than the cost of capital is considered a worthwhile investment.

If two investments have equal lifetimes, both IROR and NPV methods will yield the same result. If investment lifetimes vary, however, these methods require additional assumptions to yield a cor-

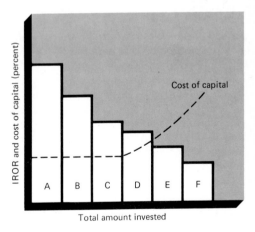

FIGURE S7.1 Investment projects.

rect answer. The additional assumptions must specify what is done after the lifetime of the shortest investment. Is the capital invested in a riskless investment, a like investment, a technologically superior alternative, or what? The answer to these questions will affect the ranking of the alternatives.

A series of applications of the above investment methods will be described next. In each case, not only the numerical analysis but also other factors in the decision will be discussed.

PURCHASE OF A NEW MACHINE

The operations department is considering the installation of a machine to reduce the labor required in one of its processes. The machine will cost $50,000 and have a 5-year life, with a salvage value of $10,000 at the end of 5 years. The pretax cash-flow savings in labor which will accrue over the cost of operating the machine is $11,000 per year. Assume a 50 pecent tax bracket, straight-line depreciation, and a 10 percent investment tax credit. What is the NPV of the investment at a 15 percent hurdle rate after tax? What IROR does the investment provide?

In all investment problems first the cash flow must be determined on an annual basis. In this case, the annual cash flow is

Cash flow—pretax	$11,000
Depreciation	8,000
Net income	$3,000
Additional taxes	1,500

Since the additional taxes paid are $1500 per year, the cash flow after tax is $9500 per year ($11,000 − $1500). In the first year, there is an additional tax credit of $5000 (10 percent of $50,000). The net cash flow in the first year is therefore $14,500 = ($9500 + $5000). The after-tax cash flows— assuming that all of these occur at the end of the year—are shown in Figure S7.2. Here, investments and cash outflows are shown as negative numbers while cash inflows and salvage values are shown as positive numbers. It is always helpful to draw one of these cash-flow diagrams prior to making NPV or IROR calculations.

The NPV at 15 percent cost of capital is

$$NPV = -\$50,000 + \left[\frac{\$14,500}{1 + .15} + \frac{\$9500}{(1 + .15)^2} + \frac{\$9500}{(1 + .15)^3} + \frac{\$9500}{(1 + .15)^4} + \frac{\$19,500}{(1 + .15)^5}\right]$$

$$NPV = -\$50,000 + \$41,165$$
$$NPV = -\$8835$$

Since the NPV is negative, the investment is not worthwhile at 15 percent.

The IROR is obtained by inserting i in place of .15 in the above equation and solving for an NPV = 0. Thus the IROR must satisfy the following equation:

$$0 = -\$50,000 + \left[\frac{\$14,500}{1 + i} + \frac{\$9500}{(1 + i)^2} + \frac{\$9500}{(1 + i)^3} + \frac{\$9500}{(1 + i)^4} + \frac{\$19,500}{(1 + i)^5}\right]$$

Since the NVP at 15 percent was negative, we know that $i < .15$. As a trial value select $i = .10$ and plug into the right-hand side of the above equation. At $i = .10$, we have NPV = −$3232. Since NPV is still negative, try a smaller interest rate, say 5 percent, which yields an NPV of $3727. Since this NPV is positive, the interest rate must lie between 5 and 10 percent. By interpolation:

$$i = 5 + \frac{\$3727}{\$3232 + \$3727}(10 - 5) = 7.7\%$$

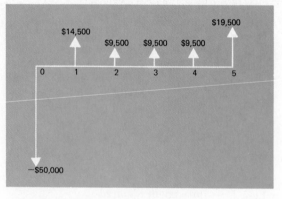

FIGURE S7.2   Cash flow, example 1.

The IROR is thus estimated to be 7.7 percent.

In this case, there are other factors to be considered in the decision, such as a possible loss of flexibility after converting to the machine and more consistent quality due to the machine. Since the ROI is so low, these factors will probably not be overriding.

MACHINE REPLACEMENT

The second example is the well-known machine-replacement problem, where the decision is whether or not to replace a current machine with a new model. Suppose for the sake of this example that we have a 5-year-old car and are considering whether to replace it with a "new" one (only 2 years old). If the car is not replaced now, assume it will be driven for another 3 years. For each alternative, the following costs are given:

Year			
Keep old car	1	2	3
Maintenance	$ 200	$250	$ 300
Tires	200	—	—
Gas and oil	600	600	600
Insurance and license	150	125	100
Total	$1150	$975	$1000

Buy new car			
Maintenance	$ 50	$150	$200
Tires	—	—	—
Gas and oil	400	400	400
Insurance and license	250	200	150
Total	$700	$750	$750

The new car is expected to get better gas mileage, as reflected in the above costs of gas and oil. The new car will have higher insurance and license costs but lower maintenance and tire costs, also as shown in the above numbers. The net result·is that the new car will be less expensive to operate than the old one.

Assume that the new car will cost $5000 ($2000 with the trade-in) and it will be worth $3000 at the end of 3 years. Also assume that the old car is worth $3000 now and will be worth $1400 in 3 more years.

The cash-flow pattern for the difference between these two alternatives is shown in Figure S7.3. The new-car alternative requires a new investment of $2000 at time zero, including the trade-in. The new-car alternative will save $450 in the first year, $225 in the second year, and $250 in the third year. In addition, the salvage value of the new car will be $1600 ($3000 − $1400) more than the old car's salvage value at the end of 3 years. Since this is a personal decision, there will be no depreciation and no tax consequences.

As in the previous example, two questions can be asked: (1) is the new car worth the investment at some given rate of interest, perhaps 15 percent, and (2) what rate of interest does the investment earn? The first question can be answered by computing the net present value of the cash flow shown in Figure S7.3.

$$NPV = -\$2000 + \frac{\$450}{1.15} + \frac{\$225}{(1.15)^2}$$
$$+ \frac{\$250}{(1.15)^3} + \frac{\$1600}{(1.15)^3}$$

$$NPV = -\$2000 + \$1778 = -\$222$$

Since the net present value of the investment is negative, it is not worthwhile to buy the new car at 15 percent return on capital.

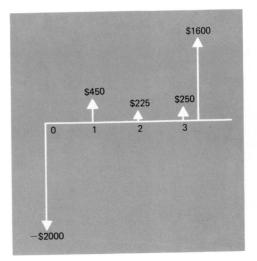

FIGURE S7.3

Cash flow, example 2. The cash flows reflect the net difference between purchasing the new car and keeping the old car.

The IROR is the interest rate which makes the above net present value equal to zero. By iteration, we find that IROR = 9.6 percent.

In this example, there are several additional questions of interest. First, what is the value of capital to the car buyer? If the buyer takes the money out of a savings account, the after-tax value of capital might be about 7 or 8 percent. At this rate the investment would clearly be worthwhile, since the IROR is 9.6 percent. If the capital were diverted from other personal investments, which could earn, say, 15 percent after tax, then the investment would not be worthwhile.

The new-car buyer would also want to consider the intangible value of having a new car. The buyer might have fewer repair problems, there might be less squeaks and rattles, and there would be an aesthetic value to owning the new car. It would be difficult to put a dollar figure on such intangible benefits, and they would probably have to be incorporated subjectively in the decision. One way to evaluate these intangibles, however, is to compute their dollar value. If capital is worth 15 percent, the intangibles would have to be worth more than $222 (the negative amount of present value) to go ahead with the decision.

Similar problems are encountered in process technology choice when a current machine is being replaced by a new one. The new machine will require additional investment, but it will probably reduce annual operating costs. The new machine will also provide intangible benefits, as does the new car, such as fewer production disruptions through greater reliability.

The examples illustrate two different types of decisions on choice of process technology. The first example was a choice between an existing manual technology and a proposed new automated technology. The second example was one of technology replacement. In practice, there are other variations of these problems, but the basic principles still apply.

QUESTIONS

1. What are the advantages and disadvantages in using the payback method?
2. Under what conditions would you use the IROR or NPV method?
3. What problems are created by unequal investment lives? How are these problems handled?
4. Precisely how does depreciation affect cash flow?
5. Under what conditions would you choose an investment which does not meet the hurdle rate?

PROBLEMS

1. A factory is considering the installation of a new machine which will replace three workers who have been doing the job by manual methods. The combined wages and benefits of the three workers are $45,000 per year. The new machine will be run by a single operator paid $15,000 a year in wages and benefits; it will also require $5000 a year for maintenance and utilities expense. The machine will provide the same output as the manual method, but the investment and installation will be $60,000. For tax purposes, the machine can be depreciated over a 5-year period using a double declining balance. Assume a 50 percent tax rate, a 10 percent investment credit, and no salvage value.
   a. Is the machine a good investment at a 15 percent interest rate? Use a 10-year machine life.
   b. Calculate the IROR for this decision.
   c. What other issues are important in this process technology decision?
2. A laundromat is considering replacing its washers and dryers. Two options are available. *Option A:* A new machine will cost $11,000 initially and $12,000 per year to operate.

Expected life for taxes and operations purposes is 5 years.

Option B: The new machines will cost $14,000 initially and $11,000 per year to operate. Expected life for taxes and operations purposes is 10 years.

   a. Using straight-line depreciation, determine which option is the best at a 10 percent interest rate. Assume a 50 percent tax rate.

   b. What is the break-even interest rate, where the two options have equal present values?

3. A machine has been used in production for 5 years and is being considered for replacement. At the present time the machine is fully depreciated but could be sold for $8000. The firm pays tax on half of all capital gains. The new machine being considered will cost $30,000 and will have a 5-year life for both tax and cash-flow considerations. The new machine will require one less operator at a savings of $12,000 per year in wages and benefits. Assume no salvage value, a 50 percent corporate income tax, and straight-line depreciation.

   a. What is the NPV of the investment at 10 percent, 15 percent, and 20 percent?

   b. What is the IROR at these same percentages?

   c. What additional factors would you consider in this decision?

4. The ABC Company is considering whether to lease or own its automobiles. If an automobile is purchased, it will cost an average of $12,000. It will be driven for 20,000 miles a year and can be sold for $5000 at the end of 3 years. Assume that the out-of-pocket expenses for gasoline, oil, and repairs are 22 cents per mile. Also assume that straight-line depreciation is used with a 3-year life and $5000 salvage value. If the leasing option is used, the lease will cost 30 cents per mile driven. This cost includes the car plus all gas, oil, and repairs.

   a. If the cost of capital is 12 percent, should the company buy or lease the cars? Assume a 50 percent tax rate.

   b. What is the IROR of this investment?

   c. What are the intangible factors in this decision?

5. A company is considering installation of a new flexible manufacturing system. The system will be able to make some of the company's existing parts at lower costs, thereby saving $700,000 per year. The product line will also be redesigned to use fewer parts at a saving of $200,000 per year. Faster throughput and higher quality will also be possible. The expected profits from the additional business gained from these advantages will be $800,000 per year. The FMS will cost $4 million to install and $800,000 per year to operate. An expected lifetime of 10 years can be assumed. Straight-line depreciation is used, and corporate income taxes are 35 percent. Assume a 5 percent future inflation rate per year in future savings and costs.

   a. At a hurdle rate of 15 percent, is the investment worthwhile?

   b. What IROR does this project earn?

   c. If the profits from the additional business are ignored, is the investment still worthwhile at 15 percent?

6. A factory that makes piano parts has been operating at the same site for 50 years. While the equipment has been upgraded (the last time was 10 years ago), management thinks it is now time to build a new factory. Competition has recently entered the market and is now producing piano parts more cheaply and selling them at lower prices. As a result, the company has lowered its prices and is taking lower profit margins than in the past. If the new factory is not built, management projects that market share and profitability will continue to erode, ultimately putting the company out of business. The new factory will have a lower manufacturing cost (expressed as a percentage of sales) due to moderniza-

tion. It will also have higher sales (in millions of dollars) due to retention of the market, as shown below:

Year	Old factory		New factory	
	Sales	Mfg. cost	Sales	Mfg. cost
1	100	70%	100	60%
2	80	75%	90	65%
3	60	80%	80	70%
4	40	90%	70	70%
5	0	0%	70	70%

a. The new factory will cost $20 million to build. After 5 years it will have a salvage value of $10 million. The old factory has no salvage value at the present time. Should the new factory be built at a hurdle rate of 20 percent? Assume straight-line depreciation and income tax rates of 35 percent.

b. Instead of using a salvage value for the new factory, assume that its lifetime is 20 years at the same sales level and manufacturing cost as at the end of year 5. At the end of 20 years there is no salvage value. Should the new factory be built on the basis of these assumptions?

7. The ACE machine shop is considering reorganizing its production into a cell using the principles of group technology. As a result of this change the following savings are estimated. A savings of $1 million in inventory initially and continuing savings of $300,000 per year in inventory carrying costs. The parts made in the cell will have the same direct labor costs, but overhead will be much less, resulting in a savings in $100,000 per year. The overhead savings is due to simplified production control, less supervision, and better quality control. The use of the cell will also permit much faster throughput of production orders. As a result, new business will be gained, resulting in additional profits of $100,000 per year. To organize the cell will require some additional equipment at a cost of a $2 million initial investment and $150,000 per year operating cost. The equipment can be depreciated over a 5-year period, and corporate tax rates are 35 percent. Assume a 5 percent inflation rate per year in future savings and costs. Use straight-line depreciation with no salvage value.

a. Is it worthwhile to form this cell using a 15 percent hurdle rate? Also, try a 20 percent hurdle rate.

b. What is the internal rate of return from this project?

c. The additional business gained from the cell is considered a "soft" estimate. What effect does leaving this estimate out of the calculations have on the answers to part a?

8. Two different machines are being considered for a production job, with the following characteristics:

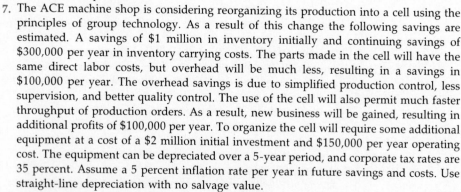

	Machine A	Machine B
Initial cost	$10,000	$7000
Op. cost/year	$ 2,000	$1500
Lifetime	10 years	5 years

a. Which machine is the better buy at a 15 percent discount rate? Assume that machine B is replaced by another one of the same type at the end of 5 years. Also assume that depreciation is straight line, income taxes are 35 percent, and inflation is 5 percent per year.

SELECTED BIBLIOGRAPHY

ANTHONY, ROBERT N., and GLENN A. WELSCH: *Fundamentals of Management Accounting,* Homewood, Ill.: Irwin, 1974.

GRANT, EUGENE L., W. GRANT IRESON and RICHARD LEAVENWORTH: *Principles of Engineering Economy,* 7th ed., New York: Wiley, 1982.

VAN HORNE, JAMES C.: *Financial Management and Policy,* 5th ed., Englewood Cliffs, N.J.: Prentice-Hall, 1980.

WELSCH, GLENN A., and ROBERT N. ANTHONY: *Fundamentals of Financial Accounting,* Revised ed., Homewood, Ill.: Irwin, 1977.

CHAPTER 8
Process-Flow Analysis

In the last three chapters, we dealt with macro-level decisions in process design. These macro decisions determine the type of process selected and the type of technology used. Once the macro design decisions are made, we can proceed with the micro-level process design decisions, which are process-flow analysis and facilities layout.

These micro-level decisions affect decisions in other parts of operations, including scheduling decisions, inventory levels, the types of jobs designed, and the methods of quality control used. Therefore, micro decisions about process design should always be made with the effects on other parts of operations in mind.

The study of process flows deals directly with the transformation process itself which can be viewed as a series of flows connecting inputs to outputs. In studying process flows, we will be analyzing how a good is manufactured or how a service is delivered. When the sequence of steps used in converting inputs into outputs is analyzed, better methods or procedures can usually be found.

At the heart of process-flow analysis is the flowchart. The idea of describing process flows in flowchart form is quite powerful and aids the search for better procedures and methods.

Throughout the first part of this chapter, different types of flowchart methods will be described. In the second part, flowchart analysis is extended to the mathematical modeling of process flows. A model can be used to describe a transformation process in more precise terms than is possible with a simple flowchart. Thus mathematical models are an extension of the flowchart analysis described in the first part of the chapter.

8.1 SYSTEMS THINKING

A prerequisite to process-flow analysis is defining the operations transformation process as a system. This requires identification of the relevant system to be analyzed by defining a systems boundary and identification of the appropriate inputs, outputs, and systems flows. Some orientation toward general systems thinking is therefore provided before moving to more detailed flowcharting topics.

A system is usually defined as a collection of interrelated elements whose whole is greater than the sum of the parts. The human body is a system. It consists of interrelated organs including the lungs, heart, muscles, etc. But the human body as a whole is certainly more than the sum of the individual parts. By itself, the heart is merely a pump. The brain cannot function without the heart and lungs. Each part of the body contributes to the functioning of the whole.

A business organization is a system. Its parts are the functions of marketing, operations, finance, and so on. But the business as a system accomplishes more as a whole than the individual functions could accomplish. A single function accomplishes nothing by itself. A business cannot sell a product which it cannot produce. It does no good to produce a product which cannot be sold. When the different parts of a system work together, a synergistic effect is achieved where the output of the system is greater than the sum of the individual contributions.

Every operation can be viewed as a system by identifying a transformation or conversion process, as described in Chapter 1. The transformation process must be isolated from its environment and defined in terms of inputs, outputs, and the transformation method used. The most difficult part of using the systems approach for process analysis, however, is defining the system boundary which separates the operations system from its environment. The boundary tells us, for purposes of analysis, how large or small the system is. The selection of a boundary is arbitrary; the system can be as large or as small as desired, depending on the particular process problem being studied. The boundary should encompass all important interactions within the system, but it is always difficult to define exactly what should be included or excluded.

In operations process analysis, the largest system ordinarily considered is the entire operations function. Whenever a larger system needs to be considered, the decision will usually concern general management as well as operations management. In process analysis, managers also consider subsystems which are only a part of operations. Examples include the production and inventory control subsystem, the quality subsystem, and so on.

To illustrate these ideas regarding systems and process analysis, consider a typical small bank, which we shall call the First City Bank. This bank is located in a community of 100,000 people, and there are five other banks in the town. First City Bank employs twenty people: seven employees work as cashiers, including a drive-up window cashier; six employees record transactions from checking, savings, and loan accounts; two employees work with new-customer accounts; and five work in the loan department. The bank utilizes the services of a computer through a correspondent bank, which processes transactions and keeps the bank's books.

The bank is considering the installation of a new automatic teller. What would the relevant system for this decision be? Applying the principles that we have just discussed, all parts of the business affected by this decision should be included in the systems definition. The new teller machine will affect the cashiering function, since cash will be distributed directly to customers and deposits will be taken by the new machine. We can safely assume that the loan department is outside the system boundary, since loans are not affected. New accounts are affected, since new customers will probably be offered the services of the automatic teller when they come to the bank. Accounting is not affected, assuming the transactions coming from the machine teller will be exactly the same as those that come from human tellers.

The systems approach to process analysis thus helps us define the system boundary and identify those parts of operations and the business which are affected by the proposed decision. In a similar way, we would proceed to identify the effect of the decision on the inputs, outputs, and transformation process of operations. These effects in First City Bank include effects on labor skills and on the services offered to the customer. Maintenance skills will be required to keep the automatic teller in operating condition. Services from the automatic teller can be offered outside normal business hours. All these effects and others must be identified as part of the process analysis. See Box 8.1 for a continuation of this example including a discussion of flowcharting.

BOX 8.1
TYPICAL DECISION PROBLEM

Section 8.1 describes First City Bank's effort to decide whether to install a new automatic teller. In connection with this decision, Sally Jones, manager of cashier operations, decided to conduct a process-flow analysis. This analysis required Sally to trace the flow of paperwork for the new teller and the flow of customers through the bank.

The decision concerning the automatic teller will affect the waiting time of customers as they stand in line for service. Sally reasoned that the average time a customer waits in line will depend on both the arrival rate of customers and the service time of the automatic teller. If customers arrive at a fast rate, there will be more waiting time than in slack periods. If the automatic teller can handle customers rapidly, the waiting time will be reduced. To evaluate these effects quantitatively, Sally decided to construct a queueing model of the automatic teller and the waiting line. This model would provide estimates of waiting times and teller capacity for typical bank conditions.

As part of the process-flow analysis, Sally also decided to trace the flow of paperwork required to operate the automatic teller. To do this, she constructed a flowchart and documented the procedures required at each step of the way. Although much of the procedure was the same as for the human teller, a few steps were different. This flowchart helped Sally to understand how the new automatic teller would affect daily cashier operations, and she felt more confident that she could describe the effect to others.

8.2   FLOWCHART ANALYSIS

Flowcharts are used to describe and improve the transformation process in productive systems. In improving the effectiveness or efficiency of productive processes, some or all of the following process elements might be changed:

1. Raw materials
2. Product (output) design
3. Job design
4. Processing steps used
5. Management control information
6. Equipment or tools

Process analysis can, therefore, have a wide effect on all parts of operations.

Process-flow analysis is heavily dependent on systems thinking, described above. In order to analyze process flows, a relevant system is selected, and the inputs, outputs, boundaries, and transformations are described. In effect, the process-flow problem is described as a system.

Using the systems approach, the following steps are then taken in a process flowchart analysis:

1. Decide on the objectives of the analysis, e.g., to improve efficiency, throughput time, effectiveness, capacity, or worker morale.
2. Select a relevant productive process (or system) for study, e.g., the whole operation or some part of it.
3. Describe the existing transformation process by means of flowcharts and efficiency measurements.
4. Develop an improved process design by revising the process flows and/or inputs used. Usually the revised process is also described by a flowchart.
5. Gain management approval for the revised process design.
6. Implement the new process design.

Notice that this method assumes an existing process. If there is no existing process, steps 3 and 4 are combined to describe the desired process, but the rest of the method is still used. This general method of flowchart analysis will be illustrated below for specific situations.

In Section 8.3, material flows will be treated in detail. This will be followed by analysis of information flows. One of our objectives is to show how these two types of process flows can be analyzed by the same procedure even though they are often thought of as being different.

8.3   MATERIALS-FLOW ANALYSIS

The analysis of materials flows in factories was one of the first applications of process-flow-analysis ideas. These ideas were developed in the early 1900s by industrial engineers applying the principles of Taylor's scientific management. First they broke down the manufacturing process into detailed elements, and then they carefully studied each element and the interrelationship between elements in order to improve overall process efficiency.

Today, materials-flow analysis has come back into vogue through emphasis on reducing manufacturing throughput time (cycle time)—the total time to order, manufacture, and distribute a product from beginning to end. This is being done by seeking to reduce waste in the process. Waste is defined as any operation which does not add value during the production process, including the time the product sits in storage, the time the product is being moved from one location to another, inspection time, etc. Only actual processing time of the material by machine or by labor adds value. The tools for eliminating waste through analyzing materials flows are described next. Much more is said about eliminating waste in Chapter 16 where just-in-time concepts are discussed.

As part of materials-flow analysis, it is necessary to describe the flow of materials in great detail. This is done in manufacturing through four principal types of documents: assembly drawings, assembly charts, routing sheets, and flow-process charts.

An assembly drawing is used to specify how the parts in a manufactured item should be assembled. These drawings are developed by the engineering department and given to manufacturing. An example of an assembly drawing for a child's tricycle is shown in Figure 8.1

In order to show the exact sequence of operations used to assemble a product, an assembly or "Gozinto" (goes into) chart is prepared from the assembly drawing. This chart shows each step in the assembly process and the parts which go into the final product, as illustrated for the tricycle in Figure 8.2.

A routing sheet (or operations process sheet) is even more detailed than an assembly chart because it shows the operations and routing required for an individual part. Each machine or labor operation is listed, along with the tools and equipment needed. In some cases the production times for each operation are also listed. A routing sheet for the rear wheel of the tricycle is shown in Figure 8.3.

Taken together, the assembly drawings, assembly charts, and routing sheets will completely specify how a product is to be manufactured. These documents

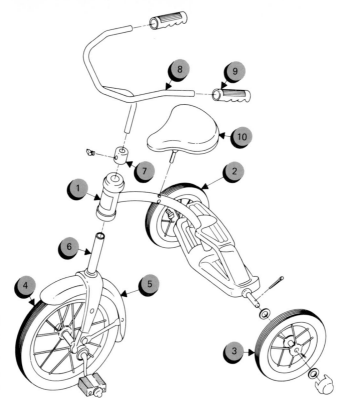

FIGURE 8.1
Assembly drawing
for a tricycle.
*Source: The Murray
Ohio Manufacturing
Company,
Lawrenceburg,
Tenn.*

are all derived from the blueprints and the bill of materials which specify the original design of the product.

One would expect to find assembly drawings, assembly charts, and routing sheets as part of normal manufacturing documentation. Although these documents help describe the process flow, they do not provide all that is needed for analysis and improvement. For analysis purposes, a flow-process chart (or, more simply, a process chart) is usually constructed; it breaks the process down in terms of the symbols shown in Figure 8.4.

The flow-process chart is illustrated by an operation in which groceries are selected, assembled, and delivered in response to customer telephone orders. As the first step in the process, orders are received by phone from customers and punched directly into a computer. The computer then generates picking lists for each of the various aisles (dry groceries, produce, meat, dairy, etc.) in the grocery warehouse. The items are picked by employees in each aisle and then assembled into a complete order for delivery to the customers.

Figure 8.5 is a flow-process chart for a portion of this operation, which includes the groceries that are picked from the produce, dairy, and meat aisles. Notice the use of the special symbols for operations, transportation, inspection, delays, and storage. Only the operations activity adds value to the product. The other activities (transportation, inspection, delays, and storage) are considered as waste,

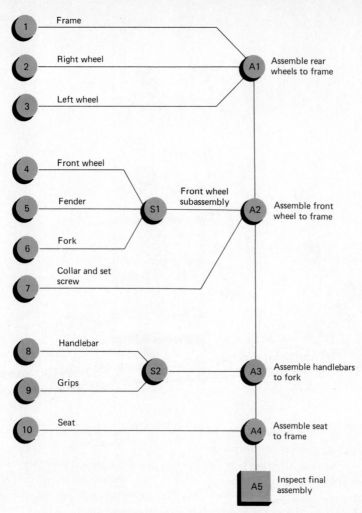

FIGURE 8.2
Tricycle assembly
chart.

or non–value-adding activities, and should be reduced or eliminated. In Figure 8.5, the time and the distance are not noted on the chart, but these quantities were measured in the study in order to identify and assess possible improvements.

The flow-process chart is a key tool for improving the flow of materials. After examining it, the manager may be able to combine certain operations, eliminate others, or simplify operations to improve overall efficiency. This may, in turn, require changes in layout, equipment, and work methods and possibly even changes in product design.

But it is not enough simply to draw flow-process charts. A key to analyzing these charts is to ask the following types of questions:

1. *What.* What operations are really necessary? Can some operations be eliminated, combined, or simplified? Should the product be redesigned to facilitate production?

Operation	Description	Dept.	Tools/Equipment
Part Name	Rear Tricycle Wheel	Date	9/8/78
Assembly	A2936	Issued by	RGS
Part Number	261982		
1	Cut wires for spokes (10 qty.)	06	E10 Shear
2	Cut tubing for axle	06	F2 Hacksaw
3	Cut flat steel for rim	02	F1 Shear
4	Stamp end caps for spokes	03	A7 Press
5	Form steel for rims	03	A4 Press
6	Weld rim together	01	U9 Welder
7	Weld caps to axle tube	01	U9 Welder
8	Weld spokes to axle and rim	01	U7 Welder
9	Cut rubber tire to size	06	E7 Shear
10	Fix rubber tire on rim	09	C6 Press

FIGURE 8.3
Routing
(operations
process) sheet.

2. *Who.* Who is performing each operation? Can the operation be redesigned to use less skill or less labor hours? Can operations be combined to enrich jobs and thereby improve productivity or working conditions?

3. *Where.* Where is each operation conducted? Can the layout be improved to reduce distance traveled or to make the operations more accessible?

4. *When.* When is each operation performed? Is there excessive delay or storage? Are some operations creating bottlenecks?

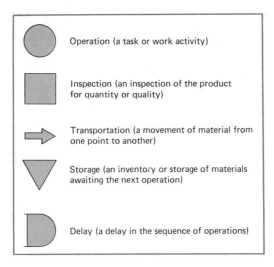

FIGURE 8.4
Symbols used in
a flow-process
chart.

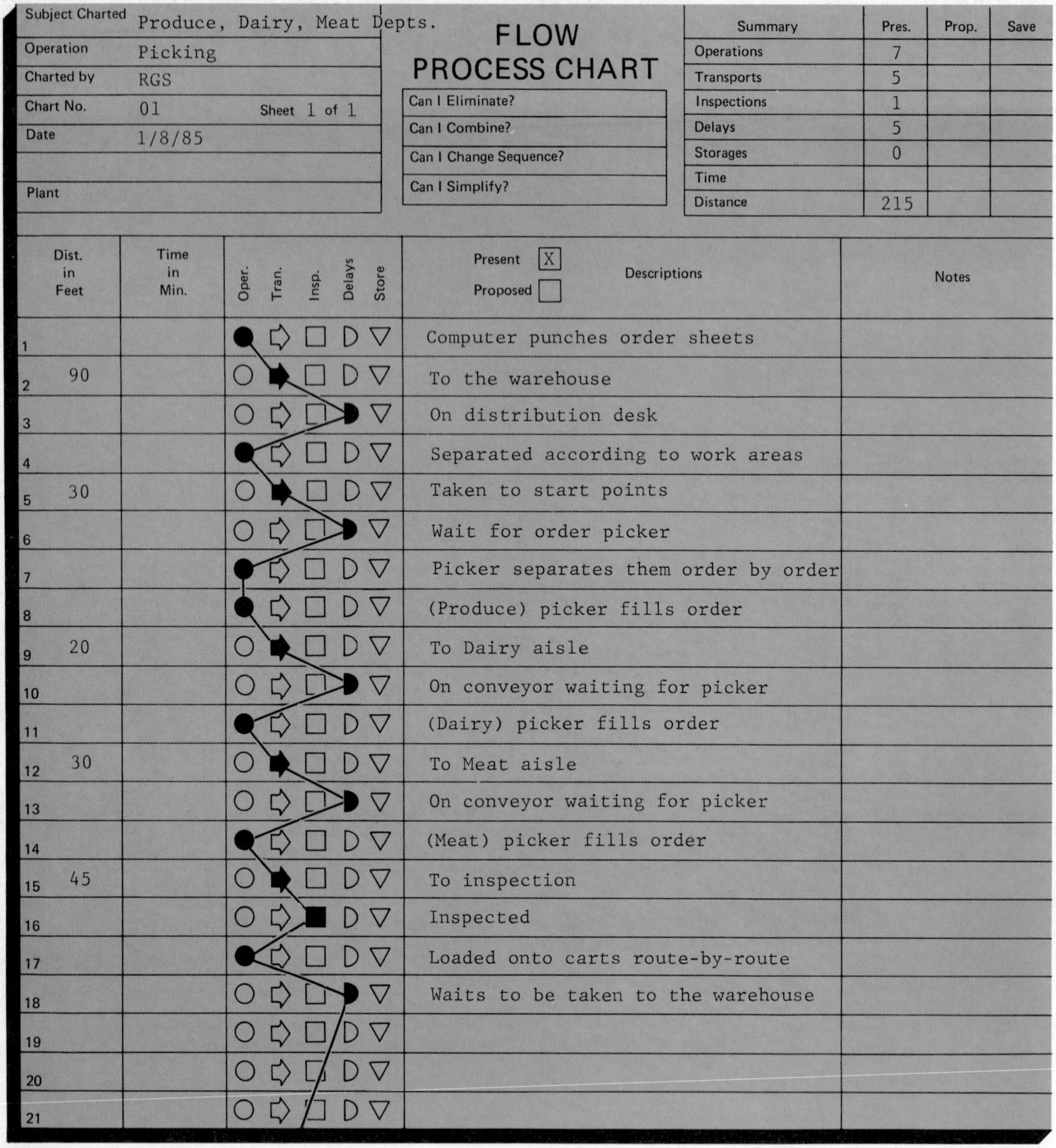

Subject Charted	Produce, Dairy, Meat Depts.	FLOW PROCESS CHART		Summary	Pres.	Prop.	Save
Operation	Picking			Operations	7		
Charted by	RGS			Transports	5		
Chart No.	01 Sheet 1 of 1	Can I Eliminate?		Inspections	1		
Date	1/8/85	Can I Combine?		Delays	5		
		Can I Change Sequence?		Storages	0		
Plant		Can I Simplify?		Time			
				Distance	215		

Dist. in Feet	Time in Min.	Oper.	Tran.	Insp.	Delays	Store	Present [X] Proposed [ ] Descriptions	Notes
1		●	⇨	□	D	▽	Computer punches order sheets	
2	90	○	◤	□	D	▽	To the warehouse	
3		○	⇨	□	D	▽	On distribution desk	
4		●	⇨	□	D	▽	Separated according to work areas	
5	30	○	◤	□	D	▽	Taken to start points	
6		○	⇨	□	D	▽	Wait for order picker	
7		●	⇨	□	D	▽	Picker separates them order by order	
8		●	⇨	□	D	▽	(Produce) picker fills order	
9	20	○	◤	□	D	▽	To Dairy aisle	
10		○	⇨	□	D	▽	On conveyor waiting for picker	
11		●	⇨	□	D	▽	(Dairy) picker fills order	
12	30	○	◤	□	D	▽	To Meat aisle	
13		○	⇨	□	D	▽	On conveyor waiting for picker	
14		●	⇨	□	D	▽	(Meat) picker fills order	
15	45	○	◤	□	D	▽	To inspection	
16		○	⇨	■	D	▽	Inspected	
17		●	⇨	□	D	▽	Loaded onto carts route-by-route	
18		○	⇨	□	D	▽	Waits to be taken to the warehouse	
19		○	⇨	□	D	▽		
20		○	⇨	□	D	▽		
21		○	⇨	□	D	▽		

FIGURE 8.5   Flow-processing chart.

5. *How.* How is the operation done? Can better methods, procedures, or equipment be used? Should the operation be revised to make it easier or less time-consuming?

The application of these questions can be illustrated by using the grocery warehouse example. In that case, two more items of information in addition to the flow-process chart were collected as part of the analysis: a flow diagram of the facility and time study data. The flow diagram, shown in Figure 8.6, illustrates the layout of the facility and the major flow of groceries for each order. Extensive data were also collected on the time it took, for both current methods and the suggested new methods, to perform each type of picking operation.

After the data were collected and the above questions were asked, the following types of changes were made:

1. *Layout.* The layout of the facility was revised to be more efficient and compact. Some aisles were moved from one part of the warehouse to another.

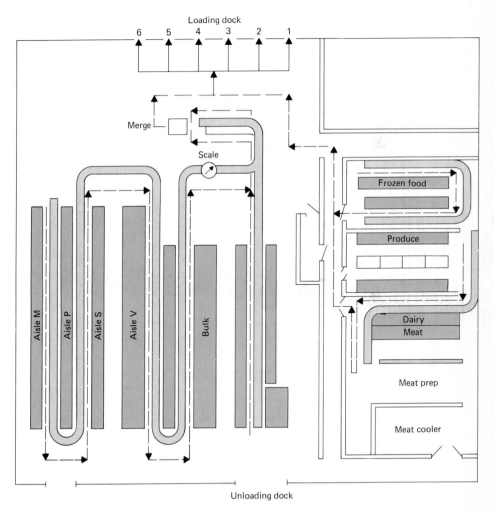

FIGURE 8.6
Initial layout of a grocery warehouse.

2. *Methods and jobs.* Methods of picking groceries were revised to reduce bottle-necks and labor.
3. *Equipment.* Special carts were designed to make loading of the delivery vans easier and faster. An overhead conveyor was also installed to consolidate orders and speed up the flow of materials.

These changes contributed significantly to better materials flow and improved efficiency. More value was added to the service produced by reducing wasted time and effort.

It should be noted that analysis of materials flow extends far beyond manufacturing. The grocery warehouse example was a service operation. Other examples of service operations with a substantial flow of materials are restaurants, laundries, the U.S. Postal Service, warehousing, and retail trade.

8.4 INFORMATION-FLOW ANALYSIS

Information flows can be analyzed in a manner analogous to that used for the flow of materials. Although information flows are sometimes recorded on a flow-process chart using the standard symbols, different forms of flowcharting are also used for information flows. However, the purpose of information-flow analysis is the same as for the analysis of materials flow: to improve the efficiency and effectiveness of the process.

There are two types of information flows. In the first, information is the product of the operation. This is typical, for example, of clerical processing in offices, where the office can be thought of as a "paperwork factory" converting the paperwork from "raw material" to "finished goods." In Chapter 6, we briefly described information-flow analysis for service operations. The emphasis was on designing the flows to be aware of customer contact points and "moments of truth." Since information is the product for many service operations, information-flow analysis becomes a key tool, much like analyzing materials flow for factories.

In the second case, the information flow is used for management or control purposes. Examples of this are order entry, purchasing documents, and paperwork used in manufacturing. In this case the paperwork is used to control the flow of materials. Although the methods of analysis are the same, the purposes of these two types of information flow are quite different.

It is usually insufficient to analyze a materials-flow process without also analyzing the flow of information. This is because the materials flow may be improved but management control of the process may still be lacking. To illustrate this concept, we have shown in Figure 8.7 the information flow from the grocery warehouse example. (See Figure 8.8 for an explanation of the symbols used. Although these are not the only symbols used in flowcharting, they illustrate the concepts involved.)

As Figure 8.7 indicates, three key types of information are used to control the flow of groceries: (1) route maps, (2) drivers' manifests, and (3) pick sheets. A route map tells the driver which route to follow in delivering the groceries for a particular run. The computer constructs the routes for each delivery on the basis of

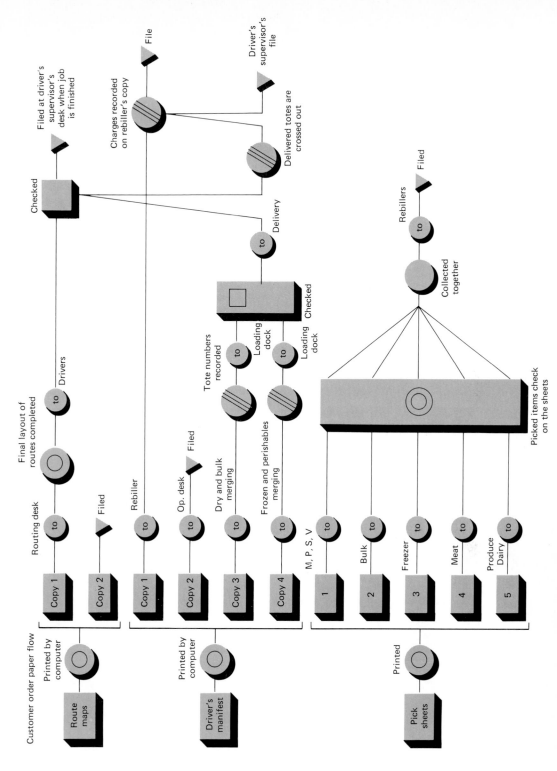

FIGURE 8.7 Information flows in a grocery warehouse.

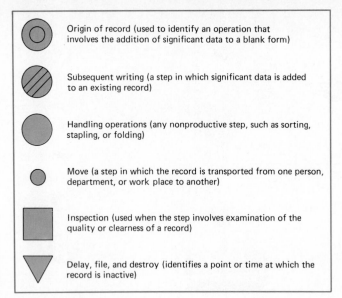

FIGURE 8.8
Symbols used in
an information-
processing
flowchart.

the locations of the customers' homes. The driver's manifest is simply a listing of the groceries to be delivered to each customer. Finally, the pick sheets are used to list the groceries by warehouse aisle so as to facilitate picking. In this case, all these types of information are used to control the delivery of grocery services. The paperwork flow itself is not the "product."

After the information flowchart is completed, the analysis proceeds in much the same way as the analysis of materials flows. The analysis should include the five key questions of "what," "who," "where," "when," and "how." It might also include some recording of times and information-flow volumes.

As a result of the analysis, it should be possible to consolidate or simplify information flows. This may result in changes in equipment (perhaps involving the computer), in jobs, and in procedures.

The analysis of information flows is sometimes seen as different from the analysis of materials flows. This may be because industrial engineers deal with materials flows while computer systems analysts deal with information flows. As we have seen, however, systems analysts might be considered as "industrial engineers of the office."

USING PROCESS-FLOW ANALYSIS

In summary, process flowchart analysis describes the transformation process used to convert inputs into outputs. The analysis may be used to describe materials flows or information flows. First, an appropriate process or system is isolated and a flowchart is constructed of the process. After the flowchart is prepared, questions of "what," "who," "where," "when," and "how" are asked to improve the process. From the answers to these questions, improvements might be made in procedures, tasks, equipment, raw materials, layout, or management control information. Basically, the objective is to add more value to the product or service by eliminating waste or unnecessary activities at all stages. As we have shown in the examples, a variety of processes can be improved by following this relatively simple form of analysis.

To this point, process-flow analysis has been presented as primarily technological in nature. But this type of analysis also affects the design of jobs and social aspects of the work environment. Process-flow analysis can be viewed as a sociotechnical problem, but only limited work along these lines has been done to date.

In an attempt to address this problem, the author developed a combined sociotechnical approach for an office of the state of Minnesota. This approach included both a traditional analysis of process flow and a diagnosis of job and organizational attitudes, as shown in Figure 8.9. With this approach, process-flow

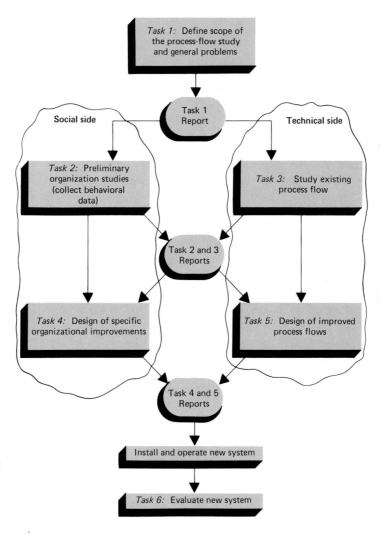

FIGURE 8.9
A sociotechnical
approach to
process-flow
analysis.

information and psychological data on workers' attitudes toward their jobs were collected. The analysis was then merged in a sociotechnical design of the new system.

It is clear that much attention needs to be given to the human element in process-flow analysis—not only in designing the new system but also in gaining acceptance for changes. Research has shown that the best way to accomplish this is to involve the persons affected in every stage of diagnosis and design. This tends to encourage individual ownership of the new system and therefore to reduce fears associated with change. It is difficult to overemphasize the need for user and worker involvement in process-flow design.

In the remainder of this chapter, we will describe a more sophisticated form of process-flow analysis which utilizes mathematical models. The basic idea is to express the process flow in terms of one or more mathematical relationships. These models can then be manipulated to analyze the effects of alternative management decisions.

 ## MODELING OF PROCESS FLOWS

A great many models—including linear programming, simulation, and queuing—are used to describe process flows. Our purpose in this section is not to explain any of these particular methodologies but rather to describe the general approach to the modeling of process flows and to show how this is useful in process design decisions. Additional materials on modeling and simulation are contained in the chapter supplement.

The first step in modeling process flows is to draw a flowchart of the process or the information flows used to control the process. Frequently, a block-diagram flowchart is useful. A block diagram consists of a series of three types of blocks: processing blocks, decision blocks, and feedback blocks, as in Figure 8.10. The processing block is represented by inputs, transformation, and outputs. It is, in effect, a small system used to convert inputs into outputs. In a decision block, the output is the result of a decision made during processing. Branches can be taken in the logic of the model depending on the decisions made. The last type of block is a feedback block; here information on the output level is fed back to control or change input values. Feedback blocks are most often used for management control purposes.

An operations process can be described as a network of processing blocks, decision blocks, and feedback blocks. Actually, a very complex system can be represented by interconnecting a large number of different blocks. As a first step in modeling, a network block diagram is drawn to isolate the processing system and the various subsystems of interest. Once this has been done, mathematical relationships for each of the blocks in the diagram can be defined. In this way a very complex system can be built up from a set of relatively simple blocks.

We will illustrate below the development of a block diagram and the subsequent use of a simulation model to improve decision making. The example is a classical job-shop simulation study.

Job-shop simulation was one of the early applications of process-flow modeling

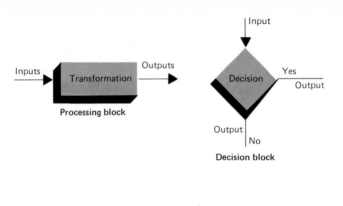

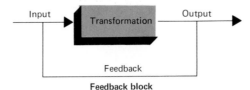

FIGURE 8.10
Types of blocks.

by simulation; an excellent example from the production of integrated circuits is given by Reitman. In Reitman's example, batches of silicon slices are processed through a number of steps including polishing, chemical etching, heating, photoengraving, and testing. The number of steps, up to a maximum of 24, varied for different circuits. The integrated circuits are microscopic in size—up to 1000 circuits may be placed on a small silicon wafer 1½ inches in diameter.

Production yields of these circuits were often quite low and unpredictable. As a result, a great deal of reprocessing was required and it was difficult to meet delivery schedules.

The sequence of events was as follows. After a new order had been taken, a check was made to see whether the order could be filled from inventory. If this could not be done, the order was added to existing batches in process before the new order was separately scheduled. Once it was in production, the order was processed at some stations in batches and at other stations as single wafers.

The decision process used to plan and control this job shop is shown by a network block diagram in Figure 8.11. Notice that this is the information control system and not the materials flow process itself.

After drawing the network block diagram, the information control system was tested by simulation. Incoming orders were accepted by the simulation model, and the resulting effect on work-in-process inventories and production schedules was determined. As a result, different scheduling rules and processing steps could be tested on the simulation model before putting them into effect.

This example illustrates how modeling can be used to test proposed changes via computer simulation. Flowcharts can be extended by use of simulation models to permit analysis of process flows. This makes it possible to study and improve the transformation system in operations by formal mathematical analysis. The supplement to this chapter provides several more examples of how this can be done.

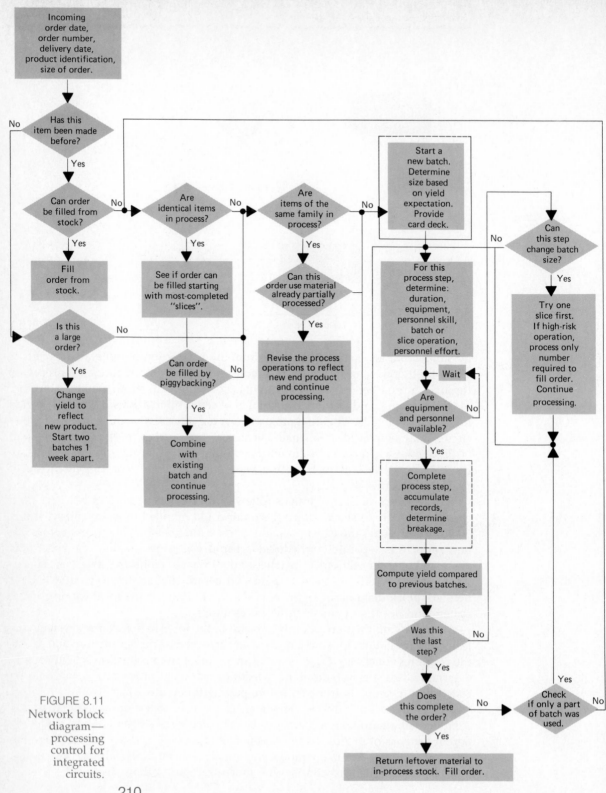

FIGURE 8.11
Network block
diagram—
processing
control for
integrated
circuits.

210

8.7 SIMULATION OF PROCESS FLOWS

While the above example illustrates the use of a block diagram to model process flows, the next example will concentrate on issues of data collection and model validation. The example is an outpatient obstetric-care facility studied by Glenn and Roberts to determine the effects of resource allocations (doctors, nurses, and rooms) on patient service. The simulation started with the flowchart shown in Figure 8.12, which describes the steps each patient goes through in the clinic.

Each patient reported to the appointment station when she entered the clinic. She then waited in the lobby until she was taken by a nurse's assistant for laboratory tests, if required, and then to an examination room where she prepared for the prenatal exam. When the doctor became available, the examination was conducted, sometimes with the assistance of a nurse's assistant. The patient then left the examining room and received information about caring for herself during pregnancy, including dietary information if needed. Finally, the patient made another clinic appointment and then left the clinic. This process is summarized in Figure 8.12.

For this simulation model, a given patient load was assumed, using levels of 20, 50, and 80 patients per day. It also was assumed that patients' visits would be scheduled to supply a continuous input to the first processing step in the flowchart. Thus, patient scheduling was not part of the model. This illustrates the proper definition of the system boundaries of interest.

Management decided to use two measures of patient service: total time to process a given number of patients (clinic duration) and average time in the clinic per patient (mean transit time). Resource utilization was measured by three variables: room utilization (percent), physician utilization (percent), and assistant utilization (percent). The purpose of the study was to determine the relationship between the amount of resources available (rooms, physicians, and assistants), the resulting utilization of resources, and the measures of patient service.

After the flowchart was drawn, the next step was to collect data on the process. Over a 7-day period, some 303 patients were observed by three data collectors at various locations in the clinic. These observers collected data on all processing times and tasks for each patient. The observers also collected data for 2 additional clinic days; these data were reserved for validation of the model.

A simulation model was developed and programmed on the computer. The user of the model specified four input variables: number of patients to be treated, number of physicians assigned, number of examining rooms assigned, and number of assistants assigned. The model used the empirical data for processing times and processing steps, along with a first-come–first-served scheduling rule to process all the hypothetical "patients" one at a time. When the last one had been processed, the computer reported statistics on clinic performance: clinic duration, mean patient transit time, and utilization of rooms, physicians, and assistants.

The model was validated using three methods. First, a logical check was made. For example, when the number of physicians was increased, with all other variables held constant, did physician utilization decrease? Second, an intuitive check of model performance was made on "standard" clinic conditions of 50

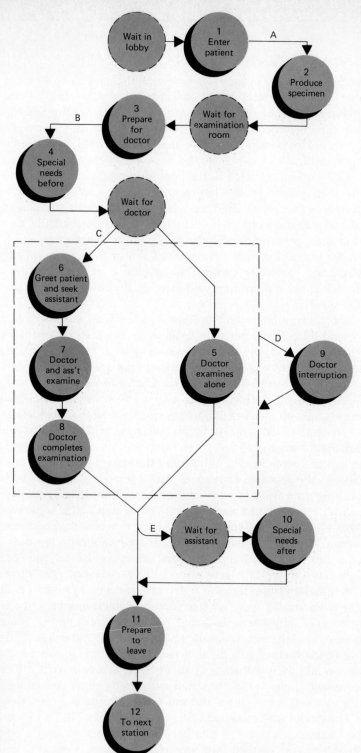

FIGURE 8.12
Flowchart model
of outpatient
clinic.
*Source: John K. Glenn
and Stephen Roberts,
"The Relationship
between Resources
and Utilization
Factors in an
Outpatient Care
System," AIIE
Transactions, vol. 5,
no. 1, March 1973,
p. 27.*

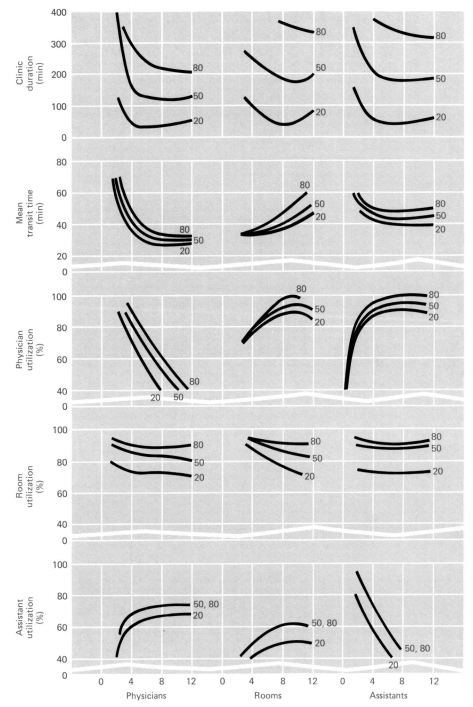

FIGURE 8.13
Outpatient clinic
results. Numbers
identifying curves
indicate patient
load (patients per
session).
*Source: John K. Glenn
and Stephen Roberts,
"The Relationship
between Resource and
Utilization Factors in
an Outpatient Care
System," AIIE
Transactions, vol. 5,
no. 1, March 1973,
p. 30.*

patients, 9 rooms, 3 doctors, and 5 assistants. The output of the simulation for these conditions was checked by clinic personnel to see if the results appeared reasonable. The third validity check utilized data for the 2 additional days which were observed. The outputs of the simulation were compared with figures actually observed and tested statistically for differences. The model passed all three of these validation tests.

The next step in the analysis was to use the simulator to develop relationships between inputs and outputs. Rather than simply running a large number of trials and plotting graphs, the investigators developed an experimental design to test different levels of each variable systematically and to develop a series of equations relating input to output.

From this part of the analysis, it was determined that output varied nonlinearly with inputs and that various resources interacted in affecting outputs. These results can be seen quite clearly in Figure 8.13, along with the general results of the study. The graphs in this figure indicate the relationship between each input and all outputs. In effect, we have described the production function[1] of the clinic through the simulation of process flows.

Clinic managers can use the information in Figure 8.13 to answer several questions. For example, what will be the effect of increasing the number of assistants from four to six? What will be the effect of an increasing patient load in the clinic if no additional resources are added? What will be the effect on clinic hours of adding two more physicians? Can the entire patient load be processed in 2 hours instead of 3?

This analysis also allows the clinic managers to identify specific bottlenecks in the process flow. A bottleneck is any operation which constrains the flow of patients to other operations in the process. Bottlenecks can be alleviated by various methods including adding resources, changing scheduling rules, or modifying process flows. The idea is to obtain a smooth flow through the entire process.

8.8 KEY POINTS

This chapter has emphasized the analysis of transformation processes used to produce goods or services. Two main types of analysis were stressed: descriptive analysis through the use of flowcharts and mathematical analysis through the use of process-flow models. Both these forms of analysis can be used to improve the delivery, costs, quality, and flexibility of the productive process.

Some of the key points stressed in the chapter are as follows:

• A systems definition is a prerequisite to process-flow analysis. Systems definition requires isolation of a system for study and identification of the boundary, inputs, outputs, and process flows.

---

[1]The term "production function" is used in the classic economic sense as a transformation function between input and output.

- Both materials and information flows can be analyzed by a common framework and common procedure: that is, to describe the flows as a system through the use of flowcharts and to ask questions regarding what is done, who does it, and where, when, and how it is done. The result of this analysis may lead to changes in any or all elements of the process (output, raw materials, tools, equipment, jobs, methods, and information).
- In analyzing materials flows, four types of documents are typically used: assembly drawings, assembly ("Gozinto") charts, routing sheets, and flow-process charts. These documents together describe exactly how the product is made and how it flows through the production process.
- Information flows can be analyzed either as the product itself or as management information used to plan and control production of the product. In the same way as materials flows, information flows are depicted in flowcharts which are then analyzed to find ways of improving the process.
- A sociotechnical approach is needed to consider physical flow design simultaneously with the design of jobs. This approach should result in processes which are both economically and humanly rewarding.
- Mathematical models can be used to study the design of production processes described in terms of input, transformation, and output. A model is used to study process design alternatives before putting them into practice. Classical applications of process design through process-flow modeling are the job-shop simulation and flows through facilities such as hospitals, restaurants, and warehouses.

QUESTIONS

1. In the following operations, isolate a system for analysis, and define what services are produced and the primary process flows.
   a. A college
   b. A fast-food restaurant
   c. A library
2. How is the analysis of material similar to and different from the analysis of information?
3. Give three reasons why the flow of materials and the flow of control information should be analyzed together, at the same time.
4. What is meant by a sociotechnical approach to process analysis? Under what circumstances should such an approach be used?
5. What kinds of problems are presented by the redesign of existing processes which are not encountered in the design of a new process?
6. How can a job shop be viewed as a "network of queues"?
7. Why are block diagrams needed to study process flows? How are they useful?
8. Describe the differences between a simulation model used to design a process initially and a simulation model used to operate and redesign the process on an ongoing basis.
9. What is meant by the statement, "A simulator describes the production function of an operation?"
10. How is the flowcharting of a process related to simulation or optimization models of the same process?
11. Discuss the methods and problems of validating process-flow models.

PROBLEMS

1. Draw a flowchart of the following processes:
   a. The procedure used to keep your checkbook
   b. College registration
   c. Obtaining a book from the library
2. Using the special symbols, draw a flow-process chart of the processes listed in Problem 1.
3. Use the key questions of "what," "who," "where," "when," and "how" on Problem 1 or 2 to suggest improvements in the process.
4. Draw an assembly chart for a double-decker hamburger.
5. Develop a routing sheet (operations process sheet) for all operations required to:
   a. Cook a hamburger
   b. Prepare a term paper
6. The following process is designed to handle 100 customers a day. The customer is "processed" through each of the three operations, A, B, and C, in sequence. The average rate at which each operation can process customers is also shown below.

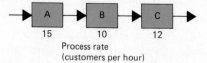

Process rate
(customers per hour)

   a. For an 8-hour day identify any bottlenecks in the process.
   b. What effect will bottlenecks have on the overall output and the other operations?
   c. Suppose that all processes are operated for 10 hours per day. Is there still a bottleneck?
   d. How will random arrivals affect the throughput and processing rate of this process? What methods can be used in this case to analyze the process?
7. Using processing blocks, decision blocks, and feedback blocks, draw a flowchart of the following processes.
   a. Check-in service at the front desk of a hotel
   b. Check-out service at the hotel
   c. Use the "what," "who," "when," and "how" questions to suggest improvements in check-out in Problem 7a.
8. Using the special operations symbols, draw a flow-process chart of the following processes.
   a. Preparing yourself for school in the morning
   b. Cleaning up your room (even if you haven't done it lately)
9. Use the "what," "who," "when," and "how" questions to make improvements in Problem 8a and 8b.
10. Draw an assembly chart for a three-ring notebook consisting of several sections which are each produced by separate departments in a company.
    a. Assume each section of the notebook is assembled independently of the others.
    b. Assume that some of the sections must be assembled together, before putting them into the notebook.

SELECTED BIBLIOGRAPHY

ACKOFF, R. L.: "Towards a System of System Concepts," *Management Science,* vol. 17, July 1971, pp. 661–667.

BOULDING, K.E.: "General Systems Theory—The Skeleton of Science," in P. P. Schroderbek (ed.), *Management Systems,* 2d ed., New York: Wiley, 1971.

CHUCHMAN, C. W.: *The System Approach,* New York: Delacorte, 1968.

EMSHOFF, JAMES R. and ROGER L. SISSON: *Design and Use of Computer Simulation Models,* New York: Macmillan, 1970.

GLENN, JOHN K. and STEPHEN ROBERTS: "The Relationship between Resource and Utilization Factors in the Outpatient Care System," *AIIE Transactions,* vol. 5, no. 1, March 1973.

NAYLOR, THOMAS H.: *Computer Simulation Experiments with Models of Economic Systems,* New York: Wiley, 1971.

REITMAN, JULIAN: *Computer Simulation Applications,* New York: Wiley, 1971.

TUZCU, ERTUGRUL: "Methods Improvement and Design of an Existing Plant," Minneapolis: University of Minnesota. Spring 1978, Plan B paper.

SUPPLEMENT
Simulation

Simulation is a technique which can be used to formulate and solve a wide class of models. The class is so broad that it has been said, "If all else fails, try simulation." Simulation models include business games, analogue simulators, and flight simulators, which all represent a real situation in terms of a model. In this supplement, however, our discussion of simulation will be limited to computer simulation of business decision problems.

Simulation is typically, but not always, used for dynamic models which include multiple time periods. Dynamic simulation models are incremented from one time period or one event to the next as the situation unfolds over time. In this way the effect of successive decisions can be evaluated.

Simulation should be used in situations where it is too expensive or too difficult to experiment in the real situation. In these cases, the effects of a decision can be tested on a simulation model before the decision is implemented. A large number of situations have been simulated in this way, including the flow of patients in clinics, the operation of physical distribution networks, the organization of curricula in colleges, factory operations, and arrivals and departures of all types (ships, aircraft, students, blood shipments, etc.), to name only a few. Simulation is frequently useful in solving queuing problems which have complicated arrival patterns, service distributions, or line disciplines. Simple queuing problems can be solved by analytical methods discussed in the supplement to Chapter 6.

We will begin this supplement with a simple example of simulation. This will be followed by a discussion of the general simulation method, and some comments on the uses of simulation in operations.

A SIMULATION EXAMPLE: BETTY'S BAKERY

Betty's Bakery orders a number of bakery products each day; these are carried in stock. One product Betty carries is a special type of whole wheat bread. Betty wanted to determine how much of this bread she should order each day to maximize her profits. If she ordered too little, she would lose sales and profit. If she ordered too much, the excess would be wasted. For simplicity, we assume that all bread not sold during the day would be given away the next day at a total loss. (In real life, the leftover bread could, perhaps, be sold as day-old bread at only a partial loss.)

Betty collected data on the daily demand for her bread for 100 days, obtaining the following demand frequencies:

Demand (loaves)	Midpoint	Frequency
20–24	22	.05
25–29	27	.10
30–34	32	.20
35–39	37	.30
40–44	42	.20
45–49	47	.10
50–54	52	.05

Betty had been managing her bread inventory by ordering an amount equal to demand on the day before. Sometimes this decision rule left her with too much bread, and sometimes she did not have enough. Therefore, Betty wondered whether there was a better decision rule that she might use. For example, how would profits be affected if she ordered an amount of bread equal to the average past usage? For this case, average past usage is equal to 37 loaves per day.

$$\overline{X} = .05(22) + .10(27) + .20(32) + .30(37) \\ + .20(42) + .10(47) + .05(52) = 37$$

To resolve this issue, we will construct a simulation model incorporating the following two decision rules:

- Rule 1: Order a number of loaves equal to demand on the previous day.

- Rule 2: Order 37 loaves each day regardless of past demand.

The best rule will be selected on the basis of maximum profit over the total number of days simulated. We will use 15 days of simulation, just for purposes of illustration. In a real application, many more days would be used to obtain reliable results.

To simulate this problem, we will generate a series of random daily demands with frequencies equal to those given above. To visualize the demand-generation procedure, imagine a large wheel of fortune with 100 positions on it. Five of those positions are labeled with a 22, corresponding to the .05 frequency above. Ten of the positions are labeled with a 27, corresponding to the .10 frequency, and so on. The wheel is spun once for each day, and where it stops determines the daily demand. As a result, provided that the wheel is truly random, random demands with the proper frequencies are generated.

Although this process of generating random demands is helpful conceptually, it can be made more efficient by using a random number table. The random number table shown in Appendix B consists of a series of random numbers arranged in rows and columns. The numbers are randomized across rows, down columns, and by digits within numbers. The table can be used by selecting an arbitrary starting point and proceeding either across rows or down columns. Some of the digits can be thrown away if they are not needed because the numbers in the table are completely randomized.

For example, suppose we wish to generate 15 two-digit random numbers for Betty's Bakery. Suppose we start in the upper left-hand corner of the table (arbitrarily) and proceed across the first row. Taking the first two digits of each number and throwing the rest of the digits away, we obtain:

27, 43, 85, 88, 29, 69, 94, 64
32, 48, 13, 14, 54, 15, 47

In this case, we could also have used all the digits in each number or proceeded down the columns instead of across rows or used any other pattern we liked as long as the pattern was consistent.

Now that we have generated 15 random numbers, we can convert them to loaves of bread demanded. This is done by associating the entire range of 100 random numbers with the demand distribution, as follows[2]:

Demand midpoint	Frequency	Random numbers
22	.05	00–04
27	.10	05–14
32	.20	15–34
37	.30	35–64
42	.20	65–84
47	.10	85–94
52	.05	95–99

The random numbers that we have generated above are converted to loaves of bread demanded, as shown in Table S8.1. For example, the first random number, 27, corresponds to a demand of 32 loaves; the second random number, 43, corresponds to a demand of 37 loaves; and so on. In this way, we can simulate the demand for bread on each of the 15 days of the problem by what is commonly called the Monte Carlo method.

The next step will be to calculate the corresponding sales and amount ordered on each day. These calculations depend on the rule chosen; therefore, two sets of calculations are shown in Table S8.1. With rule 1, the amount ordered can be filled in the table, since demand is known. Sales is then just the minimum of the amount ordered and

---

[2]In the table, 00–04—a total of 5 numbers out of 100—is assigned to the first category. Similarly, 05–14 contains 10 numbers, or a frequency of .10.

TABLE S8.1
BETTY'S BAKERY

Day	Random number	Demand	Rule 1 Amount ordered	Rule 1 Sales	Rule 2 Amount ordered	Rule 2 Sales
0		37				
1	27	32	37	32	37	32
2	43	37	32	32	37	37
3	85	47	37	37	37	37
4	88	47	47	47	37	37
5	29	32	47	32	37	32
6	69	42	32	32	37	37
7	94	47	42	42	37	37
8	64	37	47	37	37	37
9	32	32	37	32	37	32
10	48	37	32	32	37	37
11	13	27	37	27	37	27
12	14	27	27	27	37	27
13	54	37	27	27	37	37
14	15	32	37	32	37	32
15	47	37	32	32	37	37
		587	550	500	555	515

the amount demanded on each day. Betty cannot sell more than she ordered, and she cannot sell more than the demand. Similar daily calculations are made for rule 2.

The total amount ordered and the total amount sold over the 15 days are obtained in Table S8.1. These figures can be multiplied by the unit cost and selling price to derive profits. Assume that bread sells for 50 cents a loaf, and it costs 25 cents to purchase a loaf wholesale. The total profit over 15 days for each rule then is:

$$\text{Rule 1: Profit} = .50(500) - .25(550)$$
$$= \$112.50$$
$$\text{Rule 2: Profit} = .50(515) - .25(555)$$
$$= \$118.75$$

Rule 2, therefore, offers some improvement in profit contribution over rule 1.

GENERAL METHODOLOGY

The example we have just discussed represents an application of the generalized simulation method. The steps used in every simulation study are

shown in Figure S8.1 and described below; it is assumed that a computer is being used in the simulation process.

Define the Problem

A relevant decision problem must be isolated and defined for study. Considerable experience and insight are required if a problem for simulation is to be properly isolated from its environment. Problem defintion also includes deciding on the objectives, constraints, and assumptions which will be used. After the problem is defined in general terms, a specific quantitative model can be developed.

In Betty's Bakery, a problem regarding a specific type of bread was isolated. It was assumed that if the whole wheat bread was not available, the sale would be lost. Customers' substitution of other types of bread or other bakery products was not considered possible. It was also assumed that Betty's objective was to maximize profits, and a variety of other explicit or implicit assumptions were made. These assumptions collectively define the problem.

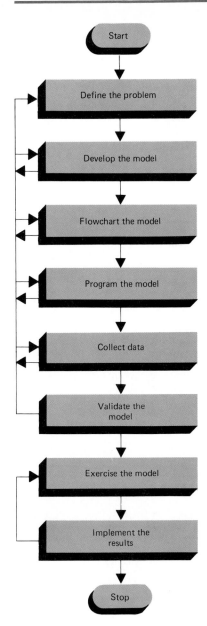

FIGURE S8.1 Simulation method.

Develop the Model

In the development of simulation models, the controllable variables, the uncontrollable variables, measures of performance, decision rules, and model functions must be defined. In this way a specific mathematical representation of the problem will be developed. Every model can be expressed in the form

$$P = f(U_i, C_k)$$

In developing the simulation model, we are simply specifying the P, f, U_i, and C_k values in the model.

In the model, the uncontrollable variables U_i, or parameters, are fixed constants which are outside the control of the decision maker. For example, in Betty's Bakery, the initial demand level, the frequency distribution of demand, the cost of purchasing bread, and the price of bread were all considered fixed values and, therefore, uncontrollable variables.

The controllable variables, or decision variables C_k, in a simulation model can be controlled by the decision maker. These variables will change in value from one run to the next as different decisions are simulated. In Betty's Bakery, the amount ordered each day was the controllable decision variable. The values of this variable were specified by a decision rule which determined the amount ordered each day.

Finally, a decision model has one or more measures of performance P and function(s) which relate the variables to performance. In Betty's Bakery, the measure of performance was profit. A specific formula was used to calculate profit as a function of the controllable and uncontrollable variables in the model.

After all the model elements have been defined, the model is ready for computer flowcharting and programming. Before a flowchart can be constructed, however, the analyst must decide whether the model will be incremented by fixed or variable time increments. Every simulation model has a "clock" which keeps track of the time increments in the model. In a fixed-time-increment model, the clock is advanced in fixed time periods (e.g., Betty's Bakery). In a variable-time-increment model, the clock is advanced to the next event. For example, if patient flows in a hospital are simulated, each arrival and departure can be treated as an event. The clock is then advanced to the next arrival or departure time, which results in variable time increments.

Flowchart the Model

A simulation model should always be flowcharted prior to computer programming. Flowcharting helps clarify the precise computational logic of the model. This facilitates computer programming and helps the model builder discover logical errors in the model.

A flowchart for Betty's Bakery is shown in Figure S8.2. The flowchart simply represents the logic used to construct the data recorded in Table S8.1. Each day of the simulation, a demand value is generated. The order quantity is then determined by using the appropriate decision rule and comparing the order quantity with the demand. If the demand is greater than or equal to the order quantity, sales are set equal to the order quantity, since Betty will sell all she has on hand. If demand is less than the order quantity, sales are set equal to demand and the rest of the available bread will be given away. Using the quantities for sales and order size, profit is then computed, and the simulation is recycled until it reaches the desired number of periods. When the simulation is finished, a report showing the various values of sales, order quantities, demands, and profit is printed.

The flowchart is a representation of the mathematical model being simulated. On each step of the simulation, we compute values for the equation $P = f(U_i, C_k)$. In the case of Betty's Bakery, we use the mathematical model already described above to compute sales and profit on each step of the flowchart.

In constructing simple flowcharts, two types of symbols are used:

□ = operation symbol

◇ Yes = decision symbol
No

An operation may consist of generating a demand, setting a value of a variable, or other tasks in

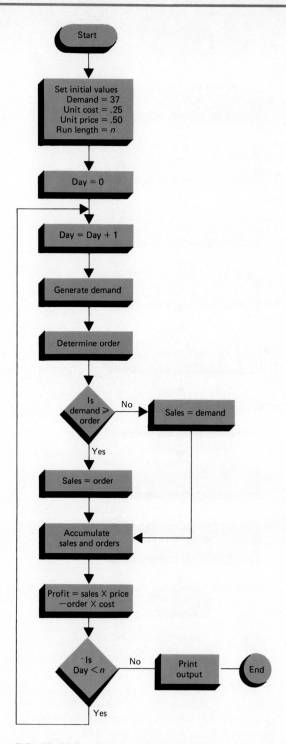

FIGURE S8.2   Flowchart for Betty's Bakery.

the simulation. A decision results in a branch in the simulation model depending on a comparison or test of variables. Flowcharts are normally drawn from top to bottom. (See Figure S8.2.)

Program the Model

A good flowchart will make it easy to program the simulation model for computer operation. For example, a simple FORTRAN program for Betty's Bakery is shown in Figure S8.3. The program uses the following fixed inputs: demand for day zero, the decision rule being used for order quantity, the demand distribution, unit cost, unit price, and run length. The output of the program when rule 1 is used is shown in Table S8.2. This table provides the same information as the data recorder we constructed earlier by hand. The advantage of the program, of course, is that we can easily change the run length and other input parameters when we are using the simulation model for decision making.

Simulation programming can be done in a variety of computer languages—general languages such as FORTRAN, PASCAL, and BASIC as well as special simulation languages such as GASP and GPSS. The advantage of the special languages is that they simplify the programming through the

use of special simulation statements. For example, GASP has statements which can be used to generate arrivals, build queues, and maintain statistics commonly used in simulation.

Collect Data

After the model is programmed, data must be collected to specify the input parameters. In the case of Betty's Bakery, data are required for unit cost, price, and the demand distribution. The unit cost might be available from the accounting department, or it might be derived from past purchase orders. The price is easily obtained from current practice. The demand data might be derived from available records or collected by a special study. A minimum of about 20 days would be needed to obtain even rough estimates of demand frequencies. It would be better to have as many as 100 days of past demand data for stable estimates of demand frequency.

The collection of data is often one of the most costly and time-consuming parts of the simulation study. Because of the time required, data collection is often done at the same time as the programming. In this case, when the programming is done, the data are also available to begin validation of the model.

TABLE S8.2
BETTY'S BAKERY OUTPUT

Day	Demand	Amount Ordered	Sales	Profit
1	37	37	37	9.25
2	52	37	37	9.25
3	42	52	42	8.00
4	32	42	32	5.50
5	37	32	32	8.00
6	22	37	22	1.75
7	32	22	22	5.50
8	32	32	32	8.00
9	42	32	32	8.00
10	37	42	37	8.00
11	27	37	27	4.25
12	42	27	27	6.75
13	37	42	37	8.00
14	27	37	27	4.25
15	32	27	27	6.75
Total	530	535	470	101.25

```
      DIMENSION D(100),Q(100),PROFIT(100),SALES(100)
C   INITIALIZE VARIABLES
      TPROF=0
      TDEMAN=0
      TSALES=0
      TQTY=0
      D1=37
      C=.25
      P=.5
      N=100
      DO 100 I=1,N
C   GENERATE DEMAND
      NX=RANF(0)*100.
      IF(NX.GE.0..AND.NX.LE.4.)    D(I)=22
      IF(NX.GE.5..AND.NX.LE.14.)   D(I)=27
      IF(NX.GE.15..AND.NX.LE.34.)  D(I)=32
      IF(NX.GE.35..AND.NX.LE.64.)  D(I)=37
      IF(NX.GE.65..AND.NX.LE.84.)  D(I)=42
      IF(NX.GE.85..AND.NX.LE.94.)  D(I)=47
      IF(NX.GE.95..AND.NX.LE.99.)  D(I)=52
C   DECISION RULE
      IF (I.EQ.1) THEN
         Q(I)=D1
      ELSE
         Q(I)=D(I-1)
      ENDIF
C   SALES
      IF(D(I).GE.Q(I)) SALES(I)=Q(I)
      IF(D(I).LT.Q(I)) SALES(I)=D(I)
C   PROFIT CALC
      PROFIT(I)=SALES(I)*P-Q(I)*C
  100 CONTINUE
C   HEADINGS
      PRINT 110
  110 FORMAT(///,1X,28X,6HAMOUNT,/,3X,3HDAY,8X,6HDEMAND,8X,7HORDERED,
     *   8X,5HSALES,10X,6HPROFIT,//)
C   SUMMATION
      DO 200 I=1,N
      TPROF=PROFIT(I)+TPROF
      TDEMAN=TDEMAN+D(I)
      TSALES=TSALES+SALES(I)
      TQTY=TQTY+Q(I)
      PRINT 180,I,D(I),Q(I),SALES(I),PROFIT(I)
  180 FORMAT(3X,I3,10X,F3.0,12X,F3.0,11X,F3.0,9X,F7.2,/)
  200 CONTINUE
      PRINT 210,TDEMAN,TQTY,TSALES,TPROF
  210 FORMAT(1X,5HTOTAL,6X,F7.0,8X,F7.0,7X,F7.0,7X,F9.2)
      STOP
      END
```

FIGURE S8.3 FORTRAN program.

Validate the Model

Validation determines whether the simulation models are a sufficiently accurate portrayal of the real world. To be useful, the model does not have to reflect every real-world condition and assumption. As a matter of fact, a simplified description of the real world is often necessary to make the model controllable and affordable. Therefore, simplifying assumptions incorporated into the model must be checked by the process of validation.

There are several types of validation: of input parameters, of outputs, and of run length. Validation of input parameters is aimed at determining whether the inputs used by the model match the correct values. For example, in the case of Betty's Bakery, we should test whether the demand distribution for bread generated by the model is a good match for the assumed distribution. Figure S8.4 shows a plot of 100 values of the demand distribution used in a simulation run versus the true values of the demand distribution. In each case, there are errors between the true demand and the observed values used in the simulation. Standard statistical tests can be used (e.g., the chi-squared test) to determine whether or not the observed distribution is a sufficiently close fit to the true distribution. If

not, perhaps more runs may be needed or there may be an error in the coding itself. Similar tests can be made on output values to determine whether the simulator is predicting properly or not. In the case of Betty's Bakery, an output test would be a comparison of actual sales and profit data with the outputs from the model under similar conditions. These output comparisons can be tested statistically in the same way as the inputs.

Finally, validity can be related to run length. In simulation, run length is set to obtain stable or realistic results. One way to determine run length is to plot the output results of the model versus run length and determine when output stability occurs. In Figure S8.5, both sales and profit are plotted as a function of run length. As may be noted, there are wide fluctuations for small run lengths, but the output stabilizes as run length increases. Often, simulators have initial starting conditions which are arbitrarily selected. Therefore, the simulator must be run long enough to arrive at steady-state results. Standard statistical tests can be run on the output to determine when stability occurs.

In order to determine model validity, it may be necessary to revise the model. Therefore, Figure S8.1 shows a feedback loop from validation to all earlier steps in the modeling process. In addition to guiding model revision, validation should help determine an appropriate run length. When validation is completed, the model is ready to be used.

Exercise the Model

To aid decision making, the simulation model is exercised or *run* through several cases of interest. In the case of Betty's Bakery, a run is made for each of the two decision rules, and the effects on sales and profits are compared. For 100 periods, the following results are obtained:

	Rule 1	Rule 2
Profit	$ 749	$ 810
Sales	$1687	$1735

In this comparison, exactly the same daily demand is used for both rules, so demand variability is the same in both cases.

In simulation studies, sensitivity analysis is required to test the sensitivity of the results to input assumptions. In the case of Betty's Bakery, for

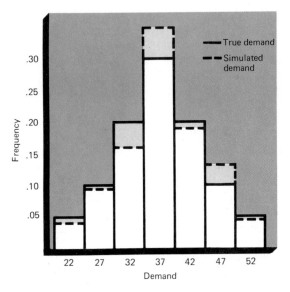

FIGURE S8.4   Betty's Bakery: True versus simulated demand.

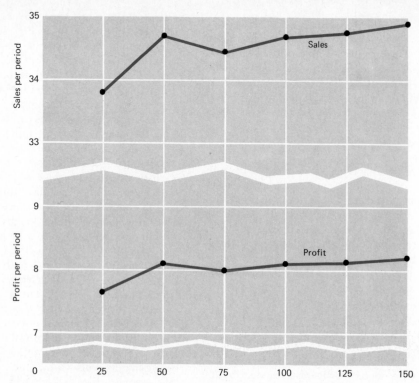

FIGURE S8.5
Outputs versus
run length.

example, there may be some uncertainty with regard to the unit cost figure. In the example, a cost of 25 cents per loaf was used, but the cost might really be 30 or 20 cents a loaf, depending on the assumptions made. Would these changes in cost affect our preference for the rule used? In order to answer this question, we make two additional calculations: one with $C = .30$ and the other with $C = .20$. The results of these calculations are:

	$C = .20$		$C = .30$	
	Rule 1	**Rule 2**	**Rule 1**	**Rule 2**
Profit	$936	$995	$561	$625

As indicated earlier, rule 2 is still preferred to rule 1 on the basis of profit.

As part of the decision-making process, similar sensitivity runs could be made for price and demand. In many cases, sensitivity runs are the most valuable part of the analysis because they give the decision maker a "feel" for the situation.

For Betty's Bakery, additional decision rules should also be investigated. For example, why should we order at the average of past demand? Should we not also consider other values of constant ordering levels? Figure S8.6 shows profit as a function of various constant ordering levels, indicating that it is most profitable to order 40 loaves a day (slightly more than the past average of demand). As part of the analysis, other rules should also be investigated.

Implement the Results

In the pursuit of model building, we sometimes forget that the simulation study is not useful until it has some impact on decision making. This means that the result of the study must cause a change in behavior or—at a very minimum—provide confirmation that the present actions are correct. In the latter case, the study may have prevented undesirable change.

Implementation, therefore, requires us to consider the behavioral reactions of decision makers and the people they manage. In the case of Betty's Bakery, rule 2 is preferred; fortunately, it has the

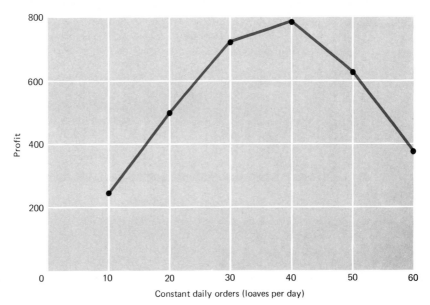

Profit

Constant daily orders (loaves per day)

FIGURE S8.6
Sensitivity
analysis.

VARIABLE-TIME-INCREMENT SIMULATION

As we have already indicated, variable-time-increment simulation is not based on discrete time periods; instead, the "clock" is advanced from one event to the next. As a result, the clock could read time 1, 3, 9, 12, and 17, for example, in a simulation run consisting of 5 events and 17 time units. The principles of designing a variable-time-increment simulation model are exactly the same as those of designing the fixed-time-increment model. Therefore, following the same steps in model design, we will provide a variable-time-increment example as follows.

Suppose we are trying to design dock facilities for ships. Since docks are very expensive, we want to decide whether to use one or two docks in a particular harbor. To solve this problem, we need an arrival-time distribution for the ships. In particular, suppose the ships arrive at random with a specified mean time between arrivals, according to the exponential arrival distribution described in the supplement to Chapter 6. We also assume, for the sake of convenience, that the time to service a ship

least behavioral impact on the supplier, for a constant number of loaves is ordered each day.

is a constant number of days, such as 5. Service in this case involves unloading a ship and refueling it at a dock. Under these conditions, we are interested in how long the ships will have to wait in the harbor before they are unloaded. After finding the waiting time, we might convert waiting time to waiting cost in order to trade off the cost of the waiting ships with the cost of the additional dock.

In developing this model, we need to generate exponential ship arrivals. When we assume an average time of 6 days between ship arrivals, the exponential distribution of arrival times is as shown in Figure S8.7. These times are derived from the following formula[3]:

$$y = P(x \le t) = 1 - e^{-\lambda t} \qquad (S8.1)$$

where

x = interarrival time
y = probability $x \le t$
t = time
λ = mean rate of arrivals, $\lambda = \frac{1}{6}$
$1/\lambda$ = mean time between arrivals = 6 days

Random times for ship arrivals can be generated by using the discrete probability distribution shown in

[3]This formula is the exponential distribution which specifies the time between arrivals for a Poisson arrival distribution. See page 152 for more details.

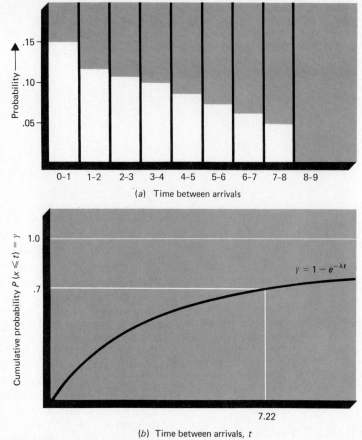

FIGURE S8.7
Distribution of
arrival times.

Figure S8.7*a* or the continuous distribution shown in Figure S8.7*b*. The discrete distribution is used in the same way as in the previous example, by assigning random numbers to the distribution.

The continuous distribution is used by generating a random number for the *y* axis between 0 and 1 and computing the corresponding *t* coordinate from the inverse of the exponential equation. The inverse equation is obtained from the exponential formula [Equation (S8.1)] by solving for *t* in terms of *y*. This is done by first expressing Equation (S8.1) in the following form:

$$1 - y = e^{-\lambda t}$$

Then, taking the natural logarithm of both sides yields

$$\ln (1 - y) = -\lambda t$$

Solving for *t* gives

$$t = (-1/\lambda)\ln (1 - y) \tag{S8.2}$$

Various values of *y* between 0 and 1 are generated at random and plugged into Equation (S8.2) to give the corresponding value of *t*. For example, if $y = .7$ is generated, this corresponds to a ship arrival time of $t = 7.22$ days between ships.

$$t = -6 \ln (1 - .7) = 7.22$$

This computation is shown in Figure S8.7*b*, where the $y = .7$ value is projected onto the *t* axis.

The arrival times generated with the continuous exponential distribution are shown in Table S8.3, which also shows the corresponding times the ship

TABLE S8.3
SHIP EXAMPLE

Arrival number	Arrival time	Enter service	Service time	Depart service	Ship waiting time	Server idle time
1	3.5	3.5	5	8.5	0	0
2	4.7	8.5	5	13.5	3.8	0
3	8.3	13.5	5	18.5	5.2	0
4	12.8	18.5	5	23.5	5.7	0
5	13.7	23.5	5	28.5	9.8	0
6	28.7	28.7	5	33.7	0	0.2
7	34.7	34.7	5	39.7	0	1.0
8	52.1	52.1	5	57.1	0	12.4
9	59.9	59.9	5	64.9	0	2.8
10	65.0	65.0	5	70.0	0	0.1

enters and leaves service. For the single dock, if another ship is in the dock when an arrival occurs, the ship joins the waiting line and waits until the preceding ship is finished. As a result, the waiting time for each ship can be calculated from the table.

The remaining steps in using an event-oriented model, flowcharting, programming, data collection, validation, experimentation, and implementation, are exactly the same as with the time-oriented model described above.

For this example, the problem would also be simulated using two docks and the same ship arrival times. Then the solutions with one dock and two docks would be compared. A decision could be based on differences in costs, waiting times, and other factors of importance.

APPLICATIONS OF SIMULATION IN OPERATIONS

Applications of simulation in operations are numerous. Well-known applications include the following:

1. **Facilities design.** These applications are related to the size of facilities or the number of servers required. Examples include the number of checkout counters in a supermarket, the number of runways in an airport, and the number of toll booths on a freeway. Simulation models are useful in queuing situations, such as these, with complex conditions.

2. **Aggregate planning.** Where an operation's ag-

gregate capacity must be determined, simulation models are used to find the cost of alternative plans. Specific aggregate planning decisions that may involve simulation are described in Chapter 11.

3. **Scheduling.** Simulation has been used in the evaluation of alternative scheduling rules. In scheduling patients for surgery, for example, should the longest operation be scheduled first or last? In Chapter 12, the scheduling of jobs in a machine shop is discussed and alternative dispatching rules are evaluated by simulation.

4. **Inventory.** Many inventory models are evaluated by simulating the effects of ordering rules. In complex inventory situations, it is often necessary to simulate proposed rules before they are put into effect to determine the impact on customer service and cost.

5. **Materials requirements planning.** When materials requirements planning (MRP) is used to plan and control manufacturing, simulation is used to evaluate proposed changes in the manufacturing plan before the changes are put into effect. As a result, "what if" questions can be asked by management before decisions are made. These applications are described in greater detail in Chapter 15.

Simulation is a broad methodology which has wide applicability to operations decisions. As the book develops, many other applications of simulation will be cited.

QUESTIONS

1. Discuss the differences between fixed- and variable-time-increment simulation models. When would one model or the other be preferred?
2. Suppose you are simulating the arrival of customers at a barbershop so as to determine the number of chairs needed. Develop an approach to model validation in this case.
3. How should you decide how long to run a simulation model?
4. Show how random times can be developed from a normal distribution using the cumulative normal distribution function.
5. Discuss the advantages and disadvantages of making a simulation model completely realistic.
6. Sketch out a flowchart for the ship-arrival simulation problem described in the supplement.
7. What is the purpose of using sensitivity analysis in simulation studies?
8. Contrast and compare the use of simulation and analytical methods for solving queuing problems.

PROBLEMS

1. The owner of the ABC grocery store is trying to decide whether to install one or two check-out counters. The time between customer arrivals is exponentially distributed with an average of 18 minutes between arrivals. The time to service a customer is also exponentially distributed with an average of 10 minutes per customer. Customers are served on a first-come–first-served basis.
   a. Simulate this problem either by writing a computer program or by doing it manually. If the simulation is done manually, use 10 arrivals.
   b. Calculate the average waiting time of the customer and the percentage of idle time of the server or servers.
   c. How would you decide between the alternatives?
2. An inventory of a certain repair part is maintained in a garage. At present, when the supply of the part drops to 30 units, an additional 40 units are ordered. It takes 2 days to get the parts after they are ordered. The daily demand is exponentially distributed with a mean of 13 units. Assume a starting inventory of 35 units.
   a. Simulate this problem by writing a computer program or doing it by hand. For hand computations, use 20 days of simulated demand.
   b. How many orders are placed, how much inventory is carried on average, and how many stockouts occur?
   c. How would you validate your model in this case?

3. An assembly operation requires processing through two stations in sequential order. The amount of time required for processing at each station is a random variable, as shown in the following table. Assume that station 2 must wait whenever there is no work available from station 1. Also assume that there is no buffer between the stations.
   a. How long will it take to process 10 jobs through both stations, assuming the stations are empty when starting?
   b. How much time do stations 1 and 2 spend waiting?
   c. What is the effect on waiting time of placing a buffer between the two stations?

Station 1		Station 2	
Minutes	Probability	Minutes	Probability
1.7	.1	1.6	.2
1.8	.2	1.7	.2
1.9	.4	1.8	.2
2.0	.2	1.9	.2
2.1	.1	2.0	.2

4. A florist is trying to decide how many bouquets of fresh flowers to cut for each day. Any flowers cut and not sold during the day are thrown away. The variable cost of growing and cutting flowers is $4 per bouquet, and the price is $6 per bouquet. The following demand distribution has been observed in the past:

Number of bouquets	Probability
45	.1
50	.2
55	.4
60	.2
65	.1

The florist would like to evaluate policies of cutting 55 and 60 bouquets each day.
   a. Simulate each policy for 20 days.
   b. Which policy maximizes profit?

5. A laundromat is considering installation of 10 washers and 5 dryers. On average, a customer arrives at the laundromat every 12 minutes with one or more baskets of clothes. The time between arrivals is distributed according to the exponential distribution. The number of washer loads per customer is distributed as follows:

Loads	Probability
1	.2
2	.3
3	.3
4	.2

Each dryer will handle two loads from the washer. It takes 15 minutes to wash a load of clothes and 30 minutes to dry a load.
   a. Simulate the operation of this laundromat for 4 hours. Build a table to describe the status of the washers, the dryers, and the waiting loads.
   b. How much idle time is there for the washers and dryers? How much waiting time for customers?
   c. What actions might be suggested by your simulation?

6. A repairer tends three different machines. Each machine has an exponential distribution of time between failures, with a mean of 100 minutes. When the machine fails, it takes an average of 20 minutes to repair it with an exponential service time. Assume all machines are in operation at the beginning of the simulation.
   a. Simulate the problem for a total of 8 hours.
   b. How much idle time is there for the machines and for the repairer?

c. If the repairer is paid $10 per hour and lost machine time costs $30 per hour, evaluate the suggestion to add another repairer.

7. At an airport, aircraft wait in a holding pattern whenever the runway is busy or temporarily closed for bad weather. After 20 minutes in the holding pattern, a plane must be diverted to an alternate field for landing. Planes arrive at the field at an average rate of one plane every 5 minutes according to the Poisson distribution. Landing takes a constant time of 3 minutes for each plane.

a. Simulate 10 landings at the airport.

b. How long do planes wait on the average? Are any planes diverted to another field?

c. What is the average utilization of the runways?

d. Suppose planes arrive at a rate of one every 4 minutes. What effect will this have on your answers?

8. In order to reduce congestion, it has been proposed that a second runway be opened to landings at the airport described in Problem 7.

a. Simulate 10 landings with the two runways in operation.

b. What improvements are made in average landing times?

c. What percentage of the time are both runways busy?

9. Patients arrive at a hospital emergency room for x-rays. The arrivals occur at random according to a Poisson distribution with an average of 30 minutes between arrivals. Service is provided by x-ray technicians who take an average of 20 minutes per patient, but service time varies exponentially.

a. Simulate the arrival and service of 20 patients at the x-ray room.

b. Compute the average waiting time, the average number of patients in line, and the percentage of idle time of the x-ray machine.

c. Compute the same statistics as in part b using the queuing formulas from the supplement to Chapter 6. Compare the results and explain differences.

10. A repairer fixes a total of 500 different major appliances in an apartment complex. Each appliance operates an average of 900 hours between failures using an exponential distribution. It takes the repairer an average of 25 minutes to get to the site, fix the machine, and return to base. The repair times follow a uniform probability distribution with a minimum of zero and a maximum of 50 minutes per repair.

a. Simulate 15 machine failures and repairs.

b. How busy is the appliance repairer? How long is the average appliance out of service for repair?

c. The company is considering adding 200 more appliances to the repair load. What will the effect be on the statistics in part b?

d. What if the repairer can fix the machines in a maximum of 40 minutes using the uniform distribution of repair times?

SELECTED BIBLIOGRAPHY

Conway, Richard, William Maxwell, John McClain and Steven Worona: *Users Guide to XCELL & Factory Modeling System*, Palo Alto, CA: Scientific Press, 1987.

Gordon, Geoffrey: *The Application of GPSS V to Discrete System Simulation*, Englewood Cliffs, N.J.: Prentice-Hall, 1975.

Hershauer, James C., and Ronald G. Egert: "Search and Simulation Selection of a Job-Shop Sequencing Rule," *Management Science*, vol. 21, no. 7, March 1975, pp. 833–843.

Kwak, N. K., P. J. Kuzdrall, and Homer H. Schmitz: "The GPSS Simulation of Scheduling Policies for Surgical Patients," *Management Science*, vol. 22, no. 9, May 1976, pp. 982–989.

LAW, AVERILL M., AND W. DAVID KELTON: *Simulation Modeling and Analysis*, New York: McGraw-Hill, 1982.

NANDA, R.: "Simulating Passenger Arrivals at Airports," *Industrial Engineering*, vol. 4, no. 3, March 1972, pp. 12–19.

NEW, C. C.: "Matching Batch Sizes to Machine Shop Capabilities: An Example in Production Scheduling," *Operations Research Quarterly*, vol. 23, no. 4, December 1972, pp. 561–572.

PEGDEN, C. DENNIS: *Introduction to SIMAN*, Systems Modeling Corp, 1986.

PETERSEN, CLIFFORD C.: "Simulation of an Inventory System," *Industrial Engineering*, vol. 5, no. 6, June 1973, pp. 35–44.

ROCHETTE, RENE, and RANDALL P. SADOWSKI: "A Statistical Comparison of the Performance of Simple Dispatching Rules for a Particular Set of Job Shops," *International Journal of Production Research*, vol. 14, no. 1, 1976, pp. 63–75.

SCHRIBER, THOMAS J.: *Simulation Using GPSS*, New York: Wiley, 1974.

SHANNON, ROBERT E.: *Systems Simulation: The Art and Science*, Englewood Cliffs, N.J.: Prentice-Hall, 1975.

WYMAN, F. PAUL, and GERALD CREAVEN: "Experimental Analysis of a GPSS Simulation of a Student Health Center," *Socio-Economic Planning Science*, vol. 6, no. 5, October 1972, pp. 489–499.

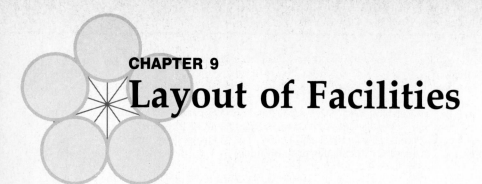

CHAPTER 9
Layout of Facilities

$\mathbf{I}$n the last chapter we considered the analysis and modeling of process flows. One type of modeling, however, has been reserved for this chapter—modeling for decisions on the layout of physical facilities. In this chapter we will be discussing layout decisions and models for all types of facilities: those using line, intermittent, and project processes. Box 9.1 describes layout practices used by typical Japanese factories.

In Chapter 5 the process selection decision from among line, intermittent, and project processes was discussed. Because the pattern of flow is so different in each type of process, the layout decisions will also differ for each. In this chapter we will assume that the process selection decision has been made and that we are dealing with the layout of a specific type of process.

In Section 9.1, layout decisions for intermittent processes are discussed. Following sections deal with line-flow and project layouts. As the chapter

BOX 9.1
JAPANESE FACTORY LAYOUTS

The Japanese are masters at the layout of factories. They tend to select very efficient and compact layout designs. The typical Japanese factory takes only one-third the space required by a comparable U.S. or European factory.

Just-in-time (JIT) production practices have resulted in compact Japanese factory layouts. The JIT system ensures that work-in-process (WIP) inventory is minimized. This reduces the floor space required to store parts which are in the process of production. As a result of much lower WIP inventories, machines can be moved closer together. This in turn facilitates visual control of manufacturing and makes for a smooth flow of materials through the plant in a small amount of space.

Western companies are now adopting JIT practices and the more compact and efficient layouts which result. This has drastically reduced space requirements and increased capacity (by as much as a factor of 2 or 3) for existing plants. Western companies are realizing that layout is not an independent decision, but rather highly related to practices followed in quality control, maintenance, and production scheduling which are all changed by a JIT philosophy. These practices should, therefore, be carefully evaluated before layouts are fixed.

Source: Schonberger, Richard, *World Class Manufacturing*, New York: Free Press, 1986.

develops, exactly how these layout decisions are related to one another will become clear.

9.1 LAYOUT OF INTERMITTENT PROCESSES

It will be recalled that in intermittent operations, the flow pattern is jumbled because different products or customers flow through the facility along different paths. From a layout standpoint, the intermittent operation is called a process layout because similar equipment processes or similar worker skills are grouped together by department (or work center). Each product or customer being processed then flows through some departments and skips others, depending on processing requirements. If these concepts are not clear, they can be reviewed in Chapter 5, Section 5.1.

In the intermittent-flow layout problem it is likely that flows between some departments may be very heavy, while those between others are very light. In a hospital, for example, the flow of patients between the orthopedic and x-ray departments may be very heavy because most bone fractures require an x-ray before treatment. Other departments, such as pediatrics and geriatrics, may have very little patient or doctor flow between them. Because of such differences in flow volumes, an economical flow of traffic can be obtained by locating departments with a heavy flow of traffic adjacent to each other while those with light traffic are placed farther apart.

In a nutshell, the intermittent-flow layout decision determines the relative location of processing centers (departments) to achieve a stated decision criterion within certain layout constraints. Examples of decision criteria for the layout decision include minimizing materials-handling costs, minimizing distance traveled by customers, minimizing employee traveling time, and maximizing the proximity of related departments. The most common constraints include limitations of space, the need to maintain fixed locations for certain departments (e.g., shipping, and receiving), the limited weight-bearing capacity of certain floor areas, safety regulations, fire regulations, and aisle requirements. The problem is to find the best layout or at least a satisfactory layout which meets all the applicable constraints.

Intermittent-flow layout problems fall into two basic categories: (1) those involving quantitative decision criteria and (2) those involving qualitative criteria. The quantitative-criteria problems call for decisions which can be expressed in measurable terms such as materials-handling costs, travel time of customers, or distances. In qualitative-criteria layout decisions, it may not be possible to identify a specific, measurable flow of materials, customers, or employees. Instead, qualitative criteria may be stated. For example, it may be highly desirable to keep the welding and paint departments apart for fire-safety reasons, or a noisy department must be kept away from a quiet area. These qualitative relationships cannot be handled by the same methods used to solve quantitative problems.

Quantitative Criteria

Various types of intermittent layout problems can be formulated with quantitative criteria. These include the minimization of materials-handling costs in factories and warehouses and the minimization of employee or customer traveling time in service operations. A choice of criteria, of course, always requires a decision on the objectives of the operation; i.e., is it more important to minimize doctor or patient traveling time in a hospital, or should the sum of both times be minimized?

Many quantitative-criteria problems concerning the location of facilities can be expressed in the following form:

$$C = \sum_{i=1}^{N} \sum_{j=1}^{N} T_{ij} C_{ij} D_{ij} \tag{9.1}$$

where T_{ij} = trips between department i and department j
  C_{ij} = "cost" per unit distance per trip traveled from i to j
  D_{ij} = distance from i to j
  C = total cost
  N = number of departments

Notice that T_{ij} and C_{ij} are fixed constants and do not depend on the location of departments i and j. Thus, D_{ij} is the only variable in Equation (9.1) which depends on location decisions. In concept, then, we are searching for the particular D_{ij} combination, or layout plan, which results in minimum value of C.

The cost in Equation (9.1) can be considered in dollars or time units, to accommodate either materials-handling or traveling-time criteria. Actually any

TABLE 9.1

DEPARTMENTS IN A FACTORY MAKING LAWN MOWERS AND SNOW BLOWERS

Department number	Department name	Area (m^2)
1	Painting	500
2	Metal shearing	350
3	Welding	600
4	Small engines	225
5	Metal working	600
6	Controls	275
7	Tires and wheels	500
8	Final assembly	600

resource-based criteria can be handled by considering the "cost" as some scarce resource which is being conserved or minimized by the layout decision.

From Equation (9.1), it is apparent that the cost criterion has been expressed as a linear function of distance.[1] This has mathematical advantages, but it also has practical disadvantages. For example, the layout of a school district which has 50 students each of whom lives a mile from the school is considered equivalent to a layout with one student living at a distance of 50 miles and 49 students at zero distance.[2]

The mathematical location problem is to minimize C by determining the values of D_{ij} in Equation (9.1). To illustrate this problem, consider a factory which makes snow blowers and lawn mowers using the departments shown in Table 9.1. Assume that the objective in this problem is to minimize the cost of moving materials from one department to the next as the products are made in the intermittent operation. In describing this example, we will simply list the steps required to define T_{ij}, C_{ij}, and D_{ij} for Equation (9.1).

The first step in solving this problem is to determine the number of trips between each pair of departments. This number can be estimated from the routing sheets for each of the various product types and estimates of future product volumes. Information on the number of materials-handling trips is shown in Figure 9.1, where the entries in the matrix are interpreted as the total number of trips per week between department i and department j *in both directions*.[3] The weekly volume was simply chosen for convenience; any time period—such as daily, monthly, or yearly—could be used.

The next step is to determine the cost of materials handling per unit of distance traveled on each trip. This cost might vary between department pairs because of different materials-handling methods. For example, forklifts might be used to

---

[1]Cost is a linear function since T_{ij} and C_{ij} are constants, the D_{ij} variables are to the first power, and the terms are additive.

[2]The solution methods described in this section can easily be extended to nonlinear functions if desired.

[3]It is also possible to formulate the problem by separating trips between i and j from those between j and i. The formulation presented here combines trips in both directions simply for convenience.

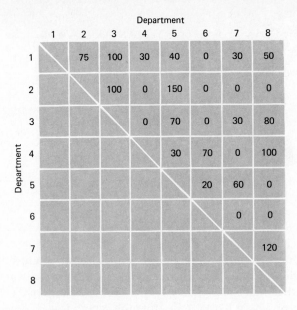

FIGURE 9.1 Trip matrix. Matrix entry T_{ij} is the number of materials-handling trips per week between department i and department j in both directions.

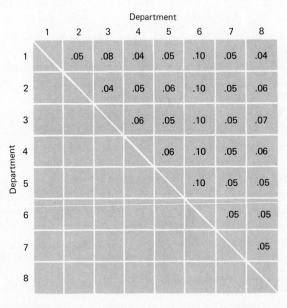

FIGURE 9.2 Unit materials-handling costs. Matrix entry C_{ij} is the materials-handling cost in dollars per meter per trip between department i and department j.

Painting 1	Small engines 4	Metal working 5	Tires and wheels 7	*Receiving dock*
Aisle				
Metal shearing 2	Welding 3	Controls 6	Final assembly 8	*Shipping dock*

FIGURE 9.3
Initial layout.

move materials between the engine department and the final assembly department, while material might be moved by handcarts between controls and welding. For the sake of this example, the materials-handling costs per meter per trip are shown in Figure 9.2.

The next step in the analysis is to determine the distances between each pair of departments. These distances will depend on the layout chosen, and we will assume the layout shown in Figure 9.3 as an initial solution. With this layout, the distances between each pair of departments can be found, as shown in Figure 9.4.

We have now specified the number of trips (T_{ij}) matrix, the cost (C_{ij}) matrix, and the distance (D_{ij}) matrix for a particular layout. With these data, it is possible to compute the total materials-handling cost for each pair of departments. In Figure 9.5, each cell in the total-cost matrix is computed by multipying $T_{ij} D_{ij} C_{ij}$ from each

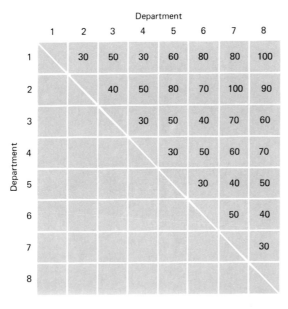

Department

	1	2	3	4	5	6	7	8
1		30	50	30	60	80	80	100
2			40	50	80	70	100	90
3				30	50	40	70	60
4					30	50	60	70
5						30	40	50
6							50	40
7								30
8								

FIGURE 9.4 Initial interdepartmental distances. Matrix entry D_{ij} is the materials-handling distance (per trip) between department i and department j in meters.

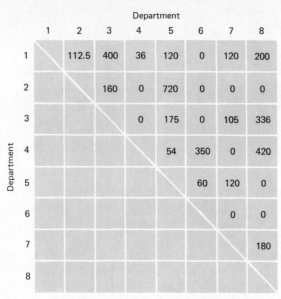

Total cost = $3668.50 per week ($190,762 per year)

FIGURE 9.5 Total-cost matrix. Each matrix entry is the product of $T_{ij} C_{ij} D_{ij}$ from Figures 9.1, 9.2, and 9.4. The resulting entries are the cost in dollars of materials flows between each pair of departments.

of the three previous matrices. For departments 1 to 2, for example, the cost of materials handling is $(75)(.05)(30) = \$112.50$. After these costs have been calculated, all cells in Figure 9.5 are added to yield $C = \$3668.50$ per week. This completes the evaluation of Equation (9.1) for a particular layout plan.

Given the total cost of an initial layout, we might wonder whether improvements can be made to reduce C. This question can be answered by considering exchanges in pairs of departments. Suppose, for example, that departments 4 and 5 were exchanged in the initial layout. Recalculating the cost matrix in Figure 9.5 (or evaluating the cost changes), we get $C = \$3144.50$, a reduction of $524 per week. The revised costs of the affected cells are shown in Figure 9.6. By considering other possible exchanges of departments, we might be able to reduce cost even further. However, one cannot expect to arrive at an optimal solution by this method unless every possible combination of departments is evaluated.

For small problems it may be feasible to enumerate all possible layout combinations. For example, if there are nine departments, there are $9! = 362,880$ possible location combinations, since there are nine choices of location for the first department, eight for the second, seven for the third, and so on. However, some of these 9! locations are mirror images of the others. There are only $9!/8 = 45,360$ layout combinations which differ in relative locations. For 20 departments, for example, there are 608 trillion combinations of layouts, which is too many to enumerate even by the fastest computer. There are, however, computer methods

Department	1	2	3	4	5	6	7	8
1				72	60			
2				0	450			
3				0	105			
4						210	0	300
5						100	180	0
6								
7								
8								

FIGURE 9.6 Adjusted costs due to department 4 to 5 swap.

for approximating a solution to these larger problems; these will be discussed later.

In summary, then, the quantitative layout problem for intermittent operations can often be expressed as a linear function of distance between departments. The required data are the number of trips between departments per time period, the "cost" per unit of distance traveled on each trip, and the distance between departments for any particular layout. These data permit the total cost of a particular layout plan to be evaluated. Improved layouts can then be determined by considering exchanges between pairs of departments. However, in most cases of practical interest, there are so many possible exchanges that all possibilities cannot be evaluated; therefore special methods are needed to arrive at an optimal or near-optimal (minimum cost) solution for these problems.

Qualitative Criteria

Layout problems involving qualitative criteria occur when relationships between departments in intermittent-flow facilities are specified in qualitative terms (e.g., the desirability of locating one department near another or at a distance from another). In some cases, these qualitative criteria may be more readily available or more appropriate than quantitative criteria.

The qualitative location problem has been studied in depth by Muther and Wheeler, who have proposed a method of formulation and solution called SLP (systematic layout planning). According to Muther's and Wheeler's approach, the desirability of locating a given department next to any other department is rated by one of the following terms: "absolutely necessary," "especially important," "important," "ordinary closeness okay," "unimportant," and "undesirable."

These qualitative ratings may be based on safety considerations, customer convenience, or approximate flows between departments. For example, it might be desirable to locate the baby food department near the milk department in a supermarket for convenience of shopping; it might also be desirable to locate the heavy items near the supermarket door to reduce carrying distance; and expensive items should perhaps be located near the cash registers to reduce pilferage. These kinds of qualitative relationships can be specified using SLP, as shown in Figure 9.7 for a typical supermarket example. Notice how the relationships are arranged in a matrix format similar to that for the quantitative layout problem.

After the qualitative relationships are specified, it is necessary to find a way to solve the problem. For small problems, this can be done by visual inspection, as shown in Figure 9.7. One simply attempts to locate all the absolutely essential departments next to each other; the especially important relationships are also satisfied by adjacent departments, if possible, or by departments at a separation distance of one department, and so on, until the undesirable departmental relationships are satisfied by departments as far apart as possible. The solution shown in Figure 9.7 is not necessarily an "optimal" solution but simply a good solution chosen for purposes of illustration.

When the relationships have been decided, the layout problem is still not solved. This is because the entire layout must usually fit within a rectangular or other geometric shape. Figure 9.7 shows how the layout is converted from a block diagram to a final layout plan. At this point, it may be helpful for the reader to study all the steps used in Figure 9.7 to arrive at a solution.

For larger problems, the solution cannot be obtained by inspection but must depend on computerized methods which attempt to consider all the specified relationships and arrive at an optimal (or satisfactory) solution. These methods require that qualitative relationships be converted to a numerical scale; the resulting problem is then solved by a mathematical algorithm. Because of the conversion process, the solution obtained may not accurately reflect the qualitative relationships originally specified. In this case the solution must then be adjusted accordingly. Some of these computerized methods will be described below.

The qualitative layout formulation has been applied to many types of situations including factories, warehouses, offices, and service operations. This method can be used for any layout problem because qualitative relationships between departments can always be specified. Qualitative layout problems are frequently encountered in the service industries, where customers interact with the facilities. In this case, customer preference for relative location of facilities becomes an important qualitative consideration.

Computerized Layout Planning

Computerized layout planning of intermittent-process facilities has been evolving since 1963, when CRAFT, the first practical program, was developed. Today, as catalogued by the Center for Environmental Research, some 80 computer programs are available. We will examine two widely known programs: CRAFT for quantitative criteria and ALDEP for qualitative criteria.

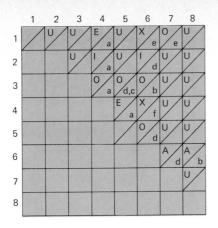

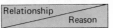

	Department	Area (m²)
1	Meats and produce	1900
2	Frozen foods	1700
3	Dry groceries	2300
4	Receiving	1000
5	Canned foods	1500
6	Checkout area	1100
7	Breads/snacks	900
8	Nonfood	800

Rating	Relationships Definition	Symbol
A	Absolutely necessary	≡≡≡
E	Especially important	≡≡
I	Important	═
O	Ordinary closeness OK	—
U	Unimportant	
X	Undesirable	-----

Reason for relationship

Code	Reason*
a	Materials handling
b	Ease of supervision
c	Common personnel
d	Customer convenience
e	Improve sales
f	Appearance

*Others may be added

(a)

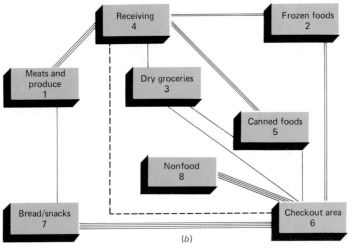

(b)

(c)

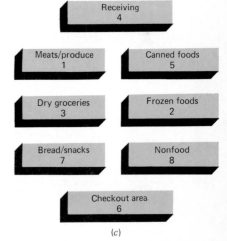

(d)

FIGURE 9.7
Grocery store example: Qualitative layout. (a) Initial information; (b) diagram of relationships; (c) block layout; (d) final layout.

243

CRAFT (Computerized Relative Allocation of Facilities). CRAFT was developed by Armour and Buffa and later refined by Buffa, Armour, and Vollmann. It uses a quantitative-criterion layout formulation and can solve problems with up to 40 departments or activity centers.

The input to CRAFT is a matrix of unit costs and an initial layout plan. The unit-cost matrix is the product of the T_{ij} and C_{ij} matrices described earlier. The initial layout plan may be an existing layout or an arbitrary starting layout. Then, using the initial layout provided, the computer determines the distances between centroids of departments.

The next step in the program is to calculate the cost of the initial layout by using the unit-cost matrix and the computed distances from the initial layout. In effect, the CRAFT program evaluates Equation (9.1), just as in the previous example.

The CRAFT program then determines whether the initial total cost can be reduced by exchanging departments in pairs.[4] Each possible pair of departments is exchanged, and the cost, whether an increase or a decrease, is computed and stored in the computer's memory. When all pairs of exchanges have been considered, the lowest-cost exchange is selected and these departments are exchanged in the initial layout.[5] If the cost is reduced, the resulting cost and the new layout are then printed out, and the procedure is repeated for a second exchange of departments. A new layout and lower cost are printed out on each successive round of exchanges until no further cost reduction is obtained.

The final solution reached by CRAFT is often sensitive to the initial layout input. Thus, to reduce the effect of bias, several different starting layouts should be selected. CRAFT does not provide a minimum-cost solution. CRAFT is a heuristic program which provides a very good solution but not a guaranteed optimal solution . (See Box 9.2 on heuristics.) In practice, however, the lack of a truly optimal solution is not a severe limitation—any improvement over the present layout or over other layout methods is useful.

CRAFT has been applied in practice to a large number of different layout problems. According to Buffa, it has been used by four aircraft plants, two of the largest automobile companies, two computer manufacturing operations, a pharmaceutical manufacturer, a meat packer, a precision machine shop, a movie studio, and a hospital. Since the program is in wide circulation, it has, no doubt, been used for other applications as well.

ALDEP (Automated Layout Design Program). ALDEP was developed by IBM in 1967 and originally described by Seehof and Evans (1967). The ALDEP program handles only qualitative-criteria layout problems.

The inputs of ALDEP include a relationship matrix, as shown in Figure 9.7, and constraints such as building size, fixed locations of departments, stairwells, etc. The ALDEP program begins by randomly selecting a department and placing it in the layout plan. In the second step, all remaining departments are scanned and one with a high closeness-relationship rating (such as A or E) is arbitrarily selected

---

[4] In a more advanced version of CRAFT, departments are also exchanged three at a time.

[5] All together, $\binom{n}{2} = \dfrac{n(n-1)}{2}$ pairs of exchanges are considered on each round for n departments.

BOX 9.2
HEURISTIC DECISION RULES

The word "heuristic" is derived from the Greek *heuriskein*, meaning "to discover." Heuristics are decision rules which are discovered, usually by trial and error, to solve problems. Sometimes these rules come very close to providing an optimal solution to mathematical problems, and sometimes the rules are not so good.

We use heuristics, or rules of thumb, in everyday life. For example, we decide to start looking for a gas station when the tank reaches ¼. We decide to invest in the stock market when the price of our favorite stock stops dropping and rises for the second day in a row.

Heuristics are used to solve decision problems when optimal techniques are not available or too cumbersome or too expensive to use. In this chapter we will use such heuristic rules of thumb to solve both layout problems and assembly-line balancing problems. In practice, these heuristics are sometimes quite good and lead to improved solutions for decision problems even though the optimal or best solution may not be reached.

and placed in the layout next to the first department. If a high closeness rating cannot be found, a department is selected at random and placed in the layout. This selection process continues until all departments have been placed in the layout plan. A total score for the layout is then computed by converting each closeness relationship to a numerical scale and adding the values of those relationships in the layout plan. The entire process is repeated many times starting with a different random department as the first step each time. Each iteration results in one more layout plan being generated.

The ALDEP program is useful for generating a large number of good layouts for examination. The program can be controlled so that only layouts with a specified score or better are printed out. This has the effect of reducing the number of layouts which must be examined. While ALDEP is a useful heuristic for generating good layouts, it does not produce optimal solutions except by accident.

ALDEP saves much of the tedious work involved in layout, but it still requires judgment to arrive at a final solution. The ALDEP program is designed to handle up to 63 departments and a three-story building.

Layout Decisions

We have been emphasizing the analytical aspect of layout decisions. However, behavioral factors must also be considered. Layout models locate people based on quantitative or qualitative criteria with little consideration of human factors, such as social contact, degree of privacy, and sense of ownership. But layout affects the behavior of people and their perception of the job, ultimately affecting job performance, motivation, and satisfaction. "A work station may be reorganized in a way that is theoretically very efficient, but less work will actually be done if the user hates being there and seizes every opportunity to leave the station" [Steel (1973), p. 16].

According to a study by Schuler, Ritzman, and Davis (1981), the most important behavioral factors in layout are privacy and proximity to others who work on related tasks. Privacy is important since it allows one to regulate control of interpersonal interactions. Proximity to others with whom people work is facilitated by appropriate spatial arrangements. Easier access to others saves travel time and improves communications, which increases work performance.

The results of the Schuler, Ritzman, and Davis study support the idea that layout decisions should be based not only on efficiency considerations but also on the relative location of people who depend on each other and the degree of control that people have over their interactions with others. Layout decisions will be more effective when they consider the effect on people's behavior, motivation, and performance. The paper by Stone and Luchetti (1985) suggests ways that human factors should be considered in layout designs.

LAYOUT OF LINE PROCESSES

The layout of line processes differs greatly from the layout of intermittent processes. These differences arise because the sequence of processing activities in the line processes is fixed by the product design as the product is made sequentially from one step to the next along the line of flow. While the layout of line flows does not affect the direction of flow of the product, it does affect the efficiency of the line and the jobs assigned to individual workers.

The classic case of line-flow operations is the moving assembly line. This form of production results in great efficiency, as we noted in Chapter 5. At the same time, the assembly line seems to have serious side effects in terms of job boredom, absenteeism, and turnover. Thus the design of assembly lines and alternatives to the traditional assembly line should be carefully considered by management.

In the first part of this section it is assumed that a traditional moving assembly line is being used, and we will consider the problem of assigning tasks (operations) to workers along the assembly line so that the work is evenly divided among workers. This is the classic problem of assembly-line balancing. In the second part of this section, we will consider alternative forms of assembly-line layout including two or more smaller lines and work group or team assembly.

Assembly-Line Balancing

The problem of assembly-line balancing can best be described by example. Suppose an assembly line is being designed where the maximum time that any worker on the line can spend on the product is specified to be 60 seconds (this is called the cycle time). Now visualize a number of workers along this line, each working on the product for a maximum of 60 seconds and then passing the product along to the next worker.

In balancing the assembly line we ask: How should individual operations (or tasks) be assigned to these workers? If we assign the first worker on the line a discrete number of operations, the total time assigned may add up to slightly less than the 60 seconds available, because there may be no combination of operations which need to be done at the first work station that add up exactly to the cycle time. Similarly, the second worker may also be assigned less than 60 seconds of work, and so on down the line. It is very possible that, owing to the product structure and the discrete nature of operation times, some workers may have substantially less than 60 seconds of work.

Therefore the problem of assembly-line balancing is as follows: given a cycle time, find the minimum number of work stations or workers required. In this case, each worker will have a minimum amount of idle time consistent with the product structure, and the line will use as few people as possible. In rare cases, a perfect balance will be achieved, where each worker has no idle time and the line is 100 percent efficient.

Another way to state the assembly-line balancing problem is to minimize the cycle time for a given number of work stations. These problems are mirror images of each other. It just depends on whether we are given the cycle time or the number of work stations to start with.

The following symbols and definitions will be used in discussing the assembly-line balancing problem:

N = number of work stations along the line. Usually a work station is the space occupied by a single worker. A work station could, however, have more than one worker assigned, or one worker could handle more than one work station. We will assume, however, that each work station has exactly one worker unless otherwise noted.

C = cycle time, the maximum time allowed at any work station. The cycle time will also be the time between production of successive finished units by the line.

t_i = operation time for the ith operation on the product. Each operation is assigned to one and only one work station.

Σt_i = total work content of the product. This is the total labor required to produce one unit.

There are some important relationships between these variables. First of all, it is common for output rate (units per day) to be given. The cycle time can then be derived from the output rate by the equation $C = 420/\text{output rate}$, C being expressed in minutes. This formula assumes that there are 420 productive minutes (7 hours) in a day.

Once C is known, we can derive the minimum number of stations required on the line (assuming 100 percent efficiency, or perfect balance).[6]

$$N_{\min} = \left\langle \frac{\Sigma t_i}{C} \right\rangle$$

This formula is based on the idea that the total work-content time must be provided by workers who put in a time of C units each with perfect balance. Whether a balance can then be found with the minimum number of stations

---

[6]The symbol $\langle \rangle$ denotes the next integer greater than the quantity in brackets. The minimum number of stations is thereby rounded up to an integer value.

depends on the particular precedence constraints and task times in the problem under consideration.

After balancing the line, the efficiency of the balance is computed as follows:

$$\text{Efficiency} = \frac{\Sigma t_i}{NC}$$

This formula is based on the notion that NC is the actual time spent on each product including idle time, but Σt_i is the productive time spent. The opposite of efficiency has been termed "balance delay" in the literature of assembly-line balancing.

Balance delay $= 1 - \text{efficiency}$

The following example will illustrate the procedure used for assembly-line balancing and also the calculation of the above quantities. Suppose that a line is being designed to assemble the tricycle shown in Figure 8.1. To start, we would need assembly drawings and an assembly chart of the type shown in Figures 8.1 and 8.2. As a matter of fact, because operations will be grouped into work stations, we will need to have the operations defined at the most detailed level possible, as in Table 9.2. This table defines each assembly operation required and the associated operation times (t_i). As can be seen, the maximum t_i is 18 seconds. Since these operations cannot be subdivided further, 18 seconds will be the minimum cycle time unless two workers are assigned to some work station. Furthermore, the cycle time cannot exceed the total work content of the product. Thus we have

$$\text{Max } [t_i] \leq \text{cycle time} \leq \Sigma t_i$$

Suppose we decide initially to balance this tricycle line at 20 seconds. Notice that this will be a very fast line made up of exceedingly boring and repetitive tasks (e.g. putting the left wheel on the axle).

At this cycle time of 20 seconds, 1260 tricycles (420/.333) will be produced per day. The minimum number of stations is 13.

$$N_{\min} = \langle 253/20 \rangle = \langle 12.65 \rangle = 13$$

Certain technological constraints must be observed in assembling the tricycle; e.g., the inside washer must be put on before the wheel, and the seat must be inserted before the seat bolt is tightened. The technological constraints are shown in Figure 9.8. Actually, these constraints are slightly more restrictive than necessary. For example, the seat can be put on the tricycle at the same time as the rear wheels. This might result, however, in a work station which inserts one washer on a rear axle, inserts the seat, and puts one handle grip on the handle bar. To avoid such mixed jobs Figure 9.8 requires that both rear wheels be put on before proceeding to the seat and front fork assemblies.

The precedence diagram in Figure 9.8 shows which operations must precede other operations. In the diagram, all tasks at the tail of an arrow must be completed before tasks at the head of the arrow. Thus, the sequence of assembly operations required on the left rear wheel is washer, wheel, washer, cotter key,

TABLE 9.2
TRICYCLE ASSEMBLY OPERATIONS

Operation number	Description*	Time (seconds)
1	Starting point	0
	LEFT WHEEL	
2	Fit washer on left axle	10
3	Fit left wheel on axle	18
4	Fit washer on left axle	10
5	Insert and fasten cotter key	15
6	Insert and fasten hub cap	17
	RIGHT WHEEL	
7	Fit washer on right axle	10
8	Fit right wheel on axle	18
9	Fit washer on right axle	10
10	Insert and fasten cotter key	15
11	Insert and fasten hub cap	17
12	Dummy operation	0
	FRONT-WHEEL ASSEMBLY	
13	Insert front-wheel fork in frame	18
14	Fit collar on front-wheel fork	11
15	Insert handle bars into fork	15
16	Tighten front wheel collar	18
17	Attach left handle grips	12
18	Attach right handle grips	12
	SEAT ASSEMBLY	
19	Insert seat into frame	9
20	Tighten seat set screw	18
21	End point	0
	Total	253

*Operations 1, 12, and 21 are added for purposes of computer convenience. The computer requires a single beginning and ending point in the diagram.

hubcap. However, these operations can be intermixed between the left and right rear wheels since the two rear-wheel sequences are in parallel. Assembly of the seat and front fork can also be intermixed, but—according to the diagram—not with assembly of the rear wheels.

With the 20-second cycle time, the operations times, and the precedence diagram, operations can be assigned to work stations to minimize the number of work stations required. There are a great number of possible assignments to consider. If precedence constraints are ignored, there are 18! ways of assigning the 18 operations to work stations. Since we cannot enumerate all possibilities in real-world cases, assembly-line balancing methods have been devised to solve this problem.

The best methods currently available are heuristic methods, which do not

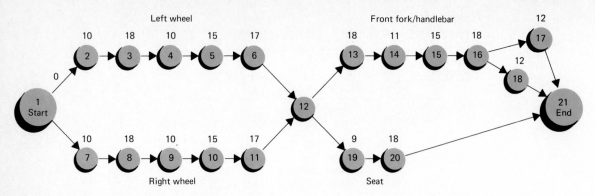

FIGURE 9.8   Tricycle precedence diagram.

necessarily find the minimum number of work stations but do usually find solutions which are close to the optimum. It is not our intention to present all the various heuristic assembly-line balancing methods here. Rather, we will simply present two methods for illustrative purposes.

One way to solve the problem at hand is to begin the assignment of operations with the one that has the least number of predecessors and then to move on to those with more predecessors.[7] In Table 9.3, the tricycle operations are rank-ordered in terms of their number of predecessors, starting with the least number of predecessors. The operations are then assigned to work stations, moving down the list until a maximum of 20 seconds is reached. If there is a tie in precedence, the longest operation time is assigned first so as to save short operations until the end and to pack stations as tightly as possible in the beginning. If an operation with the next-highest precedence does not fit in the work station's available time, then we move down the precedence list to find an operation that does fit in the available time. If none is found, the work station is left partly idle.

As a result of applying this rule, 15 stations are required, as shown in Table 9.4. The resulting efficiency of this balance is 84 percent, or a balance delay of 16 percent.

$$\text{Efficiency} = \frac{\Sigma t_i}{NC} = \frac{253}{15(20)} = .84$$

In solving practical assembly-line balancing problems, computer methods are necessary. Hoffmann's method, for example, requires three types of inputs common to all assembly-line balancing problems: precedence relationships, operations time, and cycle time. The output is an assignment of operations to work stations, the theoretical minimum number of stations, and the efficiency of the balance. A sample output from Hoffmann's method is shown in Figure 9.9.

Hoffmann's method attempts to assign to the first station those operations which would result in the least idle time at that station. This is done by

---

[7]This method was first suggested by Kilbridge and Wester (1961).

TABLE 9.3

TRICYCLE OPERATIONS RANKED BY NUMBER OF PREDECESSORS

Operations	Number of predecessors	t_i
1	0	0
2	1	10
7	1	10
3	2	18
8	2	18
4	3	10
9	3	10
5	4	15
10	4	15
6	5	17
11	5	17
12	11	0
13	12	18
19	12	9
14	13	11
20	13	18
15	14	15
16	15	18
17	16	12
18	16	12
21	20	0

TABLE 9.4

LEAST PREDECESSOR RULE LINE BALANCE

20-second cycle time		
Stations	Operations	Idle
1	1, 2, 7	0
2	3	2
3	8	2
4	4, 9	0
5	5	5
6	10	5
7	6	3
8	11	3
9	12, 13	2
10	19, 14	0
11	20	2
12	15	5
13	16	2
14	17	8
15	18, 21	8

```
TOTAL ELEMENT TIME =253.0000
NUMBER OF ELEMENTS IS    21
NUMBER OF PRECEDENCE RESTRICTIONS IS    23
 WHAT IS THE CYCLE TIME        ? 20
                      ASSEMBLY LINE BALANCE
                      CYCLE TIME = 20.0000

STATION              SLACK
NUMBER               TIME        ELEMENT NUMBERS

   1                    0     1     2    7
   2                2.0000     3
   3                2.0000     8
   4                    0     4     9
   5                5.0000     5
   6                3.0000     6
   7                5.0000    10
   8                3.0000    11    12
   9                2.0000    13    12
  10                    0    14    19
  11                2.0000    20
  12                5.0000    15
  13                2.0000    16
  14                8.0000    17
  15                8.0000    18    21

TOTAL SLACK TIME =47.0000             EFFICIENCY = 84.33  PER CENT

THEORETICAL MINIMUM NUMBER OF STATIONS IS    13
```

FIGURE 9.9 Sample assembly-line balancing program.
Source of program: Thomas R. Hoffman, "Assembly Line Balancing with a Precedence Matrix," Management Science, *vol. 9, no. 4, July 1963, pp. 551–562.*

enumerating all feasible solutions from the precedence graph. If a solution with no idle time is found, the enumeration is stopped. A similar procedure is followed for the second station, the third station, and so on, until all operations have been assigned. The assembly line is then also balanced backward on the precedence graph, and the best forward and backward solution is taken as the final balance.

We could go on to describe several of the other methods available, but this is not our main objective. Rather, our purpose is to describe the principles of assembly-line balancing and the implications for management. Other methods have been surveyed and compared in the literature by Baybars (1986), Johnson (1988), Mastor (1970), and Talbot and Gehrlein (1986).

The assembly-line balancing problem has been greatly simplified in our discussion. In practice, several considerations complicate the problem and sometimes require more sophisticated solutions. Some of these include:

1. **Variability of operations times.** The time required for humans to perform a task will often vary depending on such factors as materials problems, fatigue, and improper alignment. As a result, buffers of materials may be required between stations, the whole assembly line may be slowed down to accommodate these variations, or some items may be only partially completed on the line.

2. **Multiple products.** It is quite common for mixed models or products to be made

on the same assembly line. The result of this is a balance which is not optimal for any one of these products.

3. *Zoning constraint.* In some cases certain operations must be done together because similar skills are required or certain operations, such as painting and sanding, must be separated. To reflect these conditions, zone constraints are added to the precedence diagram and operations must be completed within their assigned zones.

4. *Social factors.* The effect of short cycle times on worker attitudes and job performance has already been noted. Some alternatives for addressing this problem will be described below.

Despite all the work which has been done on assembly-line balancing, these methods are not widely used in practice. In an excellent survey of 90 companies, Chase found that 80 used manual methods, 7 used computer methods, and 3 used combined computer and manual methods. Chase attributes lack of use primarily to unfamiliarity with formal published methods (57 percent of the respondents were unfamiliar with published techniques). For those who were familiar with the methods, the lack of use was attributed to the time it takes to use them and their perceived inflexibility. From an educational and management perspective, there remains a great deal of room for improvement of practice in industry.

One of the most important implications of our discussion on assembly-line balancing is that output rate cannot be varied up and down in line-flow operations. If management decides to change the output rate or model mix, the line must be rebalanced. After the balance is changed, it will take a period of time for the workers to learn their new jobs and for efficiency to return. Therefore the output rate and product mix are kept as stable as possible while demand variations are absorbed by a buffer of finished-goods inventory. In his survey, Chase noted that the average assembly line was rebalanced three times per year and that it took an average of 5.4 days to reach full production after a major rebalance.

Alternatives to Traditional Assembly Lines

The study by Chase also gathered some information on the effects of assembly lines on the work force. The study indicates that personnel turnover averages 28.9 percent per year, with a range from 3.5 to 46.3 percent, depending on the company. The average number of formal grievances per 100 workers per year is 51.9. This is evidence of considerable turmoil on the part of at least some assembly-line workers. It behooves management, therefore, to consider alternatives to traditional, rigidly paced assembly lines.

Alternatives which should be considered are as follows:

1. Several assembly lines producing the same product, each with longer cycle times and thus more task variety than a single line.

2. Assembly lines which permit group organization and teamwork, thus allowing more social interaction between workers while on the job.

3. Assembly lines which permit more self-pacing through buffers of materials

between work stations. The product in this case would not be rigidly fixed to the assembly line but would move along at variable rates.

4. Mixed model assembly lines where workers are not always making the same product. In these cases, model A is followed by model B, then model C and so forth.

The use of the first type of assembly-line alternative would be rather expensive in capital-intensive industries because it requires the duplication of equipment and tools. There are, however, many highly labor-intensive assembly lines which could easily adopt this approach. For example, in the assembly of the tricycle, which is primarily labor-intensive, several small lines could be used.

The second approach has been tried in Europe by Volvo [Gyllenhammar (1977)] for the assembly of automobiles. In Volvo's plan, a group of employees is assigned the automobile for a block of time. For example, an upholstery group might work as a team to install all the interior upholstery. The team decides who does what jobs, and the members can rotate work assignments provided the team completes the upholstery in the assigned block of time. This approach enriches the social interaction between workers and allows job rotation and job variety. General Motors is now using this team approach at its joint-venture plant with Toyota in Fremont, California, and plans to use it in the new Saturn automobile plant [see *Business Week* (1987)].

The third approach has been tried by General Electric in its modernization of the Louisville dishwasher plant. In this case dishwashers are automatically moved from one station to the next on dollies, which are used to build up a buffer of a few dishwashers between work stations. As a result, workers can emphasize quality by having some additional time, if needed, to finish a unit [Wheelwright and Hayes (1985)]. For the results of a similiar approach using buffers at Saab, see Box 9.3.

The fourth approach, mixed-model production, has gained great popularity in just-in-time production systems. At the Kawasaki plant in Lincoln, Nebraska, motorcycles are made on a line which intermixes the various models, as noted by Schonberger (1986). This method provides more variety in workers' tasks and reduces inventory, since the model mix more nearly approximates final demand.

As can be seen, there are many ways to organize assembly work once some of the traditional assumptions are brought into question. These options can be illustrated a little more clearly by again using the tricycle example.

Suppose we want to assemble 575 tricycles per day (in 8 hours). This amounts to a 50-second cycle time if a single-paced line is used. Using Hoffmann's method, we will need six stations. The first person's job will involve putting the left wheel and three washers in place, the second person will complete the left wheel assembly and put on the right wheel, and so on for the other workers. These are obviously quite finely divided jobs.

Another way to organize assembly of 575 tricycles a day is to set up two-person teams. In this case, one person can put on the right wheel while the other puts on the left wheel. One person can put on the seat while the other inserts the front fork, and they can both complete the front fork and put on the handle grips. As a

BOX 9.3
SAAB

The automobile industry is well known for its continued use of automated line-flow process. The trend in the industry has been toward the use of additional automation. Saab is an exception to this trend. They have moved away from the use of automation.

Saab began the move away from a heavy dependence upon the assembly line in an attempt to decrease their firm's high level of worker discontent and the associated cost. The source of the discontent was the worker's impression that work on the assembly line was too rigid and its tempo too fast. The effects of the discontent were increases in the level of worker absenteeism, in the rate of employee turnover, and in the rate of employee accidents. An additional problem was the firm's decreasing level of product quality.

Saab eliminated the use of the assembly line and replaced it with semiautonomous work groups separated by buffers of inventory. Each work group had members who performed assembly work as part of a pair and an additional member who was the team coordinator. The members of each group maintained their own buffer stocks, which allowed them to work at their own pace without affecting the workers who performed the preceding or succeeding steps on the product.

While the use of these semiautonomous work groups decreased costs due to worker discontent, the system also resulted in some cost increases for the following reasons: The buffer significantly increased the work-in-process inventory costs. Labor costs also increased. Since workers' jobs expanded in scope, their pay was increased by 21 cents per hour.

Even though these cost increases were significant, the cost decreases were of greater magnitude. It was estimated that the gains exceeded the added costs by a factor of 5.

Source: John Logue, "Semi-autonomous Groups at Saab: More Freedom, High Output," *Management Review,* vol. 71, no. 9, September 1982, pp. 32–33.

matter of fact, each team could organize its own work in precisely the fashion it wished. A manager should expect the same productivity, perhaps more, from these teams as from the single assembly line. For the same productivity, there should be three two-person teams and each team should produce 192 tricycles per day with a cycle time of 150 seconds per tricycle. For many workers, this method of assembly might be much more desirable than the single-paced line with shorter cycle time and less opportunity for human interaction. From an efficiency standpoint, it makes no difference as long as the same number of tricycles are produced by the same number of employees.

Another way to organize the assembly of tricycles would be to have two small assembly lines, each with three work stations. These smaller assembly lines would have a cycle time of 100 seconds, thus permitting more job variety for each worker.

We could go on with still other alternatives, but the point should be clear. There are many options which need to be considered carefully if management is to design assembly lines from both the social and technical viewpoints. The problem of assembly-line layout is not merely one of balancing single-paced lines.

 ## 9.3 LAYOUT OF PROJECTS

A project is a one-time activity which produces a unique product. The uniqueness of the product is one of the primary reasons why project layouts are different from intermittent or line layouts. Some examples of project-layout problems may be helpful at the outset. After reviewing these examples, we will summarize the key principles of project layout.

One category of projects is the construction of buildings, highways, dams, and so on. In construction projects, materials-handling costs is an important consideration; therefore much attention is paid to the efficient layout and staging of materials during construction. An attempt will usually be made to locate high-usage materials near the construction site and lower-usage materials at greater distances. This materials-handling problem can be formulated in a manner similar to that of the CRAFT model used for intermittent layouts.

Another key factor in determining the layout of construction projects is technological precedence. Materials will be staged according to whether they are used early or later in the project. This factor is especially important when space is limited. A related factor here is scheduling, which also determines the timing of project activities and thus establishes a basis for layout of the construction facility.

A second category of projects is manufacturing in fixed position. Large items are usually manufactured in this way, including ships, aricraft, locomotives, and space vehicles. In this type of project, materials are often located in concentric circles, with the product at the center. On the inner rings of the circle are those items used most often—such as rivets, bolts, or fasteners—while unique items are located further out from the center. This principle of concentric circles is used by both construction and fixed-manufacturing projects to reduce materials-handling costs.

The third category is multiple projects undertaken at the same site. Examples are projects for advertising agencies, research and development departments, and movie lots. Each project executed by these operations is unique, but the same type of project is repeated by using an intermittent process. For example, movie lots are organized by wardrobe shop, scenery shop, prop shop, and so on. The multiple-project layout problem can thus be thought of as intermittent production with a batch size of one unit each. Therefore the principles of intermittent-process layout apply in this case There will, however, be difficulty in forecasting flows of materials because of the uniqueness of projects.

What, then, do these operations have in common? First of all, materials handling is often an important consideration; however, a regular flow pattern cannot easily be established for project layouts. The second feature is that layout is dictated to a large extent by technological and scheduling considerations. This is especially relevant as the timing of a project becomes an important factor in the staging of materials. In summary then, materials handling, technological considerations, and scheduling are all important factors in project layouts.

Although we have considered project layouts in general terms, there is not a great deal of research on the subject. Perhaps the layout of project operations is difficult to study because of project uniqueness. Furthermore, there has been a preoccupation with scheduling problems in project operations which may have precluded the study of other problems, such as layout.

9.4 KEY POINTS

We have seen in this chapter that layout decisions are highly dependent on the process selection decision which we assumed has been made prior to layout decisions. Layout is then concerned with the arrangement of the physical processing facilities within a given type of process (intermittent, line, or project). Service and manufacturing layout decisions are treated within a common framework. Thus, the same general principles, concepts, and methods are used for both services and manufacturing; but the application of these ideas may be slightly different, as we have noted.

Key points covered in the chapter are as follows:

- Intermittent operations present a challenging layout problem. In this case, the physical arrangement of departments or processing activities must be determined to achieve stated criteria within physical constraints. We have discussed both quantitative decision criteria and qualitative criteria and the different methods used to solve each case.
- Intermittent-process layout problems of practical size usually require computer-assisted solutions. CRAFT and ALDEP are heuristic methods used in practice to solve intermittent-process layout problems.
- The line-flow layout problem is quite different from that involving intermittent flows because the direction of the flow of product has already been decided. The physical arrangement of processing facilities is dictated for line flows by the product technology. There does remain, however, a problem of assigning operations (processing tasks) to work stations.
- In the single-paced assembly line, the primary problem of layout is assembly-line balancing. Here the objective is to minimize the number of workers for a given cycle time or vice versa. The solution to this problem can be approximated by various heuristic methods which assign individual operations to workers. Management should not arbitrarily specify cycle times because small changes in cycle time can greatly affect the efficiency of the balance.
- With regard to assembly-line layout, perhaps the greatest problems facing operations management today are the high levels of boredom, turnover, absenteeism, and dissatisfaction among workers. A possible solution is to consider alternative types of assembly lines. For example, cycle time can be increased using two or more assembly lines instead of one. If the process is labor-intensive, this is a practical alternative and can reduce the problems mentioned. Management

should also consider various forms of group or team assembly and assembly using flexible, buffered lines which allow more individual pacing.

- The third type of layout problem is the project process. For projects, the product is unique, but similar projects can be conducted at the same site. The layout problem is highly dependent on technological precedence and project scheduling, since this determines the order in which materials and skills are used. A principle of concentric circles was described for fixed-location manufacturing and construction, where the product is in the center and material with high usage is staged in the inner circles while materials with lower usage are placed in the outer circles.
- Layout decisions still present a substantial challenge for management. Many layout decisions have long-term effects which cannot be easily reversed. These decisions determine the efficiency of operations as well as the design of jobs. It is thus important to improve the practice of layout by using the best approaches available.

QUESTIONS

1. In considering layout decisions, why do we assume that the decision about which process to use has already been made?
2. Consider a layout decision which has been made in your residence or at work. How was the decision made? What were the important factors?
3. What relationships exist between layout decisions, capacity decisions, and scheduling?
4. How, specifically, do layout problems differ between intermittent, line, and project flows?
5. Suppose you were asked to lay out a department store.
   a. What questions would you ask management?
   b. What data would you need to collect, and where do you think you would get the data?
   c. How would you analyze the data to arrive at a recommendation?
6. In a few sentences state the intermittent-process layout problem.
7. In laying out a hospital, do you think it is appropriate to minimize the sum of distances walked by all patients and staff? Suggest some other criteria that you might use.
8. What type of decision criterion do you think would be appropriate for the following types of layout situations?
   a. Cafeteria line
   b. Hotel rooms
   c. Golf course
   d. Office
   e. Factory
   f. School rooms
9. Compare and contrast the quantitative and qualitative layout problem for intermittent-process facilities. Which type of criterion is best?
10. What differences are there between the layout design of a new facility and the revised layout of an existing facility?
11. Identify behavioral factors which may be important in making layout decisions. Do these factors differ between the various types of layout problems?
12. Compare and contrast CRAFT and ALDEP.
13. While the departments in a factory were being located, the comment was overheard

that CRAFT would not be a suitable method because it considers only materials-handling costs and ignores other tangible and intangible factors. Comment on this statement.

14. In a few sentences, define the assembly-line balancing problem.
15. Several alternatives to single-paced assembly lines were suggested. Which of the alternatives might be appropriate for:
    a. Capital-intensive operations
    b. Labor-intensive operations

PROBLEMS

1. Suppose that four departments (A, B, C, and D) are located on a grid, as shown in the diagram. Show that there are 24 possible locations of departments but only three location plans with different relative locations of departments. [Adapted from Buffa (1977).]

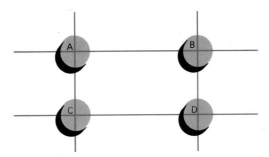

2. A small manufacturing company has four departments between which the following loads are transported:

		To			
		A	B	C	D
	A		30	35	60
	B	15		25	35
From	C	25	30		50
	D	52	15	24	

Assuming that all departments are the same size and that materials-handling cost is a linear function of distance, find the location plan which minimizes total materials-handling cost. (Hint: See Problem 1.)

3. A medical clinic is trying to locate the following departments: x-ray, orthopedics, pediatrics, and laboratory. An inital layout of these departments and the associated distance matrix is shown below, along with the number of trips per day between each pair of departments. Assume that a patient can travel at the rate of 150 feet per minute when walking between departments.
    a. Determine the total travel time of all patients for the layout shown below.
    b. Find the best layout to minimize total patient travel time. Hint: Only three alternative layouts need to be considered.
    c. What factors other than patient travel time should be considered in this case?

Feet per trip

	A	B	C	D
A		100	100	200
B			200	100
C				100
D				

X-ray A	Orthopedics B
Pediatrics C	Laboratory D

Trips per day

	A	B	C	D
A		50	20	30
B			10	25
C				40
D				

4. A manager is trying to determine the best layout for her office. The following information has been collected on the average number of trips per day by various types of persons from and to their own offices. It is also known that executives are paid $200 per day, staff people are paid $110 per day, and secretaries are paid $70 per day. The manager would like to minimize the cost of lost time due to trips between various locations in the office.

	From/to trips per day		
Department	Executives	Secretaries	Staff
A. Mail room	0	40	10
B. Secretarial office	15	0	20
C. Conference room	30	10	25
D. Coffee room	5	35	20
E. Executive offices	0	40	40
F. Staff offices	20	30	0

Assume that a trip between adjacent offices takes 5 minutes traveling time in both directions. If the trip is between nonadjacent offices, the traveler must move in rectangular directions along the hallways between offices. Thus, the traveling times for the layout shown are given below.

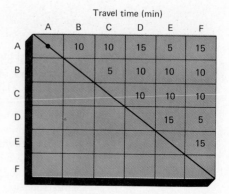

a. Evaluate the total cost of this layout plan.
b. Develop a layout plan with lower cost.
c. What additional factors other than travel cost might be important in this problem?

5. From the information given in Table 9.1 and Figures 9.1 to 9.5, find the cost of an exchange between departments 7 and 8.

6. In an outpatient clinic, the relative desirability of locating departments near each other has been rated as shown below. These ratings are based on such factors as patient travel, staff travel, safety and fire hazards, preference of doctors and nurses, etc. Using ALOEP, generate a layout for the clinic. Limit your search to three different layouts.

	X-ray	Orthopedics	Pediatrics	Gynecology	Lab	General
X-ray		A	U	I	U	O
Orthopedics			U	E	U	O
Pediatrics				U	E	O
Gynecology					I	I
Lab						E
General						

A = Absolutely necessary
E = Especially important
I = Important
O = Ordinary closeness OK
U = Unimportant
X = Undesirable

7. A police station is trying to utilize its space in the best possible way. The relationship matrix for various police departments is shown below.

Department	Front desk	Precinct office	Toilets	Detention	Interrogation
Front desk		I	U	U	O
Precinct office			X	U	U
Toilets				A	O
Detention					E
Interrogation					

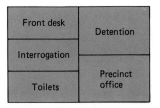

a. Evaluate the layout given above. Use A=5, E=4, I=3, O=2, U=1, X=0.
b. Suggest a better layout plan.
c. Using ALDEP, put the front desk in the location shown above. Then select the next department with the highest closeness relationship and put it in the layout. Continue this procedure until all departments are located. What is the resulting total numerical value of the layout?
d. Identify the weaknesses in using ALDEP to solve this problem.

8. The tricycle example described in the chapter (Table 9.2) has been given a cycle time of 30 seconds.

a. How many stations are needed to obtain a balance using Hoffmann's method?
b. Use the least-number-of-predecessors rule to arrive at a balance and compare it with the answer to part a.
c. Suggest two alternative types of assembly lines which have the same output rate per day. Discuss the pros and cons of each of these alternatives.

9. An enterprising college student has received a contract to deliver 400 submarine sandwiches per day to a cafeteria. The student expects to assemble these sandwiches on an assembly line using the following times and precedence relationships.

Task	Description	Seconds	Precedences
A	Spread both buns (butter)	25	—
B	Put on lettuce	15	A
C	Put on meat	13	A
D	Put on cheese	15	A
E	Put on tomato	12	A
F	Wrap finished sandwich	20	A, B, C, D, E

a. For a 40-second cycle time, balance the assembly line using the least-number-of-predecessors rule. How many stations are required and what operations are assigned to each?
b. What is the minimum number of stations for a 40-second cycle time? What is the efficiency of the balance obtained in part a? How long will it take to produce the 400 sandwiches a day?
c. Suggest alternative ways to organize the assembly of these sandwiches using the same amount of labor. Which method do you prefer?

10. Develop your own heuristic rule to balance the line given in Problem 9.

11. The following precedence diagram and times are given for the assembly of a hydraulic valve. (Times are shown above the circles.)

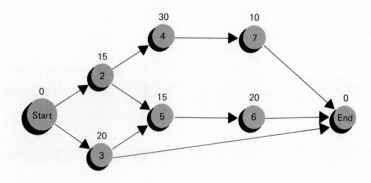

a. Given a cycle time of 45 seconds, balance the line using the least-number-of-predecessors rule.
b. How many valves are produced in 8 hours?
c. If you were given three stations to use, what cycle time would be best?
d. Use Hoffmann's method to balance the line with a cycle time of 45 seconds.

12. A hand-held calculator is assembled as shown below by the precedence network. The times (in seconds) for each operation are also shown on the diagram.

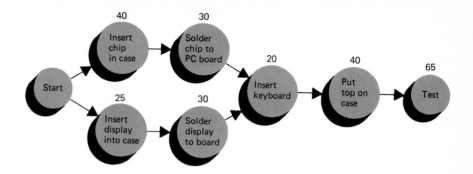

a. What is the minimum number of stations that can be used for an output of 100 calculators per hour?

b. Obtain a line balance using the least-number-of-predecessors rule and a cycle time of 70 seconds. How many stations are needed?

c. What is the efficiency of the balance obtained in part b?

d. What cycle time is needed to obtain a balance for four stations?

SELECTED BIBLIOGRAPHY

ARMOUR, G. C., and E. S. BUFFA: "A Heuristic Algorithm and Simulation Approach to Relative Location of Facilities," *Management Science,* vol. 9, no. 1, 1963, pp. 294–309.

BAYBARS, ILKER: "A Survey of Exact Algorithms for the Simple Assembly Line Balancing Problem," *Management Science,* vol. 32, no.8, August 1986, pp. 909-932.

BUFFA, ELWOOD S.: *Modern Production Management: Managing the Operation Function,* 5th ed., New York: Wiley, 1977.

———, G. C. ARMOUR, and T. E. VOLLMANN: "Allocating Facilities with CRAFT," *Harvard Business Review,* vol. 42, no. 2, 1964, pp. 136–159.

Business Week, "General Motors: What Went Wrong," Mar. 16, 1987.

CHASE, RICHARD B.: "Strategic Considerations in Assembly Line Selection," *California Management Review,* Fall 1975, pp. 17–23.

———: "Survey of Paced Assembly Lines," *Industrial Engineering,* vol. 6, no. 2, February 1974, pp. 14–18.

DENHOLM, D. H., and G. H. BROOKS: "A Comparison of Three Computer Assisted Plant Layout Techniques," *Proceedings of the American Institute of Industrial Engineers, 21st Annual Conference and Convention,* Cleveland, 1970.

FRANCIS, RICHARD L., and JOHN A. WHITE: *Facility Layout and Location: An Analytical Approach,* Englewood Cliffs, N.J.: Prentice-Hall, 1974.

GEHRLEIN, WILLIAM, and JAMES PATTERSON: "Balancing Single Model Assembly Lines: Comments on a Paper by E. M. Dar-El (Mansoor)," *AIIE Transactions,* March 1978, pp. 109–112.

GYLLENHAMMAR, PEHR: "How Volvo Adapts Work to People," *Harvard Business Review,* July–August 1977.

HELGESON, W. B., and D. P. BIRNIE: "Assembly Line Balancing Using the Ranked Positional Weight Technique," *Journal of Industrial Engineering,* vol. 12, no. 6, November–December 1961, pp. 394–398.

HOFFMANN, THOMAS R.: "Assembly Line Balancing with a Precedence Matrix," *Management Science,* vol. 9, no. 4, July 1963, pp. 551–562.

IGNALL, EDWARD: "A Review of Assembly Line Balancing," *Journal of Industrial Engineering,* vol. 16, no. 4, July–August 1965, pp. 244–252.

JOHNSON, ROGER V.: "Optimally Balancing Large Assembly with 'Fable', " *Management Science,* vol. 34, no. 2, Feb. 1988, pp. 240-253.

KAIMAN, LEE: *Computer Architecture Programs*, Boston: Center for Environmental Research, 1970 (3 vols., looseleaf).

KILBRIDGE, MAURICE, and LEON WESTER: "A Heuristic Method of Assembly Line Balancing," *Journal of Industrial Engineering*, vol. 12, no. 4, July–August 1961, pp. 292–298.

MASTOR, ANTHONY: "An Experimental Investigation and Comparative Evaluation of Production Line Balancing Techniques," *Management Science*, vol. 16, no. 11, July 1970, pp. 728–746.

MOORE, J. M.: "Computer Program Evaluates Plant Layout Alternatives," *Industrial Engineering*, vol. 3, no. 8, 1971, pp. 19–25.

MUTHER, RICHARD: *Practical Plant Layout*, New York: McGraw-Hill, 1955.

―――― and JOHN D. WHEELER: "Simplified Systematic Layout Planning," *Factory*, vol. 120, nos. 8, 9, 10, August, September, October 1962, pp. 68–77, 111–119, 101–113.

SCHONBERGER, RICHARD J.: *World Class Manufacturing*, New York: Free Press, 1986.

SCHULER, RANDALL, LARRY P. RITZMAN, and VICKI DAVIS: "Merging Prescriptive and Behavioral Approaches for Office Layout," *Journal of Operations Management*, vol. 1, no. 3, February 1981, pp. 131–142.

SEEHOF, J. M., and W. O. EVANS: "Automatic Layout Design Program," *The Journal of Industrial Engineering*, vol. 18, no. 12, December 1967, pp. 690–695.

SOMMERS, M. S., and J. B. KERNAN: "A Behavioral Approach to Planning Layout and Display," *Journal of Retailing*, Winter 1965–1966, pp. 21–27.

STEEL, F. J.: *Physical Settings and Organizational Development*, Reading, Mass.: Addison-Wesley, 1973.

STONE, PHILIP, J., and ROBERT LUCHETTI: "Your Office Is Where You Are," *Harvard Business Review*, March–April 1985.

TALBOT, F. BRIAN AND WILLIAM V. GEHRLEIN, "A Comparative Evaluation of Heuristic Line Balancing Techniques," *Management Science*, vol. 32, no. 4, Apr. 1986, pp. 430-454.

VOLGYESI, A. S.: "Toronto General: The Hospital That Computers Built," *Computer Decisions*, September 1969.

VOLLMANN, THOMAS E., and ELWOOD BUFFA: "The Facilities Layout Problem in Perspective," *Management Science*, vol. 12, no. 10, June 1966, pp. B450–B458.

―――――, C. E. NUGENT, and R. L. ZARTLER: "A Computerized Model for Office Layouts," *Journal of Industrial Engineering*, vol. 19, July 1968, pp. 321–327.

WHEELWRIGHT, STEVEN C., and ROBERT HAYES: "Competing through Manufacturing," *Harvard Business Review*, January–February 1985.

PART THREE

CAPACITY PLANNING AND SCHEDULING

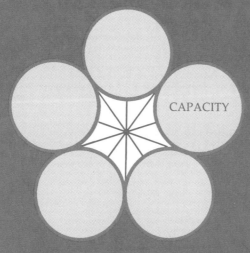

CAPACITY

- **FACILITIES DECISIONS**
- **AGGREGATE PLANNING**
- **SCHEDULING OPERATIONS**
- **PROJECT SCHEDULING**

Operations managers are responsible for providing sufficient capacity to meet their firm's needs. Capacity decisions should be made by forecasting demand and by developing plans to provide sufficient capacity for the long, medium, and short time ranges. The disaggregation of capacity plans from long-range facility planning through medium-range aggregate planning and then to short-range scheduling provides the organizing principle for Part 3. One chapter is devoted to each of the long-, medium-, and short-range capacity decisions.

Long-range facilities decisions typically extend 2 years or more into the future and constrain all shorter-range capacity decisions. Facilities planning naturally leads to questions of how much capacity is needed, when is it needed, and where the facilities should be located.

The term "aggregate planning" is used to describe planning for all product lines gathered together over approximately 1 year into the future. As a result of aggregate planning, decisions should be made regarding the size of the work force, overtime, subcontracting, and overall inventory levels. In the chapter on aggregate planning, a variety of methods are reviewed for making this decision in both manufacturing and service industries.

Scheduling involves short-range capacity decisions allocating available resources to jobs, orders, activities, or tasks. While facility planning and aggregate planning are resource-acquisition decisions, scheduling allocates available resources. The result of scheduling is a time schedule which describes exactly when each activity will be started and completed. Scheduling should also be used to help predict the load on facilities and to control the relationships between the operation's input and output. An organizing principle of the scheduling chapters is the separation of line, intermittent, and project scheduling problems.

As a result of the entire range of capacity decisions, the output of the operations function should closely match the customer needs. This will require accurate demand forecasting and numerous tradeoffs between the conflicting goals of good customer service, low inventories, and low costs of operations. It will also require a hierarchy of interlocked capacity decisions from long to medium to short range.

The decision-making framework can be used to describe the interaction between capacity decisions and all other decisions in operations. As we have already noted, capacity decisions affect the type of process used and the degree of process automation as well as the details of process design. Capacity decisions also affect the level of inventory through capacity-inventory tradeoffs. Scheduling decisions are of great importance in managing the work force; they affect output, quality, and the morale of workers. Capacity decisions should, therefore, be made with the impact on other parts of operations in mind.

Facilities Decisions

Facilities decisions are of great importance to the business and to the operations function. These decisions place physical constraints on the amount that can be produced, and they require investment of scarce capital. Therefore, facilities decisions are often made at the highest corporate level, including top management and the board of directors.

Facilities decisions occur at one end of a hierarchy of capacity decisions ranging from long-term to short-term. The facilities commitment is the longest-range in nature and thus constrains all the other capacity decisions. After the facilities decisions have been made, the remaining capacity decisions must be made within the facilities available. These remaining short- and medium-range capacity decisions are discussed in the next three chapters.

Because of construction lead times, facilities decisions often require up to 5 years of lead time, but they can also require as little as 1 year. The 1-year time frame refers to buildings and equipment which can quickly be constructed or leased. The 5-year time frame refers to large and complex facilities such as oil refineries, paper mills, steel mills, and electricity generating plants.

In facilities decisions, there are three crucial questions:

1. *How much* capacity is needed?
2. *When* is the capacity needed?
3. *Where* should the capacity be located?

The question of how much, when, and where can be separated conceptually, but they are often intertwined. As a result, facilities decisions are exceedingly complex and difficult to analyze.

In this chapter the above three types of facilities decisions will be considered in detail. We begin with the notion of a facilities strategy and its relationship to business strategy. Then, analysis for facilities decisions is presented, followed by a detailed discussion of facilities location decisions.

FACILITIES STRATEGY

Chapter 2 noted that a facilities strategy (or policy) is one of the major parts of an operations strategy. Since major facilities decisions affect competitive success, facilities decisions need to be considered as part of the total operations strategy and not simply as a series of incremental capital budgeting decisions. This point of view also applies to other major strategic decisions in operations, as we have already noted, for certain process design decisions.

As indicated above, a facilities strategy typically considers the amount of capacity, the timing of capacity, and the location of capacity needed for the long run. These elements of a facilities strategy need to be considered in an integrated fashion and are affected by the following factors.

1. *Predicted demand.* Formulating a facility strategy requires a forecast of demand, even if the variance is quite large. Techniques for making these forecasts were considered in Chapter 3.
2. *Cost of facilities.* Cost will enter into the facility strategy in considering whether large or small facilities should be built. Cost also affects the amount of capacity added at any one time, the timing, and the location of capacity.
3. *Likely behavior of competitors.* A slow expected competitive response may lead the firm to add capacity to "grab" the market before competitors become strong.

On the other hand, a fast expected competitive response may cause the firm to be more cautious in expanding capacity.

4. *Business strategy.* The business strategy may dictate that a company put more emphasis on cost, service, or flexibility in facilities choices. For example, a business strategy to provide the best service can lead to facilities with some excess capacity or market locations for fast service. Other business strategies can lead to cost minimization or other types of facilities choices.

5. *International considerations.* As markets become more global in nature, facilities must be located on a global basis. This involves not merely chasing "cheap labor," but locating facilities globally for the best strategic advantage. International aspects of capacity will be described in detail in Chapter 22.

Amount of Capacity

One part of a facilities strategy is the amount of capacity provided in relation to expected demand. This can best be described by the notion of a "capacity cushion," which is defined as follows:

Capacity cushion = capacity − average demand

Since the capacity cushion is expressed relative to the average demand level, a positive cushion provides excess capacity over the average demand and a negative cushion means that average demand will exceed capacity. Of course, we would ideally like to provide no capacity cushion, but this is impossible in the face of uncertain demand.

Three strategies can be adopted with respect to the amount of capacity cushion [see Hayes and Wheelwright (1984)].

1. *Try not to run out.* In this case a positive capacity cushion is used. The firm would be trying to go beyond the average demand forecast and provide some additional capacity. Such a strategy would be appropriate when there is an expanding market, or when the cost of building and operating capacity is inexpensive relative to the cost of running out of capacity. Electric utilities seem to adopt this approach, since blackouts or brownouts are generally not acceptable. Companies in growing markets may also adopt a positive capacity cushion, since it allows them to capture market share ahead of their competitors. Also, in growth markets there is less risk of having idle capacity for long, since the market is expanding.

2. *Build to average forecast.* In this case the firm is more conservative with respect to capacity provided. Building to average forecast will provide a 50 percent probability of running out of capacity and a 50 percent probability of having excess capacity.[1] This strategy would be used when the cost (or consequences) of running out is approximately in balance with the cost of excess capacity.

3. *Maximize utilization.* In this case a small or negative capacity cushion would be planned to maximize utilization. This strategy is appropriate when capacity is very expensive, relative to stockouts, as in the case of oil refineries, paper mills, and

---

[1] This, of course, assumes a symmetrical probability distribution of demand.

other capital-intensive industries. These facilities operate profitably only at very high capacity rates approaching 90 to 100 percent. This strategy would tend to maximize short-run earnings, but could, however, damage the long-run market share, especially if competitors adopt larger capacity cushions and demand develops in excess of capacity.

An approach for determining the amount of capacity cushion will be described in the next section.

Size of Units

After deciding on the level of capacity to be provided, a facility strategy must also address the question of how large each unit of capacity should be. This is, of course, a question involving economies of scale. Scale economies are based on the notion that large units are more economical because fixed costs can be spread over more units of production. These economies occur for several reasons. First, the cost of building and operating large production equipment does not increase linearly with volume. A machine with twice the output rate generally costs less than twice as much to buy and operate. Also, in larger facilities the overhead due to managers and staff can be spread over more units of production. As a result, the *unit* cost of production falls as facility size increases, when scale economies are present, as shown in the left part of Figure 10.1.

This is a good news–bad news story. For along with the good news (economies of scale) comes the bad news (diseconomies of scale). Diseconomies occur as the facility gets larger for several reasons. First, there are transportation diseconomies present. For example, a large facility incurs more transportation costs than two smaller facilities which are closer to their markets. Diseconomies of scale also occur because communications, coordination, and control costs increase in large bureaucratic organizations. As more layers of staff and management are added to manage the organization, the cost ultimately increases faster than the output level.

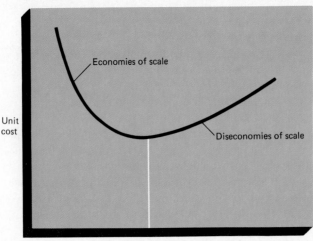

FIGURE 10.1
Optimum unit
size.

Facility size (units produced per year)

Furthermore, costs of complexity and confusion arise as more products are added and a facility becomes larger. For these reasons, the curve in Figure 10.1 rises on the right-hand side due to the diseconomies of scale.

As Figure 10.1 indicates, there is a minimum unit cost for a certain facility size. This particular optimum size will depend on how high the fixed costs are and how rapidly diseconomies of scale occur. As an example, Hewlett-Packard tends to operate small plants of less than about 300 people. This plant size is used because Hewlett-Packard wants to encourage innovation and it has many small product lines with relatively low fixed costs. On the other hand, IBM operates very large plants in the range of 5000 to 10,000 people for producing mainframe computers. IBM plants tend to be highly automated, and they use a decentralized management approach in order to minimize diseconomies of scale. Every company seems to have an "optimum" facility size depending on its cost structure, product structure, and particular operations strategy, which may emphasize cost, flexibility, or service. Cost is, after all, not the only factor which affects facility size.

Timing of Facility Additions

Another element of facility strategy is the timing of additions to capacity. There are basically two strategies here.

1. *Preempt the competition.* In this case the firm will lead the market, by building capacity in advance of the need. This strategy will tend to provide a positive capacity cushion, it may actually stimulate the market, and it could prevent competition from coming in for a while. An example of this strategy was followed by Apple Computer in the early days of the personal computer market. Apple built a factory in advance of demand and had a lion's share of the market before competitors moved in. McDonald's also followed this strategy in the early days of the fast-food industry.

2. *Wait and see.* In this case the firm will wait to add capacity until demand develops and the need is clear. As a result, the company will be following the leader and taking a lower-risk strategy. A small or negative capacity cushion could develop, and a loss of potential market share may result. However, this strategy can also be very effective, since superior marketing channels or technology can allow the follower to capture market share. For example, IBM followed the leader (Apple) in the personal computer market but was able to take away market share because of its superior brand image, size, and market presence. On the other hand, U.S. automobile companies followed the "wait and see" strategy, to their chagrin, for small compact autos. While U.S. automakers waited to see how demand for small cars would develop, the Japanese grabbed a dominant position in the U.S. small-car market.

Types of Units

The final element in facility strategy considers the question of multiple facilities. There are four different types of facility choices.

1. Product-focused (57 percent)
2. Market-focused (31 percent)
3. Process-focused (9 percent)
4. General purpose (3 percent)

The figures in parentheses indicate the percentages of companies in the Fortune 500 using each type of facility [Schmenner (1982)].

The product-focused facilities produce one family or type of product usually for a large market. An example is the Anderson Window plant which produces various types of windows for the entire United States from a single product-focused plant. Product plants are often used when transportation costs are low or scale economies are high. This tends to centralize facilities into one or a few locations. Other examples of product-focused facilities are large bank credit card processing operations and auto leasing companies which process leases for cars throughout the United States from a single site.

Market-focused facilities are located in the markets that they serve. Many service operations fall into this category, since services cannot be transported. Plants which require quick customer response or customized products or which have high transportation charges tend to be market-focused. An example is plants which produce mattresses. Due to the bulky nature of the product and high shipping charges, it makes sense to locate small mattress plants in regional markets. International facilities also tend to be market-focused because of tariffs, trade barriers, and potential currency fluctuations.

Process facilities have one or at most two technologies. These facilities frequently produce components or parts which are shipped to other facilities for further processing or assembly. This is common in the auto industry, where engine plants and transmission plants are feeder plants for the final assembly plants. Process plants can also supply plants outside the company and they can make a wide variety of products within the given process technology. As noted above, the process facility is not widely used compared with product or market facilities, but is nonetheless important in certain cases.

General-purpose facilities may produce several types of products and use several different processes. They tend to be used by thousands of small companies that do not have sufficient volume to justify more than one facility. Larger companies usually specialize their facilities according to product, market, or process. The disadvantage of the general-purpose facility, of course, is that it is unfocused, as described in Chapter 2, unless a plant-within-a-plant strategy can be used.

We have shown how a facility strategy can be constructed by considering questions of capacity, size of units, timing, and types of units. Of course, a facility strategy needs to be supported by various methods of analysis, which will be discussed in the remainder of this chapter.

ANALYSIS FOR FACILITY STRATEGY

Analysis for a facility strategy can be organized around the following steps. These steps are quite simple to describe, but difficult to implement in practice.

1. Develop a measure of facility capacity.
2. Prepare a forecast of future demand.
3. Determine facility needs.
4. Generate alternatives.
5. Evaluate alternatives.
6. Decide.

Measuring Facility Capacity

The first step in facilities analysis is quite challenging in its own right and requires a clear definition of capacity. *Capacity is the maximum output rate of an operation.* As a rate of output, capacity should always be measured in units of output per time period. Some examples of capacity measures are:

* Barrels of beer per day
* Tons of steel per year
* Patients treated per month
* Customers served per day
* Cubic yards of gravel moved per day
* Students graduated per year

One common mistake in measuring capacity is to ignore the time dimension. For example, erroneous measurements of capacity are the number of beds in a hospital, seats in a restaurant, or pupils in a school building. The number of beds in a hospital represents facilities size, not a rate of output. The number of beds should be combined with an estimated length of hospital stay to arrive at a capacity measure, such as patients treated per month. Similarly, the restaurant and school examples represent only facility size and not the maximum rate of output.

Another common mistake in measuring capacity is to confuse capacity and volume. Volume is the actual output rate over some time period, while capacity is the maximum output rate. Thus if 10,000 students were graduated from the University of Minnesota last year, this figure—unless volume happened to equal capacity—is merely a volume figure. The actual graduation volume by itself does not tell us how many students *could* have been graduated.

After capacity has been correctly defined, there are still two important measurement problems. First, an aggregate unit of capacity must be specified for facility-planning purposes. In cases where there is a single product or there are a few homogenous products, such as beer or flour, the aggregate measure is easily defined. When a complex product mix is produced from the same facility, however, capacity is more difficult to measure. As an example of a complex product mix, suppose we want to measure the capacity of a restaurant which produces hamburgers, French fries, shakes, etc. In this case, meaningful measures of aggregate capacity are customers served per day or dollars of sales per day. Most other measures one could think of would not reflect the great diversity of products. Using this same line of reasoning, airlines often measure their capacity in available seat miles (ASMs) per month.[2] This measure incorporates the effects of different types of planes, different turnaround times for maintenance, different flying speeds, etc.

In general terms, if all other measures fail, one can express capacity in terms of dollars of sales. However, more convenient physical units, such as those mentioned above, are available in many cases. In any event, the capacity will be affected by product mix; this cannot be avoided.

The second problem in measuring capacity is to assess the effect of management policy variables. One of these variables is the number of hours worked per week. This figure will vary from a normal week of 40 hours to three shifts for 7 days a week. The correct number of hours to use depends on the operating policies in effect. In a steel mill, it would be normal to base capacity on around-the-clock operations 7 days a week. In other operations, such as public schools, the normal school day might be used, although it should be noted that evening classes add to the capacity available. To handle this problem, nominal capacity is sometimes defined as the maximum output rate possible under normal operations policies. This might be one shift, two shifts, or three shifts, whatever is normal. Nominal capacity would not, however, include overtime, extra subcontracting, or crowding of the facilities.

In measuring capacity, there is one final distinction which must be made: peak capacity versus sustained capacity. Peak capacity can be sustained for only a short period of time, such as a few hours in a day or a few days in a month. Peak capacity represents the surge capability of the operation, considering, perhaps, overtime, extra workers, and special surge policies. On the other hand, the sustained capacity is a level which can be maintained over long periods of time with no adverse effects.

In planning facilities, it is often necessary to consider both peak and sustained capacities. For service industries, however, it should be noted that the peak capacity is often more important than sustained capacity, e.g., electricity generating, golf courses, restaurants, and telephone service. The greater emphasis on planning for peak capacity in service industries arises because the product cannot be stored.

In summary, measurement of capacity will require resolution of the following issues:

1. An aggregate measure
2. Product-mix effects
3. Operations policies (e.g., hours per week)
4. Sustained and peak capacity

Forecasting Demand

The second step in facilities analysis takes the capacity measure as given and proceeds to develop a forecast of demand. As noted in Chapter 3, a long-range

---

[2]An available seat mile is one seat flown for a distance of 1 mile. Multiplying the number of seats in each plane by the number of miles that can be flown will yield total ASM.

forecast will often be made by qualitative methods or causal models. For facilities analysis, the time-series models are generally less useful.

In facilities planning, great care is often taken in making the forecast, since the forecast will drive the strategy. Furthermore, it is good practice to develop a probability forecast for facilities so that the risk of the decision can be evaluated. Since forecasting was discussed at length in Part 1, we will not dwell on it further here.

Determining Facility Needs

The third step in facilities analysis is to determine the capacity needs over time. The need can be thought of as the gap between required and available capacity in the future. The required capacity, in turn, can be related to the forecast and to the degree of management risk taken in meeting the forecast.

For example, suppose that the probability forecast of demand 2 years in the future is as follows:

Demand (units per year)	Cumulative probability
≤ 10,000	.1
≤ 12,000	.3
≤ 14,000	.5
≤ 16,000	.7
≤ 18,000	.9

Management will need to study this forecast to determine the required capacity and the amount of capacity cushion required. If a 30 percent chance of demand exceeding capacity can be accepted, then the required capacity can be set at 16,000 units. If only a 10 percent risk can be taken, 18,000 units of capacity should be planned. The level of risk accepted should depend on the means available to expand capacity and the consequences of demand exceeding capacity. Thinking in these terms requires assignment of a "cost" to running out of capacity and a cost of having too much capacity. The relative values of these two costs will determine the proper level of capacity.

After the requirement has been decided upon, the available capacity is projected into the future, deducting for worn-out facilities or other reductions in capacity which will occur. The difference between the required and projected available capacity then represents the needed capacity. This need should be time-phased over several years into the future so that various alternatives for meeting future needs can be considered.

Generating Alternatives

This is perhaps the most creative step in the entire decision process and will certainly require management judgment and input. The generation of alternatives can be complex because combinations of the three basic questions ("how much," "when," and "where located") may be used. For example, in a particular situation the following alternatives might be considered:

1. Build a 40,000-unit-per-year facility now in Los Angeles.
2. Build a 40,000-unit-per-year facility now in Denver.
3. Build a 20,000-unit-per-year facility now and a 20,000-unit-per-year facility in 2 years in Los Angeles.
4. Build a 30,000-unit facility a year from now in Chicago.

Because of the combinations possible, a large number of alternatives may have to be considered. In some cases, however, management may constrain the alternatives to make the decision more manageable. This could be done by deciding on capacity, location, or timing first and thereby reducing the size of the problem. Alternatives are also constrained by developing a general facility strategy which defines, for example, the maximum size of units and the type of facility, e.g., market locations. These constraints limit the number of alternatives which must be considered.

In some cases, the number of alternatives cannot easily be enumerated. This quite commonly occurs in plant or warehouse location problems where a very large number of alternatives are available. In these cases, a mathematical model may be formulated which implicitly constrains the alternatives without enumerating each one. An example of this procedure will be given later.

In other cases, it is difficult to find one feasible alternative (to say nothing about the optimal or best alternative). This situation quite commonly occurs in public decisions involving compromise and in consensus decisions. Here the problem is to develop simply one alternative which all parties can accept.

Whether one or many alternatives present themselves, the quality of the decision will be defined in relation to the alternatives available. It is, therefore, important to expend creative effort on the generation of alternatives.

Evaluating Alternatives

The most crucial step in evaluating alternatives is to select the relevant criteria. These criteria usually include benefits and costs. If costs and benefits both vary between the alternatives, it will be difficult to evaluate them; it is much easier if the alternatives generated are either equal cost or equal benefit. For example, if all the alternatives provide the required capacity which is considered the benefit, then the evaluation is simply a cost comparison. If the alternatives generate different revenues, the most convenient evaluation measure may then be profit or return on investment. In still other cases, response time or service delivered may be an important measure of benefit.

In many facility evaluation problems, the benefits can be stated in terms of cash flow over time. If this is the case, present values, discounted cash flows, or internal rate-of-return calculations can be used as a basis for evaluation. Since we have already discussed these methods in the supplement to Chapter 7, we will use them freely in this chapter without further comment.

To illustrate the method of cash-flow analysis, suppose that alternatives 1 and 3 above are being evaluated. The cash-flow pattern for each alternative is shown in Figure 10.2. Since the alternatives each provide the same amount of total capacity,

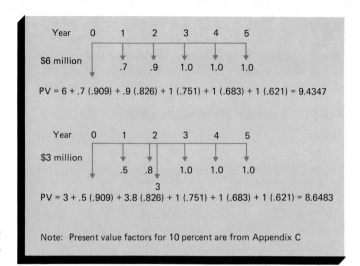

FIGURE 10.2
Present values
for capacity.

and revenue is assumed to be the same, we can simply compare present values of costs. At a 10 percent (real) discount rate the present value of alternative 1 is $9.4347 million and the present value of alternative 3 is $8.6483 million. To minimize the cost, alternative 3 should be selected.

If the alternatives include a large number of location options, it may be necessary to construct a mathematical model of the problem. These models, to be discussed later in the chapter, provide a framework for the formal evaluation of alternatives and for extensive analysis of the decision alternatives.

Although the evaluation step often receives a great deal of attention, it should be kept in perspective as only one element of the decision-making process. It should be further emphasized that managers make decisions—models do not. Therefore, the evaluation step will not automatically lead to the decision.

The Facilities Decision

In the end, facilities decisions will often be made by the chief executive and board of directors in consultation with operations and other departments in the firm. This is done to ensure that a consistent pattern of facilities decisions occurs over time. In this way a coherent facility strategy is developed. The facility decision should be seen as one which affects all parts of the organization and not just operations. Facilities decisions require capital and are thus of concern to financial managers. Facilities decisions also affect the future ability of the firm to meet customer needs and are thus of interest to marketing. Because of these multiple effects, facilities decisions are often made at the level of top management, where all facets of the problem can be properly evaluated and the decision can be integrated with corporate strategy.

In the end, the decision maker must determine whether the decision meets the objectives of the firm. If the objectives are to provide superb customer service, then some excess capacity may be provided. If the competitive situation and the firm's objectives require strict cost control, then a more conservative stance on capacity may be taken. In cases where products are rapidly changing, flexibility may be an important objective. The decision should ultimately be guided by management's assessment of how the decision meets these conflicting objectives.

10.3 FACILITY LOCATION PROBLEMS

In Sections 10.1 and 10.2 we have been treating facilities decisions in general terms, including how much, when, and where located. The methodology described is useful in many contexts, but it is limited when complex location problems are presented. We shall, therefore, expand specifically on location problems in the remainder of this chapter.

Location problems can be characterized by a choice among multiple sites. Apart from this common feature, each location decision tends to be different. In some cases, the decision criterion is cost; in others it is revenue, vehicle response time, or multiple criteria. Some location problems involve the consideration of only a few sites; others involve many. Some location problems include distribution costs from multiple plants and warehouses; others do not.

Since there are many different types of location problems, the following classification framework has been developed.

1. **Single-facility location.** In this type of location problem, only one facility which does not interact with the firm's other facilities is located. Examples include a single factory or warehouse, a government facility, and a single retail store. This type of location problem typically has multiple criteria such as labor costs, labor supply, union atmosphere, community services, and taxes. The problem is to consider all these criteria objectively.

2. **Location of multiple factories and warehouses.** In this type of location problem, total distribution costs and perhaps total production costs will be affected by the location decision. The new facility may necessitate adjustment in the shipping patterns and production levels of all other facilities. This problem is usually formulated by considering a production-distribution network of plants and warehouses with the criterion of minimizing costs.

3. **Location of competitive retail stores.** In this location problem, the revenue obtained from the retail store is affected by the relative location of competing stores. This problem is typically encountered in selecting sites for department stores, supermarkets, restaurants, etc., where the sales level is assumed to be affected by the distance customers have to travel to the new location versus the locations of competitors. Revenue is a variable that depends on where the facility is located in relation to competition.

4. **Location of emergency services.** The decision criterion in locating emergency services is often related to response time. Such problems occur in the location of police, fire, and ambulance stations. In this case the criterion has shifted from revenue to a direct measure of the service delivered.

As can be seen from Box 10.1, different operations tend to formulate their location problems in different ways. Manufacturing companies tend to fall into category 1 or 2, depending on whether single or multiple facilities are involved. Retail stores and emergency services also fall into category 1 if there is only a single site; otherwise they fall into categories 3 or 4, respectively.

BOX 10.1
EXAMPLES OF LOCATION PROBLEMS

1. Single-facility problems (multiple criteria)
     A factory or warehouse
     Government facility
     Hospital
     Electric power plant

2. Location of multiple factories and warehouses (minimize production and distribution cost)
     Multiple factories
     Multiple warehouses
     Multiple factories and warehouses

3. Location of competitive retail stores (maximize revenue)
     Banks
     Department stores
     Supermarkets
     Restaurants

4. Emergency-service location (minimize response time)
     Ambulance
     Fire station
     Police station

In the remainder of the chapter, these various types of location problems will be considered. In each case a methodology will be presented, along with examples of how the methodology can be used.

SINGLE-FACILITY LOCATION

Many location problems require the selection of a site for a single facility. These include the location of a factory, a warehouse, and a government office. A crucial assumption in these problems is that the revenue, costs, or other facility characteristics do not depend on the location of other facilities of the firm or competitors. When this is the case, the facility can be isolated for location purposes and analyzed by the methods described in this section.

Most facility location problems involve multiple criteria. In the case of the single-facility problem, several criteria can be dealt with directly. In other cases, a single criterion is often selected to simplify the analysis.

Multiple decision criteria can be classified into two types: cost and noncost factors. The cost factors can be measured objectively even though substantial uncertainties may be involved. The noncost factors include various intangibles such as community attitudes, labor relations, and government relations. Even though these factors may be intangible, they can be systematically evaluated and logically considered together with the cost factors.

The types of tangible costs usually involved in a location problem include:

1. Costs of land, buildings, and equipment
2. Transportation costs
3. Utilities costs
4. Taxes and insurance
5. Labor costs

The noncost factors which should be considered include:

1. Supply of labor
2. Labor and union relations
3. Community attitudes
4. Government regulations
5. Quality of life (climate, schools, living, recreation, etc.)
6. Environmental impact
7. Competitive reaction

One way to combine all these factors is to develop a rating scale for each one which reduces management judgment to a quantifiable score. The noncost factors can then be combined with the cost factors to arrive at one overall score for each location alternative. This method will be more completely described below by an example.

Suppose we are considering two different cities—Richmond, Virginia, and Birmingham, Alabama—for the location of a medium-sized bakery. The bakery will produce an assortment of bakery goods on site and will sell directly to retail customers as well as wholesale to grocery stores, restaurants, etc. It is expected that the bakery will employ 20 people ranging from a store manager to clerks, bakers, truck drivers, and custodians. The factors shown in Table 10.1 have been evaluated for these two sites.

A total score can be computed for each site. This is done by first converting the rating for each noncost factor to a numerical score. The conversion for the example is shown in Table 10.2 using a 10-point scale.

TABLE 10.1
BAKERY LOCATION EXAMPLE

	Richmond	Birmingham
Supply of labor	Very good	Excellent
Labor and union relations	Good	Fair
Community attitudes	Excellent	Very good
Government regulations	Poor	Good
Quality of life	Very good	Good
Annual return on investment	9%	15%

TABLE 10.2
COMPUTATION OF LOCATION SCORE

Weight		Richmond	Birmingham
15	Supply of labor	8	10
5	Labor and union relations	6	4
5	Community attitudes	10	8
5	Government regulations	2	6
10	Quality of life	8	6
60	Annual return on investment	6	10
100			

Excellent = 10, very good = 8, good = 6, fair = 4, poor = 2. Return on investment is normalized to a 10-point maximum scale, the same as the subjective ratings.

The next step is to develop a weighting scheme among the factors by rating, subjectively, the importance of each factor in relation to the others, as shown in Table 10.2. In this case, 100 points have been assigned to all the factors. However, it is not necessary that the weights add to 100 in every case; any total score can be used. If an additive scale is used, it is appropriate to multiply the weight by the factor scores to arrive at a total score for each factor. The location with the highest total score is then the best choice.

The procedure which has been described can be summarized as follows:

$$S_j = \sum_{i=1}^{m} W_i F_{ij} \quad j = 1, \ldots, n$$

where S_j = total score for location j
W_i = weight for factor i
F_{ij} = factor score for factor i on location j
n = number of locations
m = number of factors

In the example we have been using in Table 10.2, the total scores are as follows:

$S_1 = 15(8) + 5(6) + 5(10) + 5(2) + 10(8) + 60(6) = 650$
$S_2 = 15(10) + 5(4) + 5(8) + 5(6) + 10(6) + 60(10) = 900$

This scoring system, therefore, indicates that alternative 2, Birmingham, is preferred.

There are some aspects of the scoring system which need discussion. First, in the model used, several assumptions are being made to quantify and combine factor ratings. It is assumed that subjective ratings can be converted to a "ratio interval" scale where excellent (10), for example, is five times better than poor (2). It is also assumed that a linear combination of factor scores is appropriate in arriving at the total score. In this way, a low score on one factor can be "made up" by a higher score on another factor.

Some managers might argue that such assumptions cannot be defended and that therefore subjective ratings should not be converted to a quantitative score. The other side of the argument is that subjective factors cannot be meaningfully incorporated into the decision unless some basis for quantification is developed. It is often better to quantify the subjective factors even though the result may be imprecise.

In some decision settings, it is important that *all* factors have relatively high ratings for the alternative selected. In this case, a multiplicative model might be more appropriate than an additive scoring model. The score for factor *j* can then be computed as follows[3]:

$$S_j = \prod_{i=1}^{m} F_{ij}^{Wi} \quad j = 1, \ldots, n$$

With this model, any single factor with a low score will cause a low overall product score. Furthermore, the weighting is nonlinear in emphasizing the effect of a factor score through the exponent weights used. In choosing the product scoring model over the additive model, one must remember that the product model will tend to favor alternatives which do not have a low rating on any of the factor scales.

The methods which have been defined in this section can be used on almost any single-facility location problem. They have been applied to location problems for factories, hospitals, office buildings, retail stores, etc. We will turn next to location problems involving interaction and dependence between the facilities.

10.5 LOCATION OF MULTIPLE FACTORIES AND WAREHOUSES

In many plant and warehouse location problems, the primary objective is to minimize the costs of providing a given amount of supply. In other words, the capacity has been fixed and the best location plan from a distribution point of view is being sought. A simple version of this problem will be presented below, followed by a more general discussion of it.

The H. G. Hicks Company supplies lumber to three market areas from two warehouses in Chicago and Atlanta. The company is considering locating an additional warehouse in either Kansas City or Minneapolis, and it would like to evaluate these two sites based on the minimum cost of transportation. It is assumed that the new warehouse may alter the current distribution plan from the two existing warehouses. In this case, all present shipments may be rerouted to take advantage of the new warehouse configuration.

The approach used in evaluating these sites will be to consider two distribution problems. The first will assume that the Minneapolis site is used along with Chicago and Atlanta. The second will assume that the Kansas City site is used along with Chicago and Atlanta. The best of these two plans, based on minimum cost, will then be selected.

The situation using the new Minneapolis warehouse and the warehouses in Chicago and Atlanta is shown in Figure 10.3. The matrix indicates the amount available from each warehouse (per month), the amount required in each of the three markets, and the unit costs of shipping from each warehouse to each market.

---

[3]The Π sign in the equation denotes the *product* of the factors.

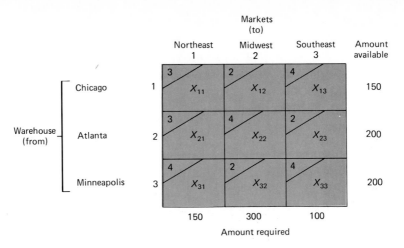

FIGURE 10.3   Transportation matrix. The number above the diagonal of each cell is the cost per unit shipped through the cell (C_{ij}). The X_{ij} value in the cell is the amount shipped through the cell.

The data are shown in the form of a transportation matrix using a "from-to" shipment conversion. In this case the product is shipped from the warehouses in the rows to the markets in the columns. Each cell in the matrix represents a possible distribution channel from a particular warehouse to a particular market.

If the total supply requirements are met, the amounts shipped through all cells in a column must add to the total required at the bottom of the column. This will ensure that each market requirement is met by shipments from one or more warehouses. If we let X_{ij} represent the amount shipped from warehouse i to market j, then the column requirement which has just been stated can be written:

$$\sum_{i=1}^{m} X_{ij} = b_j \tag{10.1}$$

where b_j = total amount required by market j.

Notice that the summation is over all rows ($i = 1, \ldots, m$) for each column j. Physically we are summing over all warehouses i for each market area j.

In a similar manner, the total amount shipped from each warehouse must be sent to some market. In this case, when we sum the amount shipped across the columns for each particular row, we will obtain the total amount shipped from each warehouse. Thus we have

$$\sum_{j=1}^{n} X_{ij} = a_i \tag{10.2}$$

where a_i = total amount available at warehouse i.

The total amount shipped to all markets must equal the amount available at each warehouse. We also require that the amount shipped be nonnegative.

$$X_{ij} \geq 0 \tag{10.3}$$

Our objective is to minimize the costs of transportation. To formulate this objective, we let C_{ij} represent the cost of shipping one unit from warehouse i to market j. By multiplying these unit costs by the amount shipped and then adding, we will arrive at the total transportation cost C. Thus we have

$$C = \sum_{i=1}^{m} \sum_{j=1}^{n} C_{ij} X_{ij} \tag{10.4}$$

The mathematical problem then is to minimize the cost given by Equation (10.4) subject to the restrictions in Equations (10.1) (10.2) (10.3).

The problem originally given in Figure 10.3 can be written in mathematical terms as shown below:

Min $\quad 3X_{11} + 2X_{12} + 4X_{13} + 3X_{21} + 4X_{22} + 2X_{23} + 4X_{31} + 2X_{32} + 4X_{33}$

Subject
to:
$$
\begin{aligned}
X_{11} + X_{12} + X_{13} &&&&&&&&&= 150 \\
X_{21} + X_{22} + X_{23} &&&&&&&= 200 \\
X_{31} + X_{32} + X_{33} &= 200 \\
X_{11} \qquad\qquad + X_{21} \qquad\qquad + X_{31} &= 150 \\
X_{12} \qquad\qquad + X_{22} \qquad\qquad + X_{32} &= 300 \\
X_{13} \qquad\qquad + X_{23} \qquad\qquad + X_{33} &= 100 \\
X_{ij} &\geq 0
\end{aligned}
$$

This is just a linear programming problem with a special structure. It can be solved by using either the simplex method described in the supplement to Chapter 11 or the special transportation algorithm described in the supplement to this chapter. The transportation algorithm is generally somewhat more efficient because it takes advantage of the special structure in the problem. It does, however, require a separate computer program.

The problem in Figure 10.3 has been solved, and the optimal solution is shown in Figure 10.4. The solution tells us that the new warehouse in Minneapolis should ship entirely to the midwest market and the Chicago and Atlanta warehouses should each split up their shipments to the two remaining markets. The total cost of this distribution plan is $1250, which is the minimum possible cost using the Minneapolis warehouse.

The result for the Kansas City warehouse is also shown in Figure 10.4. In this case the new warehouse in Kansas City ships to both the midwest and the southeast, while the Chicago warehouse ships only to the midwest and the Atlanta warehouse ships to the northeast and southeast. The cost of this optimal solution is $1400.

Since the cost of using the Minneapolis warehouse is lower, it should be given preference over the Kansas City location. We have thus solved our original location problem by using the transportation method to find the least-cost solution for each alternative. While this simple example illustrates the principles involved, it does not provide a feel for the complexities encountered in real plant and warehouse location problems. These complexities will be described below and illustrated by two real-world examples.

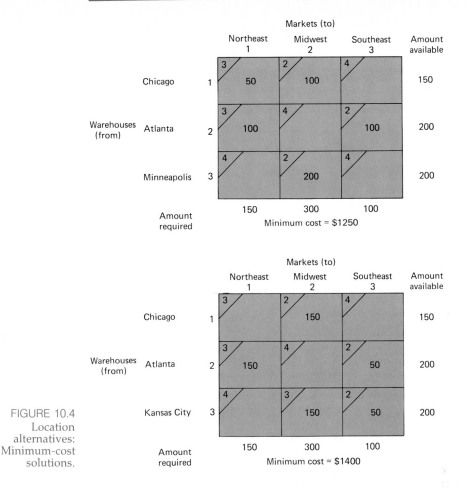

FIGURE 10.4
Location
alternatives:
Minimum-cost
solutions.

Some of the typical complexities encountered in the location of plants and warehouses are as follows:

1. There may be many plants, many warehouses, and many customer locations, leading to a very large number of variables and constraints. It would not be unusual, for example, to have 20 plants, 50 warehouses, and 150 markets, resulting in 150,000 variables and 220 constraints.

2. The number of plants and warehouses to be used may not be fixed in advance. This produces a very large number of combinations of locations to consider.

3. There may be fixed charges at each plant and warehouse plus a variable cost depending on the amount produced and shipped. This cost structure is nonlinear and therefore requires a special algorithm for solution.

4. There are usually multiple products, which increases the size of the problem.

5. It may be necessary to consider alternative inventory levels at various locations. In this case the service level is not fixed but depends on the decision parameters selected.

6. Different modes of transportation may be possible (air freight, truck, train, etc.).
7. Various customer-service policies may be stated, such as, "The customer must be served from the closest warehouse."
8. The demand may be probabilistic in nature.

These complexities all serve to make the problem more difficult to formulate and solve. Nevertheless, many of these conditions have been represented in models used in practice. The state-of-the-art in solving distribution problems has been very highly developed.

Arthur Geoffrion formulated and solved a complex distribution problem for Hunt-Wesson Foods. The original distribution system involved national distribution of several hundred distinct products from 14 plants through 12 regional distribution centers (warehouses). The purpose of the study was to determine how many distribution centers were needed, whether some of the 12 centers should be relocated, and how customers should be assigned to them. As a result of the study, five changes in the location of distribution centers were made (including movement of existing facilities to new locations and the opening of new facilities). Geoffrion reports annual cost savings from these changes to be in the millions of dollars.

This problem was formulated as a multiple-product transportation problem with 17 product classes, 14 plants, 45 distribution-center sites, and 121 customer zones defined by zip codes. A minimum-cost solution for the resulting problem was found using Bender's decomposition method and the transportation algorithm. Recent advances in operations research methods made it possible to solve such a large problem within reasonable computer cost and time. It was also possible to solve many variations on the problem for purposes of sensitivity analysis.

Another application of sophisticated modeling to real-world distribution problems was reported by Markland. In this case the problem was to determine the number of warehouses, warehouse locations, and inventory service levels for the Ralston Purina Company. The distribution network in 10 midwestern states consisted of 4 factories with associated factory warehouses, 5 field warehouses, and 137 customer shipping zones. It was possible to ship from factory warehouses or field warehouses to customers and also to transship between factory warehouses or field warehouses, depending on inventory availability and the closest point of demand.

This problem was modeled by using simulation. Since inventory levels and random demands were involved, it was necessary to use simulation rather than the transportation method. The simulation was conducted by generating demands for each product type and filling them by the closest warehouse with inventory available. If a demand could not be filled, a back order was placed and an associated back-order-cost assigned. Penalty costs were also assigned to demands not filled from the closest warehouse. Once the location of the source of shipment had been determined, the mode of transportation (truck or rail) was simulated from previously known probability distributions. Transportation costs were then charged, and the inventory was reduced by the amount shipped. This process was then continued for all products, customers, and time periods. Costs were accumulated for transportation, warehousing, and penalties to arrive at a total distribution cost.

At Ralston Purina, the costs for 5, 4, 3, 2, 1, and 0 field warehouses were computed. As a result of these calculations, it was found that 3 field warehouses was the least-cost alternative, resulting in a large annual savings over the existing 5 field warehouses. The costs were also computed for various inventory service levels. An 85 percent service level was the least-cost alternative, with a 100 percent service level costing significantly more per year.

This simulation model illustrates how one can handle nonlinear cost structures, random demands, and combined capacity and location problems. It is a classical application of simulation analysis to the study of complex management problems. For an innovative use of the warehouse location formuation in service situtions, see Box 10.2.

BOX 10.2
COMPTROLLER, STATE OF TEXAS

Up through 1980 all Texas state tax auditors with out-of-state corporate accounts were based in the auditing office located in Austin, Texas. As a result of this location, these auditors spent approximately 50 percent of their time away from their homes. When this group's turnover rate became a problem (21 percent in 1980), the use of the single facility in Austin for out-of-state auditors came under review. During 1980 the use of the Austin office for auditors with out-of-state accounts was discontinued. The decision to eliminate the office was based on the argument that locating offices outside of Texas would result in decreased travel expenses, decreased turnover of auditors, and increased voluntary compliance by the corporations based outside of Texas; and finally it would improve the taxpayer services.

Once the decision to open out-of-state offices was made, it was necessary to determine where each office should be located and the number of offices to be established. To assist in the determination of the appropriate values for these factors, a warehouse location model called LOCATE/ALLOCATE was introduced into the planning process. Generally, we might not think of the location of audit offices as a warehouse location problem. However, this problem and the general warehouse location problem have sufficiently similar characterisitics for both to be solved through the use of the same methods. For locating the audit offices, the warehouse problem characteristics had to be redefined in audit location terms. The warehouse became the audit office; audit trips were commodity demand; audit labor hours were the measure of storage capacity; facility fixed costs were defined as office rent and overhead; the state was the customer demand zone; and, finally, air fare plus per diem was used for the transportation cost.

LOCATE/ALLOCATE incorporates a network optimization algorithm that selects the locations and number of facilities that will minimize the total cost of the system. This model requires the user to define numerically the problem characteristics addressed above. In addition, the user must input the sites to be considered. In the case of the auditors' offices, some preliminary analysis had to be performed to reduce the number of possible sites to a manageable number. Since there were no existing Texas audit offices outside of the state's boundaries and since there were no special interests involved in the selection process, any site outside of Texas was a possible location. The number of potential sites was narrowed to 12, based on where the out-of-state taxpayers were concentrated. Then these sites were used as input into the LOCATE/ALLOCATE model.

The first run of the model was left unconstrained with regard to the number of auditors that could be assigned to each office. This run came up with an optimal solution that had facilities in New York City, Los Angeles, Chicago, and Tulsa and a total cost of $3,145,847. This solution was discarded owing to the agency's desire to limit the number of auditors at any one site to a maximum of 10. The original solution required 11 auditors in New York City and 16 in Chicago. A second run was made constraining the maximum number of auditors per facility to 10. The new solution differed in that either Los Angeles or San Francisco could be used as a site and Atlanta was added to the set that was suggested in the first run. The new cost was $3,158,413, an increase of $12,566. The actual set of sites used differed only slightly from the solution to the second run. The agency opened offices in both Los Angeles and San Francisco rather than selecting just one of these two sites.

Source: James A. Fitzsimmons and Lou Austin Allen, "A Warehouse Location Model Helps Texas Comptroller Select Out-of-State Audit Offices," *Interfaces*, vol. 13, no. 5, October 1983, pp. 40–46.

10.6 LOCATION OF COMPETITIVE RETAIL STORES

Many retail location problems can be formulated with the criterion of maximizing revenue. These problems typically occur for grocery stores, department stores, and fast-food restaurants, where the revenue of a particular site depends on the intensity of competition from other competitors' locations nearby. Notice how the location chosen for these service facilities has become a determinant of revenue, which was not a factor for manufacturing facilities.

Most retail location models are based on the assumption that revenue is proportional to the size of the facility and inversely proportional to the time the customer has to travel to the facility. Huff developed a model in which revenue was proportional to the ratio S/T^A, where S is the size of the retail facility in square feet, T is the travel time, and A is a parameter estimated empirically to reflect the effect of travel time on shopping preferences. Huff cites evidence that travel time and store size influence consumer behavior and may be sufficient by themselves to predict consumer preferences.

To reflect the effect of competition in a given trade area, the following model is formulated:

$$N_{ij} = P_{ij}C_i = \frac{\dfrac{S_j}{T_{ij}^A}}{\displaystyle\sum_{j=1}^{n}\frac{S_j}{T_{ij}^A}}C_i \tag{10.5}$$

where N_{ij} = number of customers in region i that are likely to travel to
  site j

P_{ij} = probability that an individual customer in region i will travel to
  site j

C_i = number of total customers residing in region i

S_j = size of the facility at site j (ft^2)

T_{ij} = customer time required to travel from region i to site j

A = parameter used to reflect effect of travel time on customer
  shopping behavior

To use this model, a trade region is first divided into customer zones. Census tracts or zip codes might be used as a convenient base to identify the number of likely customers in each zone i. The existing competitive sites in the trade area are then identified, along with their sizes, the travel times from each site to every customer zone, and an estimate of the number of customers served by each site. Using the above model, we select a value A to "tune" the model to the data collected. Notice that all values except A are known for existing sites. In a study by Huff, values of A in the range of 2.1 to 3.2 were found to work quite well for furniture stores.

After "tuning" the model to the existing sites, a new proposed site is inserted in the trade area. Travel time and the size for this new site are inserted into the model along with the previously determined value of A and the values for the existing sites. The model is solved to estimate the number of customers for the new site. Notice that the model assumes a gain of customers for the new site at the expense of the old sites through relative drawing power based on size of facilities and travel times. The model thus predicts how the available customers will be "divided up" among the stores.

As an example of this procedure, consider the situation shown in Figure 10.5. In this case assume there are two original stores at sites 1 and 2, four customer zones, and 3800 total customer trips per day for shopping purposes. Using the model given by Equation (10.5) with $A = 2$, we find that store 1, the smaller store, is expected to draw 1526 customers per day and store 2, the larger store, is expected

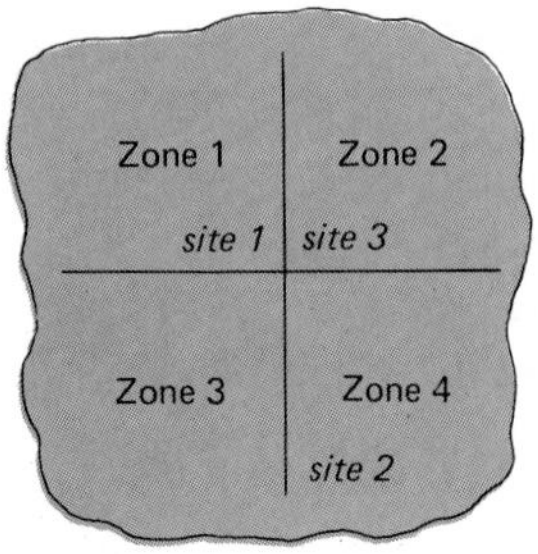

Zone i	Customers C_i	Travel times, minutes		
		T_{i1}	T_{i2}	T_{i3}
1	1000	5	15	10
2	500	10	10	5
3	1500	10	10	15
4	800	15	5	10

Store j	Size S_j(ft^2)
1	200,000
2	400,000
3	400,000

Computed P_{ij}

	Store 1	Store 2	Store 3
Zone 1	.580	.130	.290
Zone 2	.091	.182	.727
Zone 3	.257	.515	.228
Zone 4	.0425	.7665	.191

FIGURE 10.5 Simulation of distribution alternatives.

to draw 2274 customers per day. Assume these expected customer draws are close enough to actual data to validate the model.

What will happen if a new store is located at site 3 in zone 2? Using Equation (10.5) once again, this time with three stores, we find that store 1 is expected to draw 1045 customers per day, store 2 will draw 1606 customers per day, and the new store, store 3, will probably serve 1149 customers per day. Note, the new store takes customers from both the small store and the large store. The new store also draws the greatest proportion of its customers (72.7 percent) from the zone in which it is located.

Retail location models are quite useful, since they apply to a large number of situations. These models also indicate the problems faced by service industries in locating dispersed facilities. While distribution cost is not a significant factor in these cases, the effect of competition on revenue is a significant problem. In the next section we shall consider another service location problem where the criterion is not revenue but rather the service delivered. Such problems are commonly encountered in the public sector.

EMERGENCY-SERVICE LOCATION

A significant class of location problems concerns the delivery of emergency services—fire, police, and ambulance. These problems often have minimum response time as a decision criterion, since time is of the essence in delivering emergency service. As a result, these problems illustrate location decisions where a measure of service, such as response time, is the most important location criterion.

The location of emergency units can have a great impact on cost. Chaiken and Larson estimate that it takes about five people on the payroll to fill a single post around the clock. Thus the direct labor costs of operating a two-person patrol car in New York are approximately $500,000 per year; a single fire engine may cost over $1,000,000 per year to operate. If only one or two emergency units can be eliminated by the choice of location, a substantial reduction in cost will result.

Decisions regarding the location of fire, police, and ambulance units have often been made on the basis of geographical coverage. These decisions have been reinforced by government and insurance standards. For example, the American Insurance Association standard is used in most communities to establish fire insurance rates. In certain "high-value districts" the standard requires every point to be within 1 mile from an engine company and no further than 1.25 miles from a ladder company. Furthermore, there must be at least three engine companies within 1.5 miles of any point and at least two ladder companies within 2 miles.

Geographical coverage standards do not, however, consider the density of calls for emergency service. If an area has many calls, the response time will be reduced. The standard also does not consider the speed of travel possible and the availability of direct roads. Geographical standards are, therefore, poorly correlated with response time. But even response time is a surrogate measure when the purpose of emergency units is to save lives, reduce property damage, or deter crime.

Emergency response time can be estimated for different location sites by using simulation models. These models permit the incorporation of factors such as density of calls, speed of travel, dispatching rules, and number of vehicles available. Through the use of these models, it is possible to evaluate not only location sites but capacity decisions as well.

10.8 KEY POINTS

This chapter has described facilities decisions concerned with how much capacity is needed, when it is needed, and where it should be located. These decisions are on the long-range end of a hierarchy of capacity decisions which successfully constrain the capacity available to operations. Facilities decisions are crucial because they determine future availability of output and require the organization's scarce capital.

Some of the chapter's key points are:

- A facility strategy should be implemented rather than a series of incremental facility decisions. A facilities strategy answers the questions of how much, when, where located, and what type of capacity.
- The amount of capacity planned should be based on the desired risk of meeting forecasted demand. A capacity cushion will be the result of the level of risk taken. The firm can choose to either preempt the competition or wait and see how much capacity is needed.
- Both economies and diseconomies of scale should be considered when setting an optimum facility size. The type of facility selected will be focused on product, market, process, or general-purpose needs.
- A procedure was suggested for analyzing facilities decisions, including (1) measurement of capacity, (2) forecasting of demand, (3) determination of capacity needs, (4) generation of alternatives, (5) evaluation of alternatives, and (6) deciding. This procedure can be used to analyze any capacity decision or strategy.
- Facilities decisions are often made by the chief executive and the board of directors. Because these decisions are strategic in nature, they require the input not only of operations but of all other functional areas as well.
- Location problems can be classified into four basic categories: single-facility location, plant and warehouse location, retail store location, and emergency-service location. Each of these problems typically has different decision criteria and utilizes a different type of modeling approach.
- Single-facility location problems are those which do not interact with existing facilities and can therefore be isolated for purposes of analysis. These problems are also characterized by multiple criteria, and either additive or multiplicative scoring models can be used.
- Plant and warehouse location problems are often formulated to minimize distribution and production costs while providing a given amount of supply capacity. These problems can be analyzed by either the transportation method or simulation models.
- Location of retail stores may affect revenues as well as costs. The revenue can be

estimated by a drawing-power model which relates travel time and store size to store revenues. The resulting model estimates the effect of competition at any given location.

- Emergency units can be located on the basis of response time rather than revenue. There are a variety of models which can be used to locate these services.

QUESTIONS

1. Approximately how long would one need to plan ahead for the following types of facilities?
   a. Restaurant
   b. Hospital
   c. Oil refinery
   d. Toy factory
   e. Electric power plant
   f. Public school
   g. Private school
2. What problems are created by mixing the capacity questions of "how much," "when," and "where located"?
3. How could capacity be measured for the facilities listed in Question 1? What assumptions are needed about product mix, nominal capacity, and peak versus sustained capacity?
4. A school district has forecast student enrollment for several years into the future and predicts excess capacity for 2000 students. The school board has said that the only alternative is to close a school. Evaluate.
5. Why is it difficult to evaluate both costs and benefits at the same time? How does the single-facility scoring model handle this problem?
6. For each of the facilities listed in Question 1, specify one or more decision criteria which might be used.
7. Why will the facility decisions made not necessarily agree with the analysis? Is this a problem? Why?
8. Why are facilities decisions often made by top management? What is the role in these decisions of operations, marketing, finance, and personnel?
9. What are the strengths and weaknesses associated with scoring models for facility location?
10. Discuss the interactive nature of multiple facilities in plant-and-warehouse environments. How is this interaction represented by a transportation matrix?
11. How does the location problem for retail stores differ from that for factories?
12. Why is a scoring model inappropriate for the location of multiple emergency-service units?
13. How do facilities decisions for public firms differ from those for private firms?
14. In what ways does corporate strategy affect location decisions?

PROBLEMS

1. The Quickfix Hairdressing Salon is considering expanding its capacity to handle 100 more hairdos per week. Two options, both of which provide the same capacity, have been identified:

Alternative A: Build a new salon at a separate location. The cost of the building is estimated to be $200,000 with a 20-year life. The cost of the equipment is $50,000 with a 10-year life. Property taxes would be $5000 per year. Use straight-line depreciation and assume a 50 percent income tax bracket.

Alternative B: Lease a building for 5 years. The annual lease payments would be $9000. In this case the equipment would cost $60,000 and would last 10 years.

It is expected that the operating costs of these two options—including labor, supplies, and utilities—would be the same.

a. Compare the two alternatives on an after-tax basis using 10 percent real cost of capital.
b. What additional factors should be considered in this case?

2. Suppose that we are considering the question of how much capacity to build in the face of uncertain demand. Assume that the cost is $18 per unit of lost sales due to insufficient capacity. Also assume that there is a cost of $5 for each unit of capacity built. The probability of various demand levels is as follows:

Demand— X units	Probability of X
0	.05
1	.10
2	.15
3	.20
4	.20
5	.15
6	.10
7	.05

a. How many units of capacity should be built to minimize the total cost of providing capacity plus lost sales?
b. State a general rule regarding the amount of capacity to build.
c. What principle does this problem illustrate?

3. The Ace Steel mill estimates the demand for steel in millions of tons per year as follows:

Millions of tons	Probability
10	.10
12	.25
14	.30
16	.20
18	.15

a. If capacity is set at 16 million tons, how much capacity cushion is there?
b. What is the probability of idle capacity, and what is the average utilization of the plant at 16 million tons of capacity?
c. If it costs $10 million per million tons of lost business and $100 million to build a million tons of capacity, how much capacity should be built to minimize total costs?

4. The Speedy Mail Service processes millions of pieces of "junk mail" advertising each

year. The company prints, addresses, and mails literature for its customers. The costs of operating the plant are given by the following equation.

$$C(x) = x^2 - 600x + 90{,}200$$

$C(x)$ is the unit cost, and x is the volume of the plant.
a. Plot a graph of cost versus volume.
b. What is the minimum-cost point?
c. At $x = 500$, what is the dollar magnitude of the diseconomies of scale?

5. An entrepreneur would like to consider locating a gourmet restaurant in Dallas, Texas. One of the most important factors in locating this facility will be the density of customer traffic in the vicinity. Also consider the costs of construction and operation, the neighborhood surroundings, and the availability of parking. These factors have been evaluated for two sites, A and B, as follows:

	Site A	Site B
Customer traffic (customers/yr)	10,000	11,000
Costs ($/yr)	$600,000	$650,000
Neighborhood	Good	Very good
Parking	Excellent	Good

a. Use an additive model and equal weights to evaluate these two sites.
b. Does the choice of the best site change if a multiplicative model is used?

6. Two locations for the new Bay City Hospital are being considered. These locations have been rated on a number of factors, as shown below.

	Site 1	Site 2	Percent weight
Miles per month traveled			
Patients over 55	25,000	15,000	10
Patients under 55	18,000	17,000	10
Doctors and nurses	10,000	15,000	15
Costs of land and building	$4 million	$4.5 million	25
Average miles traveled per emergency	7.3	5.6	10
Support of community groups	Fair	Very good	15
Doctors' and nurses' preference	Excellent	Poor	10
Room for future expansion	Fair	Excellent	5

In brief, site 1 is closer for doctors and nurses but farther away for patients; it is cheaper but has less room for future growth.
a. Using an additive scoring model, which site is preferred? (Use excellent = 5, very good = 4, fair = 3, poor = 2.)
b. When a multiplicative scoring model is used, which site is preferred?
c. Which model (additive or multiplicative) is the best for this case?
d. What role do you think models of this type can play in actual hospital location decisions?

7. The Quicker Liquor Store is considering opening a new retail bottle shop. The store expects to draw customers from four regions as shown below. Another store already exists at site A, and Quicker Liquor is considering site B for its store.

| | Time it takes to get to store site | | |
Region	A	B	Customer visits per day
1	10	4	500
2	5	8	800
3	10	6	700
4	8	12	900
Store size (1000 ft²)	20	25	

a. What number of customers can each store expect to draw using a value of $A = 3$ in the drawing-power model?

b. Assume that it costs $4 million to build the new store and each customer yields a profit of $2.50 before taxes. Use straight-line depreciation, a life time of 20 years, and an 8 percent (real) discount factor. What is the present value of this investment if the store is open 360 days per year? Use a tax rate of 35 percent.

c. What other factors should be considered in this decision?

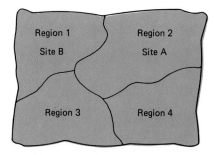

8. The Hurryback Department Store is considering a new site (site 3) in a trade area where two other stores are already located. The following data for these stores are given:

| Customer zone | Time to store site (minutes) | | | Customer visits per day |
	1	2	3	
1	10	4	12	1200
2	12	8	8	1500
3	4	9	8	1000
4	8	12	4	1600
Site size in square feet	400,000	300,000	200,000	

Zone 1 site 2	Zone 2
Zone 3 site 1	Zone 4 site 3

a. If management locates the new store at site 3, how many customer visits per day can the store expect? Use $A = 2$.

b. Suppose the average customer spends $5 per visit and the store is open 300 days per year. Also assume that it costs $3 million to build the store, that $1.5 million per year is needed to operate it, and that the store will last 20 years. What internal rate of return on the investment can the store expect before taxes?

c. What additional factors might be important in this decision?

9. The Goodfeel Shirt Company is considering a new plant location for either Denver or Phoenix. The existing plants are located in New York City and San Francisco; they ship to four national warehouses in Chicago, Atlanta, Kansas City, and Los Angeles. The unit costs of transportation, the availability of goods, and the requirements are shown below:

City of origin	Shipping costs per unit to warehouse in				Units available
	Chicago	Atlanta	Kansas City	Los Angeles	
New York	$ 6	$ 3	$ 5	$ 7	100
San Francisco	5	9	7	2	150
Denver	3	5	2	4	150
Phoenix	5	7	3	2	150
Units required	75	100	125	100	

a. To minimize the costs of transportation, where should the new plant be located—Denver or Phoenix?

b. What other factors should be considered in making this plant location decision?

10. The Funtyme toy company is considering whether it should build a new plant in Minneapolis, Minnesota, or whether it should expand the existing plants in Philadelphia or San Francisco. Actually it might do both—build the new plant and expand one or both of the existing plants. It might also rely only on plant expansions. All combinations of expansion and construction alternatives will be considered by the Funtyme company. The data follow:

Plant of origin	Shipping costs per unit to regions				Present capacity units	Maximum units available	Unit cost of production
	East	West	North	South			
Philadelphia	2	6	3	2	150	200	10
San Francisco	4	2	2	3	100	150	8
Minneapolis	3	3	1	2	0	250	6
Units required	100	75	125	50			

a. What plan should be used to minimize the total cost of production and transportation? Formulate and solve as a transportation problem.

b. What assumptions are incorporated in your answer to part a?

SELECTED BIBLIOGRAPHY

BROWN, P. A., and D. F. GIBSON: "A Quantified Model for Facility Site Selection: Application to a Multiplant Location Problem," *AIIE Transactions*, vol. 4, no. 1, March 1972, pp. 1–10.

BUFFA, ELWOOD, S.: *Operations Management*, New York: Wiley, 1976.

CHAIKEN, JAN M., and RICHARD C. LARSON: "Methods for Allocating Urban Emergency Units: A Survey," *Management Science*, vol. 19, no. 4, part 2, December 1972, pp. 110–130.

FITZSIMMONS, JAMES: "A Methodology for Emergency Ambulance Development," *Management Science,* vol. 19, no. 6, February 1973, pp. 627–636.

FULTON, MAURICE: "New Factors in Plant Location," *Harvard Business Review,* May-June 1971, pp. 4–17, 166–168.

GEOFFRION, ARTHUR M.: "Better Distribution Planning with Computer Models," *Harvard Business Review,* July-August 1976, pp. 92–99.

HAYES, ROBERT H., and STEVEN WHEELWRIGHT: *Restoring Our Competitive Edge: Competing through Manufacturing,* New York: Wiley, 1984.

HERTZ, DAVID B.: "Risk Analysis in Capital Investment," *Harvard Business Review,* September–October 1979, pp. 169–181.

HUFF, D.L.: "Determination of Intra-Urban Retail Trade Areas," Los Angeles: UCLA Graduate School of Management, 1962.

MARKLAND, ROBERT E.: "Analyzing Geographically Discrete Warehousing Networks by Computer Simulation," *Decision Sciences,* vol. 4, 1973, pp. 216–236.

RIDER, KENNETH LLOYD: "A Parametric Model for the Allocation of Fire Companies in New York City," *Management Science,* vol. 23, no. 2, October 1976, pp. 146–158.

SAVAS, E.S.: "Simulation and Cost-Effectiveness Analysis of New York's Emergency Ambulance Service," *Management Service,* vol. 15, no. 12, August 1969, pp. B-608–B-627.

SCHMENNER, ROGER W.: "Before You Build a Big Factory," *Harvard Business Review,* July–August 1976, pp. 100–104.

———: "Multiplant Manufacturing Strategies among the Fortune 500," *Journal of Operations Management,* vol. 2, no. 2, February 1982.

———: *Making Business Location Decisions,* Englewood Cliffs, N.J.: Prentice-Hall, 1982.

STUDENT, KURT R.: "Cost vs. Human Values in Plant Location," *Business Horizons,* April 1976, pp. 5–14.

SUPPLEMENT
Transportation Method

In Chapter 10, we treated location problems that involve the distribution of goods from one location to another. These problems can be formulated as transportation models where the objective is to find the lowest-cost location alternative. Even when location is not an issue, the transportation method can be used to find the best shipping routes.

In this supplement we will develop methods for solving the transportation problem. But first the transportation problem must be formulated. The general transportation problem can be described in the form of a matrix with shipments from one location to another. Suppose, for example, we have shipments from factories to warehouses, with factories represented by the rows and warehouses by the columns of the matrix. In Figure S10.1, there are three factories and four warehouses. Each cell in the matrix represents a route from a particular factory to a particular warehouse. In all there are 12 routes in this problem.

Listed on the right-hand side of the matrix are the amounts available at each factory. These amounts must be shipped to one or more warehouses. Listed on the bottom of the matrix are the amounts required at each warehouse. These amounts required must be supplied from one or more factories. For the moment, we assume that the total amount available at all factories just equals the total amount required at all warehouses.

The objective of the transportation problem is to find the shipping routes from factories to warehouses which will minimize the total cost of transportation. In each cell of the matrix the unit cost of shipping one unit through the cell or route is shown. The total cost of transportation is then the sum of the amounts shipped through each cell multiplied by the unit costs of shipping through that cell.

To describe the transportation problem mathematically, we let:

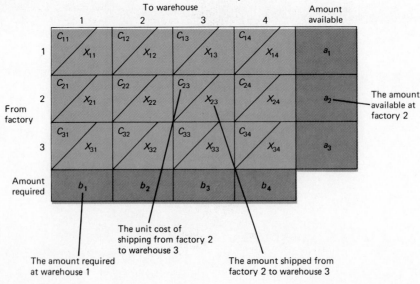

FIGURE S10.1
Transportation problem.

298

X_{ij} = amount shipped from factory i to warehouse j

C_{ij} = unit cost of shipping from factory i to warehouse j

Then the total transportation cost is

$$C = \sum_{i=1}^{m} \sum_{j=1}^{n} C_{ij}X_{ij}$$

where m is the number of factories and n is the number of warehouses.

We wish to find the values of X_{ij} which will minimize the value of C subject to the constraints

$$\sum_{i=1}^{m} X_{ij} = b_j$$

The total shipped to each warehouse j must equal the amount required at the warehouse.

$$\sum_{j=1}^{n} X_{ij} = a_i$$

The total amount shipped from each factory i must equal the amount available at the factory.

$$X_{ij} \geq 0$$

All shipments must be nonnegative.

In Figure S10.2, a particular set of costs, requirements, and availabilities is given for the three factories and four warehouses. The objective is to find a set of shipments through the cells (values of X_{ij}) which will minimize the total cost of transportation subject to the constraints on the row and column totals.

To solve a transportation problem, we first find an initial solution (values of X_{ij}), and then improve the initial solution by reducing the cost through successive iterations until the minimum-cost solution is found. The transportation method is an iterative method, which reduces the cost of the solution on each successive iteration.

THE INITIAL SOLUTION

One way to find an initial solution is to use the northwest corner rule. Using this rule, the maximum amount is shipped through the northwest cell of the matrix. Maximum shipments through other cells are then made by moving to the right and down in the matrix until all row and column requirements are met. The northwest corner assignment for the sample problem is shown in Figure S10.3.

In this case we have shipped 20 units through cell (1,1) in the northwest corner because this is the maximum amount possible. Then we move to the right and assign the remaining 5 units from row 1 to cell (1,2). Next, we move down column 2 and ship 10 units through cell (2,1), again the maximum amount possible. By continuing to move to the right and then down, all row and column totals are finally satisfied. At this point, we have an initial feasible solution to the problem.

Although the northwest corner rule results in a feasible solution to the transportation problem, the solution is often quite costly because no attention is given to costs as the solution is constructed. Therefore Vogel has developed a better method which does consider costs.[4]

The Vogel approximation method (VAM) begins by computing the difference between the lowest cost and the next-lowest cost in each row and column. The row or column with the largest cost difference is then selected for a shipment. As much as possible is shipped through the minimum-cost cell in the selected row or column. The row or column which is filled is then deleted from further

---

[4]N. V. Reinfeld and W. R. Vogel, *Mathematical Programming*, Englewood Cliffs, N.J.: Prentice-Hall, 1958.

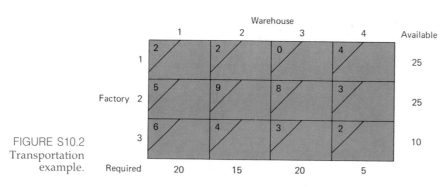

FIGURE S10.2
Transportation example.

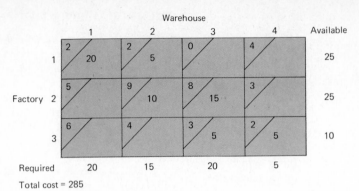

FIGURE S10.3
Northwest corner
rule.

consideration and the method is repeated. Because of the row or column deletion, at least some of the row and column differences must be recomputed at each step.

Application of the VAM to the sample problem is shown in Figure S10.4. In step 1, the largest difference between the lowest cost and next-lowest cost was found in columns 1 and 3. Since there is a tie, column 3 is selected arbitrarily for an assignment. The lowest cost in column 3 is zero in cell (1, 3); thus as much as possible should be shipped through that cell. The assignment of a value of 20 through cell (1, 3) satisfied the requirement for column 3; therefore column 3 is deleted from further consideration. The VAM differences are recomputed in step 2 and the procedure is repeated.

In the second matrix in Figure S10.4 the new VAM differences are shown. Note that the VAM differences for some of the rows have changed because column 3 was deleted, and in these cases the lowest cost or second-lowest cost was in column 3. The VAM differences for the columns did not change. Now, column 1 in the second matrix has the largest VAM difference. Therefore, column 1 is selected for an assignment in step 2. The maximum amount which can be shipped through the lowest-cost cell in this column is 5 units at a cost of 2 per unit through cell (1, 1). Row 1 is now deleted as a filled row, and the procedure is repeated in step 3. After five steps, an initial feasible solution is found.

The VAM method uses an opportunity-cost principle. At each step the difference between the lowest cost and the next-lowest cost is the oppor-

tunity cost of not making an assignment in a particular row or column. By choosing the largest difference, the largest opportunity cost is avoided. The result of the VAM method is usually a good approximation to the optimal solution; in some cases, the optimal solution itself may be found. The VAM method produces a much better starting solution than the northwest corner rule.

EVALUATION AND IMPROVEMENT

Given a starting solution, the next step in the transportation method is evaluation of the solution for optimality. The evaluation is done by assigning row and column numbers to the initial solution. This is done by selecting an arbitrary row or column and assigning a zero (or other value) to that row or column. In Figure S10.5, we have assigned a zero arbitrarily to row 1.

For each cell with a positive shipment value, the row plus column numbers must equal the unit cost in the cell. As a result of applying this rule, a 2 can be assigned to column 1 and a zero can be assigned to column 3. These numbers are obtained as follows: After row 1 is assigned a zero, look across row 1 to see that cell (1, 1) and cell (1, 3) have positive shipments through them. As a result, make an assignment of a column number to column 1 and column 3 in order to satisfy the rule that column plus row numbers must equal the cost for cells with a positive shipment. This leads to the assignment of a 2 to column 1 and a 0 to column 3. Then using the 2 assigned to column 1, a 3 must be assigned to row 2 so that the sum equals 5. Next, using row 2, a 6 must be assigned to column 2 so

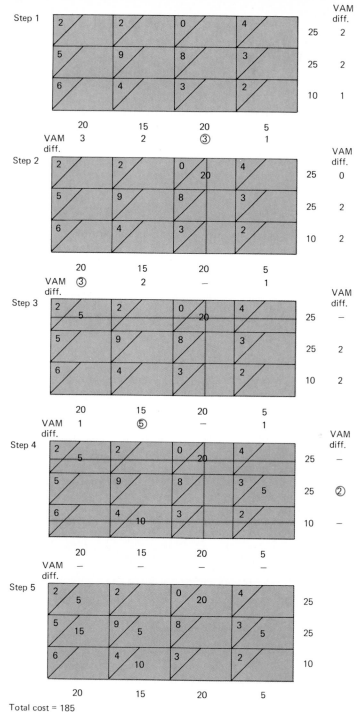

FIGURE S10.4
VAM method.

Total cost = 185

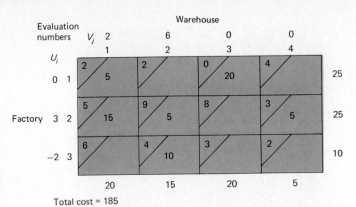

Warehouse

FIGURE S10.5
Evaluation of the
initial solution.

Total cost = 185

that the sum equals 9, the cost value of cell (2, 2). This procedure is continued until all row and column numbers are assigned.

A condition for optimality of a solution is

$$U_i + V_j \leq C_{ij}$$

where U_i = evaluation number for row i
V_j = evaluation number for column j
C_{ij} = unit cost of shipping via cell (i, j)

To check for optimality, we test whether the above optimality condition is satisfied for all cells. Notice that we have already assigned $U_i + V_j = C_{ij}$ for the cells with positive shipment values.

In Figure S10.5, the optimality condition is satisfied for all cells except cell (1, 2). For cell (1, 2) $U_1 + V_2 = 0 + 6 = 6$, which is greater than $C_2 = 2$. Therefore, the initial solution is not optimal. Furthermore, we should consider cell (1, 2) for a shipment to reduce the cost of the present solution.

To revise the solution, we ship as much as possible through cell (1, 2). This change will require an adjustment of the other shipments in our solution to maintain row and column constraints. From Figure S10.5, the most we can ship through cell (1, 2) without driving one of the current shipments negative is five units. When we set $X_{12} = 5$, both X_{11} and X_{22} will be reduced to zero. The revised solution resulting from these changes is shown in Figure S10.6.

The revised row and column numbers are also shown in Figure S10.6. These numbers were obtained in the same way as before. Assign a zero to row 1, then make the row-plus-column sum equal to the cost in each cell with a positive shipment. In this case, we find that a zero must be assigned to one of the cells in order to continue with the evaluation procedure. A zero can be assigned arbitrarily to any cell whenever it is needed to continue the evaluation algorithm. In this case we selected cell (3, 4) for a zero assignment.

The row and column numbers in Figure S10.6

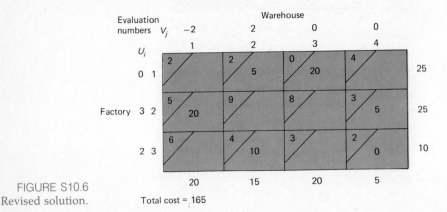

FIGURE S10.6
Revised solution.

Total cost = 165

indicate that an optimal solution has been reached, since for every cell we have

$$U_i + V_j \leq C_{ij}$$

The total cost of this optimal solution is $165. This is a substantial reduction from the northwest corner solution, which cost $285.

COMMENTS ON THE TRANSPORTATION PROBLEM

To this point we have assumed that the total amount available at the factories equals the total amount required at the warehouses. Whenever the two amounts are not equal, the problem can be solved by adding a dummy row or a dummy column. If the total amount available at the factories exceeds the total requirements at the warehouses, a dummy warehouse (column) should be added to absorb the excess supply. The costs of shipping to this dummy warehouse from any factory should be set equal to zero. The dummy warehouse serves exactly the same purpose as slack variables in the linear programming (LP) formulation.

If the total amount required at the warehouses exceeds the amount available, a dummy factory (row) should be added. The amount supplied by the dummy factory should just meet the shortage, and the shipping costs from the dummy factory should be zero.

The transportation problem can also be solved by the simplex method described in the supplement to Chapter 11, since the transportation problem is an LP problem. The simplex method, however, is not as efficient as the transportation method. The special transportation method takes advantage of the structure in the transportation problem and thus provides a more efficient solution procedure.

The transportation problem has been particularly important in operations and logistics management. Applications include efficient location of warehouses and plants, optimal shipping patterns from existing plants to warehouses, and optimal shipping patterns from existing warehouses to markets. Some of the advanced applications have included variations on the basic transportation method, including fixed charges, nonlinear cost structures, and other refinements.

PROBLEMS

1. The Staytight Door Company ships doors from three factories to three warehouses located in the Midwest. The amounts available for an average month, the amounts required, and the unit shipping costs are shown below. Find a shipping schedule that will minimize the total transportation cost.

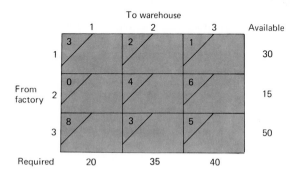

2. The Staytight Door Company in Problem 1 is considering adding a new warehouse, number 4, due to expanding sales. The new transportation problem is shown below.
   a. Find the optimal shipping plan.
   b. What effect will the new warehouse have on the optimal shipping routes found in Problem 1?

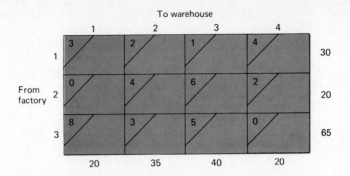

3. The ABC Freight Company ships freight from three warehouses to four markets. The transportation costs and the total amounts shipped are shown below.

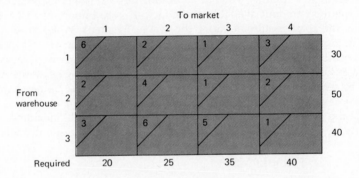

a. How much should be shipped from each warehouse to each market?
b. What is the effect of changing C_{12} from 2 to 3?
c. What is the effect of changing C_{22} from 4 to 2?

4. The Best Wooden Pencil Company is considering revising its current transportation routings to reduce costs. At present, the company has extra capacity at its factories as shown below.

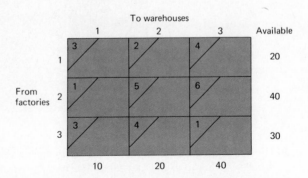

a. Add a dummy warehouse to absorb the slack in this problem.
b. How much should be shipped from each factory to each warehouse?

c. What is the effect on the optimal solution of changing the amount required at warehouse 1 from 10 to 30 units?

5. The distance that auditors must travel in auditing customer accounts (hundreds of miles) is shown as the "cost" in the following matrix. The number of hours of auditing time available in the next month from each office and the hours required by each customer are also shown.

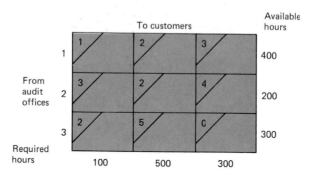

a. What is the minimum total distance assignment of auditors from offices to customers?
b. Suppose customer 2 decides to require 200 fewer hours of auditing time. What is the effect of this change?
c. Office 2 has just hired a new auditor and now has 100 additional hours of time available. Will this change the solution from part a?

6. Managers can be assigned to one of several different projects but each manager has a different effectiveness on each project (rated on a scale of 1 to 10) as shown in the matrix below.

	Project		
	1	2	3
Manager A	8	6	4
Manager B	9	7	3
Manager C	6	5	7

a. Assign the managers to the projects in order to maximize total effectiveness. Hint: Each row and column should sum to 1.
b. The effectiveness of manager A has just been reevaluated on project 3 to be 9 instead of 4. Will this change the assignment?

CHAPTER 11

Aggregate Planning

Aggregate planning is concerned with matching supply and demand of output over the medium time range, up to approximately 12 months into the future. The term "aggregate" implies that the planning is done for a single overall measure of output or, at the most, a few aggregated product categories. The aim of aggregate planning is to set overall output levels in the near to medium future in the face of fluctuating or uncertain demand.

As a result of aggregate planning, decisions and policies should be made concerning overtime, hiring, layoff, subcontracting, and inventory levels. Aggregate planning determines not only the output levels planned but also the appropriate resource input mix to be used.

Aggregate planning might seek to influence demand as well as supply. If this is the case, variables such as price, advertising, and product mix might be used. If changes in demand are considered, then marketing, along with operations, will be intimately involved in aggregate planning.

In this chapter, we will be using a broad definition of the term "aggregate planning." There are also narrow definitions which limit aggregate planning to particular types of mathematical formulations. These formulations might include, for example, supply variables only, a specific objective of cost minimization, or particular mathematical forms.

In the broad sense of the definition, the aggregate planning problem has the following characteristics:

1. A time horizon of about 12 months, with updating of the plan on a periodic basis (perhaps monthly).
2. An aggregate level of product demand consisting of one or a few categories of product. The demand is assumed to be fluctuating, uncertain, or seasonal.
3. The possibility of changing both supply and demand variables.
4. A variety of management objectives which might include low inventories, good labor relations, low costs, flexibility to increase future output levels, and good customer service.
5. Facilities that are considered fixed and cannot be expanded.

Aggregate planning forms an important link between facilities planning on the one hand and scheduling on the other. Facilities planning determines the physical capacity which cannot be exceeded by aggregate planning. Thus facilities planning extends further into the future than aggregate planning and constrains the aggregate planning decisions.

Scheduling, on the other hand, refers to the short range (a few months or less) and is constrained by aggregate planning decisions. While aggregate planning deals with the acquisition of resources, scheduling is concerned with allocating available resources to specific jobs and orders. Thus a basic distinction should be made between acquiring resources through aggregate planning and later allocating them through scheduling.

This hierarchy of capacity decisions is shown in Figure 11.1 and is discussed in more detail in the introduction to this part of the book. Notice that the decisions proceed from the top down and that there is also a feedback loop from the bottom up. Thus, scheduling decisions often indicate a need for revised aggregate planning, and aggregate planning may also uncover facility needs.

Aggregate planning is closely related to other corporate decisions, involving, for example, budgeting, personnel, and marketing. The relationship to budgeting is a particularly strong one. Most budgets are based on assumptions about aggregate output, personnel levels, inventory levels, purchasing levels, etc. An aggregate plan should thus be the basis for initial budget development and for budget revisions as conditions warrant.

Personnel planning is also greatly affected by aggregate planning because the results of aggregate planning include hiring, layoff, and overtime decisions. In the service industries, where inventory is not a factor, aggregate planning is practically synonymous with budgeting and personnel planning.

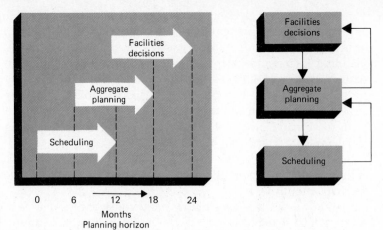

FIGURE 11.1
Hierarchy of
capacity
decisions.

Marketing must always be closely related to aggregate planning because the future supply of output, and thus customer service, is being determined. Furthermore, cooperation between marketing and operations is required when both supply and demand variables are being used to determine the best *corporate* approach to aggregate planning. Aggregate planning should be seen as an activity which is the primary responsibility of the operations function but which requires coordination and cooperation with all parts of the firm. The coordination problem in a typically aggregate planning decision is illustrated in Box 11.1.

BOX 11.1
TYPICAL DECISION PROBLEM

In January 1989, a meeting was held at the corporate offices of Farwell Enterprises, a major manufacturer of furnaces and furnace equipment. In attendance at the meeting were Marlene Lenton, president, Gretchen Davidson, vice president of operations, and Tom Christopherson, marketing vice president. Christopherson began, "I've just returned from our national sales meeting, and it appears that sales will be up even beyond my previous forecast. Last year we lost sales because of stockouts of certain key furnace models, and this hurt us more than we expected. As a result, I'm raising the forecast for fiscal 1990 (June 1990 to June 1991) from 100,000 units to 110,000 units."

Gretchen interrupted, "Tom, you've got to be kidding. Just two months ago we sat here in this office and agreed on the forecast of 100,000 units. We simply do not have the plant capacity to produce 110,000 units. And what are we going to do with all the inventory if we add the capacity and the forecast does not materialize?"

Marlene changed the subject by asking, "Suppose for a moment the forecast is correct. What are our options for more plant capacity?"

Gretchen replied, "We don't have time to build a new plant. That leaves us with four options: (1) add a night shift in the present plant, (2) work the present work force on overtime, (3) add a second assembly line using some of the present warehouse space, or (4) build up more inventory in advance of the selling season.

At the present time, the demand for furnaces is extremely seasonal, with a peak during the late summer and early fall and much lower sales the rest of the year. To meet this demand pattern, we've been using a level work force with some layoffs in the off season and some overtime in the peak season."

Marlene wanted to see these options properly evaluated and a better job of forecasting done. Accordingly, she directed Tom to prepare a detailed analysis of probable sales for each product line, using as much hard data as possible. This report would be due in 3 weeks, and the group would meet again to decide on the forecast. Marlene put Gretchen on notice that if the forecast were increased as a result of the study, she would ask for a new aggregate production plan considering all the options already outlined along with a supporting analysis and recommendation. The aggregate plan would have to specify the cost of inventory, labor, and capital equipment for each of the options. In addition, the effects on other operations objectives, delivery, flexibility, and quality would have to be evaluated.

The next section contains a detailed discussion of the options available to modify demand and supply for aggregate planning. This will be followed by the development of specific decision rules which can be used to plan aggregate output for both manufacturing and service industries. The chapter is completed with examples of aggregate planning and an evaluation of its use in practice.

11.1 DECISION OPTIONS

The aggregate planning problem can be clarified by a discussion of the various decision options available. These will be divided into two types of decisions: (1) those modifying demand and (2) those modifying supply.

Demand can be modified or influenced in several ways:

1. **Pricing.** Differential pricing is often used to reduce peak demand or to build up demand in off-peak periods. Some examples are matinee movie prices, off-season hotel rates, factory discounts for early- or late-season purchases, nighttime telephone rates, and two-for-one prices at restaurants. The purpose of these pricing schemes is to level demand through the day, week, month, or year.

2. **Advertising and promotion.** This is another method used to stimulate or in some cases smooth out demand. Advertising is generally timed so as to promote demand during slack periods and to shift demand from the peak periods to the slack times. For example, ski resorts advertise to lengthen their season, and turkey growers advertise to stimulate demand outside the Thanksgiving and Christmas seasons.

3. **Backlog or reservations.** In some cases demand is influenced by asking customers to wait for their orders (backlog) or by reserving capacity in advance (reservations). Generally speaking, this has the effect of shifting demand from peak periods to periods with slack capacity. However, the waiting time may result in a loss of business. This loss can sometimes be tolerated when the aim is to maximize

profit, although most operations are extremely reluctant to turn away customers; backlogs or reservations are preferred.

4. *Development of complementary products.* Firms with highly seasonal demands may try to develop products which have countercyclic seasonal trends. The classic example of this approach is a lawn-mower company that begins building snow-blowers. In the service industry, an example is provided by fast-food restaurants that begin to offer breakfast so as to smooth out demand and utilize capacity more fully.

The service industries, using all the mechanisms cited above, have gone much further than their manufacturing counterparts in influencing demand. This can probably be attributed to one crucial difference—the inability of service operations to inventory their product.

There are also a large number of variables available to modify *supply* through aggregate planning. These include:

1. *Hiring and layoff of employees.* The use of this variable differs a great deal between companies and industries. Some companies will do almost anything before reducing the size of the work force through layoffs. Other companies routinely increase and decrease their work forces as demand changes. These practices affect not only costs but also labor relations, productivity, and worker morale. As a result, company hiring and layoff practices may be restricted by union contracts or company policies. One of the purposes of aggregate planning, however, is to examine the effect of these policies on costs or profits.

2. *Using overtime and undertime.* Overtime is sometimes used for short- or medium-range labor adjustments in lieu of hiring and layoffs, especially if the change in demand is considered temporary. Overtime usually costs 150 percent of regular time, with double time on weekends or Sundays. Because of its high cost, managers are sometimes reluctant to use overtime. Furthermore, workers are reluctant to work more than 20 percent weekly overtime for a duration of several weeks. "Undertime" refers to planned underutilization of the work force rather than layoffs or perhaps a shortened workweek. Undertime can be thought of as the opposite of overtime. Another term for undertime is "idle time."

3. *Using part-time or temporary labor.* In some cases it is possible to hire part-time or temporary employees in order to meet demands. This option may be particularly attractive because part-time employees are often paid significantly less in wages and benefits. Unions, of course, frown on the use of part-time employees, because the latter often do not pay union dues and may weaken union influence. Part-time employees are, however, essential to many service operations, such as restaurants, hospitals, supermarkets, and department stores. These operations are highly dependent on their ability to attract and utilize part-time and temporary workers for periods of peak demand.

4. *Carrying inventory.* In manufacturing companies, inventory can be used as a buffer between supply and demand. Inventories for later use can be built up during periods of slack demand. Inventory thus uncouples supply from demand in manufacturing operations, thereby allowing for smoother operations. Inventory

can be viewed as a way to store labor for future consumption. This option is, of course, not available for service operations (excluding facilitating goods) and leads to a somewhat different and more difficult aggregate planning problem for them.

5. *Subcontracting.* This option, which involves the use of other firms, is sometimes an effective way to increase or decrease supply. The subcontractor may supply the entire product or only some of the components. For example, a manufacturer of toys may utilize subcontractors to make plastic parts during certain times of the year. The manufacturer may furnish the molds and specify the materials and methods to be used. Service operations may subcontract for secretarial help, catering services, or facilities during peak periods.

6. *Making cooperative arrangements.* These arrangements are very similar to subcontracting in that other sources of supply are used. Examples include electric utilities which are hooked together through power-sharing networks, hospitals which send their patients to other hospitals for certain specialized services, and hotels or airlines which shift customers among one another when they are fully booked.

In considering all these options, it is clear that the aggregate planning problem is extremely broad and affects all parts of the firm. The decisions which are made must, therefore, be strategic and reflect all the firm's objectives. If aggregate planning is considered narrowly, suboptimization may occur and inappropriate decisions may result. Some of the multiple tradeoffs which should be considered are customer service level (through back orders or lost demand), inventory levels, stability of the labor force, and costs. All these conflicting objectives and tradeoffs are sometimes combined into a single cost function. A method for evaluating cost will be described in the next two sections.

BASIC STRATEGIES

Two pure operations strategies can be used, along with many combinations in between, to meet fluctuating demand over time. One pure strategy is to *level* the work force, and the other is to *chase* demand with the work force. With a perfectly level strategy, the rate of regular-time output will be constant. Any variations in demand must then be absorbed by using inventories, overtime, temporary workers, subcontracting, cooperative arrangements, or any of the demand-influencing options. What has essentially been done with the level strategy is to fix the regular work force by using one of the above 10 variables available for aggregate planning.

With the pure chase strategy, the work force level is changed to meet (or chase) demand. In this case, it is not necessary to carry inventory or to use any of the other variables available for aggregate planning; the work force absorbs all the changes in demand.

Of course, these two strategies are extremes; one strategy makes no change in the work force and the other varies the work force directly with demand changes. In practice, many combinations are also possible, but the pure strategies help focus on the basic issues.

Consider, for example, the case of a brokerage firm which utilized both strategies. The data processing department maintained a capacity to process 17,000 transactions per day, far in excess of the average load of 12,000. This capacity allowed the department to keep a level work force of programmers, systems analysts, computer operators, and keypunchers, even though capacity exceeded demand on many days. Because of the skilled work force, the high capital investment, and the low marginal cost of additional capacity, it made sense for the data processing department to follow this strategy.

Meanwhile, in the cashiering department, a chase strategy was being followed. As the transaction level varied, part-time workers, hiring, and layoffs were used. This department was very labor-intensive, with a high personnel turnover and a low skill level. The manager of the department commented that the high turnover level was an advantage, since it helped facilitate the reduction of work force in periods of low demand.

It can be seen from this situation that the characteristics of the operation seem to influence the type of strategy followed. Sasser has generalized this observation to the factors shown in Box 11.2. While the chase strategy may be more appropriate for low-skilled labor and routine jobs, the level strategy seems more appropriate for highly skilled labor and complex jobs.

BOX 11.2
COMPARISON OF CHASE VERSUS LEVEL STRATEGY

	Chase demand	Level capacity
Level of labor skill required	Low	High
Job discretion	Low	High
Compensation rate	Low	High
Working conditions	Sweatshop	Pleasant
Training required per employee	Low	High
Labor turnover	High	Low
Hire-fire costs	High	Low
Error rate	High	Low
Amount of supervision required	High	Low
Type of budgeting and forecasting required	Short-run	Long-run

These strategies, however, cannot be properly evaluated unless specific decision criteria are stated. One way to do this is to reduce all the most important criteria to cost, as described in the next section.

11.3 AGGREGATE PLANNING COSTS

Most aggregate planning methods determine a plan which minimizes costs. These methods assume that demand is fixed; therefore strategies for modifying demand are not considered. If both demand and supply were simultaneously modified, it would be more appropriate to maximize profit.

When demand is considered given, the following costs should be considered.

1. *Hiring and layoff costs.* The hiring cost consists of the recruiting, screening, and training costs required to bring a new employee up to full productive skill. For some jobs, this cost might be only a few hundred dollars; for more highly skilled jobs, it might range up to several thousand. The layoff cost includes employee benefits, severance pay, and other costs associated with layoff. The layoff cost may also range from a few hundred dollars to several thousand dollars per person. In some cases, where an entire shift is hired or laid off at one time, a "shift" cost can be included.

2. *Overtime and undertime costs.* The overtime costs often consist of regular wages plus 50 to 100 percent premium. The cost of undertime is often reflected by use of employees at less than full productivity.

3. *Inventory carrying costs.* Inventory carrying costs are associated with maintaining the product in inventory; they include the cost of capital, variable cost of storage, obsolescence, and deterioration. These costs are often expressed as a percentage of the dollar value of inventory, ranging from 15 to 35 percent per year. This cost can be thought of as an "interest" charge assessed against the dollar value of inventory held in stock. Thus, if the carrying cost is 20 percent and each unit costs $10 to produce, it will cost $2 to carry one unit in inventory for a year.

4. *Subcontracting costs.* The cost of subcontracting is the price that is paid to a subcontractor to produce the units. Subcontracting costs can be either more or less than the cost of producing units in house.

5. *Part-time labor costs.* Because of differences in benefits, the cost of part-time or temporary labor will probably be less than that of regular labor. Although part-time workers often get no benefits, a maximum percentage of part-time labor may be specified by operational considerations or by union contract. Otherwise, there might be a tendency to use all part-time or temporary labor. However, the regular labor force is essential to the effective utilization of part-time and temporary personnel.

6. *Cost of stockout or back order.* The cost for taking a back order or for a stockout should reflect the effect of reduced customer service. This cost is extremely difficult to estimate, but it can be related to the loss of customer goodwill and the possible loss of future sales. Thus we may think of stockout or back-order costs in terms of foregone future profits.

Some or all of these costs may be present in any particular aggregate planning problem. The applicable costs will be used to "price out" alternative strategies. In the example below, only a few strategies will be priced out. In later mathematical models, a very large number of strategies will be considered.

11.4 EXAMPLE OF COSTING

The Hefty Beer Company is constructing an aggregate plan for the next 12 months. Although several types of beers are brewed at the Hefty plant and several container sizes are bottled, management has decided to use gallons of beer as the aggregate measure of capacity.

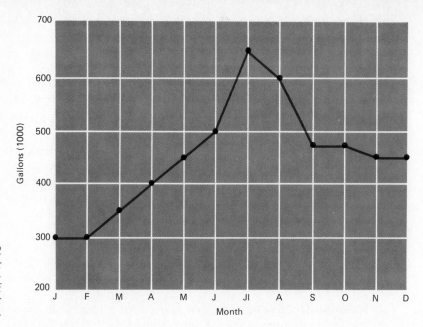

FIGURE 11.2
Hefty Beer
Company—
Forecast of
demand for
beer.

The demand for beer over the next 12 months is forecast to follow the pattern shown in Figure 11.2. Notice how this demand usually peaks in the summer months and is decidedly lower in the winter.

The management of the Hefty brewery would like to consider three aggregate plans:

1. *Level work force.* Use inventory to meet peak demands.
2. *Level work force plus overtime.* Use 20 percent overtime along with inventory, as necessary, in June, July, and August to meet peak demands.
3. *Chase strategy.* Hire and lay off workers each month as necessary to meet demand.

To evaluate these strategies, management has collected the following cost and resource data.

1. Each worker can produce 10,000 gallons of beer per month on regular time. On overtime, the same production rate is assumed, but overtime can be used for only 3 months during the year. Assume the starting work force is 40 workers.
2. Each worker is paid $1000 per month on regular time. Overtime is paid at 150 percent of regular time. A maximum of 20 percent overtime can be used in any of the 3 months.
3. It costs $1000 to hire a worker, including screening costs, paperwork, and training costs. It costs $2000 to lay off a worker, including all severance and benefit costs.

4. For inventory valuation purposes, beer costs $2 a gallon to produce. The cost of carrying inventory is assumed to be 3 percent a month (or 6 cents per gallon of beer per month).

5. Assume that the starting inventory is 50,000 gallons. The desired ending inventory a year from now is also 50,000 gallons. All forecast demand must be met; no stockouts are allowed.

The next task is to evaluate each of the three strategies in terms of the costs which have been given. The first step in this process is to construct charts like those shown in Tables 11.1 through 11.3, which show all the relevant costs: regular work force, hiring/layoff, overtime, and inventory. Notice that subcontracting, part-time labor, and back orders/stockouts have not been allowed as variables in this case.

In evaluating the first option, we must calculate the size of the work force required to meet the demand and inventory goals. Since ending and beginning inventories are assumed to be equal, the work force must be just large enough to meet total demand during the year. When the monthly demands from Figure 11.2 are added, the annual demand is 5,400,000 gallons. Since each worker can produce $10,000(12) = 120,000$ gallons in a year, a level work force of $5,400,000 \div 120,000 = 45$ workers is needed to meet the total demand. On the basis of this work force figure, the inventories for each month and the resulting costs have been calculated in Table 11.1.

The second strategy is a bit more complicated since some overtime can be used. If X is the work force size for option 2, we must have

$$9(10,000X) + 3[(1.2)(10,000X)] = 5,400,000$$

For 9 months we will produce at 10,000X gallons per month, and for 3 months we will produce at 120 percent of this rate, including overtime. When the above equation is solved for X, we have $X = 43$ workers on regular time. In Table 11.2 we have once again calculated the inventories and resulting costs for this option.

The third option requires the work force be varied in each month to meet the demand by hiring and laying off workers. Straightforward calculations produce the number of workers and associated costs for each month. In this case, notice that a constant level of 50,000 units in inventory is maintained as the minimum inventory level.

The annual costs of each strategy are collected and summarized in Box 11.3. Based on the assumptions used, strategy 3 is the least-cost strategy, but cost is not the only consideration. For example, strategy 3 requires building from a minimum work force of 30 to a peak of 65 workers, and then layoffs are made back down to 45 workers. Will the labor climate permit this amount of hiring and layoff each year, or will this lead to unionization and ultimately to higher costs of labor? Maybe a two-shift policy should be considered for part of the year and one shift for the remainder of the year. These ideas—and others—should be considered in attempting to evaluate and possibly improve on the chase strategy.

TABLE 11.1
AGGREGATE PLANNING COSTS—STRATEGY 1*

Level work force	Jan.	Feb.	Mar.	Apr.	May	June	July	Aug.	Sept.	Oct.	Nov.	Dec.	Total
Resources													
Regular workers	45	45	45	45	45	45	45	45	45	45	45	45	
Overtime (%)	—	—	—	—	—	—	—	—	—	—	—	—	
Unit produced	450	450	450	450	450	450	450	450	450	450	450	450	5400
Sales forecast	300	300	350	400	450	500	650	600	475	475	450	450	5400
Inventory (end of month)	200	350	450	500	500	450	250	100	75	50	50	50	
Costs													
Regular time	$45	$45	$45	$45	$45	$45	$45	$45	$45	$45	$45	$45	$540.0
Overtime	—	—	—	—	—	—	—	—	—	—	—	—	
Hire/layoff	5	—	—	—	—	—	—	—	—	—	—	—	5.0
Inventory carry	12	21	27	30	30	27	15	6	4.5	3	3	3	181.5
Total cost	$62	$66	$72	$75	$75	$72	$60	$51	$49.5	$48	$48	$48	$726.5

*All costs are expressed in thousands of dollars. All production, inventory, and sales figures are in thousands of gallons. Starting inventory is 50,000 gallons in each case.

TABLE 11.2
AGGREGATE PLANNING COSTS—STRATEGY 2*

Use of overtime	Jan.	Feb.	Mar.	Apr.	May	June	July	Aug.	Sept.	Oct.	Nov.	Dec.	Total
Resources													
Regular workers	43	43	43	43	43	43	43	43	43	43	43	43	—
Overtime (%)	—	—	—	—	—	20	20	20	—	—	—	—	
Units produced	430	430	430	430	430	510	510	510	430	430	430	430	5400
Sales forecast	300	300	350	400	450	500	650	600	475	475	450	450	5400
Inventory (end of month)	180	310	390	420	400	410	270	180	135	90	70	50	—
Costs													
Regular time	$43	$43	$43	$43	$43	$43	$43	$43	$43	$43	$43	$43	$516.0
Overtime	—	—	—	—	—	12.9	12.9	12.9	—	—	—	—	38.7
Hire/layoff	3	—	—	—	—	—	—	—	—	—	—	—	3.0
Inventory carry	10.8	18.6	23.4	25.2	24.0	24.6	16.2	10.8	8.1	5.4	4.2	3.0	174.3
Total cost	$56.8	$61.6	$66.4	$68.2	$67.0	$80.5	$72.1	$66.7	$51.5	$48.4	$47.2	$46.0	$732.0

*All costs are expressed in thousands of dollars. All production, inventory, and sales figures are in thousands of gallons. Starting inventory is 50,000 gallons in each case.

TABLE 11.3

AGGREGATE PLANNING COSTS—STRATEGY 3*

Chase demand	Jan.	Feb.	Mar.	Apr.	May	June	July	Aug.	Sept.	Oct.	Nov.	Dec.	Total
Resources													
Regular workers	30	30	35	40	45	50	65	60	48	48	45	45	
Overtime (%)	—	—	—	—	—	—	—	—	—	—	—	—	
Units produced	300	300	350	400	450	500	650	600	475	475	450	450	5400
Sales forecast	300	300	350	400	450	500	650	600	475	475	450	450	5400
Inventory (end of month)	50	50	50	50	50	50	50	50	50	50	50	50	
Costs													
Regular time	$30	$30	$35	$40	$45	$50	$65	$60	$48	$48	$45	$45	541
Overtime	—	—	—	—	—	—	—	—	—	—	—	—	
Hire/layoff	20	—	5	5	5	5	15	10	24	—	6	—	95
Inventory carry	3	3	3	3	3	3	3	3	3	3	3	3	36
Total cost	$53	$33	$43	$48	$53	$58	$83	$73	$75	$51	$54	$48	$672

*All costs are expressed in thousands of dollars. All production, inventory, and sales figures are in thousands of gallons. Starting inventory is 50,000 gallons in each case.

318

BOX 11.3
COST SUMMARY

Strategy 1
Regular-time payroll	$540,000
Hire/layoff	5,000
Inventory carrying	181,500
Total	$726,500

Strategy 2
Regular-time payroll	$516,000
Hire/layoff	3,000
Overtime	38,700
Inventory carrying	174,300
Total	$732,000

Strategy 3
Regular-time payroll	$541,000
Hire/layoff	95,000
Inventory carrying	36,000
Total	$672,000

In aggregate planning, it is sometimes useful to compare cumulative demand against cumulative production plus initial inventory, as shown in Figure 11.3 on page 320. The difference between these curves will then be the inventory (or backlog) at any given time. The inventory buildup rates and inventory levels can be seen at a glance from these cumulative curves.

We have shown how to compare costs in a very simple case of aggregate planning for a few strategies. In Section 11.5, many other strategies and more complex cost structures will be considered by formulating the aggregate planning problem as a series of mathematical models.

11.5 MATHEMATICAL MODELS

A wide variety of aggregate planning models have been developed over the years. In this section we will formulate the general mathematical model for aggregate planning and then discuss three alternative solution approaches: decision rules, simulation, and linear programming.

General Model

The aggregate planning problem has three general variables:

P_t = the amount produced during period t

I_t = the inventory level at the end of period t

F_t = the forecasted demand for period t

We can define the inventory at the end of period t in terms of these variables.

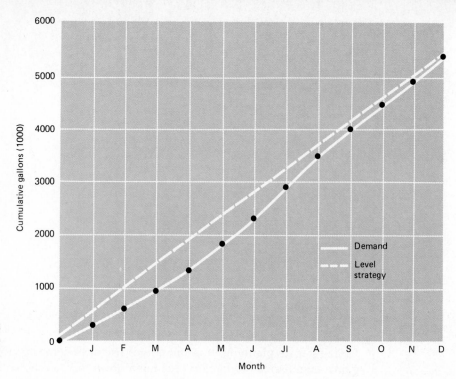

FIGURE 11.3
Cumulative
demand and
production.

$$I_t = I_{t-1} + P_t - F_t \qquad t = 1, 2, \ldots, N \tag{11.1}$$

The inventory at the end of any period t is just the inventory at the end of the preceding period, plus the production during the period, minus the demand during the period. We have, of course, been calculating the inventory in precisely this fashion in the Hefty Beer Company example. We also want to specify that the inventory and the production levels will not be chosen as negative values:

$$I_t, P_t \geq 0 \tag{11.2}$$

We need a cost function to evaluate the various production strategies used. A cost function for the aggregate planning problem is as follows:

$$\text{Cost} = \sum_{t=1}^{N} f(I_t, P_t, F_t) \tag{11.3}$$

The cost is a function of the inventory carried, the production rate, and the forecasted demand over all periods.

Now we can state the mathematical problem as finding that set of variables (P_t and I_t), given (F_t), which will minimize the cost given by Equation (11.3), subject to the constraints given by Equations (11.1) and (11.2).

The chase strategy and the level strategy, which we have been working with, will be two particular (feasible) solutions to this problem. For the chase strategy, we set $P_t = F_t$ for all values of t; the production level is just equal to the forecast.

And for the level strategy, we set P_t = a constant value for all periods; the production level does not vary. The mathematical model will allow us to evaluate the cost of these strategies and any other strategies that we may choose. It will also allow us to find, under certain conditions, an optimal strategy which minimizes the total cost equation.

Decision Rules

One approach to solving the above problem is to construct a decision rule which specifies the value of production for each period as a function of the forecast, inventory levels, and other parameters of interest. A manager can use such a decision rule to determine production levels dynamically at any time t. For example, we can specify the following decision rule:

$$P_t = P_{t-1} + A(F_t - P_{t-1}) \qquad \text{for } t = 1, 2, \ldots, N \tag{11.4}$$

where A is a smoothing constant $0 \leq A \leq 1$.

For this rule, if we set $A = 0$, we will get the level strategy ($P_t = P_{t-1}$), and if we set $A = 1$, we will get the chase strategy ($P_t = F_t$). Values of A in between 0 and 1 will produce various other decision rules. Note the similarity of this rule to the exponential smoothing approach used for forecasting. This particular decision rule will simply smooth out production over time to respond to changes in the forecast.

Many other decision rules have been proposed in the literature. The first study of aggregate planning, done in a paint factory in 1955, used the so-called linear decision rule [Holt, Modigliani, and Simon (1955)]. In this case the cost function was quadratic in nature, and the resulting optimal decision rules were linear in terms of forecasted demand, inventory, and previous production levels. Later studies, such as those by Jones (1967) and Mellichamp and Love (1978), considered more general cost functions and other types of decision rules.

Mellichamp and Love observed that managers seem to favor one large change in the work force (and production level) rather than a series of smaller continuous changes. As a result, Mellichamp and Love formulated a three-level decision rule for production with levels of high, medium, and low. This production switching rule determines when to jump from one production level to the next. As a result, production increases and decreases in a series of steps.

Simulation

Another technique which can be used to evaluate the models described above is simulation. This technique can be used to rapidly evaluate a large number of different decision rules or production choices. The first application of simulation to aggregate planning was in 1966 by Vergin. He showed how complex cost structures could be used and how simulation could be controlled to systematically search for a "good" solution.

In 1986 Schroeder and Larson reformulated the aggregate production planning problem in terms of random demands. This was done since most practical problems have unpredictable future demands. In addition, management seems to be primarily concerned with evaluating the probabilities of stockouts and associated inventory levels for a few feasible strategies. Management needs to know how any given strategy will affect probable inventory levels and the ability to meet demand estimates. This problem was solved through the use of simulation.

Today, the availability of commerical spreadsheets, such as Lotus® 123,® VisiCalc, and Multiplan, has made simulation easy to use for aggregate planning problems. Spreadsheet models can be easily built, and many alternatives can be evaluated. Lotus 123 spreadsheets have been provided for some of the problems at the end of this chapter in the software which accompanies this text.

Linear Programming

In 1960 Hanssmann and Hess proposed the use of linear programming to solve aggregate planning problems. This method offers powerful solutions provided that costs can be expressed in a linear or piecewise linear form. A linear programming formulation is provided below, and the simplex method for solving linear programming problems is given in the supplement to this chapter.

For the linear programming formulation we will need several additional variables for regular time, overtime, and subcontracting. Accordingly, let

$$P_t = R_t + O_t + S_t$$

where R_t = production by regular-time workers
O_t = production by overtime workers
S_t = production by subcontractors

Then we can rewrite the inventory equation (11.1) in the following form:

$$I_t = I_{t-1} + R_t + O_t + S_t - F_t \qquad t = 1, 2, \cdots, N \tag{11.5}$$

We will also usually want to constrain overtime to some percentage of regular time, such as 20 percent. Thus we have

$$O_t \leq .2R_t \tag{11.6}$$

And similarly we can also constrain the amount of subcontracting if desired.

In order to reflect changes to the regular work force through hiring and layoffs in any period, we will need the following equation:

$$R_t = R_{t-1} + H_t - L_t \tag{11.7}$$

where H_t = the amount of production added through hiring in period t
L_t = the amount of production reduced through layoffs in period t

We need to ensure that all variables are nonnegative, and so we have

$$I_t, R_t, O_t, S_t, H_t, L_t \geq 0 \tag{11.8}$$

The objective function in this case is the total cost of regular time, overtime, subcontracting, inventory carrying, hiring, and layoff. This cost can be expressed by the following equation.

$$\sum_{t=1}^{N} aR_t + bO_t + cS_t + gI_t + hH_t + lL_t \tag{11.9}$$

The constant terms in the equation are simply the unit costs associated with each variable. For example, a is the cost of producing one unit on regular time.

The linear programming formulation is to minimize the cost equation (11.9) subject to the constraints given by Equations (11.5) to (11.8). This is a standard problem which can be quite easily solved by the simplex method. As a matter of fact, in the supplement you will be asked to solve this problem for Hefty Beer and compare the solution with the alternatives evaluated above. The Hefty Beer problem is formulated in Box 11.4.

BOX 11.4

HEFTY BEER COMPANY LINEAR PROGRAMMING FORMULATION

Hefty Beer can be formulated as a linear programming problem in order to find the strategy which minimizes total costs. To formulate this problem we will start with the objective function which consists of several cost terms. We are told that regular time costs $1000 per worker per month, and so we write $1000\,R_t$ as the first cost term in the objective function. We are also told that overtime costs 150 percent of regular time, and so we have $1500\,O_t$ as the second cost term. We know that it costs 6 cents to carry a gallon of beer per month, and so we have $.06\,I_t$ as the cost of carrying inventory. This assumes, of course, that I_t is measured in gallons. Next, we include the hiring and layoff costs by writing $1000\,H_t$ and $2000\,L_t$ as cost terms, since it costs $1000 to hire each worker and $2000 to lay off each worker. Adding all these terms together, we get the total cost function for Hefty Beer as follows: (Note: We must also add the costs over all 12 time periods.)

$$\sum_{t=1}^{12} 1000\,R_t + 1500\,O_t + .06\,I_t + 1000\,H_t + 2000\,L_t$$

Next, we will formulate the constraints. For inventory we have

$$I_t = I_{t-1} + 10{,}000\,(R_t + O_t) - F_t \qquad t = 1, 2, \ldots, 12$$

The figure 10,000 in the above constraint is multiplied by $(R_t + O_t)$, since each regular or overtime worker can produce 10,000 gallons of beer per month. We also must subtract the forecasted demand during the month and add the beginning inventory to arrive at the inventory for the end of the period t.

The Hefty Beer problem states that overtime is constrained in June, July, and August to be less than or equal to 20 percent of regular time. This constraint is written mathematically as

$$O_t \le .2\,R_t \qquad t = 6, 7, 8$$

Here we have used $t = 6$, 7, and 8 to represent the months of June, July, and August.

Finally, we must connect the regular-time variables and the hiring and layoff variables from period to period. Thus we have the constraints

$$R_t = R_{t-1} + H_t - L_t \qquad t = 1, 2, \ldots 12$$

This problem can be solved by the simplex method described in the chapter supplement. All variables will be automatically maintained at nonnegative values. The minimum-cost solution and the optimal values of each variable will be found. This will provide the lowest-cost strategy for Hefty Beer to follow in terms of the number of people to hire and lay off each period, the overtime to plan, and the resulting inventory and production levels.

Linear programming makes it possible to evaluate an infinite number of production strategies and find the minimum-cost alternative. It provides a powerful methodology for not only solving the problem, but evaluating other solutions which might be suggested, relative to the best one.

Linear programming has also been extended to more complex situations. Lee and Moore (1974) have suggested that a goal programming formulation be used. They used an example with multiple goals specified in the following priority order.

P_1 = operate within the limits of productive capacity

P_2 = meet the contracted delivery schedule

P_3 = operate at a minimum level of 80 percent of regular-time capacity

P_4 = keep inventory to a maximum of a given number of units

P_5 = minimize total production and inventory costs

P_6 = hold overtime production to a minimum

The solution procedure seeks satisfaction of these goals, starting with P_1 and proceeding to P_2, P_3, etc. Through the use of this approach, tradeoffs can be made between the goals of capacity, delivery schedule, stable work force, production, inventory, and overtime cost. This makes it possible to consider a richer goal structure than cost alone.

11.6 AGGREGATE PLANNING APPLICATION

To illustrate the use of aggregate planning, an application for service operations will be reviewed. This classic application was done by Taubert in a research laboratory which employed approximately three hundred scientists and a hundred support employees. Research for both company projects and outside government contracts was done. However, there was considerable fluctuation in the load on the laboratory due to the changing nature of goverment contracts.

The aggregate planning problem was to determine each month the size of the scientific and support staffs as well as an allocation of the scientific staff to government contracts, company research programs, and overhead. The purpose of the overhead allocation was to retain scientists temporarily until future work developed. The aggregate planning problem was therefore formulated in terms of the following four variables for each month of a 6-month planning horizon:

1. Staff allocated to government contracts
2. Staff allocated to corporate research programs
3. Staff allocated to overhead
4. Size of support staff

Taubert formulated the cost structure of this laboratory in terms of the 12 cost functions, shown in Figure 11.4. These cost functions included linear, piecewise linear, and nonlinear costs. The objective was to choose the 24 variables which would minimize the overall cost. The minimization was achieved by using a search pattern method. This method establishes a search procedure based on past

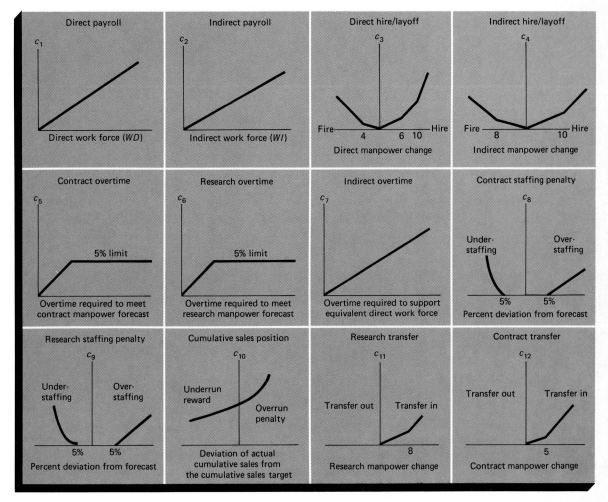

FIGURE 11.4   Research laboratory cost model.
Source: W. H. Taubert, "The Search Decision Rule Approach to Operations Planning," Ph.D. dissertation, University of California at Los Angeles, 1968.

patterns of step size and direction which have reduced the cost function. Through successive steps, the procedure can arrive at an approximate local minimum of the cost function. Taubert used this procedure to evaluate the variables in his model with good results and a minimum amount of computer time.

Taubert validated the model over a 5-year period. When compared with management decisions, the model's results showed fewer fluctuations in the work force level from month to month. More importantly, the analysis indicated that costs could have been reduced by 12 percent through use of the model.

It should be noted that Taubert's search model is very similar to the manufacturing problem except that it has no inventory and it uses multiple manpower categories. It is interesting that four types of staff were used instead of one overall aggregate manpower category. This example illustrates the need to tailor a model to the specific decision problems faced by management.

11.7 EVALUATION OF AGGREGATE PLANNING

Now that several methods have been reviewed, what can be said about these methods and their use in business? First, it should be observed that some of the methods incorporate the concept of a decision rule. This concept is fundamental to aggregate planning and should be clearly understood.

Second, there has been a tendency over time for the methods to become more powerful in handling general cost structures. While the early methods were restricted to quadratic and linear costs, more recent methods can handle any desired cost function. The more recent methods have also been designed to handle multiple criteria through goal programming or simulation methods.

Although there has been a vigorous development of methods, there have been only a few studies of how well these methods perform in practice. One study of note is the original paint factory study, which showed a possible cost reduction of 8.5 percent. Twenty years later, however, Schwartz and Johnson showed that much of this reduction was attributable to aggregate inventory policy, not detailed aggregate planning rules.

Lee and Khumawala reported on a study comparing several decision rules with management practice in a job shop. The results indicate that profits could have been improved 13.6 percent by the best decision rule. This was an impressive saving of over $600,000 per year.

Although there is good evidence that aggregate planning methodologies can improve profits or reduce costs in practice, the implementation record has been poor. An *ongoing* use of aggregate planning methods is rarely reported in the literature. Even in the original paint company, only a part of the linear decision rule was implemented. In most other cases, the company was used as an example of what could have been done, not what actually was done over a period of time. Why has this occurred with a methodology which is rather well developed and apparently has the potential to improve profits substantially? Shouldn't management be anxious to adopt these methods?

A study done by Shearon helps to shed some light on these questions. In his survey of aggregate planning in industry, Shearon surveyed 100 companies from which he received 48 replies. These companies were all included in the Fortune 500 listing of the largest industrial companies in the United States.

Shearon's survey indicates that production managers are typically responsible for aggregate planning decisions but general managers often review and approve large changes in inventories or work force. The study also indicates that the aggregate decisions are fragmented, with marketing controlling variables which influence demand and operations controlling supply variables. There is little coordination between marketing and operations strategies.

Of the 48 firms that responded, 42 indicated that they preferred to maintain a level work force whether demand was fluctuating, seasonal, or uncertain. This preference seemed to be influenced by the fact that labor is becoming more of a fixed cost. In half the cases, the firms were required to pay supplemental unemployment benefits. These benefits ranged up to 90 percent of take-home pay for up to 26 weeks while a worker was on layoff, making layoff and rehire very expensive propositions.

Operations managers were also asked how they were evaluated on job performance. Meeting schedules was clearly the most important criterion, followed in order of importance by controlling direct costs, controlling indirect costs, inventory turnover, and labor relations. These criteria seemed to help explain the types of aggregate decisions which were made. In periods of increasing demand, operations managers added overtime first, followed by increases in the work force. The typical manager will use up to 8 hours overtime per week for 12 weeks before adding employees. Reductions in inventories or increased back orders are clearly secondary options when demand increases. On the other hand, when demand decreases, inventories are allowed to increase and layoffs in labor are considered only as a last resort. This behavior can perhaps be explained by the greater emphasis on schedule than on costs or inventory turnover.

Vollmann also sheds some light on aggregate planning in industry by his study of a furniture manufacturer. In this case Vollmann was part of a research team which developed an aggregate planning model similar to Taubert's search model. Although the managers were very pleased with the results, they were not inclined to use the model. It appeared to management that other short-range scheduling problems were more pressing. To gain user support, the research team then shelved the aggregate planning model and proceeded to develop a computerized scheduling system. After some time, this scheduling system was successfully implemented.

Upon returning to the aggregate planning problem, Vollmann and his associates discovered that the managers still did not want to use the original model. The company did not really do aggregate planning in the classical sense. First of all, planning was done by several major product groups, since these groups were produced on separate assembly lines. Planning was not done by one overall measure of aggregate capacity. Second, management did not think that all its objectives could be combined into a single cost objective; management felt, instead, that the objectives should be treated separately. As a result, the research group developed a simulation model which was tailor-made for the problem faced by management.

The model projected inventories and back orders into the future for 36 months by each product line, using demand forecasts and current work force, overtime, and subcontracting levels. The model permitted management to evaluate suggested changes in capacity variables in terms of their effect on projected inventory and back-order levels, and the model was programmed for computer time sharing so that the user could easily manipulate the variables and receive the results. Managers found this model useful because it clearly addressed the decisions they had to make.

In summary, these studies seem to indicate some guidelines for using aggregate planning in industry:

1. Management may not perceive the existence of an aggregate planning problem. The decisions on work force and inventories may be made on a reactive week-by-week basis through scheduling. If this is the case, management will need to establish an aggregate planning function and assign the responsibility to a manager before quantitative techniques will be useful.

2. Management may not understand the value of a quantitative approach. In Vollmann's case study, the lack of familiarity with quantitative approaches required solution of the scheduling problem before the more general aggregate planning problem was attacked. Vollmann argues that modeling efforts must be oriented toward user problems if implementation is to succeed.

3. Aggregate planning models should be tailor-made for the particular situation. It may be necessary to include more than one aggregate product type in the model, or to consider product allocation decisions between plants, or to work with multiple objectives—not only costs. The management problem should always be considered carefully first, and alternative formulations should be explored, rather than force-fitting a particular model to the situation.

4. In some companies, aggregate planning is highly constrained by a policy such as maintenance of a level work force. In this case, the aggregate planning problem might be viewed as a one-time policy-evaluation effort rather than an ongoing model for making monthly decisions.

5. Before a company accepts an aggregate planning approach, the model's capacity to provide better decisions should be demonstrated. This can often be done by comparing past management performance with the results which could have been achieved by the model. If the results are not improved, a better model should be built or the present methods continued in use.

It should be possible to improve aggregate planning practice in many companies. The potential improvement has been shown in a few cases. A vast array of standard techniques have been developed. The opportunity and challenge is to demonstrate that practice can, in fact, be broadly improved.

11.8   KEY POINTS

Aggregate planning serves as a link between facilities decisions and scheduling. The aggregate planning decision sets overall output levels for the medium time range. As a result, decisions regarding aggregate inventory levels, work force size, subcontracting, and back-order levels are also made. These decisions must fit within the level of facilities available, and they constrain the resources which will be available for scheduling.

The following key points are made in the chapter:

- Aggregate planning is concerned with matching supply and demand over the medium time range. In the aggregate planning problem, the overall output level is planned so as to use the best possible mix of resource inputs.
- Supply variables which may be changed by aggregate planning are hiring, layoff, overtime, idle time, inventory, subcontracting, part-time labor, and cooperative arrangements. Variables which are available to influence demand are pricing, promotion, backlog or reservations, and complementary products.
- When demand is given, two pure strategies are available for adjusting supply: the chase strategy and the level strategy. There are also many mixed strategies between these two extremes. A choice of strategy can be made by determining the total cost of each of the strategies available.
- Many models for aggregate planning have been proposed. The three most widely known model types utilize decision rules, simulation, or linear programming as a solution methodology.
- Despite the number of models available and the favorable results in a few cases, aggregate planning models have not gained widespread acceptance in industry. A more concerted implementation effort may be needed which includes careful definition of the decision problem in each case, tailor-made models, and demonstration of improved planning results.

QUESTIONS

1. A definition of aggregate planning by another author is given here. Contrast and compare this definition to the one given in the text. "*Aggregate* planning or scheduling refers to planning in general terms—considering product groups, special promotions, trends in work-force availability, changes in resource suppliers, etc. The objective of aggregate planning is to effectively allocate system capacity—men, materials, and equipment—over some time horizon." (Richard B. Chase and N. J. Aquilano, *Production and Operations Management*, rev. ed., Homewood, Ill.: Irwin, 1977, p. 227.)

2. Aggregate planning is sometimes confused with scheduling. What is the difference?

3. The XYZ Company manufactures a seasonal product. At the present time, the company uses a level labor force as a matter of company policy. The company is afraid that, if it lays off workers, it will not be able to rehire them or to find qualified replacements. Does this company have an aggregate planning problem? Discuss.

4. It has been said that aggregate planning is related to personnel planning, budgeting, and market planning. Describe the nature of the relationship between these types of planning.

5. Every company has multiple objectives such as good labor relations, low operation costs, high inventory turnover, and good customer service. What are the pros and cons of treating these objectives separately in an aggregate planning problem versus combining them all into a single measure of cost?

6. How is the choice between a level strategy and a chase strategy influenced by the skill

level of the work force and the degree of automation? After all, isn't the choice between these strategies just a matter of the lowest cost?

7. What factors are important in choosing the length of the planning horizon for aggregate planning?

8. What are the cost factors that should be included in calculating the total cost of an aggregate strategy?

9. Provide a definition of a decision rule. Is a decision rule always required in an aggregate planning model?

10. What assumptions are used in deriving the linear programming model?

11. What are the advantages and disadvantages of the following aggregate planning methods?
   a. Linear decision rule
   b. Linear programming
   c. Simulation
   d. Search decision rule
   e. Goal programming

12. What problems are being experienced in using aggregate planning in history? How can these problems be overcome?

13. A barbershop has been using a level work force of barbers 5 days a week, Tuesday through Saturday. The barbers have considerable idle time on Tuesday through Friday, with certain peak periods during the noon hours and after 4 p.m. each day. On Friday afternoon and all day Saturday, all the barbers are very busy, with customers waiting a substantial amount of time and some customers being turned away. What options should this barbershop consider for aggregate planning? How would you analyze these options? What data would be collected and how would the options be compared?

PROBLEMS

1. The Zoro Company manufactures fast-cutting lawn mowers. The company has devised the following decision rule.

$$P_t = P_{t-1} + A (F_t - P_{t-1})$$

   a. If at the present time Zoro has a production level of 1000 units, a forecast for next period of 1500 units, and a smoothing constant of .5, what should the production level be for the next period?
   b. Suggest a procedure for bringing inventory into the above equation.

2. The Chewy Candy Company would like to determine an aggregate production plan for the next 6 months. The company makes many different types of candy but feels it can plan its total production in pounds provided the mix of candy sold does not change too drastically. At the present time, the Chewy Company has 70 workers and 9000 pounds of candy in inventory. Each worker can produce 100 pounds of candy a month and is paid $5 an hour (use 160 hours regular time per month). Overtime, at a pay rate of 150 percent of regular time, can be used up to a maximum of 20 percent in addition to regular time in any given month. It costs 80 cents to store a pound of candy for a year, $200 to hire a worker, and $500 to lay a worker off. The forecast sales for the next 6 months are 8000, 10,000, 12,000, 8000, 6000, and 5000 pounds of candy.
   a. Determine the costs of a level production strategy for the next 6 months, with an ending inventory of 8000 pounds.
   b. Determine the costs of a chase strategy for the next 6 months.

    c. Calculate the costs of using the maximum overtime for the 2 months of highest demand.

    d. Formulate this as a linear programming problem.

3. Draw a cumulative graph of demand and of the three production strategies given in Problem 2.

4. A company produces to a seasonal demand, with the forecast for the next 12 months as given below. The present labor force can produce 500 units per month. Each employee added can produce an additional 20 units per month and is paid $1000 per month. The cost of materials is $30 per unit. Overtime can be used at the usual premium of time and a half for labor up to a maximum of 10 percent per month. Inventory carrying cost is $50 per unit per year. Changes in production level cost $100 per unit due to hiring, line changeover costs, etc. Assume 200 units of initial inventory. Extra capacity may be obtained by subcontracting at an additional cost of $15 per unit over and above producing them yourself on regular time. What plan do you recommend? What is the incremental cost of this plan?

Month	J	F	M	A	M	J	J	A	S	O	N	D
Demand	600	700	800	700	600	500	600	700	800	900	700	600

5. Approximately 40 percent of a medical clinic's weekly incoming calls for doctor's appointments occur on Monday. Due to this large work load, 30 percent of the callers receive a busy signal and have to call back later. The clinic now has one clerk for each two doctors to handle incoming calls. Each clerk handles calls for the same doctors all week long and thus is familiar with the doctors' hours, scheduling practices, and idiosyncrasies. Consider the following alternatives to solve this problem:

    • Continue the present system, which results in some customer inconvenience, loss of business, and perceived poor service. About 1000 patients attempt to call the clinic on Mondays. The clinic has 50,000 patients in all.

    • Expand the phone lines and add more people to handle the peak load. Estimated cost to add five more lines and five clerks is $50,000 per year.

    • Install a computer to speed up appointments. In this case, the peak load could be handled with present personnel. Estimated cost to lease and maintain the equipment and programs is $25,000 per year.

    • Expand the phone lines and ask people to call back later in the week for an appointment. Add five lines and five phone-answering clerks part time at $30,000 per year.

    a. Analyze these options from the standpoint of an aggregate planning problem. What are the pros and cons of each option?

    b. Which option do you recommend? Why?

    c. How does this problem differ from the other aggregate planning problems given above?

6. The Restwell Motel in Orlando, Florida, would like to prepare an aggregate plan for the next year. The motel has a maximum of 300 rooms which are fully utilized in the winter months but largely vacant in the summer, as shown by the forecast below. The motel requires one employee, paid $800 per month, for each 20 rooms rented on regular time. It can utilize up to 20 percent overtime at time and a half and can also hire part-time workers at $700 per month. The regular-time workers are hired at a cost of $500 and laid off at a cost of $200 per worker. There is no hiring and layoff cost for the part-time workers.

Month	J	F	M	A	M	J	J	A	S	O	N	D
Demand (rooms)	185	190	170	160	120	100	100	80	100	120	140	160

a. With a regular work force of six employees and 20 percent overtime when needed, how many part-time workers are required in each month and how much does this strategy cost per year?

b. What is the best strategy to follow if a level work force of six regular workers is used? You may use various amounts of overtime and part-time workers.

c. Formulate this as a linear programming problem.

7. The Bango Toy Company produces several types of toys to seasonal demand. The forecast for the next six months in thousands of dollars is given below:

	July	Aug.	Sept.	Oct.	Nov.	Dec.
Forecast	$1000	$1500	$2000	$1800	$1500	$1000

A regular employee can produce $10,000 worth of toys per month, and the company has 80 regular employees at the end of June. Regular-time employees are paid $1500 per month (including benefits). On overtime an employee produces at the same rate as regular time but is paid 150 percent of regular pay. Up to 20 percent overtime can be used in any one month. A worker can be hired for $1000, and it costs $2000 to lay off an employee. Inventory carrying costs are 30 percent per year. The company wishes to end the year with 80 employees. Beginning inventory of toys is $900,000.

a. Calculate the cost of a chase strategy.

b. What is the cost of a level strategy?

c. Using the Lotus 123 software, simulate several other strategies.

d. Determine the effect on the chase strategy, in part a, of changing the hiring cost to $1500, $2000, and $2500. What do these changes suggest the relationship is between hiring cost and total cost?

e. Use the Lotus 123 software to study the effects of changes in demand, by assumed percentages, on the total cost of the chase strategy.

8. A small textile company makes various types of sweaters. Of course, demand is very seasonal, as shown by the following quarterly demand estimates. Demand is estimated in terms of standard hours of production required.

	Fall	Winter	Spring	Summer
Forecast	10,000	15,000	8000	5000

An hour of regular time costs the company $8. Employees are paid $12 per hour on overtime, and labor can be subcontracted from the outside at $10 per hour. A maximum of 1000 overtime hours is available in any given month. A change in the regular level of production (either increase or decrease) incurs a one-time cost of $5 per hour for adding or subtracting an hour of labor. It costs 2 percent per month to carry an hour of labor in inventory. Materials and overhead costs in inventory are equal to the direct labor costs. At the beginning of fall quarter, there are 5000 standard hours in inventory and the work force level is equivalent to 10,000 standard hours.

a. Suppose managment sets the level of regular workers for the year equal to the average demand and subcontracts out the rest. What is the cost of this strategy?

b. What is the cost of a chase strategy?

c. What is the cost of the best strategy from a linear programming solution? How much was saved over part a?

9. Beth's Broasted Chicken shop offers a variety of fast-food items. Beth uses regular and part-time workers to meet demand. The demand for the next 12 months has been forecast in thousands of dollars as follows:

	J	F	M	A	M	J	J	A	S	O	N	D
Demand	25	33	40	55	50	58	50	44	37	33	28	32

Assume that each employee can produce $5000 worth of demand in a month. The company pays regular workers $7 per hour (including benefits) and part-time workers $5 per hour. Of course, management would like to use as many part-time workers as possible, but must limit the ratio to 1 regular worker to 1 part-time worker in order to provide adequate supervision and continuity of the work force. Demand cannot be inventoried and must be met on a month-by-month basis. It costs $500 to hire a regular worker and $200 to lay off a regular worker. No costs are associated with hiring and layoff of part-time workers. A maximum of 20 percent slack is allowed in months where the company would prefer to not lay off people and rehire them in the following months. In other words, the regular and part-time work force cannot exceed 120 percent of demand in any given month.

a. Develop a strategy for this problem by using the maximum amount of part-time workers and by not laying off people when they would be needed the following month. What is the cost of this strategy?

b. Simulate several other strategies using the Lotus 123 software.

c. Formulate and solve as a linear programming problem. Compare your solution to your answers for parts a and b.

10. Valley View Hospital faces a somewhat seasonal demand. Patients defer elective surgery in the summer and in the holiday season at the end of the year. As a result, the forecast of patient days of demand is as follows (a patient day is one patient staying for one day in the hospital):

	Spring	Summer	Fall	Winter
Forecast	90,000	70,000	85,000	65,000

The hospital uses regular nurses, part-time nurses (when the hospital can get them), and contract nurses (who are not employees). Contract nurses work a number of hours which varies depending on their contract established with the hospital. Regular nurses are paid a sum of $5000 per quarter for 60 days of work; part-time nurses are paid $2000 per quarter for 30 days of work. Contract nurses get an average of $6000 per quarter for 60 days of work. It costs $1000 to hire or lay off any of these three types of nurses.

a. Suppose that regular nurses are set at a level of 800 nurses for the year. Each regular nurse works the equivalent of 60 days per quarter. The remainder of the demand is made up by 50 percent part-time and 50 percent contract nurses on a quarter-by-quarter basis. What is the cost of this plan starting at the beginning of spring with a level of 800 regular nurses, 200 part-time nurses, and 200 contract nurses? Assume it takes 0.8 nurse days to provide around-the-clock care for each patient day.

b. Formulate and solve with linear programming.

SELECTED BIBLIOGRAPHY

ABERNATHY, WILLIAM J., et al: "A Three-Stage Manpower Planning and Scheduling Model—A Service Sector Example," *Operations Research,* vol. 21, May–June 1973, pp. 693–711.

Bowman, E. H.: "Consistency and Optimality in Managerial Decision Making," *Management Science*, vol. 9, January 1963, pp. 310–321.

———: "Production Scheduling by the Transportation Method of Linear Programming," *Operations Research*, vol. 4, February 1956, pp. 100–103.

Buffa, Elwood S.: *Modern Production Management*, 5th ed., New York: Wiley, 1977.

Colley, John L., Jr., Robert Landel, and Robert R. Fair: *Production Operations Planning & Control*, San Francisco: Holden-Day, 1977.

Eilon, Samuel: "Five Approaches to Aggregate Production Planning," *AIIE Transactions*, vol. 7, no. 2, June 1975, pp. 118–131.

Fuller, Jack A.: "A Linear Programming Approach to Aggregate Scheduling," *Academy of Management Journal*, vol. 18, no. 1, 1975, pp. 129–137.

Galbraith, Jay R.: "Solving Production Smoothing Problems," *Management Science*, vol. 15, no. 12, August 1969, pp. B665-B673.

Hanssmann, F., and S. W. Hess: "A Linear Programming Approach to Production and Employment Scheduling," *Management Technology*, vol. 1, January 1960, pp. 46–52.

Holt, C., et al: *Planning Production Inventories and Work Force*, Englewood Cliffs, N.J.: Prentice-Hall, 1960.

———, Franco Modigliani, and Herbert Simon: "A Linear Decision Rule for Production and Employment Scheduling," *Management Science*, vol. 2, no. 1, October 1955, pp. 1–30.

Jones, Curtis H.: "Parametric Production Planning," *Management Science*, vol. 13, no. 11, July 1967, pp. 843–866.

Krajewski, L. J., and H. E. Thompson: "Efficient Employment Planning in Public Utilities," *The Bell Journal of Economics and Management Science*, Spring 1975.

Lee, S. M.: "An Aggregative Resource Allocation Model for Hospital Administration," *Socio-Economic Planning Sciences*, vol. 7, 1973, pp. 381–395.

——— and L. J. Moore: "A Practice Approach to Production Scheduling," *Production and Inventory Management*, 1st quarter, 1974, pp. 79–92.

Lee. W. B., and B. M. Khumawala: "Simulation Testing of Aggregate Production Planning Models in an Implementation Methodology," *Management Science*, vol. 20, February 1974, pp. 903–911.

Mellichamp, Joseph, and Robert Love: "Production Heuristics for the Aggregate Planning Problem," *Management Science*, vol. 24, no. 12, August 1978, pp. 1242–1251.

Sasser, W. Earl: "Match Supply and Demand in Service Industries," *Harvard Business Review*, November–December 1976, pp. 133–140.

Schroeder, Roger G.: Resource Planning in University Management by Goal Programming," *Operations Research*, vol. 22, July–August 1974, pp. 700–710.

——— and Paul Larson, "A Reformulation of the Aggregate Planning Problem," *Journal of Operations Management*, vol. 6, no. 3, May 1986, pp. 245–256.

Schwarz, Leroy B., and Robert E. Johnson: "An Appraisal of the Empirical Performance of the Linear Decision Rule for Aggregate Planning," *Management Science*, vol. 24, no. 8, April 1978, pp. 844–849.

Shearon, Winston T.: "A Study of the Aggregate Planning Production Problem," Ph.D. dissertation, the Colgate Darden Graduate School of Business Administration, University of Virginia, 1974.

Silver, Edward A.: "A Tutorial on Production Smoothing and Work Force Balancing," *Operations Research*, November–December 1967, pp. 985–1011.

Taubert, W. H.: "A Search Decision Rule for the Aggregate Scheduling Problem," *Management Science*, vol. 14, no. 6, Feburary 1968, pp. B343–B359.

———: "The Search Decision Rule Approach to Operations Planning," Ph.D. dissertation, University of California at Los Angeles, 1968.

Vergin, R. C.: "Production Scheduling under Seasonal Demand," *Journal of Industrial Engineering*, vol. 17, May 1966.

Vollmann, Thomas E.: "Capacity Planning: The Missing Link," *Production and Inventory Management*, 1st quarter, 1973, pp. 61–73.

SUPPLEMENT
Linear Programming

In the preceding chapter we described a linear programming formulation of the aggregate planning problem. This problem, and many others, can be solved by the methods described in this supplement. The supplement begins with a formulation of the product-mix problem and then provides graphical and simplex methods for solution of linear programming problems.

PRODUCT-MIX PROBLEM

For the sake of simplicity, suppose a furniture company can make only two types of products: tables and chairs. The company has limited resources of lumber, labor, and finishing capacity with which to produce these items. The management of the company would like to determine the best mix of products to make: all chairs, all tables, or some mix of chairs and tables. Management defines the best mix of products as the one which maximizes the total contribution to profit and overhead subject to the limited availability of resources already mentioned.

The product-mix problem can be formulated in mathematical terms as follows:

Let: X_1 = the number of tables produced
X_2 = the number of chairs produced

Both X_1 and X_2 are unknown variables to be determined by the solution of the linear programming problem. Also assume that the following unit production technology matrix is given. This matrix describes the transformation process used to convert the scarce resources (lumber, labor, and finishing capacity) into tables or chairs. For example, it takes 30 board feet to make one table and 20 board feet to make one chair. We also assume that the amount of scarce resources available is given: 120 board feet of lumber, 9 hours of labor, and 24 hours of finishing capacity.

RESOURCES USED PER UNIT PRODUCED

	Tables	Chairs
Lumber, board feet	30	20
Labor, hours	2	2
Finishing capacity, hours	4	6

If we multiply the values in the unit production technology matrix by the number of units produced and add over both products, we will obtain the total resources of each type required. These requirements must be less than the amount of resources available. Thus we have:

$$30X_1 + 20X_2 \leq 120$$
$$2X_1 + 2X_2 \leq 9$$
$$4X_1 + 6X_2 \leq 24$$

Since 30 board feet are required for each table, 30 X_1 board feet will be required for X_1 tables, as shown in the first constraint above. Likewise, $20X_2$ board feet are required to produce X_2 chairs. The total amount of lumber required for both tables and chairs ($30X_1 + 20X_2$) must be less than or equal to the amount available (120). A similar logic can be used to derive the second two constraints.

Management wishes to find the values of X_1 and X_2 which will maximize the contribution to profit and overhead. To formulate this objective function, we assume that each table contributes \$10 and each chair \$8 to profit and overhead. Then the total contribution for X_1 tables and X_2 chairs is:

$$10X_1 + 8X_2$$

Finally, we require that X_1 and X_2 be nonnegative values, since we cannot produce a negative number of tables or chairs. Gathering together the constraints and objective function that we have specified, the product-mix problem can be summarized as follows:

Objective: max $10X_1 + 8X_2$
Subject to: $30X_1 + 20X_2 \leq 120$
                     $2X_1 + 2X_2 \leq 9$
                     $4X_1 + 6X_2 \leq 24$
                     $X_1 \geq 0, X_2 \geq 0$

When this problem is solved by the methods described below, optimal values of X_1 and X_2 will be found. These optimal values, however, are a solution to the mathematical problem as stated and not necessarily a solution to the manager's original decision problem. The mathematical problem is always an abstraction of the manager's real problem; therefore the optimal solution must be carefully evaluated before a decision can be made.

In practice, a series of product-mix problems may be formulated and solved before the manager is satisfied. For example, suppose the optimal solution to our problem is to produce all tables and no chairs. Also assume that this solution conflicts with the marketing strategy in the company. Therefore, either the marketing strategy must be modified or the production constraints altered or other changes made in the formulation to make the mathematical solution consistent with the real decision problem. Even though the optimal solution to the product-mix problem is not implemented, it may provide important insights into possible coordination problems between marketing and production, possibly leading to further analysis and ultimate solution of the decision problem.

GENERAL LP PROBLEM

The problem that we have just formulated is a member of a class of general problems—called linear programming, or LP, problems—the notation for which follows:

Objective:
    max $C_1X_1 + C_2X_2 + \cdots + C_nX_n$
Subject to:
    $a_{11}X_1 + a_{12}X_2 + \cdots + a_{1n}X_n \leq b_1$
    $a_{21}X_1 + a_{22}X_2 + \cdots + a_{2n}X_n \leq b_2$
        .   .   .   .
        .   .   .   .
        .   .   .   .
    $a_{m1}X_1 + a_{m2}X_2 + \cdots + a_{mn}X_n \leq b_m$
    $X_1 \geq 0, X_2 \geq 0, \ldots, X_n \geq 0$

In this formulation the C_j, a_{ij}, and b_i values are given constants and the X_j are called decision variables.

The problem is to find the values of the n decision variables $(X_1, X_2 \ldots, X_n)$ which maximize the objective function subject to the m constraints and the nonnegativity conditions on the X_j variables. The resulting set of decision variables which maximizes the objective function is called an optimal solution. In this problem "max" may be replaced by "min" and $\leq$ may be replaced by $\geq$ or $=$ signs to obtain the general set of LP problems.

The general LP problem as formulated above is based on the following four assumptions:

1. *Linearity.* Both the objective function and the constraints must be linear functions of the X_j. This implies that no cross products, powers of X_j, or other nonlinearities are permitted in the problem. It also implies that resource utilization is proportional and additive, e.g., if it takes 2 hours to produce one table, it will take 4 hours to produce two tables.

2. *Divisibility.* The X_j variables are permitted to take on continuous values. Thus we can obtain a solution to the product-mix problem, for example, of 20.5 chairs and 30.2 tables. Sometimes the continuous solution can be rounded off or interpreted as the average production per day. In other cases, special integer programming problems must be formulated to provide integer solutions.

3. *Nonnegativity.* The decision variables must have nonnegative values. In many problems this assumption is natural and presents no difficulties. If negative values are needed, however, the LP formulation can be modified to handle these cases.

4. *Certainty.* All constants C_j, a_{ij}, and b_i are assumed to have certain values. If these values are probabilistic, other special chance-constrained or stochastic programming problems can be formulated.

Although LP problems have some rather restrictive assumptions, a large class of real decision problems can still be solved by LP methods. In addition, LP methods sometimes form the nucleus for more advanced nonlinear, stochastic, or integer programming methods.

Linear programming can be used to solve a general class of resource-allocation problems including product-mix, blending, and scheduling problems. All these decision problems are concerned with finding the best allocation of scarce resources. In the product-mix problem, the scarce resources are allocated to the products; in the blending problem, the best mix of resource inputs to meet a prescribed product blend is determined; and in scheduling problems, available machine times may be allocated to the required products. Even in the aggregate planning problem, resources are allocated to regular time, overtime, inventory, or subcontracting in order to minimize the costs of meeting required demand. In each of these cases, scarce resource inputs are allocated among several economic activities. This is a general characteristic of most, if not all, LP problems.

Graphical Solution Method

The graphical solution method may be used to solve LP problems with two variables. Although two variables are not enough to describe real problems, the graphical method provides important insights into LP solution procedures. For illustration purposes, we will solve the product-mix problem formulated above.

The first step in the graphical procedure is to plot the constraint equations. The three constraints from the product-mix example are shown in Figure

S11.1 Each constraint is plotted on the figure by first considering the $\leq$ sign as an $=$ sign. The first constraint is thus plotted as the equation $30X_1 + 20X_2 = 120$. By setting $X_1 = 0$ in this equation, we have $X_2 = 6$; and by setting $X_2 = 0$, we have $X_1 = 4$. These two coordinates are placed on the graph and connected with a straight line. The original constraint equation, however, includes all points smaller than or equal to the right-hand side. Thus all points to the left of the lines in Figure S11.1 are permitted by the constraints.

The intersection of points from all three constraint equations plus the nonnegativity conditions forms the feasible region shown in white in Figure S11.1. All points within this feasible region *simultaneously* satisfy all the LP constraints. The problem then is to find the one or more points (or solutions) in the feasible region which maximize the original objective function. This point(s) will be the optimal solution(s).

The optimal solution is found by graphing the objective function on the same graph as the feasible region. For illustration purposes, we have drawn the feasible region again in Figure S11.2 and plotted a series of objective functions or isoprofit lines on the graph. Each isoprofit line is obtained by setting the objective function equal to an arbi-

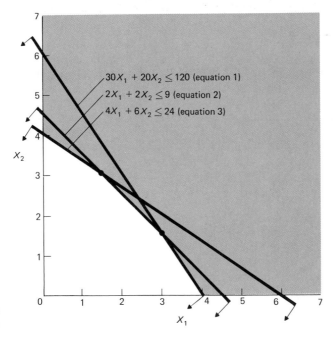

FIGURE S11.1
Product-mix
problem.

$30X_1 + 20X_2 \leq 120$ (equation 1)

$2X_1 + 2X_2 \leq 9$ (equation 2)

$4X_1 + 6X_2 \leq 24$ (equation 3)

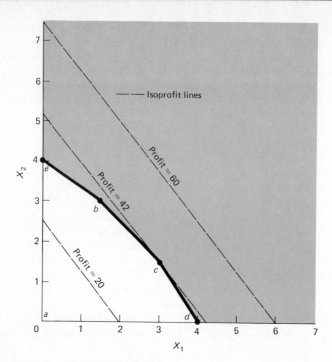

FIGURE S11.2
Product-mix
problem solution.

trary value. For example, suppose we arbitrarily set the objective function equal to 60. Then the line $10X_1 + 8X_2 = 60$ is plotted just as we plotted the constraints. Since the value of the objective function is unknown, a series of arbitrary values is selected to generate a series of parallel isoprofit lines, as shown in Figure S11.2.

The problem now is to find the isoprofit line which has the largest profit and is still in the feasible region. This can be done by starting at the origin or any other point inside the feasible region and moving the isoprofit line out away from the origin parallel to itself until the last point in the feasible region is reached. In this example the last feasible point is the corner labeled c ($X_1 = 3$, $X_2 = 1.5$), which maximizes the value of the isoprofit line and is therefore the optimal solution to the LP problem.

The exact coordinates of the optimal solutions may be found by solving for the intersection of equations 1 and 2, which define the optimal corner c. These two equations in two unknowns are solved simultaneously for the values of X_1 and X_2. As a result, we find $X_1 = 3$ and $X_2 = 1.5$. Although X_2 is a fractional number of chairs, this solution might still be perfectly realistic. For example, sup-

pose we produce 3 tables and 1.5 chairs a day over a period of several weeks. The 1.5 chairs can then be interpreted as an average production rate per day.

The optimal solution will always occur on at least one corner point (or extreme point) of the feasible region. In the example, there was only one optimal solution because a single corner point was reached. If the isoprofit line had been parallel to a side of the feasible region, then two corner points and all the points in between would have been optimal solutions. In this case, we would have had alternate optimal solutions, different values of X_1 and X_2 which yield the same value of the objective function.

The fact that the optimal solution occurs at one or more extreme points is exploited in LP methods. The simplex method, described next, is an adjacent-extreme-point method. It moves from one corner point to the next until an optimal solution is found. Since there are only a finite number of corner points but an infinite number of feasible solutions inside the feasible region, the general solution to linear programming problems is greatly simplified when only adjacent extreme points are examined.

SIMPLEX METHOD

The simplex method is a general algebraic method which can be used to solve LP problems with a very large number of variables and constraints. When more than a few variables and constraints are involved, the computerized simplex method is required. Nevertheless, for purposes of instruction, we shall illustrate the simplex method by hand computations. An understanding of the simplex method's mechanics facilitates interpretation of LP results.

With the simplex method, the problem must be put in a special format and specific computational rules must be followed. To illustrate, we will use the product-mix problem which has already been solved graphically.

The first step in the simplex method is to convert the LP problem to the proper format by changing all the inequality constraints into equalities. This is done by adding a slack variable to each constraint inequality, as shown below.

Objective:
$$\max 10X_1 + 8X_2 + 0X_3 + 0X_4 + 0X_5$$
Subject to:
$$30X_1 + 20X_2 + 1X_3 + 0X_4 + 0X_5 = 120$$
$$2X_1 + 2X_2 + 0X_3 + 1X_4 + 0X_5 = 9$$
$$4X_1 + 6X_2 + 0X_3 + 0X_4 + 1X_5 = 24$$
$$X_1 \geq 0, X_2 \geq 0, X_3 \geq 0, X_4 \geq 0, X_5 \geq 0$$

In the first constraint, variable X_3 is added to the left-hand side to take up the slack between the value of the original left-hand side and the right-hand side of the inequality. Then X_3 must also be restricted to be nonnegative, so that it properly

represents the slack on the left-hand side of the first constraint. Similarly, X_4 and X_5 are added as slack variables to the second and third constraints, respectively. Since we do not want these slack variables to affect the profit, they are entered with zero coefficients in the objective function. The revised problem will have exactly the same optimal solution for X_1 and X_2 as the original problem.

Now that the problem is in the required form for the simplex method, we can construct the first tableau. The term "tableau" refers to the special simplex tables which are constructed to keep track of the computations. The first tableau is shown in Figure S11.3.

The tableau is constructed by detaching the coefficients from the variables and displaying the resulting coefficients by themselves in the appropriate rows and columns of the tableau. For example, the first row in the body of the tableau is the first constraint equation, the second row is the second equation, and so on. In the right-hand column of the tableau, the right-hand side of the constraints is placed under the heading "Solution quantity." In every tableau, this column will represent the values of the X_j variables for the current solution. The particular X_j variables in the solution are shown in the box labeled "Solution variables" on the left-hand side of the tableau. For example, the initial solution is $X_3 = 120$, $X_4 = 9$, $X_5 = 24$. All variables not in the solution are always assumed to have zero values. Thus, $X_1 = 0$ and $X_2 = 0$ in the first tableau.

On the very top row of the tableau, the objective function coefficients are displayed corresponding

C_j		10	8	0	0	0	
	Solution variables	X_1	X_2	X_3	X_4	X_5	Solution quantity
0	X_3	30	20	1	0	0	120
0	X_4	2	2	0	1	0	9
0	X_5	4	6	0	0	1	24
	Z_j	0	0	0	0	0	0
	$C_j - Z_j$	10	8	0	0	0	

FIGURE S11.3
First tableau—product-mix problem.

to the columns represented by each X_j variable. For example, the profit coefficient of X_1 is 10, which is written directly above the symbol X_1. The values of the C_j which correspond to the solution variables are listed to the left of the solution variables in the tableau. In the first tableau, these C_j values are all zero, since only slack variables are in the initial solution.

Finally, the tableau has two rows on the bottom labeled Z_j and $C_j - Z_j$. The Z_j row is computed by multiplying the C_j values on the left by the coefficients in each column and adding. For example, Z_1 is computed as follows:

$$Z_1 = 0(30) + 0(2) + 0(4) = 0$$

In the first tableau, the resulting values of Z_j are zero, since all the C_j values are zero.

The last row in the tableau, $C_j - Z_j$ is the result of subtracting the Z_j value we have just computed from C_j at the top of the tableau.

The Z_j values can be interpreted economically as the gross profit due to introducing *one* unit of the corresponding X_j variable. For example, in column 1, if one unit of X_1 is introduced to the solution, the value of X_3 must be reduced by 30 to maintain the equality in the first row, X_4 must be reduced by 2 to maintain the equality in the second row, and X_5 must be reduced by 4 to maintain the equality in the third row. Therefore, the coefficients in the X_1 column represent the physical rates of substitution between X_1 and each of the variables in the solution. When these substitution rates are multiplied by their respective profit coefficients, the result is Z_1, the gross profit lost when one unit of X_1 is introduced. The profit gained by introducing one unit of X_1, however, is the value $C_1 = 10$. Therefore, the value $C_1 - Z_1$ represents the *net* profit gained by introducing one unit of X_1. It stands to reason, then, that introducing either X_1 or X_2 into the solution of the first tableau will improve the net profit because the $C_1 - Z_1$ and $C_2 - Z_2$ values are positive.

All the facts required to solve the LP problem are represented in the tableau: the current solution values on the right, the substitution ratios of each variable for the others in the tableau body, and the net profit contribution for increasing the value of each variable on the bottom.

As we mentioned earlier, the simplex method works by moving from one corner of the feasible region to an adjacent corner. The first tableau represents corner *a* at the origin in Figure S11.2, because we have $X_1 = 0$, $X_2 = 0$, in the tableau. All three constraints have slack in them ($X_3 = 120$, $X_4 = 9$, and $X_5 = 24$) at the origin. There are only two possible ways to move from the origin to an adjacent extreme point without "cutting across" the feasible region. One way to move is to increase X_1 until we reach corner *d*, at a value of $X_1 = 4$. At this point, we will also have $X_3 = 0$, since there will no longer be slack in constraint number 1. The other adjacent extreme point can be reached by increasing X_2 until $X_2 = 4$ at corner *e*. In this case $X_5 = 0$, since constraint 3 no longer has slack.

The simplex method selects between these two options on the basis of the largest net profit contribution per unit ($C_j - Z_j$). Since $C_j - Z_j$ is largest for X_1, the simplex method will move to corner *d* by increasing X_1 and simultaneously decreasing X_3 to zero. In the language of the simplex method, X_1 is introduced into the solution and X_3 is removed from the solution, since its new value is zero.

Without reference to the graphical picture, we can determine which variable will enter the solution and which one will leave by using the following rules:

- *Entering rule.* To enter the solution, select the variable with the largest value of $C_j - Z_j$. Call this the key column.
- *Leaving rule.* Take the ratio of the solution quantities to the key-column coefficients for those coefficients which are positive. Select the row variable with the minimum ratio to leave. Call this the key row.

In the first tableau, by application of the entering rule X_1 is chosen to enter. The application of the leaving rule produces the following ratios, one for each row: 120/30, 9/2, and 24/4. Since 120/30 is the smallest ratio for the first row, the variable represented in the first row, X_3, will be leaving the solution. Intuitively, as the value of X_1 is increased in column 1, X_3 will be the first variable in the current solution to reach zero. This fact is determined by calculating the above ratios for positive coefficients. The key column and key row are denoted in the first tableau by small arrows. The intersection of these arrows is called the "pivot element," which is circled in the tableau.

After applying the entering and leaving rules, the next step in the simplex method is to transform the tableau to the new solution by using the pivot element. This is done by the process of gaussian elimination which transforms the tableau but maintains the same solution to the constraint equations. In gaussian elimination, any row in the tableau may be multiplied or divided by a nonzero constant and placed in the new tableau. Also, any row may be multiplied by a nonzero constant and added to any other row, with the sum placed in the new tableau. What we are doing with the gaussian elimination method is solving simultaneous equations.

According to the gaussian rules, all coefficients in the key row are divided by the pivot element and the result is placed in the new tableau; see Figure S11.4. Then the key row is multiplied by a constant and added to a row other than the key row, so the result is a zero in the key column. The appropriate constant is selected for each nonkey row. For example, the constant $-2/30$ is multiplied by the key-row coefficients and added to each coefficient in the second row, with the sum placed in the second row of the new tableau. The constant value of $-2/30$ was selected so that the key column for row 2 will be zero in the new tableau. Similarly, the key row is multiplied by $-4/30$ and added to the third row to get the new third row in tableau 2. This completes the gaussian procedure which puts the second tableau in the proper format and ensures that the solution set is not changed.

After this step is completed, the values of Z_j and $C_j - Z_j$ are computed by updating the computations with the new coefficient values in tableau 2. The new tableau is exactly like the old one except that we have replaced column 3 by column 1 in the solution. Notice that column 1 in the new tableau has a 1 in the first position; the rest are zeros. At every step of the simplex, the variables in the solution have a 1 in some position and the rest zeros, yielding an identity matrix in the tableau. This makes it possible to read the solution directly from the tableau. In the second tableau, we have $X_1 = 4$, $X_2 = 0$, $X_3 = 0$, $X_4 = 1$, and $X_5 = 8$. By following the gaussian elimination rules, we are computing a solution of three equations and three unknowns for each tableau until the optimal tableau is reached.

The second tableau is not yet optimal, since a positive increase in net profit is shown in the $C_j - Z_j$ row. Since $C_2 - Z_2$ is the largest positive value, column 2 is the key column. Taking the ratios, we find that row 2 has the minimum ratio, so row 2 is the key row and X_4 leaves the solution. Pivoting on column 2 and row 2, we obtain the third tableau (Figure S11.5) by gaussian elimination. Since no values of $C_j - Z_j$ are positive, we have arrived at the optimal solution; no further improvement in net profit is possible. The optimal solution in the third tableau is $X_1 = 3$, $X_2 = 3/2$, $X_3 = 0$, $X_4 = 0$, $X_5 = 3$.

Since the simplex method is rather long, a brief recap of the main steps might be helpful.

1. Put the constraints in equality form by adding slack variables. Set up the first tableau.
2. Pick the key column to enter the solution, on the basis of largest positive, $C_j - Z_j$ value. If no $C_j -$

C_j		10	8	0	0	0	
	Solution variables	X_1	X_2	X_3	X_4	X_5	Solution quantity
10	X_1	1	2/3	1/30	0	0	4
0	X_4	0	2/3	−2/30	1	0	1
0	X_5	0	10/3	−4/30	0	1	8
	Z_j	10	20/3	10/30	0	0	40
	$C_j - Z_j$	0	4/3	−10/30	0	0	

FIGURE S11.4
Second tableau.

C_j		10	8	0	0	0	
	Solution variables	X_1	X_2	X_3	X_4	X_5	Solution quantity
10	X_1	1	0	1/10	−1	0	3
8	X_2	0	1	−1/10	3/2	0	3/2
0	X_5	0	0	6/30	−5	1	3
	Z_j	10	8	2/10	2	0	42
	$C_j − Z_j$	0	0	−2/10	−2	0	

FIGURE S11.5
Third tableau.

Z_j values are positive, an optimal solution has been reached.

3. Calculate the ratio of the right-hand side to all positive coefficients in the key column. Select the key row on the basis of the minimum ratio.
4. Transform the tableau by pivoting on the key row and key column using the gaussian elimination procedure. Recalculate the values of Z_j and $C_j − Z_j$ and then return to step 2.

The simplex solution of the product-mix problem may be interpreted in direct economic terms. The simplex method started with zero production of both products—an initial feasible solution but not a very profitable one. Product 1 was then introduced to the solution because it had the largest net profit contribution ($10 per unit versus $8 per unit). The simplex method is a method of "steepest ascent." It moves in the direction of the greatest unit profit improvement at each tableau. Then as much of product 1 as possible was introduced, until a constraint was reached. In this case the constraint on lumber was the most binding constraint and limited the amount of X_1 to four units. When four units of X_1 were produced, the profit was increased from zero to $40.

Next, a calculation was made to determine whether the profit could be improved even more by introducing some of the second product. This calculation required a substitution between product 1 and product 2. As product 2 was increased, less of product 1 was produced because the constraints limited the total amount of resources available.

The net effect on profit of increasing product 2 and decreasing product 1 is represented by the C_2 − Z_2 calculation, which indicated that profit could be improved by $4/3 per unit of X_2 produced. Next, it was found that a maximum of $1\frac{1}{2}$ units of X_2 could be introduced to the solution because of the combination of the lumber and labor constraints. Increasing the value of X_2 to $1\frac{1}{2}$ units also reduced X_1 to three units. The net effect of these changes in X_1 and X_2 was an improvement in profit to $42. At this point the simplex method determined that no further improvement in profit was possible.

In economic terms, the simplex method starts with a feasible solution and introduces one product at a time provided that profit is improved. When no further incremental improvement in profit is possible, the optimal solution is reached.

SHADOW PRICES

After the optimal solution has been computed, much information can be obtained from the final tableau. One type of data comprises "shadow prices," which are used to evaluate the scarce resources available. The precise interpretation of a shadow price is the amount of improvement in the objective function per unit change in a right-hand-side value. For example, in the product-mix problem, there are shadow prices for lumber, labor, and finishing capacity. The shadow price for each of these resources is the amount of improvement in profit possible if an additional unit of the resource is made available. One can thus use the shadow prices to evaluate proposed changes in resources as they might affect the objective function. For example, the shadow price for lumber is 20 cents per board foot; therefore any proposal to make additional lumber available at less than this price would improve profits up to the point where the constraints of labor and finishing capacity become binding. Shadow prices are used to evaluate potential right-hand-side changes. This evaluation procedure is called sensitivity analysis, since the optimal solution's sensitivity to changes in the problem formulation is being evaluated.

The shadow prices for the product-mix problem can be obtained directly from the final tableau (Figure S11.5). The negative of the shadow price appears in the $C_j - Z_j$ row under the slack variables. Since X_3 was the slack variable in the first constraint, $-(C_3 - Z_3)$ is the shadow price $\frac{2}{10}$ (or 20 cents per board foot) for lumber. Similarly, $-(C_4 - Z_4)$ is the shadow price, $2 per hour for labor, in the second constraint. The third constraint represented by the X_5 slack variable, has a shadow price of $-(C_5 - Z_5) = 0$. This value of zero is logical, since there is excess finishing capacity at the optimal solution. The economic value (or shadow price) of this resource is therefore zero.

As another illustration, suppose someone offers to work for you at $4 per hour. Since the shadow price of labor is only $2 per hour, it would not pay to use the additional labor. In this case profit is improved by only $2 per hour while the additional resource costs $4 an hour—a net loss of $2 per hour for each additional hour of labor used.

MINIMIZATION PROBLEM

Linear programming can also be used to solve minimization problems. The procedures require some modifications, however, which will be described below. As an example of a minimization problem, suppose that a machine shop has two different types of machines, machine 1 and machine 2, which can be used to make a single product. These machines vary in the amount of product produced per hour, in the amount of labor used, and in the cost of operation. Also assume that at least a certain amount of the product must be produced and that we would like to utilize at least the regular labor force. Under these conditions, how much should we utilize each machine in order to minimize total costs and still meet the requirements?

This problem can be formulated as a linear programming problem by letting:

$X_1 =$ hours of machine 1 time
$X_2 =$ hours of machine 2 time

We also assume that machine 1 can produce 20 pounds of product per hour, machine 2 can produce 15 pounds of product per hour, and at least 100 pounds of product are required from both machines. This constraint is expressed mathematically as:

$$20X_1 + 15X_2 \geq 100$$

Suppose also that 2 hours of labor are required for each hour of machine 1 operation, 3 hours of labor are required for each hour of machine 2 operation, and we must use at least the 15 hours of regular-time labor available. This constraint is expressed mathematically as:

$$2X_1 + 3X_2 \geq 15$$

Finally, we assume that it costs $25 per hour (labor and materials) to operate machine 1 and $30 per hour to operate machine 2. Our desire to minimize total costs of operation is expressed as follows:

$$\text{Min } 25X_1 + 30X_2$$

The problem as stated above, along with the $X_1 \geq 0$, $X_2 \geq 0$ constraints, is graphed in Figure S11.6. The constraints are plotted as equations just as before, but the feasible region for $\geq$ signs is to the *right* of the line, since the feasible points must exceed the line. The isoprofit lines are also shown in Figure S11.6. Since we are minimizing, the isoprofit line closest to the origin which is feasible is chosen as the minimum. This results in an optimal solution at the intersection of the two constraints. The solution of those constraints as simultaneous equations yields $X_1 = 2.5$, $X_2 = 3.33$, for the optimal solution. The corresponding minimum cost is $162.50.

This problem can also be solved by the simplex method with some minor modifications. Just as before, the first step is to convert the inequalities to equations. Since the inequalities are $\geq$, a variable must be *subtracted* from the left-hand side to make the two sides equal. This variable is called a surplus variable, but it serves the same function as the slack variable for $\leq$ signs. The resulting LP problem is:

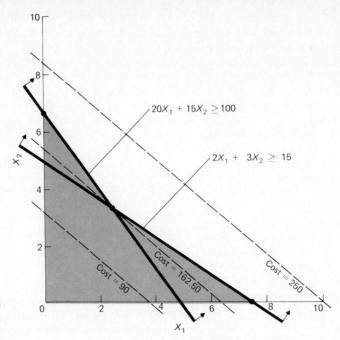

FIGURE S11.6
Minimization
problem.

Objective:
$$\min 25X_1 + 30X_2 + 0X_3 + 0X_4$$
Subject to:
$$20X_1 + 15X_2 - X_3 \qquad = 100$$
$$2X_1 + 3X_2 \qquad - X_4 = 15$$
$$X_1 \geq 0, \ X_2 \geq 0, \ X_3 \geq 0, \ X_4 \geq 0$$

The simplex method requires a nonnegative feasible solution as a starting point. If we were to set $X_1 = 0$, $X_2 = 0$, as we did before, we would have $X_3 =$

-100 and $X_4 = -15$. Since this solution violates the nonnegativity conditions, a feasible starting point is not available in this problem. To correct this situation, we add an artificial variable to each equation with a very large positive coefficient (called large M) in the objective function. Since we are minimizing costs, artificial variables will be driven out of the solution by the simplex method due to their large cost coefficients. This is, of

C_j		25	30	0	0	M	M	
	Solution variables	X_1	X_2	X_3	X_4	X_5	X_6	Solution quantity
M	X_5	20	15	-1	0	1	0	100
M	X_6	2	3	0	-1	0	1	15
	Z_j	$22M$	$18M$	$-M$	$-M$	M	M	$115M$
	$C_j - Z_j$	25 $-22M$	30 $-18M$	0 $+M$	0 $+M$	0	0	

FIGURE S11.7
First tableau—
minimization
problem.

C_j		25	30	0	0	M	M	
	Solution variables	X_1	X_2	X_3	X_4	X_5	X_6	Solution quantity
25	X_1	1	15/20	−1/20	0	1/20	0	5
M	X_6	0	3/2	2/20	−1	−2/20	1	5
	Z_j	25	75/4 +3/2M	−5/4 +1/10M	−M	5/4 −1/10M	M	125 + 5M
	$C_j - Z_j$	0	45/4 −3/2M	5/4 −1/10M	+M	5/4 +11/10M	0	

FIGURE S11.8
Second tableau.

course, just what we want, since artificial variables cannot remain in the optimal solution. The purpose of artificial variables is to provide a feasible starting point for the simplex method.

With the use of artificial variables, the LP formulation becomes:

Objective:
min $25X_1 + 30X_2 + 0X_3 + 0X_4 + MX_5 + MX_6$
Subject to:
$$20X_1 + 15X_2 - X_3 + X_5 = 100$$
$$2X_1 + 3X_2 - X_4 + X_6 = 15$$
$$X_1 \geq 0, X_2 \geq 0, X_3 \geq 0, X_4 \geq 0, X_5 \geq 0, X_6 \geq 0$$

Now we have achieved an LP formulation with an initial starting solution of $X_1 = 0$, $X_2 = 0$, $X_3 = 0$, $X_4 = 0$, $X_5 = 100$, and $X_6 = 15$. The initial cost is then $100M + 15M$, which is very large, since M is an arbitrarily large positive number. This problem is now ready to go into the first simplex tableau, shown in Figure S11.7.

With minimization, the entering variable is based on the largest *negative* $C_j - Z_j$, since we want

to reduce the objective function as much as possible on each iteration. In the first tableau, the entering column is therefore, X_1, which has the largest negative M coefficient in the $C_j - Z_j$ row. The rest of the simplex method is now applied in exactly the same way as in the maximization problem. On the basis of the minimum ratio, X_5 is the leaving variable. The pivot element is then used to perform a gaussian transformation to the second tableau, shown in Figure S11.8.

In the second tableau, X_2 is selected as the incoming variable, since it has the largest negative value of $C_j - Z_j$. Taking the minimum ratio over positive coefficients of column 2 yields X_6 as the leaving variable. Performing a gaussian transformation then yields the third tableau, shown in Figure S11.9.

The third tableau is optimal, since all $C_j - Z_j$ are positive; no further reduction in the objective function is possible. From the tableau, the optimal solution is $X_1 = \frac{5}{2}$, $X_2 = \frac{10}{3}$, and cost = \$162.50.

C_j		25	30	0	0	M	M	
	Solution variables	X_1	X_2	X_3	X_4	X_5	X_6	Solution quantity
25	X_1	1	0	−1/10	1/2	1/10	−1/2	5/2
30	X_2	0	1	1/15	−2/3	−1/15	2/3	10/3
	Z_j	25	30	−1/2	−15/2	1/2	15/2	162.5
	$C_j - Z_j$	0	0	1/2	15/2	−1/2 +M	−15/2 +M	

FIGURE S11.9
Third tableau.

The shadow prices are 50 cents for each additional pound of product produced and $7.50 for each additional hour of labor required. The marginal cost of 50 cents per pound can be used to help decide whether additional orders should be taken. The marginal labor cost of $7.50 per hour can be used to help decide whether all the labor should be utilized. For example, it will pay for some people to be idle if their wage rates are less than $7.50 per hour.

In summary, there are two main effects on the simplex method for a minimization problem. First, the entering-column criterion is the largest negative $C_j - Z_j$ instead of the largest positive $C_j - Z_j$ value. Second, the simplex method stops at the optimal solution when all $C_j - Z_j \geq 0$. Otherwise, all features of the simplex method are the same as in the maximization case.

APPLICATIONS OF LP IN OPERATIONS

LP has been applied to a wide range of decisions both inside and outside operations. Within operations, well-known applications include the following:

1. Product mix. A simplified version of the product-mix decision was formulated in the first part of this supplement, where scarce resources were allocated to products. In real situations, additional constraints—such as minimum or maximum production levels of each product and multiple time periods—may be introduced to provide more realism. As we have indicated, one benefit of the optimal-product-mix solution is to identify coordination problems between production and marketing, since the best mix of products from a production point of view is provided by the LP solution. If this optimal mix of products is not being marketed, either marketing strategy or production resources should be adjusted.
2. Blending. The blending decision determines the best resource inputs to make a blended product such as gasoline or sausage. In the sausage blending decision, certain specifications such as fat content, water content, pork percentage, and beef content are given for the final product.

These specifications are frequently stated as maximums or minimums. Several types of raw-meat stocks are available which vary in their cost and product-specification characteristics. The problem is to find the best blend of raw-meat stocks which meets the final product specifications and minimizes the cost of the product.

3. Scheduling. A wide range of scheduling decisions have been supported by LP, including the operation of blast furnaces, project scheduling, and scheduling of nurses in hospitals. Scheduling decisions typically include the assignment of available resources to jobs or tasks which must be completed. One example is a situation in which a number of blast furnaces can be used to produce several types of steel and each furnace varies in both its cost and steel output characteristics. Under these circumstances, LP is used to determine which furnaces should be scheduled for the production of each steel product in order to minimize the cost of production.
4. Distribution. LP has been applied to a wide range of distribution decisions such as optimal shipping patterns and optimal location of plants and warehouses. In these decisions, goods may be shipped from one location to another through a variety of alternate paths and locations. The best shipping paths and patterns can then be identified by an LP formulation. One simple version of this problem, the transportation problem, has been described in the supplement to Chapter 10.
5. Aggregate planning. The aggregate-planning decision, described in Chapter 11, determines the best mix of inventory, employment, subcontracting, and other resources to meet a given demand. Demand is typically specified for several months into the future on an aggregate or total basis. This decision can be formulated as an LP problem or in several other ways. LP helps select the best aggregate plan when the conditions of the problem are linear in nature.

Although only a few examples are given above, LP has been used to solve many hundreds of real problems in operations. Remember, LP did not solve these problems; it merely assisted the manager in reaching a better decision. LP did, however, solve the mathematical formulation of the manager's problem.

QUESTIONS

1. Define the following terms:
   a. Slack variable
   b. Constraint
   c. Objective function
   d. Artificial variable
   e. Extreme point
   f. Optimal solution
   g. Feasible solution
2. What information is provided by shadow prices?
3. Explain the concept of a shadow price by using the LP graph in Figure S11.2
4. The simplex method is an adjacent-extreme-point method. Explain.
5. How do we know when an optimal solution for a minimization problem has been reached by the simplex method?
6. What is the purpose of using gaussian elimination in going from one tableau to the next?
7. How are corner points represented by the simplex tableau?
8. Why is a large M value assigned to artificial variables?
9. Why does the optimal solution to an LP problem always occur at a corner point? How is this fact exploited in finding the optimal solution?
10. In the simplex method, what are the differences between minimization and maximization problems?

PROBLEMS

1. Solve the following LP problem by the graphical method:

   Objective:
   $$\max 3X_1 + 4X_2$$

   Subject to:
   $$4X_1 + 2X_2 \leq 8$$
   $$2X_1 + 5X_2 \leq 10$$
   $$X_1 \geq 0, X_2 \geq 0$$

2. Solve the following problem by the graphical method:

   Objective:
   $$\min 6X_1 + X_2$$

   Subject to:
   $$2X_1 + X_2 \geq 6$$
   $$4X_1 - X_2 \geq 6$$
   $$X_1 \geq 0, X_2 \geq 0$$

3. A company manufactures two types of toys: trucks and cars. Each truck requires 1 minute of molding time, 2 minutes of painting time, and 1 minute of packing time. Each car requires 2 minutes of molding time, 1 minute of painting time, and 2 minutes of packing time. There are a total of 300 minutes of molding time, 400 minutes of painting time, and 400 minutes of packing time available each day. Both cars and trucks contribute $1 per unit to profit.

a. Formulate this problem.

b. Solve it graphically.

c. Solve it by the simplex method.

d. If only one of the three resources can be increased in capacity, which one would you choose?

4. The x-ray department of a hospital has two machines, A and B, which can be used to develop x-ray film. The maximum daily processing capacity of these machines is A = 80 films and B = 100 films. The department must plan to process at least 150 films per day. The operating costs per film are $4 for machine A and $3 for machine B. To minimize costs, how many films per day should each machine process?

a. Solve this problem graphically.

b. Solve it by the simplex method.

c. How much would you be willing to pay for additional capacity on machine A?

5. Gasoline is blended from several stocks to obtain minimum required octane ratings. Suppose an order for 1000 gallons of 80-octane gasoline has been received. There are three blending stocks available. Stock A has 95 octane and costs $1.20 per gallon. Stock B has 70 octane and costs $1 per gallon. Stock C has 85 octane and costs $1.10 per gallon. There are only 500 gallons of stock A, 900 gallons of stock B, and 600 gallons of stock C available. Assume that octane numbers combine in proportion to the volume of the stocks which are blended together. How much stock of each type should be used to minimize the total cost of filling the order?

a. Solve this problem by the simplex method.

b. How much would you be willing to pay per additional gallon of stock A?

6. Brand X animal feed is made from a combination of wheat and corn. Wheat contains 10 percent protein, 40 percent starch, and 50 percent fiber by weight. Corn contains 15 percent protein, 50 percent starch, and 35 percent fiber by weight. The recipe for brand X feed calls for a minimum of 45 percent starch and 40 percent fiber; there is no restriction on protein. If a batch of at least 800 pounds of brand X is produced, how many pounds of corn and how many pounds of wheat should be used to minimize costs? Corn costs 5 cents per pound and wheat costs 3 cents per pound.

7. Using the formulation from Box 11.4, solve the Hefty Beer Company problem described in Chapter 11, by use of linear programming. Compare the optimal solution with the three solutions described in the chapter as follows:

a. How much improvement in cost is obtained by the optimal LP solution?

b. Does the minimum-cost LP solution result in a radically different strategy for regular time, overtime, or inventory than the best solution found in Chapter 11?

c. Describe how the Hefty Beer Company should use LP to make aggregate planning decisions.

8. The Realistic Picture Frame Company makes four different types of ready-made picture frames: rustic, modern, French, and Roman. Each frame takes the following amounts of resources in wood, labor, and machine time as shown by the unit production technology matrix below. The profit contributions per unit for each frame type are: rustic = $1.50, modern = $1.25, French = $.95, and Roman = $.80. At the present time, we have available 1000 board feet of wood, 500 hours of labor, and 100 hours of machine time.

Resources used per unit produced			
	Rustic	Modern	French	Roman
Wood, Board feet	1.0	1.5	2.0	2.0
Labor, hours	1.0	.9	.7	.6
Machine, hours	.3	.2	.1	.1

a. Formulate the problem as a linear programming problem.
b. Solve using the simplex method. What is the optimal number of frames of each type to produce, and how much profit contribution is made?
c. How much would you pay in order to make more wood, labor, or machine time available?

9. A berry farm can choose to plant four different types of strawberries. Some of the berry plants provide more fruit, but they also require more land and labor. The yields from each type of berry plant and the amount of land and labor required are shown below.

Berry type	A	B	C	D
Yield (lb/plant)	2	2.5	3	1.8
Land (plants/acre)	10,000	8000	6000	12,000
Labor (hours/plant)	.1	.15	.2	.1

At the present time, berries are selling for 50 cents a pound, and we have 10 acres of land and 10,000 hours of labor available for planting and picking the berries.
a. Formulate the problem as a linear programming problem.
b. How many berries of each type should be planted in order to maximize the revenue that we can obtain from these resources?
c. More labor can be obtained for $5 an hour, and more land can be rented for $100 per acre. Should additional resources be obtained?

SELECTED BIBLIOGRAPHY

CHARNES, ABRAHAM, and W. W. COOPER: *Management Models and Industrial Applications of Linear Programming,* New York: Wiley, 1961.

DAELLENBACH, HANS G., and EARL J. BELL: *User's Guide to Linear Programming,* Englewood Cliffs, N.J.: Prentice-Hall, 1970.

DANTZIG, GEORGE B.: *Linear Programming and Extensions,* Princeton, N.J.: Princeton University Press, 1963.

GASS, SAUL I.: *Illustrated Guide to Linear Programming,* New York: McGraw-Hill, 1970.

GRINOLD, RICHARD C.: "Input Policies for a Longitudinal Manpower Flow Model," *Management Science,* vol. 22, 1976, pp. 570–575.

LEE, SANG M.: *Linear Optimization for Management,* New York: Petrocelli/Charter, 1976.

LYONS, D. F., and V. A. DODD: "The Mis-Feed Problem," *Operational Research,* Amsterdam: North-Holland Publishing, 1975.

NAYLOR, THOMAS H., EUGENE T. BYRNE, and JOHN M. VERNON: *Introduction to Linear Programming: Methods and Cases,* Belmont, Calif.: Wadsworth, 1971.

ZIERER, T. K., W. A. MITCHELL, and T. R. WHITE: "Practical Applications of Linear Programming to Shell's Distribution Problems." *Interfaces,* vol. 6, no. 4, August 1976, pp. 13–26.

Scheduling Operations

Scheduling decisions allocate available capacity or resources (equipment, labor, and space) to jobs, activities, tasks, or customers through time. Since scheduling is an allocation decision, it uses the resources made available by facilities decisions and aggregate planning. Therefore scheduling is the last and most constrained decision in the hierarchy of capacity planning decisions.

In practice, scheduling results in a time-phased plan (or schedule) of activities. The schedule indicates what is to be done, when, by whom, and with what equipment.

Scheduling should be clearly differentiated from aggregate planning. Aggregate planning seeks to determine the resources needed, while scheduling allocates the resources made available through aggregate planning in the best manner to meet operations objectives. Aggregate planning is done on a time frame of about 1 year, while scheduling is done on a time frame of a few months, weeks, or hours.

Scheduling seeks to achieve several conflicting objectives: high efficiency, low inventories, and good customer service. Efficiency is achieved by a schedule which maintains high utilization of labor, equipment, and space. Of course, the schedule should also seek to maintain low inventories, which—unfortunately—may lead to low efficiency due to lack of available material or high setup times. Thus a tradeoff decision in scheduling between efficiency and inventory levels is required. Customer service can be measured by the speed with which customer demands are met, either through available stock or short lead times. Fast customer service is in conflict, too, with low inventories and high efficiency. The primary aim of scheduling is, therefore, to make tradeoffs between conflicting objectives so as to arrive at a satisfactory balance. One example of the conflicting objectives faced in a scheduling decision is given in Box 12.1.

BOX 12.1
TYPICAL DECISION PROBLEM

Dr. Jerome Preston, Chief of Surgery for the Crestview Hospital, faced a continual problem in scheduling the 12 operating rooms in the hospital. Sometimes all the operating rooms were busy and patients were waiting to get in; at other times all or almost all the rooms were empty. The problem was compounded by the need to reserve a certain part of the schedule for emergency operations, the difficulty of predicting how long any given operation would take, and the preferences of doctors to work only certain hours. For the doctors' convenience, it was common practice to schedule most surgery in the morning and to have the operating rooms empty during much of the afternoon.

Faced with this problem, Dr. Preston met with Sally Ames, his assistant in charge of operating room scheduling. "Sally, isn't there something we can do to improve the scheduling of operating rooms? It seems to be either feast or famine. How can the workload be predicted or leveled to achieve better utilization of the operating rooms? If this isn't done, it's possible that we'll have to add more operating rooms in the near future."

Sally proposed that several measures be taken. First, she suggested that a committee of surgeons be formed to study the situation and suggest changes in scheduling practices. She would act as a staff assistant to the committee. The committee would be shown utilization figures for the operating rooms by time of day, day of the week, and month of the year. Suggestions for changes in scheduling practice would then be taken from the committee members and evaluated by Sally as to their potential impact on operating room utilization. To do this, Sally would simulate the use of the suggested rules and practices on her personal computer. After reviewing the results of the simulations, the committee would suggest changes to Dr. Preston, who would then decide on actions to be taken. Dr. Preston agreed to form the committee to begin work on the problem.

It is not possible to treat scheduling for all types of operations as a single subject. In order to highlight the differences, scheduling can be classified by type of process: line, intermittent, and project. This chapter addresses the scheduling of ongoing line and intermittent operations. Chapter 13 addresses the scheduling of projects.

 ## 12.1 LINE PROCESSES

The scheduling of line processes is required for both assembly lines and the so-called process industries. For these line processes the scheduling problem is, at least partly, solved by the design of the process, since the product flows smoothly from one work station to another. For a single product made in one facility, there is no scheduling problem, because the flow of materials is completely determined by the design of the process. A scheduling problem exists only when multiple products are made in a single facility and thus compete for use of limited resources.

When several different products are made on the same line, each product is actually produced in a batch, and a line changeover is required for the next product. The changeover may be fairly simple, or it may be complex enough to require extensive retooling and modification of work stations. One example of line scheduling is the production of air conditioners, where a changeover from one model to another may cost several thousand dollars. Other examples include refrigerators, microwave ovens, stoves, electronic devices, tires, and most mass-produced products. These changeover problems involve scheduling, since they require the allocation of line capacity to several different products.

Recently, efforts have been made, by some companies, to greatly reduce changeover times to practically zero and thereby obtain a very flexible assembly line. In this case mixed models can be scheduled, one after another, rather than discrete batches. Mixed-model production will be discussed in Chapter 16 when we consider JIT production systems. Here, we assume that the changeover time is a significant factor and that production is scheduled in batches.

The first concern in scheduling the multiple-product batch line is to calculate economic lot sizes. This calculation requires a tradeoff between setup cost (to change over the line) and inventory carrying cost. If the setup is done often, small lots are produced and frequent setup costs are incurred, but inventories are held down. If setups are done infrequently, the opposite situation occurs, leading to less setup cost but more inventory. Thus the economic (least-cost) lot size can be determined by a balance between setup costs and inventory carrying costs. Lots which are either too large or too small are expensive. The exact formula for calculating these lot sizes is explained in Chapter 14.

Once the lot sizes for each product have been determined, on strictly economic grounds or otherwise, there is still a question of when each product should be produced. This gets to the heart of the scheduling problem, which is the sequencing of products on the line, one after another.

Sometimes the best sequence can be calculated by means of a mathematical model. However, the available mathematical formulations do not consider demand uncertainty, which is a serious problem in line scheduling. To solve this problem, a dynamic method of scheduling and continually rescheduling products is needed.

In addressing the line scheduling problem, we will assume that the line is producing to inventory, and we will develop a scheduling rule which considers current inventory levels as well as future demand rates. If the inventory for a particular product is low relative to future demand, that product should be scheduled ahead of products with larger relative inventories. A way to formalize this idea is to schedule lots on the basis of runout times.

The *runout time* for product i is defined to be

$$r_i = \frac{I_i}{d_i} \qquad i = 1, \ldots, n$$

where r_i = runout time, weeks
I_i = inventory, units
d_i = weekly demand, units

The scheduling rule is to schedule first one lot of the product with the lowest value of r_i. This will ensure that the product with the smallest runout time is placed first in the schedule. The next step is to reevaluate the runout times assuming the first lot has been completed and to repeat the process until several lots have been scheduled. By this process of simulation, a schedule can be developed for as far into the future as desired.

The following example illustrates the idea of runout-time calculations. An assembly line makes six different products to stock. The lot sizes, production rates, inventories, and forecast demand for these products are shown in Table 12.1. The runout time is calculated for each product by taking the ratio of inventory to forecasted weekly demand. The product with the lowest runout time—in this case product B with a runout time of 5.5 weeks—should be scheduled first.

We then continue to develop the entire production schedule. The lot size for product B is 450 units and the production rate is 900 units per week. Thus product B should be scheduled for 0.5 week to produce one lot. The inventories and runout times are projected forward to the end of 0.5 week, as shown in Table 12.1. Product E now has the lowest runout time at 7.0 weeks, so it is scheduled for a lot of production. This lot will take 1.0 week to produce, so the status is projected forward again until the end of week 1.5.

Now product F has the lowest runout time, so product F is scheduled next. This time the lot size will require 1.5 weeks to produce, so the status is projected forward to the end of week 3.0. Continuing this process as shown in Table 12.1, the production sequence will be B, E, F, D, C for the next 3.5 weeks.

As the calculations indicate, we should not simply make up the entire schedule from the initial runout times but rather schedule the lots one at a time while simulating the process forward. Furthermore, this schedule should be revised as actual demand data are accumulated and new forecasts are made. The runout calculation is, therefore, dynamic and continually adjusts to changing conditions.

After the scheduling is done, one should look carefully at the resulting

TABLE 12.1
RUNOUT-TIME CALCULATIONS

	Demand data			Supply data		
Product	Inventory units	Weekly demand, units	Runout time, weeks	Lot size, units	Production rate, units per week	Production time, weeks
A	2,100	200	10.5	1500	1500	1.0
B	550	100	⑤.⑤	450	900	.5
C	1,475	150	9.8	1000	500	2.0
D	2,850	300	9.5	500	1000	.5
E	1,500	200	7.5	800	800	1.0
F	1,700	200	8.5	1200	800	1.5
Total	10,175	1150				

projected inventories to see whether inventory is building up too fast or being reduced to low levels. If this is the case, a change in capacity may be needed to bring the schedule into conformity with objectives. From the example in Table 12.1, it can be seen that inventories are being reduced somewhat over the scheduling period from a starting level of 10,175 units to an ending level of 9100 units. Unless inventories were too high in the beginning, this calculation would indicate a need for aggregate planning to provide more capacity through overtime, subcontracting, hiring, etc. If an aggregate decision is made to change capacity, we would then recalculate the schedule by using the new production rates. This example illustrates clearly the interaction between scheduling and aggregate planning.

The runout method is a very simple heuristic which does not take into account inventory carrying costs, stockout costs, different demand variances, and so on. It can be improved by formulating a model which takes specific management objectives into account. Nevertheless, the runout-time calculation has intuitive appeal because it clearly illustrates the line scheduling problem.

Whatever scheduling rule is utilized, it must be embedded in a production scheduling and control system. Often the concept of a well-structured system is more important than the particular scheduling rule utilized. Later in the chapter, we will be discussing some general principles for the design of such scheduling systems.

INTERMITTENT PROCESSES

In this section much of the terminology ("shop," "job," "work center") comes from traditional manufacturing job shops. The concepts, however, apply equally to intermittent operations of all types, including factories, hospitals, offices, and schools. For service operations, the term "job" can be replaced by "customer," "patient," "client," "paperwork," or whatever flows through the process instead of materials or jobs. Furthermore, the term "work center" can be replaced by the words "room," "office," "facility," "skill specialty," or whatever the processing centers are. In this way the concepts can be generalized to all types of operations.

TABLE 12.1 (*Continued*)

End of week 0.5		End of week 1.5		End of week 3.0		End of week 3.5	
Inventory	Runout time	Inventory	Runout time	Inventory	Runout time	Inventory	Runout time
2,000	10.0	1800	9.0	1500	7.5	1400	7.0
950	9.5	850	8.5	700	7.0	650	6.5
1,400	9.3	1250	8.3	1025	6.8	950	6.3
2,700	9.0	2400	8.0	1950	6.5	2300	7.7
1,400	7.0	2000	10.0	1700	8.5	1600	8.0
1,600	8.0	1400	7.0	2300	11.5	2200	11.0
10,050		9700		9175		9100	

The intermittent scheduling problem is quite different from that for line processes. First of all, each unit flowing through an intermittent process typically moves along with many starts and stops, not smoothly. This irregular flow is due to the layout of the intermittent process by machine group or skills into work centers. As a result, jobs or customers wait in line as each unit is transferred from one work center to the next. Work-in-process (WIP) inventory builds up or people wait in lines, and scheduling becomes complex and difficult.

The intermittent scheduling problem can be thought of as a network of queues. A queue of WIP inventory is formed at each work center as jobs wait for the facilities to become available. These queues are interconnected through a network of material or customer flows. The problem of scheduling intermittent processes is how to manage these queues.

As we have noted in Chapter 5, one of the characteristics of an intermittent operation is that jobs or customers spend most of their time waiting in line. The amount of time spent waiting will, of course, vary with the load on the process. If the process is highly loaded, a job may spend as much as 95 percent of its total production time waiting in queues. Under these circumstances, if it takes a week to actually process an order, it will take 20 weeks to deliver it to the customer. On the other hand, if the process is lightly loaded, the waiting time will be reduced, since all the jobs flow through the process more rapidly. Regardless of the load on the process, the challenge is to develop scheduling procedures that will effectively manage the flow of jobs, customers, and work.

The scheduling of intermittent processes in manufacturing is closely related to materials requirements planning (MRP) systems, which are discussed in Chapter 15. Since MRP deals with a variety of topics—inventory, scheduling, and manufacturing control—the discussion of MRP is deferred until later. Much of the material discussed in this section, however, can be considered as a component of an MRP system, in addition to the broader scheduling and service-industry applications.

There are a number of scheduling problems for intermittent processes: input-output analysis, loading, sequencing, and dispatching. Each of these problems and their interrelationships will be described below.

12.3 INPUT-OUTPUT CONTROL

The purpose of input-output control is to manage the relationship between a work center's inputs and outputs. Before discussing these relationships, a definition of terms will be helpful.

1. **Input.** The amount of work (jobs) arriving at a work center per unit of time. Input may be measured in such units as dollars, number of orders, standard hours of work, or physical units (tons, feet, cubic yards) per unit of time.
2. **Load.** The level of WIP inventory or back orders in the system. Load is the total volume of work still to be processed. It may be measured in the same units as input, but load is not expressed as a rate per unit of time.
3. **Output.** The rate at which work is completed by a work center. Output rate depends on both capacity and load.
4. **Capacity.** The maximum rate of output which can be produced. Capacity is determined by a combination of physical factors and management policy, as described in Chapter 10.

The relationships between these four terms may easily be visualized by the hydraulics analogy in Figure 12.1. Input is represented by the rate at which water flows into the tank and is controlled by the input valve. Load is represented by the level of water in the tank and corresponds to WIP inventory or back orders. Output is the rate at which water flows out of the tank. Capacity is the size of the output pipe, not the size of the tank. While capacity limits the maximum rate of flow, the actual output rate may be less than capacity if the water level is low. The

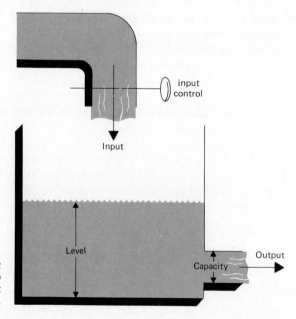

FIGURE 12.1
Hydraulic
analogy to
input-output
control.

proper way to control this tank system is to regulate the input valve so that the output and load achieve the proper levels. One cannot push more water through the tank simply by opening up the input valve, although this tactic is frequently attempted in factories and service operations. Once capacity is reached, the *only* way to get more output is to increase the size of the output pipe.

Managers are well aware of the consequences of too little input: low machine utilization, idle labor, and high unit costs. What is often not understood are the consequences of too much input. In this case working capital will rise due to a larger WIP inventory, the average processing time to complete an order will increase as orders spend more time in queues, and system performance will generally decline. It is often better to control input by backlogging orders or even turning business away, if necessary, than to make futile attempts to push more through the system.

One popular way to attempt to increase output without increasing capacity is to expedite the work in progress. Expediting is done by identifying critical jobs and rushing them through the facility. For example, an expeditor may place red tags on critical jobs which should be worked on first. This is a shortsighted solution which often does more harm than good. Every job expedited today may cause two jobs to be late tomorrow. Expediting destroys a smooth flow of work; it is the antithesis of planning. Even in the best-managed operations, a little expediting may be needed when things go wrong; but expediting should not be substituted for proper planning, scheduling, and control. One way to tell whether an operation is out of control is to count the number of jobs carrying rush stickers, red tags, or other expediting messages. Expediting indicates a failure to manage the relationships between input and output.

Some basic calculations will help explain input-output relationships. Figure 12.2 shows an input rate to an operation of $100,000 per week, or about $5 million per year. The output rate is also $100,000 per week, and WIP inventory is $2 million. Notice that the system is in steady state, with the input rate equal to the output rate.

In this condition, the average processing time for an order will be $\frac{\$2,000,000}{\$100,000} =$ 20 weeks. It would be interesting to know, in this case, what amount of time the average order spends in actual processing—perhaps 1 or 2 weeks out of the 20-week total.

FIGURE 12.2
Input-output
calculations.

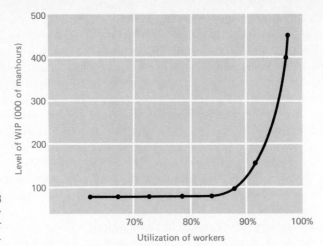

FIGURE 12.3
WIP inventory
versus labor
utilization.

There is also a relationship between utilization and WIP inventory level, but this must be expressed through complicated formulas or simulation models. Such a simulation of a typical job shop was done by Colley et al., with the results shown in Figure 12.3. In this case, various levels of WIP inventory were selected and the resulting utilization of labor and equipment was calculated. When initial levels of utilization were low, they were greatly increased by even a small increase in WIP. This occurred because machines and people—not jobs—were waiting. When utilization was high (in the 90 percent range), only a very large increase in WIP inventory could raise utilization still higher.

The tradeoff between utilization and WIP inventory can be illustrated by the following simple example. Suppose that WIP inventory can be reduced by 10 percent while utilization of labor declines by only 1 percent. Is this tradeoff worthwhile? To answer this question, we need to know that WIP inventory = $2 million, 200 people are employed at $5 per hour, and it costs 20 cents to carry $1 of inventory for a year. The annual cost of decreased labor utilization is then

$$(.01)(200)(40)(52)(\$5) = \$20,800$$

The annual savings in inventory is

$$(.1)(.20)(\$2,000,000) = \$40,000$$

Since the inventory savings is greater than the cost owing to lower labor utilization, it would pay to reduce inventories. This can be done, of course, by holding input below output for a period of time and clearing the system of some of the partially completed orders.

This discussion of input-output control can be summarized by Figure 12.4. In this case, increasing levels of WIP are seen to help in increasing throughput (output rate) to a point where the curve actually decreases because WIP inventory finally "gets in the way." At the same time, increasing WIP can also be expected to increase the average lead time (processing time) and the variance of processing time as jobs spend more time in the queues. A key to controlling lead times,

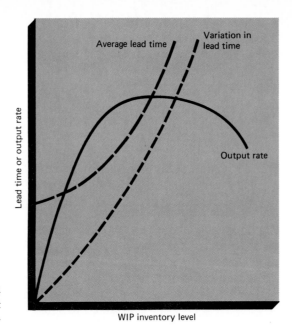

FIGURE 12.4
Input-output
relationship.

utilization, and inventories is to control input to the intermittent process. In some industries, too little attention is paid to input control; the result is high WIP inventories and long lead times.

In a factory, input is controlled by the releasing function. If the factory is in steady state, work should be released to the shop floor only in the same amount as the product is being shipped out the door. The release rate and shipment rate are frequently measured in standard labor hours of work or machine hours, whichever is the most critical resource. A job is not released to the factory simply because the materials are available or because some of the workers are idle; a like amount of work must be shipped out the other end of the factory. In a similar way, input-output control is handled in service facilities by appointment schedules. Only so much work is put into the system over a given period of time. If more customers are accepted without a corresponding change in service capacity, customers will simply wait longer to be served.

LOADING

Loading is a type of scheduling used to develop a "load" profile by work center. In loading, the total hours or number of jobs is used to obtain a rough idea of when orders can be delivered or whether capacity will be exceeded. A precise schedule or sequence for each job is not developed.

Loading uses an *average* waiting time for jobs at each work center to determine the progress of jobs through the facility. This is in contrast to detailed scheduling or sequencing, where job interference is taken into account and the waiting time of each job in each queue is precisely calculated. This type of exact sequencing will be covered in the next section. Remember, the purpose of loading is to obtain a rough idea of the load on the facilities and not an exact work schedule.

There are two types of loading: forward and backward.

1. *Forward loading.* Begins with the present date and loads jobs forward in time. The processing time is accumulated against each work center, assuming infinite or finite capacity. In this case, due dates may be exceeded if necessary. Since average waiting times are used in queues, the resulting job completion date is only an approximation of the date which might be calculated by more precise scheduling. The purpose of forward loading is to determine the approximate completion date of each job and, in the case of infinite capacity, the capacity required in each time period.

2. *Backward loading.* Begins with the due date for each job and loads the processing-time requirements against each work center by proceeding backward in time. The capacity of work centers may be exceeded if necessary. The purpose of backward loading is to calculate the capacity required in each work center for each time period. As a result, it may be decided that capacity should be reallocated between work centers or that more total capacity should be made available through revised aggregate planning. Due dates of jobs are always given for backward loading.

The techniques of forward and backward loading are best illustrated by example. Suppose we have a very simple shop with three work centers (A, B, C) consisting of one machine each and five jobs (1, 2, 3, 4, 5) to be loaded. The processing time of each job in each work center is shown in Figure 12.5. These times will be accumulated to form the load on each work center in machine hours. One could also accumulate labor hours, but that would complicate the example. We are thus assuming that machine hours is the scarce resource in this example.

A job will spend a great deal of its production time being moved and waiting in line. We will assume that move/wait time is an average of 8 hours per work center in addition to the machine processing time. In fact, waiting time depends on the loading sequence used. But we ignore this fact for the moment. The move/wait time will be incurred each time a job changes from one work center to the next. A job thus alternates between processing and waiting as it moves from one work center to the next.

Job	Work center/machine hours	Due date
1	A/2, B/3, C/4	4
2	C/6, A/4	3
3	B/3, C/2, A/1	4
4	C/4, B/3, A/3	4
5	A/5, B/3	2

FIGURE 12.5
Job data for
loading.

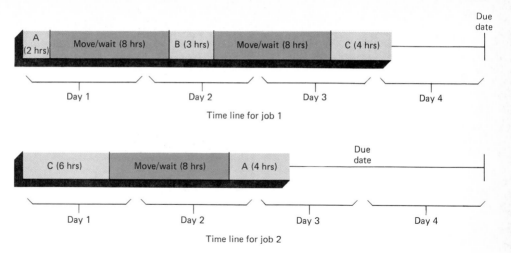

FIGURE 12.6 Time lines for forward loading.

The times shown in Figure 12.5 need some explanation. Job 1, for example, has work-center machine hours listed as follows: A/2, B/3, C/4. This means that job 1 requires 2 hours of processing time in work center A followed by 3 hours of processing time in work center B and finally 4 hours of processing time in work center C. In between each pair of work centers, 8 hours of move/wait time is assumed to occur, as noted above. Similarly, job 2 requires 6 hours of processing in work center C followed by 8 hours of move/wait time and then 4 hours in work center A.

Next, we will describe forward loading to infinite capacity using the data from Figure 12.5. The first step is to construct a time line for each job as illustrated in Figure 12.6 for jobs 1 and 2. This time line starts at time zero for each job, since we are forward-loading the work in time. The data are taken from Figure 12.5 and placed on the time line in Figure 12.6 as follows. Job 1 spends 2 hours of work time in work center A, 8 hours of move/wait time en route to work center B, 3 hours of processing time in work center B, another 8 hours of move/wait time, and finally 4 hours of processing time in work center C. The important point to note in Figure 12.6 is the relationship of processing times to days, assuming 8 hours in each day. For example, the processing time for job 1 in work center A falls entirely in day 1, the processing time for work center B is entirely in day 2, and the processing time for work center C is split into 3 hours in day 3 and 1 hour in day 4. This information will be used shortly in constructing load charts. Also, note for job 2 that the processing time in work center C is in day 1, but the processing time in work center A is split between days 2 and 3.

Next, we will take the information from the time lines and transfer it to the forward load charts shown in Figure 12.7. In this figure there is one load chart for each work center. Placing job 1 into these charts, we simply use the above time line to assign 2 hours to work center A in day 1, 3 hours to work center B in day 2, 3 hours to work center C in day 3, and 1 hour to work center C in day 4. Job 2 is forward-loaded next using its time line. The result is 6 hours in work center C in

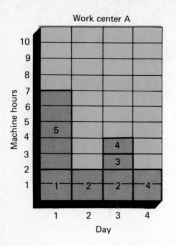
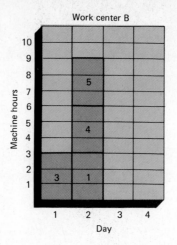
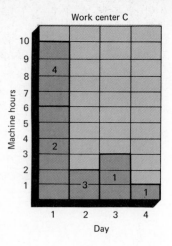

FIGURE 12.7 Forward-loading example. The numbers 1, 2, 3, 4, and 5 within the bars are job numbers.

day 1, 2 hours in work center A in day 2, and 2 hours in work center A in day 3. We continue this procedure with jobs 3, 4, and 5 until all jobs are forward-loaded.

In this case we have loaded everything to infinite capacity in order to determine the capacity required to achieve the earliest possible completion dates. As a result of the forward load, we can also predict the earliest possible delivery date for each job as follows: job 1 in day 4, job 2 in day 3, job 3 in day 3, job 4 in day 4, and job 5 in day 2 (see Figure 12.7).

The load obtained from forward loading is rather uneven. We have a very high load on work center C in day 1, followed by low loads in days 2, 3, and 4. In work center B the first period has a relatively light load followed by a heavy load in period 2. Work center A also has a somewhat uneven load. Since the delivery dates calculated by this procedure are the earliest possible, orders may be produced before they are due. This presents an opportunity for leveling the load to some extent by delaying the start of some jobs.

There is no exact method to determine which jobs should be delayed; this can be done only by inspection and heuristic analysis. Without missing the due dates, the possible delay in starting time (in hours) for each job is as follows:

Job	Possible delay
1	7
2	6
3	10
4	6
5	0

Suppose that we decide to move jobs 1 and 4 forward in time to achieve a more nearly uniform workload. When the start dates for jobs 1 and 4 are deferred until the second day, the resulting load is more level, but jobs 1 and 4 will be a day late

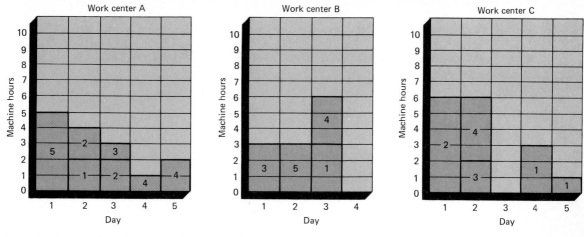

FIGURE 12.8 Load-leveling example.

(see Figure 12.8). If the customers will accept these delays, we will have achieved a much more efficient loading of the facilities.

This example illustrates how loading can be used to achieve the multiple objectives of an intermittent operation. Forward loading is done first. If a level load is obtained, and due dates are met, we will have obtained a good load on the first try. If the load is not level, perhaps the start of some jobs can be delayed to achieve a more level load. In order to get an idea of the effect of delaying the start dates, a backward load should be developed which starts each job at the latest possible time to just meet due dates.

In backward loading, we start with the due dates given in Figure 12.5 and work backward in time. First, construct a backward time line for each job, as shown in Figure 12.9 for jobs 1 and 2. Starting at the end of day 4 when job 1 is due, load 4 hours of time for work center C, the last processing step, at the end of day 4. Then move backward in time by 8 hours for move/wait time, and load 3 hours on the time line for work center B. Moving back another 8 hours of move/wait time, load 2 hours for work center A. This tells us precisely how many hours of processing time are needed in each work center in each day. Similarly, for job 2 we have started at the end of day 3, when it is due, and loaded processing times for work center A and work center C backward in time, as shown in Figure 12.9.

We can now take the time lines from Figure 12.9 and use this information to arrive at the backward load charts for each work center in Figure 12.10. The procedure for doing this is similar to the one used for forward loading. Use the job 1 backward time line to assign 4 hours to work center C in day 4, 3 hours to work center B in day 3, 1 hour to work center A in day 2, and 1 hour to work center A in day 1. Note how job 1 is split between days 1 and 2. Follow the same procedure for jobs 2, 3, 4, and 5 by transferring the time lines onto the work-center load charts until all jobs are backward-loaded.

The load obtained from backward loading in Figure 12.10 also has an uneven profile. For example, work center B has no work on day 1. It would be desirable to

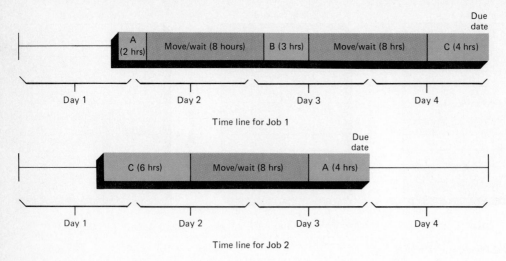

FIGURE 12.9   Job times for backward loading.

start some work earlier in order to keep work center B busy in day 1. Similarly, work center A is underloaded in day 2. In solving these two problems we could start job 1 up to 7 hours earlier and job 2 up to 6 hours earlier, as we have noted before. In this case the jobs would be finished earlier than they were really needed, but the people and machines would be kept busy. We are thus making a tradeoff between finishing the job earlier for inventory/delivery and machine/labor utilization.

Backward loading helps us determine the maximum capacity needed to meet all due dates. It can also help us visualize how to level out the workload when used in conjunction with forward loading. By working between backward and forward loading, it should be possible to achieve a satisfactory load which meets due dates

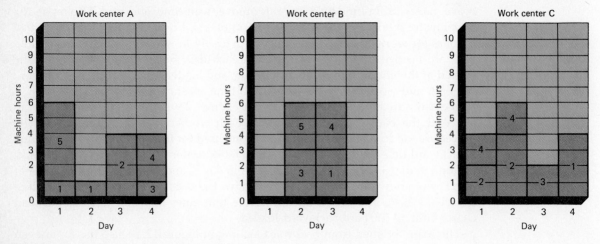

FIGURE 12.10   Backward-loading example.

but is still reasonably efficient and has low inventories. The procedure for doing this is heuristic and judgmental in nature.

It is easy to see from an understanding of loading why close liaison should be maintained between marketing and operations. Marketing should not promise arbitrary delivery dates simply on the basis of the customer's request because of the possible adverse effect on the intermittent facility's load. Perhaps a few days' difference in the delivery promise will make it possible to level out the peaks and valleys in the load. Thus, marketing should check with operations before making delivery promises, and operations should then live up to its commitments to deliver on time. This procedure is often not followed in practice, leading to a great deal of friction and poor delivery performance.

In this section we have been loading to "infinite" capacity with subsequent use of load leveling to reflect actual capacities. Forward loading can also be done to finite capacity. In this case, capacities are never exceeded, but due dates may be. Since loading to finite capacity is a straight forward extension of infinite loading, we will not discuss it further here.

12.5 SEQUENCING

Sequencing is concerned with developing an exact order (or sequence) of job processing. In sequencing, job interference and queuing times are computed by laying out a schedule for each job. An average queuing (or waiting) time is *not* assumed, as in the case of loading.

One of the oldest sequencing methods, the Gantt chart, was proposed by Henry L. Gantt in 1917. Although there are many variations of the Gantt chart, we shall restrict its use in this chapter to the sequencing problem.

The Gantt chart is a table with time across the top and a scarce resource, such as machines, people, or machine hours, along the side. In the example below, we shall assume that machines are the scarce resource to be scheduled.

For the sake of contrast, we will take the previous example and sequence the jobs with the Gantt chart. In doing this it will be assumed, as before, that each work center contains exactly one machine. Then the jobs are scheduled forward in time within the finite capacity of the one machine of each type (A, B, and C). We also assume, arbitrarily, that the jobs should be scheduled in the sequence 1, 4, 5, 2, 3.

The Gantt chart resulting from these assumptions is shown in Figure 12.11. This chart is constructed by first scheduling job 1 on all three machines. Job 1 starts on machine A for 2 hours, then is placed on machine B for 3 hours (time 2 to time 5), and is finally processed on machine C for 4 hours (time 5 to time 9). There is no idle time for the first job scheduled, since there can be no job interference or waiting. Next, job 4 is scheduled on the Gantt chart for machines C, B, and then A. Job 4 can begin immediately on machine C, since the machine is open until time 5 and only 4 hours are needed. After an idle time of 1 hour, job 4 can start on machine B. Job 4 can finally be scheduled on machine A from time 8 to 11. Next, job 5 is scheduled on the Gantt chart. Job 5 is processed on machine A first, but machine A is already scheduled until time 2. So job 5 starts at time 2 and is

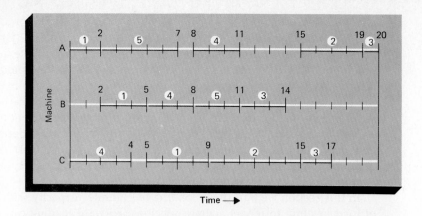

FIGURE 12.11
Gantt chart. Jobs
are sequenced in
order 1, 4, 5,
2, 3.

	Machine idle (hr)
A	5
B	8
C	4
	17

Make span = 20 hr

Job	Job idle (hr)	Delivery time (hr)
1	0	9
2	9	19
3	14	20
4	1	11
5	3	11

completed by time 7. After completion on machine A, job 5 is moved to machine B, which is busy until time 8. Job 5 is then scheduled from time 8 to 11 on machine B. This process of scheduling is continued until all jobs have been placed in the Gantt chart.

After a Gantt chart has been constructed, it should be evaluated with respect to both job and machine performance. One way to evaluate machine performance is on the basis of the time it takes to complete all work—the *make span*. In Figure 12.11 the make span is 20 hours, since it takes 20 hours to complete all the jobs.

Another measure of the Gantt chart performance is *machine utilization*. Utilization may be measured in Figure 12.11 by adding up the idle time for each machine $(5 + 8 + 4 = 17)$ and computing a utilization or idle percentage. The idle-time percentage is $17/60 = 28.3$ percent, and the utilization percentage is $43/60 = 71.7$ percent. Notice that utilization is closely related to make span. In the five jobs a total of 43 hours of processing time is required (simply add machine times for all jobs from Figure 12.5). The 43 hours of processing time is a constant regardless of the schedule used. Notice also that we have: idle time = 3 (make span) − 43. Therefore, minimizing make span will also minimize machine idle time.

A measure of job performance is the sum of the delivery times for each job. Minimizing this measure would also be equivalent to minimizing job waiting time, since the two times are complementary. In Figure 12.11 the delivery times and job-waiting times are listed for each job. These figures are obtained directly from the Gantt chart. The delivery time and waiting times will, of course, depend greatly on the job sequence used. Since job 1 was scheduled first, it has no waiting time and is completed as soon as possible, ahead of due date. Jobs 2 and 3, which were scheduled last, have considerable waiting time.

It can be seen from this example that the waiting time for jobs is highly variable and not a constant 8 hours, as we assumed for loading purposes. Loading is therefore a very rough procedure which approximates only total load and delivery times for jobs. Gantt chart scheduling is more precise, since it considers job interference and computes the waiting times for each job. Nevertheless, Gantt chart scheduling becomes very complex when there are several machines in each work center, job times are not precise, and workloads are shifting. In this case, loading gives a good forecast of capacity needs or due-date predictions, without obtaining a precise schedule.

A great deal of attention has been given in the literature to optimal job-sequencing algorithms. These algorithms typically optimize one or more measures of schedule performance, such as make span, but they utilize a highly restrictive set of assumptions, such as constant processing times, no passing of jobs, no job splitting, etc. One particular problem is called the $m \times n$ machine scheduling problem, where m is the number of machines and n is the number of jobs. To suggest the nature of the research which has been done on this problem we will review a few of the simpler algorithms below.

The $m \times n$ machine scheduling problem has been solved for $m = 1, 2, 3$ and arbitrary values of n. Efficient algorithms have not been developed for $m \geq 4$ because of the extremely large number of possible sequences. However, fairly good heuristics which seem to develop "good" solutions for any values of m and n are available. See Campbell, Dudek, and Smith.

The simplest $m \times n$ machine scheduling problem is for $m = 1$ and any n. In this simple case, the make span and utilization are fixed, since all jobs must be processed through the single facility. Make span will be the sum of the processing times and machine utilization will be 100 percent. We can, however, minimize the sum of the delivery dates or the *job* idle times. This is accomplished by scheduling the job with the shortest processing time first. By doing this, we are getting work done as fast as possible and thus reducing the time that other jobs wait for processing.

Let us assume that there are four jobs to schedule on a single machine, with processing times A = 3, B = 6, C = 2, D = 1, and that the jobs are sequenced in the order D, C, A, B. This sequencing uses shortest processing time first, then next-shortest processing time, etc. The resulting job waiting times will be D = 0, C = 1, A = 3, and B = 6, for a total of 10 hours. This is the minimum waiting time of all possible job sequences.

The $m = 2$ machine scheduling problem is slightly more complicated. First, assume that all jobs go through machine 1 and then machine 2 in the same order. Also assume that the processing times are given for each job on each machine, as shown in Figure 12.12.

The algorithm for solving this problem was first developed by S. M. Johnson (1954) and has been called the left-hand-right-hand rule by Woolsey (1975).

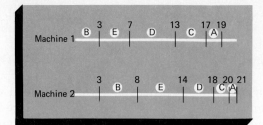

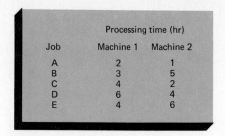

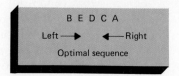

FIGURE 12.12
Two-machine
scheduling.

According to the method, the job timetable is first searched for the shortest processing time. In Figure 12.12, the shortest time is 1 hour and is on the right under machine 2. Since this time is on the right, job A is placed on the right side of the sequence and is crossed off the table. The next-shortest time is 2, which is also on the right under job C, so job C is placed on the right of the sequence next to job A and is crossed off the table. The next-shortest time is 3, which is on the left, so job B is placed on the left of the sequence and crossed off the table. The remaining jobs D and E are tied for shortest time, so we select job D arbitrarily and place it on the right. Job E remains and is placed on the left, according to its shortest time.

The resulting job sequence is B, E, D, C, A. If the jobs are processed in this order, we will achieve the minimum make span. This sequence will, of course, also minimize machine idle time, as noted above.

To compute the value of the minimum make span for this particular sequence, a Gantt chart should be constructed, as shown in Figure 12.12. The minimum make span is 21 hours. According to S. M. Johnson, this is the shortest make span among all possible job sequences (5 ! = 120 sequences in this case).

In studying the Gantt chart, one can see intuitively what is happening with Johnson's rule. A short time is scheduled first on machine 1, so that machine 2 is not kept waiting too long in the beginning. Since the shorter times in the beginning are on machine 1, on the left, machine 2 probably can be kept busy once it starts processing. At the end of the sequence the situation reverses, and the shortest times are on machine 2. This helps in the "end game" in quickly processing the remaining jobs through the second machine.

Although these sequencing rules and others have a great deal of theoretical interest, they have not been applied much in practice. This is because real sequencing problems involve a great deal of variability in processing times, multiple objectives, and other complicating factors. Nevertheless, the rules are useful for gaining insight into scheduling problems and for suggesting heuristics which might possibly be of value in practice. Some of these heuristics are reviewed in detail in the next section.

12.6 DISPATCHING RULES

In practice, schedules are difficult if not impossible to maintain because conditions often change; a machine breaks down, a qualified operator becomes ill, materials do not arrive on time, and so on. As a result, some operations are run without a detailed schedule. In this case, dispatch rules are used.

A dispatch rule specifies which job should be selected for work next from among a queue of jobs. When a machine or worker becomes available, the dispatch rule is applied and the next job selected. A dispatch rule is thus dynamic in nature and continually adjusts to changing conditions. Unlike a schedule, a dispatch rule cannot be out of date, and it answers the worker's immediate question: "What should I do next?"

A classic study of dispatch rules by Earl LeGrande evaluated six rules at Hughes Aircraft in El Segundo, California. The Hughes fabrication shop had 1000 machines, 400 to 500 workers, and 1800 to 2500 orders in process; it completed 100 to 150 shop orders per day. The performance of the rules was evaluated by simulating the shop in detail. As each job was completed on a machine, the dispatching rule was used to select the next job.

The following six rules were evaluated:

1. *MINPRT (minimum processing time).*[1] For this rule the job with the shortest processing time on the machine is selected. This rule is based on the idea that when a job is finished quickly, other machines downstream will receive work, resulting in a high flow rate and high utilization.
2. *MINSOP (minimum slack time per operation).* "Slack time" is defined as time remaining until the due date minus processing time remaining. Thus a job with zero slack would have just enough time to be completed if there were no waiting time in queues. In this rule, the slack is divided by the number of operations to normalize the slack time.
3. *FCFS (first come, first served).* This rule is based on the familiar "fairness" criterion, where the job which arrives first at the work center is processed first.
4. *MINSD (minimum planned start date).* This rule uses the results of a previous schedule to determine the planned start date for each job. The job with the minimum planned start date is processed first.
5. *MINDD (minimum due date).* By this rule, the job with the earliest due date is processed first.
6. *RANDOM (random selection).* This rule selects the next job to be processed at random. The rule would not be used in practice; it is simply a benchmark for comparison with other rules.

In order to evaluate these rules, it is necessary to develop criteria for shop performance. As previously mentioned, there are three types of criteria: efficiency

---

[1]This rule is also called SPT (shortest processing time) or SOT (shortest operation time).

TABLE 12.2

COMPARISON OF DISPATCHING RULES

Criteria*	1	2	3	4	5	6	7	8	9	10	Total relative rank
Relative weights	1	1	1	1	1	1	1	1	1	1	
MINPRT	1.00	.83	1.00	.20	1.00	1.00	.76	.91	1.00	1.00	8.70
MINSOP	.87	1.00	.63	1.00	.73	.52	.96	.99	.92	.92	8.54
FCFS	.80	.54	.54	.20	.73	.38	.84	.98	.93	.93	6.93
MINSD	.84	.48	.46	.22	.68	.36	.91	1.00	.91	.91	6.77
MINDD	.94	.62	.64	.24	.84	.51	1.00	.99	.87	.87	7.52
RANDOM	.84	.68	.79	.20	.67	.66	.80	.93	.92	.91	7.40

Source: Earle LeGrande, "The Development of a Factory Simulation System Using Actual Operating Data," *Management Technology,* vol. 3, no. 1, May 1963, p. 17.

*Key to criteria:
  1. Number of orders completed
  2. Percent of orders completed late
  3. Mean of the distribution of completions
  4. Standard deviation of the distribution of completions
  5. Average number of orders waiting in the shop
  6. Average wait time of orders
  7. Yearly cost of carrying orders in queue
  8. Ratio of inventory carrying cost while waiting to inventory cost while on machine
  9. Percent of labor utilized
 10. Percent of machine capacity utilized

of machines and labor, work-in-process inventory, and customer service. Although there are only three criteria, there are many ways to measure them. In the Hughes Aircraft simulation, 10 measures were selected, as shown in Table 12.2. The table also indicates how each rule performed on each measure. In this table, a value of 1.00 indicates the best performance on each measure, while the other values are relative measures.

The table indicates that the MINPRT rule does best on efficiency and flow-rate measures, while the MINSOP rule does best on meeting due dates. This result should be expected because the MINSOP rule incorporates due date in the rule while MINPRT does not. It should also be noted that the FCFS rule, which is quite popular in practice, performs poorly on all criteria. As a matter of fact, FCFS performs worse than the RANDOM rule.

Since the Hughes study was completed, two additional rules which are quite useful have been proposed:

1. MINPRT with truncation. In this rule the job with minimum processing time is selected next, just as in MINPRT, except when a job has waited for a specified period of time. The rule is then truncated and the job that has been waiting longest is done next. The result of this truncation is to process the long jobs sooner, with some sacrifice in efficiency. This reduces the adverse effect of the MINPRT rule, which is that long jobs wait in the queue and do not get processed.

2. Critical ratio. The critical ratio is computed as:

$$CR = \frac{\text{remaining time until due date}}{\text{remaining processing time}}$$

The job with the minimum value of CR is scheduled next. This rule calculates the ratio of demand time to supply time. When the ratio exceeds a value of 1, there is sufficient time available to complete the job if the queue times are properly managed. If the ratio is less than 1, the job will be late unless processing times can be compressed. The performance of the CR rule is similar to that of MINSOP, since they both explicitly account for due dates. However the CR rule has slightly more intuitive appeal, since the CR itself has a precise meaning; e.g., a ratio = 2 means that there is twice as much time remaining as the processing time.

Rules such as MINSOP and the CR rule are the most widely used in practice, since due dates seem to have more importance than efficiency and flow time. This is understandable because of the emphasis placed on schedule performance in industry.

In using dispatching rules, a shop-floor control system which updates the status of each job in process is needed. Using the feedback on job status, the supervisor receives a priority report each morning (or in real time). The priority report ranks all jobs waiting in that work center (or due to arrive that day) in priority order. These priorities can be calculated with any of the dispatching rules available. The supervisor then schedules work on the jobs in the work center on the basis of the priorities given. If the highest-priority job cannot be done (owing to machine breakdown, operator illness, or other reasons), the second job is done, and so on down the list. The priority list does not specify a rigid schedule and thus allows flexibility for local work-center conditions.

The use of priority rules in dispatching illustrates a very important principle stated by Plossl (1978): "Lead time is what you say it is." If a job is given a very tight due date, perhaps just a little greater than total processing time, a rule such as CR or MINSOP will speed the job through the shop because of the high priority. Of course, too many of these high-priority jobs will ruin the system. According to Plossl's rule, if a long lead time is promised, the entire time will be used since the job has a relatively low priority. With dispatching rules, lead time can be expanded or contracted by a large factor. This is one of the problems with loading calculations which assume that lead time is fixed when it is not.

It comes as a surprise to some people that lead times can be managed. The common view is that lead time is a relatively fixed or a statistical phenomenon. There is little realization that lead time is a function of both priority and capacity. If an operation is producing at near capacity, average lead times will be extended as already shown in Figure 12.4. Even though the *average* lead time is long, an individual job can still have a short delivery if its priority is high enough during dispatching. Thus, lead time is a function of both *capacity and priority* decisions.

The Japanese have recently shown us that lead times can be substantially reduced by different management practices. One way this is done is by reducing setup times and by scheduling more frequent deliveries with vendors. The resulting reduction in lead time has had dramatic effects on reducing inventories and improving customer service. Now many American companies are following the Japanese lead. More on this will be covered in Chapter 16 on JIT.

When loading is used in conjunction with input-output control and a dispatching rule, an effective dynamic scheduling system can be designed. The loading rule will serve to make the required capacity available in the work centers; the input-output rule will control the release of work to the shop so that the shop is not overloaded; and the dispatching rule will serve to manage the jobs through the operation to meet desired due dates. Notice that, in this case, a Gantt chart schedule is not maintained on individual jobs. There are cases, however, where Gantt chart sequencing is quite valuable. These cases include intermittent-process operations with relatively stable conditions. In this situation, a Gantt chart can be used to represent current conditions and thus to answer the worker's question, "What do I do next?"

PLANNING AND CONTROL SYSTEMS

As a popular TV advertisement said, "The system is the solution." This principle applies to scheduling operations, where an adequate planning and control system is needed. This scheduling system should not only facilitate the development of good schedules (planning) but also ensure that schedules are implemented and corrected as needed (control). These scheduling systems will usually incorporate some of the methods which have been described above. But without the system, the methods are useless.

There are several questions that every scheduling system should answer:

1. *What delivery date do I promise?* As discussed above, the promised delivery date should be based on both marketing and operations considerations. These considerations include available capacity, the customer's work requirements, and efficiency of operations. We have seen how the promised date can be derived for intermittent-process operations through loading or Gantt chart scheduling.
2. *How much capacity do I need?* A scheduling system can answer this question by forecasting and developing workloads for individual activities. For line-process operations, the question is answered by using runout times and projecting inventories into the future. For intermittent-process operations, this question is answered by infinite loading of the available jobs.
3. *When should I start on each particular activity or task?* This question too should be answered by all scheduling systems, but the methods used vary. In intermittent-process operations, the question is answered by using dispatching rules or a Gantt chart schedule. In line-process operations, the question is addressed directly by runout times.
4. *How do I make sure that the job is completed on time?* Dispatching helps to answer this question partially, but the answer also requires feedback on job status and constant monitoring of activity. If progress is continually or periodically evaluated, corrective action can be taken as needed to make sure that deliveries are made on time. In manufacturing, this question is answered by a shop-floor control system.

In order to illustrate the principles of scheduling and control, three examples that cover a wide range of scheduling problems will be discussed.

Courtroom Scheduling[2]

Courtroom scheduling urgently requires more systematic scheduling and control systems. Sometimes court calendars are overloaded, with the result that police officers, witnesses, lawyers, and defendants spend long times waiting. After a day in court without being heard, some witnesses will not return.

On the other hand, the same court may also suffer from case underload, with judges kept waiting and inefficient use of courtrooms. This condition occurs when cases finish early or cases scheduled to appear are delayed.

In an attempt to correct these problems, a court scheduling system was developed for the New York City Criminal Court. The system was designed to achieve the following five objectives: (1) there should be a high probability that judges will be kept busy, (2) there should be a high probability that cases will be heard when scheduled, (3) several cases should be batched together for a police officer on the same day, (4) high-priority cases should be scheduled as soon as possible, (5) and a maximum waiting-time limit should be set for all cases.

The heart of the system was a priority dispatching rule. The rule determined priorities for cases based on such factors as seriousness of the charge, whether the defendant was in or out of jail, and elapsed time since arraignment. When the priority of a case reached a certain threshold, it was inserted into the court calendar; otherwise it was returned to the unscheduled pool.

When a case was scheduled, the time required was predicted by a multiple regression equation which utilized causal variables such as plea of the defendant, seriousness of the offense, number of witnesses, and presiding judge. The predicted time was then scheduled for the first available spot on the calendar. Some slots, however, were kept open for emergencies and future rescheduling.

Each day the priorities were revised on the basis of the current conditions. Any new cases with a high enough priority were placed on the schedule with the required amount of predicted time.

The example illustrates how a service operation can use a dispatching rule as part of a logical scheduling and control system. The methods used were embedded in an information system which provided overall planning and control of the schedule. The system helped answer the crucial questions required to develop and implement the schedule.

Capacity Requirements Planning System

The capacity requirements planning (CRP) system was developed by Honeywell for use in intermittent-process manufacturing facilities. The computerized CRP system performs the following functions: (1) developing a capacity requirement plan, (2) scheduling and dispatching individual orders, and (3) shop-floor control reporting. The general outline of the system is shown in Figure 12.13.

In order to perform its functions, the system maintains several types of records, which are part of the larger Honeywell Manufacturing System data base. A

---

[2]This discussion is based on a study by Shapiro (1971).

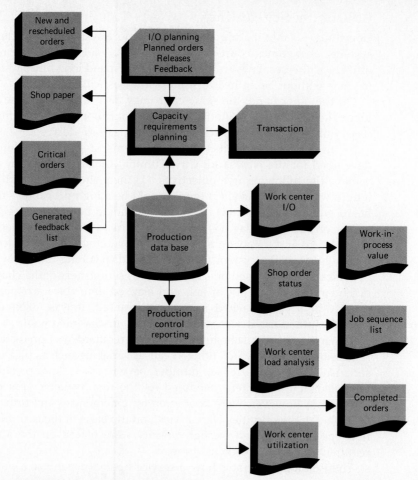

FIGURE 12.13   Overview of capacity requirements planning from the
Honeywell Manufacturing System.
Reprinted with permission, Honeywell, Inc.

work-center record is maintained for each group of similar machines. This record
contains information such as maximum machine hours available, length of
workday, cost of operations per hour, average queue time, and average move
time.

A routing record is also maintained for each job or order. This record contains a
description of all operations required, the sequence of operations, setup times, and
run times per piece (or per batch).

Finally, a work-in-process record is maintained for each order which is planned
or released. This record contains information on the status of the order, such as
current operation being worked on, expected completion date, and required
completion date.

A key part of the system is shop feedback, which is done by computer cards or at on-line terminals. If cards are used, there will be one computer card for each operation required. This pack of cards is placed in a shop packet along with shop paperwork authorizing work on the job. When each operation is completed, the card is returned to the central control office, along with information on time taken, number of pieces produced, scrap, and other items of importance. This information can also be transmitted via computer terminals.

The above information is used by the CRP system to perform scheduling, dispatching, and production reporting functions. The scheduling function is done through forward and backward loading to infinite capacity. Backward loading is done on the basis of given due dates, and forward loading is done from given start dates. The times used for loading include setup time (if required), run time per piece, average queue time for each work center, and average move time. Orders that fall behind schedule are reloaded by the system. The result of loading is a schedule for each order plus a load profile for each work center.

CRP performs the dispatching function by means of the critical-ratio rule (the ratio of total work time available to processing time remaining). These priorities are then listed for the supervisor of each work center to use in selecting jobs. In order to provide a measure of user control, the calculated ratios may be modified by user-supplied priorities. The user priorities will alter the priority of the order as the user specifies.

The production reporting function of CRP consists of a variety of status and management reports, work-center utilization records, and shop paperwork. These reports allow management to monitor the status of the system and the performance of the loading and dispatching functions.

Like the courtroom scheduling system, the CRP system provides the information environment for scheduling. The various rules and methods are the heart of the system, and the information ties the parts together into a logical whole.

Optimized Production Technology (OPT)

OPT is a computer program for scheduling manufacturing facilities which has recently gained some attention. The program was originally developed in Israel and brought to the United States in 1979. Some of the early users of OPT were General Electric and Sikorsky.

The OPT method begins by modeling an intermittent-manufacturing operation as a network of flows. The nodes in this network are machines or machine groups, and the arcs are paths from one machine to the next. Parts being processed thus proceed from one node to the next along the arcs as they flow through the facility.

The second step in OPT is to identify the bottleneck work centers in the network. A bottleneck is a machine group which must operate at greater than 100 percent capacity in order to meet the given schedule. Bottlenecks are thus scarce machine resources that will constrain or limit the flow through the shop. These bottlenecks are identified by loading a given output schedule back onto the various machine groups as we have described in this chapter.

The next step in OPT is to schedule the bottlenecks or critical resources to finite capacity. This is done by means of a computer routine which determines the batch size and the schedule for each job in order to get the most through the bottleneck operations while meeting the output schedule if possible. This program attempts to make the best use of the most critical resources.

After the bottleneck resources are scheduled to finite capacity, the remaining machines are scheduled backward in time to provide the needed parts to the bottlenecks. Nonbottleneck machines will have excess capacity and may produce in small lots to keep the bottleneck machines fully loaded. The lot sizes for transfer batches from noncritical machines may, therefore, be different from the processing lot sizes on critical machine groups.

OPT is useful in scheduling capacity-limited facilities since it will identify the bottleneck machines and attempt to make the best use of these critical resources. The program does a good job of maximizing the flow of parts through a facility without building up excess inventories.

OPT is not a tool to be used across the board for scheduling. It requires very accurate data (routings, time standards, bills of material, and capacities) and well-trained people to use it. Since the shop is being modeled at a very detailed level, the OPT schedule is only as good as the data fed into it. Nevertheless, some dramatic results (reduced inventories and better throughput) have been achieved in practice.

OPT is also useful for simulating changes in the factory. The effects of adding new machines or changing layouts to group technology or revising part routines can be evaluated in advance. Once an OPT model is in place, it has many uses for capital planning. For more information on OPT, see Fox (1983).

12.8   KEY POINTS

In this chapter, we have treated scheduling decisions for line- and intermittent-process operations. The chapter's theme is that all scheduling decisions deal with the allocation of scarce resources to jobs, activities, tasks, or customers. We assume, for scheduling purposes, that resources are fixed as a result of aggregate planning and facilities decisions.

The following are among this chapter's key points:

* Within the available resources, scheduling seeks to satisfy the conflicting objectives of low inventories, high efficiency, and good customer service. Thus, tradeoffs are always implicitly or explicitly made whenever a schedule is developed. Scheduling, however, differs between line, intermittent, and project forms of operations.
* The scheduling of line-process operations is concerned with producing multiple items on a single line. If only one product is produced on a line, there is no scheduling problem because the line is utilized to the extent needed for the single product. For multiple products, runout-time calculations can be used to determine a schedule which allocates line capacity among the products.
* There are a variety of scheduling decisions for intermittent-process operations. One of these involves regulating the input to the intermittent process. Too little input will result in low inventories, low utilization of labor and machines, and fast

customer service. Too much input will result in high inventories, high utilization, and long customer delivery times. The concepts of input-output control are used to regulate inputs in relation to outputs and available capacity.

- A second scheduling decision for intermittent-process operations is the loading of work centers. Both forward and backward loading are used to determine capacity needs, delivery due dates, and a smooth work flow. Loading utilizes average queue times and thus only approximates the aggregate load on facilities.

- For scheduling individual jobs, either sequencing or dispatching rules may be used. If sequencing is used, a Gantt chart is developed which shows exactly when each operation is planned for each job. When dispatching rules are used, jobs are selected for the next operation on the basis of prescribed priority rules. These priority rules are used to control the flow of work dynamically as it progresses through a facility. When dispatching rules are used, a Gantt chart or sequence is not constructed in advance.

- To be useful, scheduling methods must be embedded in an information system. Scheduling systems, in general, should answer the following questions: (1) what delivery date do I promise? (2) how much capacity do I need? (3) when should I start each particular activity or task? (4) how do I make sure that the job is completed on time? In order to handle constantly changing situations, these systems are usually computerized, and they require constant feedback on job status.

- Lead time is not a statistical phenomenon. Lead time is a function of both capacity and priority decisions.

QUESTIONS

1. What types of scheduling decisions is management likely to encounter in the following operations?
   a. Hospital
   b. University
   c. Movie making
   d. Military campaign
   e. Appliance factory
   f. Railroad

2. Specify the kinds of objectives that might be appropriate for each of the situations listed in Question 1.

3. What is the role of costs in the changeover and scheduling of assembly lines?

4. In making runout calculations, how far should one plan into the future?

5. Why is it important to view an intermittent-process operation as a network of interconnected queues?

6. How is the scheduling of patients in a doctor's clinic similar to or different from the scheduling of jobs in a factory?

7. What is meant by input-output control for intermittent-process operations? How is input-output control handled for line-process operations?

8. What are the effects of too little input and of too much input?

9. Under what circumstances is a combination of input-output control, loading, and dispatching more effective than precise sequencing through Gantt charts?

10. Describe the differences between forward loading and sequencing.

11. Why are there so many different types of dispatching rules?
12. What is the purpose of forward loading and backward loading?
13. How can production lead time be managed in operations? Why isn't lead time a constant value?
14. Why do you suppose that $m \times n$ machine scheduling algorithms are not widely used in practice? Should optimal rules be more widely used?
15. What is the purpose of a shop-floor control system? Can effective scheduling be done without shop-floor control?

PROBLEMS

1. An assembly line is used to make products A, B, and C. The scheduling information for these products follows:

Product	On-hand inventory, units	Production rate, units per week	Demand rate, units per week	Lot size, units
A	10,000	3000	1500	1000
B	6,000	1500	500	1500
C	9,000	4000	2000	2000

a. Calculate the production sequence (schedule) for the next 6 weeks using the runout method. Only one product can be produced at a time.
b. What is the projected inventory at the end of 6 weeks? Should capacity be adjusted?
c. Suppose capacity is increased by 25 percent for each product. What is the effect on the production sequence calculated in part a?

2. A batch process is used to make four types of cereal. The process can be changed over from one cereal to another by cleaning the cereal vats and resetting the packaging line for the new cereal. The resulting lot sizes for each cereal are shown below along with the production rates, demands, and on-hand inventories.

Product	On-hand inventory	Production rate, units per week	Demand rate, units per week	Lot size, units
Crunchies	50,000	15,000	5000	30,000
Munchies	40,000	10,000	2000	10,000
Crispies	30,000	6,000	3000	12,000
Sunshine	40,000	20,000	5000	20,000

a. Calculate the production sequence (schedule) for the next 5 weeks using the runout method.
b. What is the projected inventory at the end of 5 weeks? Should capacity be adjusted?
c. Suppose the beginning inventory of Crunchies is only 25,000. What effect does this have on the production sequence?

3. In an intermittent-process operation, work-in-process inventory can be reduced by 20 percent with a corresponding 5 percent reduction in labor utilization. Should the inventory reduction be made? The current level of WIP inventory is $10 million, carrying cost is 30 percent per year, and labor cost is $10 million per year. If the input to this operation is $1 million per week, what is the production lead time? How much will customer service be improved by the proposed inventory reductions?

4. By a creative new scheduling process it is possible to simultaneously improve labor utilization by 3 percent and reduce inventory by 10 percent. The current level of inventory is $5 million, and the labor costs are $2 million per year. It costs 30 percent per year to carry inventory.

   a. What level of savings can be expected from this program?

   b. If it costs $1 million to install the new scheduling system, what is the real IROR for a 5-year life?

5. The following information is given for four jobs and three work centers:

Job	Work center/machine hours	Due date, days
1	A/3, B/2, C/2	3
2	C/2, A/4	2
3	B/6, A/1, C/3	4
4	C/4, A/1, B/2	3

   Assume there are 6 hours of move and queue time between work centers for each job.

   a. Perform a backward load of all jobs.

   b. Forward-load all jobs.

6. Sequence the jobs given in Problem 5 using a Gantt chart. Assume that the move time between machines is 1 hour. Sequence the jobs in priority order 1, 2, 3, 4.

   a. What is the make span?

   b. How much machine idle time is there?

   c. When is each job delivered compared with its due date?

   d. How much idle time (waiting time) is there for each job?

   e. Devise a better job sequence for processing.

7. The Security Life Insurance Company processes all new life insurance policies through three departments, incoming mail (I), underwriting (U), and policy control (P). The incoming mail department receives applications and customer payments and then routes the files to the underwriting department. After checking on the applicants' qualifications for life insurance, the underwriting department forwards the file to policy control for the issue of the policy. At the present time, the company has five new policy applications waiting to be processed. The time required for processing in each department is shown below.

Policy	Department/hours
1	I/3, U/6, P/8
2	I/2, P/10
3	I/1, U/3, P/4
4	I/2, U/8, P/6
5	I/1, P/6

   a. Perform a forward load to infinite capacity for each policy. Assume there are 8 hours of move/wait time between departments.

   b. Prepare a Gantt chart schedule for these policies. Compare the Gantt chart with the forward load. Which is best? Why?

8. At the University Hospital, five blood samples must be scheduled through a blood testing laboratory. Each sample goes through up to four different testing stations. The times for each test and the due dates for each sample are as follows:

Sample	Test station/hours	Due date hours
1	A/1, B/2, C/3, D/1	10
2	B/2, C/3, A/1, D/4	6
3	C/2, A/3, D/1, C/2	8
4	A/2, D/2, C/3, B/1	12
5	D/2, C/1, A/2, B/4	14

a. Using a Gantt chart, schedule these five samples; schedule them in priority order of earliest due date first.

b. Prepare a backward load of these samples. Use a move/wait time of 1 hour between test stations.

c. Prepare a forward load.

d. Analyze the backward and forward loads in order to suggest a new load. Which is more level?

9. Students must complete two activities in order to register for class: registration and payment of fees. Because of individual differences, the processing time (in minutes) for each of these two activities varies as shown below for five students:

Student	Minutes	
	Registration	Pay fees
A	12	5
B	7	2
C	5	9
D	3	8
E	4	6

a. What sequence should be used to process the students in order to maximize utilization of the registration process? Hint: Use the left-hand–right-hand rule.

b. Construct a Gantt chart to determine the total time required to process all five students.

c. What problems might be encountered in using this approach for registration in colleges?

10. Six jobs must be processed through machine A and then B as shown below. The processing time for each job is also shown.

Job	Machine, min	
	A	B
1	10	6
2	6	12
3	7	7
4	8	4
5	3	9
6	6	8

a. Using the left-hand–right-hand rule, what sequence should be used to minimize the make span?

b. Develop a Gantt chart to determine the total time required to process all six jobs.

11. Several dispatching rules are being considered by a secretary for purposes of typing term papers. The following information is given on jobs which are waiting to be typed.

Paper	Hours until due date	Total remaining processing time, hours*	Processing time, typing hours	Remaining number of operations	Order of arrival
A	20	14	10	2	4th
B	19	15	15	1	3d
C	16	9	6	3	2d
D	10	5	5	1	1st
E	18	11	7	2	5th

*Includes typing, corrections, and copying.

Use the following dispatching rules to determine the order of processing by the typing activity.

a. MINPRT   d. MINDD

b. MINSOP   e. CR

c. FCFS

12. Suppose that you are in charge of dispatching for the University Hospital laboratory described in Problem 8. Use the following dispatching rules for the first station (A) at the beginning of processing to determine which job should be processed first through station A. Hint: Decide between jobs 1 and 4.

a. MINPRT   c. MINDD

b. MINSOP   d. CR

SELECTED BIBLIOGRAPHY

BAKER, KEN: *Introduction to Sequencing and Scheduling*, New York: Wiley, 1974.

BEDWORTH, DAVID, and JAMES BAILEY: *Integrated Production Control Systems*, 2d ed., New York: Wiley, 1987.

BUFFA, ELWOOD S., MICHAEL J. COSGROVE, and BILL J. LUCE: "An Integrated Work Shift Scheduling System," *Decision Sciences*, vol. 7, no. 4, October 1976, pp. 620–630.

BULKIN, MICHAEL L., JOHN L. COLLEY, and HARRY W. STEINHOFF, JR.: "Load Forecasting, Priority Sequencing, and Simulation in a Job Shop Control System," *Management Science*, vol. 13, no. 2, October 1966, pp. B29–B51.

CAMPBELL, H. G., R. A. DUDEK, and M. L. SMITH: "A Heuristic Algorithm for the *n* Job *m* Machine Sequencing Problem," *Management Science*, vol. 16, no. 10, June 1970, pp. B630–B637.

COLLEY, JOHN L., ROBERT LANDEL, and ROBERT FAIR: *Production Operations Planning and Control*, San Francisco: Holden-Day, 1977.

CONSTABLE, C. J., and C. C. NEW: *Operations Management: A Systems Approach through Text and Cases*, New York: Wiley, 1976.

CONWAY, R. W., WILLIAM L. MAXWELL, and LOUIS W. MILLER: *Theory of Scheduling*, Reading, Mass.: Addison-Wesley, 1967.

FETTER, R. B., and J. D. THOMPSON: "The Simulation of Hospital Systems," *Operations Research*, vol. 13, no. 5, September–October 1965, pp. 689–711.

FOGARTY, DONALD W., and THOMAS R. HOFFMANN: *Production and Inventory Management*, Cincinnati, Oh.: South-Western, 1983.

FOX, BOB: "OPT—An Answer for America," Part IV, *Inventories and Production*, vol. 3, no. 1, March–April 1983, pp. 12–22.

HONEYWELL INFORMATION SYSTEMS, INC.: *Honeywell Manufacturing System: Summary Description*, 1986.

JOHNSON, S. M.: "Optimal Two-Stage and Three-Stage Production Schedules with Setup Times Included," *Naval Research Logistics Quarterly*, vol. 1, no. 1, March 1954, pp. 61–68.

JONES, C. H.: "An Economic Evaluation of Job Shop Dispatching Rules," *Management Science*, vol. 20, no. 3, November 1973, pp. 293–307.

LEGRANDE, EARL: "The Development of a Factory Simulation System Using Actual Operating Data," *Management Technology*, vol. 3, no. 1, May 1963, pp. 1–18.

MABERT, VINCENT A., and ALAN R. RAEDELS: "Detail Scheduling of a Part-Time Work Force," *Decision Sciences*, vol. 8, no. 1, January 1977, pp. 109–120.

MATHER, HAL, and GEORGE PLOSSL: "Priority Fixation versus Throughput Planning," *Production and Inventory Management*, vol. 19, no. 3, 3d quarter, 1978.

SHAPIRO, SAMUEL: "An Automated Court Scheduling System," presented at the 12th American Meeting of the Institute of Management Sciences, Detroit, Mich., September 1971.

VOLLMANN, THOMAS E., WILLIAM L. BERRY, and D. CLAY WHYBARK: *Manufacturing Planning and Control Systems*, Homewood, Ill.: Irwin, 1984.

WEMMERLÖV, URBAN: *Capacity Management Techniques*, American Production and Inventory Control System, 1984.

WOOLSEY, R. D., and H. S. SWANSON: *Operations Research for Immediate Application, A Quick & Dirty Manual*, New York: Harper & Row, 1975.

CHAPTER 13

Planning and Scheduling Projects

In the last three chapters, we have discussed capacity planning and scheduling for ongoing operations, but we have omitted one important type of operation—the project. As originally defined in Chapter 5, the project form of operations is used to produce the unique product, a single unit. Because of this, the management of a project is quite different from that of an ongoing operation.

Although there are many decisions in projects that differ from those in ongoing operations, our main concern in this chapter will be with project planning and scheduling decisions. In the first part of the chapter, a broad framework for project planning will be established; this will include the objectives of projects and the planning and control activities they require. In the last part of the chapter, specific scheduling methods—PERT and CPM—will be described in detail.

TABLE 13.1
EXAMPLES OF PROJECTS

Building construction
New-product introduction
Research and development
Computer system design
Installation of equipment
Space shots
Fund raising
Movie making
Teaching a course
Designing an advertising campaign
Startup or shutdown of a plant
Manufacture of aircraft, ships, and large machines
Auditing accounts
Planning a military invasion

Projects include a wide range of manufacturing and service activities. Large objects such as ships, passenger aircraft, and missile launchers are manufactured on a project basis. Each unit is made as a unique item, and the manufacturing process is often stationary, so that materials and labor must be brought to the project. The construction of buildings is typically organized on a project basis. Services such as movies, R&D, and fund raising are also delivered on a project basis. Table 13.1 lists a wide range of manufacturing and service activities which are managed as projects. Box 13.1 describes a typical scheduling decision for a movie studio.

BOX 13.1
TYPICAL DECISION PROBLEM

Carrie James, a recent graduate from a prestigious business school, had just been hired by International Pictures Studio to work in the project management area. Her boss, Arthur Broberg, director of the studio, was describing the current method of project management used. "Carrie, as you know, each movie we produce is established as a separate project. In the beginning, the producer determines an overall schedule and budget for the picture. The producer then develops a detailed work breakdown and a bar-chart schedule of all activities required to produce the movie. Although these activities and schedules are unique for each movie, they bear some resemblance to those for other movies which we have produced in the past. A detailed budget is also established by the producer and time-phased to correspond to the time schedule. When these planning and scheduling activities are completed, the project begins, with initial casting and work on the script, the scenery, and the costumes."

Mr. Broberg continued by discussing several problems that he had with the present project management system: "The individual movie schedules do not consider the load on common facilities such as scenery shops, the film editing department, and costume shops. As a result, these shops are frequently overloaded and the schedules cannot be met."

Mr. Broberg also observed that "the schedule we set initially is often out of date. We try to revise the schedules for each movie monthly, but due to changing priorities and time estimates, we cannot seem to stay on schedule. Carrie, as you know, movie stars are sometimes fickle and difficult to work with; therefore, certain shots may take longer than expected. On other occasions, we shoot a scene successfully the first time, and then we are ahead of schedule. We need a better method to handle the variability in schedule times."

Broberg went on to describe the method used to run the weekly schedule. "Each Monday morning, we have a meeting of all the shop superintendents and directors. All the scheduling problems that directors are having are discussed at the meeting and decisions are made on the spot. Sometimes these meetings last for three or four hours. There must be a better way to handle these problems. Frequently a crisis atmosphere prevails. Would you please review these problems and give me your analysis and suggestions in writing by a week from Friday? We will then meet again to discuss your report."

As she left the meeting, Carrie wondered whether the problems could be solved with a better project scheduling technique such as PERT or whether a completely fresh approach was required.

OBJECTIVES AND TRADEOFFS

In projects, there are usually three distinct objectives: cost, schedule, and performance. The project cost is the sum of direct and allocated costs assigned to the project. The project manager's job is to control those costs which are directly controllable by the project organization. These costs typically cover labor, material, and some support services. Ordinarily, the project manager will have a project budget which includes the costs assigned to the project.

The second objective in managing projects is schedule. Frequently a project completion date and intermediate milestones are established at the outset. Just as the project manager must control the project costs within budget, so the project manager must control the schedule to meet established dates. Frequently, the budget and schedule conflict. For example, if the project is behind schedule, overtime may be needed to bring it back on. But there may be insufficient funds in the budget to support the overtime costs. Therefore, a tradeoff decision between time and cost must be made. Management must determine whether the schedule objective is of sufficient importance to justify an increased cost.

The third objective in project management is performance, that is, the performance characteristics of the product or service being produced by the project. If the project is research and development on a new type of machine, "performance" refers to the performance specifications of the new machine. If the project is a movie, "performance" refers to the quality of the movie produced and its subsequent box-office receipts. In this case, performance may be specified by a variety of movie standards regarding casting, sound, filming, and editing. Performance for a service project, such as a movie, is ordinarily much more difficult to specify than for a manufactured product.

Performance may also require tradeoffs with both schedule and cost. In a movie, for example, if the picture is not meeting performance expectations, additional shots or script revisions may be required. These performance requirements may, in turn, cause cost and schedule changes. Since it is rarely possible to predict performance, schedule, and cost requirements accurately before a project begins, numerous tradeoffs may be required while the project is under way.

PLANNING AND CONTROL IN PROJECTS

A general sequence of management decisions required in all projects is planning, scheduling, and control decisions. "Planning" refers to those decisions, required in the beginning of a project, which establish its general character and direction. Generally speaking, project planning establishes the major project objectives, the resources required, the type of organization used, and the key people who will manage and implement the project. Project planning is usually a function of top and middle managers. When completed, project planning should be documented by a project authorization form or letter which is used to initiate further project activities. The project authorization form should specify all the planning decisions listed in part A of Table 13.2.

The scheduling phase of project management specifies the project plan in more detail. This phase begins with the construction of a detailed list of project activities, called a work-breakdown structure. A detailed time schedule for each

TABLE 13.2
PROJECT MANAGEMENT ACTIVITIES AND DECISIONS

A. PLANNING

Identify the project customer
Establish the end product or service
Set project objectives
Estimate total resources and time required
Decide on the form of project organization
Make key personnel appointments (project manager, etc.)
Define major tasks required
Establish a budget

B. SCHEDULING

Develop a detailed work-breakdown structure
Estimate time required for each task
Sequence the tasks in the proper order
Develop a start/stop time for each task
Develop a detailed budget for each task
Assign people to tasks

C. CONTROL

Monitor actual time, cost, and performance
Compare planned to actual figures
Determine whether corrective action is needed
Evaluate alternative corrective actions
Take appropriate corrective action

activity in the work-breakdown structure is then established, using the methods described later in this chapter. When the time schedule is completed, a time-phased budget, which is keyed to the start and completion times of each of the project activities, can be developed. Finally, the project personnel can be assigned to individual project activities.

Project control is maintained by monitoring each activity as the work is performed on the project. Activities should be monitored for time, cost, and performance in accordance with the project plan. When a significant discrepancy exists between actual results and the plan, corrective action should be taken. These corrective actions might include revision of the plan, reallocation of funds, personnel changes, or other changes in resources. As a result of corrective actions, the plan should once again be feasible and realistic.

The study of project management should ideally treat all aspects of planning, scheduling, and control, including both behavioral and quantitative issues. Owing to space limitations, however, the remainder of this chapter will be restricted primarily to quantitative scheduling methods.

SCHEDULING METHODS

Several types of scheduling methods are in use. These may be generally classified as Gantt chart or network methods. The Gantt chart methods utilize a bar or milestone chart as shown in Figure 13.1. The network methods use a graph or network to show precedence relations.

The Gantt chart method of scheduling has a great deal in common with Gantt chart scheduling for intermittent processes, described in Chapter 12. In each case,

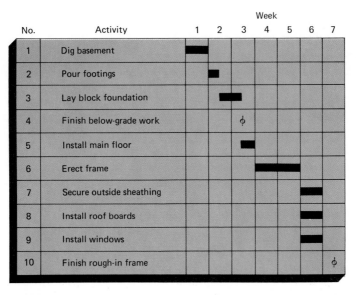

FIGURE 13.1
Gantt chart
project example.

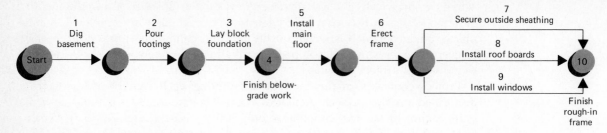

FIGURE 13.2 Network project chart.

the activity durations are shown on the chart by a bar or line. These charts also show when each activity is scheduled to begin and when it will be completed.

Figure 13.1 is a simplified Gantt chart for the construction of a house. Time is shown across the top, and activities are shown down the side. Each activity in the project is shown as a bar on the chart over the period of time for which the particular activity is scheduled. Notice that activities 1, 2, and 3 are scheduled in a sequence. That is, activity 1 is completed before activity 2 begins, and activity 2 is completed before activity 3 begins. The chart also indicates that activities 7, 8, and 9 are done in parallel at the same time. The Gantt chart, therefore, shows not only how much time is required for each activity but also when each activity takes place.

In addition to activities, Gantt charts can also show milestones (or events). A milestone is an instant in time, while an activity is a task with a certain duration of time. A milestone is often used to signal the beginning or end of one or more activities. In Figure 13.1, one milestone indicates the completion of all below-grade work, and another milestone indicates the completion of all rough-in framing.

Gantt charts are very commonly used in project scheduling because they are easy to use and quite widely understood. In complex projects, however, a Gantt chart becomes inadequate because it does not show the interdependencies and relationships between activities. For complex projects, it is difficult to schedule the project initially and even more difficult to reschedule it when changes occur. The network method of project scheduling overcomes these difficulties.

Figure 13.2 is a network diagram for the same house construction project shown in Figure 13.1. In the network chart, activities are shown as arrows, while milestones (or events) are shown as circles.[1] Notice that the network diagram clearly shows precedence relationships between the activities. The convention used in drawing these network diagrams is that all arrows leading into a circle (event) must be completed before any arrows leading out of the circle can begin. All arrows leading into a circle are then called predecessors, and all arrows leading

---

[1]This notation is called the activity on arrow (AOA) convention. There is also the activity on node (AON) convention, which is the opposite. When the AON convention is used, the activities are denoted by circles (or nodes) and the precedence relationships between activities are indicated by arrows. The AON convention is discussed later in the chapter.

out of the circle are called successors. All predecessor activities must be completed before any of the successors can begin.

The advantage of the network methods over the Gantt chart is that the precedence relationships in network scheduling are explicitly shown on the network. This permits development of a scheduling algorithm which accounts for all precedence relations when the schedule is developed. With Gantt charts, the precedence relations must be kept in the scheduler's head. On complex projects, this cannot easily be done, and Gantt charts become unwieldy. Furthermore, when a single activity time changes on the Gantt chart, the entire chart must be rescheduled by hand. Rescheduling can be done automatically by a network algorithm. On the other hand, networks are more complex, more difficult to understand, and more costly to use than Gantt charts. Thus networks should be used in complex projects, provided the additional cost is justified.

Network scheduling methods involve the use of some important scheduling concepts, such as critical path and slack. These network scheduling concepts will be described next by means of the constant-time network. More complicated networks, using random times, time-cost tradeoffs, and precedence diagrams will be developed later in the chapter.

13.4 CONSTANT-TIME NETWORKS

In constant-time networks, the time for each activity is assumed to be a constant. This is the simplest case from the standpoint of scheduling. Other, more complicated methods are then derived from these constant-time network methods.

A simple constant-time network is shown in Figure 13.3. In this example, the events (or milestones) are numbered in sequential order, so that the head of each

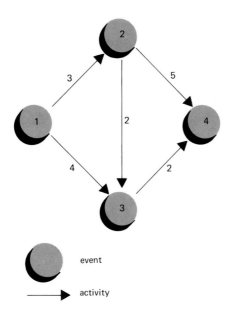

FIGURE 13.3
Network
diagram.

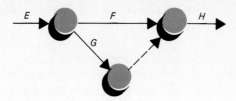

a. Activities *F* and *G* have the same predecessor (*E*) and the same successor (*H*).

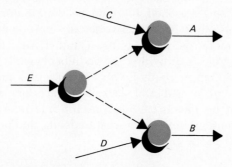

b. Activities *A* and *B* have a common predecessor (*E*), but they have different predecessors (*C* and *D*).

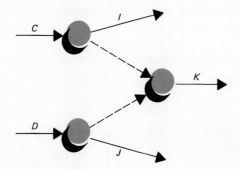

FIGURE 13.4
Dummy activity
situations.

c. Activities *C* and *D* have a common successor (*K*), but different successors (*I* and *J*).

arrow has a larger number than the tail. This will ensure that all successor activities and events have larger numbers than their predecessors. Through the use of this numbering scheme, scheduling computations can proceed in order of the numbers, and the predecessors will all be scheduled ahead of successors.

The event numbers shown in Figure 13.3 allow each activity to be identified by its tail and head number pair. Thus activity 1–2 identifies the activity or arrow going from event 1 to event 2. Other activities are also identified in a similar manner.

Some of the precedence relationships indicated in Figure 13.3 are as follows: Activity 1–2 must be completed before activity 2–4 or 2–3 can begin. Activities 1–2, 2–3, and 1–3 must all be completed before activity 3–4 can begin. In general, all predecessors must be completed before any successor activity can begin. Figure

13.3 also shows, immediately next to the arrow, the time required for the completion of each activity. For example, activity 1–2 requires 3 days, and activity 1–3 requires 4 days.

Sometimes, dummy activities are needed in order to draw the network diagram. A dummy activity has a duration time of zero and is used to indicate a precedence relationship only. For example, if two activities have identical predecessor and successor activities, a dummy activity will be needed to draw the network, since two activities cannot have identical predecessors and successors when using the normal procedure. A dummy activity is also needed when two activities have predecessor or successor sets of activities which are partially in common, but not identical. These situations are shown in Figure 13.4, where the dummy activity is shown as a dashed arrow. A dummy activity is basically a device used to resolve logical difficulties when drawing networks.

Once the network has been defined, the scheduling calculations can be made. Actually there are two types of calculations: one for event times and the other for activity times. For the sake of simplicity, event calculations will be presented first.

Event Calculations

To calculate event times, the following notation is needed:

t_{ij} = time to complete activity from event i to event j

E_j = earliest time event j can occur based on completion of all predecessor activities

L_j = latest time event j can occur without delaying the project's completion

Early event times (E_j) are calculated in a sequential fashion by starting at the beginning of the network and proceeding through the network to the end. We will illustrate this calculation by using the previous example and Figure 13.5 to compute the earliest time that each event can occur. First, assign a zero starting

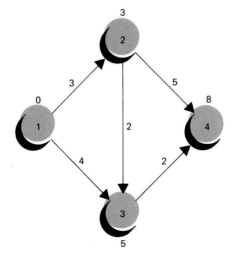

FIGURE 13.5
Network forward pass. Early occurrence, E_j, values shown above each event j.

time to the first event. Then assign a 3 to event 2, since it can occur as soon as activity 1–2 is completed, which takes 3 time units. Event 3 can occur as soon as *both* activities 2–3 and 1–3 are completed. Activity 2–3 takes 2 time units beyond event 2 (which was assigned a 3) and will be completed at time 5 = (3 + 2). Activity 1–3 is completed sooner, at time 4. Since event 3 cannot occur until both activities are completed, it occurs at time 5, the maximum of its two predecessor times. Similarly, event 4 can occur at the maximum of (3 + 5) and (5 + 2), or at time 8. This method hinges on the fact that no event can occur until *all* of its immediate predecessors are completed. Thus the maximum of preceding times is used when calculating E_j's. The forward computational pass we have just described will be used to calculate the earliest event times (E_j) for each event j. This is done by means of the following algorithm:

1. Set $E_1 = 0$ for the starting event.[2]
2. Set $E_j = \max_i (E_i + t_{ij})$ where the maximization occurs over all events i which are immediate predecessors of event j.

This algorithm proceeds sequentially from one event to the next beginning with event 1.

As the algorithm proceeds, each event j is labeled with the value of its earliest start time E_j. In Figure 13.5, the values of E_j are shown next to each event, using the example from Figure 13.3. In this example, event 1 is labeled with time zero as the time. Event 2 is then labeled with the time $0 + 3 = 3$ by using the activity time from 1 to 2. To label event 3, both activity times 2–3 and 1–3 must be considered, as we have shown above.

$$E_3 = \max (3 + 2, 0 + 4) = 5$$

Also, the earliest occurrence time of event 4 is computed by taking the maximum of event 2 plus activity 2–4 and event 3 plus activity 3–4. Thus we have

$$E_4 = \max (3 + 5, 5 + 2) = 8$$

We label event 4 with the value 8. Since event 4 is the last event in the network, the earliest completion of the entire project will also be 8 days. This is the earliest completion time of the project considering the precedence and times of all activities in the network.

In summary, we have computed the earliest time that each event can occur by considering all the immediate predecessors of each particular event. The forward pass utilizes the maximum time of all predecessor combinations since, by definition, an event cannot occur until all its predecessors are completed.

In network calculations, a backward pass is also made to derive the latest time that each event can occur without delaying completion of the project. The algorithm for computing these latest times is:

Define $L_n = E_n$

---

[2]Arbitrary starting times other than zero can also be used.

where n represents the last event in the network, and then let

$$L_i = \min_j (L_j - t_{ij})$$

where the minimization occurs over all events j which are immediate successors of event i.

The above times are computed by starting with the last event in the network, representing completion of the project, and proceeding in reverse order, backward, through the network.

The latest event times for the example are shown in Figure 13.6. In this example, we set $L_4 = E_4 = 8$ for the last event. Then there is only one successor for event 3, so:

$$L_3 = L_4 - t_{34} = 8 - 2 = 6$$

We label event 3 with a 6 for its latest occurrence time. For event 2, we have two successor events, 3 and 4. Therefore we have

$$L_2 = \min (8 - 5, 6 - 2) = 3$$

We have taken the minimum in this case, rather than the maximum on the forward pass, because all the successor events must occur before their latest times. Event 2 is labeled with a latest time of 3 days.

The latest time for event 1 is computed in a similar way as that for event 2. Since event 1 has two successor events,

$$L_1 = \min (3 - 3, 5 - 4) = 0$$

It should always turn out that the latest and earliest occurrence times of the first event are the same. This fact can be used as a partial check on the arithmetic used in the calculations.

With the backward pass, we have computed the latest time that each event can occur without delaying the project. In this calculation, all the immediate succes-

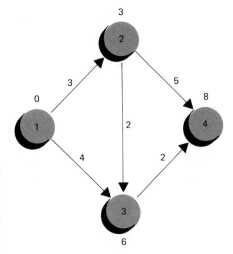

FIGURE 13.6
Network
backward pass.
Latest occurrence,
L, values shown
above each
event i.

sors of each event were considered. The minimum time of all successor combinations was taken since any delay in event occurrence beyond the minimum of these times would delay the project completion time.

The information calculated from the forward and backward pass can be used for several managerial purposes: (1) identifying the critical path, (2) calculating slack, and (3) determining the final completion date of the project. A path is any sequence of activities which connects the starting and ending events of the network. The *critical path* is defined as the *longest-time* path through the network. The critical path, therefore, constrains the completion date of the project, since it is the longest path of activity times from the start to the end of the network.

In the example from Figure 13.3, there are only three paths through the network: 1–2–4, 1–2–3–4, and 1–3–4. The length of these paths is 8, 7, and 6, respectively. These lengths are obtained by adding the times along the activities on each path. It is apparent from these calculations that path 1–2–4 is the longest of the three and is therefore the critical path. Notice that the length of the critical path is 8, which is also the earliest completion time (E_4) of the project that we have just computed. The forward pass, therefore, immediately provides the length of the critical path as the project completion time.

In large examples, it is not possible to evaluate all paths, as we have just done, to find the longest path, because there are simply too many. Therefore, the forward and backward passes are used directly to find the critical path. In general, the critical path connects those events with $E_i = L_i$. These events are critical since their earliest and latest occurrence times are the same. In the example, events 1, 2, and 4 have $E_i = L_i$; therefore the critical path is 1–2–4.

In managing a project, all activities and events on the critical path must be carefully monitored. If any of the critical activities slips (takes more time than planned), the completion date of the project will slip by a like amount. In a typical project, with a few hundred activities, only 5 to 10 percent of all activities are on the critical path. Therefore the monitoring of critical activities and events provides a significant reduction in managerial effort.

The information computed from the forward and backward passes also allows for the calculation of event slack. The slack for event i, S_i, is defined as follows:

$$S_i = L_i - E_i$$

The slack is, therefore, the precise amount that the event occurrence time can slip before affecting the project completion date. Observe that all events on the critical path should have slack equal to zero. This is another, equivalent way of defining the critical path.

In the example we have been using, the event slack = 0 for events 1, 2, and 4, and slack = 1 for event 3. Thus the occurrence time of event 3 can slip by 1 day before the completion time of the project is affected. This slip of 1 day could occur by an increase of either 1 day in activity 2–3 or 2 days in activity 1–3. In this case, there are two different activities which can consume the event slack.

The third use of the forward and backward pass computations is to establish a completion date for the project. If the date calculated from the forward pass is not satisfactory, perhaps activities along the critical path can be extended or shortened to obtain an acceptable date. In this case, tradeoffs may have to be made between cost, performance, and time. The network calculations help to evaluate these tradeoffs since they provide a precise determination of the effect of each proposed change on the completion date of the project.

It is now apparent that network calculations have several advantages over the Gantt chart. Networks allow precise determination of the critical path and slack, and they allow the rapid evaluation of proposed schedule changes. In addition, the ideas of critical path and slack are important conceptual notions in their own right.

Activity Calculations

Up to this point we have concentrated on calculating event times. But there are similar calculations for activity start and finish times. In managing networks, it is sometimes important to know the scheduled times for both activities and events. In this section, we will be concentrating on scheduling the arrows (activities) rather than scheduling the circles (events).

To calculate activity start and finish times, the following notation is needed:

$ES(a)$ = early start of activity a

$EF(a)$ = early finish of activity a

$LS(a)$ = late start of activity a

$LF(a)$ = late finish of activity a

Each activity has four scheduled times, as defined above. These times may be calculated by a forward and backward pass of the type used for event times, or they may be calculated directly from the event schedule.

To calculate the four activity times directly from the network, a forward activity pass is made by the following method:

$ES(a)$ = 0 for starting activities

$EF(a)$ = $ES(a) + t(a)$

$ES(a)$ = max [EF (all predecessors of a)]

where $t(a)$ denotes the duration of activity a.

On the basis of the example from Figure 13.3, the forward-activity pass computations are made; they are shown in Figure 13.7. The early start and early finish for each activity are placed on the top of each arrow, as shown.

As an example, the earliest start time of activity 3–4 is computed as the maximum of the earliest finish of activities 2–3 and 1–3. The maximum is used because both these predecessors must be completed before activity 3–4 can begin. The early start time of activity 3–4 is therefore the maximum of (4, 5), which is 5. The earliest finish of activity 3–4 is just its early start time of 5 plus the duration of 2 days. In a similar way, the ES and EF times for all other activities are computed.

A backward pass is also needed to calculate the late start and late finish times. The backward-activity pass is based on the following calculations:

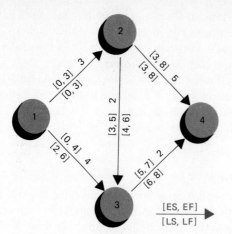

FIGURE 13.7
Activity start and
finish times.

$$LF(a) = min [LS \text{ (all successors of a)}]$$
$$LS(a) = LF(a) - t(a)$$

These late times are computed by starting with the last activities in the network and proceeding backward through the entire network in numerical order. The project completion time is set equal to 8, based on the forward pass, and used as the LF times for all ending activities.

In the example in Figure 13.7, the LS and LF times are placed on the bottom of each activity arrow, as shown. To illustrate the computations, the latest finish for activity 2–3 is time 6, since there is only one successor of activity 2–3 which has a latest start of 6. In the case of activity 1–2, there are two successors; the latest finish of activity 1–2 is therefore the minimum of the latest starts for the two successors.

The start and finish times for each activity are summarized in Table 13.3, along with two types of activity slack (or float)—total slack and free slack. The definitions of these activity slack times are:

$$\text{Total slack} = LS(a) - ES(a) = LF(a) - EF(a)$$
$$\text{Free slack} = min [ES \text{ (all successors of a)}] - EF(a)$$

The total slack is the amount of time that an activity duration can be increased without delaying the project completion. All activities on the critical path will, therefore, have a total slack of zero. This is shown in Table 13.3 by zero total slack for activities 1–2 and 2–4. Note that LS = ES and LF = EF for these activities on the critical path. Activities not on the critical path have slack as determined by the difference between LS and ES or between LF and EF. See Table 13.3.

Free slack is the amount of time that an activity time can be increased without delaying the start of the *very next activity*. The slack is free in the sense that the next activity is not delayed due to other precedence relationships in the network. On

TABLE 13.3
ACTIVITY TIMES

Activity	ES	EF	LS	LF	Total slack	Free slack
1–2	0	3	0	3	0	0
1–3	0	4	2	6	2	1
2–3	3	5	4	6	1	0
2–4	3	8	3	8	0	0
3–4	5	7	6	8	1	1

the other hand, use of the total slack early in a project network will reduce the slack in successor activities later in the project. Use of total slack in one activity may therefore affect the start dates of successor activities throughout the network, but the final completion date of the project will not be affected. Use of free slack will not affect any of the start dates in the network.

The free slack in activity 1–3 is 1 day as indicated in Table 13.3. Note that a delay of 1 day in activity 1–3 will not delay the start of its successor, activity 3–4, because activity 3–4 cannot start until day 5 at the earliest anyway. In this case activity 3–4 is constrained by the path 1–2–3, which has a length of 5 days. Thus, activity 1–3 can be extended in this network by 1 day without any effect whatsoever on its successor. A similar argument holds for activity 3–4, which also has 1 day of free slack.

The results of the activity-time calculations are used in the same way as the event-time calculations. The critical path can be identified, the slack times are available, the total project completion date is known, and one can identify the effect on the project completion of reducing or increasing the time for any particular activity. In principle, then, the management information available from activity or event computations is the same.

In summary, it is possible to define early occurrence time, late occurrence time, and slack for each event. These quantities are calculated by a forward and backward pass on event times. We have also shown how it is possible to compute early start, late start, early finish, late finish, total slack, and free slack for each activity. These activity times are computed by a forward and backward pass on activity times. Actually it is possible to compute all these times with only one forward and backward pass. In this case, the activity times ES, LS, EF, LF can be computed directly from the early occurrence and latest occurrence times of the event without doing a separate forward and backward pass. While this procedure is easier computationally, it is more difficult to understand conceptually.

13.5 PERT NETWORKS

Program evaluation review technique (PERT) is a network method for project scheduling that was first developed in the mid-1950s for the Polaris submarine project. [See PERT (1958).] The technique was used to schedule over 3000 contractors, suppliers, and agencies, and it is credited with bringing the Polaris submarine project in ahead of schedule by up to 2 years.

PERT, as originally defined, required three time estimates for each activity: an optimistic time estimate T_o, a most likely time estimate T_m, and a pessimistic time estimate T_p. These three estimates recognize the uncertainty in activity time which is typical of R&D projects. The PERT technique also assumes that the actual activity times are distributed according to the beta probability distribution. The beta distribution is skewed to the right with time estimates that are more likely to exceed the average than to be less than the average (see Figure 13.8 for the typical shape of the beta distribution).

Based on experience, time estimates often exceed the most likely time or best estimate in project activities because people tend to be optimistic in their time estimating. This leads to a distribution which is skewed to the right, as shown in Figure 13.8. Actual time exceeds most likely time more frequently than it comes before it.

From the beta distribution, it is possible to convert the PERT network into a constant-time network. This is done by using the expected times T_e for each activity. According to a beta distribution, the average or expected time can be computed as follows:

$$T_e = \frac{T_o + 4T_m + T_p}{6}$$

In this formula, the most likely time is weighted four times more heavily than the optimistic or pessimistic times. The value of T_e is then used as the single constant-time value for each activity. With these expected times, the constant-time methods of the last section can be used in forward and backward passes to compute all event and activity times.

But one cannot eliminate the problem of uncertainty in activity times so easily. When the individual activity times are uncertain, the total project completion time will also be uncertain. To deal with this problem, PERT calculations assume that the variance in total project completion time can be computed by adding the variances along the critical path. This is a reasonable assumption when there are no other near critical paths in the network. In this case, the variance (var_i) for each activity i on the critical path is estimated as follows:

$$var_i = \left(\frac{T_p - T_o}{6}\right)^2$$

This formula is based on the assumption that the pessimistic and optimistic times will cover six standard deviations on the beta distribution.[3] The variance is then the square of the standard deviation.

If we let T be the total completion time of the project, we can then compute:

---

[3]This assumption, in turn, implies that T_o should be set at about the first percentile, while T_p is set at the 99th percentile.

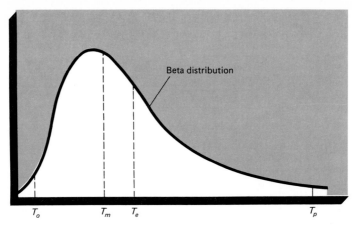

FIGURE 13.8
PERT activity
times.

$$E(T) = \sum_{\substack{\text{critical} \\ \text{path}}} T_e$$

$$\text{var}(T) = \sum_{\substack{\text{critical} \\ \text{path}}} \text{var}_i$$

where $E(T)$ denotes the expected value of T and var(T) denotes the variance of T.

We also assume that the distribution of project completion times is normal. This assumption is based on the central limit theorem, which assures us that the sum of random times will tend to a normal distribution under rather general conditions. Since we know the mean and variance of the normal distribution of project completion times, it is possible to compute the probability of completing the project by any given date. This is done by standardizing the normal variable and using a table of normal probabilities. See Box 13.2 for an example of these calculations.

BOX 13.2
PERT EXAMPLE

The PERT network and three time estimates for each activity are given below. Compute the probability that the project will be completed by time 13.

Using the formulas given in the text, the expected time and variance for each activity are computed as follows:

Activity	T_e	Activity variance
1–2	4.33	1.000
2–3	4.50	.694
1–3	2.00	.111
2–4	4.17	.694
3–4	3.00	.444

Using the values of T_e, a forward pass is made to calculate the expected project completion time of 11.83 as follows:

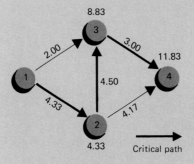

The variance of project completion time (2.138) is the sum of the variances along the critical path.

var = 1.0 + .694 + .444 = 2.138

The project completion time is assumed to have a normal distribution with mean = 11.83 and standard deviation = $\sqrt{2.138}$ = 1.462. The probability that the project completion time will be 13 days or less is obtained by calculating the standard normal variate, which is

$$Z = \frac{13 - 11.83}{1.462} = .8002$$

From a table of normal probabilities, the probability of completion by time 13 (for Z = .8002) is .788. The diagram below shows the probability area under the normal curve.

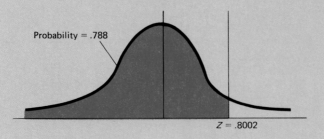

Dealing with the uncertainty or randomness of individual time estimates is the essence of the PERT network. When the individual activity times are random, the project time will also be random. It is therefore not appropriate, in this case, to set concrete project completion dates. Each completion date will have a certain probability of being met, which is a function of the uncertainties in the individual activities and the precedence relationships. From a management standpoint it is much better to recognize the uncertainty in completion dates than to force the problem into a constant-time framework.

Another concept which emerges from the PERT network is the idea of a probabilistic critical path. Following PERT logic, there is no certain critical path. Rather, each activity has a probability of being on the critical path, some activities having probabilities near zero and others near one. The critical path itself is random when activity times are uncertain.

PERT calculations have been extended to reduce the assumptions inherent in the PERT methodology. One way to do this is to simulate the network by sampling random times for each activity. As a result, an exact distribution of project completion time and a probability that each activity is on the critical path can be computed. [See Wiest and Levy (1977) for more details.]

13.6 CRITICAL PATH METHOD

The critical path method (CPM) was developed by E. I. du Pont de Nemours & Co. as a way to schedule the startup and shutdown of major plants. Since these plant activities were repeated frequently, the times were fairly well known. However, the time of any activity could be compressed by expending more money. Thus CPM assumes a time-cost tradeoff rather than the probabilistic times used in PERT.

The CPM method of project scheduling uses a time-cost function of the type shown in Figure 13.9 for each activity. The activity can be completed in

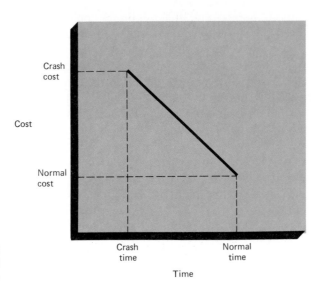

FIGURE 13.9
CPM time-cost
tradeoff.

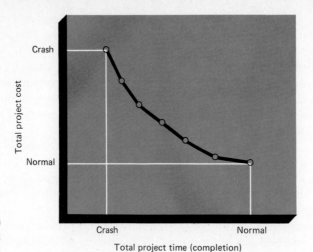

FIGURE 13.10
CPM time and
cost.

proportionally less time if more money is spent. To express this assumed linear time-cost relationship, four figures are given for each activity: normal time, normal cost, crash time, and crash cost.

The project network is solved initially by using normal times and normal costs for all activities. If the resulting project completion time and cost are satisfactory, all activities will be scheduled at their normal times. If the project completion time is too long, the project can be completed in less time at greater cost.

For any given project completion time that is less than the normal time, a great number of network possibilities exist, each at a different total cost. This occurs because a variety of different activity times can be decreased to meet any specified project completion time. All these possibilities can be evaluated by means of a linear programming problem. The LP problem is used to find the solution representing the minimum total project cost for any given project completion time. [For details on this formulation, see Wiest and Levy (1977).]

To illustrate the principles involved, an example is shown in Box 13.3. The example shows how to calculate normal times and normal costs and how to determine the best way to reduce project completion by 1 day. Although this simple example is easily evaluated, it will, as the network becomes more complex, be necessary to use linear programming to evaluate all the combinations.

Note from Box 13.3 that the project completion time can be decreased one unit at a time by incurring more cost. This can be continued until all activities on the critical path are "crashed" to their minimum times. Other activities can have some slack in them. A diagram of the type shown in Figure 13.10 will be obtained indicating the total project cost for any given project duration between normal time and crash time. Management can use this curve to make an appropriate tradeoff between time and cost.

BOX 13.3
CPM EXAMPLE

A project network—along with activity times and costs—is given below. Calculate the normal project time and normal cost. Also calculate the least-cost way to reduce the normal project completion time by 1 day.

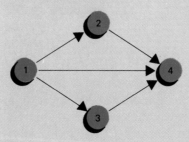

Activity	Normal time	Normal cost	Crash time	Crash cost
1–2	3	$40	1	$80
1–3	2	50	1	120
1–4	6	100	4	140
2–4	4	80	2	130
3–4	3	60	1	140

The normal project completion time is computed by setting all activities at their normal times and making a forward pass. The resulting normal project completion time = 7. See the event time calculations below.

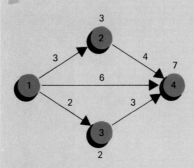

The normal project cost is the sum of normal costs for all activities, which equals $330. The project completion time can be reduced to 6 days by crashing either activity 1–2 or 2–4 by one day. It costs $20 per day, $(80 − 40)/2$, to crash activity 1–2 and $25 per day, $(130 − 80)/2$ to crash activity 2–4. Therefore it is less costly to crash activity 1–2 by 1 day in order to achieve an overall project completion time of 6 days.

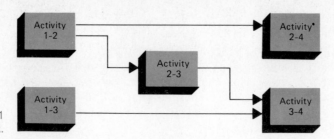

FIGURE 13.11
PDM network.

PRECEDENCE DIAGRAMMING METHOD

A method of network scheduling which has been gaining more and more popularity in recent years is the precedence diagramming method (PDM). Using PDM, an activity on node presentation method is used where the activities are displayed on the nodes (or circles) rather than on the arrows. This presentation completely reverses the convention that we have been using. In PDM, arrows represent precedence relationships between activities.

A PDM network is shown in Figure 13.11 for the problem from Figure 13.3, which we have been using in this chapter. Figure 13.11 is constructed by drawing the activities as boxes and then describing the precedence relationships between each set of activities.

One important advantage of the PDM network is that it allows the network schedule to be drawn to scale, as shown in Figure 13.12. This permits the users to see visually the times when activities are scheduled to occur, as well as how long

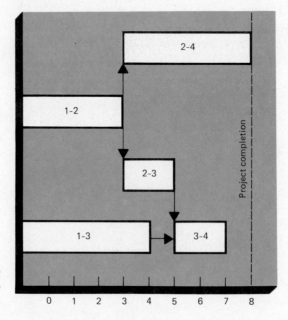

FIGURE 13.12
PDM time
schedule.

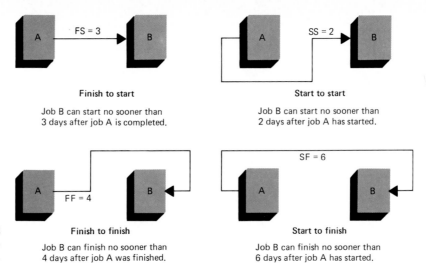

Finish to start

Job B can start no sooner than
3 days after job A is completed.

Start to start

Job B can start no sooner than
2 days after job A has started.

Finish to finish

Job B can finish no sooner than
4 days after job A was finished.

Start to finish

Job B can finish no sooner than
6 days after job A has started.

FIGURE 13.13
PDM precedence
relationship.

they will last and their precedence relationships. This form of presentation is easier to use and explain than conventional network diagrams.

It is clear from Figure 13.12 that activities 1–2 and 2–4 form the critical path since there is no slack in these activities—they completely fill the time from zero to eight. On the other hand, activities 2–3 and 3–4 each have 1 day of slack while activity 1–3 has 2 days of total slack, as can be readily seen from Figure 13.12. It is quite easy to also visualize, from this figure, the effect of activity slippages on the project schedule. For example, if activity 1–3 slips by 1 day, it will not delay the start of activity 3–4. Thus, activity 1–3 has 1 day of free slack.

In addition to their convenient format, precedence diagrams can be used to represent complex precedence relationships. For example, a start-to-start relationship can be represented in PDM where one activity cannot start until another has also started. Start-to-finish and finish-to-finish relationships can also be represented in these networks in addition to the more conventional finish-to-start relationships of PERT and CPM networks. In the finish-to-start case, the next activity cannot start until the preceding activity has finished.

All these cases, along with time delays, are shown in Figure 13.13. A time delay simply means that an activity cannot start or finish until a certain number of days before or after its predecessor starts or finishes. Notice in this figure that the conventional PERT or CPM network would be represented by a finish-to-start relationship with $FS = 0$.

These additional relationships could be used, for example, in the case of pouring a cement floor. All the forms need not be put into place before cement pouring begins. However, the forms must be started before any cement can be poured, and the forms must be finished before cement pouring can be finished. In Figure 13.14, this situation is shown with 1 day provided after beginning form installation before cement can be poured. This is done quite simply with a start-to-start and a finish-to-finish relationship. See Wiest (1981) for more complex examples.

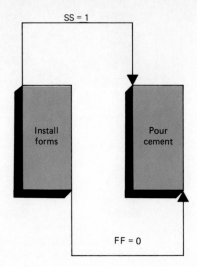

FIGURE 13.14
Cement floor
example.

The precedence diagramming method, because of its flexibility, allows more complex situations to be easily represented. Owing to this feature and the presentation advantages already discussed, PDM is being more and more widely used for project scheduling. Most computer codes allow PDM networks as well as conventional network presentations.

 ## USE OF PROJECT MANAGEMENT CONCEPTS

Project management requires a great deal more than scheduling. Planning for the project is required before the scheduling begins, and control is required after the schedule is developed. Project management requires a blend of behavioral and quantitative skills. Thus scheduling methods should be seen as only one part of a complete approach to project management.

In selecting project scheduling methods, a conscious tradeoff should be made between sophisticated methods and cost. Gantt chart methods should not be seen as outdated or naïve. Rather, Gantt charts are justified for projects where the activities are not highly interconnected or for small projects. In these cases where the Gantt chart is warranted, a network method may not provide enough additional benefits in relation to its costs.

If a network method is justified, a choice must be made between constant time, PERT, CPM, PDM, or more advanced methods. The constant-time method is adequate for cases where activity times are constant or nearly so. If activity times are random, a PERT network should be chosen to reflect the uncertainty directly. PERT may therefore be applied to situations such as R&D, computer system design, and military invasions, where activity times are expected to vary.

CPM methods, on the other hand, should be used where activity times are fairly constant but can be reduced by spending more money. CPM might apply in cases such as construction projects, installation of equipment, and plant startup and shutdown. More advanced network methods include generalized networks and resource-constrained situations. These methods are still in development and have not been widely used in practice. See Davis (1976) for more details on advanced scheduling methods.

The PDM method has been gaining in use because of its ability to display schedules conveniently and to represent complex precedence relationships. In practice, PDM has been found to be easy to use and easy to explain to people who are not familiar with networks.

Network scheduling methods are usually computerized in practice. A large number of different standard software packages are available to cover the entire range of scheduling methods. These packages not only support scheduling but also assist in project accounting and in controlling progress.

KEY POINTS

The planning and scheduling of projects is concerned with the unique, one-time production activity. Because projects are unique, the scheduling problem is quite different from that of ongoing operations.

The key points covered in this chapter include the following:

- The three objectives in projects are time, cost, and performance. Because these objectives are conflicting, tradeoffs between them must constantly be made in the course of managing projects.
- All projects go through three phases: planning, scheduling, and control. The planning phase establishes the objectives, organization, and resources for the project. The scheduling phase establishes the time schedule, cost, and personnel assignments. The control phase monitors the progress of the project in cost, time, and performance; it also corrects the plan as necessary to achieve project objectives.
- The Gantt chart is a scheduling method for displaying project activities in a bar-chart format. The Gantt chart is useful for small projects or projects where activities are not highly interrelated.
- There are three network scheduling methods: constant-time, PERT, and CPM. All these methods rely on a network or graph to represent the precedence relationship between activities.
- A network allows one to identify the critical path, slack, and activities which need to be rescheduled. The critical path is the longest time path of activities from the beginning to the end of the network. Activities on the critical path have zero slack—they must be completed on time to prevent slippage of the project completion date. Slack is the amount of time that an activity or event can be extended, while still allowing the project to be completed on time.
- The earliest and latest occurrence time for each event is computed by means of a forward and backward pass through the network. The early start, late start, early finish, and late finish times for each activity can also be computed by means of a forward and backward pass.
- PERT is a network-based project scheduling method which requires three time estimates for each activity: optimistic, most likely, and pessimistic. Using these

three time estimates, a probability of project completion by any specified date can be computed, along with the standard start and finish times for each activity or event.

- CPM is a network-based method which uses a linear time-cost tradeoff. Each activity can be completed in less than its normal time by crashing the activity for a given cost. Thus if the normal project completion time is not satisfactory, certain activities can be crashed to complete the project in less time.
- PDM is a network method which shows activities on nodes. Relationships between nodes are indicated by arrows, which can depict a variety of start-and-finish relationships.

QUESTIONS

1. How, precisely, does project scheduling differ from the scheduling of ongoing operations?
2. How would you, after the fact, audit a project to determine whether it was successful or not?
3. Give three examples of projects not given in the text. Are these projects unique, or are they repeated in some way?
4. Contrast and compare CPM and PERT as project scheduling techniques.
5. Define the terms "critical path," "event slack," "free slack," and "early start."
6. What is the management significance of finding the critical path through a network?
7. What statistical assumptions are made in PERT? Under what conditions are those assumptions realistic?
8. An R&D manager has told you that the statistical part of PERT seems complicated and perhaps too complex for scheduling R&D. What would your response be?
9. What cost-time assumptions are made for the CPM method?
10. How is the Gantt chart used as a scheduling tool? When should the Gantt chart be used in preference to network-based methods?
11. Is it possible to have multiple critical paths in the CPM method? How will this occur?
12. Suppose a particular activity has a very high variance in a PERT chart. How will this affect the result?

PROBLEMS

1. A public accounting firm requires the following activities for an audit:

Activity	Immediate predecessor	Immediate successor	Activity time
a	—	b, e	3
b	a	d, f	2
c	—	d, f	4
d	b, c	g	2
e	a	g	5
f	b, c	—	6
g	e, d	—	5

a. Prepare a Gantt chart for this project.
b. Draw a network for this project. Label the events in sequential order.
c. Draw a PDM network.
d. Make a forward and backward pass for events.

   e. What is the critical path and the project completion time?
   f. If the project completion must be reduced by 2 days, which activities might be affected?
2. The following activities are required in starting up a new plant:

Activity	Immediate predecessor	Immediate successor	Activity time
a		c	3
b		d,e	2
c	a	f,g	1
d	b	f,g	4
e	b	g	4
f	c,d		2
g	e,c,d		3

   a. Prepare a Gantt chart for this project.
   b. Draw a network (AOA) for this project.
   c. Draw a PDM network.
   d. Make a forward and backward pass for activities to determine ES, LS, EF, LF.
   e. Calculate total slack and free slack.

3. A construction project has the following network and activity times:

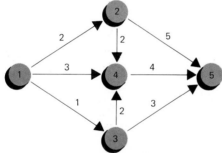

   a. Prepare a Gantt chart for this project.
   b. Make a forward and backward pass on the activity times.
   c. Find the total slack and free slack for each activity.
   d. Activity 1–4 will be delayed by 1 day. What effect will this have on the project?
   e. Draw a PDM network.
4. An advertising campaign uses a PERT network as shown below:

Activity	T_o	T_m	T_p
1–2	4	5	6
1–3	3	4	8
2–4	1	2	5
2–5	5	6	9
3–4	2	3	4
3–5	2	3	6
4–6	4	5	6
5–6	3	4	8

a. Draw a network and label each activity with its expected time and variance.

b. Calculate the expected completion time and variance for the entire project.

c. What is the probability that the project is completed in 18 days?

d. Are the PERT assumptions used to calculate the probability in part c realistic in this case? Why or why not?

e. What is the effect of the large variance in activity 1–3?

5. An R&D project has the following PERT network with the three time estimates shown on each arrow.

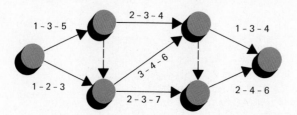

a. Calculate the expected time and variance for each activity.

b. Calculate the expected completion time and variance for the entire project.

c. What is the probability the project can be completed in 10 days?

6. A plant startup is based on the following CPM network:

Activity	Immediate predecessor	Immediate successor	Normal time	Normal cost	Crash time	Crash cost
a	—	d, e	4	$100	2	$150
b	—	g	8	80	2	140
c	—	f	2	40	1	60
d	a	g	3	80	2	120
e	a	—	5	80	3	140
f	c	—	5	60	1	100
g	b, d	—	6	120	2	160

a. Draw the network for this project and label the events.

b. What is the normal project completion time and normal cost?

c. Identify the critical path.

d. How much will it cost to crash the project completion by 1 day? by 2 days?

e. What is the minimum time for project completion?

7. An entrepreneur is starting a new business. The activities and times required are given below:

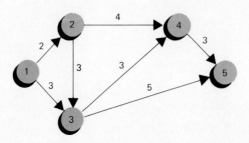

a. Find the critical path and the project completion time.
b. What is the ES, LS, EF, and LF for each activity?
c. How much total slack and free slack is there in activity 2–4?
d. Suppose the project completion must be reduced by 1 day. The costs of expediting various activities are shown below. What should be done and how much will it cost?

Activity	Expediting cost per day
1–2	$50
2–3	30
2–4	40
3–4	20
4–5	20
3–5	50

8. In preparing to teach a new course, the professor has estimated the following expected activity times and variances. On each arrow, the expected time is given, followed by the variance.

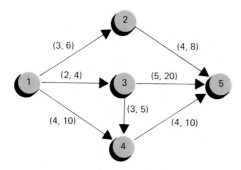

a. Find the expected completion time of the project and the variance of completion time.
b. What is the probability that the class will be ready by time 12?
c. What will the effect of the large variance be on activity 3–5?
d. Are the PERT assumptions justified in this case? Explain. What is the effect of the PERT assumptions on the probability calculated in part c?

9. A project has the following activities and precedence relationships as shown by the PDM activity-on-node diagram. The duration of each activity is also shown inside each box.

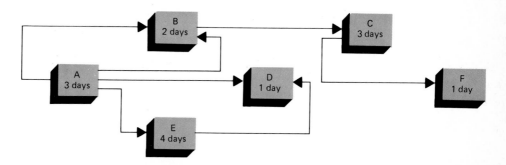

a. Describe the start-and-finish relationships shown by the above diagram; e.g., B cannot start until A starts.

b. Calculate the early start and early finish time of each activity by making a forward pass.

c. Calculate the latest start and latest finish time for each activity by making a backward pass.

SELECTED BIBLIOGRAPHY

DAVIS, EDWARD W. (ed.): *Project Management: Techniques, Applications, and Managerial Issues,* monograph no. 3, Production Planning and Control Division, American Institute of Industrial Engineers, 1976.

KELLY, JAMES E., JR., and MORGAN R. WALKER: "Critical Path Planning and Scheduling," *Proceedings of the Eastern Joint Computer Conference,* Boston, Mass., 1959, pp. 160–173.

MACCRIMMON, K. R., and C. A. RYAVEC: "Analytic Studies of the PERT Assumptions," *Operations Research,* vol. 12, no. 1, January–February 1964, pp. 16–37.

MALCOLM, DONALD G., et al.: "Applications of a Technique for Research and Development Program Evaluation," *Operations Research,* vol. 7, no. 5, September–October, 1959, pp. 646-669.

MARTIN, CHARLES C.: *Project Management: How to Make It Work,* New York: AMACOM, a division of American Management Associations, 1976.

MEREDITH, JACK R., and SAMUEL J. MANTEL, JR.: *Project Management,* New York: Wiley, 1985.

PERT, Program Evaluation Research Task, Phase I Summary Report, Special Projects Office, Bureau of Ordinance, Department of the Navy, Washington, D.C., July 1958, pp. 646–669.

WIEST, JEROME D.: "Precedence Diagramming Method: Some Unusual Characteristics and Their Implications for Project Managers," *Journal of Operations Management,* vol. 1, no. 3, February 1981.

———— and FERDINAND LEVY: *A Management Guide to PERT/CPM,* 2d ed., Englewood Cliffs, N.J.: Prentice-Hall, 1977.

PART FOUR

INVENTORY MANAGEMENT

INVENTORY

- **INDEPENDENT-DEMAND INVENTORY**
- **MATERIALS REQUIREMENTS PLANNING**
- **JUST-IN-TIME**

One of the oldest decision areas addressed by operations managers is the scientific management of inventories. In a manufacturing company, inventory and capacity are two sides of the same coin; they must be managed together. In Part 3, the primary focus was on capacity, with inventory treated as a related variable. In Part 4, the primary focus will be on inventory, with capacity as a related variable.

The basis for organizing Part 4 is the distinction between independent- and dependent-demand inventories. Independent demand is subject to market forces and is thus independent of operations. Finished goods and spare parts are independent-demand inventories. Dependent demand is derived from the demand for another part or component; thus work-in-process inventory and raw materials inventories have dependent demand. In automobile production, the demand for finished automobiles is independent, and the demand for parts which go into the automobile is dependent on the demand for automobiles (e.g., one steering wheel, four wheels, and one engine per car).

Chapter 14, on independent-demand inventory, focuses on the different types of models which can be used to replenish inventories. These models help the inventory manager answer the questions of how much and when to order to meet customer-service goals at the lowest possible cost. Some examples of computer systems for controlling independent-demand inventories are also given.

Dependent-demand inventories are controlled by materials requirements planning (MRP) systems described in Chapter 15. These systems support the planning and control of inventories and capacity in manufacturing companies. This is done by developing a master schedule of planned output and exploding it into all the parts and components required in a time-phased materials plan. As a result, purchase orders and shop orders are released at the right time and capacity is managed to meet delivery promises.

Chapter 16 describes the use of just-in-time (JIT) inventory systems for dependent demand. This approach, used in manufacturing companies, views inventory as waste and attempts to eliminate inventories completely. This is done by streamlining material flows and producing parts only when absolutely needed. As a result, inventory turns for raw materials and work-in-process inventories in repetitive manufacturing can approach 50 or 100 turns a year.

The distinction between independent and dependent demand has yielded great improvements in the management of inventories and in production control. By utilizing the concepts in Part 4, managers will find it possible to meet customer service goals while holding down the costs of inventory and production.

CHAPTER 14

Independent-Demand Inventory

Inventory management is among the most important operations management functions because inventory requires a great deal of capital and affects the delivery of goods to customers. Inventory management has an impact on all business functions, particularly operations, marketing, and finance. Inventories provide customer service, which is of vital interest to marketing. Finance is concerned with the overall financial picture of the organization, including funds allocated to inventory. And operations needs inventories to assure smooth and efficient production.

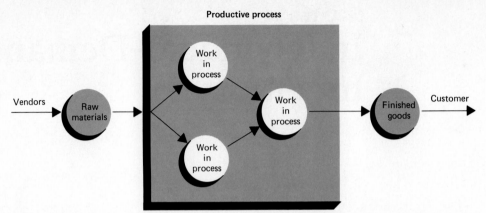

Productive process

FIGURE 14.1
A materials-flow
process.

There are, however, conflicting inventory objectives within the firm. The finance function generally prefers to keep the level of inventories low to conserve capital, marketing prefers high levels of inventories to enhance sales, while operations prefers adequate inventories for efficient production and smooth employment levels. Inventory management must balance these conflicting objectives and manage inventory levels in the best interests of the firm as a whole. This chapter provides a basis for such an overall approach to inventory management.

It is, perhaps, best to begin our discussion with a definition of inventory. An *inventory* is a stock of materials used to facilitate production or to satisfy customer demands. Inventories typically include raw materials, work in process, and finished goods. This definition fits nicely with the view of operations as a transformation process. In Figure 14.1, an operation is shown as a materials-flow process with raw materials inventories waiting to enter the productive process, work-in-process inventories in some intermediate stage of transformation, and finished goods inventories already completely transformed by the production system.

Our definition of inventory as a stock of materials is narrower than that given by others. Some authors define inventory as an idle resource of any kind which has potential economic value. This definition allows one to consider equipment or

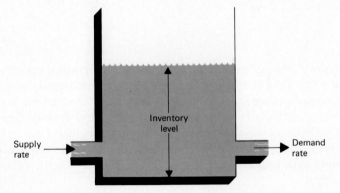

FIGURE 14.2
A water tank
analogy for
inventory.

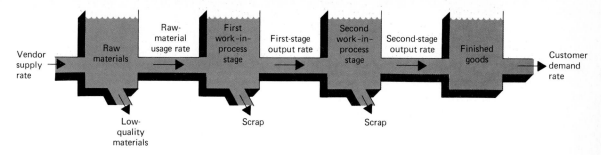

FIGURE 14.3 A water tank system analogy.

idle workers as inventory, but we consider all idle resources other than materials as capacity. From a management and accounting perspective, it is important to distinguish between inventory and capacity. Capacity provides the potential to produce, while inventory, as defined here, is the product at some point in the conversion and distribution process.

Inventory stocks are located at various points in the productive process, with flows connecting one stock point to another. The rate at which a stock can be replenished is the supply capacity, and the rate of stock depletion is demand. Inventory acts as a buffer between the different demand and supply rates.

The water tank shown in Figure 14.2 is a good analogy for these concepts of flows and stocks. In this figure, the level of water in the tank corresponds to inventory. The rate of flow into the tank is analogous to supply capacity, and the rate of flow out corresponds to demand. The water level (inventory) is thus a buffer between supply and demand. If demand exceeds supply, the water level will drop until the demand and supply rates come back into balance or until the water is depleted. Likewise, if supply exceeds demand, the water level will rise.

Imagine a number of these tanks connected together, each with varying inputs and outputs. This situation, illustrated in Figure 14.3, is a good analogy to a single-product inventory-management problem. Here, one tank represents raw materials, while there are two tanks for work in process and one for finished goods. The tanks serve as buffers to absorb variations in flow rates within the system. In Chapter 16 we will show how the size of the buffers (inventory levels) can be drastically reduced by smoothing out flow rates and reducing variations in the production system through a just-in-time approach.

PURPOSE OF INVENTORIES

The primary purpose of inventories is to uncouple the various phases of operations. Raw materials inventory uncouples a manufacturer from its vendors; work-in-process inventory uncouples the various stages of manufacturing from each other; and finished goods inventory uncouples a manufacturer from its customers.

Within the overall uncoupling purpose, there are four reasons to carry inventory:

1. To protect against uncertainties. In inventory systems, there are uncertainties in supply, demand, and lead time. Safety stocks are maintained in inventory to protect against those uncertainties. If customer demand were known, it would be feasible—although not necessarily economical—to produce at the same rate as consumption. In this case, no finished goods inventory would be needed; however, every change in demand would be immediately transmitted to the productive system in order to maintain customer service. Instead of such tight coupling, safety stocks of finished goods are maintained to absorb changes in demand without immediately changing production. In a similar way, safety stocks of raw materials are maintained to absorb uncertainties in delivery by vendors, and safety stocks of in-process inventories are maintained to allow for poor maintenance, unreliable workers, or fast schedule changes. In general, inventory carried to absorb uncertainty is called safety stock. If these sources of variations can be reduced, however, safety stock and inventories can be correspondingly reduced. Much unnecessary safety stock is carried because variations in vendor delivery times and production processes are too high.

2. To allow economic production and purchase. It is often economical to produce materials in lots. In this case, a lot may be produced over a short period of time, and then no further production is done until the lot is nearly depleted. This makes it possible to spread the setup cost of the production machines over a large number of items. It also permits the use of the same productive equipment for different products. A similar situation holds for the purchase of raw materials. Owing to ordering costs, quantity discounts, and transportation costs, it is sometimes economical to purchase in large lots, even though part of the lot is then held in inventory for later use. The inventory resulting from the purchase or production of material in lots is called cycle inventory, since the lots are produced or purchased on a cyclic basis. There is a trend under way in industry today, however, to reduce setup times and costs drastically by altering the product or process. This will result in smaller lot sizes and much lower inventories. In some cases the setup time can be reduced so that the economical lot size is 1 unit. This possibility will be discussed further in Chapter 16 on just-in-time manufacturing.

3. To cover anticipated changes in demand or supply. There are several types of situations where changes in demand or supply may be anticipated. One case is where the price or availability of raw materials is expected to change. Companies often stockpile steel prior to an expected steel industry strike. Another source of anticipation is a planned market promotion where a large amount of finished goods may be stocked prior to a sale. Finally, companies in seasonal businesses often anticipate demand in order to smooth employment, as discussed in Chapter 11. For example, a producer of air conditioners may select a nearly uniform rate of production, although a great deal of the product is sold in the summer.

4. To provide for transit. Transit inventories consist of materials that are on their way from one point to another. These inventories are affected by plant location decisions and by the choice of carrier. Technically speaking, inventories moving between stages of production, even within a plant, can also be classified as transit inventories. Sometimes the inventory in transit is called pipeline inventory because it is in the "distribution pipeline."

The first two categories of inventory will be treated extensively in this chapter, while the remaining two categories are treated in other parts of the book. The reasons for carrying inventory will influence the methods used for inventory management. This will become clearer as the chapter develops.

14.2 DECISION PROBLEMS

There are a number of different decision problems in inventory management:

1. Which items should be carried in stock?
2. How much should be ordered?
3. When should an order be placed?
4. What type of inventory control system should be used?

Question 1 deals with whether the item will be made to stock or made to order. It also deals with the issue of whether existing items should be continued in stock or discontinued. Many inventories include numerous obsolete or "insurance" items for which there is very little demand. Should these items be kept, salvaged, written off the books, or replenished?

Questions 2 and 3 are the classical inventory questions. There have probably been more papers published on these two questions than any other topics in business administration. Question 2 is concerned with the order quantity, given that an order is placed. Question 3 is concerned with the timing of the order—when should it be placed? Answers to both of these questions provide a decision rule which specifies when to order and how much to order. Several decision rules will be examined later.

To make sure that the right amount is ordered at the right time, an inventory control system is needed. This system should keep accurate records, trigger orders when needed, and track the flow of materials in and out of inventory. An answer to Question 4 matches the right kind of computer or manual system to the inventory problem.

A typical inventory control system is described in Box 14.1. Notice how this problem is related to the aggregate planning problem discussed in Chapter 11.

BOX 14.1
BLUE BELL TRIMS ITS INVENTORY

Blue Bell is one of the world's largest apparel manufacturers, with over $1 billion in sales, 95 plants, and 49 distribution centers worldwide. Some of the popular products made by Blue Bell are Wrangler jeans and Jantzen swimwear and sweaters. By implementing modern inventory control systems, Blue Bell reduced its inventory by more than 31 percent, from $370 to $250 million, while improving service delivered to customers.

This tremendous improvement in inventory, over a period of 2 years, was made possible by implementing a series of forecasting, inventory, and scheduling models. The sales forecasting model provides an estimate of monthly customer demands for the next year. To provide a high level of customer service a safety stock must be added to the forecast to hedge against demand uncertainty. In calculating safety stock, the model incorporates production lead time, target service level, and the standard deviation into its calculations.

Next, the product-line planning model determines the amount of production which should be scheduled each month by product line in order to meet forecast needs while smoothing employment levels (aggregate planning). The results of this model are broken down into specific sizes and types of garments which are needed each week. The existing inventories and WIP are subtracted in order to arrive at the amount of each stock-keeping unit which should be scheduled. Finally, the specific garments are arranged into economical cutting patterns so as to minimize wasted material while meeting the required schedule.

This inventory control system for managing independent-demand inventories was programmed specifically for Blue Bell's computers. It was then pilot-tested and implemented one product line and then one plant at a time throughout the entire company. The system made possible large savings in inventory and working capital while improving customer service.

Source: Jerry Edwards, et al., "Blue Bell Trims Its Inventory", *Interfaces,* vol. 15, no. 1, January–February 1985.

14.3 INVENTORY COST STRUCTURES

Many inventory decision problems can be solved by using economic criteria. One of the most important prerequisites, however, is an understanding of the cost structure. Inventory cost structures incorporate the following four types of costs:

1. Item cost. This is the cost of buying or producing the individual inventory items. The item cost is usually expressed as a cost per unit multiplied by the quantity procured or produced. Sometimes item cost is discounted if enough units are purchased at one time.

2. Ordering (or setup) cost. The ordering cost is associated with ordering a batch or lot of items. Ordering cost does not depend on the number of items ordered; it is assigned to the entire batch. This cost includes typing the purchase order, expediting the order, transportation costs, receiving costs, and so on. When the item is produced within the firm, there are also costs associated with placing an order which are independent of the number of items produced. These so-called setup costs include paperwork costs plus the costs required to set up the production equipment for a run. In some cases, setup costs can amount to thousands of dollars, leading to significant economies for large runs. Later, we will discuss how setup times can be reduced by changes in the production system or the product. Setup cost is often considered fixed when, in fact, it can be reduced by changing the way operations are designed and managed.

3. Carrying (or holding) cost. The carrying or holding cost is associated with keeping items in inventory for a period of time. The holding cost is typically charged as a percentage of dollar value per unit time. For example, a 15 percent annual holding cost means that it will cost 15 cents to hold $1 of inventory for a year. In practice, holding costs typically range from 15 to 30 percent per year.

The carrying cost usually consists of three components:

- *Cost of capital.* When items are carried in inventory, the capital invested is not available for other purposes. This represents a cost of forgone opportunities for other investments, which is assigned to inventory as an opportunity cost.
- *Cost of storage.* This cost includes variable space cost, insurance, and taxes. In some cases, a part of the storage cost is fixed, for example, when a warehouse is owned and cannot be used for other purposes. Such fixed costs should not be included in the cost of inventory storage. Likewise, taxes and insurance should be included only if they vary with the inventory level.
- *Costs of obsolescence, deterioration, and loss.* Obsolescence costs should be assigned to items which have a high risk of becoming obsolete; the higher the risk, the higher the costs. Perishable products should be charged with deterioration costs when the item deteriorates over time, e.g., food and blood. The costs of loss include pilferage and breakage costs associated with holding items in inventory.

4. Stockout cost. Stockout cost reflects the economic consequences of running out of stock. There are two cases here. First, suppose items are back-ordered or backlogged for the customer and the customer waits until the material arrives. There may be some loss of goodwill or future business associated with each back order because the customer had to wait. This opportunity loss is counted as a stockout cost. The second case is where the sale is lost if material is not on hand. The profit is lost from the sale, and goodwill, in the form of future sales, may also be lost.

Inventory costs are often difficult to assess, but with persistence they can be estimated accurately enough for most decision-making purposes. The item cost can usually be estimated directly from historical records. Item cost is one inventory cost on which estimation accuracy is normally good.

The ordering (setup) cost can also be determined from company records. However, difficulties are sometimes encountered in separating fixed and variable ordering-cost components. The ordering cost should include only the costs which vary with the number of orders placed.

The carrying cost is more difficult to determine accurately. First of all, the cost of capital is an opportunity cost which cannot be derived from historical records. One can, however, determine an appropriate cost of capital on the basis of financial considerations. The rest of the carrying costs—storage, deterioration, obsolescence, and losses—can be based on company records plus special cost studies. For more detail on the measurement of carrying cost, see Rhodes (1981).

Stockout cost is the most difficult of all inventory costs to estimate. Estimates can be based on the concept of forgone profits; in practice, however, the problem is often handled indirectly by specifying an acceptable stockout risk level. This practice can be costly; it may imply very high stockout costs, as will be demonstrated later. The problem of stockout-cost measurement does not have a satisfactory solution. More theoretical and practical research work is needed.

14.4 INDEPENDENT VERSUS DEPENDENT DEMAND

A crucial distinction in inventory management is whether demand is independent or dependent. *Independent demand* is influenced by market conditions outside the control of operations; it is therefore independent of operations. Finished goods inventories and spare parts for replacement usually have independent demand. *Dependent demand* is related to the demand for another item and is not independently determined by the market. When products are built up from parts and assemblies, the demand for these components is dependent on the demand for the final product.

A toy wagon can be used to illustrate the difference between independent and dependent demand. The demand for wagons is independent because it is influenced by the market. The demand for wagon wheels is dependent because it is mathematically related to the demand for wagons; it takes four wheels to complete each wagon produced. Likewise, the demand for wagon handles is dependent on the demand for finished wagons.

Independent and dependent demands exhibit very different usage or demand patterns. Since independent demand is subject to market forces, it often exhibits some fixed pattern while also responding to random influences which usually stem from a great many different customer preferences. On the other hand, dependent demand exhibits a lumpy, on-again, off-again pattern because production is typically scheduled in lots. A quantity of parts is required when a lot is made; then no parts are required until the next lot is made. These demand patterns are shown in Figure 14.4.

Different demand patterns call for different approaches to inventory management. For independent demand, a *replenishment* philosophy is appropriate. As the stock is used, it is replenished in order to have materials on hand for customers. Thus, as inventory begins to run out, an order is triggered for more material and the inventory is replenished.

For dependent-demand items, a *requirements* philosophy is used. The amount of

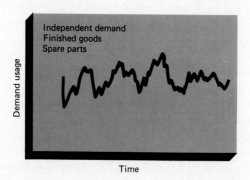
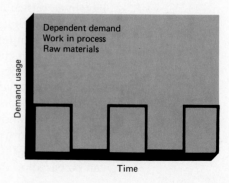

FIGURE 14.4
Demand patterns.

stock ordered is based on requirements for higher-level items. As one begins to run out, additional raw material or work-in-process inventory is *not* ordered. More material is ordered only as required by the need for other higher-level or end items.

The nature of demand, therefore, leads to two different philosophies of inventory management. These philosophies, in turn, generate different sets of methods and computer software systems. In this chapter, the independent-demand case will be covered, including the following types of inventories:

1. Finished goods inventories and spare parts in manufacturing companies
2. Retail and wholesale finished goods
3. Service-industry (e.g., hospitals, schools, etc.) inventory

In Chapters 15 and 16, we will study the management of dependent-demand inventories.

ECONOMIC ORDER QUANTITY

In 1915, F. W. Harris developed the famous economic order quantity (EOQ) formula. Later, this formula gained wide use in industry through the efforts of a consultant named Wilson. Thus, the formula is often called the Wilson EOQ even though it was developed by Harris. The EOQ and its variations are still widely used in industry for independent-demand inventory management.

The derivation of the EOQ model is based on the following assumptions:

1. The demand rate is constant, recurring, and known. For example, demand (or usage) is 100 units a day with no random variation, and demand is assumed to continue into the indefinite future.
2. The lead time is constant and known. The lead time, from order placement to order delivery, is therefore always a fixed number of days.
3. No stockouts are allowed. Since demand and lead time are constant, one can determine exactly when to order material to avoid stockouts.
4. Material is ordered or produced in a lot or batch, and the lot is placed into inventory all at one time.
5. A specific cost structure is used as follows: The unit item cost is constant, and no discounts are given for large purchases. The carrying cost depends linearly on the average inventory level. There is a fixed ordering or setup cost for each lot which is independent of the number of items in the lot.
6. The item is a single product; there is no interaction with other products.

Under these assumptions, the inventory level over time is shown in Figure 14.5. Notice that the figure shows a perfect "sawtooth" pattern, because demand is constant and items are ordered in fixed lot sizes.

In choosing the lot size, there is a tradeoff between ordering frequency and inventory level. Small lots will lead to frequent reorders but a low average inventory level. If larger lots are ordered, the ordering frequency will decrease but

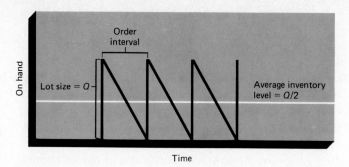

FIGURE 14.5
EOQ inventory
levels.

more inventory will be carried. This tradeoff between ordering frequency and inventory level can be represented by a mathematical equation using the following symbols:

D = demand rate, units per year
S = cost per order placed, or setup cost, dollars per order
C = unit cost, dollars per unit
i = carrying "interest" rate, percent of dollar value per year
Q = lot size, units
TC = total of ordering cost plus carrying cost, dollars per year

The annual ordering cost is:

Ordering cost per year = (cost per order) (orders per year) = $S \dfrac{D}{Q}$

In the above equation, D is the total demand for a year, and the product is ordered Q units at a time; thus D/Q orders are placed in a year. This is multiplied by S, the cost per order placed.

The annual carrying cost is:

Carrying cost per year = (annual carrying rate) (unit cost) (average inventory)

$$= \frac{iCQ}{2}$$

In this equation, the average inventory is $Q/2$. A maximum of Q units is carried just as a batch arrives; the minimum amount carried is zero units. Since the stock is depleted at a constant rate, the average inventory is $Q/2$. The carrying rate per year i times the unit cost C gives the cost of holding *one* unit in inventory for a year. This unit charge multiplied by the average inventory level gives the total carrying cost on an annual basis.

The total annual cost of inventory is then[1]:

Total cost per year = ordering cost per year + carrying cost per year

$$TC = \frac{SD}{Q} + \frac{iCQ}{2} \tag{14.1}$$

---

[1]Notice that the item cost of procurement is the constant CD, which is independent of Q and can therefore be removed from further consideration. It will not affect the minimum of TC.

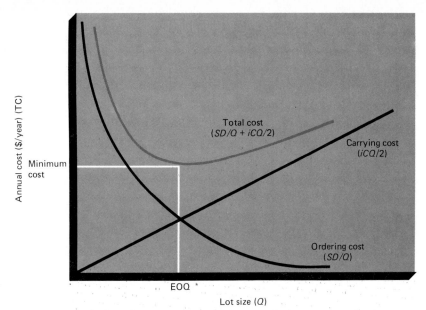

FIGURE 14.6
Total cost of
inventory.

Figure 14.6 is a plot of TC versus Q, with each component of TC shown separately along with the total. As Q increases, the ordering-cost component decreases because fewer orders are placed per year; at the same time, however, the carrying-cost component increases because more average inventory is held. Thus, ordering and carrying costs are offsetting; one decreases while the other increases. This is precisely the tradeoff between ordering and carrying costs which we mentioned earlier. Because of this tradeoff, the function TC has a minimum.

Finding the value of Q which minimizes TC is a classic problem in calculus.[2] We take the derivative of TC, set it equal to zero, and then solve for the resulting value of Q.

$$\text{TC}' = -\frac{SD}{Q^2} + \frac{iC}{2} = 0$$
$$\frac{SD}{Q^2} = \frac{iC}{2}$$
$$Q^2 = \frac{2SD}{iC}$$
$$Q = \sqrt{\frac{2SD}{iC}} \tag{14.2}$$

Equation (14.2) is the classic Wilson economic order quantity, which minimizes the cost of operating the inventory. Although we have minimized cost on an

---

[2]Without the use of calculus, the EOQ formula can be rationalized as follows: Observe from Figure 14.6 that the minimum of TC occurs where the two curves intersect. Determine this intersection by setting $SD/Q = iCQ/2$ and solve for the resulting value of Q. This approach is not generalizable but works in this case due to the special nature of the functions involved.

annual basis, any unit of time can be used provided the demand rate and interest rate are compatible. For example, if demand is expressed on a monthly basis, the interest rate must also be expressed on a monthly basis.

To illustrate the use of the EOQ formula, suppose we were managing a carpet store and wanted to determine how many yards of a certain type of carpet to buy. The carpet has the following characteristics:

D = 360 yards per year
S = $10 per order
i = 25% per year
C = $8 per yard

Thus

$$Q = \sqrt{\frac{2(10)(360)}{.25(8)}} = \sqrt{3600} = 60$$

The manager should order 60 yards of carpet at a time. This will result in $360/60$ = 6 orders per year, or one order every 2 months.

The minimum cost of operating this inventory will be $120 per year.

$$TC = 10(360/60) + .25(8)(60/2) = 60 + 60 = 120$$

Notice that the minimum cost occurs when the ordering-cost component equals the carrying-cost component.

Table 14.1 shows that the total-cost curve for the carpet inventory is very flat in the neighborhood of the minimum. For example, if 50 or 70 units instead of 60 are ordered, the cost change is very slight, about a 1 percent increase. Even if 80 units are ordered instead of 60, the cost increase is about 4 percent. Thus the manager can adjust the order quantity by a fair amount if necessary, with little effect on the cost of operating the inventory.

Likewise, the cost of ordering and holding need not be exact because the EOQ is fairly insensitive to these parameters. For example, if the cost of ordering is increased by 50 percent, the EOQ increases by only 22.5 percent due to the square-root effect.

TABLE 14.1
INVENTORY COST VERSUS ORDER QUANTITY

Q	TC
10	$370
20	200
30	150
40	130
50	122
60	120
70	121.4
80	125
90	130
100	136

The EOQ formula has many limitations. Some of the most serious ones are the following:

1. Demand is assumed constant, while in many real situations demand varies substantially. In the next sections, random demand will be considered.
2. The unit cost is assumed to be constant, but in practice there are often quantity discounts for large purchases. This case requires a modification of the basic EOQ model and is treated in the chapter supplement.
3. The material in the lot is assumed to arrive all at once, but in some cases material will be placed in inventory continuously as it is produced. This case is also treated in the supplement.
4. A single product is assumed, but sometimes multiple items are purchased from a single supplier and they are all shipped at the same time. This case is treated later in the chapter.
5. The setup cost is assumed to be fixed when, in fact, it can often be reduced. This case is treated in Chapter 16 on JIT.

Even though the EOQ formula is derived from rather restrictive assumptions, it is a useful approximation in practice. The formula at least "puts you in the ball park," provided the assumptions are reasonably accurate. Furthermore, the total-cost curve is rather flat in the region of the minimum; thus the EOQ can be adjusted somewhat to conform to reality without greatly affecting the costs.

The EOQ formula can also provide insight into economic behavior of inventories. For example, traditional turnover arguments suggest that inventory should increase directly with sales if a constant turnover ratio is desired. Since turnover is the ratio of sales to inventory, a doubling of sales will allow a doubling of inventory if the turnover rate is held constant. But the EOQ formula suggests that inventory should increase only with the square root of sales. This indicates that it is not economical to maintain a constant turnover ratio as sales increase; a higher turnover is indeed justified.

Despite this caveat, managers continue to place undue reliance on turnover criteria. Although turnover may "suggest" that inventories are too high or too low, inventory policy should *not* be based on turnover ratios. In Section 14.8 a rational basis for inventory policy which considers both costs and desired service levels will be discussed.

The most important idea in this section is not the EOQ at all, but rather the concept of total cost. Regardless of the situation, if one can identify the relevant total-cost equation, then an economic lot size can be found. The idea of a total-cost equation is basic to all lot-sizing formulas and situations.

CONTINUOUS REVIEW SYSTEM

In practice one of the most serious limitations of the EOQ model is the assumption of constant demand. In this section, we will relax this assumption and allow random demand. The result will be a model which is sufficiently flexible to use in practice for independent-demand inventory management. All other EOQ assumptions except constant demand and no stockouts will remain in effect. In this section, we will be assuming that the stock level is reviewed continuously; in Section 14.7, a periodic review model will be developed.

In inventory work, decisions to reorder stock are based on the total on-hand plus on-order quantity. On-order material is counted the same as on-hand for reorder decisions because the on-order material is scheduled to arrive, even if nothing more is done. The total of on-hand and on-order material is called stock position (or available stock). One should be careful on this point. A common mistake in inventory problems is failure to consider amounts already on order.

In a continuous review system, the stock position is monitored after each transaction (or continuously). When the stock position drops to a predetermined order point (or reorder point), a fixed quantity is placed on order. Since the order quantity is fixed, the time between orders will vary depending on the random nature of demand. The continuous review system is sometimes called the Q system or the fixed-order-quantity system.

A formal definition of the Q-system decision rule follows:

> Continually review the stock position (on hand plus on order). When the stock position drops to the reorder point R, a fixed quantity Q is ordered.

A graph of the operation of this system is shown in Figure 14.7. The stock position drops on an irregular basis until it reaches the reorder point R, where an order for Q units is placed. The order arrives later, after a lead time L, and the cycle of usage, reorder, and stock receipt is then repeated.

The Q system is completely determined by the two parameters Q and R. In practice, these parameters are set by using certain simplifying assumptions. First, Q is set equal to the EOQ value from Equation (14.2) by using the average demand for D. In more complicated models, Q and R must be determined simultaneously. Using the EOQ formula for Q is, however, a reasonable approximation provided that demand is not highly uncertain.

The value of R can be based on either stockout cost or stockout probability. Formulations which utilize stockout cost, however, become quite complicated

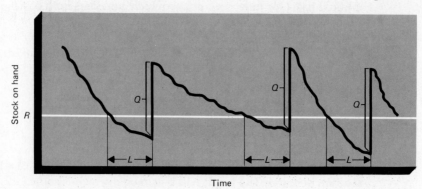

FIGURE 14.7
A continuous review (Q) system. (R = reorder point; Q = order quantity; L = lead time.)

mathematically and the stockout cost is difficult to estimate anyway. Therefore, stockout probability is commonly used as a basis to determine R.

A widely used term in inventory management is service level, which is the percentage of customer demands satisfied from inventory. A 100 percent service level thus represents meeting all customer demands from inventory. The stockout percentage is equal to 100 minus service level.

There are several different ways to express service level:

1. Service level is the probability that all orders will be filled from stock during the replenishment lead time of one reorder cycle.
2. Service level is the percentage of demand filled from stock during a given period of time (e.g., a year).
3. Service level is the percentage of time the system has stock on hand.

Each of these definitions of service level will lead to different reorder points. Furthermore, one must determine whether to count customers, units, or orders when applying any of these definitions. In this text, for the sake of simplicity, only the first definition of service level will be used.[3] For more definitions of service level, see Fogarty and Hoffmann (1980).

The reorder point is based on the notion of a probability distribution of demand over the lead time. When an order has been placed, the inventory system is exposed to stockout until the order arrives. Since the reorder point is usually greater than zero, it is reasonable to assume that the system does not run out of stock unless an order has been placed; the only risk of stockout is during replenishment lead time.

Figure 14.8 shows a typical probability distribution of independent demand over lead time. The reorder point in the figure can be set sufficiently high to reduce the stockout probability to any desired level. However, in calculating this probability, it will be necessary to know the statistical distribution of demand over the lead time. In the remainder of this discussion, we will assume a normal distribution of demand. This assumption is quite realistic for many independent-demand inventory problems.

The reorder point is defined as follows:

$$R = m + s \qquad (14.3)$$

where R = reorder point
m = mean (average) demand over the lead time
s = safety stock (or buffer stock)

We can express safety stock as

---

[3]In this case, the percentage of orders filled from stock during a given period of time will be a function of the reorder frequency.

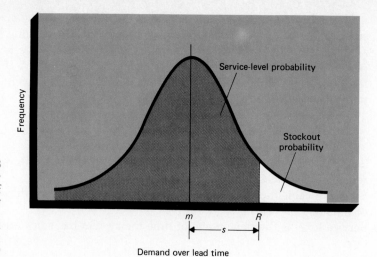

FIGURE 14.8
Probability
distribution of
demand over
each time. (m =
mean demand; R
= reorder point;
s = safety stock.)

$$s = z\sigma$$

where z = safety factor

σ = standard deviation of demand over the lead time

Then we have

$$R = m + z\sigma$$

Thus the reorder point is set equal to the average demand over lead time m plus a specified number of standard deviations σ to protect against stockout. By controlling z, the number of standard deviations used, one can control not only the reorder point but also the service level. A high value of z will result in a high reorder point and a high service level.

The percentages in Table 14.2 are from the normal distribution. These percentages represent the probability that the demand will fall within the specified number of standard deviations from the mean. Given a particular service level desired, it will be possible to determine z and then the reorder point from Table 14.2.

An example might help cement some of these ideas. Suppose we are managing a warehouse which distributes a certain type of breakfast food to retailers. The breakfast food has the following characteristics:

Average demand = 200 cases per day
Lead time = 4 days for resupply from the vendor
Standard deviation of daily demand = 150 cases
Desired service level = 95%
S = \$20 per order
i = 20% per year
C = \$10 per case

Assume that a continuous review system will be used and also assume that the

TABLE 14.2

NORMAL DEMAND PERCENTAGES

z	Service level, percent	Stockout, percent
0	50.0	50.0
.5	69.1	30.9
1.0	84.1	15.9
1.1	86.4	13.6
1.2	88.5	11.5
1.3	90.3	9.7
1.4	91.9	8.1
1.5	93.3	6.7
1.6	94.5	5.5
1.7	95.5	4.5
1.8	96.4	3.6
1.9	97.1	2.9
2.0	97.7	2.3
2.1	98.2	1.8
2.2	98.6	1.4
2.3	98.9	1.1
2.4	99.2	.8
2.5	99.4	.6
2.6	99.6	.5
2.7	99.6	.4
2.8	99.7	.3
2.9	99.8	.2
3.0	99.9	.1

warehouse is open 5 days a week, 50 weeks a year, or 250 days a year. Then average *annual* demand = 250(200) = 50,000 cases per year.

The economic order quantity is

$$Q = \sqrt{\frac{2(20)(250)(200)}{10(.20)}} = \sqrt{10^6} = 1000 \text{ cases}$$

The average demand over the lead time is 200 cases a day for 4 days; therefore $m = 4(200) = 800$ cases. The standard deviation of demand over the lead time is $\sqrt{4}(150) = 300$ units.[4]

The 95 percent level requires a safety factor of $z = 1.65$ (see Table 14.2). Thus we have

$$R = m + z\sigma = 800 + 1.65(300) = 1295$$

The Q-system decision rule is to place an order for 1000 cases whenever the stock position drops to 1295 cases. On average, 50 orders will be placed per year,

---

[4]The standard deviation of demand over the 4-day lead time can be computed from the daily standard deviation by assuming that the daily demands are independent. In this case the variance is additive and the variance for 4 days is four times the daily variance. This equates to $\sigma^2 = 4(150)^2$ or $\sigma = \sqrt{4}(150)$.

and there will be an average of 5 working days between orders. The actual time between orders will vary, however, depending on demand.

To complete this example, Box 14.2 simulates the operation of the Q-system decision rule. Here a series of random demands were generated on the basis of an average of 200 cases per day and a standard deviation of 150 cases per day. It is assumed that 1100 units are on hand at the beginning of the simulation and none are on order. An order for 1000 cases is placed whenever the stock position reaches 1295 units. The stock position is reviewed each day, as demands occur, for a possible order. The result is that orders are placed in periods 1, 7, 10, and 15. The lowest inventory level is 285 units at the beginning of day 10. It will be good practice to verify the numbers in part of the box.

BOX 14.2

A Q-SYSTEM EXAMPLE*

Day	Demand	Beginning period on hand	Beginning period on order	Beginning period stock position	Amount ordered	Amount received
1	111	1100	—	1100	1000	—
2	217	989	1000	1989	—	—
3	334	772	1000	1772	—	—
4	124	438	1000	1438	—	—
5	0	1314	—	1314	—	1000
6	371	1314	—	1314	—	—
7	135	943	—	943	1000	—
8	208	808	1000	1808	—	—
9	315	600	1000	1600	—	—
10	0	285	1000	1285	1000	—
11	440	1285	1000	2285	—	1000
12	127	845	1000	1845	—	—
13	315	718	1000	1718	—	—
14	114	1403	—	1403	—	1000
15	241	1289	—	1289	1000	—
16	140	1048	1000	2048	—	—

*For this box we have used $Q = 1000$ and $R = 1295$.

A PERIODIC REVIEW SYSTEM

In some cases the finished goods stock position is reviewed periodically rather than continuously. Suppose a supplier will only take orders and make deliveries at periodic intervals, for example, every 2 weeks, as his truck makes the rounds to your store. In this case, the stock position is reviewed every 2 weeks and an order is placed if material is needed.

In this section we are assuming that the stock position is reviewed periodically and the demand is random. All EOQ assumptions in Section 14.5 except constant demand and no stockouts will remain in effect.

In a periodic review system, the stock position is reviewed at fixed intervals. When the review is made, the stock position is "ordered up" to a target inventory level. The target level is set to cover demand until the next periodic review plus the delivery lead time. A variable quantity is ordered depending on how much is needed to bring the stock position up to target. The periodic review system is often called the P system of inventory control, the fixed-order-interval system, the fixed-order-period system, or simply the periodic system.

A formal definition of the P-system rule follows:

Review the stock position (on hand plus on order) at fixed periodic intervals P. An amount equal to target inventory T minus the stock position is ordered after each review.

A graph of the operation of this system is shown in Figure 14.9. The stock position drops on an irregular basis until the fixed review time is reached. At that time, a quantity is ordered to bring the stock position up to the target level. The order arrives later, after a lead time L; then the cycle of usage, reorder, and stock receipt repeats.

The P system functions in a completely different manner than the Q system because (1) it does not have a reorder point but rather a target inventory; (2) it does not have an economic order quantity, since the quantity varies according to demand; and (3) in the P system, the order interval is fixed, not the order quantity.

The P system is completely determined by the two parameters, P and T. An approximation to the optimal value of P can be made by using the EOQ formula in Equation (14.2). Since P is the time between orders, it is related to the EOQ as follows:

$$P = \frac{Q}{D}$$

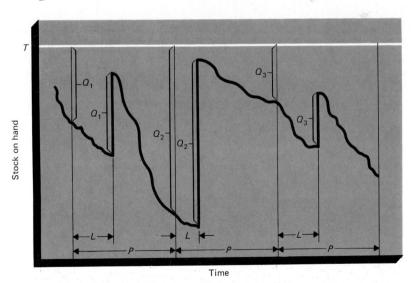

FIGURE 14.9
A periodic review system.

Then, substituting the EOQ formula for Q, we have

$$P = \frac{Q}{D} = \frac{1}{D}\sqrt{\frac{2DS}{iC}} = \sqrt{\frac{2S}{iCD}} \qquad (14.4)$$

Equation (14.4) provides an approximately optimal review interval P.[5]

The target inventory level can be set by a specified service level. In this case the target inventory is set high enough to cover demand over the lead time plus review period. This coverage time is needed because stock will not be ordered again until the next review period, and that stock will take the lead time to arrive. To achieve the specified service level, demand must be covered over the time $P + L$ at the average level plus a safety stock. Thus we have

$$T = m' + s' \qquad (14.5)$$

where T = target inventory level
   m' = average demand over $P + L$
   s' = safety stock

The safety stock should be set high enough to assure the desired service level. For safety stock, we have

$$s' = z\sigma'$$

where σ' = the standard deviation over $P + L$
   z = safety factor

By controlling z, we can control the target inventory and the resulting service level provided.

To illustrate, we will use the breakfast food example from the last section. Recall that the EOQ was 1000 cases and the daily demand 200 cases. The optimal review interval is then

$$P = \frac{Q}{D} = \frac{1000}{200} = 5 \text{ days}$$

The formula for target inventory is

$$T = m' + z\sigma'$$

In this case, m' is the average demand over $P + L = 5 + 4 = 9$ days. Thus we have $m' = 9(200) = 1800$. The standard deviation σ' is for the period $P + L = 9$ days. Thus we have $\sigma' = \sqrt{9}(150) = 450$, where 150 is the daily standard deviation and 9 the number of days.

Therefore,

$$T = 1800 + z(450)$$

For a service level of 95 percent, we need $z = 1.65$. Thus,

$$T = 1800 + 1.65(450) = 2542$$

---

[5]When demand is highly uncertain, the approximation may be quite poor. See Starr and Miller (1962), p. 129.

The P-system decision rule is to review the stock position every 5 days and order up to a target of 2542 cases.

It is interesting to note, at this point, that the P system requires $1.65(450) = 742$ units of safety stock, while the same service level is provided by the Q system with only $1.65(300) = 495$ units of safety stock. A P system always requires more safety stock than a Q system for the same service level. This occurs because the P system must provide coverage over a time of $P + L$, while the Q system must protect against stockout only over the time L.

This example is completed by Box 14.3, which uses the same demand figures as Box 14.2. Here, however, the review is periodic instead of continuous. A review is made in periods 1, 6, 11, and 16—that is, every five periods. The amounts ordered are 1442, 786, 1029, and 1237. While the review period is fixed, the amount ordered is not.

BOX 14.3
A P-SYSTEM EXAMPLE*

Day	Demand	Beginning period on hand	Beginning period on order	Beginning period stock position	Amount ordered	Amount received
1	111	1100	—	1100	1442	—
2	217	989	1442	2431	—	—
3	334	772	1442	2214	—	—
4	124	438	1442	1880	—	—
5	0	1756	—	1756	—	1442
6	371	1756	—	1756	786	—
7	135	1385	786	2171	—	—
8	208	1250	786	2036	—	—
9	315	1042	786	1828	—	—
10	0	1513	—	1513	—	786
11	440	1513	—	1513	1029	—
12	127	1073	1029	2102	—	—
13	315	946	1029	1975	—	—
14	114	631	1029	1660	—	—
15	241	1546	—	1546	—	1029
16	140	1305	—	1305	1237	—

*For this box we have used $P = 5$ and $T = 2542$.

USING P AND Q SYSTEMS IN PRACTICE

In industry, both Q and P systems as well as modifications of them are in wide use for independent-demand inventory management. The choice between these systems is not a simple one and may be dictated by management practices as well as economics. There are, however, some conditions under which the P system may be preferred over the Q system:

1. The P system should be used when orders must be placed and/or delivered at specified intervals. An example is weekly order and delivery of canned goods to a grocery store.
2. The P system should be used when multiple items are ordered from the same supplier, and delivered in the same shipment. In this case the supplier would prefer consolidation of the items into a single order. An example is different colors of paint which might be ordered from a paint supplier. The supplier would then deliver at fixed times instead of delivering the different colors of paint at different times.
3. The P system should be used for inexpensive items which are not maintained on perpetual inventory records. An example is nuts or bolts used in a manufacturing process. In this case, the bins may be filled up daily or weekly. The bin size determines the target inventory, and the bin is filled up to target at fixed time intervals. No records need be kept of each disbursement and receipt into inventory.

In sum, the P system provides the advantage of scheduled replenishment and less record keeping. It requires, however, a somewhat larger safety stock than the Q system, as the last example illustrates. Because of this larger safety stock, the Q system is often used for expensive items where it is desirable to hold down the investment in safety stock inventory. The choice between the Q and P systems should, therefore, be made on the basis of timing of replenishment, the type of record-keeping system in use, and the cost of the item.

In practice, one also finds hybrid systems which are a mixture of P and Q inventory rules. One of these systems is characterized by min/max decision rules and periodic review. In this case, the system has both a reorder point (min) and a target (max). When the periodic review is made, no order is placed if the stock position is above the min. If the stock position is below min, an order is placed to raise the stock position to the max level.

Use of Forecasts

The issue of forecasting is important for both the P and Q systems. These systems have been derived under the assumption of a constant average demand level with random variation around the average. When this is the case, it is only necessary to forecast the average demand level and to monitor the actual demands for a possible change in the average. When such a change is detected (by statistical methods), the model should be reset on the basis of the new average demand observed. If no change in average is detected, the model should remain in effect.

In many cases, however, independent demand is subject to either a trend or a seasonal pattern; i.e., the average demand is not constant. Then the P and Q formulas from the last section are inadequate and must be modified. Equation (14.3) for the reorder point is modified by using *forecast* demand over lead time for m in place of *average* demand over lead time. The forecast demand for the future lead-time period will include a trend or seasonal adjustment. Thus the reorder point will be dependent on the forecast and will change after each new forecast is made. Conceivably, the reorder point could change after each inventory transaction, when a new demand is observed and a new forecast is computed. In the same way the order quantity could be recomputed after each new forecast is made.

In the case of the P model, a modification to the target inventory equation—Equation (14.5)—is needed. In this case, the *forecast* demand over $P + L$ should be substituted for the *average* demand over $P + L$. This change will have the effect of introducing a changing target level each time a new forecast is made.

The simple example in Box 14.4 illustrates these ideas. In this case, a P system with a review interval of two periods and a lead time of one period is being used. Upon review of inventory levels, a forecast is made for three periods $(P + L)$ and this forecast is used to set the new target level. The forecast utilizes second-order exponential smoothing with $\alpha = .2$, a starting level of 50, and a starting trend of 50.[6] The changing target level is needed because finished goods demand is clearly exhibiting an upward trend of about 50 units per period. As indicated, the revised target adjusts quickly to the changing demand levels. The low point reached is five units in week 9. For practice, one might construct a similar table using the Q method of inventory control.

BOX 14.4
P SYSTEM FOR INCREASING DEMAND

Period	Demand	Three-period second-order forecast	Target*	Beginning on hand	End on hand	Amount ordered	Amount received
1	100	450	500	200	100	300	—
2	140	—	—	400	260	—	300
3	200	742	792	260	60	532	—
4	230	—	—	592	362	—	532
5	290	1027	1077	362	72	715	—
6	350	—	—	787	437	—	715
7	410	1325	1375	437	27	938	—
8	460	—	—	965	505	—	938
9	500	1649	1699	505	5	1194	—
10	535	—	—	1199	664	—	1194
11	590	1940	1990	664	74	1326	—

*Target = three-period forecast + s', $s' = 50$, review interval = 2, lead time = 1 period.

In addition to expected demand, one must also estimate the standard deviation of demand σ. Recall that the standard deviation is used to set the safety stock in both the P and Q systems. The forecast standard deviation is also sometimes called the "forecast error." These forecasts of error or standard deviation are automatically made by exponential-smoothing systems. The forecast standard deviation is, however, produced for the same period of time as the demand interval. For example, with daily demand data, the forecast standard deviation

---

[6]See Chapter 3 for details on second-order exponential smoothing.

will be for one day. This standard deviation must be adjusted to L periods, since we need the standard deviation over the lead time ($L + P$ in the case of the P model). The adjustment can be made by using the procedure described above.

Service Level and Inventory Level

There is an important tradeoff between service level and inventory level. In the management of independent-demand inventories, one of the key considerations is customer-service levels. But customer-service levels must be balanced against investment in inventory, since higher customer service levels require higher inventory investments.

The average inventory level I is given by

$$I = \frac{Q}{2} + z\sigma$$

The reasoning behind this formula is that $Q/2$ units are carried on average owing to ordering in lots of size Q, and $z\sigma$ units are carried on average owing to safety stocks. (In the case of the P system, use σ' in place of σ.) Thus the inventory level is the sum of cycle stock and safety stock components.

For a fixed Q, the inventory level will be a function of z, which, in turn, also determines the service level. Thus, for given values of z, one can plot service level versus the average inventory required. Such a plot is shown in Figure 14.10.

The figure indicates that an increasing inventory level is required to achieve higher service levels. As the service level approaches 100 percent, very large inventories are required. This happens because we are assuming normally distributed demand over the lead time, and we must cover very unlikely events as the probability approaches 100 percent.

Due to the highly nonlinear relationship, it is crucial for management to compare the service-level graph with that of the inventory level before setting a service level. Selection of an arbitrary service level may be very costly, since the difference of a few percentage points in service level could substantially increase the required inventory level. For instance, in Figure 14.10, an increase in service level from 95 to 99 percent (four percentage points) requires a 32 percent increase

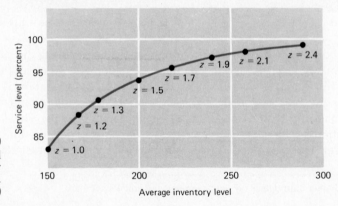

FIGURE 14.10
Service level versus inventory level. ($Q = 100$. $\sigma = 100$.)

in inventory. It is, therefore, essential that management study the service level and inventory tradeoffs in each situation.

The relationship between service level and inventory level helps to determine appropriate inventory turnovers. Suppose a firm is compared with its industry or with itself over time and turnover is now low. This lower turnover could be explained by either higher service levels or different ordering and holding costs. Management should look beyond turnover to the service-level policy or the cost structure inherent in the situation. On the basis of better customer service or different cost structures, management may prefer a policy which leads to turnovers that are lower than the industry norm.

Multiple Items

Most inventory situations involve multiple items. If P and Q systems are used for these, the resulting inventories could exceed available space or the quantities required could exceed purchasing budgets. On the other hand, if no constraints, budgets, or inventory policies are violated, then the P and Q models derived in the earlier discussion can be used directly for multiple items. In this case, the multiple-item inventory problem is simply a composite of all the single items considered one at a time.

If constraints are violated, then adjustments must be made to the P or Q model in use. There are two cases of interest here. First, assume that a budget, investment level, or space constraint has been violated. In this case, a higher value of carrying cost i should be used to reduce the values of Q, or lower service levels should be used. Whether one or both of these adjustments should be used will depend on the types of constraints violated and the effect of each adjustment. Higher-level management should then be made aware of the resulting service levels and required value of carrying cost. This could result in a reassessment of the situation and perhaps a change in the constraints.

This discussion indicates that the inventory carrying charge i can be viewed as a policy variable. If management specifies certain constraints on space or budget, they have in fact implicitly set a value of i (or service level). Such constraints should not be applied blindly but always evaluated in light of their effect on inventory. [See Schroeder (1974) for more details on this subject.]

The second case, where multiple items may interact, is the case of a single supplier of multiple items. In this case the supplier may offer substantial discounts if a truckload lot is ordered at one time, owing to the transportation economics involved. The question then becomes: Under what circumstances would it be economical to place a single order for all the different items to take advantage of the lower freight rate? This question can be answered by comparing the total cost of ordering the items together, in one shipment, with the sum of the total cost for ordering them separately. The option with the lower total inventory cost is preferred.

A similar problem occurs when several items can be produced from a single machine setup. In this case it may cost a great deal to set up the machine for the group of items but only a small amount to shift over from one item to the next. The question in this case is the same: When is it economical to schedule the group of items together rather than independently? The answer here also depends on a comparison of total setup plus holding costs for the two options.

Multiple items may, therefore, require modification of the basic inventory formulas to reflect the interaction among items. Although we have not presented the new formulas in detail, they are available in the literature for many different cases. [See Silver and Peterson (1985).]

 14.9 INVENTORY CONTROL SYSTEMS

To this point, we have been concentrating on decision rules which can be used to determine when and how much to order. In operations, these rules need to be embedded in an inventory control system. In addition to calculation of the decision rules, the system should include a way to record inventory transactions and a way to monitor inventory management performance.

An inventory control system can be either manual or computerized or a combination of the two. Nowadays many inventory systems are computerized, the exceptions being those with a small number of items or inexpensive items. For these cases, the cost of a computerized system may be greater than its benefits.

In a modern inventory control system, the following functions should be performed:

Transaction counting. Every inventory system requires a method of record keeping, which must support the accounting needs of the organization and the inventory management function. Sometimes this requires that perpetual records be kept by recording every disbursement and receipt. In other cases, periodic (e.g., annual) counts of the inventory will suffice. Whatever the exact method used, every inventory control system requires a suitable transaction subsystem.

The accuracy of inventory records is of such importance that it can hardly be overemphasized. Many systems do not respond properly because the records of on-hand or on-order inventory are inaccurate. In Chapter 15, we will discuss cycle counting as a way to control the accuracy of inventory records.

Inventory decision rules. An inventory system should incorporate decision rules to determine when and how much to order. In this chapter, we have developed the periodic and continuous decision rules at length. Whatever rules are used, the system should implement them automatically. In many systems, the computer can also automatically generate purchase orders based on the decision rules in use.

Exception reporting. When inventory decision rules are automatically incorporated in a system, exceptions should be reported to management. These exceptions might include situations in which the forecast is not tracking accurately with demand, a very large purchase order has been generated, stockouts have reached an excessive level, and so on. The purpose of exception reporting is to alert management to changing assumptions. In practice, however, many systems do not incorporate sufficient exception reporting. Such systems have a tendency to run out of control and to generate inventory orders which are not economical.

Forecasting. Inventory decisions should be based on forecast demand. In Chapter

3 we developed exponential smoothing, which is a useful technique for forecasting inventory demands. Inventory decisions should not be based purely on hunches from the marketing department or the inventory manager; a quantitative technique should be incorporated into the system. Judgment should play a role in forecasting, however, to modify the quantitative forecasts for unusual events.

Top-management reporting. An inventory control system should generate reports for top management as well as for inventory managers. These reports should measure the overall performance of inventory, and they should assist in making broad inventory policy. Such reports should include service level provided, costs of operating the inventory, and investment levels as compared with other periods. Too much reliance is often placed on turnover ratios as the only performance measure, resulting in inadequate information for inventory policy making. In practice, most systems provide very poor information for top management.

As can be seen, a good inventory control system should go far beyond mere record keeping. It should provide for management decision making while also controlling inventory levels.

Types of Control Systems

Many types of inventory control systems are in use. These four are typical:

1. **Single-bin system.** In a single-bin system, the bin or shelf is filled up periodically. Examples of this are shelves in retail stores, automobile gas tanks, and small-parts bins in factories. The single-bin system is a P system. The size of the bin is the target, and the inventory is brought up to target periodically by filling the bin. In this type of system, records of each receipt or disbursement are not kept. However, purchase orders are usually kept, so that usage between any two physical counts of inventory can be determined.

2. **Two-bin system.** To understand the two-bin system, visualize a bin with two compartments. The front compartment contains material which is issued, and the back compartment is sealed. When the material in the front compartment is gone, the back compartment is opened for use and an order for new material is placed. Thus the back compartment must contain enough material to last throughout the replenishment lead time with high probability. This is a Q system of inventory control with the back compartment containing stock equal to the reorder point. The record-keeping aspects of this system are the same as those of the one-bin system.

3. **Card-file system.** With this system, a card file—usually containing one card for each inventory item—is kept. As items are sold, the corresponding cards are located and updated. Similarly, the cards are updated when new material arrives. They may also contain decision rules for either the P or Q system. The card-file system might be appropriate for small inventories with not too many transactions.

4. **Computerized system.** A record on computer-readable storage is maintained for each item. Transactions are posted against this record as items are disbursed or received. The computer applies either the P or Q decision rules, forecasts demand,

TABLE 14.3

ANNUAL USAGE OF ITEMS BY DOLLAR VALUE

Item	Annual usage in units	Unit cost	Dollar usage	Percentage of total dollar usage
1	5,000	$ 1.50	$ 7,500	2.9
2	1,500	8.00	12,000	4.7
3	10,000	10.50	105,000	41.2
4	6,000	2.00	12,000	4.7
5	7,500	.50	3,750	1.5
6	6,000	13.60	81,600	32.0
7	5,000	.75	3,750	1.5
8	4,500	1.25	5,625	2.2
9	7,000	2.50	17,500	6.9
10	3,000	2.00	6,000	2.4
Total			$254,725	100.0

and monitors performance of the inventory system. The computer system reduces clerical effort and also provides better management control of inventories.

The choice between these four systems depends on the relative costs and benefits. Generally speaking, the cost-benefit ratio for medium and large inventories favors the computer. With the advent of the personal computer, even many small inventory systems can be economically computerized.

ABC Inventory Management

In 1906, Vilfredo Pareto observed that a few items in any group constitute the significant proportion of the entire group.[7] At that time he was concerned that a few individuals in the economy seemed to earn most of the income. It can also be observed that a few products in a firm result in most of the sales and that, in volunteer organizations, a few people do most of the work. The law of the significant few can be applied to inventory management as well.

In inventories, a few items usually account for most of the inventory value as measured by dollar usage (demand times cost). Thus, one can manage these few items intensively and control most of the inventory value. In inventory work, the items are usually divided into three classes: A, B, and C. Class A typically contains about 20 percent of the items and 80 percent of the dollar usage. It therefore represents the most significant few. At the other extreme, class C contains 50 percent of the items and only 5 percent of the dollar usage. These items contribute very little of the dollar value of inventory. In the middle is class B, with 30 percent of the items and 15 percent of the dollar usage. The classification of inventory in this way is often called ABC analysis or the 80-20 rule. [See Dickie (1951).]

Table 14.3 is an example of an inventory with 10 items. In this case, items 3 and 6 account for a great deal of the dollar usage (73.2 percent). On the other hand, items 1, 5, 7, 8, and 10 are low in dollar usage (10.5 percent). The ABC principle,

---

[7]Vilfredo Pareto, *Manual of Political Economy*, Ann A. Schwier (trans.), New York: A. M. Kelly, 1971.

TABLE 14.4
ABC CLASSIFICATION

Class	Item numbers	Percentage of total items	Percentage of total dollar usage
A	3, 6	20	73.2
B	2, 4, 9	30	16.3
C	1, 5, 7, 8, 10	50	10.5
Total		100	100.0

therefore, applies to this small example. The percentages in each category are summarized in Table 14.4.

The designation of three classes is arbitrary; there could be any number of classes. Also, the exact percentage of items in each class will vary from one inventory to the next. The important factors are the two extremes: a few items which are significant and a large number of items which are relatively significant.

Most of the dollar usage in inventory (80 percent) can be controlled by closely monitoring the A items (20 percent). For these items, a tight control system including continuous review of stock levels, less safety stock, and close attention to record accuracy might be used.

On the other hand, looser control might be used for C items. A periodic review system could be used to consolidate orders from the same supplier, and less record accuracy might be sufficient. Even manual systems might be used for C items. The B items require an intermediate level of attention and management control.

With computerized systems, a uniform level of control is sometimes used for all items. Nevertheless, the management of inventories still requires the setting of priorities, and the ABC concept is often useful in doing this.

14.10 KEY POINTS

Inventory management is a key operations responsibility because it greatly affects capital requirements, costs, and customer service. This chapter provides an overview of inventory management together with specific methods for the management of independent-demand inventories.

The chapter's major points include the following:

- Inventory is a stock of materials used to facilitate production or to satisfy customer demands. Inventories include raw materials, work in process, and finished goods.
- Decision problems in inventory management include what to carry, how much to order, when to order, and what type of control system to use. A decision rule specifies how much to order and when. In the calculation of decision rules, there are four types of inventory costs to consider: item cost, ordering (or setup) cost, carrying (or holding) cost, and stockout cost. The relevant costs to include are those which vary with the decision to be made.
- The economic order quantity (EOQ) assumptions include a constant demand rate, constant lead time, fixed setup time, no stockouts, lot ordering, no discounts, and a

single product. Within the assumptions made, the EOQ formula minimizes both holding and ordering costs.

- A continuous review system provides one way to handle random demand. When the stock position drops to the reorder point R, a fixed quantity Q is ordered. The time between orders will vary depending on actual demand. The value of Q is set equal to the EOQ. The value of R is based on the service level desired.

- A periodic review system provides another way to handle random demand. The stock position is reviewed at fixed intervals P, and an amount is ordered equal to the target inventory T minus stock position. The amount ordered at each review period will vary depending on actual demand. The value of P is set by use of the EOQ, and the value of T is based on the service level desired.

- The choice between P and Q systems should be based on the timing of replenishment, type of record keeping, and cost of the item. A periodic system should be used when inventory orders must be regularly scheduled.

- High service levels require high investment levels. Management should, therefore, study the service level and investment relationship before setting the service levels desired. The optimal turnover in inventory should be based on the service level desired and the problem's cost structure. Comparisons of turnover ratios, do not, by themselves, provide an adequate basis for decisions on inventory level.

- An inventory control system should do five things: count transactions, implement inventory decision rules, report exceptions, forecast, and report to top management. There are four basic types of inventory control systems: single-bin, two-bin, card-file, and computerized. The choice between the systems should be based on a cost-benefit comparison.

- The ABC inventory concept is based on the significant few and the insignificant many. The concept should be used to carefully control the significant A items and to spend less effort and cost on the B and C items.

QUESTIONS

1. Identify the different types of inventories (raw materials, work-in-process, and finished goods) carried in the following organizations: gas station, hamburger stand, clothing store, and machine shop. What functions (purposes) do these inventories perform?

2. Consider the following types of items carried in a retail store: light bulbs, phonograph records, and refrigerated drugs. Discuss the probable cost structure for each of these items including item cost, carrying cost, ordering cost, and stockout cost.

3. Why is stockout cost difficult to determine? Suggest an approach which might be used to estimate it.

4. Why can the item cost be dropped from the simple EOQ formula? Are item costs important when quantity discounts are given? Why?

5. What is the difference between a requirements philosophy and a replenishment philosophy of inventory management? Why is this difference important?

6. Compare and contrast the management of finished goods inventory in a manufacturing company with that in a retail or wholesale firm.

7. For a given service level, why will a P system require a larger inventory investment than a Q system? What factors affect the magnitude of the difference?

8. Suppose you were managing the Speedy Hardware Store. Give examples of items

which might be managed by a P system and other items which might use a Q system. How do these items differ?

9. How should a manager decide on the appropriate service level for finished goods items? Should some items have a 100 percent service level?

10. A manager was heard to complain, "I have some items which have a 2-week review interval, and it takes 4 weeks for resupply. Every 2 weeks, I place orders based on the on-hand quantity in stock. Now I seem to have too much inventory." What went wrong?

11. A student was overheard saying, "The EOQ-model assumptions are so restrictive that the model would be hard to use in practice." Is it necessary to have a different model for each variation in assumptions? Why or why not?

12. What is the appropriate role of turnover criteria for managing inventory? Under what circumstances is high turnover detrimental to the firm?

13. How should forecasting be used in an inventory control system? Under what circumstances would forecasts be unnecessary?

14. Suppose you were managing a chain of retail department stores. The inventory in each store is computerized, but there are a large number of different items. As a top manager, how would you measure the overall inventory management performance of each store? How would you use this information in your relationship with the individual store managers?

15. Why should exception reporting be included in an inventory control system? What types of exceptions would you want reported?

16. Visit a department store, a local garage, or a fast-food outlet. Determine the type of inventory control system used, including forecast methods, decision rules, exception reporting, record keeping, and management reports.

PROBLEMS

1. The Speedy Grocery Store carries a particular brand of coffee which has the following characteristics:

   Sales = 10 cases per week
   Ordering cost = $10 per order
   Carrying charge = 30 percent per year
   Item cost = $80 per case

   a. How many cases should be ordered at a time?
   b. How often will coffee be ordered?
   c. What is the annual cost of ordering and carrying coffee?
   d. What factors might cause the company to order a larger or smaller amount than the EOQ?

2. The Grinell Machine Shop makes a line of metal tables for customers. Some of these tables are carried in finished goods inventory. A particular table has the following characteristics:

   Sales = 200 per year
   Setup cost = $1200 per setup (this includes machine setup for all the different parts in the table)
   Carrying cost = 20 percent per year
   Item cost = $25

   a. How many of these tables should be made in a production lot?
   b. How often will production be scheduled?

c. What factors might cause the company to schedule a different lot size than you have computed?

3. What is the effect on EOQ and total cost of the following types of errors for the data in Problem 1?

   a. A 50 percent increase in demand

   b. A 50 percent increase in carrying charge

   c. Use Lotus to study the relationship between lot size and carrying cost.

4. The famous Widget Company sells widgets at the rate of 100,000 units per year. Each widget sells for $100, and it costs 30 percent to carry widgets in inventory for a year. The process of widget production has been automated over the years, and it now costs $1000 to change over the widget production line to other products which are made on the same line.

   a. What is the economical lot size for production of widgets?

   b. How many lots will be produced each year?

   c. What is the annual cost of carrying widgets and the annual cost of changeover?

   d. What factors or changes in assumptions might cause the Widget Company to produce a larger lot than the economic lot size calculated in part a?

5. The Harvard Coop orders sweatshirts with the Harvard University emblem on them for sale at $25 each. During a typical month, 1000 sweatshirts are sold (this includes all styles and sizes ordered from a particular supplier). It costs $25 to place an order (for multiple sizes and styles) and 25 percent to carry sweatshirts in inventory for a year.

   a. How many sweatshirts should the Coop order at one time?

   b. The supplier would like to deliver sweatshirts every week in smaller lot sizes than the optimal order size. How much will this cost the Coop per year? Under what conditions would you agree to the supplier's proposal?

   c. Suppose that sales increase to 1500 sweatshirts per week, but you decide to keep the lot size the same as in part a. How much will this decision cost the Coop per year?

6. The Coop in Problem 5 has discovered that it should establish a safety stock for its sweatshirts. It wants to use a reorder point system with a 2-week lead time. The demand over a 2-week interval can be assumed to have an average of 500 units and a standard deviation of 250 units.

   a. What reorder point should the Coop establish to ensure a 95 percent service level for each order placed?

   b. What reorder point should be established to ensure that no more than one stockout occurs in the course of a year?

   c. How much average inventory will the Coop carry for part b? Include both cycle inventory and safety stock in your answer.

   d. How often will the Coop turn over its inventory using the results from part c?

7. An appliance store carries a certain brand of TV which has the following characteristics:

   Average annual sales = 200 units
   Ordering cost = $25 per order
   Carrying cost = 25 percent per year
   Item cost = $400 per unit
   Lead time = 4 days
   Standard deviation of daily demand = .1 unit
   Working days per year = 250

   a. Determine the EOQ.

   b. Calculate the reorder point for a 95 percent service level, assuming normal demand.

   c. State the Q rule for this item.

   d. Study the effect on reorder point of changes in lead time or in standard deviation.

8. For the data given in Problem 7:
   a. Determine a P system of inventory control for a 95 percent service level. Compute the values of P and T.
   b. Compare the inventory investment required for the P system and the Q system from Problem 7 for various values of service level.
   c. Why does the P system require a higher inventory investment?

9. The Suregrip Tire Company carries a certain type of tire with the following characteristics:
   Average annual sales = 500 tires
   Ordering cost = $40 per order
   Carrying cost = 25 percent per year
   Item cost = $40 per tire
   Lead time = 4 days
   Standard deviation of daily demand = 1 tire
   a. Calculate the EOQ.
   b. For a Q system of inventory control, calculate the safety stock required for service levels of 85, 90, 95, 97, and 99 percent.
   c. Construct a plot of inventory investment versus service level.
   d. What service level would you establish on the basis of the graph in part *c*? Discuss.

10. For the data in Problem 9:
    a. Calculate the annual turnover as a function of service level.
    b. If sales were to increase by 50 percent, what would happen to the turnover at a 95 percent service level?

11. Assume that the Suregrip Tire Company described in Problem 9 faces an increasing demand trend. They have been using second-order exponential smoothing, which has predicted a current daily average of 2 units, with an increasing trend of ½ unit per day.
    a. Calculate the reorder point for a 99 percent service level.
    b. What service level would be obtained if the reorder point were calculated by ignoring the trend?

12. The Easyfoot Carpet Company carries three types of carpet with the following characteristics:

Type	Annual demand, yards	Item cost per yard
A	300	$10
B	200	8
C	100	6

Assume that the items are to be ordered together from the same supplier at an ordering cost of $20 per order and an annual carrying cost of 20 percent. Also assume 300 working days in a year.
    a. Using a P system, what is the optimal ordering interval in days?
    b. How much of each type carpet would be ordered when a combined order is placed?
    c. What is the effect on ordering interval of changing the carrying cost to 25, 30, and 35 percent?
    d. Why can't these carpets be ordered by a Q system?

13. Suppose that you are the supplier of the Easyfoot Carpet Company described in Problem 12. It costs $2000 each time you change over your carpet-producing machine from one type of carpet to another (A, B, or C). Assume that your carrying cost is 30 percent and the other data are as given in Problem 12.

a. What lot sizes would the supplier of carpet prefer to make for types A, B, and C?

b. How would you reconcile the lot sizes which the supplier would like to produce and those which the Easyfoot Carpet Company would like to buy? Mention several ways that these two differing lot sizes can be reconciled.

*14. Suppose that, for Problem 1, the Speedy Grocery Store is offered a discount if more than 50 cases are ordered at a time. The unit item costs are $80 a case for 0 to 49 cases and $76 a case for 50 cases or more. This price of $76 applies to the entire order.

a. Should the grocery store take the discount offer?

b. What discount is required before the store is indifferent between taking the discount or ordering the EOQ?

*15. A supplier has come to you and offered the following deal. If you buy 29 cases or less of cleaning solution, the cost will be $25 for the case. If you buy 30 or more cases, the cost will be $20 per case. Assume your cost of carrying inventory is 15 percent a year, it costs $20 for you to reorder the material, and you use 50 cases per year.

a. How many cases should you order?

b. Would you negotiate with this supplier for a further discount? Explain the quantities and prices that you would negotiate for and why these quantities and prices were selected.

*16. For Problem 2, suppose the Grinell Machine Shop produces its tables at a rate of 2 per day. (250 working days per year.)

a. What is the optimal lot size?

b. Draw a graph of on-hand inventory versus time.

c. What is the maximum value of inventory?

*17. A producer of electronic parts wants to take account of both production rate and demand rate in deciding on lot sizes. A particular $50 part can be produced at a rate of 1000 units per month, and the demand rate is 200 units per month. The company uses a carrying charge of 24 percent a year, and the setup cost is $200 each time the part is produced.

a. What lot size should be produced?

b. If the production rate is ignored, what would the lot size be? How much does this smaller lot size cost the company on an annual basis?

c. Draw a graph of on-hand inventory versus time.

SELECTED BIBLIOGRAPHY

Brown, Robert G.: *Decision Rules for Inventory Management*, New York: Holt, 1967.

Buffa, E. S., and W. H. Taubert: *Production-Inventory Systems: Planning and Control*, rev. ed., Homewood, Ill.: Irwin, 1972.

Chase, Richard B., and Nicholas Aquilano: *Production and Operations Management: A Life Cycle Approach*, rev. ed., Homewood, Ill.: Irwin, 1977.

Dickie, H. Ford: "ABC Inventory Analysis Shoots for Dollars Not Pennies," *Factory Management and Maintenance*, July 1951.

Fogarty, Donald W., and Thomas R. Hoffmann: "Customer Service," *Production and Inventory Management*, First Quarter, 1980, pp. 71–80.

——— and ———: *Production and Inventory Management*, Cincinnati, Oh: South-Western, 1983.

Green, James H.: *Production and Inventory Control*, Homewood, Ill.: Irwin, 1974.

Plossl, George: *Production and Inventory Control: Principles and Techniques*, 2d ed., Englewood Cliffs, N.J.: Prentice-Hall, 1985.

Rhodes, Phillip: "Inventory Carrying Costs May Be Less than You've Been Told," *Production & Inventory Management Review and APICS News*, October 1981, pp. 35–36.

*The supplement is required to work these problems.

SCHROEDER, ROGER G.: "Managerial Inventory Formulations with Stockout Objectives and Fiscal Constraints," *Naval Research Logistics Quarterly,* vol. 21, no. 3, September 1974, pp. 375–388.

———: "Return on Investment as a Criterion for Inventory Models," *Decision Sciences,* vol. 7, no. 4, October 1976, pp. 697–704.

SHORE, BARRY: *Operations Management,* New York: McGraw-Hill, 1973.

SILVER, E.H., and R. PETERSON: *Decision Systems for Inventory Management and Production Planning,* 2d ed., New York: Wiley, 1985.

VOLLMANN, THOMAS E., WILLIAM L. BERRY, and D. CLAY WHYBARK: *Manufacturing Planning and Control Systems,* 2d ed., Homewood, Ill.: Irwin, 1988.

Advanced Models

This supplement presents two additional models which are useful for independent inventory demands. The first model applies to outside procurement where price discounts are given, while the second applies to a gradual fill of inventory when the lot arrives uniformly over time—not all at once.

PRICE BREAKS

Outside suppliers often offer price discounts for large purchases. These discounts may be given at different procurement levels, and they may apply either to the whole order or only to the increment purchased. In this supplement, we assume that the price discounts apply to the entire procurement order. For example, the procurement price may be $2 per unit for 0 to 99 units and $1.50 per unit for 100 units and up. The cost of the units thus exhibits a jump or discontinuity at 100 units. For 99 units, the cost of the procurement order is $198, and for 100 units the cost is $150.

In order to solve for the economic order quantity, the procedure is to first calculate the EOQ for each different procurement price. Some of these EOQs may not be feasible because the EOQ falls outside the range of the price used to compute it. The infeasible EOQs are eliminated from further consideration. The total procurement and inventory operating cost for each feasible EOQ and each price-break quantity is then computed. The feasible EOQ or price break which results in the lowest total cost is then selected as the order quantity.

Consider the following example:

D = 1000 units per year
i = 20 percent per year
S = \$10 per order
C_1 = \$5 per unit for 0 to 199 units
C_2 = \$4.50 per unit for 200 to 499 units
C_3 = \$4.25 per unit for 500 units or more

First calculate the three EOQs corresponding to the three values of C_i. We then obtain Q_1 = 141, Q_2 = 149, and Q_3 = 153. In this case, Q_2 and Q_3 are infeasible, and they are eliminated from further consideration. We then compute the total cost of procurement and inventory at the remaining EOQ and at the two price breaks. These total costs are as follows[8]:

$$\text{TC} = S(D/Q) + iC(Q/2) + CD$$
$$\text{TC}(141) = 10(^{1000}\!/_{141}) + .20(5)(^{141}\!/_2) + 5(1000)$$
$$= 5141$$
$$\text{TC}(200) = 10(^{1000}\!/_{200}) + .20(4.50)(^{200}\!/_2)$$
$$+ 4.50(1000) = 4640$$
$$\text{TC}(500) = 10(^{1000}\!/_{500}) + .20(4.25)(^{500}\!/_2)$$
$$+ 4.25(1000) = 4482$$

Since TC(500) is the lowest annual cost, 500 units should be ordered.

The cost behavior for the example is shown in Figure S14.1. Notice that at each price break the total cost is reduced. Therefore the quantity at the highest price break is selected.

It is not always necessary to calculate all the EOQs and the cost at each point. A more efficient procedure is to first calculate the EOQ for the lowest cost per unit (the largest price-break quantity). If this EOQ is feasible, i.e., above the price break, then the most economical quantity has been found. If the EOQ is not feasible, use the next-lowest price and continue calculating EOQs until a feasible EOQ is found or until all prices have been used. Then calculate the total cost of the EOQ, if found, and the total cost at all the *higher* price breaks. The minimum of these total costs indicates the most economic order quantity. In the above example, this procedure would have resulted, by coincidence, in the same amount of calculation.

---

[8]Note that the annual cost CD of buying the units has been added to this cost equation, since this cost will be affected by the discount.

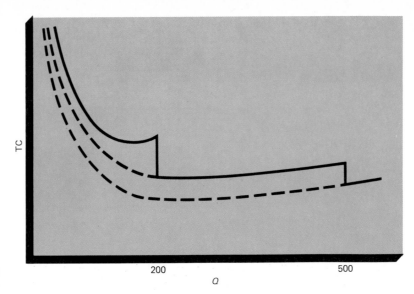

FIGURE S14.1
Inventory cost
with price breaks.

UNIFORM LOT DELIVERY

In some cases, the entire lot is not placed in inventory at one time but is delivered gradually. An example is a manufacturer who builds inventory at a constant production rate. Another example is a retailer who takes the lot in several shipments over a period of time.

The effect of this delivery condition on inventory is shown in Figures S14.2. The inventory level builds up gradually as both production and consumption occur. Then the inventory level is depleted as only consumption takes place.

The effect of gradual delivery is to reduce the maximum and average inventory level over that obtained in the simple EOQ case. Suppose units are produced at a rate of p units per year and consumed at a rate of D units per year (where $p > D$). Then the average inventory level will be

$$\frac{Q}{2}\left(1 - \frac{D}{p}\right)$$

This formula can be derived with the use of geometry by reference to Figure S14.2.

The above expression for average inventory is used in place of $Q/2$ in Equation (14.1). By mini-

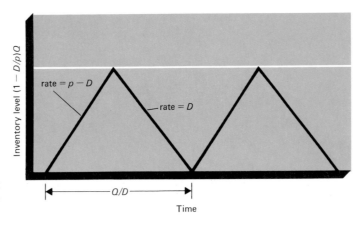

FIGURE S14.2
Uniform lot
delivery.

mizing the resulting expression for TC, the following EOQ formula is obtained:

$$Q = \sqrt{\frac{2SD}{iC(1 - D/p)}}$$

The EOQ in this case will always be somewhat larger than the ordinary EOQ because the factor $(1 - D/p)$ is less than 1. As p approaches D, the EOQ becomes very large, which means that production is continuous. When p is very large, the above EOQ formula approaches the ordinary EOQ. In deriving the ordinary EOQ, we assumed the entire lot arrived in inventory at once, which is equivalent to an infinite production rate p.

CHAPTER 15

Materials Requirements Planning

Many manufacturing operations are managed in a more or less chaotic way. Inventories are swollen, parts are being expedited to get orders out on time, and a pressure-cooker atmosphere prevails. It is now possible to remedy this situation through use of a computerized planning and control system called materials requirements planning (MRP).

MRP derives its power from the very important distinction between independent- and dependent-demand inventories. In Chapter 14 we defined independent-demand inventories as those which are subject to market conditions and are thus independent of operations. Examples of independent-demand inventories are finished goods and spare parts in a manufacturing company that are used to satisfy final customer demand. These inventories should be managed by the order-point methods described in the last chapter.

Dependent-demand inventories, on the other hand, are not subject to market conditions. They are dependent on demand for higher-level parts and components up to and including the master production schedule. Examples of dependent-demand inventories are raw materials and work-in-process inventories used in manufacturing companies to support the manufacturing process itself. These inventories should be managed by an MRP system or by the just-in-time (JIT) systems described in Chapter 16.

An MRP system is driven by the master schedule which specifies the "end items" or output of the production function. All future demands for work in process and raw materials should be dependent on the master schedule and derived by the MRP system from the master schedule. When raw materials and work-in-process inventories are being planned, all past history of demand is irrelevant unless the future is exactly the same as the past. Since conditions are usually changing, the master schedule is a far better basis than past demand for planning raw materials and work-in-process inventory.

Using MRP, the master schedule is "exploded" into purchase orders for raw materials and shop orders for scheduling the factory. For example, suppose the product in the master schedule is a hand-held calculator. The process of parts explosion will determine all the parts and components needed to make a specified number of calculator units. This process of parts explosion requires a detailed bill of materials which lists each of the parts needed to manufacture any given end item in the master schedule. The required parts may include assemblies, subassemblies, manufactured parts, and purchased parts. Parts explosion thus results in a complete list of the parts which must be ordered and the shop schedule required.

In the process of parts explosion, it is necessary to consider inventories of parts which are already on hand or on order. For example, an order for 100 end items may require a new order of only 20 pieces of a particular raw material because 50 pieces are already in stock and 30 pieces are on order.

Another adjustment made during parts explosion is for production and purchasing lead times. Starting with the master schedule, each manufactured or purchased part is offset (i.e., ordered earlier) by the amount of time it takes to get the part (the lead time). This procedure ensures that each component will be available in time to support the master schedule. If sufficient manufacturing and vendor capacity is available to meet the orders resulting from parts explosion, the MRP system will produce a valid plan for procurement and manufacturing actions. If sufficient capacity is not available, it will be necessary to replan the master schedule or to change the capacity. Methods for doing this will be described in detail later. A typical MRP installation is described in Box 15.1.

15.1 DEFINITIONS OF MRP SYSTEMS

Although MRP is easy to understand conceptually, it can be used in a variety of different ways. This leads to the three different types of MRP systems described as follows:

BOX 15.1
CORNING GLASS WORKS

By the middle of the 1970's, Corning Glass Works found they were unable to meet the demand for their products. The problem they were facing was not one of insufficient plant capacity but one of unbalanced production. They did not have a materials management system that assured all components would be available at the time they were needed and in the quantity required. The management at Corning recognized the need for a new method for managing production. In 1978 they went on-line with Arista, Xerox's MRP package. Their first successes were with their installations in Greencastle, Harrodsburg, and Martinsburg.

The Greencastle facility's operations are restricted to the packaging and warehousing of goods shipped to them from other plants. By 1981 the Greencastle facility alone had increased inventory accuracy by 17 percentage points to 86 percent, reduced inventory by $2 million, achieved an improvement of 1.2 inventory turns a year, moved from a 71 percent schedule compliance to 90 percent, increased on-time deliveries to 91 percent (a 27 percent increase), improved long-term scheduling to the point where workers knew of work force changes 6 months prior to their occurrence. Major benefits were also achieved during that period at the Harrodsburg and the Martinsburg plants.

The conversion attempt suffered many of the classic problems that result when attempting to install an MRP system. Just a few of these problems are as follows. One plant had an increase in inventory levels rather than a decrease. This was caused by the plant's increasing production of the needed components prior to the disposal of the unnecessary units. Top management almost stopped the system owing to an inaccurate estimate of a system's development time. That system had a promised delivery time of 1 year, but actual development took 4 years. Finally, a low level of inventory accuracy was in effect in one plant when they installed their MRP system. This resulted in a larger problem than expected with the plant's inventory.

Corning's success, however, was due in part to the backing of top management. The individuals behind the installation of the system were aware of other firm's MRP disasters. To reduce the potential for problems affecting the acceptance of MRP in their organization, they used a novel approach to install their system, which is named EPIC (efficient production inventory control). Plant managers were not required to convert to the EPIC system. Instead, Corning management decided to present the arguments for EPIC to the plant managers through presentations by the managers of plants that had successfully converted. Another factor was that Corning's operations were well suited to MRP. They had diverse product offerings in both their consumer and industrial lines. In addition, the demand patterns for their products were not constant over time. For example, in the consumer product area, the pattern was highly seasonal with peaks around Christmas, Easter, and Mother's Day.

Source: Bruce Horovitz, "Why Corning Is Sticking with MRP," Industry Week, vol. 212, no. 2, January 25, 1982, pp. 44–48.

Type I: An inventory control system. The type I MRP system is an inventory control system which releases manufacturing and purchase orders for the right quantities at the right time to support the master schedule. This system launches orders to control work-in-process and raw materials inventories through proper timing of order placement. The type I system does not, however, include capacity planning.

Type II: A production and inventory control system. The type II MRP system is an information system used to plan and control inventories and capacities in manufacturing companies. In the type II system, the orders resulting from parts explosion are checked to see whether sufficient capacity is available. If there is not enough capacity, either the capacity or the master schedule is changed. The type II system has a feedback loop between the orders launched and the master schedule to adjust for capacity availability. As a result this type of MRP system is called a closed-loop system; it controls both inventories and capacity.

Type III: A manufacturing resource-planning system. The type III MRP system is used to plan and control all manufacturing resources: inventory, capacity, cash, personnel, facilities, and capital equipment. In this case the MRP parts-explosion system also drives all other resource-planning subsystems in the company.

A closed-loop (type II) MRP system can conveniently be described by Figure 15.1. At the top of the figure is the master production schedule, which is determined by customers' orders, aggregate production planning, and forecasts of future demand. The parts-explosion process, at the heart of the system, is driven by three inputs: master production schedule, bill of materials, and inventory records. The result of the parts-explosion process is two types of orders: purchase orders which go to vendors and shop orders which go to the factory. Before shop orders are sent to the factory, however, a check is made on whether sufficient capacity is available to produce the parts required. If capacity is available, the shop orders are placed under control of the shop-floor control system. If capacity is not available, a change must be made in the capacity or in the master schedule through the feedback loop shown. Once the shop orders are under the shop-floor control system, the progress of these orders is managed through the shop to make sure that they are completed on time.

Figure 15.1 represents MRP as an *information system* used to plan and control inventories and capacity. Information is processed through the various parts of the system to support management decisions. If the information is accurate and timely, management can use the system to control inventories, deliver customer orders on time, and control the costs of manufacturing. In this way the materials conversion process will be continually managed in a dynamic and changing environment.

Joseph Orlicky, in his pioneering book on MRP [(1975), p. 158], has defined three principal functions of MRP as follows:

Inventory
- Order the right part
- Order in the right quantity
- Order at the right time

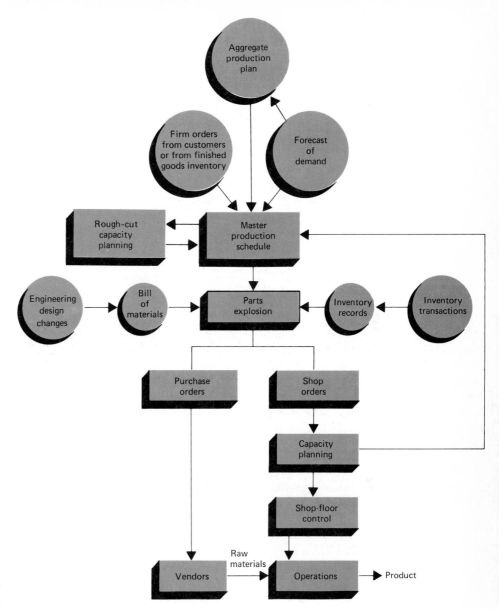

FIGURE 15.1
A closed-loop
MRP system.

Priorities
- Order with the right due date
- Keep the due date valid

Capacity
- A complete load
- An accurate (valid) load
- An adequate time span for visibility of future load

If the closed-loop system in Figure 15.1 is used properly, all of Orlicky's three functions can be achieved.

Since MRP is a simple and logical concept, one might wonder why it was not introduced earlier. The chief reason was the lack of computer technology until the mid-sixties. Today, further advances in computer technology are making MRP systems practical even for the small business. Although the technology is in hand, substantial implementation problems still exist in industry. These problems will be discussed in detail later in the chapter; also see Box 15.2.

BOX 15.2
LONG-HELD ATTITUDES IN MANUFACTURING COMPANIES

- "You can't forecast our business out that far."
- "We in Sales are not interested in your Manufacturing problems; we have enough of our own."
- "Don't ask me which customer order I want shipped first. I want them all now."
- "You can't lock up any part of this master production schedule" [sales talking]. Or, "You can't change any of this schedule within the first six months" [manufacturing talking].
- "That new system just can't react fast enough. We need Ed to ramrod through extra orders from time to time."
- "If I want 100 units a month out of this plant, I know from long experience I have to ask for 150."

Source: G. W. Plossl, *Newsletter #18*, September 1975.

MRP VERSUS ORDER-POINT SYSTEMS

MRP calls into question many of the traditional concepts used to manage inventories. The order-point systems discussed in Chapter 14 do not work well for the management of inventories which are subject to dependent demand. Prior to the advent of MRP, however, there was no choice; the typical manufacturing company managed *all* inventories with order-point systems.

Some of the key distinctions between MRP and order-point systems are summarized in Table 15.1. One distinction is the requirements philosophy used in MRP systems versus a replenishment philosophy used in order-point systems. A replenishment philosophy indicates that material should be replenished when it runs low. An MRP system does not do this. More material is ordered only when a need exists as directed by the master schedule. If there are no manufacturing requirements for a particular part, it will not be replenished, even though the inventory level is low. This requirements concept is particularly important in manufacturing because demand for component parts is "lumpy." When a lot is scheduled, the component parts are needed for that lot, but demand is then zero until another lot is scheduled. If order-point systems are used for this type of lumpy demand pattern, material will be carried on hand during long periods of zero demand.

Another distinction between the two systems is in the use of forecasting. For

TABLE 15.1
COMPARISON OF MRP AND ORDER-POINT SYSTEMS

	MRP	Order point
Demand	Dependent	Independent
Order philosophy	Requirements	Replenishment
Forecast	Based on master schedule	Based on past demand
Control concept	Control all items	ABC
Objectives	Meet manufacturing needs	Meet customer needs
Lot sizing	Discrete	EOQ
Demand pattern	Lumpy but predictable	Random
Types of inventory	Work in process and raw materials	Finished goods and spare parts

order-point systems, future demand is forecast based on the past history of demand. These forecasts are used to replenish the stock levels. In MRP systems, past demand for component parts is irrelevant. The ordering philosophy is based on requirements generated from the master schedule. MRP is future-oriented; it derives the future demand for component parts from higher-level demand forecasts.

The ABC principle also does not work well for MRP systems. In manufacturing a product, C items are just as important as A items. For example, an automobile cannot be shipped if it lacks a fuel line or radiator cap, even though these items are relatively inexpensive C items. Therefore it is necessary to control all parts, even the C items, in manufacturing.

The time-honored square-root EOQ is not useful in MRP systems, although modified lot sizing formulas are available. The assumptions used to derive the traditional EOQ are badly violated by the lumpy demand patterns for component parts. Lot sizing in MRP systems should be based on discrete requirements. For example, suppose that the demand for a particular part by week is 0, 30, 10, 0, 0, 15. Further assume that the EOQ is calculated to be 25 parts. With the EOQ or multiples of the EOQ, we could not match the requirements exactly and would, therefore, end up with remnants in inventory. These remnants from the EOQ cause unnecessary inventory carrying costs. It would be far better to base lot sizes on the discrete demand observed. For example, with a lot-for-lot policy, we could order 30 units for the second week, 10 for the third week, and 15 for the sixth week, resulting in three orders and no carrying costs. We could also order 40 units for the second and third weeks combined, thereby saving one order but incurring a small carrying cost. With MRP systems, various discrete lot sizes need to be examined. (See Orlicky for further details.)

The objective in managing independent-demand inventories with reorder-point rules is to provide a high customer service level at low inventory operating costs. This objective is oriented toward the customer. On the other hand, the objective in managing dependent-demand inventories with MRP is to support the master production schedule. This objective is manufacturing-oriented—it focuses inward rather than outward.

It should now be evident that MRP systems differ from order-point systems in almost every important dimension, and it should not be surprising that poor results are usually obtained when order-point systems are used to manage raw materials or work-in-process inventories. These poor results can include late delivery of customer orders, excessive inventory levels, poor conversion efficiency due to lack of parts, and a great deal of fire fighting in production. Because of the differences, Joseph Orlicky has called MRP "a new way of life in the management of a manufacturing business."

 15.3 ## MRP EXAMPLE

The easiest way to understand MRP is to focus on the parts-explosion process itself. After describing this process below, by example, we will discuss the remaining elements of the MRP system.

Suppose that tables of the type shown in Figure 15.2 are being manufactured. The finished table consists of a top and a leg assembly. The leg assembly, in turn, consists of four legs, two short rails, and two long rails. In this particular example, leg assemblies are built in advance and stored in inventory. This procedure permits the table to be produced faster, as orders are received, than it could be if the table were completely assembled from individual parts. It is common practice in manufacturing companies to build assemblies for inventory in order to reduce total production lead time and to save setup costs.

The bill of materials (BOM) for this table is shown schematically in Figure 15.3. The finished table is at the first level of the bill. The leg assembly and tabletop are at the second level, since these parts are assembled together to produce a finished table. The pieces which go into the leg assembly are all listed at the third level. We are assuming that the parts for this table are purchased from outside; otherwise there would be a fourth level in the BOM for the wood used to make the legs, rails, and top.

Another piece of information needed prior to parts explosion is the planned lead times for manufactured and purchased parts, as shown in Table 15.2. For planning purposes, it takes 1 week to assemble the finished table from the leg assembly and top. This planned lead time includes average waiting time due to interference from other jobs, which is usually much longer than the actual

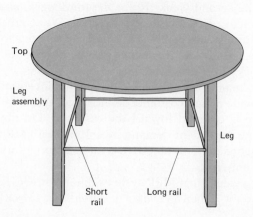

FIGURE 15.2
Table example.

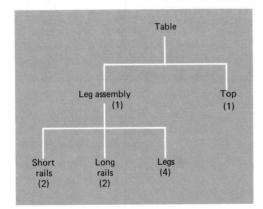

FIGURE 15.3
Bill of materials.
(Quantity per
unit shown in
parentheses.)

working time. If the finished tables were urgently needed on a priority basis, they could be assembled in a few hours. Similarly, Table 15.2 shows that 2 weeks are planned for purchase of a tabletop from the time the order is placed until the tabletop is in the factory. This planned lead time could also be compressed, to as little as a day or two if the tops were given high priority by the vendor.

It is now possible, using parts explosion, to construct a materials plan for the finished tables and all parts. The resulting materials plan is shown in Table 15.3. The master schedule in this case contains the demand for finished tables: 200 in week 4, 150 in week 5, and 100 in week 6. These quantities are listed as gross requirements for complete tables. As shown in the materials plan, there are 50 tables on hand at the present time (all figures in Table 15.3 are assumed to occur at the beginning of the week). Thus, we can subtract these available tables from the gross requirement to arrive at the net requirement. Then the net requirement is offset by 1 week, due to the planned lead time for table assembly, to arrive at planned order releases. Therefore, to meet the gross requirements of the master schedule, shop orders must be released to assemble 150 tables in week 3, 150 in week 4, and 100 in week 5.

Next, the planned order releases for tables are used to calculate gross requirements for tops and leg assemblies at the next level down in the BOM. The final

TABLE 15.2
PLANNED LEAD TIMES

	Weeks
Assemble table*	1
Finished leg assembly†	1
Purchase legs	1
Purchase short rails	1
Purchase long rails	1
Purchase top	2

*Assume the tabletop and complete leg assembly are available.

†Assume the legs, short rails, and long rails are available.

TABLE 15.3
MATERIALS PLAN—PARTS EXPLOSION

	Week					
	1	2	3	4	5	6
Tables						
Gross requirements	—	—	—	200	150	100
On-hand/scheduled receipts	50	—	—	—	—	—
Net requirements	—	—	—	150	150	100
Planned order releases	—	—	150	150	100	—
Tops						
Gross requirements	—	—	150	150	100	—
On-hand/scheduled receipts	50	50	—	—	—	—
Net requirements	—	—	50	150	100	—
Planned order releases	50	150	100	—	—	—
Leg assembly						
Gross requirements	—	—	150	150	100	—
On-hand/scheduled receipts	100	—	—	—	—	—
Net requirements	—	—	50	150	100	—
Planned order releases	—	50	150	100	—	—
Leg						
Gross requirements	—	200	600	400	—	—
On-hand/scheduled receipts	150	100	—	—	—	—
Net requirements	—	—	550	400	—	—
Planned order releases	—	550	400	—	—	—
Short rail						
Gross requirements	—	100	300	200	—	—
On-hand/scheduled receipts	50	—	—	—	—	—
Net requirements	—	50	300	200	—	—
Planned order releases	50	300	200	—	—	—
Long rail						
Gross requirements	—	100	300	200	—	—
On-hand/scheduled receipts	—	—	—	—	—	—
Net requirements	—	100	300	200	—	—
Planned order releases	100	300	200	—	—	—

planned order releases for tables are transferred to gross requirements for tops and leg assemblies on a one-for-one basis, since it takes one tabletop and one leg assembly to make a table. The on-hand inventory and scheduled receipts are subtracted from the gross requirements to arrive at net requirements. The net requirements are offset by lead time to arrive at planned order releases for tabletops and leg assemblies. Notice that in Table 15.3 there are 50 tabletops currently on hand and 50 scheduled to arrive at the beginning of week 2. The scheduled order for 50 tops was placed a week ago under a previous materials plan. Since there is a 2-week lead time, these tops will arrive at the beginning of week 2. All materials on hand and on order must be included when doing parts explosion.

The planned order releases for leg assemblies are then used to compute gross requirements for legs, short rails, and long rails. The planned orders for leg assemblies are multiplied by 4 for legs, by 2 for short rails, and by 2 for long rails to arrive at gross requirements. A gross requirement at any level is the amount of material required to support planned orders at the next-highest level. The gross to net calculation and the offset for lead time is then performed for each of the three remaining parts to arrive at planned order releases. This completes the parts explosion.

Table 15.3 has been constructed from the master schedule down, one level at a time, through the BOM. The materials plan for each level in the BOM was completed before moving down to the next level. For each part, the gross requirements have been reduced by on-hand and on-order inventory to arrive at net requirements. The net requirements have been offset (planned earlier) by the lead time to arrive at planned order releases. By the process of netting and offsetting, the master schedule is converted to planned order releases for each part required.

What does the materials plan in Table 15.3 tell us? First, we should immediately release purchase orders to our vendors for 50 tops, 50 short rails, and 100 long rails since these are the planned orders at the beginning of week 1. The materials plan also gives us the planned order releases for each week in the future. If the master schedule and all other conditions remain constant, these planned orders will be released when the time comes. For example, in week 2 we plan to release an order to the shop to complete 50 leg assemblies. If the materials arrive as planned, we should have on hand the legs and rails needed for this shop order: 200 legs, 100 short rails, and 100 long rails. In addition to the shop order for 50 leg assemblies, we plan to release, in week 2, purchase orders for 150 tops, 550 legs, 300 short rails, and 300 long rails. These materials will be needed to support future leg-assembly and table-assembly shop orders.

This example illustrates the construction of a time-phased materials plan. All purchase orders and shop orders are interrelated to provide materials when needed. If the actual lead times can be managed to meet the planned lead times, there will be no unnecessary inventory accumulations or wasted time waiting for materials in the shop, and the orders for delivery of finished tables will be shipped on time.

As an exercise, the projected inventories which will result from this materials plan have been calculated and are shown in Table 15.4. Notice that the initial inventory of parts and finished product is worked off as the plan progresses. The only inventory provided by this materials plan is due to initial on-hand inventory, previously scheduled orders, and planned work-in-process inventories. If this plan does not provide sufficient inventory to cover future demand uncertainty, inventory can be added to the plan in the form of safety stocks, or safety capacity can be added.

The numbers in Table 15.4 were calculated by projecting the inventory forward in time. Starting with the beginning inventory for each item, we add receipts and subtract disbursements in each time period. The result is the new projected inventory balance for the next week. Note that no *finished goods* inventory is provided after week 4. This is because we have planned production to just equal final demand. Likewise, no purchased parts inventories are planned after initial

TABLE 15.4
PLANNED INVENTORIES*

	Week					
	1	2	3	4	5	6
Tables finished	50	50	50	—	—	—
Tables being assembled	—	—	150	150	100	—
Tops	50	100	—	—	—	—
Leg assemblies in process	—	50	150	100	—	—
Leg assemblies finished	100	100	—	—	—	—
Legs	150	50	—	—	—	—
Short rails	50	—	—	—	—	—
Long rails	—	—	—	—	—	—

*All inventories at beginning of week.

inventories are depleted. These calculations illustrate that an MRP system really cuts things close. Unless safety stocks are added for uncertainties or inventories are added to smooth out production levels, no inventory will be carried except work-in-process required for assembly or fabrication. The MRP logic assumes parts are available exactly when they are needed to support the production plan.

15.4 MRP ELEMENTS

Although parts explosion is the heart of MRP, it takes a good deal more to make an MRP system work. The other MRP system elements are described in this section.

Master scheduling. The purpose of master scheduling is to specify the output of the operations function. Master scheduling drives the entire materials planning process. The master schedule has been described by George Plossl as "top management's handle on the business" [Plossl (1974)]. By controlling the master schedule, top management can control customer service, inventory levels, and manufacturing costs. Top managers cannot perform the master-scheduling task by themselves because there are too many details. However, top management can review the master schedule that has been created and they can set master-scheduling policy, thereby controlling the materials-planning function.

Top management should also interface with manufacturing through the aggregate production plan shown in Figure 15.1. The aggregate production plan deals with families of products or product lines, not specific products, models, or options which are in the master schedule. For example, if the manufacturer makes tractors, the aggregate production plan might contain various types of tractors, but not the particular size of engine, hydraulics options, or other features which can be selected by the customer. The aggregate production planning process, described in Chapter 11, is usually part of the annual budgeting and strategic planning process. It seeks to make the resources (capacity), people, equipment, and facilities available for the future. As such, the master scheduling process must then work within the overall aggregate production plan, which has already been established, or seek to modify this plan if necessary.

The parts-explosion process assumes that the master schedule is feasible with respect to capacity. Using the master schedule as input, parts are exploded to produce shop orders and purchase orders. In type II and III systems, the shop orders are put into a capacity planning routine to determine whether sufficient capacity is available. If sufficient capacity is not available, then either capacity or the master schedule must be changed until the master schedule is feasible.

One of the functions of master scheduling is to make sure that the final master schedule is not inflated and reflects realistic capacity constraints. All too often the master schedule is inflated in practice on the assumption that operations will produce more output if the pressure is kept on. (This is not unlike the approach of some college professors who assign students too much homework in hopes that the students will learn more.) As a result of an inflated master schedule, the order priorities (due dates) are no longer valid. The formal MRP system then quickly breaks down and the informal planning and control system takes over. The result is many past-due orders, expediting, and stock chasing to get the product out the door. Nothing is more insidious than an inflated master schedule which leads to invalid order due dates.

The master schedule is often developed in terms of weekly output requirements or so-called weekly time buckets. In this case an entire week's production is represented by one column of the materials plan. The master schedule is also frequently updated on a weekly basis. Each week after the new master schedule is developed, the parts-explosion program is run to generate new requirements. This is a so-called regenerative MRP system.

Another form of MRP is the net-change system, where changes can be made as they occur on a real-time basis. The net-change systems are continually kept up to date; this is done in preference to using a massive regeneration run. Although net-change systems have more current data, they are sometimes "nervous" in terms of constant order changes.

The master schedule might extend into the future for a year or more. It must extend at least beyond the longest cumulative production lead time to ensure that sufficient time is available to order all parts. Generally speaking, the master schedule should be frozen inside the production lead time to prevent unnecessary scrap and expediting due to changes during the production cycle.

Rarely is the master schedule a reflection of future demand forecasts. Rather, the master schedule is a forecast of what will be produced. It is a "build" schedule. Finished goods inventory is a buffer between the master schedule and final customer demand, smoothing out work loads and providing fast customer service.

Bill of materials (BOM). The BOM is a structured list of all the materials or parts needed to produce a particular finished product, assembly, subassembly, manufactured part, or purchased part. The BOM serves the same function as a recipe used for cooking: it lists all the ingredients. It would be foolish to allow errors to creep into your favorite cooking recipes. The same is true for a BOM. If there are errors in the BOM, the proper materials will not be ordered and the product cannot be assembled and shipped. As a result, the other parts which *are* available will wait in inventory while the missing parts are expedited. Management must, therefore, insist that all BOMs are 100 percent accurate. From experience it has been found that it is not too costly to have 100 percent accuracy; rather, it is too costly to tolerate imperfect BOMs.

Some companies have several BOMs for the same product. Engineering has one BOM, manufacturing has a different version, and cost accounting has still another. An MRP system requires a single BOM for the entire company. The BOM in the computer must be the correct one, and it must represent how the product is manufactured. In companies where the BOM has been used as a reference document and not a materials-planning tool, this concept of a single bill is very difficult to implement.

BOMs are constantly undergoing change as products are redesigned. Thus, an effective engineering-change-order (ECO) system is needed to keep the BOMs up to date. Usually an ECO coordinator must be appointed and charged with the responsibility for coordinating all engineering changes with the various departments involved.

Inventory records. The contents of a typical computerized inventory record are shown in Figure 15.4. The item master data segment contains the part number, which is the unique item identifier, and other information such as lead time, standard cost, and so on. The inventory status segment contains a complete

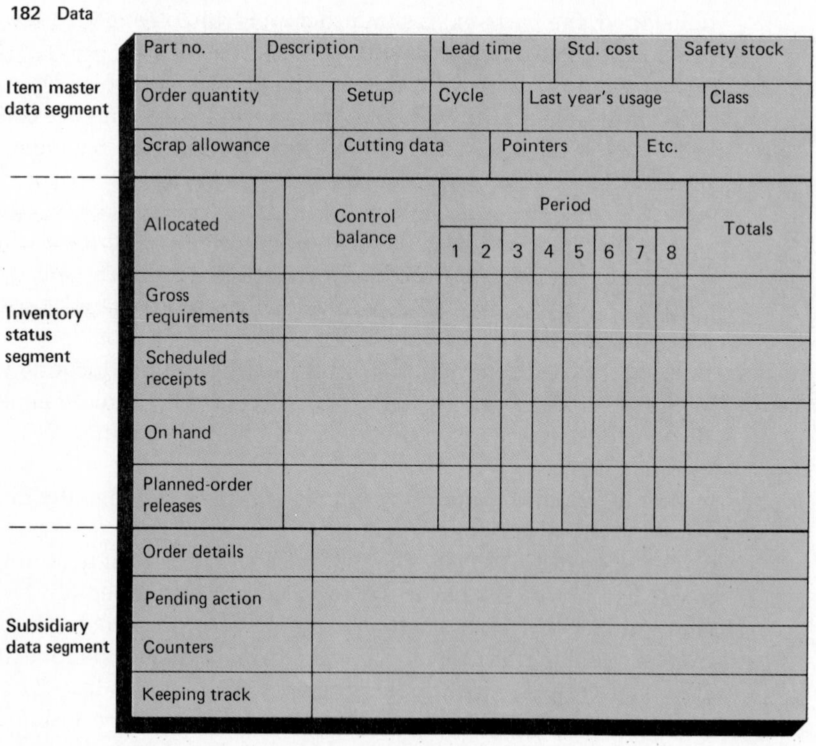

182   Data

FIGURE 15.4 Typical inventory record.
Source: Joseph Orlicky, Materials Requirements Planning, *New York: McGraw-Hill, 1975, p. 182.*

materials plan for each item over time. Finally, the subsidiary data segment contains information concerning outstanding orders, requested changes, detailed demand history, and the like.

In practice, constant effort is required to keep inventory records accurate. Traditionally, inventory accuracy has been assured by the annual physical inventory count, where the plant is shut down for a day or two and everything is counted from wall to wall. It has been found that, because inexperienced people are doing the counting, as many errors are introduced by this procedure as are corrected. After the inventory is taken, the total inventory in dollars is accurate for financial purposes because the plus and minus errors cancel out. But the counts of individual items are usually not accurate enough for MRP purposes. As a result, cycle counting has been developed as a substitute for the annual physical inventory.

With cycle counting, a small percentage of the items are counted each day by storeroom personnel. Errors are corrected in the records, and an attempt is made to find and correct the procedure which caused them. By developing a high regard for accuracy and adopting daily cycle counting, most errors in inventory records can be eliminated. [See Tallman (1976).] The result is so reliable that many auditors no longer require an annual physical inventory when an effective cycle-counting system is in place.

Capacity planning. The necessary elements for an order-launching MRP system (type I) have been described above. This system requires master scheduling, a BOM, inventory records, and parts explosion. The resulting order-launching system will determine correct due dates (order priorities) if sufficient capacity is available. If sufficient capacity is not available, inventories will rise, past-due orders will build up, and expediting will be used to pull orders through the factory. To correct this situation, a capacity planning subsystem is needed.

The purpose of capacity planning is to check on the validity of the master schedule. There are two ways this can be done: rough-cut capacity planning (also called resource planning) and shop loading. In rough-cut capacity planning, approximate labor hours and machine hours are calculated directly from the master schedule to project future capacity needs without going through the parts-explosion process. When sufficient capacity is not available, the master schedule is adjusted or capacity is changed to obtain a feasible schedule. When the master schedule is feasible, then the full parts explosion is run.

When shop loading is used, a full parts explosion is run prior to capacity planning. The resulting shop orders are then loaded against work centers through the use of detailed parts-routing data. As a result, work force and machine hours for each work center are projected into the future. If sufficient capacity is not available, either capacity or the master schedule should be adjusted until the master schedule is feasible. At this point a valid materials plan is available.

Rough-cut capacity planning requires less detailed calculation but is not as accurate as shop loading. Either of these methods or both of them can be used, depending on individual conditions and circumstances. The important point is that capacity planning should be used to close the loop in the MRP system.

Purchasing. The purchasing function is greatly enhanced by the use of an MRP system. First, past-due orders are largely eliminated because MRP generates valid due dates and keeps them up to date. This permits purchasing to develop credibility with vendors, since the material is really needed when purchasing says it is.

By developing and executing a valid materials plan, management can eliminate much of the order expediting which is usually done by purchasing. This allows the purchasing managers to concentrate on their prime function: qualifying vendors, looking for alternative sources of supply, and maintaining low purchasing costs.

With an MRP system, it is possible to provide vendors with reports of planned future orders. This gives vendors time to plan capacity before actual orders are placed. The practice of giving vendors planned orders more closely interlocks them with the company's own materials plan. [See Papesch (1978).] Some firms have gone so far as to insist that their vendors also install MRP systems so that the vendors' delivery reliability can be more readily assured.

Shop-floor control. The purpose of the shop-floor control subsystem is to release orders to the shop floor and to manage the orders on their way through the factory to make sure that they are completed on time. The shop-floor control system helps management adjust to all the day-to-day things which go wrong in manufacturing: absenteeism among workers, machine breakdowns, loss of materials, and so on. When these unplanned complications arise, decisions must be made about what to do next. Good decisions require input-output control and information on job priorities from the shop-floor control system.

The purpose of input-output control, as described in Chapter 12, is to ensure that materials are available and that the factory is not overloaded. For each work center, the amount of work put into the work center on a daily or weekly basis is compared with the amount of work produced by the work center (usually measured in standard labor hours and standard machine hours). Generally speaking, no more should be put into the work center than is taken out unless work-in-process inventories or utilization is too low. Furthermore, the material availability of each job is monitored by the shop-floor control system to ensure that both capacity and material are available as the job progresses through the shop. If the job is moving too slowly or too rapidly through the factory, this can be controlled by job priorities.

Job priorities are frequently calculated by dispatching rules of the type discussed in Chapter 12. When these rules are used as part of the shop-floor control system, it is possible to adjust to changing conditions and still get the work out on time. Through the use of dispatching rules, a job's production lead time can be drastically cut or increased as it goes through the shop. This is possible because a job normally spends as much as 90 percent of its time waiting in queues. If a job is behind schedule, its priority can be increased until it gets back on schedule. Similarly, a job can be slowed down if it is ahead of schedule. It is the function of the shop-floor control system to provide information to managers so that they can manage production lead time dynamically.

The old notion of an accurate or good lead time must be discarded. Lead times can be managed by expanding or contracting them on the basis of priority. George Plossl has expressed this by saying, "Lead time is what you say it is." This is a very difficult concept to accept when managers are used to thinking in terms of fixed lead time or lead times as random variables.

It is possible through a shop-floor control system to deexpedite orders—that is, to slow them down. This is not done in normal manufacturing, where orders are expedited but never deexpedited. Orders should be slowed down when the master schedule is changed or when other parts will not be available on time. This results in the minimum inventory consistent with MRP timing requirements.

To do its job properly, a shop-floor control system requires feedback reports on all jobs as they are processed. Typically, a worker notifies the system as each processing step is completed. This may be done through a computer terminal on the shop floor or by information submitted to a central office. The computer system then produces a dispatching list for each supervisor each day. The list shows the priority of each job in the work center, and—if possible—the supervisor works on the highest-priority job. If materials, labor, or machines are not available for the highest-priority job, then the job that is next highest in priority is done, and so on down the list.

A shop-floor control system requires valid due dates on orders. If the master schedule is inflated and the shop is overloaded, no shop-floor control system will get the work out on time. The shop-floor control system is highly dependent on proper priority and capacity planning.

OPERATING AN MRP SYSTEM

There is much more to MRP than just installing the proper computer modules. Management must operate the system in an intelligent and effective way.

One of the decisions management should make is how much safety stock to carry. To the surprise of many managers, little safety stock is needed if MRP is properly used. This is due to the concept of lead-time management, where both purchasing and shop lead times are effectively controlled within small variances. In purchasing, this is done by developing relationships with vendors who provide reliable deliveries. In the shop, lead times can be managed by a shop-floor control system as described above. Once the uncertainty in lead time is reduced, there is much less need for safety stock.

If safety stock were carried at the component-part level, a great deal of it would be needed to be effective. Suppose, for example, that 10 parts are required to make an assembly and each part has a 90 percent service level. The probability of having all 10 parts on hand when needed is only 35 percent.[1] It is much better, therefore, to plan and control the timing of the 10 parts than to cover all contingencies with safety stock.

When safety stock is carried, it is often added at the master-schedule level. This ensures that matched sets of components, not simply an assortment of various

---

[1]Probability $= (.9)^{10} = .35$, assuming parts availabilities are independent events.

parts, are available for final products. The purpose of safety stock at the master-schedule level is to provide flexibility to meet changing customer requirements.

Safety lead time is a concept that should be considered for component parts. If a vendor is unreliable and the situation cannot be remedied, then the planned lead time can be lengthened by adding safety lead time. This will add to inventories, however, when the vendor delivers the parts earlier than planned.

A third way of handling uncertainty is to plan for "safety capacity." This approach has much merit because the spare capacity can be used to make the right parts when the need becomes known. The problem with safety stock is that it is frequently available for the wrong parts—too much of one part and too little of another. Thus, serious consideration should be given to safety capacity as an alternative to safety stock; this has not been widely done in industry. Rather, safety stock (inventory) has been considered an asset (even if it is never used) and capacity utilization of 100 percent is a desirable goal, even if excess inventories result.

Another problem in operating an MRP system is the constant danger that the informal system will drive out the formal system. If the formal MRP system is not used by management, the informal system will rapidly take over as material is expedited, past-due orders build up, and an atmosphere of crisis develops. The informal system is always "lurking in the wings" to take over. It is necessary, therefore, that management strive to maintain data accuracy, user education, and system integrity so that the formal MRP system is used to manage the company.

If an MRP system is operating properly, it can be more than just a production and inventory control tool. The MRP system can support planning and control in all parts of the company (a type III system). For example, it can be used to drive financial planning systems—to project future total inventories, forecast purchasing budgets, and plan needs for equipment and facilities. An MRP system used for the physical control of materials can be expanded to provide the basis for financial planning and control. MRP users are beginning to realize that detailed physical planning can be the basis for improved financial planning.

Financial planning and control are derivatives of an MRP system, being merely measured in different units—dollars instead of physical units. For too long, financial systems have been driven by transactions and assumptions different from material control systems. The tools now exist to tie MRP and financial systems together by a simple conversion from physical units to dollars and vice versa. Physical control thus becomes the basis for financial control. It can be argued that true financial control can exist only if there is first physical control of the production process. Only the best-managed companies have made this linkage between physical control and financial control.

An MRP system can also be extended to support product costing and cost accounting. When an accurate bill of material is in the computer, it is a relatively simple matter to calculate product costs from the labor and materials cost of the component parts. As a matter of fact, a costing module is sometimes provided as part of the MRP software.

An MRP system can also be expanded into personnel planning by using a bill of labor. In this case all the labor skills for each product are listed on the bill of labor. The labor requirements are then exploded from the master schedule in a similar way as materials requirements. This makes it possible to forecast labor requirements and to tie together labor and materials needs.

The possibilities for making MRP more than just a tool for production and inventory control are appealing. These possibilities have not been achieved in very many companies to date because most companies are still in the first phases of MRP implementation. Once these organizations have achieved materials control, they can widen the applicability of their MRP systems to the planning and control of other resources.

15.6 THE CHANGING ROLE OF PRODUCTION AND INVENTORY CONTROL MANAGERS

The advent of MRP systems has drastically changed the role of production and inventory control managers in industry. Traditionally, there has been a split between inventory managers and production control managers. The inventory manager was in charge of issuing orders for more material, usually by means of order-point systems. This amounted to pushing material into the factory. The production control manager determined the real priorities through expediting and pulling material through to final assembly.

MRP is a comprehensive production and inventory control system. The MRP system, however, does not make decisions. Orders are still released by the inventory control manager based on the MRP system's advice. More importantly, the inventory control manager is responsible for seeing that the assumptions and information in the system are accurate. For example, is the lot size for a particular order correct or have conditions changed? Has an engineering change order been properly entered into the system, so that the new materials are ordered? Has a new vendor lead time taken effect? As long as all the information in the system is current, orders will be placed by the system at the right time.

Similarly, the production control manager should have much less expediting to do in the shop. More time should be spent by the production control manager on master scheduling and capacity planning and on keeping the shop-floor control system up to date.

With the advent of MRP, production and inventory control managers have become planners and users of information systems rather than order writers, stock chasers, and expediters. As Oliver Wight (1974), a noted consultant, has said: "The job of production and inventory management is to generate plans that other people can be held responsible for executing. Plans are made and performance is monitored against these plans in order to manage production and inventories." This role requires a great deal more education and a change toward professionalism in the production and inventory control field.[2]

In some organizations, MRP has led to a new management position called the materials manager. In the organizational hierarchy, purchasing, inventory control,

---

[2]The transition to professionalism has been greatly aided by the American Production and Inventory Control Society, a national professional organization of about 60,000 members.

and production control all report to the materials manager, thereby improving the integration of materials flow. The materials manager's position represents an attempt to apply the systems philosophy of integration across the entire materials conversion process. [For further details, see Miller and Gilmore (1979).]

15.7 THE SUCCESSFUL MRP SYSTEM

It takes a great deal of effort to make MRP successful. As a matter of fact, research indicates that five elements are required for success:

1. Implementation planning
2. Adequate computer support
3. Accurate data
4. Management support
5. User knowledge

Implementation planning should be a prerequisite to any MRP effort. Unfortunately, too many companies jump in and start implementing MRP without adequate preparation. Later, confusion and misunderstanding occur as problems arise. Implementation planning can help smooth out implementation efforts by advance planning and problem prevention efforts. Implementation planning should include education of senior management, selection of a project manager, appointment of an implementation team representing all parts of the company, preparation of objectives, identification of expected benefits and costs, and a detailed action plan. Only after this plan is prepared should selection of hardware and software, improvement of data accuracy, and other implementation activities begin. Details on how to do this kind of planning are given in Wight (1981) and Gray (1987).

An adequate computer system is probably one of the easiest elements of MRP to implement. Today, there are approximately 200 MRP software packages on the market. Many companies use these standard packages rather than writing their own computer programs. A flowchart for a typical software package is shown in Figure 15.5. See *PIM Review* (1987) for a listing of available software packages.

An MRP system requires accurate data, which are very difficult to obtain. Many companies are accustomed to lax record keeping in manufacturing because the company has always been managed by the informal system. But accurate data are required when decisions are made from information supplied by the computer.

A company that does not have an MRP system will need to create accurate BOMs as a first step. In some cases, the BOMs are in such poor condition that the company literally has to start over from the beginning. In other cases, the BOMs may be relatively accurate and require only some updating.

Once the BOMs are accurate, a system will be needed to keep them that way. This will require an engineering change coordinator who is in charge of all changes to the BOM.

Inventory records must also be accurate to support the MRP system. The initial accuracy of inventory records may be somewhat better than the BOMs, but

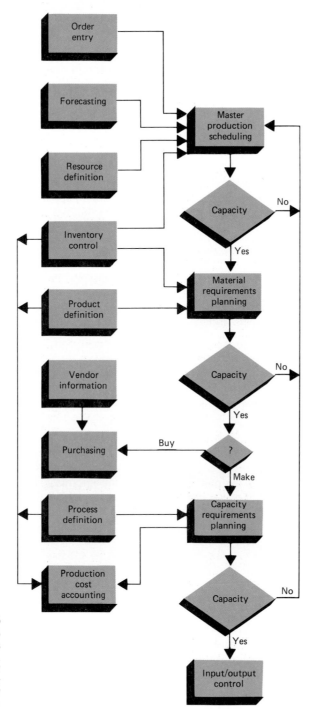

FIGURE 15.5
Honeywell HMS
systems
flowchart.
Source: Honeywell
Manufacturing
System: Summary
Description, 1982.

inventory record keeping will need improvement too. The best way to improve and maintain the accuracy of inventory records is to install a system of cycle counting.

All other MRP system data—such as shop routings, shop-floor status, and costs—must be initially screened for errors and then maintained in an acceptable state of accuracy. Keeping MRP data accurate for system integrity is one of the most important tasks in operating an MRP system. (See Box 15.3.)

BOX 15.3
MISCONCEPTIONS ABOUT MRP

1. *MRP is a computer system.* It's really a *people* system made possible by the computer. The computer does nothing but generate paper or put an image on the tube; it's what people do with that information that makes things happen in a factory.

2. *MRP primarily affects production and inventory control people.* We call it *Manufacturing Resource Planning* today because it is a company plan, a way to tie together the activities of marketing, manufacturing, and engineering so that schedules for all of these activities can be coordinated to get the best overall results for the company. Obviously, a company game plan isn't going to work very well if all of the players aren't tuned in to it.

3. *Each company requires a unique "system"* designed for them to solve their unique problems. In practice the problems of scheduling a factory, scheduling the vendors, and coordinating the activities of marketing, engineering, manufacturing, and finance are not particularly unique company to company. There is a standard logic for MRP, and we have yet to see a company that had to reinvent this logic, or, for that matter, one that tried to reinvent it and made it work.

4. *The MRP installation problems are going to be in the computer area.* The computer end of MRP installation is usually the most straightforward. The real problems come in getting basic data like inventory records and bills of material accurate enough to support MRP. Under the informal system—the shortage list—accurate bills of material were not particularly significant. If the formal system is going to work for people, these numbers have to be right. And that involves instilling a new set of values in a large group of people in the organization. And, of course, that's the real problem. MRP can provide the tools to run a business differently. The trick is in teaching people to install and use these tools effectively.

Source: Newsletter from Oliver Wight, 1977.

The importance of management support to the successful MRP system can hardly be overemphasized. Many studies have shown that top-management support is the key to successful implementation of systems. [See, for example, Hall and Vollmann (1978) and Hall (1977).] But management support requires more than lip service and passive support on the manager's part. "Management participation" or "leadership" would be a better phrase. Top managers must be actively involved in installing and operating the MRP system. They must give their time and they must change the way they operate the company. If top managers change, then the climate is set for other managers also to make the changes required by the MRP system. The ultimate change required by management at all levels is to use the system and not to override it by using the informal system.

The final requirement for the successful MRP system is user knowledge at all levels of the company. An MRP system requires an entirely new approach to manufacturing. All company employees must understand how they will be affected and grasp their new roles and responsibilities. When MRP is first being installed, only a few key managers need to be educated. But as the system begins to be used, all supervisors, middle managers, and top managers need to understand MRP, including managers inside and outside of manufacturing. As the MRP system is broadened in scope, the level of education within the company must be broadened too.

If an effective MRP system is installed according to the above guidelines, what benefits and costs can be expected? Table 15.5 helps answer this question by showing the benefits from a survey by Schroeder et al. (1981). The average company reported an improvement in inventory turnover from 3.2 to 4.3, while future improvement to 5.3 is expected when the MRP system is fully implemented. Similarly, benefits are shown in the table for reduced delivery lead time, increasing the percentage of delivery promises met, reducing the percentage of orders split because of unavailable material, and reducing the number of expediters needed. It should be noted that these are average benefits; some companies obtain fewer benefits and others obtain more.

The benefits obtained from MRP are quite substantial. Since the average company in the above study had $15 million invested in inventory, the current improvement in inventory turnover represents a reduction of $4 million in inventory with another $2 million reduction expected when MRP is fully implemented. This improvement in inventory is matched by equally impressive gains in customer service and in efficiency operations.

As far as the cost of MRP is concerned, the average company in the study by

TABLE 15.5
MRP BENEFITS

	"Pre-MRP" estimate	Current estimate	Future estimate
Inventory turnover	3.2	4.3	5.3
Delivery lead time (days)	71	59	44
Percentage of delivery promises met	61%	76%	88%
Percentage of orders requiring "splits" because of unavailable material	32%	19%	9%
Number of expediters	10	6	5

Source: Schroeder et al. (1981), p. 2.

TABLE 15.6
ESTIMATED COST OF MRP INSTALLATION

	Average	Standard deviation
Current cost	$375,000	$ 600,000
Eventual cost	618,000	1,137,000

Annual sales	Cost of MRP installation (thousands of dollars)	
	Current cost	Eventual cost
Under $10 million	$ 93	$ 194
$ 11-25 million	210	385
$ 26-50 million	298	560
$ 51-100 million	511	912
$101-500 million	565	800
Over $500 million	1633	2237

Source: Schroeder et al. (1981), p. 3.

Schroeder et al. reported spending $375,000 on MRP system installation to date, with an eventual cost of $618,000 when the MRP system is fully developed. These installation costs included people, software, hardware, and training for development of the system. The installation costs were found to be highly variable by size of company, as shown in Table 15.6.

Many companies apparently believe that the cost of MRP is worthwhile, since the number of MRP companies has rapidly expanded from only a few in 1965 to many thousands. There are still, however, some companies that have not implemented MRP. As more managers become aware of MRP in the future, the number of MRP companies can be expected to grow.

There are some MRP companies that are not gaining the maximum benefit from their MRP systems or that have failed in implementing MRP. The reasons for this are usually a lack of management support for the system and a failure in communications within the company. As a result, the informal system is in use, and the formal MRP system is in danger of failing or has already failed. Some companies are even considering reimplementing their MRP systems, that is, starting over again, because their approach to using MRP provides so little benefit.

The range of success with MRP systems has been defined by Oliver Wight (1981) in terms of class A, B, C, or D companies as shown in Box 15.4. As indicated in the box, a class A company has a full closed-loop system (type II or type III) *and* uses it to manage the company. The only difference between a class A and a class B company is in the use of MRP; the software is the same. Class C companies have an order-launching (type I) system, and in class D companies the system exists in data processing only. The study by Anderson, et al. (1981) showed that only 10 percent of companies were class A; 29 percent were class B; 48 percent were class C; and 13 percent were class D. Apparently, there is much room for improvement in industry. Effective implementation is the key to gaining maximum results from MRP systems.

BOX 15.4
USE OF MRP SYSTEMS

Class A: Closed-loop system, used for priority planning and capacity planning. The master production schedule is leveled and used by top management to run the business. Most deliveries are on time, inventory is under control, and little or no expediting is done.

Class B: Closed-loop system with capability for both priority planning and capacity planning. In this case, the master production schedule is somewhat inflated, top management does not give full support, some inventory reductions have been obtained, but capacity is sometimes exceeded, and some expediting is required.

Class C: Order-launching system with priority planning only. Capacity planning is done informally with a probably inflated master production schedule. Expediting is used to control the flow of work; a modest reduction in inventory is achieved.

Class D: The MRP system exists mainly in data processing. Many records are inaccurate. The informal system is largely used to run the company. Little benefit is obtained from the MRP system.

Source: Oliver Wight (1981).

15.8 WHO CAN BENEFIT FROM MRP?

It has been demonstrated in practice that most manufacturing companies can benefit from an MRP system *if it is properly installed and utilized.* Successful companies range from the small single-plant manufacturer to the large multiple-plant conglomerates. There are successful companies in all industries—including automobiles, metalworking, electronics, and the process industries.

While some companies may benefit from a very elaborate MRP system, others may need only a simple system. Each company should determine the scope of the MRP system needed on the basis of the incremental costs and benefits. Starting with a minimum system, a company can add features and determine whether the additional cost is justified by the additional benefits. By using this approach, each company can arrive at the type of MRP system which is best suited to its needs.

Some people feel that a company must have a fixed master schedule and fixed lead times to use MRP. Change does not destroy an MRP system, since MRP is designed to adjust to changing conditions. However, those companies that have a fixed master schedule or fixed lead times can operate their MRP systems with less inventory than those that must add safety lead time or safety stock to cover uncertainties in supply or demand. Therefore variable lead time does not destroy MRP, but it does require more inventory and results in less benefit.

Users of MRP systems can be classified by the type of BOM they have. Figure 15.6a shows a BOM for a process company, where a given input is split into

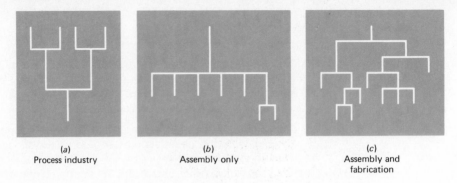

(a)	(b)	(c)
Process industry	Assembly only	Assembly and fabrication

FIGURE 15.6   Types of BOM structures.
Source: Adapted from Elwood S. Buffa and Jeffrey Millwe, Production Inventory Systems Planning and Control, *3d ed., Homewood, Ill.: Irwin, 1979.*

several different outputs. This occurs, for example, during the cracking and distillation of petroleum and during food processing. Figure 15.6b shows a BOM for a company which is in the assembly business. All parts are purchased, and the company is not vertically integrated. Finally Figure 15.6c is a BOM for a company which has both fabrication and assembly operations. This company—which might be a machinery or appliance manufacturer—is vertically integrated through all stages of manufacturing. Generally speaking, the most benefit from MRP is achieved by companies of the third type, which have the most complex bills of materials.

There is tremendous room for the application of MRP concepts in the service industry. If the bill of materials is replaced by a bill of labor or a bill of activities, one can explode the master schedule of output into all the activities and personnel required to deliver a particular mix of services. Some service operations will also require a bill of materials where materials are an important part of the goods-services bundle.

As an example, one electric utility has been using the MRP concept for several years in the electric hookup part of its business. When a new customer requests electrical service, a planner enters the request into a computer system for the type of service required. The computer then explodes this service request into detailed labor, material, and work activities. Each of these requirements is time-phased and accumulated over all jobs to determine whether sufficient capacity is available. When the time comes, the utility hookup crews are given work orders from the computer system, and work accomplishment is reported back to the computer. The "MRP" system then drives billing, labor-reporting, and other accounting systems.

The MRP concept is only beginning to be applied to service industries. There is potential in every phase of service operations including restaurants, hotels, legal offices, health care, and many others.

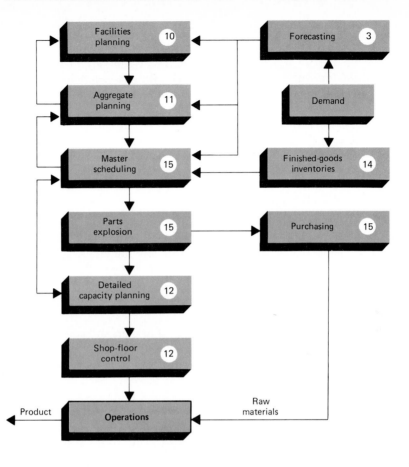

FIGURE 15.7
Integration of materials decisions. (Numbers within circles indicate chapters in the text.)

15.9 INTEGRATION OF MATERIALS PLANNING AND CONTROL

In a manufacturing company, one of the most important problems is the integration of all facets of materials planning and control. This integration can be achieved through a comprehensive information system; through a materials manager position, as described above; and through coordinated decision making. Figure 15.7 shows how the decisions described in past chapters are interrelated in a manufacturing environment.

At the top of the figure, facilities planning and aggregate planning set physical capacity and inventory levels over the medium- to long-range time frame. These decisions constrain the amount of capacity available to the master schedule and the aggregate amount of finished goods inventory available.

Demand is entered into the master schedule through finished goods inventory when finished goods exist. Demand also drives forecasting, which may be used at any of three levels: facilities, aggregate planning, and master scheduling. Master scheduling is followed by the parts-explosion process, described in this chapter. Detailed or rough-cut capacity planning (or loading) is then done to determine whether or not sufficient capacity exists at the level of the master schedule. If insufficient capacity is available, the master schedule is adjusted through a feedback loop which may, in turn, affect aggregate planning or facilities planning. If sufficient capacity is available, the operations are scheduled and purchasing actions take place. The orders are then monitored through the shop-floor control system.

 ## KEY POINTS

Materials requirements planning is based on the concept of dependent demand. By exploding the master schedule through the BOM, it is possible to derive demand for component parts and raw materials. The MRP system can then be used to plan and control capacity, and it can be extended to resource planning throughout a manufacturing firm.

This chapter's key points include the following:

- MRP is an information system used to plan and control manufacturing. There are three types of MRP systems: type I, an inventory control system (order launching); type II, a production and inventory control system (closed loop); and type III, a manufacturing resource planning system. Each of these systems expands the scope and use of MRP.
- The parts-explosion process has three principal inputs: master schedule, BOM, and inventory records. There are two principal outputs: purchase orders and shop orders. Parts explosion is the heart of the MRP system.
- MRP uses a requirements philosophy where parts are ordered only as required by the master schedule. Past demand for parts is irrelevant, and component inventories are *not* replenished when they reach a low level.
- Master schedules should be based on both marketing and production considerations. They should represent a realistic build plan within factory capacity. Top management should use the master schedule to plan and control the business.
- The BOM contains the list of parts used to make the product. To maintain the accuracy of the bill of materials, an engineering-change-order (ECO) system is needed.
- The accuracy of inventory records should be maintained through cycle counting. Daily cycle counting can be used in place of annual physical inventories.
- Shop-floor control is used to control the flow of materials through the factory. This is done by managing lead times dynamically as the product is manufactured. If lead times are properly managed, much safety stock can be eliminated.
- A successful MRP system requires (1) adequate computer support, (2) accurate data, (3) management support, and (4) user knowledge. Both system and people problems must be solved to use MRP successfully. When this is done, benefits include reduced inventory, increased customer service, and improved efficiency.

- All manufacturing and service companies can benefit from MRP if it is properly installed and operated. This includes large and small companies and all industries.

QUESTIONS

1. In what ways do independent-demand inventories differ from dependent-demand inventories?
2. Why is demand history irrelevant for the management of raw materials and work-in-process inventories?
3. A vendor has quoted a lead time of 10 weeks for delivery of a part. Your purchasing manager says the part can be delivered in 3 weeks if necessary. Of course, the vendor disagrees. Who is correct? Explain.
4. It has been said that MRP is an information system which does not rely on sophisticated mathematical models. Discuss the historical significance of this statement.
5. With regard to inventory management, discuss the difference between a replenishment philosophy and a requirements philosophy.
6. Can the ABC principle be applied to manufacturing component inventories? Discuss.
7. How much safety stock should be carried in an MRP system? What is the role of safety stock in MRP systems? Where should safety stock be carried?
8. What are the potential effects of an inflated master schedule?
9. Describe the advantages of cycle counting over an annual physical inventory.
10. Under what circumstances is a shop-floor control system needed?
11. Is it possible to control financial totals without physical control of materials in manufacturing?
12. How is the role of the production and inventory control manager changed by an MRP system?
13. A company president said his company was too small to afford an MRP system. Discuss.
14. A materials manager said that her company needed only an order-launching system. Should the loop be closed?
15. Describe how MRP concepts could be used for the following service operations:
    a. Hotel
    b. Legal office

PROBLEMS

1. The following information is given for a particular part. Using a lead time of 2 weeks, complete the table.

	Week				
	1	2	3	4	5
Gross requirements			100	300	200
On-hand/scheduled receipts	80	50			
Net requirements					
Planned order releases					

 2. The Old Hickory Furniture Company manufactures chairs on the basis of the BOM shown below. At the present time, the inventories of parts and lead times are as follows:

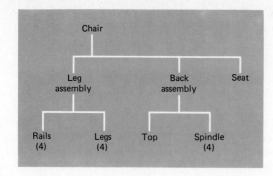

	On hand	Weeks lead time
Chairs	100	1
Leg assembly	50	2
Back assembly	25	1
Seat	40	3
Rails	100	1
Legs	150	1
Top	30	2
Spindles	80	2

The company would like to produce 500 chairs in week 5 and 300 chairs in week 6.
a. Develop a materials plan for all the parts.
b. What actions should be taken now?
c. What is the effect of changing the master schedule to 300 chairs in week 5 and 400 chairs in week 6?
d. Suppose it takes 1 hour to assemble backs, 1 hour to assemble legs, and 2 hours to finish completed chairs. Also assume that total assembly time for all three types of assembly is limited to 1000 hours per week. Will this capacity constraint cause a bottleneck in assembly? If it does, what can be done?

3. Product A consists of subassemblies B and C. Subassembly B requires two parts of D and one part of E. Subassembly C requires one part of D and one part of F.
a. Draw a product structure tree (BOM) for this product.
b. How many parts are needed to make 200 units of finished product?

4. The BOM for product A is given below:

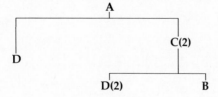

Part	On hand	Weeks lead time
A	75	1
B	100	2
C	50	1
D	125	2

Assume that the master schedule calls for 200 units of product A in week 5 and 250 units in week 6.
a. Develop a materials plan for this product.

b. What actions should be taken immediately?

c. Project the inventory ahead for each part.

d. If you were suddenly notified that part D will take 3 weeks to get instead of 2 weeks, what actions would you take?

5. The master scheduler in the ABC Widget Company is in the process of revising the master schedule. At the present time, he has scheduled 400 widgets for week 5 and is considering changing this to 500 widgets.

a. What information would you need to decide if you should make this change?

b. Suppose that each widget takes 1 hour of press time and 3 hours of assembly time, 3 weeks prior to delivery. Can the additional 100 widgets be made in view of the following shop loadings?

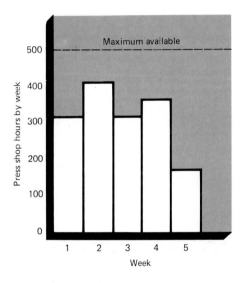 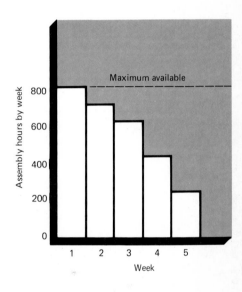

c. If the additional widgets cannot be made in part b above, what actions might be taken to make it possible to produce the required widgets?

6. A scissors company makes a basic scissors which consists of three parts: the left side, the right side, and the screw which holds the sides together. At the present time, the company has the following numbers of parts on hand and on order. The lead times for reorder of each part are also shown along with a BOM and a sketch of the scissors.

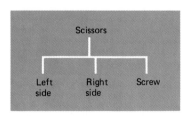 

	On hand	Weeks lead time	Scheduled receipts
Scissors	100	1	
Left side	50	2	100 in week 2
Right side	75	2	200 in week 2
Screw	300	1	200 in week 1

a. Assume the master schedule calls for 300 scissors to be shipped in week 4 and 400 in week 5; work out a complete materials plan.

b. Suppose the supplier of right-hand sides calls to say that deliveries of the 200 parts on order will be 1 week late. What effect will this have on the materials plan?

c. If demand for scissors is uncertain and has a standard deviation of 50 units, what would you recommend the company do in order to maintain a 95 percent service level for scissors?

d. If the delivery of the scissors parts is unreliable and the standard deviation of delivery lead time is 1 week for each of the parts, what would you recommend the company do to maintain its production schedule?

7. A lamp consists of a frame assembly and a shade as shown below in the sketch and the bill of materials. The frame assembly is made from a neck, a socket, and a base which are assembled together from purchased parts. A shade is added to the frame assembly in order to make the finished lamp. The number of parts on hand, the parts scheduled to arrive, and the lead times to obtain more parts are shown below.

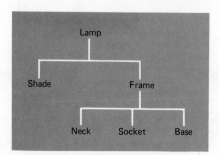

	On hand	Weeks lead time	Scheduled receipts
Lamp	200	1	
Frame	100	2	
Neck	0	3	
Socket	300	2	
Base	200	3	
Shade	400	3	

a. Assuming 1000 finished lamps are required in week 7 and 1500 in week 8, construct a complete materials plan for the lamp. What actions should be taken immediately to implement the plan?

b. If it takes 15 minutes of assembly time to assemble the parts into the frame and 5 minutes to assemble the shade and frame into a finished lamp, how much total assembly time is required in each week? What can be done if insufficient time is available in any given week?

c. If the lead time for assembly of lamps is extended from 1 week to 2 weeks, what changes will be needed in the materials plan to adjust for this change?

8. A telephone is assembled from a handset and a base. The handset in turn is assembled from a handle and a cord; and the base is assembled from a case, a circuit board, and a face plate. A BOM and a sketch of the phone, along with the numbers of parts on hand and lead times, are shown below.

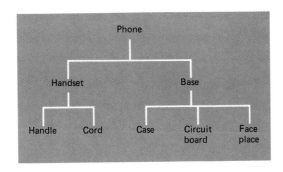

	On hand	Weeks lead time
Phone	200	1
Handset	300	1
Handle	200	2
Cord	75	2
Base	250	1
Case	200	2
Circuit board	150	1
Face plate	300	2

a. Management would like to start assembling phones as soon as possible. How many phones can be made from the available parts, and when can they be delivered? Construct a materials plan to show your answer.

b. For the materials plan constructed in part *a*, develop an inventory projection of parts and finished goods on a week-by-week basis.

c. Suppose another 100 circuit boards can be obtained within 1 week. What effect will this have on your answer for part *a*?

SELECTED BIBLIOGRAPHY

ANDERSON, JOHN C., ROGER G. SCHROEDER, SHARON E. TUPY, and EDNA M. WHITE: "Material Requirement Planning Systems: A Study of Implementation and Practice," APICS, 1981.

APICS: "Capacity Planning and Control Study Guide," *Production and Inventory Management*, vol. 16, no. 1, 1975, pp. 1–16.

BELT, BILL: "The New ABC's of Lead-Time Management," *Production and Inventory Control Management*, vol. 15, no. 2, 1974, pp. 81–91.

BEVIS, GEORGE E.: "A Management Viewpoint on the Implementation of a MRP System," *Production and Inventory Management*, vol. 17, no. 1, 1976, pp. 105–116.

FOGARTY, DONALD W., and THOMAS R. HOFFMANN: *Production and Inventory Management,* Cincinnati, Oh.: South-Western, 1983.

GRAY, CHRISTOPHER: *The Right Choice: A Complete Guide to Evaluating, Selecting & Installing MRP II Software,* Essex Junction, Vt.: Oliver Wight Ltd., 1987.

HALL, ROBERT: "Getting the Commitment of Top Management," *Production and Inventory Management,* vol. 18, no. 1, 1977, pp. 1–19.

——— and THOMAS E. VOLLMANN: "Planning Your Material Requirements," *Harvard Business Review,* September–October 1978, pp. 105–112.

HONEYWELL, INC.: *Honeywell Manufacturing System: Summary Description,* 1986.

HOYT, JACK: "Dynamic Lead Times That Fit Today's Dynamic Planning," *Production and Inventory Management,* vol. 19, no. 1, 1978, pp. 63–70.

MILLER, JEFFREY G.: "Fit Production Systems to the Task," *Harvard Business Review,* January–February 1981, pp. 145–154.

——— and PETER GILMORE: "Materials Managers: Who Needs Them," *Harvard Business Review,* July–August 1979, pp. 143–153.

——— and LINDA G. SPRAGUE: "Behind the Growth in Materials Requirements Planning," *Harvard Business Review,* September–October 1975, pp. 83–91.

ORLICKY, JOSEPH: *Materials Requirements Planning,* New York: McGraw-Hill, 1975.

PAPESCH, ROGER M.: "Extending Your MRP System into Your Vendor's Shop," *Production and Inventory Management,* vol. 19, no. 2, 1978, pp. 47–52.

PLOSSL, GEORGE: *Production and Inventory Control: Principles and Techniques,* 2d ed., Englewood Cliffs, N.J.: Prentice-Hall, 1985.

———: "Tactics for Manufacturing Control," *Production and Inventory Management,* vol. 15, no. 3, 1974, pp. 21–34.

Production and Inventory Management Review, APICS, July 1987, pp. 124–202.

SCHROEDER, ROGER G., JOHN C. ANDERSON, SHARON E. TUPY, and EDNA M. WHITE: "A Study of MRP Benefits and Costs," *Journal of Operations Management,* vol. 2, no. 1, October 1981, pp. 1–9.

SCHULTZ, TERRY: "MRP to BRP: The Journey of the 80's," *Production and Inventory Management Review and APICS News,* October 1981, pp. 29–32.

SMOLENS, R. W.: "Master Scheduling: Problems and Solutions," *Production and Inventory Management,* vol. 18, no. 3, 1977, pp. 32–38.

TALLMAN, JACK: "A Practical Approach to Installing a Cycle Counting Program," *Production and Inventory Management,* vol. 17, no. 4, 1976, pp. 1–16.

VOLLMANN, THOMAS E., WILLIAM L. BERRY, and D. CLAY WHYBARK: *Manufacturing Planning and Control Systems,* Homewood, Ill.: Irwin, 1984.

WALKER, JOHN, and FREDERICK HILLS: "The Key to Success or Failure of MRP: Overcoming Human Resistance," *Production and Inventory Management,* vol. 18, no. 4, 1977, pp. 7–16.

WALLACE, THOMAS: *MRP II: Making It Happen,* Essex Junction, Vt., Oliver Wight Ltd., 1985.

WIGHT, OLIVER W.: *Production and Inventory Management in the Computer Age,* Cahners Books International, CBI Publishing Co., Boston, 1974.

———: *MRP II Unlocking America's Productivity Potential,* CBI Publishing Co., Boston, 1981.

CHAPTER 16

Just-in-Time Manufacturing

In this chapter the just-in-time (JIT) philosophy of manufacturing will be described. JIT is called a philosophy because it goes far beyond inventory control and encompasses the entire system of production. In a nutshell, JIT is an approach which seeks to eliminate all sources of waste, anything which does not add value, in production activities by providing the right part at the right place at the right time. Parts are therefore produced just in time to meet manufacturing requirements rather than by the traditional approach, which produces parts just in case (JIC) they are needed. The JIT system results in much less inventory, lower costs, and better quality than the JIC approach.

In this chapter, the JIT philosophy is discussed in detail and compared with MRP approaches. Even though JIT goes far beyond inventory control, JIT is described at this point in the book as an alternative to MRP systems for certain types of production and as a bridge to management of the work force described in the next section. We also describe some concrete results which have been achieved from JIT systems and an implementation approach designed to gain maximum benefit from JIT.

16.1 PHILOSOPHY OF JIT

The JIT system was developed at the Toyota Motor Company in Japan. Even though Schonberger (1982) indicates that JIT might be traced back 20 years or more to the Japanese shipbuilding industry, the modern application of JIT was popularized in the mid-1970s at Toyota by Mr. Taiichi Ohno, a Toyota vice president, and several of Mr. Ohno's colleagues. The JIT concept was then apparently first transferred to the United States about 1980 at Kawasaki's Lincoln, Nebraska plant. Since then, many of the best corporations in the United States have been implementing JIT, including those in the automotive and electronics industries. JIT is achieving widespread use in American industry today.

The roots of the JIT system can probably be traced to the Japanese environment. Owing to a lack of space and lack of natural resources, the Japanese have developed an aversion to waste. They view scrap and rework as waste and thus strive for perfect quality. They also believe that inventory storage wastes space and ties up valuable materials. Anything which does not contribute value to the product is viewed as waste. U.S. companies, in contrast, with wide open spaces and a vast supply of raw materials, have not viewed waste in the same way. As a result, it was natural for the JIT philosophy to develop in Japan. Yet, as will be seen in this chapter, there is nothing culturally inherent in the JIT system which prevents U.S. companies from using JIT or improving on it. Many U.S. companies are committed to making JIT work as a matter of economic survival![1]

In addition to eliminating waste, JIT has another major tenet in its philosophy—utilizing the full capability of the worker. Workers, in the JIT system, are charged with the responsibility for producing quality parts just in time to support the next production process. If they cannot meet this responsibility, workers are required to stop the production process and call for help. In addition to greater responsibility for production, workers are also charged with improving the production process. Through quality circles, suggestion systems, and other forms of participation, workers offer improvements to the process of production. Thus, the capability of the worker is used to a much greater extent in the JIT system than in traditional production approaches.

The objective of the JIT system is not, however, worker participation; rather it is to improve profits and return on investment through cost reductions, inventory reductions, and quality improvements. The means for achieving these objectives are eliminating waste and involving workers in the production process. How this is done is summarized by the basic elements of JIT described in the next section.

We are emphasizing the use of JIT for repetitive manufacturing, which is approximately the same as mass production. Repetitive manufacturing is the production of standardized discrete products in high volume. However, some of

---

[1]For more details on the history of JIT, see Hall (1981) and Hall (1987).

the JIT concepts can also be applied to job lot production, which is inherently nonrepetitive in nature. Nevertheless, the major application to date of JIT has been in repetitive industries: auto, electronics, machinery, appliances, motorcycles, and so on. A typical use of JIT concepts is given in Box 16.1.

BOX 16.1
IBM AUSTIN PLANT

IBM has instituted Continuous Flow Manufacturing (CFM), IBM's term for JIT, at its Austin, Texas plant which produces printed circuit boards for personal computers and other IBM products. The objectives of this JIT effort were to: (1) Reduce inventory and other waste, (2) Improve quality to zero defects, (3) Improve flexibility by reducing queues, setup times, and lot sizes, (4) Revise the production flow process, (5) Establish simple, visible controls, and (6) Develop a habit of continuous improvement. These objectives were accomplished by establishing a number of implementation teams. The teams were charged with not only defining the JIT improvement plan, but in educating employees, and in carrying out the plan.

Education was accomplished by presentations of JIT concepts to all employees and by in-depth courses for those assigned to the improvement teams. Implementation utilized process analysis which included flow charting, and data analysis of all manufacturing processes. As a result, benchmarks were established for each process in terms of cycle time, WIP level, and capacity by modeling the processes. JIT was accomplished by instituting a pull-system for material movement; previous systems had utilized forward scheduling and kitting to push parts into assembly. Small lot sizes and daily releases replaced weekly releases of parts. Kanban containers were used to organize material flow into small lots with frequent replenishment. Test and repair stations were integrated into the production lines so that immediate feedback occurred. The teams also instituted management by sight through the use of electronic display boards, and status boards which indicated quality levels, problems, process changes, and other information needed to provide fast feedback to operators.

As a result of these changes, significant results were achieved. Cycle time was reduced by 50 percent, quality was improved by 30 percent, productivity was improved by 10 percent, and inventory was reduced by 40 percent. These results were achieved only through the extensive education and involvement of all people in the plant. Continuing improvements are being made as part of the JIT philosophy, which has been put in place.

Source: Spencer, Duin, et al., "Case Studies of JIT Implementation at Westinghouse and IBM," Washington, D.C.: APICS, 1986.

16.2 ELEMENTS OF A JIT SYSTEM

Before going into detail about the JIT system, we will briefly summarize how the system works as a whole. This will be done by starting with the master schedule and working backward through the production process to the vendors.

In JIT the master schedule (or final assembly schedule) is planned for 1 to 3 months into the future to allow work centers and vendors to plan their respective work schedules. Within the current month the master schedule is leveled on a daily basis. In other words, the same quantity of each product is produced each day for the entire month. Furthermore, small lots (preferably lot size equals 1) are scheduled in the master schedule to provide a uniform load on the plant and vendors during each day. The advantage of this kind of master scheduling is that it provides nearly constant demands on all downstream work centers and vendors.

JIT uses a simple parts withdrawal system (called Kanban) to pull parts from one work center to the next.[2] Parts are kept in small containers, and only a specific number of these containers are provided. When all the containers are filled, the machines are shut off, and no more parts are produced until the subsequent (using) work center provides another empty container. Thus, work-in-process inventory is limited to available containers, and parts are only provided as needed. The final assembly schedule pulls parts from one work center to the next just in time to support production needs. If a process stops because of machine breakdown or quality problems, all preceding processes will automatically stop when their parts containers become full.

The objective of JIT is to produce parts in a lot size of 1. In many cases, this is not economically feasible because of the cost of setup compared with inventory carrying cost. The JIT solution to this problem is to reduce the setup time as much as possible, ideally to zero. The setup time is not taken as given, but rather considered a cause of excess inventory. Low setup times result in small, economical lot sizes and shorter production lead times. Driving down the setup time for machines is a key to the JIT system. With shorter lead times and less material in process, the production system is also much more flexible to changes in the master schedule.

With an emphasis on quick changeovers and smaller lots, the multifunction worker is required. Cross-training is needed so that a worker can switch from one machine to the next and so that workers can perform their own setup and maintenance. This requires a broader range of skills than traditional manufacturing. JIT requires not only broader skills, but much greater teamwork and coordination since inventory is not available to cover up problems in the system. The entire production system must be more closely coordinated by the workers.

The layout of the plant is much different with JIT since inventory is held on the shop floor and not put in a storeroom between processes. Inventory is kept out in the open, so it is readily available to the next process. Since inventory is typically kept low—only a few hours of supply—plants can be kept much smaller because of the reduced storage space needed. One comparison showed only one-third the space was needed when compared with conventional plants.[3]

Quality is absolutely essential with a JIT system. Not only do defects produce waste, but they can also grind the production process to a halt. Since there is no inventory to cover up for mistakes, perfect quality is required by a JIT system. JIT,

---

[2]*Kanban* means "card" or "signal" in Japanese, since cards or other methods are used to signal the need for more production.

[3]William Harahan, Ford Motor Company, in a speech given to the Minnesota Executive Program, October 1982.

however, facilitates very good quality since defects are quickly discovered by the next process. Quality problems rapidly gain plantwide attention as the production line stops when problems occur. A JIT system is designed to expose errors and get them corrected rather than covering them up with inventory.

Finally, vendor relations are radically changed by a JIT system. Vendors are asked to make frequent deliveries (as many as four times per day) directly to the production line. Vendors receive Kanban containers, just as inplant work centers do, since vendors are viewed as an extension of the plant. Changes in shipping procedures and close proximity of vendors are often required to integrate vendors effectively with JIT procedures. Vendors are also required to deliver perfect quality. A revolution is required in the way that we usually think of vendors; we need to think of them as partners rather than as adversaries.

As can be seen, JIT affects practically every aspect of plant operations: lot sizing, scheduling, quality, layout, vendors, labor relations, and so on. While the effects are far-reaching, so are the potential benefits. Inventory turns of 50 or 100 times per year, superior quality, and substantial cost advantages (15 to 25 percent less) have been reported. The objective of JIT, however, is to improve return on investment (ROI) as shown in Figure 16.1. ROI is increased by increases in revenues, cost reductions, and less investment. A JIT system can increase revenue by improving quality, as we have already discussed, or by giving better delivery service. Better service is provided by shorter lead times, which allow faster response to customer needs, and by better conformance to schedule commitments. Cost reductions can be obtained in materials (less scrap and rework), labor, and overhead. Finally, investment is reduced by less inventory and greater throughput of plant and equipment. When JIT is evaluated, its effect on the bottom line and on investment should be the ultimate test.

Figure 16.1 also shows how the various elements we have been describing (small lots, stable master schedule, etc.) contribute to JIT production. The most important thing to note, however, is that problem-solving activities by management and workers drive the whole system. These problem-solving activities are driven, in turn, by removing inventory, which is viewed as the "root of all evil." The JIT production system is, therefore, built on a philosophy of constant improvement.

An analogy for JIT is illustrated by Figure 16.2. Production is viewed as a converging system of streams, as we have previously noted in Chapter 14. The water level in the streams is viewed as inventory. At the bottom of each stream are rocks, which represent problems relating to quality, vendor delivery, machine breakdowns, etc. The traditional approach is to hold inventory high enough to cover up the rocks and thereby keep the stream flowing. The JIT approach is the opposite; the water level is lowered to expose the top of the rocks. When these rocks have been pulverized (i.e., the problems solved), the water is lowered again and more rocks are exposed. This process is repeated until all rocks are turned into pebbles and the stream flows smoothly at a low level.

This analogy is very good because it highlights the problem-solving approach, which is at the heart of JIT. How this works will be described next in some detail by discussing each of the major elements of a JIT system.

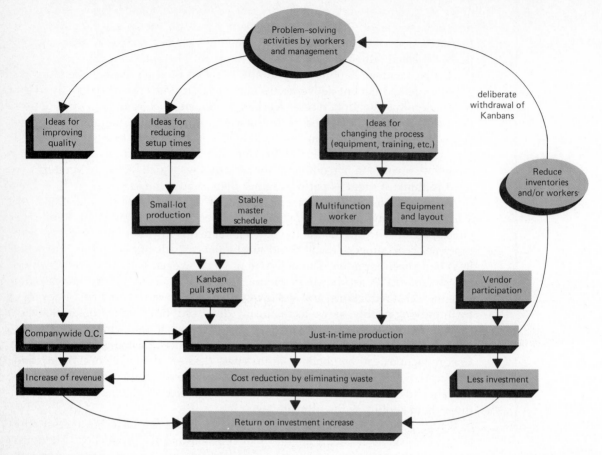

FIGURE 16.1 JIT system. *Adapted from Monden (1983), p. 3, and Schronberger (1982), p. 26.*

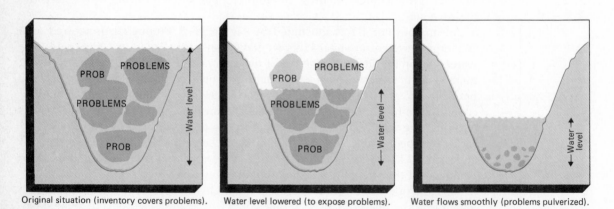

Original situation (inventory covers problems).   Water level lowered (to expose problems).   Water flows smoothly (problems pulverized).

FIGURE 16.2 Stream analogy.

16.3 STABILIZING THE MASTER SCHEDULE

The process of production planning starts with a long-range production plan, which is then broken down into annual, monthly, and daily plans. This process is shown schematically in Figure 16.3. At each point in the process, sales are considered, profit planning is done, and capacity is planned. This planning process starts with an aggregate production plan and successively refines it into specific models and products.

Master scheduling is done at the monthly and daily level so as to achieve a uniform load. The production horizon for specific models must be set at least 1 month in advance and possibly 2 or 3 months in advance, depending on lead times for production, purchasing, and capacity changes. Let's assume for the purpose of discussion that a 1-month rolling schedule is used, where 1 month of production is scheduled in advance. Also assume that the schedule calls for 10,000 units of product A, 5000 units of product B, and 5000 units of product C. If there are 20 days of production in the month, then the daily schedule will call for 1/20 of each model produced in each day: 500A, 250B, 250C. Furthermore, the individual units will be mixed as they go down the production line. The sequence will be |AABC|AABC|AABC|. Note how 2 units of A are produced for every unit of B and C. Then the sequence is continually repeated.

The reason why production is leveled to this extent is that it creates a uniform load on all work centers which support final assembly. This sequence presumes, of course, that the changeover cost between models is zero or nearly so. If this is not so, the final assembly line should be redesigned to achieve a very low setup cost. How this can be done will be described later.

In some cases, it will not be possible or economical to achieve perfectly mixed production on the final assembly line. In this case, very small lots should be scheduled, the lot size depending on the tradeoff between setup and inventory carrying costs. The objective of single-unit production, however, should not be abandoned since it ordinarily leads to the lowest system costs. An actual example of how scheduling is done for Toyota is given in Box 16.2 on page 495.

Once the monthly master schedule has been set, this information must be transmitted to all work centers and vendors. They will then plan their capacity in terms of numbers of workers needed, overtime, subcontracting, and possibly new equipment. Enough lead time must be given to them to obtain the resources they need to do the job.

The JIT system does not allow overproduction once the daily quota has been set. For example, if the daily quota is met in 7 hours, production is stopped, and production workers do maintenance or have quality circle meetings. Similarly, if production falls behind, it is usually made up by overtime the same day. This is facilitated by shift scheduling, which allows some time between shifts. For example, a two-shift operation might be scheduled from 7 a.m. to 3 p.m. and from 5 p.m. to 1 a.m. Maintenance and overtime are then scheduled between shifts. The objective of the JIT system is to produce the right quantity each day—no more and no less.

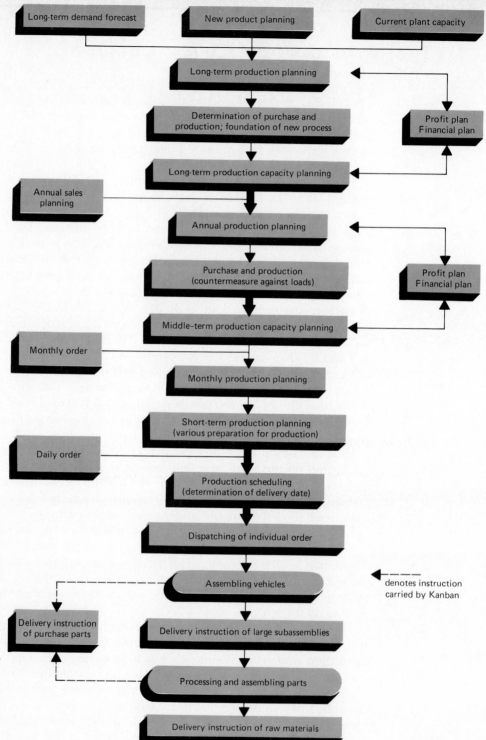

Long-term demand forecast

New product planning

Current plant capacity

Long-term production planning

Determination of purchase and production; foundation of new process

Profit plan
Financial plan

Long-term production capacity planning

Annual sales planning

Annual production planning

Purchase and production (countermeasure against loads)

Profit plan
Financial plan

Middle-term production capacity planning

Monthly order

Monthly production planning

Short-term production planning (various preparation for production)

Daily order

Production scheduling (determination of delivery date)

Dispatching of individual order

Assembling vehicles

denotes instruction carried by Kanban

Delivery instruction of purchase parts

Delivery instruction of large subassemblies

Processing and assembling parts

Delivery instruction of raw materials

FIGURE 16.3
Structure of production planning.
Source: Y. Sugimori, K. Kusonoki, F. Cho, and S. Uchikawa, "Toyota Production System and Kanban System Materialization of Just-in-Time and Respect for Human System," International Journal of Production Research, *vol. 15, no. 6, pp. 553–564, 1977.*

BOX 16.2
TOYOTA MONTHLY PRODUCTION PLANNING

The Toyota Motor Company has a yearly production plan which shows how many cars to make and sell in the current year. It also has a two-step monthly production plan. First, car types and quantities are suggested two months before, and then the detailed plan is determined one month before the particular month in question. Such suggested and determined information is also communicated to the subcontracting companies at the same time. From this monthly production plan, the daily production schedule is particularly important because the concept of smoothed production is incorporated into this schedule.

Smoothed production must extend into two areas: the averaged total production of a product per day and the averaged quantity of each variety of product within the greater total. For example, in Toyota's factory, there are many final assembly lines—the Corona line, the Crown line, the Celica line, etc. Suppose the Corona line has to produce 20,000 units in a month of 20 operating days. This means that 1,000 Coronas must be produced per day. This is a smoothing of production in terms of the daily production quantity, i.e., averaging the total quantity to be produced per day.

But at the same time, the Corona line has to be averaged in terms of the various Coronas available. The Corona line assembles about 3,000 or 4,000 kinds of Coronas, which are differentiated by the different combinations of engines, transmissions, accelerators, number of doors, outside and inside colors, tires, and various options. Each of these different types of Coronas must also be averaged for daily production.

Source: Yasuhiro Monden, *Toyota Production System: Practical Approach to Production Management,* Industrial Engineering and Management Press, Institute of Industrial Engineering, 1983, p. 57.

Master scheduling, as we have described it, has the advantage that it closely resembles customer demand on a daily basis. This minimizes finished goods inventory since the production output is closely matched to demand. As we shall see, this type of master schedule also helps reduce work-in-process and raw materials inventories. Stabilizing the master schedule is the key to stabilizing all other production processes and vendor requirements.

THE KANBAN SYSTEM

Kanban is the method of production authorization and material movement in the JIT system. As noted earlier, Kanban, in the Japanese language, means a marker (card, sign, plaque, or other device) used to control the sequencing of jobs through a sequential process. Kanban is a subsystem of JIT; the two terms are not synonymous as some authors have indicated.

The purpose of the Kanban system is to signal the need for more parts and to ensure that those parts are produced in time to support subsequent fabrication or

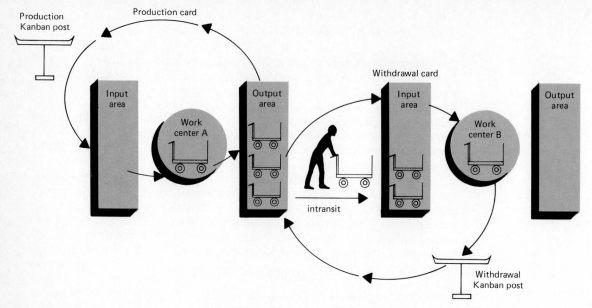

FIGURE 16.4 Kanban system.

assembly. This is done by pulling parts through from the final assembly line. Only the final assembly line receives a schedule from the dispatching office, and this schedule is nearly the same from day to day. All other machine operators and vendors receive production orders (Kanban cards) from the subsequent (using) work centers. If production should stop for a time in the using work centers, the supplying work centers will also soon stop since they will no longer receive Kanban orders for more material.

The Kanban system is a physical control system consisting of cards and containers. Let's assume for the purposes of discussion that eight containers are used between work centers A and B (A supplies B), and each container holds exactly 20 parts. The maximum inventory which can exist between these two work centers is then 160 units (8 × 20) since production at work center A will stop when all containers are filled.

In the normal course of events, the eight containers might be distributed as shown in Figure 16.4. Three containers are located at work center A in the output area filled with parts. One container is presently being filled at work center A by the machine. One full container is being moved from A to B, two full containers are sitting in the input area of work center B, and one container is being used at B. These eight containers are needed since work center A also produces parts for other work centers, machines at A may break down, and move times from A to B are not always exactly predictable.

To control movement of the containers, there are two main types of Kanban cards, production cards, and withdrawal (move) cards.[4] These cards are used to

---

[4]There are several types of Kanban cards. For information on these, see Monden (May 1981).

authorize production and to identify parts in any container. Kanban cards may be made of paper, metal, or plastic, and they generally contain the information shown in Figure 16.5. Kanban cards take the place of shop paperwork used in traditional repetitive manufacturing.

Here is how the Kanban system works, assuming containers are moved one at a time. When a container of parts is emptied at work center B, the empty container and associated withdrawal card are taken back to work center A. The production card from a full container of parts is removed from its container and replaced by the withdrawal card. The production card is then placed in the Kanban receiving post at work center A, thereby authorizing production of another container of parts. The empty container is left at work center A.

The full container of parts and its withdrawal card are moved to work center B and placed in the input area. When this container of parts is eventually used, its withdrawal card and the empty container are taken back to work center A, and the cycle is repeated.

The significant thing about the Kanban system is that it is visual in nature. All parts are neatly placed in containers of a fixed size. As empty containers accumulate, it is clear that the producing work center is getting behind. On the other hand, when all containers are filled, production is stopped. The production lot size is exactly equal to 1 container of parts.

The number of containers needed to operate a work center is a function of the demand rate, container size, and the circulating time for a container. This is illustrated by the following formula.

$$n = \frac{DT}{C}$$

where n = total number of containers

D = demand rate of the using work center

C = container size in number of parts, usually less than 10 percent of daily demand

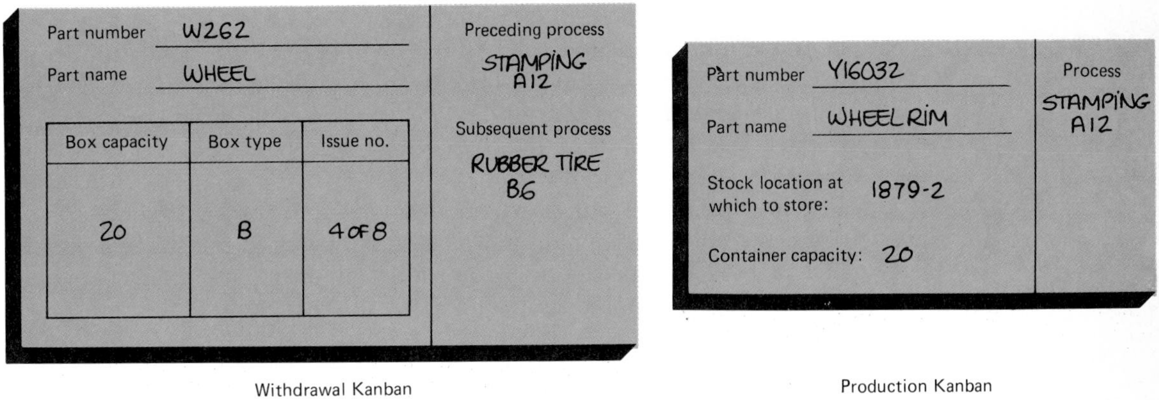

Withdrawal Kanban

Production Kanban

FIGURE 16.5 Kanban cards.

T = time for a container to complete an entire circuit: filled, wait, moved, used, and returned to be filled again. This is also called lead time.

Suppose that demand at the next work center is 2 parts per minute and a standard container holds 25 parts. Also assume that it takes 100 minutes for a container to make a complete circuit from work center A to work center B and back to A again including all setup, run, move, and wait time. The number of containers needed in this case is 8.

$$n = \frac{2 \times 100}{25} = 8$$

The maximum inventory is equal to the container size times the number of containers = $8 \times 25 = 200$ units, since the most we can have is all containers filled.

Maximum inventory = $nC = DT$

Inventory can be decreased by reducing the size of the containers or the number of containers used. This is done by reducing the time required to circulate a container including its machine setup time, run time, wait times, or move times. When any of these times has been reduced, then management can remove Kanban cards from the system and a corresponding number of containers. It is the responsibility of managers and workers in a JIT system to reduce inventory by a constant cycle of improvement. Reducing lead time is the key, as we have already stressed in Chapter 15.

Kanban links all work centers in a production facility and the vendors as shown in Figure 16.6. All material is pulled through by the final assembly schedule, based on a highly visible shop floor and vendor control system.

REDUCING SETUP TIME AND LOT SIZES

Reducing setup time is important since it increases available capacity, increases flexibility to meet schedule changes, and reduces inventory. As setup time approaches zero, the ideal lot size of 1 unit can be reached.

In conventional repetitive production, we have concentrated on reducing run times per unit and more or less ignored setup time. When long runs of thousands of units are anticipated, run times naturally are of more importance than setup times. A better solution is to concentrate on reducing both setup times and run times. This requires additional attention by engineers, managers, and workers to the setup process itself.

Since setup time has received so little attention, phenomenal reductions are possible. For example, at General Motors, the time required to change a die in a large punch press was reduced from 6 hours to 18 minutes.[5] This allowed dramatic reductions in inventory from $1 million to $100,000, reductions in lead times, and greater utilization of capacity.

---

[5] *APICS Conference Proceedings,* Los Angeles, July 1983.

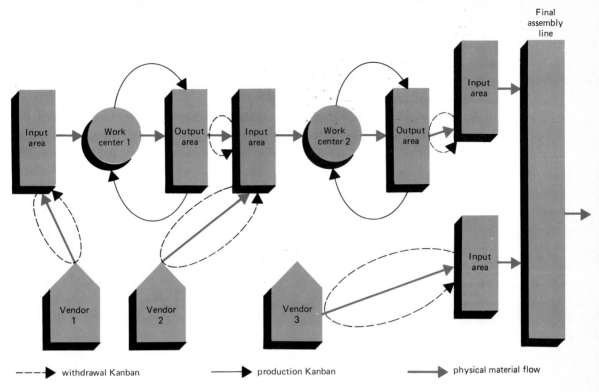

FIGURE 16.6   Complete Kanban system.
Source: Robert W. Hall, Driving the Productivity Machine: Production Planning and Control
in Japan, *American Production and Inventory Control Society, 1981.*

Single setups are being sought in many companies. Single setup refers to a setup time that has a single digit in minutes. One-touch setups are also being pursued, which refers to a setup with less than 1 minute. These low setup times can be achieved by two steps. First, external and internal setups are separated. The term "internal setup" refers to actions that require the machine to be stopped, while external setups can be done while the machine is operating. After separating internal and external setups, as much of the setup as possible is converted from internal to external. This is done, for example, by using two sets of dies, one inside the machine and one outside; by having quick change adjustments; and by employing cleverly designed tools and fixtures. Once the machine is stopped, it can then be quickly converted to the new product since internal setup has been minimized. Much can be done once people realize the importance of quick changeover. In some companies the workers even practice setups in order to reduce the time.

Reducing setup times, lot sizes, and lead times is the engine which drives JIT. These reductions make it possible to remove Kanban cards and thus decrease inventory on a continual basis.

16.6   **LAYOUT AND EQUIPMENT**

Installation of a JIT system has a natural effect on layout and equipment. The plant evolves toward a more streamlined flow and automated plant because lot sizes are reduced and problems are constantly resolved making automation possible.

The effect of JIT on layout is shown in Figure 16.7. In part *a* of the figure, an initial layout is shown in which suppliers deliver to a stockroom and parts are placed in stockrooms after certain stages of production are completed. In part *b* of the figure, a JIT system has been implemented, and all stockrooms have been eliminated. In this case, all stock is kept on the shop floor as part of the JIT system. Part *c* of the figure shows that JIT has evolved to a group technology (GT) layout. In this case, the work centers have been redefined so that parts can flow smoothly

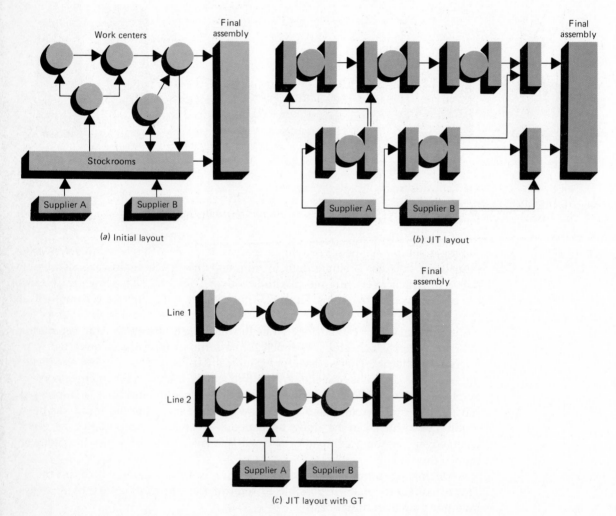

FIGURE 16.7 Effect of JIT on layout. JIT layout with GT.

from one work station to the next. Most of the inventory buffers, next to each machine, have been eliminated as the parts flow from one station to the next. It is a natural consequence of JIT to evolve toward GT and feeder-line types of layouts. More automation is also possible as lot sizes approach 1 unit.

With a JIT system, superb maintenance of equipment is required. Since inventories have been cut to the bone, equipment must be kept in a good state of repair. Workers take responsibility for most of their own maintenance, which gives them more control over production. Maintenance time is also provided between shifts for routine and preventive maintenance actions.

 EFFECT ON WORKERS

One of the critical things needed to make a JIT system work is multifunction workers. In most cases, each worker must be able to operate several machines in a group, going from one to the next to make the parts required. Since parts are not produced unless they are needed, the worker must be able to shut off the machine and move on to another job where parts are needed. The worker must also be able to set up machines, do routine maintenance, and inspect the parts. This ordinarily requires workers who are cross-trained in several different skills.

Moving toward a flexible work force may require changing the way workers are paid and rewarded. Pay is often based on seniority and job skill level. New pay systems are needed which reward workers on the basis of the number of different jobs they can perform. This will encourage workers to learn more skills and to become more flexible.

It can be difficult, but not impossible, to use JIT in a union environment. Unions often are organized along skill or craft lines, and they do not tend to encourage flexibility in the work force. As a result, management will need to work closely with unions to develop the kind of work force needed for JIT.

Methods are needed to engage the workers and engineers actively in problem-solving activities. In JIT systems, quality circles and suggestion systems are used for this purpose. An environment of participation must be created in order to get all employees to contribute toward problem solving on the shop floor.

JIT cannot be implemented without full worker understanding and cooperation. Management must ensure that workers understand their new roles and accept the JIT approach to manufacturing. So many changes are required, as indicated above, that JIT cannot possibly succeed without the active and enthusiastic support of all managers and employees. JIT is not simply another program but a whole new approach to manufacturing.

 VENDORS

Just as employees are required to change, so are the company's vendors. Under JIT, vendors are treated much as internal work centers are treated. Vendors receive Kanban cards and special containers, and they are expected to make frequent deliveries just in time for the next production stage. Vendors are viewed as the external factory and as part of the production team.

With a JIT system, as many as four deliveries are required each day, provided the vendor is located in the same vicinity. Vendors located at a distance may have local warehouses where they receive bulk shipments and then break them down for frequent deliveries to the customer. This is not desirable, however, since too much inventory builds up in the pipeline and reaction time is too long. Local vendors with short lead times are preferred.

Vendors are given specific delivery times rather than shipment dates. For example, a vendor may be required to deliver parts at 8 a.m., 10 a.m., 12 noon, and 2 p.m. On each delivery, the vendor picks up the empty containers and associated withdrawal Kanban cards. Only that number of containers is filled for the next delivery. Deliveries are made directly to the assembly line without receiving or inspection. This requires complete confidence in the vendor's quality. It also greatly reduces paperwork, lead time, inventory, the number of receiving areas, and required storage space.

In some cases, where it is too expensive to make several deliveries each day, vendors may get together and make round-robin deliveries. In this case, for example, one vendor may go to three other vendors plus his own shop for the 8 a.m. delivery. Another vendor will make the 10 a.m. run and so on. This method can save on transportation expenses for small-lot deliveries.

With the JIT system there is a tendency to use single-source vendors. This is done in order to establish a long-term relationship with the vendor and to ensure the quality of parts needed. A complete reversal of thinking is needed here since we would ordinarily assume that the single vendor might price-gouge the customer and more than one source is needed to keep the vendors honest. Single-vendor prices, however, can be kept in line provided the vendors have a long-term contract and price stability is negotiated as part of the contract. This requires a totally different type of vendor-customer relationship than we have had in the past.

As an example, General Motors has established an "integrated supplier program" in order to move toward a JIT system.[6] The features of this program are as follows:

1. *Early vendor selection.* Vendors are selected before the part reaches final design, so the design can be worked out completely with the vendor.
2. *Family of parts sourcing.* A vendor takes responsibility for an entire family of parts, thereby allowing the vendor to establish group technology layouts and economic volumes.
3. *Long-term relationship.* An exclusive contract for the life of the part is given to the vendor in exchange for a specific price schedule over the life of the part. Sometimes future price reductions or increases are specified in the schedule.
4. *Cost-analysis-based price negotiations.* Since the market does not operate in the usual sense, negotiations for the price are based on costs.
5. *Paperwork reduction in receiving and inspection.* This results in a direct savings to the customer and the vendor.

---

[6]APICS Los Angeles Conference, July 1983.

Changing vendor relations is one of the most important aspects of a JIT system.

16.9 COMPARISON WITH MRP SYSTEMS

There are many differences between JIT and MRP systems. Some of the most important differences are as follows:

MRP uses a planning philosophy. The emphasis is on constructing a valid material plan and then executing according to that plan. In contrast, JIT emphasizes eliminating waste and control of the shop floor. This is done by reducing inventories, exposing problems, and pulling materials through the plant. MRP takes the plant as given; JIT does not.

While MRP utilizes computers and sophisticated information processing, JIT uses a simple visual control system. MRP produces shop orders, purchase orders, exception notices, and a great deal of paperwork to control the plant. JIT has reusable Kanban cards, which serve as shop orders or purchase orders. JIT has minimum paperwork and does not require computerization, although computers can be used in combination with JIT concepts.

JIT requires a stable master schedule which is uniform from day to day and hour to hour. MRP allows a highly variable master schedule. Of course, one can use a JIT-type schedule with an MRP system, but then all the computer power is not needed.

JIT seeks to achieve low setup times to make small lot sizes economical. MRP takes setup times as given. With MRP systems, either lot sizes are set by edict or the tradeoff between setup and carrying cost is given consideration. Long runs and large lot sizes are considered acceptable in traditional MRP approaches.

With JIT, vendors are considered part of the team. Long-term relationships are encouraged, and frequent deliveries are expected. With MRP, vendors are often treated as adversaries. Single sourcing is frowned upon, and vendors are pitted against each other for the best prices.

With JIT systems, workers are responsible for producing quality parts just in time to support the next process. Workers participate in problem solving and are charged with improving productivity and quality. With MRP, workers are a part of the system. They are controlled and specialized to a single job. The worker's role is to follow the plan.

MRP and JIT systems are different in almost every respect. Goddard (1982) has summarized these differences in Box 16.3.

Despite the differences, both MRP and JIT systems have their particular areas of usefulness. In repetitive production, JIT probably gives the best results, provided the environmental conditions required by a JIT system can be achieved (stable master schedule, cooperative vendors, multifunction workers, etc.). MRP systems give the best results for the job shop or small batch environment, where production is nonrepetitive in nature. In a semirepetitive environment, perhaps a combination of JIT and MRP systems will be the most effective. In this case, MRP is used to plan materials in advance, and JIT is used to control the shop floor. This type of combined MRP and JIT system, called Syncro MRP, has been pioneered by

BOX 16.3
COMPARISON OF JIT AND MRP SYSTEMS

	JIT philosophy	MRP systems
Inventory	A liability. Every effort must be extended to do away with it.	An asset. It protects against forecast errors. Some safety stock is needed to cover uncertainties.
Lot sizes	Immediate needs only. A minimum replenishment quantity is desired for both manufactured and purchased parts.	Necessary to scheduling. Select a lot size to balance setup cost against holding cost as a general principle. The lot size should not be too large or too small.
Setups	Make them insignificant. This requires either extremely rapid changeover to minimize the impact on production or the availability of extra machines already set up. Fast changeover permits small lot sizes to be practical and allows a wide variety of parts to be made frequently.	Low priority. Maximum output is the usual goal. Rarely does similar thought and effort go into achieving quick changeover.
Queues	Eliminate them. When problems occur, identify the causes and correct them. The correction process is aided when queues are small. If the queues are small, it surfaces the need to identify and fix the cause.	Necessary investment. Queues permit succeeding operations to continue in the event of a problem with the feeding operation. Also, by providing a selection of jobs, the factory management has a greater opportunity to match up varying operator skills and machine capabilities, combine setups and thus contribute to the efficiency of the operation.
Vendors	Co-workers. They're part of the team. Multiple deliveries for all active items are expected daily. The vendor takes care of the needs of the customer, and the customer treats the vendor as an extension of his or her factory.	Adversaries. Multiple sources are the rule, and it's typical to play them off against each other.
Quality	Zero defects. If quality is not 100 percent, production is in jeopardy.	Tolerate some scrap. We usually track what the actual scrap has been and develop formulas for predicting it.
Equipment maintenance	Constant and effective. Machine breakdowns must be minimal.	As required. But not critical because we have queues available.
Lead times	Keep them short. This simplifies the job of marketing, purchasing, and manufacturing as it reduces the need for expediting.	The longer the better. Most supervisors and purchasing agents want more lead time, not less.
Workers	Management by consensus. Changes are not made until consensus is reached whether or not a bit of arm twisting is involved. The vital ingredient of "ownership" is achieved.	Management by edict. New systems are installed in spite of the workers, no thanks to the workers. Then we concentrate on measurements to determine whether or not they're doing it.

Source: Adapted from Walter E. Goddard, "Kanban Versus MRP II—Which is Best for You?" *Modern Materials Handling,* November 1982.

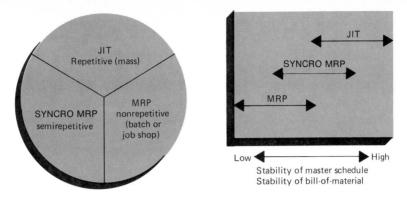

FIGURE 16.8   Uses of MRP and JIT.
Source: J. Nakane and Robert W. Hall, "Japanese Production Systems," in Lee and Schwendiman (eds.), Management by Japanese Systems, *New York: Praeger Publications, 1982.*

the Yamaha Motor Co. [see Hall (1981)]. Figure 16.8 summarizes the use of JIT and MRP.

IMPLEMENTATION OF JIT

The first and most successful application of JIT systems was at the Toyota Motor Company in Japan. As we have mentioned, Kawasaki U.S.A. in Nebraska started implementation of JIT in 1980. Implementation has been achieved in many other U.S. companies, including Ford, General Electric, General Motors, Eaton, Motorola, Black & Decker, Briggs and Stratton, Hewlett-Packard, IBM, John Deere, Bendix, Mercury Marine, Omark, Rockwell, Westinghouse, Tennant, 3M, and Honeywell.[7]

The full effect of JIT is still unknown, but some preliminary results are available. In the auto industry, inventory turns of 50 to 100 are possible compared with 10 to 20 for traditional approaches [Sugimori et al. (1977)]. In motorcycle production, JIT has given inventory turns of about 20 compared with 3 to 5 in traditional companies [see Pegels (1982)]. JIT has also improved quality, reduced costs, and improved flexibility in these same companies.

Implementation of JIT, however, is a difficult proposition. To facilitate implementation, Hall (1982) has suggested the following approach:

1. Obtain commitment from top management. Make sure that they know what changes will be required and that they will provide the leadership to adopt the JIT approach. Prepare a plan for implementation.
2. Gain the cooperation of the work force. Strong leadership is needed on the shop floor to make JIT work. Guarantee stable employment, engage in training, and encourage participation. Small-group improvement activities such as quality circles should be used to get all employees involved in problem solving. Begin cross-training the work force.

---

[7]APICS Los Angeles Conference, July 1983, and Schonberger (1986).

3. Start with the final assembly line. Level production to be almost identical every day. Reduce setup times until models can be mixed. Use standard containers for parts, and make them readily accessible to the assembly line.

4. Working backward from final assembly, reduce setup times and lot sizes in fabrication areas to match the lot sizes needed in final assembly. Remove inventory from the storerooms, and put it on the shop floor.

5. Balance fabrication rates with final assembly production rates. This may require correction of capacity shortfalls. Provide spare capacity in all areas. If any work center falls behind, it will need some spare capacity in order to catch up.

6. Extend JIT to the vendors. First, stabilize their delivery schedule, and then ask for frequent deliveries. Remove the inventory needed to cover long times and variances. Help vendors with quality assurance to meet your specifications. Negotiate long-term contracts with vendors.

It appears that JIT is gaining popularity as the preferred method for repetitive production. JIT has such a major impact that it's being compared with the Ford moving assembly line and the Taylor system as great innovations in production management. The assumptions of the JIT system are certainly opposed to most of the traditional assumptions about repetitive manufacturing. It will take a great deal of effort to implement JIT systems, but there is no choice for economic survival in many repetitive industries.

16.11   KEY POINTS

The JIT system was described in this chapter as a major approach to repetitive manufacturing. We have seen how parts should be produced just in time rather than just in case they are needed. This is accomplished by a simple visual system of production control and dedication toward constant reductions in inventories.

Key points covered in the chapter are these:

- The JIT system is based on a philosophy of eliminating waste and utilizing the full capability of each worker. This system was originally developed in Japan but is now being used in the United States.
- The objective of JIT is to improve return on investment. This is done by increasing revenues (through quality, delivery, and flexibility improvements), reducing costs, and reducing the investment required.
- To use JIT, the master schedule must be stabilized and leveled. This requires constant daily production, within the time frame of the master schedule, and mixed model assembly. As a result, the demand on preceding work centers is nearly constant.
- The Kanban system is used to pull parts through to meet the master assembly schedule. A fixed number of containers is provided for each part required. When these containers are full, no more parts are produced, thus limiting the inventory of each part. Constant improvement activities are encouraged by workers and management to reduce the number of containers, size of containers, and inventory.

- Reducing lot sizes, setup times, and lead times is the key to decreasing inventories in a JIT system. The objective is a lot size of 1 unit. This is done through small-group improvement activities and management and labor cooperative efforts.
- JIT affects plant layout by requiring much less space and encouraging movement toward group technology layouts.
- JIT requires multifunction workers who can operate several machines and perform setup, maintenance, and inspection activities. Moving toward a flexible work force will require changing the way workers are selected, trained, evaluated, and rewarded.
- New vendor relationships must be established to make JIT work. Frequent deliveries and reliable quality are required. Often, long-term single-source contracts will be negotiated with vendors.
- JIT systems are best suited to repetitive manufacturing. MRP is suited to job shop or batch production, and mixed MRP-JIT systems are best for semirepetitive manufacturing.
- Implementation of JIT systems requires a staged progression of activities. Top management must provide leadership and support. The final assembly schedule must be leveled, followed by leveling of fabrication processes and vendor schedules. Lot sizes and lead times must be reduced on all stages of production. Intensive education of workers and management at all levels is needed.

QUESTIONS

1. Visit a repetitive manufacturing facility in your area. What are the major causes of inventory? Be sure to ask about lot sizes and setup times. Would a JIT system work in this facility? Why or why not?
2. Why did the JIT approach evolve in Japan and not in the western countries?
3. Define repetitive manufacturing, and compare it with job lot or batch manufacturing.
4. Why is a stable master schedule required for JIT systems? How stable do you think the master schedule must be?
5. How can lot sizes and inventories be reduced in a JIT system? Mention specific approaches.
6. Why has repetitive manufacturing tended to use long runs and large lot sizes in the past?
7. Describe vendor relations both before and after installation of a JIT approach.
8. What are the effects of a JIT system on workers and managers?
9. Contrast and compare JIT and MRP systems.
10. What are the most critical things needed to implement JIT? Compare these things to implementation of an MRP system.
11. Will the EOQ formula work in a JIT environment? Discuss.
12. Discuss how JIT reduces costs (material, labor, overhead)—not including inventory. Be specific.
13. Are there repetitive manufacturing firms that should not use JIT? Describe them.

PROBLEMS

1. Calculate the daily production quantities and sequences from the following monthly requirements. Assume the month has 20 production days.

a. 5000 A, 2500 B, and 3000 C
b. 2000 A, 3000 B, and 6000 C

2. Suppose a JIT work center is being operated with a container size of 25 units and a demand rate of 100 units per hour. Also assume it takes 180 minutes for a container to circulate.
   a. How many containers are required to operate this system?
   b. How much maximum inventory can accumulate?
   c. How many Kanban cards are needed?

3. Suppose a work center has a setup plus run time of 30 minutes to make 50 parts. Also assume it takes 10 minutes to move a standard container of 50 parts to the next work center, and the demand rate is 1 part per minute throughout the day.
   a. Schedule this situation by drawing a picture of when work center A should be producing and idle and when movements of containers take place from A to B, the using work center.
   b. How many standard containers are needed for this part to circulate from the picture in part a.
   c. Use the formula $n = \dfrac{DT}{C}$ to calculate the number of containers.

4. For a particular operation, the setup time is 10 minutes at a cost of $15 in lost machine time and labor. The run time is 50 minutes to produce a standard lot of 400 parts. Assume a holding cost of $2 per part per month and a demand rate of 20,000 parts per month. It takes 3 hours to circulate a container of parts.
   a. Calculate the EOQ for this part.
   b. How many standard containers are needed?
   c. If the setup time can be cut to 1 minute, recalculate the lot size and number of containers needed.

5. A company is in the business of machining parts which go through various work centers. Suppose work center A feeds work center B with parts. The following times (in minutes) are given for each work center.

	Work center	
	A	B
Setup time	3	2
Run time (per part)	0.5	0.1
Move time	6	8

A standard Kanban container holds 50 parts which are transferred from work center A to work center B. The demand rate at work center B is 4 parts per minute.
   a. How many Kanban containers are needed for this situation?
   b. If move time is cut in half, what does this do to the number of containers needed? How much will this change reduce inventory?

6. A machine currently has a setup time of 2 hours and a setup cost of $10 per hour in labor and lost machine time. It costs 25 percent to carry parts in inventory for a year, and 100 parts are produced per hour by the machine. Assume that the plant operates 2000 hours per year and that the circulation time for each Kanban container is 24 hours. Each part costs $50 to make. The demand rate for parts is 100,000 units per year.
   a. What is the EOQ for this part?
   b. How many Kanban containers are needed using the lot size calculated in part a.

c. What would be the effect of reducing the setup time in this case to 10 minutes? Recalculate the EOQ and the number of Kanban containers needed.

7. Suppose that a JIT work center is being operated with a lot size of 50 units. Assume 200 parts are being demanded per hour and it takes 3 hours to circulate a container including all setup, run, move, and idle time.

a. Calculate the number of Kanban containers required.

b. What is the maximum inventory which will accumulate?

c. What can be done to reduce the inventory level? Suggest alternatives.

SELECTED BIBLIOGRAPHY

GODDARD, WALTER E.: "Kanban versus MRP II—Which Is Best for You?" *Modern Materials Handling,* November 1982.

———: *Just-in-Time: Surviving by Breaking Tradition,* Essex Junction, Vt.: Oliver Wight, Ltd., 1986.

HALL, ROBERT W.: *Driving the Productivity Machine: Production Planning and Control in Japan,* American Production and Inventory Control Society, 1981.

———: "The Toyota Kanban System," in Sang Lee and Gary Schwendiman (eds.), *Management by Japanese Systems,* New York: Praeger Publications, 1982, pp. 144–151.

———: *Attaining Manufacturing Excellence,* Homewood, Ill.: Dow Jones–Irwin, 1987.

———: *Zero Inventories,* Homewood, Ill.: Dow Jones–Irwin, 1983.

MONDEN, YASUHIRO: "Adaptable Kanban System Helps Toyota Maintain Just-in-Time Production," *Industrial Engineering,* May 1981, pp. 29–46.

———: "How Toyota Shortened Supply Lot Production Time, Waiting Time, and Conveyance Time," *Industrial Engineering,* September 1981, pp. 22–30.

———: "Smoothed Production Lets Toyota Adapt to Demand Changes and Reduce Inventory," *Industrial Engineering,* August 1981, pp. 42–51.

———: *Toyota Production System: Practical Approach to Production Management,* Industrial Engineering and Management Press, Institute of Industrial Engineering, 1983.

NAKANE, J., and ROBERT W. HALL: "Management Specs for Stockless Production," *Harvard Business Review,* May–June 1983.

NELLEMANN, DAVID O., and LEIGHTON SMITH: "Just-in-Time vs. Just-in-Case Production/Inventory Systems: Concepts Borrowed Back from Japan," *Production and Inventory Management,* vol. 23, no. 2, 2d quarter 1982, pp. 12–21.

PEGELS, C. CARL: "The Kanban Production Management Information System," In Sang Lee and Gary Schwendiman (eds.), *Management by Japanese Systems,* New York: Praeger Publications, 1982, pp. 152–164.

RICE, JAMES W., and TAKEO YOSHIKAWA: "A Comparison of Kanban and MRP Concepts for the Control of Repetitive Manufacturing Systems," *Production and Inventory Management,* vol. 23, no. 1, 1st quarter 1982, pp. 1–14.

SCHONBERGER, RICHARD J.: *Japanese Manufacturing Techniques: Nine Hidden Lessons in Simplicity,* New York: Free Press, 1982.

———: "KANBAN ("Just-in-Time") Application at Kawasaki, USA," *APICS Conference Proceedings,* 1981, pp. 188–191.

———: "Selecting the Right Manufacturing Inventory System: Western and Japanese Approaches," *Production and Inventory Management,* vol. 24, no. 2, 2d quarter 1983, pp. 33–44.

———: *World Class Manufacturing,* New York: Free Press, 1986.

SHINGO, SHIGEO: *A Revolution in Manufacturing: The SMED System,* Stamford, Conn.: Productivity Press, 1985.

SUGIMORI, Y., K. KUSUNOKI, F. CHO, and S. UCHIKAWA: "Toyota Production System and Kanban System Materialization of Just-in-Time and Respect for Human System," *International Journal of Production Research,* vol. 15, no. 6, 1977, pp. 553–564.

PART FIVE

WORK FORCE MANAGEMENT

WORK
FORCE

- **MANAGING THE WORK FORCE IN OPERATIONS**
- **JOB DESIGN**
- **WORK MEASUREMENT**

Part 5 deals with one of the most important responsibilities of operations managers: managing the work force. A broad view is taken toward the subject, beginning with a discussion of managing people for performance and proceeding through job design and work measurement. The discussion is based on the idea that work should be managed from a sociotechnical perspective and that management should include the process considerations first described in Part 2 as well as the behavioral considerations developed here. The combined management of both technical and behavioral aspects of work can result in operations which are socially stimulating as well as productive.

Chapter 17 presents an approach to managing the people

assigned to operations. The performance objective of operations is described, and some management principles which should lead to improved performance in operations are defined. The chapter ends with examples of how these principles of work force management have been applied in practical situations.

Chapter 18 focuses on job design decisions related to managing the work force. A sociotechnical approach is utilized which combines the technical and human aspects of job design. The principles of Frederick Taylor's scientific management approach are described in some detail, as are the various approaches to job enrichment. By properly combining these two approaches, a sociotechnical job design can be achieved.

After jobs are designed, a critical element in managing the work force is the measurement of productivity and work. In Chapter 19, various approaches to work measurement, productivity measurement, and methods improvement are described. It is suggested that the selection of an appropriate measurement technique should depend on its intended use, its cost, and the behavioral reactions of the workers. The conditions under which one measurement approach or another might be preferred are explained.

Managing the work force is always a central responsibility of the operations function. How well it is managed determines the quality, flexibility, delivery, and cost of operations. It is only through the effective management of people that goods and services are produced and the objectives of operations met.

Managing the Work Force in Operations

When operations managers are asked, "What is your greatest responsibility or your most important problem?" the usual reply is, "Management of our people." Yet the work force is one of the most poorly managed resources in operations.

In the past, the literature of operations management has paid little attention to management of the work force in operations. Instead, the attention has been directed to quantitative models and the technical aspects of operations. At the same time, psychologists and organizational theorists have conducted a great deal of research on how humans behave in organizations. There is now a need for more application of this behavioral research in the operations function, along with an operations management point of view regarding management of the work force. Such a viewpoint will necessarily draw heavily on psychology and organizational behavior as underlying disciplines.

Today's work force consists of not only blue-collar workers, but white-collar professionals as well. In many manufacturing organizations there are more white-collar workers than blue-collar workers. Sometimes work force has the connotation of blue collar only, but we use the term "work force" in the broader sense to include both white-collar and blue-collar workers.

The purpose of this chapter is to develop a broad perspective regarding management of the work force in operations. It will also provide a point of departure for the more detailed issues of job design and work measurement to be discussed in the next two chapters. This chapter begins with a discussion of objectives and standard work force management approaches. New approaches to managing the work force, including ideas from Japanese companies and the best managed American companies, are then described. The chapter concludes with ideas on how a philosophy of work force management can be developed. What the Ford Motor Company has done to improve its work force management is described in Box 17.1.

BOX 17.1

THE FORD MOTOR COMPANY

In the early 1980s Ford found itself in trouble with large financial losses and a questionable management style. The autocratic management style of Henry Ford I and II was rampant throughout the organization. Now, however, Ford is being hailed for its product quality and sleek cars, particularly with the Taurus and the Sable. Moreover, huge profits are being made and productivity is up.

To achieve this turnaround, Ford reluctantly acknowledged that some of its problems were rooted in the management style being used. Management had maintained a culture built on top-down directives and suppression of any ideas that had not originated at the top. Bosses were supreme and departments did not work well together.

Ford executives discovered that management style can determine the success of an organization to a great degree. Overhauling its corporate culture wasn't an act of idealism. It was one of many techniques the company used to meet global competition and become a low-cost, high-quality producer.

The process of change started with a diagnostic tool that measures the actual versus the potential level of participation, commitment and creativity in a given organization. These three factors collectively make up a measure of corporate competence. In one division, for example, Ford found that competence was extremely low. The division's actual competence index fell in the 16th percentile of a normative sample of 1,300 individuals who had rated their own business organizations. The division had the potential to have a competency rating in the 84th percentile.

In terms of participation—defined as the extent to which people are actively engaged in planning, decision-making, and day-to-day problem solving in their own work—the division scored in the 14th percentile. The commitment scale—the feeling on the part of individuals that their ideas, opinions and thoughts count—registered another poor 14th percentile. Creativity—a measure of the opportunity to exercise one's creative talent, novel insights, and ingenuity in daily problem solving was better, but only slightly, falling in the 21st percentile. The results were a real eye opener. The division vice president observed, "they were devastating. We thought we were real good managers, but that's not exactly how our employees perceived us."

Ford developed an elaborate training program to teach managers and workers how to improve competence. This involved educating 20,000 managers and 10,000 non-managers in the concepts and techniques for improving participation, creativity, and commitment. As a result, subsequent measurement showed that competence had greatly improved to nearly its full potential.

Extracted from Brian Moskal, "Glasnost in Dearborn," *Industry Week*, Sept. 21, 1987.

17.1 OBJECTIVES IN MANAGING THE WORK FORCE

Since many of the controversies regarding specific approaches to managing the work force are related to differences concerning objectives, our discussion begins with the objectives of work force management. In operations, the most important objective of work force managers must be achievement of performance. The performance objective is sometimes stated as productivity, but the term "productivity" is too narrow. Performance includes all the objectives in operations including cost, quality, delivery, and flexibility, as originally defined in Chapter 2.

The mention of performance in operations sometimes conjures up the image of a "slavedriver" who cares little about people. This image implies that the best way to get performance from people is to drive them. But the objective of performance in operations implies nothing about how the objective is to be achieved. As a matter of fact, a "people-oriented" approach *may* result in more performance than the "slavedriver" approach.

It should also be stated, at the outset, that the objective of work force management is not to *maximize* performance. Rather, the objective of the work force manager is to maximize performance within the applicable constraints. The constraints tend to prevent the operations work force manager from pursuing undesirable social, psychological, or environmental solutions which may not be represented by the performance objective itself.

Another view of the work force objective is that of satisfactory performance rather than maximum performance; Herbert Simon (1960) calls this "satisficing." Satisfactory performance can be defined as that level of performance which permits the organization to stay in business and attract the people, capital, governmental support, and customers that it needs to survive. Satisfactory performance is therefore related to long-run survival of the organization rather than to maximum performance per se.

It should be clear that the satisfaction or happiness of the work force is not the organization's *primary* objective. If the work force is happy but the organization ceases to survive, there will be no jobs. This is not to say that both objectives—performance and satisfaction—cannot be achieved simultaneously. As a matter of fact, in many cases this can be done by a proper management approach. But satisfaction of the work force should be viewed as a means, not as an end in itself.

For many years, a satisfaction-performance controversy has been reported in the literature of organizational behavior. Some have theorized that satisfaction caused performance, and that therefore satisfaction could be pursued as an end in its own right. This thinking led to the cliché that "a happy worker is a productive worker."

More recent behavioral research suggests that satisfaction does not cause performance and that probably the reverse is true. It follows that operations managers should not pursue satisfaction of the work force as an objective, hoping that performance will automatically follow. Rather, the manager should pursue an acceptable performance level, and satisfaction will follow if the worker is properly rewarded for the performance achieved. [See Lawler (1977) for a review of this issue.]

WHO MANAGES THE WORK FORCE?

The immediate answer to the question "Who manages the work force?" is "The supervisor." But the full answer is somewhat more complicated. The personnel office has a great deal of influence on what can and cannot be done in managing the work force, top management often becomes involved in work force management decisions, and all levels of operations managers are involved (top, middle, and lower). Thus, while the supervisor may be *responsible* for managing the work force, many others are also involved.

The responsibility of the supervisor is to manage the work force within the constraints imposed by the organization. Because of multiple and conflicting constraints, the supervisor's role may be nearly impossible to fulfill. As a result, the first-level supervisor can be a person caught in the middle. In some cases, top management has become the worker's manager by usurping the supervisor's authority. Unions are the first to recognize this. They view supervisors as powerless and realize that they must bypass the supervisory level to get things done. This is a reflection of the fact that top management is making the crucial decisions in managing the work force. In these cases, top management has failed to properly delegate responsibility to lower levels of work force management. As a result, the supervisor is caught in the middle between top management and the worker.

The number of staff specialists has been continually increasing in business. These specialists include engineers, accountants, lawyers, personnel staff, quality-control staff, and data processing staff. The role of the staff should be to support and assist the line managers. However, staff specialists who have channels to top or middle management can cause problems for first-line supervisors rather than helping them. For example, staff reports may be developed without the knowledge or participation of supervisors. When these reports are given to upper management, supervisors are asked to explain or defend themselves to their bosses. The supervisor is once again caught in the middle between the staff and upper management.

This situation is, of course, not typical of all organizations. Many managers, recognizing the pressures on first-level supervisors, have aligned responsibility and authority at the first level of supervision. Thus the first-level supervisor's role is expanded to a professional management job which is respected and viewed as a key managerial position. Under these circumstances, a proper relationship between line and staff is established and the work force managers are given the authority they need to achieve the expected results. Such a supervisor's job is demanding and can lead to a position in general management.

Also, in some cases the traditional supervisor has been eliminated. The supervisor is replaced by a team leader, who may be elected by the workers. The role of supervisor is drastically changed from one of control to one of coaching and team building. While the role of the supervisor is changed in this model, the importance is not diminished. Good supervisors are needed no matter what the organizational arrangement might be [Klein and Posey (1986)].

Now that we have identified the objectives and managers involved in managing the work force, we will turn to work force principles. These classic principles are defined in terms of basic management concepts. After defining these principles, we will discuss some new ways of thinking about work force management.

17.3 PRINCIPLES OF WORK FORCE MANAGEMENT

In managing the work force, there has been a tendency to follow fads, such as these:

- Human relations of the 1930s and 1940s
- Participative management of the 1950s
- T groups of the 1960s
- Job enrichment of the 1970s
- Quality circles of the 1980s

This is not to say that the above approaches to work force management are not useful. On the contrary, each of these approaches is useful under a particular set of circumstances. The problem is that some managers have applied these behavioral methods as a panacea.

Rather than advocating any specific behavioral approach to work force management, we shall propose a broad set of principles that can be used in a wide variety of situations. These principles are derived from organizational theory and modern management thinking. In practice, many work force managers follow them instinctively.

The proposed principles of good work force management are as follows:

1. Match the worker and the job. This principle implies that people should be selected for jobs on the basis of their individual differences and preferences for work. It also implies that jobs should be designed for the work force that is available. If the work force is well educated, intelligent, and able to accept responsibility, broad jobs should be designed. Individuals should also be counseled to accept jobs which meet their personal needs.

This principle implies that jobs can be overdesigned as well as underdesigned. In other words, some people might be asked to accept too much responsibility while others are asked to accept too little. How the worker and the job can be matched is described in Chapter 18.

2. Clearly define responsibilities of the worker. When job responsibilities are unclear or constantly changing, workers feel frustrated. The result can be poor quality, low productivity, and conflict between individuals. Therefore, one of the principles of good work-force management is to define job responsibilities clearly for all workers. This would normally be done through written job descriptions or statements of objectives which are kept up to date.

3. Set standards of performance. Standards of performance should be developed for all jobs. These specify what the worker is expected to accomplish and make it possible to decentralize more control to the worker on the basis of performance. When performance standards are not set, workers can become confused about their responsibilities and overly dependent on the supervisor for job direction. Several techniques for standard setting and work measurement are described in Chapter 19.

4. Ensure communications and employee involvement. People need to be informed about company policies, and they need to feel that they can influence policies through participation in decision making. The idea of participative management (or employee involvement) has been widely supported by research studies as a way to gain improved performance. Performance is also improved when two-way communications are established between management and workers.

5. Provide training. Often training is viewed as a perk in organizations. When budgets are reduced, training is the first thing to be cut back. Training should begin the first day on the job to ensure that the employee is competent in the work to be performed before beginning work. Although this may sound like an obvious idea, trial-and-error learning on the job is widely practiced. Employee development should be continued through training and education so that successive career advancement is possible. Training must be continuous in nature in today's world where knowledge is rapidly changing.

6. Ensure good supervision. As we have noted above, there is nothing more fundamental to the worker than good supervision. A supervisor should be competent in both technology and management skills and should possess a sense of fairness in dealing with people. The supervisor should also be genuinely concerned with the welfare of each individual employee while also emphasizing performance and results. According to behavioral theory, when the workers know what performance is expected and participate in developing those expectations, they will be motivated to perform. The supervisor should make sure that this type of performance climate exists.

7. Reward people for performance. When performance standards have been set, it is possible to reward people on the basis of performance. According to behavioral theory, this leads to further performance in expectation of further rewards. [See Nadler and Lawler (1977).] Since the work force manager's primary responsibility is to obtain results, the giving of rewards for performance constitutes the prime method of motivating people toward goals. Rewards can include all forms of compensation (pay, promotion, status, a pat on the back, etc.). Several incentive schemes are described in Chapter 23.

If these principles are followed, the work force will be well managed. High performance and a satisfied work force should result. Of course, the principles will need to be tailored to each situation, as we shall discuss in the remainder of this chapter.

17.4 JAPANESE WORK FORCE MANAGEMENT

An example of the application of work force management principles is the Japanese management approach. Although limited space does not allow us to discuss the entire Japanese approach to management, some of the concepts that are most relevant to management of the work force will be described.[1]

The Japanese have evolved a very interesting concept of worker responsibility. In Japan, the worker is directly responsible for the work methods used. For example, after an industrial engineer has studied a job, the final decision on whether or not the job should be changed rests with the worker. The industrial engineer is a consultant and an adviser to the worker. Because of this relationship, industrial engineers in Japan complain that they are too busy. The workers willingly call the industrial engineers to study their jobs because they are not threatened by change.

A second tradition in some Japanese companies is lifelong employment. With the exception of women and part-time workers, employees stay with the same company for their entire lifetime. This practice, however, applies to only about one-third of all Japanese workers, those employed by the large trading companies [Modic (1987)]. As a result of lifelong employment, the commitment to the company is clear. If employees are not productive, they will not receive wage increases. Management also knows that each employee must be helped to perform, since the company cannot simply replace an unsatisfactory worker. Although lifelong employment has disadvantages too, it establishes a clear relationship between the employees' welfare and that of the company.

Another interesting Japanese practice involves the idea of continuous training. Each Japanese worker is assigned to a group or circle which meets periodically to discuss work-related matters. These training circles are run by the workers, not management. The purpose of the circle is to facilitate communications within the work force, not to solve problems or make decisions. At one meeting, a worker may describe new products which are being developed. At another meeting, a worker might describe scheduling practices used in the company. And at yet another meeting, a worker might describe his or her own job. These circles help expand the worker's vision of the work place, they provide knowledge outside the worker's specialty, and they help integrate the organization. The Japanese also have separate training sessions to enhance and improve each worker's particular

---

[1]The material in this section is largely derived from Drucker (1971) and Lee and Schwendiman (1982).

specialty. But the chief aim of continuous training is to teach the worker more about other jobs in his or her circle.

Japanese companies also tend to promote people primarily on the basis of length of service. An engineer, for example, who starts with the company after college, would be promoted in step along with his or her peers. It is only when the executive level is reached that promotions are based on merit or performance.

Recently, these Japanese practices have begun to be questioned in both Japan and the United States. Shimada (1987) and Ohmae (1987) argue that managers in Japan will need to drastically change some of their practices to succeed in the future. They foresee more job mobility in Japan, and less dependence on consensus management as Japanese culture changes. Also, the Japanese practices may need to be modified in order to work in plants located in the United States and Europe. Japanese management practices should not be seen as a panacea, but should be adapted to the situation and changing conditions.

One of the myths of Japanese management is that it is culture-dependent and cannot be used in the west. The fact that over 600 Japanese plants are being operated in the United States speaks to the increasing use of Japanese management practices in this country. Most of these plants have been very successful with American workers and managers. See Box 17.2 for an example of how Japanese practices are being used by Nissan in Tennessee.

BOX 17.2
NISSAN MOTOR COMPANY

It's 7:25 A.M. at Nissan Motors Company's new truck assembly plant in Smyrna, Tennessee. Rows of autoworkers clad in pale blue work shirts and dark blue trousers (uniforms provided gratis by the company) limber up with five minutes of light calisthenics performed to the taped accompaniment of soothing piano music.

Leading the enlightenment is a former Ford Motor Company executive named Marvin Runyon, 58, who, as Nissan's president of U.S. Operations, has abandoned a jacket and tie in favor of a blue-collar outfit. One and all call him "Marvin."

Runyon's strategy is to boost productivity by encouraging employee participation in day-to-day decision making. "Most U.S. companies operate autocratically from the top down. We try to manage from the bottom up."

To help along change, Runyon has slashed the number of management levels from Detroit's standard 12 to five. He has eliminated executive washrooms, reserved parking spaces, and private dining rooms.

Nissan workers avoid assembly-line drudgery by alternating tasks and by acting as their own inspectors. During breaks and "after hours" employees enjoy the 52 ping-pong tables as well as 27 golf, baseball, basketball, and volley ball teams.

Absenteeism and tardiness are nearly nonexistent, where an honor system prevails. "It blows my mind that I don't have to punch a time clock."

As one worker summarizes, "It's a pleasure to come to a job where everyone pulls together. I go home a lot more peaceful."

Source: The newsletter of the Minnesota chapter of the American Society of Performance Improvement, vol. 4, no. 10, November 1983.

It appears that Japanese practices can be successfully used in the west when they are suitably applied. Although it is difficult to see how the idea of lifelong employment can be implemented, some companies (e.g., 3M, IBM, Hewlett-Packard, and Delta Airlines) have a policy of very low turnover and no layoffs. This is a "best effort" on the part of the company to avoid work force reductions through growth and commitment to people, rather than any guarantee of lifelong employment. Other Japanese practices, such as quality circles, continuous training, and worker responsibility, have been widely applied in the United States.

17.5 NEW APPROACHES TO MANAGING PEOPLE AND ORGANIZATIONS

Recently, a whole new paradigm for management has been emerging. This new school of thought might be characterized as a back-to-the-basics movement—a shift away from the rational management school of thought. According to this new thinking, there has been too much emphasis on planning, analysis, control systems, and the like; and too little emphasis on simplicity, entrepreneurship, values, people, and the customer. As a result, we have developed a bias toward "management by the numbers" rather than action-oriented, hard-hitting, entrepreneurial management in sales and operations.

Perhaps the best-known proponents of this school of thought are Peters and Waterman (1982), who describe the following rational model of management in their best-selling book, *In Search of Excellence.*

1. Big is better because there are economics of scale. As the organization gets larger, carefully coordinate, avoid overlap, and control waste.
2. Planning is needed to ensure profitability and achievement of corporate objectives. Do extensive market research to know what the customer wants, and carefully analyze return-on-investments for all R&D projects. Prepare large and elaborate planning documents.
3. Decision making is the manager's job. Make the correct decisions; then delegate implementation. Replace the whole management team, if necessary, to get implementation right.
4. Control everything. Write elaborate job descriptions. Develop large staffs to set standards, monitor variances, and report deviations. People are an "economic factor" in production.
5. Reward people with monetary incentives. Give the best people large rewards. Weed out the 10 percent to 20 percent who are dead wood and nonperformers.
6. All businesses are essentially the same. Concentrate on the financial reports. The people, products, and equipment are simply those resources you have to align to get results. Above all, don't let quarterly earnings drop.
7. Inspect to control quality. Quality is like everything else—order it to be done. Increase the size of the quality control department, and make it report to the president.

Peters and Waterman develop a contrasting point of view to the rational school of management. Their view is based on studies of 43 medium-to-large successful companies. These excellent companies have performed in the top half of their industries for over 20 years on several measures of performance, including profitability, sales growth, and return on capital. The eight principles which all of these companies seem to pursue are as follows:

1. A bias for action. The excellent companies have a philosophy of "do it–fix it–try it" rather than excessive planning or analysis. They tend to be fluid, recognizing that Murphy's law will certainly creep in and adjustments will be needed. This is done by allowing for mistakes and not insisting on the perfect solution before anything is done. Action is favored over analysis. Their motto is make a little, sell a little, make a little more. There is a tendency toward keeping things simple and driving out complexity. At Procter & Gamble, for instance, the one-page memo is famous.[2]

2. Close to the customer. Everyone talks about customer orientation, but few companies do it. The excellent companies actually stay close to the customer, with an obsession. Everyone has customer contact, corporate staff, engineers, operations, even accountants—not just sales. Service and quality are dominant values in these companies because that is what the customers want most. The service overkill at Frito-Lay (99.5 percent) and at IBM is well known. Most of the excellent companies, but not all of them, emphasize service and quality over low cost. The customer and the market will tell you how much service and quality are required.

3. Autonomy and entrepreneurship. The best companies have found that R&D is a numbers game. To foster innovation, you must be sure that you generate enough failures. Most good ideas get killed at least once, only to come back to life again. Some of the best ideas have been developed despite corporate orders to stop the project. Planning for innovation tends to stifle it. The best way to ensure innovation is to develop product champions. These are people who are full-time, committed fanatics who will pursue and develop new ideas. The traditional form of hierarchical organization is hopeless. Only a fluid, loose organization with information task teams, product champions, and zealots seems to work.

4. Productivity through people. Just as every company says their customers are key, they also say that people are their most important resource. Most companies, however, do not follow through on the people promise. They don't treat people as adults who can be trusted. On the contrary, many companies attempt to control and manage people. The excellent companies, however, have respect for the individual, they turn the average person into a winner, and they give people control over their own destinies. People—not capital—are treated as the primary source of productivity potential. Employment stability and training are emphasized, and people are involved in solving problems on the job. The excellent companies are also tough. They are performance-oriented, but this is born out of mutual respect—not table pounding. The key to a people orientation is trust, open communication, and a great number of "people" programs. For more on this, also see *Theory Z* by Ouchi (1981).

---

[2]Peters and Waterman (1982), p. 50.

5. Hands-on value driven. The excellent companies have identified their basic values—what they stand for. Management and workers at all levels understand these values through constant communication and reinforcement. Most everyone at IBM, for example, knows what service means—trouble-free computing for the user. Top management communicates the central values through several levels of management by constant travel and exposure in the field. At one company this is called (MBWA) Management by Wandering Around. This results in hands-on management of the basic values of the company.

6. Stick to the knitting. "Never acquire a business you don't know how to run" is an axiom in the excellent companies. Most acquisitions go awry because the acquired company has different values and cannot be easily assimilated. In addition, the executives of the acquired company may leave, and all that is left is a shell with some capital, equipment, and inventory.

A *Forbes* article describes Heublein's initial failure in controlling its Colonel Sanders acquisition. Says a Heublein executive, "In the wine and liquor business it doesn't matter what the liquor store looks like. Smirnoff vodka doesn't get the blame if the floor is dirty. And you can control your product at the factory. We simply bought a chain of five thousand little factories all over the world, and we didn't have the experience in handling that kind of operation."[3]

The organizations that branch out but stick to their knitting seem to outperform the others. For example, 3M is organized around the coating and bonding technology with a tremendous range of products and markets, but the basic technology is the same.

7. Simple form, lean staff. Many companies respond to complexity in kind by designing complex systems and structures. The excellent companies, however, strive to deal with complexity with simple organization forms and small staffs. Most of these companies have very few people at the corporate level (less than 100 people in a multibillion dollar company). These companies are also highly decentralized by divisions, and they tend to have fewer middle managers. For example, the typical American company has 15 layers of management between the CEO and line supervisor while Toyota has five levels.[4] The divisions tend to use project teams or product champions rather than complex matrix organization structures. These ad hoc coordinating mechanisms help integrate the hierarchical structure.

Above all else, the excellent companies stress "small is beautiful." Plants are kept at 500 people or less; seldom does a plant have 1000 people even when economics of scale predominate. Divisions are kept small, there is frequently less than $50 or $100 million in sales, and product development teams are kept at 10 or 20 people instead of massive 50- to 100-person projects. These small organizations may actually be more efficient because they are easier to control and manage.

---

[3]Ibid., p. 292.

[4]Ibid., p. 313.

8. Simultaneous loose-tight properties. Rather than have oppressive control systems, the best companies develop controls to manage a few critical variables. The organization is guided by the shared values rather than by elaborate procedure manuals and extensive information systems which monitor every aspect of operations. When rules are formulated, they tend to have a positive cast to reinforce the central values rather than the negative connotations we find in many companies. This type of control system is tight with respect to central values and loose on other dimensions.

Organizations which are managed by the above principles contrast sharply with those managed by the rational philosophy. This "back-to-the-basics" movement emphasizes quality, innovation, informality, customer service, and people. It is action-oriented and flexible rather than overplanned and overcontrolled. This type of an organization, of course, puts operations management and sales "back in the driver's seat." It emphasizes producing value for the customer as the basic goal of the corporation. It stands in contrast to the overemphasis on financial wheeling and dealing, analysis paralysis, and elaborate strategic planning. [See also Hayes and Abernathy (1980).]

The excellent companies are good with numbers, too, but in a different way. They understand that the product and the customer come first, that line managers must have control over the staff, and that too much planning can stifle the organization. Thus, planning and analysis are put in their proper place as supportive to the basic values and purpose of the business. Peters has expanded his original ideas with two more recent books, *A Passion for Excellence* (1985) and *Thriving on Chaos* (1987). These books continue to emphasize innovation and management of change as the new way of life.

17.6 TOWARD A WORK FORCE PHILOSOPHY

There seems to be a trend toward a much different type of work place than we have had in the past. As noted in the books *In Search of Excellence* and *Theory Z*, many of the *best* companies in the United States and Japan have already achieved the new work-place design.

The most striking thing about all these developments is the need for a coherent policy or philosophy about the work force. A program here or an experiment there will not do it. Management must develop a vision of the business and then of the associated role of people. Only when the basic values and policies have been developed should management proceed to implement specific people-oriented programs, for example, quality circles.

This is not being done in some companies—apparently, they are applying the "quick fix" or the latest fad. These companies have not taken the time to understand fully the effects of turnover, absenteeism, layoffs, skill levels, specialization, and other human factors on their business. As a result, no coherent philosophy toward people and the organization exists.

It should be pointed out that this work force philosophy can only be developed and implemented by line management—operations management and general managers. The philosophy should not be developed solely by the human resource office or corporate planners. Line management must provide the leadership to establish a coherent philosophy toward people and then instill the resulting values on a day-to-day basis. This philosophy should, of course, be developed with the assistance of the staff and middle and lower management, but leadership must come from senior line managers.

An example of a coherent work force philosophy and how it is developed might be helpful. Suppose that a business produces telephones and associated electronics for the U.S. market. This business is in repetitive manufacturing and competes on the basis of cost and quality. The competition comes not only from U.S. companies but from offshore. The company has decided to produce only high-volume products with a JIT production system. What kind of a work force policy should this company adopt to be consistent with its business, manufacturing, and marketing policies?

First, the company will need a flexible work force where workers are cross-trained to support the JIT concept. The company may need to pay people based on the number of skills learned rather than only on seniority and traditional job classifications. If a union is involved, negotiations will be needed to gain more flexibility in traditional work force rules and to gain union support for flexibility in skills. Without flexibility, the JIT system will simply not work.

Extensive work force training should be undertaken to give the workers "productivity improvement tools." The workers should be taught problem-solving skills, data analysis techniques, and industrial engineering skills so that they can uncover problems and develop solutions. This is, after all, needed to use a JIT system.

Workers must also be given assurances that they will not be laid off because of productivity improvement. This, too, is part of the work force policy—stable employment—to retain people with a high level of training and to discourage fears about layoffs. This creates an environment where important work force values and skills are retained by the company.

If workers are to be actively involved in productivity improvement, a climate of openness, trust, and participation must be developed. Workers' ideas for improvement should be actively sought, perhaps through a suggestion system or quality circles, and management must seek to implement these ideas whenever possible. Barriers between management and workers must be broken down so that an atmosphere of teamwork can develop. This is all necessary for a JIT system to work effectively.

Finally, the work force must be made responsible for quality. They should understand that quality is essential for JIT to work. Machines should be shut off immediately if there are quality problems and perfect quality must be the goal.

In summary, we have developed a work force philosophy with the following characteristics:

- flexible skills
- training in "productivity improvement tools"

- stable employment
- a climate of openness, trust, and participation
- work force responsibility for perfect quality

This philosophy was developed from the particular circumstances and situation of the company. It is needed in order to compete and to implement the business strategy. Each company will have a somewhat different philosophy depending on its circumstances, but the important point is that each company should have a work force philosophy. The philosophy should be lasting and long-lived. It should not change with each change of top management. The work force philosophy should be changed only when the basic nature of the business changes. It is the responsibility of operations to ensure that such a work force policy is developed and implemented in the company.

17.7 KEY POINTS

The thrust of this chapter is to provide a broad perspective regarding management of the work force in operations. The key points are as follows:

- The work force manager's primary objective should be performance (quality, cost, flexibility, and delivery). Worker satisfaction is not, by itself, a primary objective, but satisfaction may be achieved along with performance.
- Many people are involved in managing the work force: top managers, supervisors, middle managers, unions, and staff specialists. As a result, the supervisor can be caught in the middle between opposing interests. To prevent this situation, work force managers should have authority consistent with the responsibility assigned to them.
- The principles of work force management are: match the worker and the job, set standards of performance, clearly define responsibilities, ensure communications and employee involvement, provide training, ensure good supervision, and reward people for performance. These principles are derived from behavioral theory and management practice.
- The Japanese style of work force management utilizes worker responsibility for production, lifetime employment, continuous training, and uniform promotion. Some of these approaches are being used in the United States.
- A new philosophy of management is emerging which is entrepreneurial and action-oriented in nature. It emphasizes hands-on management which is close to the customer and can achieve productivity through people. It deemphasizes rigid control, elaborate planning, or excessive analysis.
- This chapter emphasizes the need for a coherent philosophy about the work force. The philosophy should be oriented toward the business environment and the operations strategy. This vision of the business and the associated role of people should be in place before specific people-oriented programs are pursued, for example, quality circles.

QUESTIONS

1. Why is the happy worker not necessarily the most productive worker?
2. Should the work force manager be concerned about worker satisfaction? Discuss.
3. The teachers' union in a local school district has advocated that all teachers be paid on the basis of seniority and education. Is this a good basis for rewarding teachers?
4. Susan works in a typing pool. What kinds of rewards might be available for her? How could Susan's performance be measured? Suggest some possible measures.
5. In the ABC Tire Company, the production workers are highly dissatisfied (50 percent say they do not like their jobs). Productivity has been dropping (10 percent decrease last year), and many tires are rejected due to poor quality. As a work force manager, what approach would you take to rectify the situation?
6. East-West Airlines would like to set up a continuous training program for its aircraft maintenance workers. Describe how such a program might work. What would the expected results be?
7. How does the Japanese relationship between line and staff differ from the line-staff relationship in the United States?
8. The employees in the XYZ Company have asked you, as their supervisor, to explain their responsibilities. What would you tell them?
9. Would the answer to Question 8 be any different if the employees were professors, doctors, or lawyers? Explain.
10. For a work force management situation that you are familiar with, describe the important work force management decisions and who makes each of them.

SELECTED BIBLIOGRAPHY

DRUCKER, PETER F.: *Management: Tasks, Responsibilities, Practices,* New York: Harper & Row, 1973.
————: *The Practice of Management,* New York: Harper & Row, 1954.
————: "What We Can Learn from Japanese Management," *Harvard Business Review,* March–April 1971.
FOULKERS, FRED K.: "How Top Nonunion Companies Manage Employees," *Harvard Business Review,* September–October 1981, pp. 90–96.
HAYES, ROBERT: "Why Japanese Factories Work," *Harvard Business Review,* July–August 1981.
HAYES, ROBERT H., and WILLIAM J. ABERNATHY: "Managing Our Way to Economic Decline," *Harvard Business Review,* July–August 1980, pp. 67–77.
HERZBERG, FREDERICK: "One More Time: How Do You Motivate Employees?" *Harvard Business Review,* vol. 46, no. 1, 1968, pp. 53–62.
KLEIN, JANICE A., and PAMELA A. POSEY: "Good Supervisors Are Good Supervisors—Anywhere," *Harvard Business Review,* November–December 1986, pp. 125–128.
LAWLER, EDWARD E. III: "Satisfaction and Behavior," in J. Richard Hackman, Edward E. Lawler III, and Lyman W. Porter (eds.): *Perspectives on Behavior in Organizations,* New York: McGraw-Hill, 1977.
LEE, SANG M., and GARY SCHWENDIMAN (eds.): *Management by Japanese Systems,* New York: Praeger, 1982.
MOSKAL, BRIAN S.: "Glasnost in Dearborn," *Industry Week,* Sept. 21, 1987.
MODIC, STANLEY: "Myths about Japanese Management," *Industry Week,* Oct. 5, 1987.
NADLER, DAVID A., and EDWARD E. LAWLER III: "Motivation: A Diagnostic Approach," in J. Richard Hackman, Edward E. Lawler III, and Lyman W. Porter (eds.): *Perspectives on Behavior in Organizations,* New York: McGraw-Hill, 1977.
OHMAE, KENICHI: *Beyond National Borders: Reflections on Japan and the World,* Homewood, Ill.: Dow Jones-Irwin, 1987.

Ouchi, William: *Theory Z: How American Business Can Meet the Japanese Challenge,* Reading, Mass.: Addison-Wesley, 1981.

Peters, Thomas J., and Robert H. Waterman, Jr.: *In Search of Excellence: Lessons from America's Best-Run Companies,* New York: Harper & Row, 1982.

————: *Thriving on Chaos,* New York: Knopf, 1987.

———— and Nancy Austin: *A Passion for Excellence,* New York: Random House, 1985.

Porter, Lyman W., and Edward E. Lawler III: "What Job Attitudes Tell about Motivation," *Harvard Business Review,* January–February 1968.

Shimada, Haruo: *The Management Challenge: Japanese Views,* Cambridge, Mass.: MIT Press, 1987.

Simon, Herbert A.: *The New Science of Executive Decision Making,* New York: Harper & Row, 1960.

Sirota, David: "Job Enrichment—Is It for Real?" *S.A.M. Journal,* vol. 38, no. 2, April 1973, pp. 22–27.

Skinner, Wickham: "Big Hat, No Cattle: Managing Human Resources," *Harvard Business Review,* September–October 1981, pp. 56–66, 106–114.

Steers, Richard M., and Lyman W. Porter: *Motivation and Work Behavior,* New York: McGraw-Hill, 1975.

Walton, Richard E.: "From Control to Commitment in the Workplace," *Harvard Business Review,* March–April 1985, pp. 77–84.

CHAPTER 18
Job Design

Boredom and lack of job satisfaction are widespread in American industry. The woes of assembly-line workers and clerical workers are widely publicized and well known. Lack of job fulfillment also extends to managers and professionals, but is not as well documented. Many have argued that the solution to these problems is to adopt new approaches to job design. In this chapter several of these approaches will be explored.

Job design can be defined as the synthesis of individual tasks or activities into a job which is assigned to an individual worker or to a group of workers. The job design should specify what tasks will be done, who will do them, and what results are expected. The job design completely specifies the work content and the worker's job responsibilities.

Before job design begins, the product is generally specified. Sometimes the technology or the process is given as well. When this is the case, very little flexibility remains, since the job is almost completely specified by the process technology. In our discussion below, we will assume that the technology or process is not specified prior to job design but rather that the technology and the job are designed together.

Job design is a complex subject because it requires an understanding of both technical and human (social) variables. All too often in the past, either the human or the technical variables have been ignored, leading to jobs which were boring or did not utilize the proper technology. One of the aims of this chapter is to emphasize the sociotechnical approach to job design, which requires joint optimization of both social and technical variables. Box 18.1 illustrates a comprehensive approach to sociotechnical design used at General Electric.

BOX 18.1
GENERAL ELECTRIC

Can a company install the latest manufacturing technology and reap the full benefit of that technology without making corresponding changes in its labor-management organization? A report on a relatively new plant built by Canadian G.E. in Bromont, Quebec, suggests that state-of-the-art technology is most effective when teamed with an equally modern plant organizational structure. It says: to stay competitive in today's marketplace, a company must not only be ready to invest in the latest and best technology, but must also be willing to discard concepts of plant organization that have served well in the past in favor of ideas more attuned to today's needs and realities.

Canadian G.E.'s Bromont plant was designed and built to manufacture compressor blades and vanes for the new CFM-56 jet engine, manufactured by G.E.'s Aircraft Engine Business Group. The plant was designed to be one of the most sophisticated manufacturing operations in North America.

G.E. planners knew that a highly motivated workforce would be essential to the success of the operation. A rigid, hierarchical plant organization would work against enthusiasm for the new technology. Operators, foremen, supervisors and those further up the organizational ladder, would be so busy protecting their turfs, and spend so much time worrying about losing their jobs to a computer, that they would actually frustrate the steady implementation of new technology planned for the operation. What was needed was a plant organizational structure that would encourage and motivate the workers.

The plant was divided into separate businesses, forging, "pinch and roll," and machining; this reflected the major operations performed in the plant. Each was set up as a separate "business" consisting of an A-team that provides administrative expertise, and a B-team involved in the manufacturing operations. Maintenance, tool room and manufacturing & quality engineering teams serve the production "businesses." A senior management team oversees the operation of the entire plant and caps the organizational structure. And that's it. No foremen, no supervisors, no inspectors . . . in fact, there's very little resemblance between the traditional hierarchical management structure, and Canadian G.E.'s new management structure.

The businesses are given as much responsibility as they can handle. The goal is to pass as much of it as possible from senior management to the A-teams and the producers on the shop floor. Each business operates more or less independently. Decision-making is done by consensus rather than by a hierarchy of command.

B-team members are not allowed to vegetate once they have mastered their entry-level jobs; opportunities beckon. An elaborate job training program in place permits employees to move to a new job with greater responsibilities at regular intervals. Every B-team member has the opportunity to learn every position within his business, with corresponding increases in pay. Once he has mastered the jobs in his own area, he can "graduate" to another business—even apply for an A-team position. And as the workers learn the additional skills that make them more valuable to the company, their skills in participative management also increase, enabling them to handle increased responsibility and make judgments on questions traditionally reserved for supervisors.

Source: National Productivity Report, vol. 15, no. 7, Apr. 15, 1986. Reprinted with permission.

SOCIOTECHNICAL APPROACH

The sociotechnical approach to job design was originated by Eric Trist and his associates in studies of coal mining in England. [See Trist (1963).] They discovered that new coal mining technologies which were being considered did not dictate the type of work organization required. Rather, there were a variety of social and organizational choices that could be made for any given technology. Furthermore, there were a variety of technical alternatives which could be used to achieve both economic and social objectives. This realization led to the development of sociotechnical theory as a basis for job design.

The sociotechnical concept is described in Figure 18.1. The left-hand circle represents the set of all jobs which are feasible from a technical viewpoint. Similarly, the right-hand circle represents all feasible job designs from a social point of view, considering both the psychology and the sociology of the human worker. The intersection of these two circles then contains the set of job designs which satisfy both social and technical requirements. The best sociotechnical design lies somewhere within this intersection.

The value of sociotechnical theory lies in its emphasis on both technical and social variables in relation to job design. This approach leads to the development of jobs that do not merely represent the most economic technology under the assumption that humans are a part of the machine. Instead, this view takes into

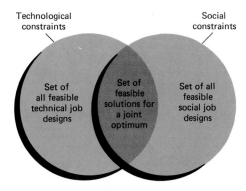

FIGURE 18.1
Sociotechnical
design.

account the possible costs of turnover, absenteeism, and boredom in relation to the choice of technology, so that the human factor is not overlooked.

When a job is designed from a strictly technological point of view, ignoring the social aspects, the result is called technological determinism. In this case the technology determines not only the task to be done but the social system as well. Then job designers have also become, in effect, social designers.

The sociotechnical design approach does not only involve jobs but also includes the design of the entire organization, as shown in Figure 18.2. The technical variables available for design purposes are shown on the left-hand side of the figure and the social variables on the right. Connecting them are various organizational design mechanisms which can affect the productivity and the quality of working life.

The broad view of organizational design shown in Figure 18.2 is particularly important when alternatives to changes in job design are being considered. When productivity or the quality of work life is too low, they might be improved by changes in supervision, in the type of workers selected, in the reward structures, or in any of the other variables. Thus, job design is only one of the many available design mechanisms which can be used to reach the same result, as we have noted in the last chapter.

The sociotechnical approach will be used as a framework for job design in this chapter. In Section 18.2 the technical approach as exemplified by scientific management will be discussed. This will be followed by a discussion of the social approach, exemplified by job enrichment. The entire discussion will demonstrate how the two approaches can be linked together under the sociotechnical umbrella.

18.2 SCIENTIFIC MANAGEMENT

Scientific management is the oldest method of job design, but it is still widely applied in today's world. It is also a method which has aroused a great deal of

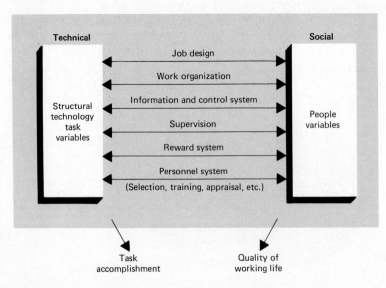

FIGURE 18.2
Organizational
design.
*Source: Raymond E.
Miles,* Theories of
Management:
Implications for
Organizational
Behavior and
Development, *New
York: McGraw-Hill,
1975.*

controversy and misconception. Because of these misunderstandings, scientific management will receive a detailed discussion here.

Scientific management was developed by Frederick W. Taylor starting in 1882 at the Midvale Steel Company. The method was later refined and applied by Frank and Lillian Gilbreth and Henry L. Gantt, along with hundreds of other managers and scientists. The initial period of active development and application of scientific management extended until about 1912, by which time it had become a widely established practice.

In industry, there is almost universal acceptance among both workers and management of restricted output. When a person first begins work, other workers generally make clear to the new worker the norm or socially acceptable rate of work output. Workers who exceed this unwritten norm often receive group reprisals and are soon conditioned to conform to it.

Taylor believed that restriction of output was due to two reasons: the workers' fear of loss of their jobs and management's unwillingness to pay for higher output levels. Workers are understandably afraid of losing their jobs or of imposing such a loss on fellow workers. Although it has been shown in many cases that increased productivity creates more jobs, not less, the worker's fear of unemployment persists.

In the second place, management has not always shared increased productivity directly with the workers. Workers, therefore, may restrict their output because their efforts benefit the company by improved profits but bring no gains to the workers themselves. To resolve this problem, Taylor advocated a wage incentive (piecework) system so that workers were automatically paid higher wages for higher output. Taylor believed that workers would not increase their productivity unless they were sure they would benefit from it economically.

There are many misconceptions about scientific management. Some people view it as a piece-rate system, time study, or use of efficiency experts. However, none of the particular techniques or factors, by themselves, are the essence of scientific management.

Taylor saw the essence of scientific management as a revolutionary change in the mental attitude of workers and management. He argued that both sides must join together and eliminate waste in order to boost output. The best method for each job must be developed on the basis of scientific study of the work, and management and workers must cooperate in using the new method to boost output without demanding increased effort from the workers. The additional output is achieved by improved methods, not harder work. As a result of applying this approach, both profits and wages are increased. According to Taylor, if economic benefits do not flow to both workers and management, scientific management will fail.

Taylor specified four principles for the application of scientific management.

1. Study the job scientifically. This requires experimentation, time study, and a search for the best method of work. Workers' suggestions are solicited and tested along with suggestions from industrial engineers and management. The resulting

method is not based on opinion but on research to discover the most economical method of work.

2. Select and train workers in the new method. It is known that all workers do not perform equally well on a given job. Each job makes its own peculiar demands on the individual and each individual has his or her own preference and ability for work. This principle of scientific management, therefore, requires the selection of a worker who is matched to the type of work designed, and this must be followed by the careful training of each worker in the new method. If a given worker is not well suited for the new method, it is management's responsibility to find alternative work for him or her. If workers are not carefully selected, productivity will fall to the lowest common denominator rather than reaching a high level.

3. Install the new method in operations. This principle calls upon both management and the workers to change procedures and methods as needed to make the new method work. Careful attention must be paid to following the method or adjusting it as required in order to install it over a period of time. The new method will not be accepted automatically; the change process itself must be carefully managed.

4. Develop teamwork between management and the workers. Taylor stressed that scientific management requires close coordination and cooperation to improve output. He used the example of a baseball team to illustrate the point. Each player may know his own job, but if the team does not work together, a winning record cannot be achieved. This principle is the hardest for management to implement because management must become the facilitator for the worker. Management must accept responsibility for proper planning, timing, and work coordination to remove unnecessary restrictions to output.

An example from the early days of scientific management may help to illustrate how these four principles are applied. One of the jobs Taylor studied was shoveling in the coal yards at Bethlehem Steel, where various types of iron ore, coal, and other materials were shoveled by hand from one place to another. Prior to the application of scientific management, each worker brought his own shovel to work, and the pace of shoveling was more or less dictated by group norms. Upon studying this job, Taylor discovered that work output was maximized (in terms of tons shoveled per day) when the shovel held a certain weight of material (21 pounds). If only 10 to 15 pounds were lifted per shovel, the worker had to shovel too fast to maintain the same output. If 30 to 40 pounds per shovel were moved, the load was too heavy and output also dropped. Although shoveling had been done for hundreds of years, no one had discovered the "science of shoveling" prior to Taylor's experiments.

After the new shoveling method was specified, workers were trained in it. Those workers who could not adjust to the new method were transferred to other jobs. After selection and training, each shoveler was put on a piece-rate system and the amount shoveled per day was recorded. When the amount fell below the standard, the worker was notified and wages were reduced. When the amount shoveled was above the standard, wages were increased. Management was also reorganized to provide centralized planning and control of the shoveling yard.

The central control office kept track of schedules and the amount produced by each worker each day. The results of this application of scientific management were striking. Wages increased by 63 percent per worker and the average cost of handling a ton of coal dropped by 54 percent.

It is interesting to note that Taylor developed his method as a result of labor-management strife. As a supervisor, Taylor saw the conflict between managers who wanted to drive the workers toward more output and workers who restricted output levels. This resulted in constant tension between management and labor because the only way that productivity could be improved was by pushing the workers to try harder. Taylor saw that both productivity and wages could be significantly improved and labor-management tensions reduced through the use of scientific management.

Scientific management has come under much criticism, some of it justified by inherent weaknesses in the method or by its misapplication. One such criticism is that scientific management creates boring, repetitive, and highly specialized jobs. Repetitive jobs, however, are created by work specialization and division of labor, which started well before Taylor's time.

Another criticism is that scientific management treats people like machines. This criticism is at least partly justified because scientific management does not consider psychological or social variables in the search for a better method. There is an implicit assumption in scientific management of the economic individual; that people work purely for economic rewards. The sociotechnical approach to work design is intended to correct this defect and broaden Taylor's theory.

Scientific management is sometimes criticized by labor as a speedup campaign. This reflects a misunderstanding of the method. The emphasis is to eliminate wasted motions and thereby accomplish work in a more efficient manner without calling upon people to work harder.

Students often wonder whether scientific management is still applicable today. The answer is that the principles still apply, but some modifications must be made in their application. No longer can jobs be merely the result of technology. Meaningful jobs should be synthesized after using Taylor's method to study the individual work elements. Work should still be divided into its basic elements and each element studied scientifically to eliminate wasted motion. But, after the basic elements have been studied, jobs should be synthesized from these elements through the consideration of economic, social, and technical requirements. A worker may, for example, be assigned more work elements than are dictated by strict economic efficiency; thus the skill variety or the wholeness of the job might be improved. JIT approaches may require broader jobs in the interest of total efficiency, not just labor efficiency. The work place may be designed so that people can converse while at work and develop stronger social relationships. These additional considerations can result in greater productivity because of a better-balanced job design. In Taylor's time, economic reward was considered the only motivator. Now, social and psychological factors are known to affect worker motivation also. A theory of job design which emphasizes these social and psychological factors is described next.

JOB-ENRICHMENT APPROACHES

In 1959, Frederick Herzberg and his associates published a famous research study which showed that intrinsic job factors (e.g., achievement, responsibility, and work itself) are potential satisfiers, while extrinsic job factors (e.g., supervision, pay, and working conditions) are potential dissatisfiers. Herzberg argued that satisfaction and dissatisfaction are not opposites on a single continuum but two distinct scales. The opposite of satisfaction is no satisfaction, and the opposite of dissatisfaction is no dissatisfaction. By this reasoning, improvement in an extrinsic factor such as pay might reduce dissatisfaction but not produce satisfaction. According to Herzberg, the only things that would satisfy workers were factors intrinsic to the job itself. Since Herzberg and his colleagues associated satisfaction with motivation, they argued that jobs should be enriched by adding intrinsic factors. Presumably this would increase not only job satisfaction but productivity as well.

Herzberg used the term "job enrichment" to refer to vertical loading—increasing the intrinsic factors in a job. Vertical loading adds decision-making responsibility, autonomy, and planning to the job. He also used the term "horizontal loading" to refer to adding skill variety to the job but not including additional decision-making responsibilities. Horizontal loading adds more skills by rotation among jobs at the same organizational level. Some psychologists, however, use the term "job enlargement" to refer to both vertical and horizontal loading. Others use the term "job enrichment" to refer to both types of loading. We shall follow the latter convention in the rest of this chapter.

Job enrichment has been carefully specified in a theoretical framework proposed by Hackman and Oldham (1975). In Figure 18.3, the framework begins on the right with a listing of certain personal and work outcomes which result from job enrichment. Proceeding to the left we find critical psychological states, core job dimensions, and implementing concepts. According to the theory, all these factors are linked together in a causal chain.

As far as personal and work outcomes are concerned, high internal work motivation means that the worker will put a great deal of effort into the job. High-quality work performance means that productivity will be high and quality will meet customer expectations. High satisfaction with the work, low absenteeism, and low turnover are self-explanatory as work outcomes. Of course, all these outcomes are desirable as the ultimate result of work.

According to the framework, the work and personal outcomes are determined by the following three critical psychological states:

- *Experienced meaningfulness of work.* The work must be perceived as important by a system of values accepted by the worker.
- *Experienced responsibility for work outcomes.* The worker must accept personal responsibility for work outcomes.
- *Knowledge of results.* The worker must be able to determine on some fairly regular basis whether or not the work outcomes are satisfactory.

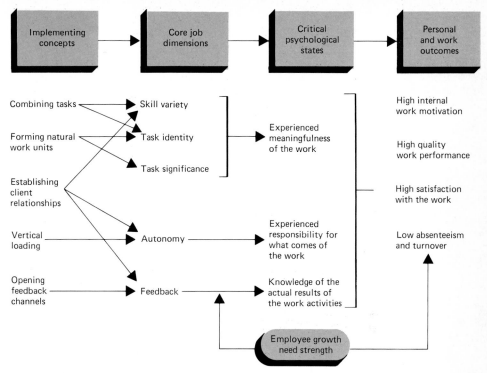

FIGURE 18.3
Hackman-Oldham
job-enrichment
framework.
*Source: J. Richard
Hackman et al., "A
New Strategy for Job
Enrichment,"*
California
Management
Review, *Summer
1975, reprinted by
permission of the
Regents.*

According to the Hackman-Oldham theory, when these three psychological states are present in the worker, there will be high internal motivation; the worker will be "turned on." The result should be greater performance in terms of personal and work outcomes. Hackman and Oldham use the example of a golfer to describe the three psychological states. The golfer experiences meaningfulness, since the golfer considers the game important by a system of values he or she accepts. If this psychological state is not present, the golf clubs will soon be put away or sold and other activities pursued. The golfer experiences responsibility for the outcome even though the weather and the course are sometimes blamed for poor results. And the golfer has knowledge of actual good or bad results.

The three critical psychological states can be achieved by five core job dimensions, also shown in Figure 18.3. For example, the theory states that experienced meaningfulness of work results from skill variety, task identity, and task significance. Skill variety is job enlargement—working at a number of different tasks which require different skills. This produces less boredom and less repetition. Task identity is associated with wholeness in the job, producing an identifiable end product or unit which the worker can identify with. In the golf game, task identity is assured because the golfer plays all strokes on all holes. Task significance is associated with a task the worker considers valuable and important to the customer or client. Surgeons tend to perceive high task significance. A person who packs parachutes would tend to feel a greater sense of task significance than another worker who packs ordinary parcels. If these three core dimensions appear in a job, the worker should experience a high degree of meaningfulness in the work.

Hackman and Oldham also postulate that autonomy in a job will affect the workers' feeling of responsibility for work outcomes. Autonomy can be achieved by giving the worker more decision-making authority. This can be done, for example, in the case of data entry by providing more scheduling authority, more authority for error correction, and so on.

Feedback is the fifth core job dimension; it provides knowledge of actual results. The best feedback is that which is built into the job itself. If a data entry operator works directly with the user, feedback on errors or good performance will come directly to the operator from the user. This type of feedback allows the worker to assess job performance continually.

The five core job dimensions have been combined into a motivating potential score (MPS). If skill variety, or task identity, or task significance is high, and autonomy is high, and feedback is high, then the MPS will be high. Jobs such as those of doctors, lawyers, and professors tend to have high MPS scores. Jobs such as those of assembly-line workers, telephone operators, and toll collectors tend to have very low MPS scores.

The MPS score is formally defined by the following formula:

$$\text{MPS} = \left(\frac{\text{skill variety} + \text{task identity} + \text{task significance}}{3} \right) (\text{autonomy})(\text{feedback})$$

Hackman and Oldham (1974, 1975) have also developed a questionnaire, the Job Diagnostic Survey (JDS), which can be used to determine the MPS for any job. The instrument has been validated by use on over 1000 different workers from 100 different jobs in a dozen organizations. In one study, for example, computer programmers had an MPS of 157, while data entry workers had an MPS of only 55. [See Couger and Zawacki.] One of the major contributions of Hackman and Oldham to the job-enrichment literature is the idea that jobs should be carefully diagnosed prior to enrichment through use of the JDS.

Is job enrichment good for everybody? Apparently not. The motivating effect of a job is dependent on the individual's growth need. This is shown by the moderating arrows on the bottom of Figure 18.3. When a job has a low MPS *and* the individual has high growth needs, then job enrichment is likely to produce favorable outcomes. If the worker has low growth needs, the job should not be enriched. In the Hackman-Oldham theory individual differences in growth needs are considered. Many of the earlier theories implied that job enrichment was for everyone.

There are also five implementing concepts which the Hackman-Oldham theory identifies. Work is sometimes assigned to individuals in a highly fractionalized and specialized way. For example, several different typists might work on the same report. As a result, the individual typist may have difficulty identifying with the final product and seeing the significance of the entire result. An implementing concept which corrects this situation is the formation of natural work units. In this case, a typist would be assigned the entire report or a specific section of the report. In this way the typist would be able to identify directly with the end product. The arrows in Figure 18.3 indicate that task identity and task significance should result when this is done.

The second implementing concept is combining tasks. This is traditionally a part of job enlargement, where the worker is given more task variety through horizontal loading. Typing-pool jobs, for example, could be enriched by eliminating the pool concept and designing jobs that require more than one skill. According to the classical economic theory of division of labor, breakup of the typing pool may result in less efficiency. But the classical theory ignores the effect of boredom and dissatisfaction on the workers' output and the costs of turnover and absenteeism. When *all* the costs are considered, less job specialization may be more efficient and at the same time more satisfying to the individual.

Another consequence of extreme division of labor is that workers have little contact with the client, user, or customer. This can be corrected by the third implementing concept: establishing client relationships. The result can be simultaneous improvement in three core job dimensions: feedback increases because the employee receives feedback directly from the customer instead of through a supervisor or intermediary; skill variety increases because the worker must develop interpersonal skills; and autonomy increases because the worker is often given discretion in dealing with the customer. The contact between the worker and the customer should be as frequent as necessary to do the job. Any form of contact is desirable: face to face, through letters, or by telephone.

Traditionally, the split between planning and doing has been designed into jobs. The implementing concept of vertical loading can be used to reverse this trend and give more decision-making responsibility to the worker. Vertical loading is perhaps the most important of all the implementing concepts because it leads to autonomy, responsibility, and a high degree of internal work motivation. If none of the other implementing concepts can be used in a particular situation due to technological considerations, vertical loading would still do a great deal to enrich the job. Vertical loading can be increased through a variety of actions such as assigning scheduling responsibility to the worker, assigning troubleshooting responsibility (most workers are told to contact their supervisor immediately if something goes wrong), or assigning responsibility for training new workers.

The last implementing concept is to open feedback channels and thereby improve knowledge of the actual results of the work activity. Feedback information is already available in many organizations, but it is not routinely given to the workers. For example, performance reports are sent to the supervisor and up the chain of command. Only indirectly does the worker learn about these reports. Quality control information is kept separate from the workers, errors are reported directly to the supervisor, and sometimes the supervisor even corrects errors without telling the employee. A great deal more can be done to ensure self-control of workers by giving feedback directly to them and by using feedback from the work itself whenever possible.

The Hackman-Oldham theory has been verified and tested by several research studies. It provides not only a conceptual view of job enrichment but also a practical method of job diagnosis to determine whether job enrichment is needed and how to go about enriching the job.

18.4 NEW PLANT DESIGNS

Job enrichment is sometimes constrained to a great extent by the existing technology. The design of new plants and offices provides the opportunity to choose the technology and the social system together. These opportunities have been utilized by some companies, including General Foods, PPG Industries, Procter & Gamble, Sherwin Williams, TRW, H. J. Heinz, Dana Corporation, Rockwell, General Motors, The Mead Corporation, and Cummins Engine. [See Lawler (1978) and Walton and Susman (1987).] Some of these organizations have started not only one new plant but two, three, or four. No one knows for sure how many new plant designs there are, but today there are, perhaps, several hundred in operation.

The new plants differ in almost every major respect from traditional factories. Some of the main differences are as follows:

Employee selection. In the new plants, a process of matching the employee and the work group is used. The prospective employee is interviewed by the work group, and both the employee and the work group decide whether there is a good match. The employees in the work group make the final decision on who will be hired.

Design and layout. Employees participate in plant layout and in the selection of equipment and machines. The emphasis is on ensuring that the technical and social systems are coordinated. There is also much more emphasis on equal facilities for workers and managers. There is usually one set of bathrooms, one cafeteria, and one parking lot with equal access to all. This is done to promote an atmosphere of teamwork between management and the workers.

Job design. Every effort is made to use the job-enrichment principles described in the last section. A great deal of emphasis is placed on teams or work groups. Each person is expected eventually to learn all the jobs in the group. The group is expected to function on a semiautonomous basis by making most of its own decisions, e.g., who does what on a given day. The group is also designed to be responsible for its own purchasing, quality control, and other staff functions. This reduces overhead and integrates the support needed into each group. Often the groups are designed to mix interesting and boring jobs, e.g., maintenance and warehousing. This ensures that everyone must share in the undesirable work. In one new plant, for example, there were no janitors; everyone took their turn at sweeping the floor.

Pay. In traditional plants, pay is often based on a job evaluation. In new-design plants, pay is based on the number of different jobs learned. This encourages each employee to keep learning on the job, and it creates a flexible labor force. In some of the new plants, group wage incentives or group profit sharing is used as a direct incentive to encourage productivity.

Organizational structure. The flat organizational structure used in the new plants represents perhaps the most striking difference by comparison with traditional plants. In some cases, there is no supervisor, merely an elected group leader. One supervisor may handle several groups, and there are often only two levels between the worker and the plant manager. In other cases, there may be a group supervisor, but he or she acts more as a facilitator and group leader. Whenever possible, the groups tend to be organized on a product basis so that they can identify with a whole unit of work. This contrasts sharply with the traditional functional organization of maintenance, quality, and so forth.

Management style. There is a definite effort to decentralize decision making to the work group level whenever possible. There is less staff and more line responsibility, since the line people carry out some of their own staff functions. There is much less division of labor, more group decision making, and more responsibility placed on the workers themselves.

In a study of 16 plants with advanced technology (CAD/CAM, CIM, or robotics), Walton and Susman (1987) found that these plants were also using the new human resource practices described above. These new human resource practices seem to be very compatible with the new technology and, in fact, may be required to ensure the effectiveness of the technology. Adoption of advanced technology in these plants had the following consequences:

- Closer interdependence among activities
- Different skill requirements—usually higher than average skills
- More immediate—and more costly—consequences of any malfunction
- Higher sensitivity of output to variations in human skills and knowledge, and to mental efforts rather than physical efforts
- More dynamism, that is, continual change and development
- Higher capital investment per employee and fewer employees responsible for a particular product, part, or process

These aspects of technology were found to be very compatible with the following organizational innovations, typically adopted by the plants:

- A highly skilled, flexible, coordinated, and committed work force
- A flat organizational structure and lean staff
- A commitment to low turnover and to promotion from within
- A strong partnership between management and labor unions
- Broader jobs to motivate workers and enhance operational flexibility
- Fewer job classifications—as few as two or three classifications
- Use of work team structure and employee involvement

By revising both the technology and the organization, these advanced technology plants have utilized the principle of sociotechnical design to achieve a proper fit between the social and technical systems.

KEY POINTS

- This chapter presents a sociotechnical view of job design. Under the sociotechnical approach, several technical alternatives are examined for their social impacts, and the best alternative considering both social and technical factors is selected. As a result, the job should provide higher productivity and satisfaction than when only one set of factors is considered.
- "Job design" refers to the assignment of specific tasks and activities to an individual or group of workers. The job or jobs involved should be completely specified as to content and responsibilities by job design.
- Job design is only one organizational design mechanism which affects productivity and the quality of working life. Thus, one should examine the possible effects of supervision, pay, personnel selection, and other factors before redesigning jobs.
- Scientific management, a method for designing jobs, stresses research to discover the best work method, worker selection, training, and management and labor cooperation to install the new method. To utilize the scientific management approach, management must share productivity gains with the workers and must ensure job security. Under these conditions, workers will usually no longer restrict output and will accept scientifically developed methods.
- Job enrichment is an approach to job design which stresses the motivating potential in the work itself. According to Hackman and Oldham, several different implementing concepts can be used to improve personal and work outcomes provided that the individual has a sufficiently high growth need. The implementing concepts are: combining tasks, forming natural work units, establishing client relationships, adding vertical loading, and opening feedback channels. The use of these implementing concepts should lead to changes in core job dimensions, critical psychological states, and—finally—personal and work outcomes.
- Prior to job enrichment, a formal job diagnosis should be made. The diagnosis should determine whether job enrichment is needed and, if so, what implementing concepts should be used.
- New plants have been designed which utilize different approaches to employee selection, job design, pay, organization structure, and management style. These approaches, when combined with advanced technology, can be used to obtain a sociotechnical system design for a new or upgraded plant.

QUESTIONS

1. From your own experience, describe a job which is boring and repetitive. What could be done to enrich this job?
2. Rate the following jobs in terms of skill variety, task identity, task significance, autonomy, and feedback.
   a. Highway toll collector
   b. Bank guard
   c. Surgeon
   d. High school teacher
   e. Truck driver

3. At the Midwest Telephone Company, telephone books are prepared in an assembly-line fashion. One person is in charge of receiving changes in name and address, another person checks the input forms for errors, a third person keypunches the information on computer cards, a fourth checks for computer errors, etc. Describe how these jobs could be enriched by using the five implementing concepts of Hackman and Oldham.

4. How would you use scientific management principles to improve your own study habits?

5. A person works in a cafeteria serving food to customers. Describe how scientific management principles could be used to improve this job.

6. A typing pool contains extremely specialized jobs. Describe how these jobs could be enriched.

7. What are the advantages of a new plant design over enrichment of present jobs?

8. A consultant has suggested that typing-pool jobs be enriched. What questions would you ask prior to approval of this project?

9. What organizational design mechanisms are available for improving productivity and the quality of working life other than job design?

10. At Volvo, the assembly line is broken up into a number of semiautonomous work groups. Each car is placed on an individual conveyor which is moved from group to group. Individuals rotate jobs within these groups from time to time. A group is responsible for a particular phase of automobile assembly such as body, upholstery, etc. Describe the core job dimensions which are affected in this case.

11. It has been said that scientific management leads to "robot"-type jobs. Discuss.

12. Scientific management is sometimes viewed as the opposite of job enrichment. Comment.

13. To what degree do workers restrict their output in the following types of jobs?
    a. Government bureaus
    b. College teaching
    c. Assembly lines
    d. Construction

14. To what degree does a baseball player experience each of the three critical psychological states defined by Hackman and Oldham?

15. Compute the MPS score for the following job: skill variety = 3, task identity = 4, task significance = 6, autonomy = 5, feedback = 6. Is this a highly motivating job?

16. It has been said that scientific management should not deal with job synthesis. What is meant by this statement?

SELECTED BIBLIOGRAPHY

COUGER, J. DANIEL and ROBERT A ZAWACKI: "Something's Very Wrong with DP Operations Jobs," *Datamation*, March 1979, pp. 149-158.

DAVIS, LOUIS E., and ALBERT CHERNS (eds.): *The Quality of Working Life*, New York: The Free Press, 1975, vols. 1 and 2.

FEIN, MITCHELL: "Job Enrichment: A Reevaluation," *Sloan Management Review*, vol. 15, no. 2, Winter 1974, pp. 69–88.

FORD, ROBERT N.: "Job Enrichment Lessons from AT&T," *Harvard Business Review*, January–February 1973, pp. 96–106.

GYLLENHAMMAR, PEHR G.: "How Volvo Adapts Work to People," *Harvard Business Review*, July–August 1977, pp. 102–113.

HACKMAN, J. RICHARD: "Is Job Enrichment Just a Fad?" *Harvard Business Review*, September–October 1975, pp. 129–138.

—— and GREG R. OLDHAM: "Development of the Job Diagnostic Survey," *Journal of Applied Psychology,* vol. 60, 1975, pp. 159–170.

—— and ——: "The Job Diagnostic Survey: An Instrument for the Diagnosis of Jobs and the Evaluation of Job Redesign Projects," Technical Report no. 4, New Haven, Conn.: Yale University, May 1974.

—— and ——: "Motivation through the Design of Work: Test of a Theory," *Organizational Behavior and Human Performance,* vol. 16, 1976, pp. 250–279.

——, JANE L. PEARCE, and JANE CAMINS: "Effects of Changes in Job Characteristics on Work Attitudes and Behaviors: A Naturally-Occurring Quasi-Experiment," Technical Report no. 13, New Haven, Conn.: Yale University, December 1976.

—— et al: "A New Strategy for Job Enrichment," *California Management Review,* Summer 1975, pp. 57–71.

HERZBERG, F.: "One More Time: How Do You Motivate Employees?" *Harvard Business Review,* January–February 1968, pp. 53–62.

LAWLER, EDWARD E. III: "The New Plant Revolution," *Organization Dynamics,* Winter 1978, pp. 3–12.

MIRVIS, PHILLIP H., and DAVID BERG (eds.): *Failures in Organization Development and Change,* New York: Wiley, 1977.

MORSE, JOHN J.: "A Contingency Look at Job Design," *California Management Review,* vol. 16, no. 1, Fall 1973, pp. 67–75.

OLDHAM, GREG R., J. RICHARD HACKMAN, and JONE L. PEARCE: "Conditions under Which Employees Respond Positively to Enriched Work," *Journal of Applied Psychology,* vol. 61, no. 4, 1976, pp. 395–403.

PETERS, TOM: "A World Turned Upside Down," *The Academy of Management EXECUTIVE,* vol. 1, no. 3, August 1987, pp. 233–243.

PETERSON, RICHARD B.: "Swedish Experiments in Job Reform," *Business Horizons,* June 1976, pp. 13–22.

REIF, WILLIAM E., and FRED LUTHANS: "Does Job Enrichment Really Pay Off?" *California Management Review,* vol. 15, no. 1, Fall 1972, pp. 30–37.

——, DAVID N., FERRAZZI, and ROBERT J. EVANS, JR.: "Job Enrichment: Who Uses It and Why?" *Business Horizons,* February 1974, pp. 73–78.

SIROTA, DAVID: "Job Enrichment—Is It for Real?" *S.A.M. Journal,* vol. 38, no. 2, April 1973, pp. 22–27.

TAYLOR, FREDERICK WINSLOW: *Scientific Management,* New York: Harper, 1911.

TRIST, E. L., et al.: *Organization Choice,* London: Tavistock Institute, 1963.

UMSTAT, DENIS, CECIL BILL, JR., and TERENCE MITCHELL: "Effects of Job Enrichment and Task Goals on Satisfaction and Productivity: Implications for Job Design," *Journal of Applied Psychology,* vol. 61, no. 4, 1976, pp. 379–394.

WALTON, RICHARD E.: "How to Counter Alienation in the Plant," *Harvard Business Review,* November–December 1972, pp. 70–81.

——: "From Control to Commitment in the Workplace," *Harvard Business Review,* March–April 1985, pp. 77–84.

—— and GERALD I. SUSMAN: "People Policies for the New Machines," *Harvard Business Review,* March–April 1987, pp. 98–106.

WANOS, JOHN P.: "Who Wants Job Enrichment?" *S.A.M. Advanced Management Journal,* Summer 1976, pp. 257–263.

WHITSETT, DAVID A.: "Where Are Your Unenriched Jobs?" *Harvard Business Review,* January–February 1975, pp. 74–80.

WOODMAN, RICHARD W., and JOHN SHERWOOD: "A Comprehensive Look at Job Design," *Personnel Journal,* August 1977, pp. 384–390.

CHAPTER 19
Work Measurement

Dost thou love life? Then do not squander time, for that's the stuff life is made of."[1] Benjamin Franklin admonishes us to conserve time, to use it wisely. This can be done by measuring the work that we do and by devising better work methods. As a result, our efforts should be more productive and efficient.

Work measurement and methods study have their roots in the scientific management movement. Frederick Taylor improved work methods through detailed motion studies, and he was the first to use the stopwatch for work measurement. Another of Taylor's contributions was the idea that a standard of

---

[1]Benjamin Franklin, *Poor Richard's Almanac,* June 1746.

output (e.g., minutes per piece) should be set for each job. A standard determines the amount of output expected of a worker and is used to plan and control direct labor costs.

Work measurement continues to be a useful but controversial practice. For example, work measurement is often a point of friction between labor and management. If the standards are "too tight," they can result in grievances, strikes, or poor labor relations. On the other hand, if standards are "too loose," they can result in poor planning and control, high costs, and low profits.

Work measurement today involves measuring not only traditional blue-collar work, but white-collar work as well. In many organizations a very large percentage of the work force is white collar. Thus, we will be considering the measurement of white-collar, as well as blue-collar, work in this chapter.

In an age where more control is being given to the workers and new systems of operations, such as JIT and CIM, are being used, new ways must be found to measure work and improve methods. No longer can management simply assume that it should set standards for a job which lacks motivating potential. Also, standards can get in the way of today's JIT and CIM systems, and sometimes the cost to set the standards may be more than the value of the direct labor being controlled. Thus management must continuously look for the appropriate use of work-measurement techniques. As the chapter proceeds, we will be examining some of these issues more carefully; but first a complete description of methods study is given and different approaches to work measurement are reviewed. A typical decision problem which utilizes work measurement is described in Box 19.1.

BOX 19.1
TYPICAL DECISION PROBLEM

After further study, Radarwave, Inc., decided to install a modified assembly line that would meet both social and technical considerations. This presented a new problem to Mary Lipton, in the work-measurement area. In order to design the new process in detail, time standards would be needed for each job. Accordingly, Mary contacted Ronald Belfy in the industrial engineering department. She asked Ron to develop a system of time standards by working together with Roger Kirk. She specifically wanted Roger involved in this effort in order to preserve the sociotechnical concepts which had already been incorporated in the design.

The first problem that confronted Ronald and Roger was how to develop standards for nonexistent jobs. The work could not be timed with a stopwatch in the usual fashion. To solve this problem, Ronald suggested that predetermined time data be used. With the help of tables listing predetermined data, time standards could be "built up" from elementary motions to the complete job. Ronald observed, "Predetermined time data should be sufficiently precise to permit a complete design of the line, and the resulting time standards can also be used during actual production." Since the speed of the line and the general types of jobs had already been determined by Roger's analysis, work could proceed on the careful definition of each job and development of the associated time standard.

The work content and time standard would be specified so that each worker could complete the job in the assigned time while working at a normal pace. No worker would be asked to produce more than could be expected from a "normal" person working under the prescribed conditions. Although these standards did not allow a great deal of individual variation, some slack time was included in each job, and buffers between work stations were provided to allow some variability in time. As a result, the time standard was an average time which did not have to be precisely met on each unit.

19.1 PURPOSES OF WORK MEASUREMENT

Work measurement can be used for a variety of different purposes. As a result, controversies about techniques and standards are often rooted in the very purpose of work measurement. It is the operations manager's responsibility to define this purpose and to ensure the use of appropriate work-measurement techniques.

Work-measurement techniques can be used for the following purposes:

1. *Evaluate a worker's performance.* This is done by comparing actual output over a given period of time with the standard output determined from work measurement.
2. *Plan work-force needs.* For any given level of future output, work measurement can be used to determine how much labor input is required.
3. *Determine available capacity.* For a given level of work force and equipment availability, work-measurement standards can be used to project available capacity. This purpose is just the reverse of the one listed in number 2.
4. *Determine price or cost of a product.* Labor standards, obtained through work measurement, are one ingredient of a costing or pricing system. In most organizations, the successful pricing of products is crucial to the survival of the business. This activity, in turn, rests on work measurement whenever cost is a basis for pricing.
5. *Compare work methods.* When different methods for a job are being considered, work measurement can provide the basis for economic comparison of the methods. This is the essence of scientific management—to devise the best method based on rigorous time and motion studies.
6. *Facilitate operations scheduling.* One of the data inputs to all scheduling systems is time estimates for work activities. These estimates are derived from work measurement.
7. *Establish wage incentives.* Under wage incentives, workers receive more pay for more output. Underlying these incentive plans is a time standard which defines 100 percent output.

Since there are so many different uses for work measurement, management must decide which of them will be selected. If work measurement is used for wage incentives, for example, one of the more accurate methods, such as the stopwatch, should be used and standards should be updated frequently. If work measurement is used for estimating capacity or planning work force needs, not as much accuracy is required in each individual time estimate and other work-measurement methods can therefore be used.

Management may decide not to set standards or to use work measurement, in the traditional sense, for two reasons. First, the cost of setting and maintaining the standards may be higher than the benefit. For example, in a highly automated manufacturing company, the cost of direct labor is typically less than 10 percent of the cost of producing the product. To track the direct labor cost of every operation performed on the product may cost more than the value of any labor saved. Direct labor should then be controlled on a more aggregate basis than through the use of detailed time standards for every operation on the product routing. Some suggestions on how to do this are given below.

The second reason that management may choose not to use time standards is to avoid interference with general plant performance. Time standards are not useful when they interfere with the production systems or strategy in use. For example, in JIT installations, a worker is required to stop work when the using work centers no longer call for parts. In this case the worker may be idle or may shift to another job for a period of time. If direct labor is measured to the individual worker level, the wrong signals will be sent. Direct labor utilization may actually drop in a JIT plant, but the overall performance is improved through reductions in inventory and overhead. Hewlett-Packard has already abandoned the use of time standards in its plants that use JIT systems. Instead, the company has adopted an aggregate approach to direct labor measurement.

The point of this discussion is that work measurement must be compatible with the needs of the organization and the specific uses being considered. The purpose of work measurement is, after all, to contribute to an improvement in overall organization performance. The methods must, therefore, be used in situations where they fit. Assuming for the moment that one of these situations is presented, we will describe the development of time standards next.

TIME STANDARDS

The principal result of some types of work-measurement activity is a production standard, also called a time standard or simply a standard. A standard can be formally defined as the amount of time it should take to execute a task or activity when a trained operator working at a normal pace uses a prescribed method. This definition includes several key features that require further clarification.

First, a standard is normative. It defines the amount of time which *should* be required for work under certain conditions. A standard is not merely the average of past times, because past averages reflect how much time a job has taken, not necessarily how much time it *should* have taken. Later, it will be shown, however, how actual time observations can be adjusted to arrive at a standard.

A standard also requires that a method be prescribed for the work or activity.

Usually the "best" method is developed to eliminate wasted motions and to streamline the work whenever possible. The prescribed method is ordinarily put in written form.

Finally, a standard requires that a trained operator be doing the work at a normal pace. An operator who is suited for the type of work involved should be selected and this operator should be carefully trained to follow the method. A "normal pace" means that the operator is working neither too fast nor too slow but at a pace which could be sustained by most workers over an entire day.

A standard thus implies a number of conditions which must be met. If a worker cannot achieve the standard, any of the following causes might be identified. Perhaps the material has changed, the product has been redesigned, the worker has not been properly trained, or the individual's abilities do not match the job. When the cause of the deviation from standard has been found, action can be taken to correct the situation.

A standard can be expressed in two ways: as either the time required per unit of output or the reciprocal, output per unit of time. Examples are minutes per piece or pieces per minute. In complex cases where the job is a task or activity for which there is no convenient unit of output, a standard must be defined as the time required to complete the task or activity.

19.3 METHODS STUDY

Most of the improvements resulting from work measurement stem from the underlying methods studies, which precede the time studies themselves. Although time standards are used for management control purposes, the standards alone do not improve efficiency. A great source of productivity improvement during the twentieth century has been the application of methods studies.

A typical methods study proceeds along the following lines:

1. Define the objectives and constraints of the study.
2. Decide on the study approach to be used.
3. Announce the study to the workers.
4. Break the job into elements.
5. Study the method through the use of charts.
6. Decide on a method for each work element.

The objectives of the study might be to improve productivity by 50 percent or, alternatively, to increase efficiency using the present machines. Management must clearly define the objectives of the study, since so many possibilities exist.

The approach selected, in the second step, might consist of a very elaborate motion study, with filming or extensive visual observation, or a "quick and dirty" study which takes only a short time. The approach might include worker responsibility for the study, with industrial engineers as the advisers, or the reverse situation. The approach might use any number of different work-measurement techniques.

In the third step, the study is announced to the workers. A methods study should never be sprung on the work force as a surprise. Normally, workers should be informed of the study in writing or at a meeting where they have a chance to ask questions. When informing the workers, management should address the objectives and planned approach for the study along with issues of job security, work pace, and worker benefits.

The fourth step in a methods study is to break the job into elements.[2] This is done to facilitate analysis, because each element will require a specific method. If the job being analyzed is typing a specified business letter, for example, the following elements might be defined:

- Read rough draft
- Correct errors
- Set up typewriter
- Type letter
- Proofread letter
- Correct errors
- Type envelope
- Get signature
- Mail letter

Each job element is then studied through observation and the use of charts. The purpose of the methods analysis is to devise a method which is efficient and economical while also considering the workers' social and psychological needs. Some of the method analysis charts which can be used are described below.

Finally, the job is designed by selecting a method for each work element. The decision may be made by the industrial engineer, the worker, or a manager. Which of these individuals holds final authority depends on the behavioral theory used by the firm. More on this issue will be presented later in the chapter.

Several different charts are used in studying work methods. The first type of chart is the process flowchart discussed in Chapter 8. The process flowchart describes the entire process and the interrelationships between jobs and activities. After the process flowchart has been constructed, attention shifts to the micro level of motion study for a particular job or work element. Three principal types of charts are used at the micro level of analysis: activity chart, operations chart, and Simo (simultaneous motion) chart.

The activity chart (also called a "man-machine" chart) shows the relationship between the operator and machine. As an example, Figure 19.1 is an activity chart for the job of making drinks in an automatic blender at a bar. The chart shows what the machine is doing and what the operator is doing at each point in time. From this chart it is possible to determine idle time of the operator and the machine and to identify the operator- and machine-paced elements. With this

---

[2]An element is a part of a job which contains a closely related set of motions, activities, or tasks.

Operator	Time*		Machine	Time*	
Take customer order	.3		Idle	.3	
Load blender	.5		Load blender	.5	
Idle	.6		Run blender	.6	
Empty blender	.2		Empty blender	.2	
Serve drink	.5		Idle	.5	

FIGURE 19.1
Activity chart for mixing a drink in a blender.

*Time in minutes

information, one can determine whether the operator can operate another machine, or whether some changes in method are possible to utilize the machine or worker more efficiently.

The operation chart shows the detailed motions of a worker's hands during each step of a job. The operation chart in Figure 19.2 is intended to show the

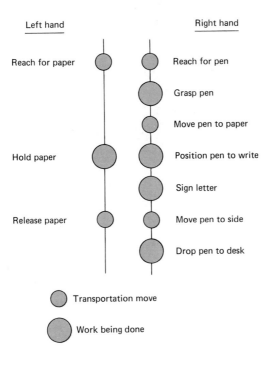

FIGURE 19.2
Operation chart (signing a letter).

motions of the left hand and the right hand during the job of signing a letter. The small circles in the figure represent a transportation move, while the large circles represent work being done on the job.

By first describing the current method in detail through use of an operations chart, one should be able to develop an improved method. This is done by analyzing the operations chart with regard to three aspects of the job: use of the human body, arrangement of the work place, and design of tools and equipment. These three aspects of method design are embodied in the principles of motion economy shown in Table 19.1. Through application of these principles, first developed by Frank and Lillian Gilbreth, it is possible to greatly simplify many jobs.

Another type of motion study chart, which is similar to the operation chart, is the Simo chart. The Simo chart also shows the motions of the left hand and right hand, but it includes the time for each movement using the standard Therblig symbols. In studying work, the Gilbreths determined that all hand motions could be divided into 17 distinct types. Each of these motions was called a Therblig (Gilbreth spelled backward with the t and h interchanged). The Gilbreths also stressed analysis of the time for each motion, usually determined by counting frames on a motion picture of the job. With this technique it was possible to combine, eliminate, or change the basic motions to develop an improved method. See Figure 19.3 for an example of a Simo chart for signing a letter.

The results of methods study can be dramatic. For example, on the basis of Gilbreth's 3-year study of bricklaying methods, the number of bricks laid per hour was increased from 120 to 350. This result was achieved by a new bricklaying

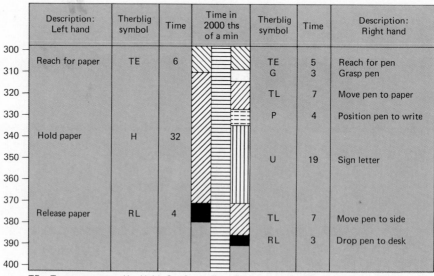

	Description: Left hand	Therblig symbol	Time	Time in 2000 ths of a min	Therblig symbol	Time	Description: Right hand
300	Reach for paper	TE	6		TE	5	Reach for pen
310					G	3	Grasp pen
320					TL	7	Move pen to paper
330					P	4	Position pen to write
340	Hold paper	H	32				
350					U	19	Sign letter
360							
370							
380	Release paper	RL	4		TL	7	Move pen to side
390					RL	3	Drop pen to desk
400							

TE = Transport empty; H = Hold; G = Grasp; TL = Transport loaded; P = Position;
U = Use; RL = Release

FIGURE 19.3
Simo chart
(signing a letter).

TABLE 19.1
PRINCIPLES OF MOTION ECONOMY

A check sheet for motion economy and fatigue reduction
These twenty-two rules or principles of motion economy may be profitably applied to shop and office work alike. Although not all are applicable to every operation, they do form a basis or a code for improving the efficiency and reducing fatigue in manual work.

Use of the human body	Arrangement of the work place	Design of tools and equipment
1. The two hands should begin as well as complete their motions at the same time.	10. There should be a definite and fixed place for all tools and materials.	18. The hands should be relieved at all work that can be done more advantageously by a jig, a fixture, or a foot-operated device.
2. The two hands should not be idle at the same time except during rest periods.	11. Tools, materials, and controls should be located close to the point of use.	19. Two or more tools should be combined wherever possible.
3. Motions of the arms should be made in opposite and symmetrical directions, and should be made simultaneously.	12. Gravity-feed bins and containers should be used to deliver material close to the point of use.	20. Tools and materials should be pre-positioned whenever possible.
4. Hand and body motions should be confined to the lowest classification with which it is possible to perform the work satisfactorily.	13. Drop deliveries should be used wherever possible.	21. Where each finger performs some specific movement, such as in typewriting, the load should be distributed in accordance with the inherent capacities of the fingers.
5. Momentum should be employed to assist the worker whenever possible, and it should be reduced to a minimum if it must be overcome by muscular effort.	14. Materials and tools should be located to permit the best sequence of motions.	22. Levers, crossbars, and hand wheels should be located in such positions that the operator can manipulate them with the least change in body position and with the greatest mechanical advantage.
6. Smooth, continuous, curved motions of the hands are preferable to straight-line motions involving sudden and sharp changes in direction.	15. Provisions should be made for adequate conditions for seeing. Good illumination is the first requirement for satisfactory visual perception.	
7. Ballistic movements are faster, easier, and more accurate than restricted (fixation) or "controlled" movements.	16. The height of the work place and the chair should preferably be arranged so that alternate sitting and standing at work are easily possible.	
8. Work should be arranged to permit easy and natural rhythm wherever possible.	17. A chair of the type and height to permit good posture should be provided for every worker.	
9. Eye fixations should be as few and as close together as possible.		

Source: Ralph M. Barnes, *Motion and Time Study: Design and Measurement of Work,* 6th ed., New York: Wiley, 1968, p. 220.

method which reduced the number of motions per brick from 18 to 5. Through the use of special scaffolds, more consistent mortar, and prearranged bricks, this new method eliminated much of the stooping, bending, and lifting that had formerly been associated with bricklaying. Thus the workers were able to lay more bricks in a day while using about the same number of total motions, so that the new method actually represented a better use of human effort—not a speedup. As a catch phrase goes, "The bricklayers worked smarter, not harder."

 ## TYPES OF WORK MEASUREMENT

After the methods study is completed, work measurement can begin. There are several types of work-measurement techniques, each suited to different uses and each with different accuracies and costs. The work-measurement methods which have been most widely used and will receive primary attention in the rest of this chapter are the following:

1. Time study
2. Predetermined time data
3. Standard data
4. Historical data
5. Work sampling

A study by Rice (1977) provides some interesting data on how these methods are used in industry. According to Rice, different methods are used to study direct and indirect labor. While direct labor is studied primarily by the first three methods, indirect labor is studied by the last two. This is because of the repetitive nature of direct labor and the greater accuracy required in direct-labor standards.

 ## TIME STUDY

The time study approach to work measurement uses a stopwatch or other timing device to determine the time required to complete given tasks. Assuming a standard is being set, the worker must be trained and must use the prescribed method while the study is being conducted.

To make a time study, one must:

1. Break the job into elements.
2. Develop a method for each element.
3. Select and train a worker or worker(s).
4. Time-study each element.
5. Set the standard.

To illustrate these steps, let us use the typing job previously described and assume that the first three steps have already been completed according to the discussion of Section 19.3. The remaining tasks are to record time and set a standard. Figure 19.4 is a typical time study chart used to record the data taken during a time study. Along the left side of the sheet is each element in the job. Along the top is each

Sheet: 1 of 1 sheets							Date: 10/9/80					
Operation: Prepare letter							Part no.:					
Operator's name: L. Lamkin							Part name:					
Observer: N. A. Jones							Shift: 1					
Begin: 9:30	Finish: 3:30		Units Finished: 10				Time in min.:					
Elements	1	2	3	4	5	6	7	8	9	10	Rating	Normal time
1. Read rough draft	.73	.85	.97	.65	.78	.84	.69	.74	.95	.88	95	.77
2. Correct errors	.30	.40	.21	.35	.25	.37	.41	.43	.48	.31	100	.35
3. Set up typewriter	.51	.63	.42	.30	.67	.51	.56	.40	.38	.41	105	.50
4. Type letter	1.65	2.03	2.15	1.50	2.20	1.80	1.93	1.75	1.76	1.85	110	2.05
5. Proofread letter	.60	.65	.50	.55	.67	.73	.69	.59	.68	.71	100	.64
6. Correct errors	.85	.90	.93	.70	.97	.71	.83	.76	.87	.91	105	.88
7. Type envelope	.60	.51	.54	.56	.63	.65	.68	.48	.46	.61	110	.63
8. Get signature	—	—	—	—	—	—	—	—	—	—		
9. Mail letter	.21	.20	.19	.18	.23	.21	.22	.23	.21	.19	100	.21
Allowances:							Total normal					6.03
Personal and fatigue 10% Delays 5%				15% Allowance			X1.15 Standard					6.93

FIGURE 19.4
Time-study
observation sheet.

cycle or observation which is made. The time study person would observe several cycles of work being performed and record the time for each element from a stopwatch. As a result, the times shown in Figure 19.4 are recorded.

The next step in the time study is to determine the rating for each job element. A rating is an estimate of work speed. A rating of 100 percent represents a normal work pace. A high percentage of trained workers should be able to work at 100 percent during the entire day or to exceed 100 percent without abnormal exertion or effort. If a worker is rated at 125 percent, more work is done in a given amount of time (i.e., the worker is working faster than normal).

On the basis of the rating factor (RF) for each element, observed times (OT) are converted to normal times (NT) by the following conversion formula:

NT = OT (RF/100)

For example, if the observed time is 1 minute and the rating factor is 120, then the normal time is 1.2 minutes. The normal time is the time it should take to do the job working at 100 percent, or normal pace.

The definition of the rating factor does not include allowances for unavoidable delays, rest for fatigue, personal time (e.g., washroom, coffee breaks), and so on. In other words, the normal time assumes that the person stays on the job the entire day, does not talk to the supervisor or take coffee breaks, and does not need to rest at intervals. To compensate for these additional factors, an allowance is provided. The allowance (A) is added to normal time (NT) to arrive at standard time (ST) as follows:

$$ST = NT (1 + A/100)$$

For example, if the allowance is 15 percent and the normal time is 20 minutes, then the standard time is 23 minutes.

Allowances vary depending on the type of working conditions. If the work is heavy or hot and requires frequent rest, allowances may be as much as 50 percent. An example of this is shoveling dirt on a construction site. For work under ideal conditions, allowances may be as low as 10 or 15 percent. Sometimes allowances are determined by separate work-sampling studies, and some allowances are even subject to union negotiations. Allowances are usually applied to the entire job and do not differ from one work element to the next. [See Niebel (1976), p. 365, for typical allowances.]

After applying allowances, the final standard is finished. A trained worker using the prescribed method should be able to meet or exceed this standard on a daily basis without overexertion. Standard time is used as a basis for judging worker output.

One question which arises in time study is how many observations will be needed. Generally speaking, the more variability in the time of an element, the more observations will be required to achieve a desired accuracy level. This idea can be reduced to a formula for computing the number of observations for any particular case. [See Barnes (1968), pp. 359–360.]

Another question which arises in time study concerns the matter of rating. Rating is a controversial issue which raises questions about the validity of time study itself. The untrained person is very poor at rating work pace. For example, if a number of untrained people observe the same person working at a normal pace, their rating estimates will usually vary from about 70 to 130 percent of normal. This is significant because many managers form instinctive judgments about work pace around the office and in other work settings. With this much variation between individuals, judgments are often wrong.

Industrial engineers who have been trained in the rating of work pace will achieve more uniform ratings. In this case, the variation may be about ± 10 percent. One method used to achieve accuracy in ratings is to have time study people watch movies of work which has previously been rated. These movies show people doing various types of jobs at various rates. Another method used to achieve accuracy in ratings is to establish benchmarks. For example, walking at a rate of 3 miles per hour is considered a 100 percent work pace by the industrial engineers. This is not an exceptionally fast rate of walking. Most people can walk at a speed of 4 miles per hour (133 percent) without undue exertion. An absolute maximum of about 5.4 miles per hour (180 percent) can be achieved without running. To the surprise of some people, it also takes a great deal of effort to walk at too slow a pace. At 2 miles per hour (66 percent), each foot must be carefully placed, since the muscles are being held back. Walking is typical of industrial work paces which range from 70 percent to about 140 percent in practice. For short periods of time, paces of 180 percent may be observed.

Another benchmark established by industrial engineers is dealing cards to represent hand-motion activity. A deck of 52 cards can be dealt into four piles on a table in 30 seconds at a 100 percent pace. You can test your own concept of normal pace by trying this experiment.

Despite its limitations, time study is a reasonably accurate method of work measurement. Because of its accuracy, it is widely used as a basis for incentive plans and in cases where disputes arise over standards. The principal disadvantage of time study is its psychological effect on workers. Some workers object to having a watch used on them while they are working. As a result, they may slow down, change methods, or use other means to manipulate the standards. Fortunately, methods which can eliminate the need for the stopwatch have been developed. These methods are described in the remainder of this chapter.

19.6 PREDETERMINED DATA

Predetermined data are based on the clever idea that all work can be reduced to a basic set of motions. Times can then be determined for each of the basic motions—by means of a stopwatch or motion pictures—to create a bank of time data. Using the data bank, a time standard can be built up for any job that involves the basic motions.

Several predetermined time systems have been developed, the most common ones being work factor, basic motion time study (BMT), and methods time measurement (MTM). As an example, the "reach" motion from MTM is shown in Table 19.2. The other motions used in the MTM system are "grasp," "move," "turn," "apply pressure," "position," and "disengage." A very large percentage of industrial and clerical work can be described in terms of these seven basic motions.

The procedure used to set a standard from predetermined time data is as follows. First, each job element is broken down into its basic motions. Next, each basic motion is rated as to degree of difficulty. A reach to an object in a variable location, for example, is more difficult and takes more time than a reach to an object in a fixed location. Once the time required for each basic motion has been determined from the predetermined-time tables, the basic motion times are added to yield total normal time. An allowance factor is then applied to obtain standard time.

Some industrial engineers who have used predetermined times find that they are more accurate than stopwatch times. The improved accuracy is attributed to the large number of cycles used in building the initial predetermined-time tables.

However, some difficulties are involved in using predetermined-time methods. To set a standard, the analyst must break a job into basic motions and assign a degree of difficulty to each motion. Different analysts will develop different basic motions and assign different degrees of difficulty to each one. This results in some variation in standards for the same job.

The greatest advantages of predetermined-time systems is that they do not

TABLE 19.2
MTM PREDETERMINED TIME DATA FOR "REACH"

Distance moved, inches	Time TMU				Hand in motion		Case and description
	A	**B**	**C or D**	**E**	**A**	**B**	
¾ or less	2.0	2.0	2.0	2.0	1.6	1.6	A Reach to object in fixed location, or to object in other hand or on which other hand rests.
1	2.5	2.5	3.6	2.4	2.3	2.3	
2	4.0	4.0	5.9	3.8	3.5	2.7	
3	5.3	5.3	7.3	5.3	4.5	3.6	B Reach to single object in location which may vary slightly from cycle to cycle.
4	6.1	6.4	8.4	6.8	4.9	4.3	
5	6.5	7.8	9.4	7.4	5.3	5.0	
6	7.0	8.6	10.1	8.0	5.7	5.7	
7	7.4	9.3	10.8	8.7	6.1	6.5	C Reach to object jumbled with other objects in a group so that search and select occur.
8	7.9	10.1	11.5	9.3	6.5	7.2	
9	8.3	10.8	12.2	9.9	6.9	7.9	
10	8.7	11.5	12.9	10.5	7.3	8.6	
12	9.6	12.9	14.2	11.8	8.1	10.1	
14	10.5	14.4	15.6	13.0	8.9	11.5	D Reach to very small object or where accurate grasp is required.
16	11.4	15.8	17.0	14.2	9.7	12.9	
18	12.3	17.2	18.4	15.5	10.5	14.4	
20	13.1	18.6	19.8	16.7	11.3	15.8	
22	14.0	20.1	21.2	18.0	12.1	17.3	E Reach to indefinite location to get hand in position for body balance or next motion or out of way.
24	14.9	21.5	22.5	19.2	12.9	18.8	
26	15.8	22.9	23.9	20.4	13.7	20.2	
28	16.7	24.4	25.3	21.7	14.5	21.7	
30	17.5	25.8	26.7	22.9	15.3	23.2	
Additional	0.4	0.7	0.7	0.6			TMU per inch over 30 inches.

Source: Copyrighted by the MTM Association for Standards and Research. No reprint permission without written consent from the MTM Association, 16-01 Broadway, Fair Lawn, N.J. 07410.

require rating or the use of stopwatches; they are also frequently less expensive. The ratings, based on a large number of observations of different people, are already built into the tables. There are, however, some jobs which do not fit into the framework of predetermined-time systems. Examples are jobs which are not highly routine in nature. Standards for these jobs must still be set by stopwatch. It is also common practice in companies that use predetermined-time systems to occasionally check some predetermined standards with a stopwatch.

STANDARD DATA

The use of standard data also involves the concept of a data bank, but the data comprise larger classes of motion than predetermined data. For example, a standard-data system may contain data on the time required to drill various-size holes through certain materials. When a standard is needed for a drilling operation, the standard data are used to estimate the required time. With standard data, it is not necessary to measure every different type of drilling operation; only a standard set of drilling operations are included in the data bank and formulas or graphs are provided to approximate other conditions.

Standard data are derived from either stopwatch data or predetermined-time data. Using standard data is quite popular for measuring direct labor. This is because a large number of standards can be derived from a small standard-data set. Typically, each company will develop its own standard-data system.

Standard-data systems are useful when there are a large number of repetitive operations which are quite similar. For example, in a furniture factory, the time required to varnish a piece of furniture could probably be based on the number of square feet of surface area. In a typing pool, the time required for typing a letter could be related to the number of words in the letter plus a fixed time for the heading and signature blocks. By using relationships of this type in setting standards, a great deal of effort can be saved.

Standard-data systems have some of the same advantages as predetermined-time data. No stopwatch is needed; the data can be used to study new operations; and accuracy can be assured through continued use and refinement of the data.

19.8 HISTORICAL DATA

The use of historical data is perhaps one of the most overlooked approaches to work measurement. This is so because methods are not controlled with historical data and it would therefore be impossible to set a standard in the usual sense of the word. But with historical data a different approach to work measurement can be taken.

To measure work on the basis of historical data, each employee or the supervisor records the time required to complete each job. For example, if the job is to drill a certain type of hole in 100 pieces, the time per piece would be recorded. Later, if the job were done again, the time per piece would also be recorded and compared with the earlier data. In this way it is possible to keep continuous track of the time required per unit of work and to control departures from the historical average.

For some jobs the approach of using historical data may be preferable because the work itself is used to develop a "standard." No stopwatch is required, and flexibility in the method is permitted, encouraging innovation without the need to set a new standard. This approach can be especially effective when it is coupled with a wage incentive plan, where the objective is to make continual improvements over the historical levels.

Historical data can also be used to develop time estimates for complicated jobs. Suppose, for example, that the time it takes for a worker in a laundry to iron a basket of clothes has been recorded in the past. The basket, however, never contains the same types and amounts of clothes. In this case a regression formula can be developed which relates the time it takes to iron the clothes to the number of shirts, pairs of trousers, and dresses in the basket. The regression equation coefficients will provide estimates of the time per shirt, the time per pair of trousers, and the time per dress. These unit times could be used for costing, scheduling, or other planning needs. The regression equation could also be used to predict the amount of time it should take to iron the contents of any given clothes basket. For control purposes, the predicted time could then be compared with the actual time.

WORK SAMPLING

In a large hospital, the administration planned to install a computer to reduce the paperwork done by nurses. However, the administrators were unsure how much time the nurses spent on paperwork; therefore, they could not estimate the expected savings from the new computer. To resolve this problem, a work-sampling study was done. The work-sampling study consisted of 500 observations of nurses, taken at random times. Upon observing a nurse at work, the observer recorded the nurse's activity, as shown in Box 19.2. Although only the time spent doing paperwork was needed, all other activities were also obtained from the work-sampling study.

BOX 19.2
SAMPLING OF NURSE'S WORK

Activity	Number of observations	Percentage of observations
Making bed	60	12
Attending to patient	150	30
Walking between locations	40	8
Reading chart	30	6
Talking with doctors	40	8
Talking with other nurses	20	4
On break	50	10
Doing paperwork	110	22
Total	500	100

The study indicated that 22 percent of a nurse's time was spent doing paperwork. Therefore, over the course of a 24-hour day, 5.28 nursing hours per nurse were devoted to paperwork. This figure was then used to estimate the potential savings from the computer system.

A work-sampling study can be defined as a random series of observations of work used to determine the activities of a group or individual. To convert the observed activity percentage into hours or minutes, a total amount of time worked must also be recorded or known. Notice that work sampling, like historical time estimates, does not control the method. Furthermore, the training of the worker is not controlled, so that standards cannot be established by work sampling.

Work sampling, however, can be used for a large number of other purposes. Some of the more common uses are the following:

1. To assess productive and nonproductive time, as an aid to setting allowances
2. To determine job content, as part of job analysis
3. To help managers and workers make better use of their time
4. To estimate managerial needs, equipment needs, or the cost of various activities

One of the requirements of work sampling is a fairly large sample size. Since percentages are being estimated, the sample size is a function of the accuracy and the degree of confidence required. This relationship can be expressed by the following formula, based on the normal approximation to the binomial distribution:

$$E = Z\sqrt{\frac{p(1 - p)}{n}}$$

where E = error in ± proportion
Z = confidence coefficient
p = proportion being estimated
n = sample size

Suppose that we want to estimate the percentage of time that a professor spends with students in his office. We think we will find that the percentage is about 20 percent, so $p = .2$. We want to estimate the true percentage to within ± 2 percentage points, so $E = .02$. We want a 95 percent confidence limit; therefore $Z = 1.96$ from the normal probability tables. Using these figures in the above equation, we can solve for n as follows:

$$n = \left(\frac{Z}{E}\right)^2 p(1 - p) = \left(\frac{1.96}{.02}\right)^2 .2(.8) = 1536$$

In this case, we should take 1536 observations to estimate the true percentage to within ± 2 percent with 95 percent confidence.

Before obtaining the large number of samples required in work sampling, it is important to randomize the observations properly. This should be done mechanically, through the use of random numbers, to avoid bias. The observer should also be trained to record each activity of interest carefully. Under these conditions, reliable estimates will be obtained from work sampling.

Work sampling is typically used for indirect labor studies or studies of groups of workers, such as a typing pool. When the work is repetitive and well defined, one of the first three methods discussed (time standards, predetermined times, or standard data) is often more appropriate.

19.10 TIME MANAGEMENT

As managers are becoming more concerned about the usage of their own time and professional staff time, the subject of time management has come into vogue. Obviously, time is a valuable resource for managers and professionals as well as the blue-collar work force.

Work sampling can be used to study management or professional time through the use of a recording machine which "beeps" at random times during the day. On the machine's signal, the manager depresses the "record" button and dictates the activity currently in progress. After several days of such recording, the tapes are analyzed and the manager is given a profile of how his or her time is spent. By analyzing these profiles, most managers can identify activities which are taking too much time and those which are receiving too little. By rearranging the daily routine, managers can obtain a better distribution of their time.

Studies of time utilization among executives have produced some interesting results. One of the earliest studies, by Sune Carlson (1951), contained the following data: "Managers work an average day of 10 hours with a range of 8½ to 11 hours. Managers spend 65–95 percent of their time in contact with other people. From 1⅕ to 5 hours per day is spent receiving visitors." The most surprising conclusions from Carlson's study was that the executive is interrupted on average once every 8 minutes. Since 25 to 30 minutes of uninterrupted time is needed to achieve significant results on a major problem, there is little time for problem solving.

Some of the other conclusions Carlson reached were as follows:

- Managers have little idea of how they spend their time.
- The managers' allocation of time is largely fixed and difficult to change.
- Most of the managers' time is controlled by others. There is very little discretionary time.
- "Fire fighting" tends to drive out planning.

Before the study was conducted, Carlson saw managers as controllers of the direction of the company. After the study, he saw them as puppets in a puppet show with hundreds of people pulling the strings and forcing the manager to act in one way or another.

To rectify the situation, work measurement is needed as a first step. Once the manager is conscious of how his or her time is spent, then positive actions can be formulated to rectify the situation. These actions frequently include:

- Better utilization of meetings to reduce wasted time
- Control of interruptions through secretaries and other means
- Clarification of objectives and assignment of priorities to guide time utilization
- Better use of subordinates through delegation

WHITE-COLLAR PRODUCTIVITY MEASUREMENT

White-collar productivity deserves separate consideration because of the difficulties encountered in measurement and the importance of white-collar jobs in the economy. White-collar workers now account for over 50 percent of the work force, and it is estimated that the percentage will grow to 90 percent by the year 2000. White-collar productivity affects all segments of society: manufacturing, service, and nonprofit. Many service firms employ 100 percent white-collar workers. Even in manufacturing companies, a great deal of the jobs are white collar in nature.

We distinguish between two types of white-collar workers, those who do routine work (e.g., clerical workers) and those who are knowledge workers. The later category, knowledge workers, includes managers, lawyers, doctors, computer programmers, accountants, and purchasing agents, to name just a few. We shall focus our attention on the knowledge worker here, because the methods we have already discussed can be widely applied to routine (clerical) white-collar work, as well as blue-collar work.

In measuring white-collar work it is difficult to know what to measure. Output is difficult to define. A knowledge worker is expected to be creative, not to do routine work, which can be easily defined and measured. Moreover, one must be careful to measure the effectiveness of the work, as well as the efficiency. Peter Drucker has defined effectiveness as doing the right things, and efficiency as doing things right. It does no good, for example, to measure the number of operations performed per day (efficiency) by a surgeon if the patients all died (effectiveness).

Measurement of knowledge work can be done at either the group or the individual level. Many knowledge jobs are highly interactive. In this case the group-level measures may be more important than individual measures. For example, suppose that a team is assigned to design a new product for the firm. The team consists of a marketing person, a mechanical engineer, an electrical engineer, a manufacturing manager, and a sales representative. The output of this team can be defined in terms of the ultimate market success of the product, whether the product was developed on time, whether specific product performance parameters were met, and so on. Likewise, the accomplishments of team members can be defined by accomplishment of their specific tasks. But the efforts of any individual are clearly suboptimal compared with the results of the group as a whole. The targets of the electrical engineer could be met, for example, at the expense of the mechanical engineer's targets. The point is that knowledge worker measurements must be taken at the lowest level which makes sense in the accomplishment of the organizational goals. This may require an entire team or group to be measured together and rewarded together, or work may be measured at the individual level, depending on how much interaction occurs.

A study done by Schroeder, Anderson, and Scudder (1985) defined the types of measurements which could be made of knowledge work. As a result of this study, which used extensive managerial input, the following 10 measures were defined.

A. *What is accomplished*
   1. Client satisfaction
   2. Project success
   3. Dollars generated
B. *How the work is done*
   4. Degree of innovation
   5. Handling of nonstandard situations
   6. Degree of immersion in the job
   7. Meeting of deadlines

8. Lack of surprises
9. Documentation and transferability of work
10. Adaptability to change

There are two groups of measures to consider: (1) what is accomplished and (2) how the work is done. First, we will discuss the measures of what is accomplished.

Many knowledge workers have one or more clients inside or outside the company. In these cases, client satisfaction is clearly an important measure of knowledge work. However, some clients may be dissatisfied no matter how well the work is done. For example, students are the clients of a given teacher, but student evaluations of courses and instructors often show at least one student dissatisfied with all aspects of the course. Client satisfaction is an important measure, but it is not necessarily the ultimate measure of the job. This points out the fact that the job itself must be defined before it is measured. In teaching students, learning is probably the ultimate outcome, and student satisfaction is a proxy measure. In health care, a healthy patient is more important than a satisfied patient, although both are desirable outcomes.

Project success is a useful measure, whenever white-collar work can be defined in terms of projects. Project success means that a project has met its cost, time, and performance goals. Since projects are usually team efforts, project success is an example of a group-oriented measure of white-collar productivity.

Many knowledge workers are involved in generating revenue, for example, through marketing or selling efforts. In an environment where research is one of the basic products (e.g., some engineering schools), obtaining research grants may be a measure of great importance. The performance of a partner in an accounting firm may be measured by the amount of revenue received. Measures of revenue provide a market evaluation, in a sense, of the knowledge worker's work.

There are many ways to measure how the work itself is done. One of these measures is the degree of innovation of the work. Innovation is important in knowledge work because we are looking for creativity and an ability to develop and implement new ideas. In the study by Schroeder, et al., one manager said he wanted knowledge workers to "leave new footprints in the sand."

The ability to handle nonstandard situations is a closely related, but different, measure than innovation. The ability to handle nonstandard situations is important, even though a great deal of innovation or ingenuity is not involved. In traditional work measurement, a standardized and repetitive job is assumed. In knowledge work, quite the opposite is true. The essence of most knowledge work is handling nonstandard situations. One type of nonstandard situation is a crisis. In this case a good knowledge worker will have anticipated the possibility of the crisis and will know how to handle it.

Knowledge workers should be immersed or involved in their jobs. Degree of immersion measures whether the worker is motivated by the job. This measure is clearly one of effort or efficiency, since the person may be doing the wrong thing but in a highly enthusiastic way.

Even though we have been focusing on creativity and uniqueness, most white-collar workers have deadlines to meet. Meeting deadlines is another efficiency measure, because a "deadline meeter" may have poor ideas. Nevertheless, deadlines are important particularly in an interactive environment, where others are dependent on the knowledge worker.

Lack of surprises is an important measure for some white-collar jobs. This measure relates to how thoroughly the work is done and whether the white-collar worker keeps his or her "clients" informed of the situation. Timely communication is an important part of knowledge work.

Documentation and transferability of work are useful measures in most environments. Computer programs, for example, must be clearly documented. Lawyers must leave a clear paper trail of how a particular case was handled. Engineers must carefully document their product designs. When documentation is an important part of the job, an employee could be evaluated on how easily a new person can take over the job.

A final measure that is frequently important is adaptability to change. Change is constantly occurring in any organization, and how an employee reacts to change is important to the continued success of the organization. A person who becomes very defensive and refuses to adapt to change is often unproductive. An example of the problems of adaptability can be found in companies where hard-line autocratic managers are being confronted with participatory management programs.

In any given situation, not all the above measures will be important. The above measures were only given as examples; the particular measurements used must be tailored to the job. While a single measure of knowledge work will seldom suffice, one must be careful to measure that which is truly important to the job. The principle of the vital few can be applied where 20 percent of the activities constitute 80 percent of the value of the job. In this case, knowledge work can be largely measured with only a few measures.

Sometimes things are measured because they are easy to measure rather than meaningful to the job. In one case an engineer was measured on the number of designs produced without regard for the produceability of the designs. Another famous example is measuring computer programmers on the lines of code generated. This can lead to programs with excessive code and reduced functionality. One insurance company measured its white-collar workers on the basis of client satisfaction. The company nearly went out of business when the claims department reduced its diligence in paying claims in order to satisfy customers.

In summary, knowledge worker measurement must be tailored to the situation and not be suboptimal in nature. More than one measure will usually be required. Both efficiency and effectiveness must be considered. Measures should encompass not only what is desired, but how the knowledge work is accomplished.

PROBLEMS ENCOUNTERED IN WORK MEASUREMENT

In practice, several problems are encountered in using work measurement properly. The first is the selection of an appropriate work-measurement technique (e.g., time study, work sampling, etc.). This problem can be solved by selecting a technique based on the following considerations:

1. Use
2. Cost
3. Accuracy
4. Type of work (e.g., repetitive)
5. Worker reaction

How the results of work measurement are to be used is a fundamental consideration. If the purpose is to establish wage incentive plans, a highly accurate technique such as time study, predetermined times, or standard data should be used. If a standard is to be set, an accurate technique will also be needed. If the aim is for planning and forecasting or job analysis, one of the less accurate methods can be used (e.g., work sampling or historical data).

Type of work is also an important consideration. For example, it does not usually pay to set a standard unless the work is repetitive. For nonrepetitive work, a historical data or work-sampling approach tends to be more appropriate. We have already indicated how knowledge work might be measured by some of these methods.

In addition to these considerations of use, accuracy, and type of work, the cost of work measurement should be considered. The method employing historical data is the least costly to use provided that the data are readily available. When there are many time standards to set, the use of predetermined times and standard data is less expensive than time study. In every case cost must be balanced against the use and accuracy considerations.

Finally, worker reaction to the work-measurement technique must be considered. Ordinarily, workers do not like to be timed with a stopwatch. This makes the techniques other than time study more attractive from a psychological point of view. In many cases, management is becoming more and more sensitive to worker reactions and would prefer to avoid stopwatches.

Another important issue in using work measurement is who is to set the standards. In some organizations, standards are set by industrial engineers; in others they are set by line management. Sirota and Wolfson (1972) give an interesting example of this dilemma in a large electronics manufacturing company. Faced with increasing cost competition, the company installed formal work measurement and hired a staff of industrial engineers to implement the program. Through work measurement and methods study, the industrial engineers improved efficiency by over 50 percent in a 2-year period. However, management also learned, through formal surveys before and after, that worker morale had decreased dramatically during this time.

Apparently, morale decreased because the workers considered some standards unfair and the industrial engineers were reluctant to change them. As a result, management decided to place the final decision for standards in the hands of first-level supervisors. If the supervisor felt the standard was unfair, the job could be placed "off standards" until it was studied once again by industrial engineers.

After restudying the job, the first-line supervisor decided whether to put the job back on work measurement again. This approach resulted in no loss in productivity and a sharp improvement in worker morale. It also resulted, of course, in a loss of power for the industrial engineers. In measuring knowledge work, the knowledge workers should normally be involved.

Another problem encountered in using work measurement is the maintenance of the standards. Each time a work method changes, the standard should be updated through another study. The updates, however, are not always done with a resulting deterioration of standards. In some organizations, workers typically exceed the standards by 30 to 50 percent, and all standards must be adjusted before they are used for planning. A company faced with this situation should reevaluate its whole work-measurement approach and develop a program to revise the standards systematically.

Finally, the use of standards is being called into question as companies stress improvement more than control. A standard implies that 100 percent effort is considered acceptable by management. Under this approach, workers and supervisors are not constantly challenged to make improvements in their methods of work. It is considered an engineering or management responsibility to make improvements while workers merely conform to the standard. With more responsibility being shifted to workers, this whole concept is being called into question. Workers are being asked to constantly seek productivity improvements and are, in some cases, rewarded for greater productivity. As a result, the concept of standard output takes on less meaning. It is more important to seek improvements in performance rather than to seek satisfactory performance. In other words, there is less emphasis on direct labor control and more emphasis on productivity and quality improvement.

KEY POINTS

The chapter's key points include the following:

- Work measurement can be used for various purposes including evaluating a worker's performance, planning work force needs, planning capacity, setting prices, controlling costs, selecting a work method, scheduling operations, and establishing wage incentives.
- In time studies, a trained worker who follows the prescribed method is timed by a stopwatch or other timing device for a number of work cycles. The worker is then rated for work pace, and allowances are added to arrive at a standard.
- Predetermined times and standard data are used to set standards without the use of a stopwatch. These approaches have important psychological and cost advantages.
- Work sampling and historical data can be used to study work but not to set time standards. With work sampling, random observations of an individual or group of workers lead to the development of a distribution of activity percentages. This approach often calls for a large number of observations.
- Knowledge worker productivity usually requires careful definition of more than

one measure. Several measures were suggested for evaluating what knowledge work is accomplished and how the work is done. Both effectiveness and efficiency must be measured.

• Several issues are encountered in using work measurement in practice; these involve selecting the proper method, maintaining worker morale, deciding who is to set the standards, and maintaining the standards.

QUESTIONS

1. It has been suggested that individual standards be set for each worker. Discuss the pros and cons of this idea.
2. Why is it essential to determine the uses for work measurement prior to selecting a method?
3. The ABC typing pool is considering an incentive pay system. What type of work-measurement methods might be appropriate?
4. At the Union Oil Company, a large number of complaints about standards that are "too tight" have been received. These standards have been set by industrial engineers on the basis of predetermined time systems. How would you solve this problem?
5. Why cannot work sampling and historical data be used to set standards?
6. Develop an activity chart to describe the procedure you use to start your car and drive it out of the driveway.
7. Develop an operations chart to describe the procedure used by a man to get his trousers out of the closet and to put them on.
8. What are the advantages and disadvantages of using stopwatch observations rather than predetermined times?
9. During a time study, the following times were observed: 40, 48, 48, 45, 46, and 43 seconds. Using a rating factor of 95 percent and an allowance of 20 percent, determine a time standard for this job.
10. Consider the following problems:
    a. If NT = 110 and OT = 90, what is RF?
    b. If ST = 170, A = 20%, and RF = 90, what is OT?
11. A worker was heard to complain that he cannot work for 8 hours, all day, at the 100 percent pace set by the industrial engineers. What is your reaction to this complaint?
12. Describe the differences between predetermined data and standard data.
13. We think that the workers in the shipping department spend 15 percent of their time in nonproductive activities (delays, rest, etc.). We want to use work sampling to determine the true percentage of nonproductive time to within ± 2 percent with 95 percent confidence. How many observations are needed?
14. Knowledge workers were heard to say that their work was too complicated to measure. What is your response to this comment?
15. Suggest appropriate measures for the following kinds of white-collar work.
    a. Teaching
    b. Engineering
    c. Computer programming

SELECTED BIBLIOGRAPHY

BARNES, RALPH M.: *Motion and Time Study: Design and Measurement of Work*, 6th ed., New York: Wiley, 1968.
CARLSON, SUNE: *Executive Behavior, A Study of the Workload and the Working Methods of Managing Directors*, Stockholm: Strombergs, 1951.

Harvard Business School: *Experience and Cost: Some Implications for Manufacturing Policy*, Cambridge, Mass.: Harvard Business School, ICCH 9-675-228, 1975.

Hegstad, Michael: "Executive Productivity and Time Management," graduate student paper, Minneapolis: University of Minnesota, 1979.

Heiland, Robert, and Wallace Richardson: *Work Sampling*, New York: McGraw-Hill, 1957.

Maynard, Harold, G. J. Stegemerten, and John L. Schwab: *Methods-Time Measurement*, New York: McGraw-Hill, 1948.

Mundel, Marvin E.: *Motivation and Time Study*, 5th ed., Englewood Cliffs, N.J.: Prentice-Hall, 1978.

Nadler, Gerald: "Is More Measurement Better?" *Industrial Engineering*, March 1978, pp. 20–25.

———: *Work Design*, Homewood, Ill.: Irwin, 1963.

Niebel, Benjamin W.: *Motion and Time Study*, 6th ed., Homewood, Ill.: Irwin, 1976.

Rice, Robert S.: "Survey of Work Measurement and Wage Incentives," *Industrial Engineering*, vol. 9, no. 7, July 1977, pp. 18–31.

Schroeder, Roger G., John C. Anderson, and Gary D. Scudder: "Measurement of White Collar Productivity," *International Journal of Operations and Production Management*, vol. 5, no. 2, 1985.

Sirota, David: "Productivity Management," *Harvard Business Review*, vol. 44, no. 5, September–October 1966, pp. 111–116.

——— and Alan D. Wolfson: "Work Measurement and Worker Morale," *Business Horizons*, August 1972, pp. 43–48.

Yelle, Louis E.: "The Learning Curve: Historical Review and Comprehensive Survey," *Decision Sciences*, vol. 10, no. 2, April 1979.

PART SIX

QUALITY MANAGEMENT AND CONTROL

- **MANAGING QUALITY**
- **QUALITY CONTROL**

Quality is one of the objectives of operations and one of the five decision-making responsibilities. In order to meet the quality objective, it is important to manage and control all aspects of quality. Chapter 20 begins this part with a discussion of managing quality, and Chapter 21, on quality control, completes it.

The management of quality should encompass all aspects of quality, from design of the product or service through production and use. All quality efforts should be guided by a corporate policy on quality and a planning and control system which ensures a quality product. This system should involve all individuals in the firm and stress the prevention of errors in all parts of the company.

Quality Control, described in Chapter 21, is aimed at continuous improvement of a stable process. A stable process is maintained by use of statistical process control which separates assignable causes from random causes of variation. Continuous improvement is achieved by removing causes of errors from the processes and by stressing prevention of errors. In this way variability is not only controlled, but continuously reduced. Inspection, or measurement, is used to detect errors and to find and correct causes of errors.

The main contribution of Part 6 is a broad treatment of quality, which includes management, planning, and policy concerns in addition to the more traditional statistical topics. In practice, quality is primarily a management problem, and statistical methods are used to achieve continuous improvement of a stable system.

CHAPTER 20
Managing Quality

Quality is one of the four key objectives of most operations. While it is something the whole organization must be concerned with, the operations function is charged with the responsibility of producing quality for the customer. This responsibility can be carried out only by the proper management and control of quality in all phases of operations.

This chapter is primarily concerned with the management of quality, while control of quality is discussed in Chapter 21. Since operations is so vitally involved in quality, it is somewhat surprising that the subject of quality management has been given only cursory treatment in the literature of operations management. Perhaps the explanation is the preoccupation with formulas, statistics, and quantitative methods which has characterized the quality control field. As more attention shifts to quality concerns, managing quality is, however, receiving increased emphasis. This emphasis includes continuous improvement, prevention of defects, total quality approaches, and Japanese quality. One can hardly pick up the newspaper today without reading about these subjects, which are treated in this chapter, along with other quality management issues.

The term "quality" is used in a variety of different ways; there is no clear definition of it. From the customer's viewpoint, quality is often associated with value, usefulness, or even price. From the producer's viewpoint, quality is associated with designing and producing a product to meet customer needs.

"Quality" has taken on different meanings through the years. In the early 1900s, it meant inspection. All finished products were inspected and any defects were corrected. In the 1940s, the word "quality" took on a statistical connotation. Pioneers in statistical quality control—like Shewhart, Dodge, Romig, and Nelson—developed the idea that any production process was subject to a certain level of natural variation. It was the job of quality control managers to discover this level through statistical methods and to assure control of the production process. In the 1960s, "quality" was extended outside of production to include all other functions using a concept of total quality control. With total quality control, the entire organization is mobilized to help produce a quality product. The meaning of the term "quality" is now being expanded to include zero defects, continuous improvement, and customer focus. An approach to improving quality at the Ford Motor Company is described in Box 20.1.

BOX 20.1
FORD MOTOR COMPANY

Operating principles for total quality control, from a speech by Donald E. Peterson, chairman and CEO, Ford Motor Company.

In the past, quality at Ford was looked on as a design, product engineering and manufacturing responsibility. Essentially, it meant conforming to specifications.

A total quality concept, however, requires a much more comprehensive approach. It calls for continuous improvement in everything we do, not just design, engineering and manufacturing. Essentially, everyone in the company is involved in a process that results in a product or service for a customer—whether that customer is a staff or operating function within the company or a car buyer or owner at a dealership.

Therefore, all employees must think of their jobs in terms of meeting a customer's needs and expectations and strive for continuous improvement by identifying improvement opportunities and preventing problems. That's the total quality concept.

How can we achieve total quality on a continuing basis?

First, we've got to keep every process in a dynamic condition so that change and continuous improvement can take place.

Second, we must let go of our traditional systems—many of which served us well in the past—and unleash the enormous power that people have to bring creative ideas to bear on our problems. This isn't a cop-out by management with respect to its responsibility to provide leadership. But, W. Edwards Deming points out that most of industry's problems are caused by faulty systems. Management, therefore, must establish systems that encourage employee creativity, not stifle it.

The third step is to identify the essential operating principles and process that must be present to achieve total quality, and then implement them. These elements are: (1) management commitment; (2) customer focus; (3) total organization participation through employee involvement and participative management; (4) statistical process control; (5) education and training; and (6) removing roadblocks to progress. I assure you, the numbers do not indicate an order of importance—I'd say they're all about equal.

So it is our job to create an environment that enables and encourages employees to participate in decisions affecting their jobs and the company's success. This is not cheerleading. It's not slogans. It is preparing employees to identify opportunities for continuous improvement and eliminating systems that limit their contributions.

Source: Extracted from a speech given to the Society of Automotive Engineers.

20.1 FITNESS FOR USE

"Quality" has been generally defined as "fitness for use." This means that the product or service meets the customer's needs; i.e., the product is fit for the customer's use. Fitness for use is related to value received by the customer and to customer satisfaction. Only the customer—not the producer—can determine it.

Fitness for use is a relative concept which varies from one customer to another. For example, while one customer may consider a Ford automobile perfectly fit for use, another may not. Each person defines quality in relation to his or her own needs.

From the producer's viewpoint, variation in quality cannot be tolerated. The producer must specify quality as concretely as possible and then strive to meet those specifications while improving the product over time. Whether the resulting product is fit for use or not will then be judged by the customer.

Producers should continuously strive to improve quality, that is, doing a better job of meeting customer needs and reducing variability in all processes. Continuous improvement is a never-ending process and is driven by knowledge and problem solving. As producers gain a better understanding of customer expectations, and as better technology becomes available, quality can be continuously improved.

According to Juran et al. (1988), fitness for use is based on the following five quality characteristics:

* Technological (e.g., strength and hardness)
* Psychological (e.g., taste, beauty, status)
* Time-oriented (e.g., reliability and maintainability)
* Contractual (e.g., guarantee provisions)
* Ethical (e.g., courtesy of sales personnel, honesty)

Quality for a manufactured product may be defined primarily by technological, contractual, and time-oriented characteristics, while a service product may involve all the characteristics listed above.

Quality is generally more difficult to define for services than for manufactured products. Whether the product is a service or a good, however, the following dimensions of quality may be defined:

- Quality of design
- Quality of conformance
- The "abilities"
- Field service

Quality of design is determined before the product is produced. In a manufacturing company, this determination is usually the primary responsibility of the engineering department, along with support from marketing and operations. In service organizations, quality of design is handled by marketing and operations working together to design the service.

Quality of design is determined by market research, design concept, and specifications. Market research is ordinarily aimed at determining the customer's needs. Since there are different ways to meet these needs, a particular design concept must be developed. For example, the customer may need inexpensive and energy-efficient transportation—a need that can be met by a large number of different automobiles, each representing a different design concept. The design concept then results in a set of specifications for the product, e.g., a blueprint, bill of materials, or service specification.

Quality of conformance means producing a product to meet the specifications. When the product conforms to specifications, it is considered by operations as a quality product even though the quality of design may be low. For example, an inexpensive pair of shoes will have high "quality" if they are made according to specifications, and they will have low "quality" if they do not meet specifications. Quality of design and quality of conformance thus represent two different uses of the term "quality."

Another aspect of quality involves the so-called abilities: availability, reliability, and maintainability. Each of these terms has a time dimension and thus extends the meaning of "quality" beyond the beginning or starting quality level. The addition of time to the definition of quality is, of course, necessary to reflect the fitness for continued use by the customer.

"Availability" defines the continuity of service to the customer. A product is available if it is in an operational state and not down for repairs or maintenance. In the military, availability is equated with operational readiness. Availability can be measured quantitatively as follows:

$$\text{Availability} = \frac{\text{uptime}}{\text{uptime} + \text{downtime}}$$

"Reliability" refers to the length of time that a product can be used before it fails. Formally speaking, reliability is the probability that a product will function for a specified period of time without failure. The reliability of a light bulb for 1000 hours might, for example, be 80 percent. In this case, if many light bulbs are tested for 1000 hours, 80 percent of them will burn the entire time and 20 percent will fail. The reliability of a product is also related to mean time between failure (MTBF), which is just the average time that the product functions from one failure to the next. The longer the MTBF, the more reliable the product.

"Maintainability" refers to the restoration of a product to service once it has failed. All customers consider maintenance or repairs a nuisance. Thus a high degree of maintainability is desired so that a product can be restored to use quickly. Maintainability can be measured by the mean time to repair (MTTR) the product.

Returning to availability, we see that availability is a combination of reliability and maintainability. If a product is high in both reliability and maintainability, it will also be high in availability. This relationship can be expressed formally as

$$\text{Availability} = \frac{\text{MTBF}}{\text{MTBF} + \text{MTTR}}$$

If a product has an MTBF of 8 hours and an MTTR of 2 hours each time it fails, then its availability will be 80 percent.

The last dimension of quality is field service, which represents warranty and repair or replacement of the product after it has been sold. Field service is also called customer service, sales service, or just service. Field service is intangible, since it is related to such variables as promptness, competence, and integrity. The customer expects that any problems will be corrected quickly, in a satisfactory manner, and with a high degree of honesty and courtesy. Unfortunately, field service is often one of the least well defined and most poorly controlled dimensions of quality.

The four different dimensions of quality are summarized in Figure 20.1. As can be seen, quality is more than just good product design; it extends to quality control of production, quality over the service life of the product, and quality of field service after the sale. In the next section we will show how these dimensions of quality can be specified by the process of quality planning and control.

PROCESS OF QUALITY PLANNING AND CONTROL

The process of quality planning and control requires a continuous interaction between the customer, operations, and other parts of the organization. Figure 20.2 illustrates how these interactions occur through a quality cycle. The customer specifies needs, usually through the marketing function. These needs are either expressed directly by the customer or discovered through a process of market research. Engineering, in turn, designs a product to meet those needs or works with the customer on design modifications which fit within production capabilities.

Once the design concept and specifications have been completed, the quality of design has been established. Engineering must then work with operations to produce the product specified or, if difficulties are encountered, to modify the specifications. Operations must continually ensure that the product is produced as

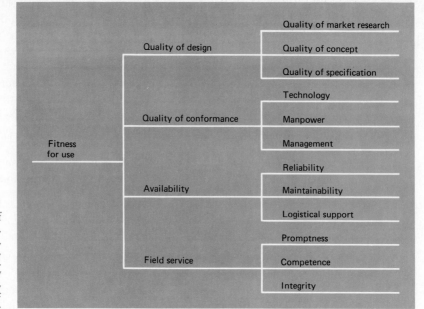

FIGURE 20.1
Different types of
quality.
*Source: J. M. Juran,
Frank M. Gryna, Jr.,
and R. S. Bingham, Jr.
(eds.), Quality
Control Handbook,
4th ed., New York:
McGraw-Hill, 1988.*

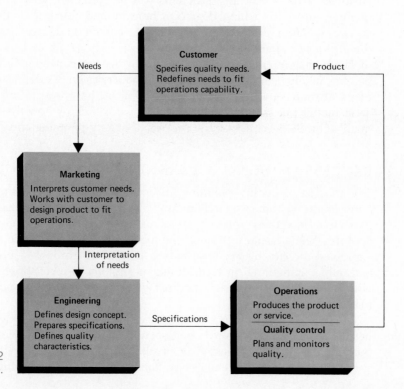

FIGURE 20.2
The quality cycle.

specified by insisting on quality of conformance. This is ordinarily done through proper training, supervision, machine maintenance, and inspection. In addition to meeting specifications, operations should strive to reduce the variance of its processes and products over time. In this way continuous improvement occurs.

Figure 20.3 is a description of the quality cycle for a mass transit system. In this case, a planning agency, in place of marketing, interprets the customer's needs. Another planner, working in greater detail, then determines the design concept and the specifications for service. The operations function delivers the service, and the public then restates its needs or confirms that the present service is satisfactory. The quality cycle should exist in every organization to ensure that all aspects of quality are planned, controlled, and continually improved.

To implement planning and control of quality through the quality cycle requires the following sequence of steps:

1. Define quality attributes.
2. Decide how to measure each attribute.
3. Set quality standards.
4. Establish an inspection program.
5. Find and correct causes of poor quality.
6. Continue to make improvements.

Planning for quality control must always start with the product attributes. The quality planner determines which attributes are important to fitness for use and which are not. For example, the manufacturer of L'eggs panty hose have determined three important quality attributes for their product: (1) a comfortable fit, (2) an attractive appearance, and (3) a wear life that is considered reasonable by the customer. They have also decided that the correct amount of material in various parts of the panty hose will provide a comfortable fit; that fabric dyed in

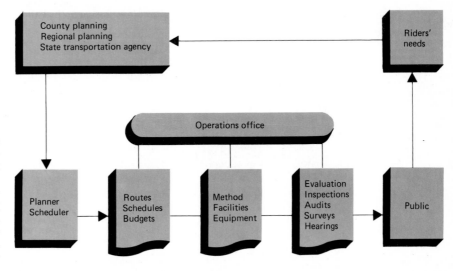

FIGURE 20.3
The quality cycle in a mass transit system.
Source: John P. Van Gigch, "Quality—Producer and Consumer Views," Quality Progress, April 1977, p. 31.

popular colors and free from defects will provide an attractive appearance; and that choice yarns and selected stitch formations will provide acceptable wear life.

A method must then be devised to test and measure quality for each of the product attributes. For example, the manufacturer of L'eggs have developed a special cross-stretcher which can be used to test the strength of their product, and this is used on a certain percentage of all their panty hose. L'eggs are also inspected visually for fabric defects, seaming defects, and shade variations.

After deciding on the measurement techniques to use, the quality planner should set standards that describe the amount of quality required on each attribute. Usually these standards are stated as tolerances (± quantities) or minimum and maximum acceptable limits. Standards can also be set as desired targets, as we shall describe in the next chapter. For example, a standard on L'eggs panty hose is the amount of pressure which the garment must withstand on the cross-stretcher.

After standards have been set, an inspection program should be established. In the case of L'eggs, this program is based on sampling procedures, since it would be far too costly to inspect each of the 120 million pairs of panty hose that are produced each year. How such inspection plans can be set up will be treated in the next chapter.

It is not enough simply to inspect the products for defects. As the saying goes, "You cannot inspect quality into a product, you must build it in." Upon discovering defects, quality personnel should find the underlying cause and correct it. Causes for poor quality could include improper raw material, lack of training, unclear procedures, a faulty machine, and so on. When the causes of poor quality are regularly found and corrected, the production system will be under constant control and improvement will be possible.

An even better approach is to prevent errors from occurring in the first place. This requires designing products and internal procedures that are "foolproof," working with suppliers to prevent errors, training employees before problems occur, and performing preventative machine maintenance. As we shall discuss later in the chapter, prevention of defects is less costly than correction of errors after the fact. Nevertheless, when errors do occur, they need to be quickly corrected and the system itself changed to prevent errors of the same type from recurring. An example of how these ideas have been used at American Express Travel Services is given in Box 20.2.

BOX 20.2
QUALITY AT AMERICAN EXPRESS TRAVEL SERVICES

Unquestionably, the success of American Express over the years has been its attention to quality service and the customer. It's been the one thing that differentiates American Express from its competitors. Since 1978 American Express Travel Services has been using the cycle of quality management to maintain and improve its quality.

Joan Simonds, director of quality assurance at American Express Travel

Services, points out that quality is measured externally by customer satisfaction. The customer determines whether travel services are delivered on time and with the required accuracy. Simonds says, "Quality from the customers' perspective is an important issue. After all, when it comes to service, do customers really care how many steps we have to go through to make travel arrangements? The customers' only concern is the end result. Our quality assurance program is, therefore, output oriented."

American Express measures its customer quality levels frequently. It determines how long it takes for new customers to receive their cards, how many errors are made in processing travel requests, how long it takes to replace a stolen credit card, etc. These measures are fed back to employees and managers for corrective action.

Quality circles have been effectively used at American Express to identify and solve problems. American Express found that quality circles minimize the anxiety that naturally occurs when introducing changes in the work place. Quality circles foster teamwork among departments. They get employees back to the basics, which is remembering there is a customer out there. Simonds says, "Anybody who works in the service industry and gets caught up in the multitude of activities that go on, knows that it is sometimes easy to lose sight of the customer."

Today, American Express Travel has about 250 people worldwide who are dedicated to measuring, monitoring, and improving service quality. Most of these employees are in the field, in operations, with just a few at the headquarters' office. Headquarters monitors global quality monthly, just like the headquarters' financial office receives monthly financial reports from all around the world. The headquarters quality group also assists in sharing information and in implementing quality programs in the divisions.

At American Express, quality has been improved by measuring quality, providing feedback to employees on quality levels, planning for quality improvement, and taking corrective action. American Express has followed the classic quality management cycle to monitor and improve quality.

Source: Joan Simonds, "Quality at American Express Travel Services," proceedings of the 4th Annual Conference of the Operations Management Association, 1985.

20.3 QUALITY POLICY

To initiate the process of quality management a quality policy should be set by top management. The quality policy, in turn, should be derived from a corporate strategy. As an aid to setting these policies and strategies, the Strategic Planning Institute has done a study called PIMS (Profit Impact of Market Strategy) [Buzzell and Gale (1987)]. The basic purpose of this study was to determine what factors affected return on investment and by how much. One of its findings was that high-quality products and services are the most profitable as shown in Figure 20.4. In this case, the quality level of the firm was defined as the percentage of the products superior to competition minus the percentage of products inferior to competition.

With respect to market position, the PIMS study demonstrated that quality and market share usually go together. Firms with high-quality products also have the

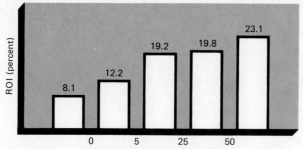

FIGURE 20.4
PIMS data.
High-quality
goods and
services are most
profitable.
*Source: PIMS Strategic
Planning Institute, no
date.*

Quality (percent of products superior to competition minus percent inferior to competition)

largest share of the market and benefit most from market growth. From the standpoint of policy, companies in a weak market position should emphasize quality as a way to build market share. They should use quality in preference to price or high marketing expenditures, since improvement in quality provides the greatest potential for ROI. The PIMS study illustrates the role of quality in strategy, which has sometimes been overlooked in the past.

Recently, the strategic importance of quality has been dramatically illustrated by global competition. High quality is a primary strategy of the Japanese and Germans in gaining a U.S. market share in industries such as autos, electronics, and machine tools, to name just a few. This is causing U.S. companies to become more aware of the strategic role that quality plays.

After considering the strategic factors, top management should set a quality policy. Garvin (1988) gives the following example of a quality policy at Corning Glass.

> It is the policy of Corning Glass Works to achieve total quality performance in meeting the requirements of external and internal customers. Total quality performance means understanding who the customer is, what the requirements are, and meeting those requirements without error, on time, every time.

This policy indicates that Corning is committed to meeting customer needs. Corning has done this by having many employees meet with the company's customers. Plant managers, engineers, and workers meet regularly with customers to determine whether the product specifications are realistic. Their aim is to eliminate or reduce tight tolerances which are unnecessary while improving or maintaining specifications which are needed.

At Corning such market sensitivity to customer needs has been coupled with internal attention to process control and improvement. Employees identify their internal customers and the needs of those customers. Corning has used statistical process control for years and aggressively pursues education of its employees in quality principles. These efforts are aimed at carrying out the Corning quality policy.

Policy statements should be followed up with detailed quality objectives set on a periodic basis, usually annually. If the company has a management by objectives

(MBO) system, the quality objectives should be incorporated into it.[1] Quality objectives should appear not only in the quality manager's MBO statement but in the statements of each manager involved in quality, e.g., operations, marketing, engineering, and field service.

Some examples of quality objectives are as follows:

- Raise the outgoing quality level to 99.999 percent (10 defects out of 1 million units) as measured by sampling procedures.
- Make sure that all managers receive a 5-day training course on quality assurance.
- Form quality control circles of workers and staff to meet weekly, to identify causes of poor quality, and to take appropriate corrective action.

Once the objectives are formulated and have been assigned to specific managers, they will provide the short-range vehicle to improve quality and to carry out the company's quality policy.

20.4 ORGANIZATION FOR QUALITY AND THE TOTAL QUALITY CONCEPT

In addition to policy and objectives, organizational structure is one of the issues that should be decided as part of quality management. In manufacturing companies, two basic types of organizational structures are used. First, the quality department may be independent of manufacturing and report directly to the general manager, as shown in Figure 20.5a. Second, the quality department may be a part of manufacturing and report to the manufacturing manager, as shown in Figure 20.5b.

Whether quality should be under manufacturing or not has raised a great deal of controversy. Those who argue for a separate quality function reporting to the general manager claim that quality should be independent to avoid compromising quality in the effort to meet schedules or to reduce costs. This view has been especially strong in companies that do government contracting. In some cases, the government insists that quality be organized separately to protect the government's interests as a customer.

Those who argue that quality should be under manufacturing point out that you cannot inspect quality into a product and that quality requires close coordination with the work force, purchasing, and all phases of operations. They argue that the manager of manufacturing is the best person to coordinate the quality department and all other departments in manufacturing which affect quality.

In recent years, as the concept of total quality has been developed, the precise organizational arrangement which is used has become less important. Using the total quality concept, the quality department is seen as the organizational coordinator for all other departments which affect quality: manufacturing, pur-

---

[1]"MBO" refers to a system where each manager agrees to written objectives with his or her supervisor, usually on an annual basis. Managerial performance is then defined in relation to the objectives which have been set.

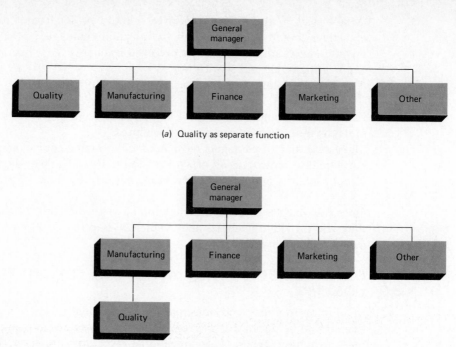

FIGURE 20.5
Organization of
quality.

chasing, marketing, and engineering. Under a total quality program, each department must identify its precise role in quality and must set objectives to maintain acceptable quality of design and conformance.

The total quality concept requires the quality department to spend more time on planning and less on inspection and control. A total quality approach stresses prevention of defects and recognizes the role of all organizational units in achieving quality goals. Prevention is not something which can be done by any one department because it requires attention to vendor relations (purchasing), training (personnel), design (engineering), customer needs (marketing), and production of the product (operations). A total systems approach is required which cuts across the entire organization. In this case, the quality department is not responsible for quality; rather, quality is everybody's responsibility. The quality department serves a coordinating role to ensure that everyone contributes to quality objectives.

Lack of a total quality concept is seen everyday in industry. When a quality problem is discovered, the general manager often turns to quality control to fix the problem. In reality, quality control can do little, since the problem was caused by engineering, manufacturing, or marketing in the first place. It is a mistake to call most problems quality problems; they should be called by the names of the departments which caused them.

It is not enough simply to recognize the importance of total quality control; rather, a positive program must be implemented throughout the organization. The program should specify how the total quality effort will be organized, how all individuals can be made aware of their role in quality, and how the results of the total quality approach will be measured.

20.5 THE DEMING APPROACH

Moving beyond strategy and organizational structure, W. Edwards Deming has emphasized the role that management should take in quality improvement. Deming defines quality as continuous improvement of a stable system. This definition emphasizes two things. First, all systems (administrative, design, production, and sales) must be stable in a statistical sense. This requires that measurements be taken of quality attributes throughout the company and monitored over time. If these measurements have a constant variance around a constant average, the system is stable. The second aspect of Deming's definition is continuous improvement of the various systems to reduce variation and better meet the customer's needs.

Deming has expressed his philosophy toward quality in his famous 14 points shown in Box 20.3 [also see Deming (1982, 1986)]. He stresses that top executives should manage for the long run and not sacrifice quality for short-run profits. Deming believes that excessive attention to quarterly profit reports and short-run objectives has distracted top management from focusing on customer service and long-run quality improvement. He also argues, as others do, that management should cease dependence on inspection to achieve quality and stress prevention of defects instead. Deming suggests that this should be accomplished by the training of all employees, good supervision, and use of statistical procedures.

Deming goes on to exhort management to break down barriers between departments and to encourage people to work together to produce quality products and services. He thinks that many of the work standards, individual performance pay systems, and quotas used by companies get in the way of cooperation among individuals and departments and thus impede quality improvement.

Deming has been a strong advocate of statistical process control ideas, which are covered in the next chapter. Quality cannot be improved by trying harder. Workers and managers must have the proper tools to identify causes of variation, to control variation, and to reduce variation in the product.

Deming has successfully taught his ideas to the Japanese and is credited, along with Juran, with helping to improve quality in Japanese industry. The Japanese attribute much of their success to American ideas, which they have thoroughly implemented. Lately, American industry is also rediscovering many of these basic ideas and is once again stressing quality as a key to survival and success.

Now that we have covered some definitions of quality, its impact on strategy, and management principles, we will move into more detail on how to manage quality. This will involve measuring the cost of quality and implementing programs to improve quality by "doing it right the first time."

20.6 COSTS OF QUALITY

A powerful idea in the area of quality is to calculate the cost of quality. This is the

BOX 20.3
DEMING'S FOURTEEN MANAGEMENT PRINCIPLES*

Requirements for a business whose management plans to remain competitive in providing goods and services that will have a market.

1. Create constancy of purpose toward improvement of products and services with the aim of being competitive and staying in business for the long-run, rather than short-run profits.

2. Adopt the new philosophy by refusing to allow commonly accepted levels of mistakes, defects, delays, and errors. Accept the need for change.

3. Cease dependence on mass inspection. Rely instead on building quality into the product in the first place and on statistical means for controlling and improving quality.

4. End the practice of awarding business on the basis of price tag alone. Instead minimize total cost. Reduce the number of suppliers by eliminating those who cannot provide evidence of statistical control of processes.

5. Improve constantly, and forever, systems of production to improve quality and productivity and thus constantly reduce costs.

6. Institute training on the job for all employees.

7. Focus management and supervisors on leadership of their employees to help them do a better job.

8. Drive out fear. Don't blame employees for "systems problem." Encourage effective two-way communications. Eliminate management by control.

9. Break down barriers between departments. Encourage teamwork among different areas such as research, design, manufacturing, and sales.

10. Eliminate programs, exhortations, and slogans that ask for new levels of productivity without providing better methods.

11. Eliminate arbitrary quotas, work standards, and objectives that interfere with quality. Instead, substitute leardership and continuous improvement of work processes.

12. Remove barriers (poor systems and poor management) that rob people of pride in their work.

13. Encourage life-long education and self-improvement of all employees.

14. Put everyone to work on implementing these fourteen points.

*Extracted from Deming (1986).

cost of not meeting the customer's requirements—the cost of doing things wrong. The cost of quality includes prevention, appraisal, and failure categories. All these are costs of not doing things right the first time. By assigning a cost to quality, it can be managed and controlled like any other cost. Since managers speak the language of money, putting quality in cost terms offers a powerful means of communication and control.

Most companies have no idea how much they spend to plan and control quality. Those who have measured them find that the costs are about 30 percent of sales, with ranges from 20 to 40 percent [Crosby (1979, 1984)]. Since these figures are greater than profit margins in many companies, a reduction in the cost of quality can lead to a significant improvement in profit. The best-managed companies have been able to reduce their costs of quality from 30 percent of sales to as little as 3 percent over a period of several years [Crosby (1984)]. This has been done while improving the quality of the product. The potential for doing this in most companies is untapped.

The cost of quality may be divided into two components: control costs and failure costs. The control costs are related to activities which remove defects from the production stream. This can be done in two ways: by prevention and by appraisal. The prevention costs include activities such as quality planning, new-product reviews, training, and engineering analysis. These activities occur prior to production and are aimed at preventing defects before they occur. The other category of control costs comprises appraisal or inspection aimed at eliminating defects after they occur but before the products reach the customer.

The failure costs are incurred either during the production process (internal) or after the product is shipped (external). The internal failure costs include such items as scrap, rework, quality downgrading, and machine downtime. The external failure costs include warranty charges, returned goods, allowances, and the like. A more complete listing of all these costs is given in Table 20.1

TABLE 20.1
COSTS OF QUALITY

PREVENTION COSTS

Quality planning: Costs of preparing an overall plan, numerous specialized plans, quality manuals, procedures.

New-product review: Review or prepare quality specifications for new products, evaluation of new designs, preparation of tests and experimental programs, evaluation of vendors, marketing studies to determine customers' quality requirements.

Training: Developing and conducting training programs.

Process planning: Design and develop process control devices.

Quality data: Collecting data, data analysis, reporting.

Improvement projects: Planned failure investigations aimed at chronic quality problems.

APPRAISAL COSTS

Incoming materials inspection: The cost of determining quality of incoming raw materials.

Process inspection: All tests, sampling procedures, and inspections done while the product is being made.

Final goods inspection: All inspections or tests conducted on the finished product in the plant or the field.

Quality laboratories: The cost of operating laboratories to inspect materials at all stages of production.

INTERNAL FAILURE

Scrap: The cost of labor and material for product which cannot be used or sold.

Rework: The cost of redoing product which can be made to conform.

Downgrading: Product which must be sold at less than full value due to quality problems.

Retest: Cost of inspection and tests after rework.

Downtime: Idle facilities and people due to quality failures.

EXTERNAL FAILURE

Warranty: The cost of refunds, repairing, or replacing products on warranty.

Returned merchandise: Merchandise which is returned to the seller.

Complaints: The cost of settling customer complaints due to poor quality.

Allowances: Cost of concessions made to customers due to substandard quality.

Source: Adapted from J. M. Juran, Frank M. Gryna, Jr., and R. S. Bingham, Jr. (eds.), *Quality Control Handbook, 4th ed.,* New York: McGraw-Hill, 1988.

The total cost of quality can thus be expressed as a sum of the following costs.

Total cost of quality = (control costs) + (failure costs)

$$= \left(\begin{array}{c} \text{prevention} \\ \text{costs} \end{array} + \begin{array}{c} \text{appraisal} \\ \text{costs} \end{array} \right) + \left(\begin{array}{c} \text{internal} \\ \text{failure} \\ \text{costs} \end{array} + \begin{array}{c} \text{external} \\ \text{failure} \\ \text{costs} \end{array} \right)$$

Prevention costs	**Control costs**	**Total cost of quality**
Appraisal costs		
Internal failure costs	**Failure costs**	
External failure costs		

The total cost of quality can be minimized by observing the relationship between cost of quality and degree of conformance to customer requirements, as in Figure 20.6. When the degree of conformance is very high (low defects), the costs of failures are low but the costs of control are quite high. When the degree of conformance is low (high defects), the opposite situation exists. Thus there is,

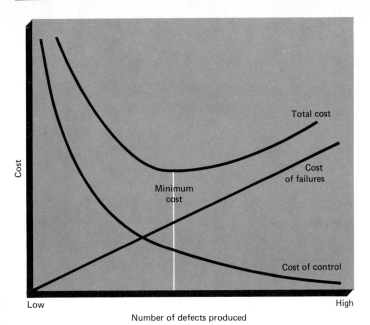

FIGURE 20.6
Cost of quality.

Cost

Total cost

Cost
of failures

Minimum
cost

Cost of control

Low

High

Number of defects produced

between the two extremes, an optimal level of conformance where total quality costs are minimized.

It is being recognized now, however, that the optimal point is close to zero defects in many cases. For example, one manufacturer of tie rods for automobiles has been producing less than one defective part per 100,000 units. This producer is now striving to reduce the defective rate to 1 defective part per million units, which the producer believes, will lower the total cost of failure and control. The optimal point is, therefore, very close to zero defects in this case.

What is at stake is not simply finding the minimum cost point for quality and operating there, but constantly reducing the cost of quality. This can be done by revising the production system including technology, training, attitudes, and management. As a result, the cost of failures and the cost of control are both reduced. This is shown in Figure 20.7.

Good quality management also requires the proper balance between appraisal and prevention costs, so that total control costs are at the minimum. Table 20.2 is a cost table from the Whirlpool Corporation showing the tradeoff between these costs. The numbers in the table are millions of dollars of total quality cost for particular expenditures on prevention and appraisal in the margins. For example, suppose $1.4 million is spent on appraisal and $1 million on prevention. Then the total cost of quality will be $18.47 million.

Most companies have a tendency to operate in the lower left-hand corner of this table by spending a great deal on appraisal and little on prevention. But the total cost is minimized in the upper right-hand corner, where more is spent on prevention and less on appraisal. The typical company would therefore benefit by reducing its appraisal costs and simultaneously increasing its prevention costs.

The costs of quality should be reported to all levels of management. There are several ways in which these costs can be tabulated:

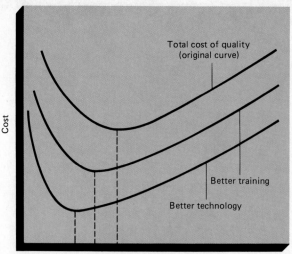

FIGURE 20.7
Reducing the cost
of quality.

- By organizational unit
- By time
- By cost-of-quality categories
- By product

Quality costs should also be normalized for volume using one or more of the following measures.

- *Per direct labor hours.* This is one of the best-known measures of volume and is readily available for calculation in most operations.
- *Per direct labor cost.* This measure has the advantage of dividing dollars by dollars and thus reducing the effects of inflation.
- *Per dollar of standard manufacturing cost.* This extends the direct labor index by adding material and overhead. The resulting index has greater stability because it is not affected as much by automation.

TABLE 20.2
TRADEOFFS IN QUALITY COSTS

		Range of prevention costs (dollars per unit)								
		0.60	0.80	1.00	1.20	1.40	1.60	1.80	2.00	2.20
Range of appraisal costs (dollars per unit)	0.60	20.05	20.29	20.18	19.40	15.90	12.22	10.09	9.82	10.22
	0.80	20.40	20.64	20.54	19.78	16.34	11.72	10.62	10.36	10.77
	1.00	20.52	20.77	20.69	19.96	16.63	12.16	11.11	10.87	11.28
	1.20	20.20	20.46	20.42	19.77	16.66	12.47	11.51	11.31	11.73
	1.40	18.08	18.40	18.47	18.03	15.58	12.25	11.56	11.50	11.95
	1.60	15.17	15.56	15.77	15.62	14.02	11.79	11.46	11.53	12.06
	1.80	14.62	15.03	15.29	15.23	13.91	12.03	11.81	11.99	12.48
	2.00	14.63	15.06	15.34	15.32	14.14	12.44	12.28	12.48	12.98
	2.20	15.09	15.52	15.80	15.80	14.64	12.98	12.83	13.04	13.54

Source: Whirlpool, *Total Quality Assurance: Total Cost of Quality,* May 1978, p. 2.

- *Per dollar of sale.* This measure has the advantage of being readily understood by top managers. It has the disadvantage of being affected by pricing changes.
- *Per equivalent unit of product.* When products are fairly homogenous, this measure is useful because it is unaffected by extraneous costs and prices.

The measures that are selected will be a function of the particular company and its reporting practices. Whatever measures are used, however, should be calculated by the accountants, just like other financial information. The accounting reports should then be interpreted by quality managers, who should also recommend appropriate actions to reduce the costs of quality.

The cost of quality can be a powerful tool for quality improvement when it is properly used. It focuses management attention on waste due to excess failures or high control costs. It also provides a quantitative basis for monitoring progress in reducing quality costs to the desired level. The cost of quality is easily understood; it brings quality out of a "goodness" or "value" area which cannot be measured to a dollars-and-cents basis.

MAKE IT RIGHT THE FIRST TIME

Suppose we find that the cost of quality is too high. How can it be reduced? What can management do? One approach is to adopt the total quality view or Deming's approach described above. Another approach is to stress prevention: to produce "zero defects" or to "make it right the first time."

It is generally accepted that there has been a reduction in craftsmanship and pride in work over the past decade. This problem is believed to stem from worker attitudes, but workers often reflect the attitudes of their managers. To reverse the decline in quality, management must be the first to change.

The advocates of the zero defects philosophy argue that we are conditioned to believe it is all right to make errors. They point to such common sayings as "To err is human," "Everybody makes mistakes," and "Nobody's perfect," all of which serve to justify the lack of conformance in the work place. The problem is further compounded by inspectors whose job it is to catch the errors made by workers.

We are conditioned to expect errors in the work place, but not in other forms of human activity. For example, when we attend a concert we do not expect the soloists to play a certain percentage of bad notes. Why should we settle for poor quality in the work place? The usual reply is that high quality costs too much. But in fact high quality may cost less. Perhaps it is cheaper to make the product right the first time than to correct errors or to pay for scrap, rework, or failures in the field.

Of course, it may be unrealistic to expect that the delivered product will literally have zero defects, but—according to the zero defects approach—everyone should strive toward this as the goal. Even when they do, however, a few defective items may be produced and shipped to the customer. As noted above, however, the defects may be measured in parts per million or parts per billion, which is nearly zero defects for all practical purposes. When the zero defects approach is being used, the work force should strive to make the product exactly to specifications or get the specifications changed. No worker should knowingly produce defects on the grounds that it is too expensive to do it right the first time.

Zero defects programs have sometimes been introduced into industry as motivational efforts. Awards and prizes are given to those workers who produce zero defects over a period of time. But prizes are not enough; the worker should be made responsible for quality. This requires the worker to do most of his or her own inspection, to receive feedback information on quality, and to accept personal responsibility for making a quality product. This can be done if management is willing to delegate authority to the line and to the work force and to expect a quality product in return.

Zero defects programs can have a dramatic effect on quality and the cost of quality. In the Martin Company, an audited savings of $1,650,000 was recorded over the first 2 years, with a 54 percent drop in defects produced. General Electric had a $2 million drop in rework and scrap during the first 2 years of its program. With respect to individual efforts, one forklift driver moved over 15 million pounds of delicate electronic hardware without a single incident of damage. A solderer made almost ½ million connections without error [Halpin (1966), pp. 16–17]. Since these studies were not controlled research efforts, it is difficult to determine the cause of the low number of defects. Nevertheless, it appears that workers are capable of delivering high quality and high productivity at the same time if the job is properly designed and management sets the climate for producing a quality product.

To implement these concepts, Philip Crosby (1979, 1984) has defined a zero defects program in terms of the following 14 steps.[2] The ingredients are management commitment, worker involvement, measurement of quality, quality improvement, and cost reduction.

Step 1: Management commitment. Ensure that senior management understands how prevention of errors can improve quality while reducing costs. Prepare a quality policy that states that each individual must perform exactly as the job requires or cause the requirement to be changed to what we and the customers really need. Agree that quality improvement is a practical way to improve profits.

Step 2: Quality improvement team. A quality improvement team is appointed consisting of one member from each department in the company. A person should be appointed who can commit the department to action, preferably the department head, the first time around. The purpose of this team is to implement the quality program throughout the company.

Step 3: Quality measurement. Establish quality measurements in all parts of the company. These measurements will be used to determine where corrective action is needed and to measure progress later on. Measurements must be established not only for the product, but for operations in the service and office areas and also for the vendors.

---

[2]This section is adapted from Philip B. Crosby, *Quality Is Free,* New York: McGraw-Hill, 1979, pp. 132–139.

Step 4: Cost of quality evaluation. The cost of quality, as defined above, must be measured. At first, the cost will be low, perhaps only 10 percent of sales, because many costs are hidden. Later, the true costs of not doing things right the first time will become apparent, perhaps 20 to 40 percent of sales. The accountants should take responsibility for the cost of quality measurement since this removes any suspected bias. Management will need to insist, however, that past accounting practices be changed to reflect the true cost of quality.

Step 5: Quality awareness. In this step employees are made aware of the quality improvement program through their supervisors. This is not a motivation program, but rather a communications effort to familiarize employees with the effects of poor quality on customers, costs, competition, and their jobs. This is the most important step of all since it prepares employees for later corrective action and error cause removal steps. All employees—office, factory, and service people— should be involved, as well as vendors.

Step 6: Corrective action. As quality problems are discussed in step 5, corrective actions will be suggested by the workers and supervisors. If upper management approval is needed, the problems should be passed up the line; otherwise, they should be solved at the lowest possible level. Weekly meetings should be held at each level to discuss quality problems. Quality circles or team meetings can be incorporated at this step, if appropriate. The habit of corrective action should begin here.

Step 7: Ad hoc committee for the zero defects program. Three or four members of the quality improvement team, established in step 2, should be assigned to an ad hoc committee to investigate the zero defects (ZD) concept and to find ways to communicate the program to all employees (e.g., signs, posters, meetings). This should not be a public relations program but rather an effort to explain why things should be done right the first time. This committee is needed to maintain momentum in the program since a year may have passed by the time ZD day is reached.

Step 8: Supervisor training. A formal program should be established to educate every manager at every level about the ZD concepts. The proof of their understanding is they can explain the concepts to others. Without management commitment at all levels, the program will fail.

Step 9: Zero defects day. A day should be set aside to explain ZD to all employees, so they all understand the concept the same way. Something should be done to signal this day, such as a special luncheon for all employees or a meeting in a large auditorium. The standard of zero defects should be firmly set on this day.

Step 10: Goal setting. The supervisor should ask each employee to set quality goals for 30, 60, and 90 days. These goals should be measurable and specific. This step helps people realize that constant progress toward improved quality is required by *them*. In some companies, a pledge is also signed for zero defects.

Step 11: Error cause removal. Each employee is asked to describe problems which prevent him or her from doing the job right the first time on a simple one-page form. This is not merely a suggestion system; it is aimed at error cause removal. The appropriate functional group is then assigned to investigate each problem and to suggest solutions. Fast feedback to the employee is necessary to maintain interest and involvement. Literally thousands of error causes must be removed in most companies to improve quality.

Step 12: Recognition. Recognition is needed in order to provide positive reinforcement for error cause removal. Various forms of recognition, such as rings, dinners, and merchandise have been used. Large monetary rewards are not as effective because recognition is sought, not rewards for suggestions.

Step 13: Quality councils. The quality professionals and team chairpersons from different parts of the company should form a quality council. They should meet periodically to share ideas and to communicate with each other about their respective programs.

Step 14: Do it over again. The typical program takes 1 year to 18 months. By that time much of the knowledge about the program has been lost owing to turnover and changing situations. Thus, the program should start again with the appointment of a new team. Zero defects day should be held each year as an anniversary. The ZD program should be continued indefinitely so that it is part of the company "culture." If quality isn't "a way of life," it will not improve.

As can be seen, this 14-step program is very extensive and time-consuming. It is not simply a motivational effort, but rather an educational program aimed at doing things right the first time. This requires not only a change in employee and vendor attitudes, but a system to identify and remove causes of errors. The ZD approach is organizationwide and improves quality while simultaneously reducing costs. This approach has been implemented in many organizations around the world with apparently good success.

20.8 QUALITY CIRCLES AND PROJECT TEAMS

Companies have found that to improve quality they must work, not only through individuals, but through groups as well. Therefore, firms have used quality circles and project teams to improve quality.

A quality circle is usually a volunteer group of employees that meets periodically to solve quality problems on the job. The leader of the quality circle may be an employee or one of the supervisors. Employees are trained in problem-solving techniques, and they actively gather data and solve problems together.

A project team is usually assigned by management to solve a particular quality problem. These teams may consist of hourly workers, staff, and managers who will collect data, suggest alternatives, and recommend a course of action to senior management. When the problem has been solved, the team will often be disbanded.

Quality circles and project teams have had success, and some failures, in improving quality. Unless management support and assistance is given, the group effort will fail. Some groups have been formed to gain employee participation, rather than to improve quality, and have not received long-term support from management. As a result, problems may be solved for a time, but then efforts lag and the group falters.

Nevertheless, quality circles and project teams are an important vehicle for identifying and solving quality problems, as well as gaining employee participation. Many problems involve people from several departments and levels. Thus groups are needed to develop solutions which can be implemented and will be supported by various parts of the organization. Most effective quality improvement programs utilize quality circles or project teams as part of the improvement effort.

When quality circles or project teams are installed at the right time and in the proper manner, they can have a dramatic and lasting impact, not only on quality, but on productivity and on the quality of work life. One operations vice president at Honeywell attributed savings in his division in excess of $1 million to the installation of quality circles. "But," he added quickly, "we don't just measure our success in terms of dollars saved or number of circles in operation. More important factors to us are the way our working style has changed and the way productivity and quality of working life have improved in our division."

 20.9 ## AMERICAN AND JAPANESE QUALITY

It is appropriate to end this chapter on quality management with a comparison of American and Japanese quality practices. The Japanese have had great successes over the last decade in producing items of high quality. Perhaps something can be learned from them.

Juran conducted an in-depth analysis of Japanese and American quality with particular attention to the color TV set. He observed the following differences in quality practices between the two countries:

1. *Scrubdown of new products.* In Japan, a very careful procedure is followed prior to the introduction of a new product to ensure the quality of design and conformance. This process of pilot production is called "scrubdown" and is aimed at getting the bugs out of the product before regular production begins. In the United States, scrubdown procedures are also used, but inevitably the conflict between the schedule and quality emerges. In most cases, the United States companies decide to go to market and meet the schedule while correcting the quality defects on the fly. In the end, the correction programs rarely materialize because of other, more pressing priorities and other new products. The Japanese scrubdown procedure is more careful and deliberate.

2. *Emphasis on quality characteristics.* A TV set has three principal quality characteristics: picture quality, cabinet appeal, and reliability. It appears that Japan has emphasized reliability to a much greater extent than the United States while competing favorably on picture quality and cabinet appeal. Juran estimates, for example, that United States color TV sets were failing in service about five times as often as Japanese sets in the middle 1970s. Although the Americans have been

attempting to close the gap, the Japanese still have the lead in quality and particularly in reliability.

3. *Marketing structure.* In Japan, the major TV producers have their own retail outlets and service shops. In Japan, their sets are not sold through huge retail chains and repaired by independent dealers, as TV sets are in the United States. The manufacturer in Japan does it all. As a result, the manufacturers pay more of the real cost of failure; logically, therefore, they stress reliability.

4. *Components.* As any TV manufacturer knows, a key to quality is the use of quality components. The Japanese carefully test all components prior to putting them in a set. They also select vendors carefully to get the best possible supplier from a quality-price standpoint. The Americans do less screening and end up with a much higher rate of in-plant failures. For example, the typical American TV manufacturer has about 150 defects per 100 sets during production while the Japanese have about 5 defects per 100 sets.

5. *Training.* The Japanese emphasize quality training at all levels. Top management attends classes on quality principles. Before receiving assignments as design engineers, engineers must all spend some time in operations to learn about the problems of production. Workers must attend training sessions (in quality circles) as a regular part of their jobs.

6. *Employee relations.* The Japanese stress teamwork and worker responsibility for quality. There is a pride in workmanship which starts with top management and permeates the entire organization. The line managers and workers are put in a decision-making role, and the staff is advisory. As a result, the work force knows it is responsible for producing a quality product and accepts that responsibility. There is a great emphasis in Japan on the total quality concept described above and on doing things right the first time.

Many people feel that the Japanese methods may be all right for Japan but that they will not work in America. This view has already been shown to be wrong in many cases. A classic example involved the Motorola (Quasar Electronics) factory which was taken over by Matsushita in 1974. Prior to the takeover, Motorola was experiencing 150 defects per 100 sets. In a relatively short period of time, the defect rate was reduced to 3 or 4 defects per 100 sets in the same factory, with the same workers, and the same quality control people. The only difference was a few Japanese managers who instituted the Japanese approach to quality management [Juran (1978), p. 14].

Americans are improving quality today as a matter of survival. Customers demand and expect better quality. Much can be learned from the Japanese, who have already succeeded in transforming their World War II image of cheap Japanese goods to the current image of cheap but *high-quality* Japanese goods.

20.10 THE INTEGRATION OF DECISION MAKING AND QUALITY

Decisions made during product and process design as well as in managing the work force directly affect quality. Product design decisions should specify quality objectives and give specifications for the product or service being designed. These product decisions can effectively reduce product liability and quality costs which might otherwise be incurred. In a similar way, the process can be designed from a quality perspective to ensure the meeting of quality objectives. A high-volume, line-flow process will ensure consistent quality, while quality is more difficult to control for intermittent and project processes. The next chapter will include detailed examples of how process design can incorporate quality considerations directly in the design of the process.

We have indicated in this chapter how work force decisions can affect product quality through training, job design, and motivation of the work force. In the case of a zero defects approach, the workers' attitude toward quality is important in reaching the quality objectives of operations. In a similar way, many work force decisions affect quality in operations.

The total approach to quality stresses the interrelationship between quality, decisions in operations, and other parts of the business. Since product design, process design, and work force management decisions affect quality, these decisions must be properly integrated with quality decisions. A summary of the effects that quality has on the entire system is given in Table 20.3.

TABLE 20.3

CHANGING QUALITY ASSUMPTIONS

From	To
Reactive	Proactive
Inspection	Prevention
AQL (acceptable quality level)	ZD (zero defects)
Product-oriented	Organization-oriented
Blame placing	Problem solving
Quality vs. operations	Quality *and* operations
Cost *or* quality	Cost *and* quality
Operations only	Product design, process design, and operations
Hunches on cost of quality	Formal reporting on cost of quality
Predominantly blue-collar caused	Predominantly white-collar caused
Defects should be hidden	Defects should be highlighted
Quality department has quality problems	Purchasing, R&D, marketing and operations have quality problems
Subordinated to management team	Part of management team
General managers not evaluated on quality	Quality performance part of general manager review
Quality costs more	Quality costs less
Meet the specifications	Continuous improvement
Quality is technical	Quality is managerial
Schedule first	Quality first

KEY POINTS

The chapter's key points include the following:

- Quality can be defined as fitness for use by the customer. There are four dimensions of quality which contribute to fitness for use: quality of design, quality of conformance, the "abilities," and field service.
- There is a cycle of product quality—from customer needs through quality of design, production, quality of conformance, and use by the customer. This cycle is controlled by specifying quality attributes, determining how to measure each attribute, setting quality standards, establishing an inspection program, and finding and correcting causes of poor quality. Continuous improvement of the system through prevention of defects is the preferred approach.
- Management should set an overall quality policy, and this should be implemented through specific objectives set by managers at all levels.
- The total quality concept utilizes a systems approach to quality by integrating quality programs and objectives across organizational lines. In most organizations a positive program is needed to implement the concept of total quality.
- Deming has argued that management needs to change in order for quality to improve. He also advocates the aggressive use of statistical quality control techniques.
- The cost of quality measures the lack of conformance to customer requirements. Quality costs can conveniently be divided into control costs and failure costs. Control costs are due to prevention or appraisal. Failure costs may be due to internal or external failures. Every company should measure and control these costs of quality.
- The philosophy that says "Make it right the first time" serves to prevent defects from occurring. The work force can be trained to reduce defects drastically if it is given the responsibility. A zero defects program can be implemented through a 14-step program which includes providing for management commitment, measurement, motivation, and rewards, and then doing it over again.
- Quality circles and project teams are an effective way to involve employees in quality and productivity improvement efforts.
- The Japanese have succeeded in using the concepts of total quality and prevention of defects. They have shown how quality improvement can be used to gain market share and improve profits.

QUESTIONS

1. How can quality be measured for the following products?
   a. Telephone service
   b. Automobile repair
   c. Manufacture of ballpoint pens
2. Describe the differences between the quality of design and the quality of conformance.
3. Product A has an MTBF of 30 hours and an MTTR of 5 hours. Product B has an MTBF of 40 hours and an MTTR of 2 hours.
   a. Which product has the higher reliability?
   b. Which product has greater maintainability?

c. Which product has greater availability?

4. Suppose you manufacture 10,000 wooden pencils per day. Describe a quality planning and control system for this product including possible attributes, measures of quality, tests, etc.

5. Suppose you own and operate a small appliance repair service. Give an example of a quality policy which addresses all the important issues.

6. Give some examples of quality objectives for Question 5.

7. Name some products or services which in your opinion have relatively poor quality.

8. Name some products which have a high degree of quality. Are these products generally associated with successful companies?

9. What are the pros and cons of placing the quality department under the operations manager?

10. The following costs have been recorded:

Incoming materials inspection	$20,000
Training of personnel	40,000
Warranty	45,000
Process planning	15,000
Scrap	13,000
Quality laboratory	30,000
Rework	25,000
Allowances	10,000
Complaints	14,000

What are the costs of prevention, appraisal, external failure, and internal failure?

11. Suppose the following cost functions are available for a particular product.

$$\text{Cost of failure } F = 1500 + 40X$$

$$\text{Cost of control } C = \frac{3080}{X}$$

where X = percent defective

What is the minimum cost of quality and the optimal percent defective?

12. How does the minimum-percent-defective philosophy agree with the idea of zero defects?

13. The cost of quality and volume figures for a hotel are as follows:

	1979	1980
Cost of quality	$100,000	$150,000
Sales	$1,000,000	$1,700,000
Number of customers	50,000	80,000
Direct labor cost	800,000	1,200,000

Has the unit cost of quality increased or decreased?

14. How could a zero defects policy be applied to student term papers?

15. Which of the Deming's 14 points do you agree with and which ones do you disagree with?

16. Contrast and compare the Deming and Crosby approaches to quality improvement.

17. Why are quality circles or teams frequently needed to improve quality?

18. Is there a cultural basis for quality which the Japanese have utilized, or is there another explanation for their success in quality improvement?

SELECTED BIBLIOGRAPHY

BUZZELL, ROBERT D., and BRADLEY T. GALE: *The PIMS Principles: Linking Strategy to Performance,* New York: Free Press, 1987.

CROSBY, PHILIP B.: *Quality Is Free,* New York: McGraw-Hill, 1979.

———: *Quality without Tears,* New York: McGraw-Hill, 1984.

DEMING, W. EDWARDS: *Quality, Productivity, and Competitive Position,* Cambridge, Mass.: MIT Center for Advanced Engineering Study, 1982.

———: *Out of the Crisis,* Cambridge, Mass.: MIT Center for Advanced Engineering Study, 1986.

FEIGENBAUM, A. V.: "Total Quality Control," *Harvard Business Review,* November–December 1956, pp. 93–101.

———: *Total Quality Control,* New York: McGraw-Hill, 1983.

GARVIN, DAVID A.: "Quality on the Line," *Harvard Business Review,* September–October 1983, pp. 64–75.

———: "Competing on the Eight Dimensions of Quality," *Harvard Business Review,* November–December 1987, pp. 101–109.

———: *Managing Quality: The Strategic and Competitive Edge,* New York: Free Press, 1988.

GRYNA, FRANK M., JR.: "Quality Costs: User vs. Manufacturer," *Quality Progress,* June 1977, pp. 10–13.

HALPIN, JAMES F.: *Zero Defects,* New York: McGraw-Hill, 1966.

HONEYWELL: "Honeywell Imports Quality Circles as Long-Term Management Strategy," *Honeywell Newsletter,* August 1980.

JURAN, J. M.: "Japanese and Western Quality—A Contrast," *Quality Progress,* December 1978.

———: *Juran on Planning for Quality,* New York: Free Press, 1988.

——— and FRANK M. GRYNA, JR.: *Quality Planning and Analysis,* 2nd ed., New York: McGraw-Hill, 1980.

———, FRANK M. GRYNA, JR., and R. S. BINGHAM, JR. (eds.): *Quality Control Handbook,* 4th ed., New York: McGraw-Hill, 1988.

LAWLER, EDWARD E. III, and SUSAN MOHRMAN, "Quality Circles after the Fad," *Harvard Business Review,* January–February 1985, pp. 65–71.

LEONARD, FRANK S., and W. EARL SASSER: "The Incline of Quality," *Harvard Business Review,* September–October 1982, pp. 163–171.

MABE, G. MIKE: "Quality Control and L'Eggs Panty Hose," *Quality Progress,* February 1978, pp. 12–14.

REDDY, JACK: "Incorporating Quality in Competitive Strategies," *Sloan Management Review,* Spring 1980, pp. 53–60.

SCHERKENBACH, WILLIAM W.: "Performance Appraisal and Quality: Ford's New Philosophy," *Quality Progress,* April 1985, pp. 40–46.

SIMONDS, JOAN: "Quality at American Express Travel Services," *Proceedings of the 4th Annual Operations Management Association Meeting,* 1985.

STRATEGIC PLANNING INSTITUTE: "PIMS-Profit Impact of Market Strategy," no date.

WILLIS, JUDITH: "Quality Circles Breed Enthusiasm," *Minneapolis Star,* Apr. 2, 1980.

CHAPTER 21
Quality Control

21.1 Design of Quality Control Systems
21.2 Statistical Quality Control
21.3 Acceptance Sampling
21.4 Process Quality Control
21.5 Continuous Improvement
21.6 Quality Control in Industry
21.7 Key Points
Questions
Problems
Selected Bibliography

As indicated in the last chapter, the field of quality control has a rich and long history. In the early 1900s, quality control was associated with inspection, which evolved from a responsibility of individual workers to that of an organized quality control department. While this evolution facilitated independent quality control, it sometimes created tension between the workers and quality control inspectors. In some organizations such tension is still evident today.

In 1924, Walter A Shewhart of the Bell Telephone Laboratories published a paper which outlined the principles of statistical quality control charts. Two other Bell System men, H. F. Dodge and H. G. Romig, further developed the theory of statistical sampling for quality control in the 1930s. However, little of this theory found its way into industry until the 1940s, when the advent of World War II created a huge demand for mass-produced goods which could only be inspected by means of statistical methods. Imagine the problems faced by the U.S. government when it ordered millions of combat boots, millions of rifles, and huge quantities of other military equipment. As a result of these difficulties, the military and the government required suppliers to use statistical sampling methods to ensure compliance with government quality standards. These government-required sampling methods then spread throughout industry to all forms of manufacturing.

The spread of quality control methods has been much slower in service industries. While some service organizations have adopted comprehensive quality control programs, others are still neglecting quality or searching for the appropriate tools and principles.

After the war, in 1946, the American Society of Quality Control (ASQC) was formed. While the initial emphasis of the society was on statistical quality control methods, the ASQC has recently addressed problems of reliability, product liability, zero defects, and total quality control. The ASQC has also made an effort to spread the use of quality control ideas throughout the service industries.

As we address the problems of quality control in this chapter, our emphasis will be on process definition, statistical quality control, and continuous improvement. We will develop the point of view that quality control is the continuous improvement of a stable process. We further advance the idea that organizations consist of many interconnected processes which need to be controlled and improved in order to produce quality products and services. An example of how this has been done at Hewlett-Packard is given in Box 21.1.

BOX 21.1
HEWLETT-PACKARD

Hewlett-Packard's Computer System Division has discovered the partnership between JIT and SQC. Two years after implementing a SQC program, Hewlett-Packard embarked on JIT. Having already established statistical control of its processes, the company found that the transition to JIT was much easier. Rick Walleigh, production manager for the division, saw the synergy between SQC and JIT. First the cycle time in the printed circuit assembly area dropped from 17 days to 6 days after 2 years of SQC implementation. Then upon implementation of JIT the cycle time was reduced to 1.6 days.

Walleigh said, "Going into JIT was simplified by the data available through SQC. Getting the quality right is the key to a successful JIT system.

"SQC distinguishes between variations in a process as a result of outside causes, and variations that are the result of inconsistencies within the process itself. Once this distinction is understood, appropriate resources can be committed to eliminate the source of the problem.

"JIT exposes problems in a less direct but often more compelling way. It strips away the mask of inventory that hides the problems of late deliveries, nonconforming raw material, processes that produce scrap, processes with unbalanced capacities, and poor production planning. Without the buffer of back-up inventory, JIT forces managers to recognize and address these problems."

Thus inventory reduction and quality improvement go hand in hand to expose and solve problems. Once JIT and SQC become a part of the manufacturing routine, continuous improvement becomes everyone's objective.

SQC and JIT have produced impressive results at the Computer Systems Division. After introducing these approaches, direct labor hours per unit dropped from 62 hours to 39 hours, nonconformities in pretest IC insertions plummeted from 1950 ppm (parts per million) to 210 ppm and are still dropping. Solder nonconformities in the wave-solder process showed the most improvement. Five months after installation of SQC and JIT, nonconformities dramatically dropped from 5200 ppm to 100 ppm. PC final assembly nonconformities started at 145 ppm and fell to 10 ppm in 10 months.

Chuck Cheshire, materials manager at Computer Systems Division, commented, "SQC and JIT allows managers to listen to operators, tap into their insights and make the system more effective while making the operators' job more interesting. Quality commitment supports individual initiative. If people have pride in their jobs, and are trained to control their jobs, they do well, and the company does well."

Extracted from "SQC and JIT: Partnership in Quality," *Quality Progress*, May 1985.

21.1 DESIGN OF QUALITY CONTROL SYSTEMS

All quality control must start with the process itself. Actually, a process of production is composed of many subprocesses, each having its own intermediate product or service. A process can be an individual machine, a group of machines, or any of the many clerical and administrative processes that exist in the organization. Each of these processes has its own internal customers and its own products or services that are produced. The customer is the next process (or processes) that receives your work output. For example, the customer of the design department is the machine shop that makes the parts. The customer of the machine shop is the assembly department that uses the parts. By breaking down a large production system into many smaller systems or processes, quality can be defined and controlled at each point along the way.

After identifying each of the processes that need to be controlled, critical control points can be identified where inspection or measurement should take place. The types of measurement or tests required and the amount of inspection required at each of these points should be determined. Finally, management should decide who will do the inspection, the work force itself or separate inspectors. Once these decisions are made, it is possible to design a complete system of quality control which ensures continuous improvement of a stable system.

The first step in designing a quality control system is to identify the critical points in each of the processes where inspection is needed. The guidelines for doing this are as follows:

1. Inspect incoming raw materials or purchased services to ensure supplier compliance with specifications. In some cases this inspection can be eliminated by certifying the supplier as a quality supplier. Supplier certification is normally granted to those suppliers who have demonstrated that they use statistical process control and other methods to achieve consistent quality performance. In this case the products or services of the supplier can be used directly by the customer without incoming inspection.

2. Inspect work in process or the service while it is being delivered. As a general rule,

the product or service should be inspected before irreversible operations take place or before a great deal of value is added to the product. In these cases the cost of inspection is less than the cost of adding more value to the product.

A precise determination of where the product should be inspected should be made from the process flowchart. One example of this procedure is shown in Figure 21.1, which makes use of symbols originally defined in Chapter 8. The flowchart defines points for lot approval, 100 percent inspection, process inspection, roving inspection, and sample inspection. It also indicates, through a combination operation and inspection symbol, where the operator uses self-inspection.

An example of process flowcharting for the drug industry is shown in Figure 21.2. In this case a very extensive quality control system is used, consisting of more than 950 analytical control tests, 130,000 visual inspections, and physical control tests to ensure the quality of drugs for human consumption. In addition, the U.S. Food and Drug Administration tests the products independently at various points in the production process.

3. The third critical inspection point is the finished product or service. In manufacturing, final products are frequently inspected prior to shipping or prior to placing the product in inventory. At one automobile assembly plant, for example, a sample of cars is taken directly off the assembly line and thoroughly inspected for appearance and function. The defects are noted and fed back to assembly-line personnel so that they can correct the underlying causes. The defects are also used to compute a quality score for comparison among assembly plants. Another form of final-product inspection at this plant involves having each supervisor in the plant drive a new car home each evening. The supervisor writes up the defects the next morning, and corrective action is taken in the daily plant meeting. These final-product checks are in addition to numerous in-process and raw materials inspections.

For services, the final product is more difficult and sometimes impossible to inspect. Since the service delivered is intangible, the customer must be asked to rate the quality of the service delivered. Hotels and restaurants typically have cards which they ask customers to complete. Many universities ask students and alumni to rate the quality of education they received. All these "inspections" are aimed at assessing the quality of the finished product or service.

It is usually far better to prevent defects from occurring rather than to inspect and correct defects after production. Nevertheless, measurement or inspection is necessary to maintain processes in a continuous state of control and to facilitate improvement. So inspection (or measurement) cannot be eliminated, but it can be reduced by a vigorous process of prevention.

The second step in designing a quality control system is to decide on the type of measurement to be used at each inspection point. There are generally two options:

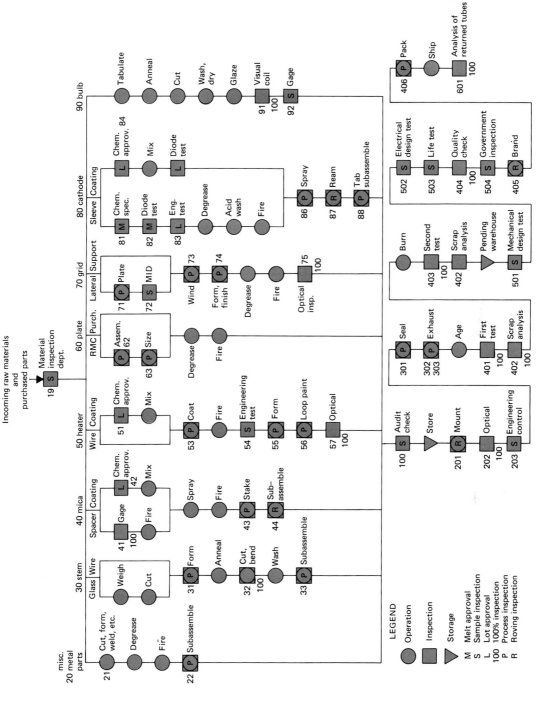

FIGURE 21.1 Quality flow diagram for electronic tubes.
Source: J. M. Juran, Frank M. Gryna, Jr., and R. S. Bingham (eds.), Quality Control Handbook, 4th ed., New York: McGraw-Hill, 1988.

605

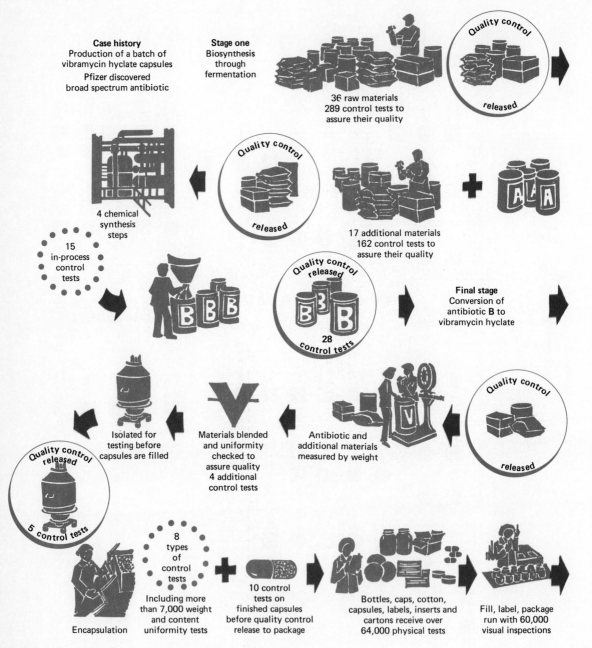

FIGURE 21.2   Controls on a drug (antibiotic) production process.
Source: J. M. Juran, Frank Gryna, Jr., and R. S. Bingham (eds.), Quality Control Handbook, *4th ed.,*
New York: McGraw-Hill, 1988.

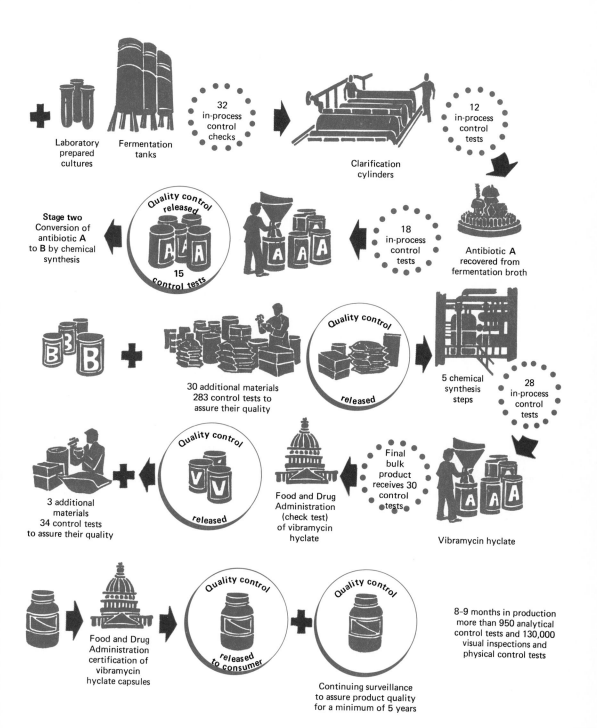

Laboratory prepared cultures

Fermentation tanks

32 in-process control checks

Clarification cylinders

12 in-process control tests

Stage two Conversion of antibiotic **A** to **B** by chemical synthesis

Quality control released

15 control tests

18 in-process control tests

Antibiotic **A** recovered from fermentation broth

30 additional materials 283 control tests to assure their quality

Quality control released

5 chemical synthesis steps

28 in-process control tests

3 additional materials 34 control tests to assure their quality

Quality control released

Food and Drug Administration (check test) of vibramycin hyclate

Final bulk product receives 30 control tests

Vibramycin hyclate

Food and Drug Administration certification of vibramycin hyclate capsules

Quality control released to consumer

Quality control

Continuing surveillance to assure product quality for a minimum of 5 years

8–9 months in production more than 950 analytical control tests and 130,000 visual inspections and physical control tests measurement based either on variables or on attributes. Variable measurement utilizes a continuous scale for such factors as length, height, and weight. Examples of variables measurement are the dimensions of parts, the viscosity of liquids, and the time that it takes to wait on tables in a restaurant.

Attribute measurement uses a discrete scale by counting the number of defective items or the number of defects per unit. When the quality specifications are complex, it will usually be necessary to use attribute measurements. In this case a complicated set of criteria can be used to define a defective unit or a defect. For example, a color TV set may be classified as defective if any of a number of functional tests fail or if the appearance of the cabinet is not satisfactory. In inspecting cloth, a defect can be defined as a flaw in the material and the number of defects per 100 yards can be counted during inspection. Determining the type of measurement to use also involves the specification of measuring equipment. A wide variety of devices are available for measurement. However the selection of these devices is beyond the scope of this text.

The third step in defining the quality control system is to decide on the amount of inspection to use. The choices are generally 100 percent inspection or a sample of a portion of the output. The guiding principle for this decision is to compare the cost of passing defects with the cost of inspection. For example, suppose that a defective unit sent to the customer costs $100 in terms of repair work, warranty, and future lost profits. Furthermore, suppose that a lot of 500 units contains an average of 2 percent defectives (10 defective units in the lot). Then the expected cost of not inspecting the lot is $1000 ($100 × 10). If it costs less than $1000 to inspect the entire lot ($2 per unit), the lot should be 100 percent inspected and the defective units screened out.[1]

There are other considerations besides cost which determine the amount of inspection. When human lives are at stake, 100 percent inspection at multiple points is often used (e.g., the drug example, Figure 21.2). When the product must be destroyed during testing, a sample must, of course, be used. Cost combined with these other considerations is used to set the proper level of inspection. Generally speaking, it is less costly to maintain processes in a stable state of statistical control by use of periodic sampling than to use 100 percent inspection to screen out defective units.

The final step in designing a quality control system is deciding who should do the inspection. Usually a combination of inspections by the workers themselves and by outside inspectors is used. If a philosophy of "zero defects" or "make it right the first time" is used, the workers will be given much of the responsibility for inspection and only a minimum of outside inspection will be used. There is much evidence to suggest that a prevention program along with a zero defects approach will be less expensive than an extensive outside inspection program.

In some cases, the customer will be involved in inspecting the product. Service customers always take this role as they receive the service. Some customers station

---

[1] This assumes that all defective units are detected by the inspection procedure.

inspectors at the vendor plants to examine and accept or reject shipments before they are sent on to the customer. The government has inspectors in a variety of industries to ensure quality in the interest of public health and safety. Thus, many people may be involved in the inspection process.

A well-designed quality control system requires a series of management judgments. The control principles themselves are elementary, requiring performance standards, measurement, and feedback of results to correct the process. The application of these principles in any given situation is complex. The guiding principle is to aim for continuous improvement of a stable system.

STATISTICAL QUALITY CONTROL

A cornerstone of quality control is the use of statistical methods to make decisions. In many cases, a great deal can be saved by taking a sample rather than making a 100 percent inspection. In other cases, there is no alternative but to take a sample (e.g., destructive testing).

Two distinct types of statistical methods are available: acceptance sampling and process control. Acceptance sampling applies to lot inspection where a decision to accept or reject a lot of material is made on the basis of a random sample drawn from the lot. This type of inspection is done after production is completed. Examples are the inspection of a railroad car of material which arrives at a factory and the auditing of accounts for a large customer.

Process control sampling is used during production while the product is being made. The decision in this case is whether to continue the process or to stop production and look for an assignable cause of defects, which may stem from the materials, the operator, or the machine. This decision is based on periodic random samples taken from the process. Once a process is brought under statistical control, it should remain there unless an assignable cause is present. By monitoring the process through sampling, a constant state of control can be maintained. Examples are the monitoring of a machine as it cuts metal parts for an engine and the monitoring of the temperature of soup produced in kettles in a school cafeteria.

These two types of statistical quality control are conceptually different. While acceptance sampling is done after production is completed, process control is done during production. These methods are not mutually exclusive, but it is usually more economical to use process control during production rather than acceptance sampling after production is completed. Nevertheless, some acceptance sampling is useful when the supplier cannot be easily certified for statistical process control or a check is needed to ensure that materials are meeting contractual or legal commitments.

Each of the two quality control methods can be used with either measurement of attributes or variables. This gives rise to four distinct cases, as shown in Figure 21.3. These four cases also give rise to different sample sizes and different philosophies of control, as will be discussed in the remainder of the chapter.

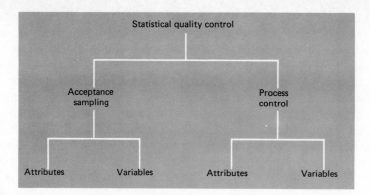

FIGURE 21.3
Statistical quality
control methods.

ACCEPTANCE SAMPLING

Acceptance sampling is defined as taking one or more samples at random from a lot of items, inspecting each of the items in the sample(s), and deciding—on the basis of the inspection results—whether to accept or reject the entire lot. This type of inspection can be used by a customer to ensure that the supplier is meeting quality specifications or by the producer to ensure that quality standards are met prior to shipment. Acceptance sampling is used in preference to 100 percent inspection wherever the cost of inspection is high in relation to the cost of passing defective items to the customer—that is, in instances where it might be too costly to inspect the entire lot.

In the following discussion, we will restrict our attention to acceptance sampling by attributes. Thus, we assume that each item inspected is classified as good or defective on the basis of quality specifications or standards.

In single acceptance sampling, one sample is taken from a lot and the decision whether to accept or reject the lot is made after the sample is inspected. Formally, we let

n = sample size
c = acceptance number
x = number of defective units found in the sample

For single sampling, the decision rule whether to accept or reject the lot after inspecting the sample is as follows:

If $x \leq c$, accept the lot
If $x > c$, reject the lot

As an example, suppose we have a lot of 10,000 items and we decide to take a random sample of 100 items ($n = 100$). We inspect the 100 items and find 3 defectives ($x = 3$). Assume the acceptance number in this case is two ($c = 2$). Therefore the lot of 10,000 items will be rejected, since the number of defective units in the sample exceeds the acceptance number ($x > c$).

Single sampling can be extended to double or multiple sampling by taking two or more separate samples. In this case, after the first sample, a decision is made whether to (a) accept the lot, (b) reject the lot, or (c) take a second sample. Multiple sampling will usually result in a smaller total sample size than single sampling, sometimes only half as large. However, it might be difficult to take more than one sample, and multiple plans are slightly more complicated to understand.

The performance of any sampling plan will depend on the quality of the items in the incoming lot or lots. If the incoming lots contain a low number of defectives, a high percentage of the lots will be accepted, which is the desired result. This occurs because the number of defectives in most samples is below the acceptance number. On the other hand, if the incoming lots contain a high number of defectives, a low percentage of lots will be accepted, which is also desirable. This occurs because most samples will have a high number of defectives and the lots will be rejected.

The precise relationship between the quality of the incoming lot or lots and the probability of accepting (P_a) any given lot is shown by the operating characteristic (OC) curve in Figure 21.4. The y axis of the OC curve represents the probability of accepting a lot (or the percentage of lots accepted for multiple lots), while the x axis shows the percentage of defective units in the incoming lot or lots. The OC curve thus shows the performance of a given sampling plan for any hypothetical incoming lot quality.

While the OC curve can be used to describe the performance of a given sampling plan (specified n and c), it can also be used to help evaluate alternative sampling plans and to select the preferred plan. To do this, management must first specify acceptable error levels. There are two types of errors: rejecting a lot which is considered to be of good quality (type I) and accepting a lot which is considered to be bad quality (type II). These errors can be specified quantitatively by selecting an acceptable quality level (AQL) and a lot tolerance percent defective (LTPD).

When incoming lots have a fraction defective less than or equal to AQL, they should be accepted. Any lot with incoming quality less than or equal to AQL which is rejected by the sampling procedure is considered a type I error. This error

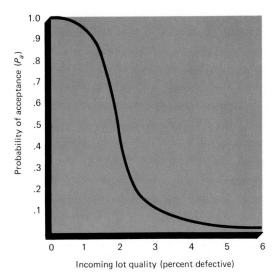

FIGURE 21.4
Operating characteristic curve.

is specified by the symbol α and is considered the producer's risk, since a good lot is rejected. Thus, we have

α = probability (reject a lot when fraction defective = AQL)

When lots have a fraction defective equal to or greater than LTPD, they should be rejected. Accepting a lot with quality $\geq$ LTPD constitutes a type II error, which is considered the consumer's risk, since a lot of bad quality is accepted. The probability of a type II error is specified by the symbol β and defined as follows:

β = probability (accept a lot when fraction defective = LTPD)

The two pairs α, AQL and β, LTPD specify two points on the OC curve, as shown in Figure 21.5. When these two points are specified, they completely determine the entire OC curve as well as the required values of n and c. The two points on the OC curve thus specify a particular sampling plan. By controlling the specification of these two error points, management will control the plan selected and the associated sampling costs.

Management should select the values of α, AQL and β, LTPD on the basis of the economics of the situation. If the cost of rejecting a good lot (with quality $\leq$ AQL) is high, then a low value of α should be selected to control the type I error. Similarly, if the cost of accepting a bad lot is high, then a low value of β should be selected to control the type II error. Whether these costs incurred by sampling are considered subjectively or mathematically, management should take them into account in selecting the α, AQL and β, LTPD parameters for a sampling plan.

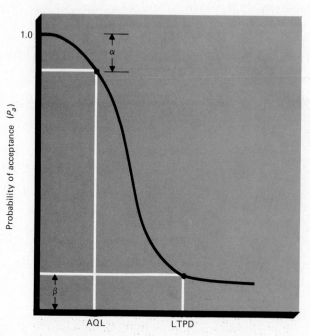

FIGURE 21.5
Error
specifications.

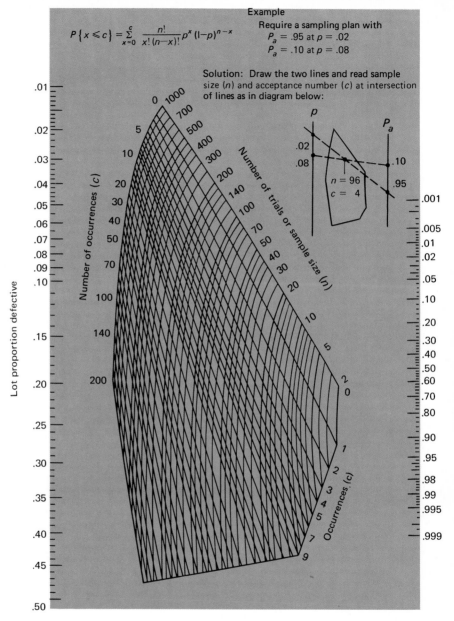

FIGURE 21.6 Nomograph of the cumulative binomial distribution.
Source: Adapted from Harry R. Larson, "A Nomograph of the Cumulative Binomial Distribution," Western Electric Engineer, *April 1965.*

A nomograph for calculating the values of n and c from the error probability pairs α, AQL and β, LTPD is given in Figure 21.6. This nomograph is based on the binomial probability distribution and provides a convenient method of computation. An example of these computations is given in Box 21.2.

BOX 21.2

COMPUTATION OF A SAMPLING PLAN FROM SPECIFIED ERROR PROBABILITIES

The ABC hardware store has just received a shipment of 1000 wrenches. If the AQL is 20 defective items in the shipment (2 percent) and the LTPD is 8 percent, find a sampling plan (n and c) which will provide a type I error of .05 and a type II error of .10.

Using the nomograph in Figure 21.6, find the lot proportion defective for AQL = .02 on the left-hand scale and the probability of acceptance $1 - \alpha = .95$ on the right-hand scale. Connect these two points with a straight line, as illustrated in the inset in Figure 21.6. Next, locate the value of LTPD = .08 on the left-hand scale and $\beta = .10$ on the right-hand scale, also illustrated in the inset. Connect these two points with a second straight line. Where the two lines intersect on the nomograph, read off the values of n and c. In this case, $n = 96$ and $c = 4$. The hardware store should inspect 96 wrenches and accept the entire lot if the number of defective units in the sample is less than or equal to 4.

The nomograph in Figure 21.6 can also be used in reverse to calculate the OC curve or type I and II errors for any given sampling plan values of n and c. This particular computation is shown in Box 21.3 (See also Figure 21.7.)

BOX 21.3

COMPUTATION OF AN OC CURVE FOR A GIVEN PLAN

Suppose the ABC hardware store decides to tighten up the inspection plan computed in Box 21.2 by making $c = 2$ while holding $n = 96$. What are the associated values of the OC curve for this revised plan? To compute the OC curve, locate the point $n = 96$, $c = 2$ on the nomograph. Pivot a ruler around this point and read off the successive pairs of values from the left-hand and right-hand scales. For example, when the lot proportion defective $p = .01$ on the left-hand scale, we have probability of acceptance $P_a = .93$ on the right-hand scale. A table of pairs of values is then as follows:

p	.01	.02	.03	.04	.05	.06	.07	.08	.09	.10
P_a	.93	.72	.48	.28	.16	.08	.04	.02	.01	.004

This OC curve is plotted in Figure 21.7. By comparison with Box 21.2, notice at p = AQL = .02 the type I error has been increased by tightening the plan to $1 - P_a = .28$. At the same time, the type II error at $p = .08$ has been reduced to $P_a = .02$.

OC curves also help the manager visualize how the performance of a sampling plan changes as the values of n and c are changed. In Figure 21.8a, OC curves are shown for various values of n, holding c constant. As n increases, the OC curve moves to the left and becomes more rectangular. When n equals the lot size (100

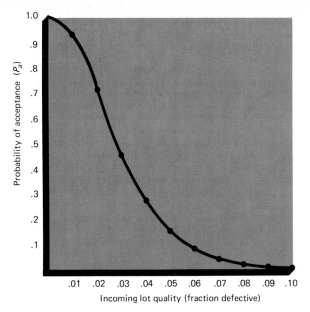

FIGURE 21.7
OC curve for Box
21.3.

percent inspection), the OC curve is a vertical line through AQL; all lots with quality less than or equal to AQL are accepted with probability = 1, and all lots with quality greater than AQL are rejected with probability = 1. Inspection of the entire lot is the case of perfect information where no statistical errors are made and the costs of errors are assumed to be infinite.

Similarly in Figure 21.8*b*, a series of OC curves is shown for constant *n* and various values of *c*. As *c* is reduced, the OC curve moves to the left and the

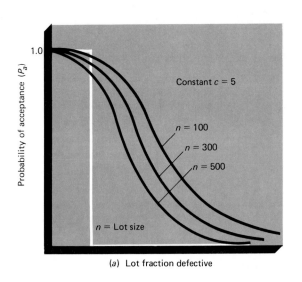

(*a*) Lot fraction defective

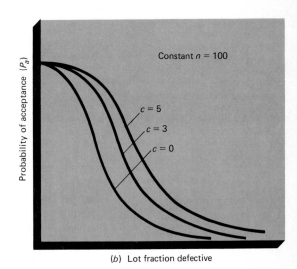

(*b*) Lot fraction defective

FIGURE 21.8   Effect on OC curves of changing *n* and *c*.

sampling plan becomes "tighter." Reducing c or increasing n has a similar effect; both tend to tighten the inspection plan.

In industry a widely accepted basis for selecting an acceptance sampling plan for attributes is Military Standard 105D. This standard consists of a set of tables which prescribes sampling plans for various lot sizes, AQLs, and other parameters; it includes double and multiple as well as single plans. Military Standard 105D is widely specified as the applicable guide for inspection in government and military contracts.

To this point, we have been discussing acceptance sampling for attributes. Acceptance sampling for variables is quite similar. There are OC curves and type I and type II errors. The main difference is that acceptance sampling for variables utilizes measurement of a continuous variable. After all items in the sample are measured, the average measurement for the entire sample is computed. If this sample average is less than an acceptance number, the lot is accepted; otherwise it is rejected. Whenever quality is measured by a continuous variable, variables acceptance sampling is the appropriate technique.

21.4 PROCESS QUALITY CONTROL

Process quality control utilizes inspection of the product or service while it is being produced. Periodic samples of the output of a production process are taken. When, after inspection of the sample, there is reason to believe that the process quality characteristics have changed, the process is stopped and a search is made for an assignable cause. This cause could be a change in the operator, the machine, or the material. When the cause has been found and corrected, the process is started again.

Process control is based on two key assumptions, one of which is that variability is basic to any production process. No matter how perfectly a process is designed, there will be some variability in quality characteristics from one unit to the next. For example, a machine filling cereal boxes will not deposit exactly the same weight in each box; the amount filled will vary around some average figure. The aim of process control is to find the range of natural variation of the process and to then ensure that production stays within this range.

The second principle of process control is that production processes are not usually found in a state of control. Due to lax procedures, untrained operators, improper machine maintenance, and so on, the variation being produced is usually much larger than necessary. The first job of process control managers is to seek out these sources of unnecessary variation and bring the process under statistical control, where the remaining variation is due to random causes.

A process can be brought to a state of control and can be maintained in this state through the use of quality control charts (also called process charts or control charts). In the control chart shown in Figure 21.9, the y axis represents the quality characteristic which is being controlled, while the x axis represents time or a particular sample taken from the process. The center line of the chart is the average quality characteristic being measured. The upper control limit represents

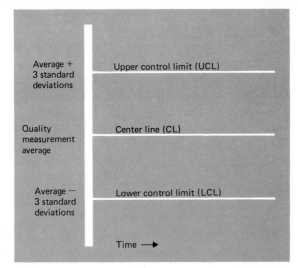

FIGURE 21.9
Process control
chart.

the maximum acceptable random variation, and the lower control limit indicates the minimum acceptable random variation when a state of control exists. Generally speaking, the upper and lower control limits are set at ± three standard deviations from the mean. If a normal probability distribution is assumed, these control limits will include 99.7 percent of the random variations observed.

After a process has been brought to steady-state operation, periodic samples are taken and plotted on the control chart; see Figure 21.10. When the measurement falls within the control limits, the process is continued. If the measurement falls

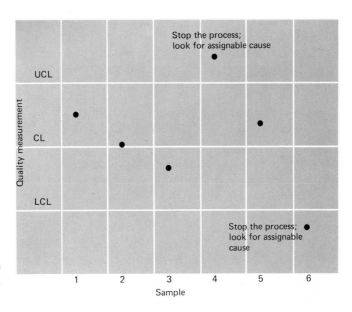

FIGURE 21.10
Quality control
chart.

outside the control limits, the process is stopped and a search is made for an assignable cause. Through this procedure, the process is maintained in a constant state of statistical control and there is only natural variation in the process's output.

Just as in the case of acceptance sampling, quality can be measured for control charts by attributes or by variables. We will cover each of these cases in turn below.

When quality is measured by attributes, the quality characteristic is the percentage of defective units in the process. This percentage is estimated by taking a sample of n units at random from the process at specified time intervals. For each sample, the observed percent defective (p) in the sample is computed. These observed values of p are plotted on the chart, one for each sample.

To get the center line and control limits of the p control chart, we take a large number of samples of n units each. The p value is computed for each sample and then averaged over all samples to yield a value $\bar{p}$. This value of $\bar{p}$ is used as the center line, since it represents the best available estimate of the true average percent defective of the process. We also use the value of $\bar{p}$ to compute upper and lower control limits as follows:

$$UCL = \bar{p} + 3\sqrt{\frac{\bar{p}(1 - \bar{p})}{n}}$$

$$LCL = \bar{p} - 3\sqrt{\frac{\bar{p}(1 - \bar{p})}{n}}$$

In this case, the process's standard deviation is the quantity under the square root sign. We are adding and subtracting three standard deviations from the mean to get the control limits. Box 21.4 gives an example of this computation for controlling computer data entry operations.

After the p control chart is constructed with its center line and upper and lower control limits, samples of the process being controlled are taken and plotted on the chart. If the sample percentage falls within the control limits, no action is taken. If the sample percentage falls outside the control limits, the process is stopped and a search for an assignable cause (material, operator, or machine) is made. After the assignable cause is found and corrected—or, in very rare cases, no assignable cause is found—the process is restored to operating condition and production is resumed.

Control charts are also used for measurements of variables. In this case a measurement of a continuous variable is made when each item is inspected. As a result, two values are computed from the sample—a measure of central tendency (usually the average) and a measure of variability (the range or standard deviation). With these values, control charts are developed for both the central tendency and the variability of the process. When the process is found to be out of control on either of these values it is stopped and a search for an assignable cause is made.

Suppose that the average $\bar{x}$ and range R are computed each time a sample is

BOX 21.4
CONTROL CHART EXAMPLE

Suppose samples of 200 records are taken from a data entry operation at 2-hour intervals to control the data entry process. The percentage of records in error for the past 10 samples is found to be .7, 1.2, 1.6, 2.0, 1.0, .8, 1.8, 1.5, .9, and 1.2 percent. The average of these 10 sample percentages yields a $\bar{p} = 1.27$ percent, which is the center line of the control chart. The upper and lower control limits are

$$UCL = .0127 + 3\sqrt{\frac{.0127(.9873)}{200}} = .0364$$

$$LCL = .0127 - 3\sqrt{\frac{.0127(.9873)}{200}} = -.0110$$

When the LCL is negative, it is rounded up to 0 because a negative percentage is impossible. Thus, we have the following chart:

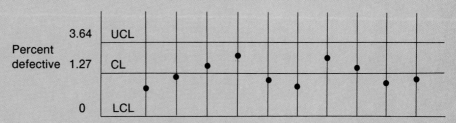

Since all sample points are found to be in control, these 10 samples can be used to establish the center line and control limits.

taken. Then a control chart for average and a chart for range will be used. The control limits for the average chart are computed as follows:

$$CL = \bar{\bar{x}}$$
$$UCL = \bar{\bar{x}} + A_2\bar{R}$$
$$LCL = \bar{\bar{x}} - A_2\bar{R}$$

where $\bar{\bar{x}}$ is the grand average of several past $\bar{x}$ averages and $\bar{R}$ is the average of several past R values. In the above formulas, A_2 is a constant which includes three standard deviations in terms of the range. Table 21.1 provides values of A_2 for various sample sizes.

The control limits for the range chart are computed as follows:

$$CL = \bar{R}$$
$$UCL = D_4\bar{R}$$
$$LCL = D_3\bar{R}$$

The constants D_3 and D_4 provide three standard deviation limits for the range. Values for these constants are also given in Table 21.1. Box 21.5 gives an example

TABLE 21.1

CONTROL CHART CONSTANTS

Sample size n	A_2	D_3	D_4
2	1.880	0	3.267
3	1.023	0	2.575
4	0.729	0	2.282
5	0.577	0	2.115
6	0.483	0	2.004
7	0.419	0.076	1.924
8	0.373	0.136	1.864
9	0.337	0.184	1.816
10	0.308	0.223	1.777
12	0.266	0.284	1.716
14	0.235	0.329	1.671
16	0.212	0.364	1.636
18	0.194	0.392	1.608
20	0.180	0.414	1.586
22	0.167	0.434	1.566
24	0.157	0.452	1.548

Source: Factors reproduced from 1950 *ASTM Manual on Quality Control of Materials* by permission of the American Society for Testing and Materials, Philadelphia.

of control by variables, illustrating how to compute control limits and how to determine whether or not a sample is in control.

There are several issues of concern in using control charts. First, the problem of sample size must be faced. For an attribute control chart, samples should be fairly large, frequently in the range of 50 to 300 observations. As a general rule, the sample must be at least large enough to allow for the detection of one defective unit. For example, if the process being controlled produces .5 percent defective units, a sample size of at least 200 should be used in order to detect one defective unit on average. Control charts for variables require much smaller sample sizes, frequently in the range of 3 to 10 items, because each variable measurement provides much more information.

The second issue is how frequently to sample. This issue is often decided on the basis of the rate of production and the cost of producing defectives in relation to the cost of inspection. A high-volume production process should be sampled frequently, since a large number of defective units could be produced between samples. When the cost of producing defectives is high in relation to the cost of inspection, the process should also be sampled frequently. An example of a costly situation is one where the entire production output must be screened when the process is found to be out of control. In these cases, samples should be taken frequently, provided that the cost of sampling is not too high.

Another issue in the use of control charts is the relationship of product specifications to control limits. If product specifications are inside the control limits, the process is being overspecified; it is simply not capable of producing to specification within its natural band of variation. In this case, the specifications

BOX 21.5
EXAMPLE OF CONTROL BY VARIABLES

The Midwest Bolt Company would like to control the quality of the bolts produced by its automatic screw machines. Each machine produces 1000 bolts per hour and is controlled by a separate control chart. Every hour, a random sample of six bolts is selected from the output of each machine and the diameter of each sample bolt is measured. From each six diameters, an average and range are computed. For example, one sample produced the following six measurements: .536, .507, .530, .525, .530, and .520. The average of these measurements is $\bar{x} = .525$ and the range is .029. We also know that the grand average of all past samples has been running $\bar{\bar{x}} = .513$ and the grand average range is $\bar{R} = .020$. From these grand averages, the control chart parameters are computed as follows (see Table 21.1):

$\bar{x}$ chart	R chart
CL = .513	CL = .020
UCL = .513 + .483(.020) = .523	UCL = 2.004(.020) = .040
LCL = .513 − .483(.020) = .503	LCL = 0(.020) = 0

On the basis of these control limits, the sample of six bolts is found to be out of control on average measurement and in control on range. We should therefore stop the process and look for an assignable cause that would tend to produce bolts which are too large in diameter.

should be relaxed, a better process used, or 100 percent inspection instituted to screen out the bad items. Control charts illustrate very clearly the need to match product specifications to the characteristics of the process. In practice, a product can be overspecified, and it will then have apparently poor quality of conformance when the process itself is inadequate.

21.5 CONTINUOUS IMPROVEMENT

We have defined quality control as continuous improvement of a stable process. As we have seen, a stable process can be maintained by the methods of process control described in the last section. Next, we will turn to approaches which are useful for achieving continuous improvement over time.

The aim of continuous improvement is to reduce variability of the product or process. This generally requires problem solving or changes in the design of the product or process itself. Such changes make it possible to make a more consistent product or service with less variation from one unit to the next.

Three techniques for continuous improvement will be reviewed in this section: Pareto analysis, cause-and-effect diagrams, and robust design. Each of these methods relies on data collection and analysis in order to improve product or process quality.

In Pareto analysis, data are collected on the various modes of failure of the product or service produced. The data are then tabulated in order to identify the most frequent modes of failure. As a result, the most important problems can be attacked first.

TABLE 21.2
DEFECTIVES IN FRONT-END LOADER HYDRAULICS

	NUMBER INSPECTED (N) = 2347	
Defective items	Number of defectives	Percent defective
O-rings missing	16	3.9%
Improper torque	25	6.1
Loose connections	193	46.8
Fitting burrs	47	11.4
Cracked connectors	131	31.8
Total	412	100.0%

In Table 21.2 reasons are given for hydraulic leaks found in assembling front-end tractor loaders in a factory. As noted in the table, the most frequent reason for a leak (defect) is loose connections, followed by cracked connectors, and so on. These data are transferred to the Pareto diagram in Figure 21.11. By graphing the reasons for leaks in decreasing order of occurrence, the Pareto diagram readily shows the importance of the various types of defects which have been found. According to Pareto's law, first discussed in Chapter 14, a few of the failure modes account for most of the defects.

The Pareto diagram shows which defects we should try to eliminate first. By reference to Figure 21.11, we should investigate loose connections first because they occur most frequently. Of course, cracked connectors is a close second and should be investigated too, especially if cracked connectors are easier or less costly to correct than loose connections. Pareto analysis is very helpful when first studying a quality problem because it helps break the problem down into smaller pieces. Leaking hydraulics has been defined as due primarily to loose connections or cracked connectors (78.6 percent combined failures).

The next step in the analysis is to take one of these failure modes, say, loose

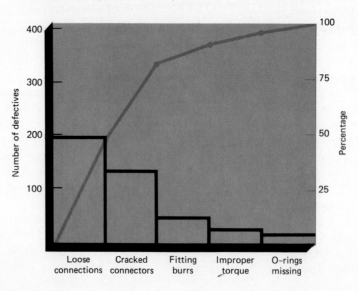

FIGURE 21.11
Pareto diagram.

connections, and to analyze the causes of failure. This is done by use of the cause-and-effect diagram, also called an Ishikawa diagram, after Dr. Ishikawa (1976) who first used these diagrams in Japan.

A cause-and-effect (CE), diagram is shown in Figure 21.12 for the loose connections. The problem itself, or the effect, is shown on the right side of the diagram. The various potential causes of this problem are shown along the spine of the diagram as materials, workers, inspection, and tools. The appearance of these diagrams suggests a fishbone analogy. The bones of the fish are common causes of quality problems, but any cause can be listed. Each of the major causes is then broken down into more detailed causes, giving rise to more bones on the fish. For example, the worker cause is split into three possibilities: inexperience, fatigue, or training. Training is in turn divided into content and knowledge.

By constructing a CE diagram, the potential causes of a problem become readily apparent. Each of these can then be evaluated one by one in order to find the true causes of the problem.

CE diagrams are frequently constructed by using quality circles or problem-solving teams. By use of brainstorming, the team will develop a wide variety of possible causes for a problem. Then the team, or an individual, can collect data to narrow down the potential causes before taking corrective action.

By using Pareto and CE diagrams, it is possible to reduce defects and thus improve quality. For example, in the case of hydraulic leaks, the loose connections may be found to be caused by the torque adjustment of the tools and the improper

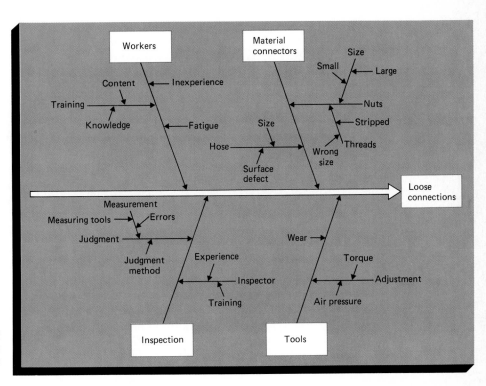

FIGURE 21.12
Cause-and-effect
diagram for loose
connections.

training of operators. After these causes are corrected, the number of defects will be reduced. It is then possible to move to the second problem, which is cracked connectors. In this way continuous improvement is achieved.

Another powerful way to reduce variability in product or process performance is through robust design. This is done by designing products and processes whose quality performance is less affected by environmental variables. Robust design can be far less expensive than attempting to control environmental sources of variation during the production process, such as temperature, light, dust, etc. It can also result in superior quality during field use where the environment is not controlled.

A story of the Japanese tile manufacturer, Ina Tile Company, may be helpful in illustrating the principles of robust design. Ina Tile Company noted that an uneven temperature distribution in the kiln that was used to bake tiles caused variation in the size of the tiles. Since uneven temperature was an assignable cause, a process quality control approach would have devised a method for controlling temperature more carefully, certainly at considerable cost. Since the company wanted to improve quality at lower cost, it tried to find a tile formulation that would be far less sensitive to uneven temperatures. Through designed experiments the company found that increasing the amount of lime in the tile formula from 1 percent to 5 percent would reduce the tile size variation by a factor of 10. This discovery was a breakthrough for the ceramic tile industry.

This example illustrates finding a set of parameters that reduces variability during production. Of far greater importance is variability of the product in the field during its life span. Robust design can be used to improve field performance and thus reduce the total cost to the customer of using the product. It can also be used to reduce variability of services delivered to the customer.

The primary causes of performance variation in operations are production imperfections and environmental variables in use. Robust design should be used to make the product as immune as possible to both production and field variation.

Robust design seeks to minimize variation around a target (or best) value of product or process performance. This assumes that any variation around the target value is undesirable. For example, suppose a cereal box should be filled with 10 ounces of cereal, the target value. Any deviation from the target has an economic cost or loss to the producer. Yet, in practice, specifications are normally set in intervals which imply that the product performance is acceptable anywhere within specifications and unacceptable the minute it falls outside. It would be far better to set a target value and associated tolerances with the objective of constantly narrowing the tolerances through continuous improvement.

The idea of designing to target has been related to loss functions. In Figure 21.13a the target value is shown along with the loss associated with deviation from the target. In this case, reduction of variance around the target would result in less loss. In Figure 21.13b a loss function is shown for the way product specifications are usually set. There is no loss if the product is within specifications, and there is infinite loss outside the specifications.

Off-line quality control refers to methods used to achieve robust designs and

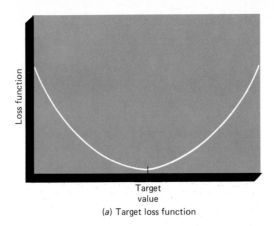

(a) Target loss function

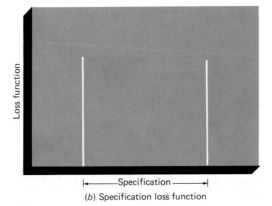

|←——————Specification——————→|

(b) Specification loss function

FIGURE 21.13
Loss functions:
(a) target loss
function; (b)
specification loss
function.

reduce potential variance before the product is made. This is done through designed experiments which use various levels of the product design parameters to determine the effect on product performance. As a result of these experiments, the product or process parameter settings can be found which are the least sensitive to manufacturing and environmental variation. Taguchi (1989) and Kackar (1985) discuss various methods for doing this.

On-line quality control refers to process control while the product is being produced. It is usually far cheaper to engage in off-line quality efforts than to try to control all sources of variation during production. Yet off-line methods of quality control are just beginning to be used in industry today.

21.6 QUALITY CONTROL IN INDUSTRY

Industry has made widespread use of the quality control methods described in this chapter as indicated by several surveys of industry practice, e.g., Saniga and Shirland (1977) and Revelle (1988). In these surveys, about three-fourths of all firms report the use of single sampling acceptance plans. Other more sophisticated multiple or sequential plans are not as widely used.

These surveys also indicate that about three-fourths of all firms use process control charts. There is greater use of $\bar{x}$ and R charts than p charts due to the small samples that are possible with variables control. Other more sophisticated charts are not as widely used as $\bar{x}$, R, and p charts.

Pareto charts and CE diagrams have also achieved significant use in industry. Recently, employees and managers at all levels have received intensive training in these techniques through quality circles and quality improvement programs. As a result, awareness of quality control ideas has increased greatly in the last 10 years in American industry.

While use of quality methods has now spread beyond operations, there is much room for further use in administrative and office functions in manufacturing firms and in service firms. Quality control education must be concentrated on all functions in the firm and on the firm's suppliers as well. Some firms have still not internalized the concept of total quality management. As a result, quality control efforts are focused primarily on production operations.

Quality control in the service industries has lagged behind that in manufacturing for several reasons. First, services are more difficult to measure because they are intangible, while the characteristics of a manufactured product can be measured and specified. For example, steel can be measured by its strength, hardness, ductility, and other properties. The quality of a service is related to intangibles such as atmosphere in a restaurant, the waiter's smile, and the customer's sense of well-being. Nevertheless, quality cannot be controlled unless it is measured. Therefore it is imperative that the service industries measure what they can and develop new, innovative measurement techniques for the "intangible" services.

Juran et al. (1988) have identified three aspects of service quality which should be measured: timeliness, consumer well-being, and continuity of service. "Timeliness" refers to the time from the customer's initiation of an order to its satisfactory delivery. The total time may be broken into components, each of which can be measured and managed independently. Consumer well-being refers to atmosphere, feeling of importance, safety, courtesy, and so on. These dimensions of service can generally be measured only by customer perceptions. To assess them, it is necessary to contact a sample of customers and ask for their evaluation of quality. Continuity of service is especially important for suppliers of services such as electricity, water, and transportation. Continuity can be measured in a similar way as reliability.

Another problem in managing quality of services is the perishability of the product, which requires that quality be controlled while the service is being delivered. As a result, a greater burden for service quality is placed on the work force, and the customer is immediately aware of it when bad quality is being delivered. Thus, service organizations should emphasize selection of the proper employees, specification of procedures whenever possible, and work force training. Of course, these are also good practices for manufacturing firms to prevent errors from occurring.

21.7 **KEY POINTS**

This chapter's key points include the following:

- Quality control is defined as the continuous improvement of a stable process. The process is actually a sequence of interconnected subprocesses, each with its own internal customers. Critical points must be defined for inspection and measurement in order to control and improve these processes.

- Inspection should be considered for the inputs, as part of the process, and for the outputs. The critical control points for inspection are best described by a flowchart of the process. As a general rule, inspection is done when the expected cost of processing defective units further through the production process exceeds the cost of inspection.

- Statistical quality control can be based on acceptance sampling or process control. With either of these approaches, measurement may be by attributes or by variables.

- In acceptance sampling, one or more samples is taken from a lot of items. If the quality measurement in the sample is found acceptable, the entire lot is accepted; otherwise the lot is rejected or another sample is selected before a decision is made. In acceptance sampling, there are two types of errors: rejecting a good lot and accepting a bad lot. These errors can be controlled to any desired level by selecting a proper sample size and acceptance number.

- In process quality control, periodic samples are taken from a continuous production process. As long as the sample measurements fall within the control limits, production is continued. When the sample measurements fall outside the control limits, the process is stopped and a search is made for an assignable cause—operator, machine, or material. With this procedure, a production process is maintained in a continual state of statistical control.

- It is preferable to use statistical process control over acceptance sampling whenever possible, because SPC is prevention-oriented. SPC can be used as a basis of achieving a certified supplier status, which requires a stable production process.

- Several methods can be used for continuous improvement of quality: Pareto charts, CE diagrams, and robust design. These methods can be used to reduce variance of a stable process or to bring a process under control.

- In industry a high percentage of manufacturing companies use acceptance sampling, process quality control, CE diagrams and Pareto charts. The use of these statistical methods has much less acceptance in the service industries.

QUESTIONS

1. Why did statistical quality control ideas catch on in the 1940s?
2. Suppose you make electronic calculators which contain a chip purchased from a local vendor. How would you decide how much inspection to perform on the chips supplied to you?
3. Draw a process flowchart for the student registration system at your college. Identify all

the current inspection points on the chart. Does the registration system use proper quality control checkpoints?

4. For the following situations, comment on whether inspection by variables or by attributes might be more appropriate.
   a. Filling feed bags to the proper weight
   b. Inspecting for defects in yard goods
   c. Inspecting appliances for surface imperfections
   d. Determining the sugar content of candy bars

5. It has been said that workers should be given more control over the inspection of their own work. Discuss the pros and cons of this proposition.

6. Is it possible to eliminate both type I and type II errors? How?

7. Contrast and compare acceptance sampling and process quality control.

8. Describe the main use of an OC chart.

9. Define type I and type II errors.

10. Your boss has suggested that the sample size on an acceptance sampling plan be increased. What will this do to the OC curve?

11. Why is it that most processes are not in statistical control when they are first sampled for control chart purposes?

12. It has been suggested that a sample of six items be taken four times a day to control a particular process. How would you go about evaluating this suggestion?

13. Define the purpose of continuous improvement of quality.

14. How can a Pareto chart be used to improve quality?

15. Which technique would be useful for each of the following situations?
    a. To rank-order the causes of a quality problem
    b. To brainstorm the various reasons why a product might have failed
    c. To find an assignable cause
    d. To determine if a process is under control in range
    e. To reduce the variability of failures found in the field under actual use of the product
    f. To achieve the smallest possible variance in the time that it takes to wait on tables in a restaurant

PROBLEMS

1. In manufacturing a small part, your customer has decided to institute an acceptance sampling plan. She will take a sample of size 100 and accept the lot if 3 or less defective units are found. Calculate the OC curve for this plan. What is your risk as a consumer when the lot quality is 8 percent defective?

2. What happens in Problem 1 when n and c are changed as follows:
   a. $n = 400, c = 3$
   b. $n = 200, c = 1$

3. Suppose you are the auditor for a bank operation. You have decided to consider error rates acceptable when there is one error or less in 100 days. You want to clear the bank (accept their procedures) with 95 percent confidence when the error rate is this low. On the other hand, if the error rate climbs to five per 100 days or more, you want to reject the bank's procedure with 90 percent probability. How many days of the bank's books should be audited? How many days can you find the bank in error and still pass it on the audit?

4. Given AQL = .02, α = .08, LTPD = .08, and β = .10, find n and c.

5. An acceptance sampling plan has $n = 100$ and $c = 3$.
   a. Draw the OC chart for values of $p = .01, .02, \ldots, .10$.

    b. What is the effect on the OC chart of changing n to 50 and n to 200? Draw the graphs for these new sample sizes and compare with the original plan.

    c. What is the effect of changing c to 2 and c to 4 while holding n at 100? Draw the graphs for these new values of c and compare.

6. A purchasing manager decided to take a sample of machined parts received from a certain supplier for acceptance sampling. She would agree to a 10 percent error of accepting the parts if the incoming lot quality were 8 defects out of 100 or worse. She would also take a 5 percent error of rejecting a good incoming lot with 2 defects out of 100 or less. Use the spreadsheet from problem 5 for this problem, parts b and c.

    a. Under these circumstances, what lot size and acceptance number are needed? Use the nomograph for this part.

    b. What would be the probability of accepting an incoming lot with 1 percent defective, 6 percent defective, and 10 percent defective?

    c. Plot the OC curve for this plan.

7. What is the effect on the OC curve in Problem 6 when n and c are changed as follows? Plot the resulting OC curves on a graph and explain the changes observed.

    a. $n = 200$, $c = 4$

    b. $n = 200$, $c = 2$

8. The U.S. government is going to set up several acceptance sampling plans to inspect different purchased materials. All these plans will have $n = 200$, but acceptance numbers may vary.

    a. If $\alpha = .05$ and AQL $= .01$, what value of c is needed?

    b. A tighter plan is also needed with $\alpha = .01$ and AQL $= .01$; what value of c is needed?

    c. If $\beta = .10$ and LTPD $= .06$, what value of c is needed?

9. We have taken 12 samples of 200 letters each from a typing pool and have found the following percentages of defective letters: .01, .02, .02, .00, .01, .03, .02, .01, .00, .04, .03, and .02. A letter is considered defective when one or more errors is detected.

    a. Calculate the control limits for a p control chart.

    b. A sample of 200 letters has just been taken, and 6 letters were found to be defective. Is the process still in control?

10. Each day 400 inventory control records are cycle-counted for errors. These counts have been made over a period of 20 days and have resulted in the following proportion of records found in error each day:

.0025	.0075	.0050	.0150	.0125	.0075	.0050	.0025	.0175	.0200
.0150	.0050	.0150	.0125	.0075	.0150	.0200	.0125	.0075	.0100

    a. Calculate the center line, upper control limit, and lower control limit for a p control chart.

    b. Plot the 20 points on the chart and determine which ones are in control.

    c. Is the process stable enough to begin using these data for quality control purposes?

11. A process for producing electronic circuits has achieved very high yield levels. An average of only 10 defective parts per million is currently produced.

    a. What are the upper and lower control limits for a sample of size 100?

    b. Recompute the upper and lower control limits for a sample size of 10,000.

    c. Which of these two sample sizes would you recommend? Explain.

12. In a control chart application, we have found that the grand average over all past samples of size 7 is $\bar{\bar{x}} = 30$ and $\bar{R} = 5$.

    a. Set up a control chart for this application.

    b. The following measurements are taken: 38, 35, 27, 30, 33, 28, and 32. Is the process still in control?

13. The producer of electronic circuits in Problem 11 has reconsidered the method of quality control and has decided to use process control by variables instead of attributes. For variables control a circuit voltage will be measured based on a sample of only five circuits. The past average voltage for samples of size 5 has been 3.1 volts, and the range has been 1.2 volts.

   a. What would the upper and lower control limits be for the resulting control charts (average and range)?

   b. Five samples of voltages are taken with the following results:

Sample	1	2	3	4	5
$\bar{x}$	3.6	3.3	2.6	3.9	3.4
R	2.0	2.6	0.7	2.1	2.3

   What action should be taken, if any?

   c. Discuss the pros and cons of using this variables control chart versus the control chart described in Problem 11. Which do you prefer?

14. A machining operation requires close tolerances on a certain part for automobile engines. The current tolerance for this measurement is 3.0 cm $\pm$ .001. The quality control procedure is to take a sample of size 4 and measure each of the parts. On the basis of past samples of size 4, $\bar{\bar{x}} = 3.0$ and $\bar{R} = .0015$.

   a. Construct an average and range chart for this part.

   b. On the basis of the following data, is the process in control?

Sample	1	2	3	4	5
$\bar{x}$	3.0005	2.9904	3.0010	3.0015	3.0008
R	0.0024	0.0031	0.0010	0.0040	0.0010

   c. Is the process running outside of its tolerances?

15. As cereal boxes are filled in a factory, they are weighed for their contents by an automatic scale. The target value is to put 10 ounces of cereal in each box. Twenty samples of three boxes each have been weighed for quality control purposes. The fill weight for each box is shown below.

	Observation		
Sample	1	2	3
1	10.01	9.90	10.03
2	9.87	10.20	10.15
3	10.04	9.89	9.76
4	10.17	9.94	9.83
5	10.21	10.13	10.04
6	10.16	10.02	9.85
7	10.14	9.89	9.80
8	9.86	9.91	9.99
9	10.18	10.04	9.93
10	9.91	9.87	10.06
11	10.08	10.14	10.03
12	9.82	9.87	9.92
13	10.14	10.06	9.84
14	10.16	10.17	10.19
15	10.13	9.84	9.92
16	10.16	9.81	9.83
17	10.20	10.10	10.03
18	9.87	9.93	10.06
19	9.84	9.91	9.99
20	10.06	10.19	10.01

a. Calculate the center line and control limits for the $\bar{x}$ and R charts from these data.

b. Plot each of the 20 samples on the $\bar{x}$ and R control charts and determine which samples are out of control.

c. Do you think the process is stable enough to begin to use these data as a basis for calculating $\bar{\bar{x}}$ and $\bar{R}$ and to begin to take periodic samples of 3 for quality control purposes?

SELECTED BIBLIOGRAPHY

DEMING, W. EDWARDS: *Out of the Crisis,* Cambridge, Mass.: MIT Center for Advanced Engineering Study, 1986.

DUNCAN, ACHESON, J.: *Quality Control and Industrial Statistics,* 4th ed., Homewood, Ill.: Irwin, 1974.

ISHIKAWA, KAORU: *Guide to Quality Control,* Tokyo: Asian Productivity Organization, 1976.

JURAN, J. M.: *Juran on Planning for Quality,* New York: Free Press, 1988.

───── and FRANK M. GRYNA, JR.: *Quality Planning and Analysis,* 2d ed., New York: McGraw-Hill, 1980.

─────, ─────, and R. S. BINGHAM, JR. (eds.): *Quality Control Handbook,* 4th ed., New York: McGraw-Hill, 1988.

KACKAR, RAGHU H.: "Off-Line Quality Control, Parameter Design, and the Taguchi Method," *Journal of Quality Technology,* vol. 17, no. 4, October 1985.

LARSON, HARRY R.: "A Nomograph of the Cumulative Binomial Distribution," *Western Electric Engineer,* April 1965.

PRIESTMAN, SARAH: "SQC and JIT: Partnership in Quality," *Quality Progress,* May 1985.

SANIGA, ERWIN M., and LARRY E. SHIRLAND: "Quality Control in Practice—A Survey," *Quality Progress,* May 1977, pp. 30–33.

TAGUCHI, G.: "Off-Line and On-Line Quality Control Systems," *Proceedings of the International Conference on Quality Control,* Tokyo, Japan, 1989.

───── and WU, Y.: "Introduction to Off-line Quality Control," Central Japan Quality Control Association (available from American Supplier Institute, 32100 Detroit Industrial Expressway, Romulus, Michigan 48174), 1980.

PART SEVEN

INTEGRATION OF OPERATIONS

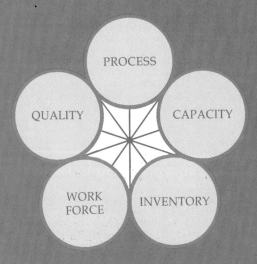

- **INTERNATIONAL OPERATIONS**
- **PRODUCTIVITY**

The two chapters in this part deal with international operations and productivity. These chapters show how decisions in operations should be integrated. The chapter on international operations describes decision making in an international environment and the effect of global markets on operations. A strategic approach is taken to facilities location, technology transfer, and outsourcing in the international arena. This chapter also shows how infrastructure should be organized, and it describes practices in German and Japanese firms.

The chapter on productivity shows how to define and measure productivity. It describes the effects of lagging productivity growth on the firm and the economy. The chapter demonstrates how the five decision-making areas in operations all affect productivity, and it provides examples of productivity improvement programs. The integration of decision making, as well as the effectiveness of individual decisions, ultimately determines the productivity of the firm.

CHAPTER 22

International Operations

International operations are becoming increasingly important in business today. One can hardly pick up the newspaper without reading about foreign competition, the trade deficit, or new international business ventures. As the world becomes smaller and business more global in nature, international operations take on a crucial role.

The purpose of this chapter is to explain the role of operations in international business and to describe the impact of international business on operations. Is there anything really different about international operations, or is it just learning how to operate a plant in Egypt, Brazil, or China? This chapter argues that international operations are indeed different for two reasons. First, the environment (cultural, economic, social, and political) is different in various countries around the world and therefore leads to different operations decisions. The impact of the international environment on decision making is discussed throughout this chapter. The second reason is that economies, and markets, are becoming more global in nature. Operations now extend across national borders, and in these cases, must be coordinated on a global basis. Businesses which do not recognize the effect that international competitors and markets have on operations will not succeed.

This chapter begins with a discussion of the nature of global markets and a comparison of the multinational firm and the truly global business. This is followed by a framework for describing the impact of international environmental variables on operations decisions and strategy. A detailed discussion is then given of various decisions in an international context, including product/process design, technology transfer, facility location, sourcing, and infrastructure. Many of these decisions have been discussed earlier in this text but are now reviewed from an international perspective. Some comparisons of Japanese, German, and U.S. operations are made, and examples are given of successful world-class competitors.

22.1   GLOBAL BUSINESS

To understand international operations you must first understand global business. The rapid advance of transportation, technology, and communications has created global markets for products and services. For example, Coca-Cola and Pepsi-Cola can be found anywhere in the world. McDonald's is on the Champs Elysees in Paris and in cities everywhere. Consulting firms have offices around the world, and communications, travel, consumer electronics, banking, and commodities have become global businesses. In a global business the world market is viewed as one entity and the product or service crosses international borders. As a result, the economies of scale are global in nature, and the competition comes from firms in any part of the globe. A firm that does not recognize the nature of global markets and products cannot effectively compete.

In contrast, the multinational firm operates in several countries around the world on a different basis. While technology and products might be shared, the multinational business is usually organized on a country-by-country basis. Each foreign subsidiary, or division, makes decisions that it feels are best for its own local markets, and the manager in each country is typically measured on a profit-and-loss basis. As a result, the multinational firm is fragmented in its approach to global markets and cannot command the resources and economies of scale of a global firm. From an operations point of view, the facilities of the multinational firm may be underutilized in one country and overutilized in another, the technology may not be transferred between countries, and the product is adapted to local tastes and customs.

Levitt (1983) argues that multinational firms can be lulled into a false sense of security by thinking they are applying the marketing concept in satisfying the needs and desires of the local market. He argues that a distinction should be made between what the customers say they want and what they will buy. A misapplication of the marketing concept gives customers what they request, rather than a product that meets their needs at a low price and consistent quality. The global firm, through its superior use of technology and economies of scale, can simultaneously make an inexpensive product available with good quality throughout the world. This global firm can drive out the multinational firms and local firms that are striving to meet local preferences.

A third type of firm that operates in international markets is one that exports products or licenses its technology for use abroad. This firm is domestically based; it does not operate foreign plants or facilities. However, it may have extensive marketing organizations in foreign countries or sell exported products through agents. These export firms can be very effective if centralized facilities can effectively meet worldwide or regional demand.

The Japanese auto companies, until recently, were export firms. Toyota, Nissan, and Honda exported into the U.S. and European markets from a domestic base in Japan. In the early 1980s these firms started to become multinational by setting up production facilities and marketing offices in foreign countries and by organizing foreign subsidiaries.[1] The Japanese firms are now operating on a global basis, to the extent that they sell the same automobiles (except for minor adaptations) throughout the world and production and sales facilities are coordinated on a global basis.

In summary there are three types of international firms:

1. *Global.* This firm markets a similar product throughout the world. It has an international network of coordinated sales and production facilities and uses a worldwide scale of operations and technology for competitive advantage.
2. *Multinational.* The multinational firm markets and produces products in the various countries, products suited to local tastes. It is usually organized with independent foreign subsidiaries, or divisions, in the separate countries.
3. *Export.* The export firm ships products to the various foreign markets from domestic facilities. It may sell through its own marketing organization or through agents, or it may license technology for use abroad.

It has been said that the global firm will be the dominant type of firm in the future. Is there still a role for the multinational firm, the export firm, and the strictly domestic firm? The answer to this question is, of course, yes. There are three basic ways to compete: low cost, differentiation, and niche markets. Worldwide "commodity" products selling at low prices favor the global firm because the basic form of competition for the global firm is standardized products and global economies of scale. Multinational and domestic firms can compete very well, however, on differentiation and niche products. Some forms of differentiation are fast service, high quality, responsiveness to customer demands, reliable deliveries, and new-product introductions. The multinational firm, by its organization and local facilities, may be able to provide better differentiated service when price is not the primary basis of competition. It can also produce products for niche markets that exist on a local basis, such as household products, branded food, pharmaceuticals, and a wide variety of industrial products and services. The

---

[1]Honda Motors built its first plant in the United States in Marysville, Ohio, in 1982.

multinational or local firm can also provide deliveries on a JIT basis, which many companies are demanding. A global firm with foreign facilities may not be able to provide JIT service at low cost.

22.2 KEY DECISIONS AND INTERNATIONAL ENVIRONMENTS

One of the key tenets of this chapter is that the international environment affects decision making in operations and the firm. These effects are illustrated by the diagram in Figure 22.1. At the center of the diagram are the various decisions in operations: process, capacity, inventory, work force, and quality. Key marketing and finance decisions are also indicated in this circle, which, of course, interact with operations decisions. Surrounding this circle are the business strategy and operations strategy, which set mission, objectives, distinctive competence, and policies for the business and for operations. The strategy is really the link between the various external environments and the internal decisions in operations and other functions. Surrounding the figure are the environments of various countries in which the firm chooses to operate. These environments are characterized by the economic, social, political, and legal systems of each of the countries. Thus operations decisions are embedded in a complex international environment consisting of more than one country.

Perhaps the effect of some of the key environmental variables on operations decisions should be explained in more detail. The effect of economic variables is quite clear. Different countries have different costs of capital and labor. As a result,

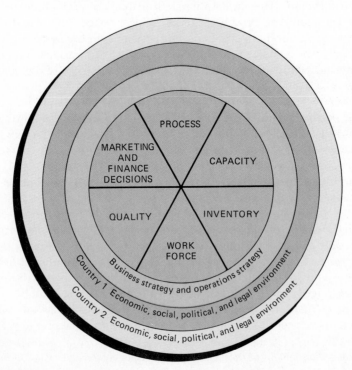

FIGURE 22.1
Operations
international
environment.

different levels of automation might be used and labor-intensive production might be moved to countries with lower labor rates. The costs, taxes, inflation rates, and currency exchange rates in various countries influence where plants are located.

Decisions are also affected by political, cultural, and legal climates around the world. An unstable political environment may contribute to an unacceptable assessment of the risk of a plant investment. Politics may also lead to trade barriers, costs, and laws which influence location or sourcing decisions. The work force is certainly affected by cultural, legal, and social factors. For example, in Japan it is practically impossible to operate a plant on a three-shift basis because women are not allowed to work after 10 p.m. In Italy, the labor redundancy laws make layoffs very expensive. Therefore, it is customary to employ many part-time workers and subcontractors in order to avoid a large permanent work force. In some European countries, employees must be represented on the board of directors. Also, in these countries you cannot close a plant without advance notice. These are just a few of the many environmental factors which affect international decisions.

In the international environment, three key regions need to be considered in the free world today. These are Europe, North America, and the Pacific Rim. Together, these regions account for 70 percent of free-world trade. When setting strategy for international operations, the environment can be simplified by thinking primarily of these three regions.

In 1992 Europe will become a totally free trade zone. All paperwork, border checks, and trade barriers will be removed within the European Common Market. This will make Europe one of the largest open markets (325 million people) in the world, even larger than the U.S. market. The Pacific Rim consists of Japan and other Asian countries, including Taiwan, Singapore, and Korea. The Pacific Rim countries export about as much each year as the U.S. and Canada combined.

The effects of international environments on operations decisions are dramatic. Before dealing with specific decisions, however, we will discuss the business and operations strategies which can be pursued on an international basis. These strategies will provide guidelines for specific decisions.

INTERNATIONAL STRATEGY

An international business strategy is a prerequisite to effective decision making in operations. A business strategy normally specifies the products and markets the firm wishes to compete in along with an indication of whether the company will pursue low cost, differentiation, or a market niche. An international business strategy is complicated by the fact that it must specify how the products, markets, and basis of competition will be handled across different countries. For example, a business could state that it wishes to market a line of textile products in Japan, the United States, and European countries on the basis of low cost. This international business strategy will in turn guide the operations strategy and specific decisions concerning operations, such as sourcing, plant location, process technology, and infrastructure. A distinctive competence, mission, and objectives will be developed for operations in order to achieve the business strategy.

FIGURE 22.2
Industry value
chain.
*Source: Michael E.
Porter,* Competitive
Advantage, *New
York: Free Press,
1985.*

Michael Porter (1986) suggests that an international strategy can be succinctly stated by use of the value chain concept. He defines the value chain as the collection of activities used to design, produce, market, deliver, and support its product. International strategy is formulated by deciding how this value chain of activities is distributed across countries.

The value chain disaggregates customers, suppliers, and the firm into discrete but interrelated activities, as shown in Figure 22.2. The value chain shows how value is created by the firm for its customers. Competitive advantage is gained whenever the firm creates value that exceeds the cost of creating it. Value is what the customers are willing to pay for, and superior value stems from lower costs for equivalent value or unique benefits that more than offset higher prices.

Value is created by the activities within the firm shown in the value chain in Figure 22.3. Some of these activities are primary; these include inbound logistics, operations, outbound logistics, marketing and sales, and service. Primary activities deal directly with production and sales of the product of the firm. There are also support activities which cut across the firm, including procurement, technical development, human resource management, and firm infrastructure (corporate finance, legal, public relations, etc.). In addition to the proficiency in conducting each activity, the linkages between these primary and support activities and the degree of coordination which exists among them create competitive advantage for the firm. The activities contribute to margin in so far as superior value is created through low costs or high differentiation by the value chain.

International strategy is determined by locating parts of the value chain for designing, producing, distributing, selling, and servicing the product on an

FIGURE 22.3
Firm value chain.
*Source: Michael E.
Porter,* Competitive
Advantage, *New
York: Free Press,
1985.*

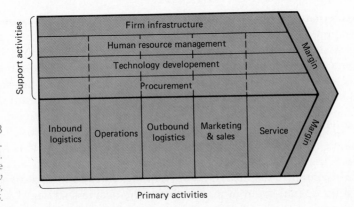

international basis. There are several options here. One is to locate all the activities in each of the countries where the firm operates. This corresponds roughly to the multinational firm described above and would be appropriate whenever the basis of competition is highly fragmented and products are localized. The firm in this case is highly decentralized, with the possible exception of firm infrastructure and some R&D.

Another option is to centralize all the value activities in one part of the world, except for sales and services. In this case the firm can export into international markets, and the firm is highly centralized, with the exception of marketing and sales.

A third option is to spread production activities throughout the world to take advantage of location costs and international sourcing. R&D could be centralized to concentrate technical expertise. All value-creating activities would be highly coordinated to achieve a worldwide competitive advantage by selling into global markets. This strategy has been described above as the global firm.

There are many other options for the location of value-creating activities. The important point is that value is created throughout the world in those locations which are best suited to meet the overall international strategy. Selecting one of the above options will provide some guidance on how the company wants to create value and competitive advantage. It will, however, still require specific decisions on exactly where to locate the facilities, where to source the components, what type of technology to use, and what kind of infrastructure to build.

Canon provides one example of how the value chain can be arranged for international strategy. Canon develops and manufactures copiers primarily in Japan, but sells and services them separately in many countries. Canon gains a cost advantage from centralizing development and manufacturing instead of performing these activities in each country. But sales and service are located in each country close to the customer for fast response.

22.4 PRODUCT AND PROCESS DESIGN

One of the decisions which must be made by the international firm is whether to standardize the products and processes of the firm on a global basis. This decision will be a result of the above strategy choices. If the choice is a multinational strategy, products and processes will be selected by each subsidiary to meet its market needs. In this case, common technology and products may still emerge, but the choice will be decentralized.

A global firm requires worldwide products and processes to compete. Selection of a global strategy specifies common products, but not the specific locations of plants or R&D centers. A global strategy could require one plant in a selected country or several plants around the world. For example, Coca-Cola is bottled in plants all over the world, because it would be too expensive to transport Coke long distances. But Coke is the same everywhere, through control of the ingredients and the recipe used.

An example of how a company can develop a worldwide product may be helpful. Black & Decker was faced with increasing world competition and the need to produce double-insulated hand tools for safety purposes.[2] The company decided to undertake a complete redesign of its consumer power tools in order to meet safety needs, to control costs, and to prevent global competition from entering its U.S. markets. Black & Decker recognized that redesign was needed for the long run, if it was to be a U.S. domestic manufacturer with aspirations to sell tools abroad. Redesign of the tools and further automation for world markets would be needed.

The strategy for worldwide product design hinged around redesign of each of the 18 tool groups to be more standardized and to use common parts whenever possible. This involved redesign of the motors in each tool to allow automation of motor production. Instead of having unique motors for each tool, a standard armature was designed which would only differ in length, not diameter, depending on the power requirements of the tool. This redesign was so efficient that motor manufacturing required only 170 people, instead of 600 people using the old designs. Nevertheless, the project required substantial investment risks—a $17 million investment with a 7-year payback.

The effect of this project on the power tools allowed Black & Decker to lower prices and capture both domestic and international market share. In the U.S. market, Black & Decker caught its competitors absolutely flat-footed. Competitors' more costly tools could not compete, and as a result Stanley, Skil, Pet, McGraw-Edison, Sunbeam, General Electric, Wen, Thor, Porter Cable, and Rockwell all left the U.S. consumer market. Only Sears & Roebuck was able to stay in the domestic market. In Europe, Black & Decker grabbed a much larger share of market by making power tools more readily available at lower prices.

The Black & Decker tool redesign also resulted in other benefits to the firm. When new products are introduced, they can be more rapidly designed using the modular motor technology. As a result of this project, manufacturing and design engineers learned to work more closely together, from the start, to design a product for produceability. And engineering and manufacturing were reorganized and put under a common vice president of operations to facilitate coordination. As products reach maturity and have to be dropped, massive write-offs are avoided, because the facilities can be used to make other tools. In short, the pace of new-product development and product retirement was greatly accelerated.

This example illustrates how global product and process standardization can be a powerful force in world markets. In this case, due to economies of scale, Black & Decker chose to export to Europe from a domestic North American base. But the principle is the same: well-designed, low-cost products often have worldwide appeal. Furthermore, continuing product and process development is supported by standardized designs and global strategies.

22.5 TECHNOLOGY TRANSFER

International operations frequently encounter the issue of technology transfer across borders. We will describe how the firm should choose to transfer its technology and what channels it should use to make the transfer.

---

[2]This example is extracted from Lehnerd (1987).

To the traditional economist the transfer of technology is simply a matter of determining the appropriate mix of labor and capital. Assuming perfect competition, homogeneous products, many firms, and economic rationality, the firm will transfer technology in order to minimize its costs. This is accomplished by choosing the mix of labor and capital which provides the lowest-cost product. The theory further holds that all firms in a given country will use the same technology and that those firms which do not use the best mix of capital and labor will be forced to leave the industry.

Studies by economists, and others, beginning in the 1970s, have shown that the classical economic theory is inadequate in explaining technology transfer. Firms in the same industry use radically different technologies, and they do not necessarily adjust labor and capital inputs from one country to the next. These departures from classical theory have been explained by several authors as follows.

In a study of 13 companies in 3 industries, Yeoman (1984) noted that two additional factors seem to influence the manager's choice of technology. If prices are very elastic and manufacturing costs are high, then managers seem to follow the classical theory. Otherwise, technology is not changed as it crosses borders. Yeoman's study also points out that firms often compete on the basis of differentiation, as we have noted above. In this case the manager may use technology to produce higher-quality products or different products which command higher prices, rather than minimizing costs.

Another study by Keddie (1984) in Indonesia indicates that the competitive model of homogeneous products had little applicability. Widespread product heterogeneity was found, and the primary reason that firms transferred technology was to gain some product advantage.

In studying the transfer of technology to Thailand, Lecraw (1984) found that the choice of technology in low-wage countries depends significantly on factors beyond the relative costs of capital and labor. His findings give strong support for factors of competition, firm strategy, and the availability of information to managers, as major determinants of technology choice. As a result of these studies, we should consider a broader theory of technology transfer than cost minimization.

Various channels for technology transfer can be used by the international firm. These include licenses, wholly owned subsidiaries, and joint ventures. A license transfer involves selling a license to use the technology to another firm in exchange for a royalty agreement. This form of transfer is common in the later stages of the product life cycle and is usually conducted by smaller firms and engineering firms. Apparently, larger firms prefer more control over their technology transfers by maintaining direct forms of ownership.

Large multinational or global firms have used wholly owned subsidiaries as a way of transferring technology in order to gain access to foreign markets. These firms tend to transfer the knowledge gained from technology after they have gained a stronghold of the domestic market. Recently, however, some global firms have introduced products on a worldwide basis right from the start. This occurred, for example, in the case of VCR technology.

The joint venture has become a very popular form of technology transfer for large multinational or global firms. These joint ventures have been formed by electronics companies, auto companies, and others to acquire a wider range of technology than the company can develop through its own R&D. As a result, technology is being transferred more rapidly and product life cycles are being shortened by these arrangements. Some of the recent joint ventures are shown in Table 22.1. See Reich and Mankin (1986) for possible dangers of joint ventures.

Teece (1981) has pointed out that technology transfer actually involves transfer of know-how and knowledge, not just equipment or product specifications. He found that well-codified knowledge is less costly to transfer than new or unproven knowledge. As a result, firms should attempt to transfer only technology which is

TABLE 22.1
JOINT VENTURES

Bendix-Murata Manufacturing Company	Machine tools
General Motors-Fujitsu Fanuc	Machine tools
Houdaille-Okuma	Machine tools
Boeing-Mitsubishi Heavy Industries	Airplanes
Boeing-Kawasaki Heavy Industries	Airplanes
Boeing-Fuji Heavy Industries	Airplanes
Armco-Mitsubishi Rayon	Lightweight plastic composites
General Motors-Toyota	Automobiles
Ford-Mazda	Automobiles
Chrysler-Mitsubishi Motors	Automobiles
Westinghouse-Komatsu	Robots and small motors
Westinghouse-Mitsubishi Electric	Robots
IBM-Sanyo Seiki	Robots
Allen Bradley-Nippondenso	Programmable controllers and sensors
General Electric-Matsushita	Disc players and air conditioners
Kodak-Canon	Copiers and photographic equipment
Sperry Univac-Nippon Univac	Computers
National Semiconductor-Hitachi	Computers
IBM-Matsushita Electric	Small computers
Honeywell-NEC	Computers
Tandy-Kyocera	Computers
Sperry Univac-Mitsubishi	Computers

Source: Robert Reich and Eric Mankin, "Joint Ventures with Japan Give away Our Future," *Harvard Business Review*, March–April 1986.

well understood or they should be prepared to pay higher costs. Even well-codified knowledge transfer will require face-to-face contact and some transfer of knowledgeable people in order to be successful. One example of how this can occur is illustrated by the following description of a Ford Motor Company investment in Spain.

> It took us just three years to the day to build a complex that includes an assembly plant, a stamping and body plant and an engine plant on a manufacturing site 2½ miles long and half a mile wide, with 55 acres under roof. The first Fiesta was driven off the assembly line well ahead of schedule. To get from farmland to an annual capacity of 250,000 cars and 400,000 engines in three years, we drew on the experience of our personnel and our technological resources from all over the world—experience and resources that couldn't be bought and that we probably wouldn't even know how to sell.

This story illustrates the important role of people and knowledge in transferring technology. The people carry the knowledge in their heads which is needed to make the technology transfer work. Not all of this knowledge is codified or understood.

Next, we will discuss facility location decisions. As we shall see, the issues involved in establishing a facility in a foreign location are closely related to those involved in technology transfer.

22.6 FACILITY LOCATION

International facility location is one of the most complex and interesting decisions that operations managers face. It involves not only questions of cost and investment, but a whole range of legal, social, and political issues. In this section we will review the location decision, first considered in Chapter 10, from an international perspective.

Kogut (1985) makes the distinction between comparative advantage and competitive advantage in locating international facilities. Comparative advantage is held by countries, not firms. A comparative advantage is usually vested in low labor or capital costs. As a result, according to the economic theory of perfect competition described before, industries and plants will be located in those countries with the lowest-cost mix of factor inputs.

Competitive advantage holds that advantage can be gained from more than costs alone. As a result of a differentiation strategy a business may locate in a country which does not have the lowest costs. But competitive advantage is gained, in this case, from the differentiation of the value chain of the business. Two bases for international facility location are described below: one where the business seeks to be the low-cost producer and the other where the business competes on a differentiation strategy.

If the business seeks to be the low-cost competitor, the choice of a niche or global strategy still needs to be made. A niche strategy, limited to one country or a region, may be appropriate if transportation costs or selling costs are high and economies of scale are low. For example, suppose the business produces a relatively bulky or heavy standard product such as beer bottles, glass jars, or automobile batteries. The business seeks to compete by charging the lowest prices among competitors and a low-cost niche strategy is desired. Even though manufacturing costs are higher in certain countries, the business should locate facilities around the world near its customers due to high transportation costs. This could include, for example, plants in each country in which the company operates.

A business choosing a low-cost strategy for a global "commodity" market will face a somewhat different situation. If transportation costs are low and economies of scale are high, it is likely that the firm will have one or a few centralized locations to serve the world. The theory of comparative advantage seems to apply here, and the business will seek to find the lowest-cost mix of input factors. Over a relatively long time period, industries may move from one country to another in search of the lowest-cost combination of factors. For example, textiles, oil, steel, and chemicals have followed global low-cost-producer strategies.

The deciding factor for the low-cost producer will be the total cost of designing, producing, distributing, and selling the product. A value chain approach can be used to think about where various value activities should be located to achieve minimum cost. Each of these value activities is located in that part of the world which results in overall lowest cost. A transportation-cost model, of the type described in Chapter 10, can be used to find plant locations which minimize the cost of production and transportation.

The second case for location is the differentiation strategy. There are several ways to differentiate, including:

1. Product innovator (this business will often be first to the market and will have many new products).
2. Flexibility (to meet changing product requirements, special customer requests, or volume changes).
3. Fast delivery (shortest lead time to supply the product from customer request to delivery).
4. Most dependable delivery (the product is delivered when promised).
5. Best product features (outperforms all other products or has features that the customer desires).
6. Consistent quality (the product consistently meets customer requirements).

Some of these differentiation strategies can only be achieved by a geographical niche strategy. For example, differentiation strategy 1 favors local R&D close to the customer because customers often help to generate many innovative ideas. Strategy 2 favors the firm which can change quickly. Small firms that are in close touch with their customers typically have the most flexibility. A large firm with centralized marketing and production would not be as competitive. Strategy 3, fast delivery, favors plants close to customers or economical air shipment of products. Strategies 4, 5, and 6 probably do not depend on location and can be executed from anywhere in the world.

JIT deserves a special word of consideration here. JIT suppliers must usually be close to customers in order to assure frequent, small shipments. One exception to this is where the product can be economically transported by air freight. Despite these exceptions, JIT affects the location decisions of international firms. JIT delivery is, after all, a form of differentiation.

Like the low-cost-producer strategy, the differentiation strategy should be analyzed on a value chain basis. Value activities are considered in terms of how much differentiation is provided by each activity. The question of where to locate each activity is analyzed in terms of how that activity can best provide differentiated value.

Location of facilities requires consideration of a broad range of quantitative and qualitative criteria. The criteria go beyond cost and include legal, political, and social factors. Many of these considerations directly affect cash flow, the risk of foreign investment, or the feasibility of a given location. Some of the factors which influence international location are discussed next.

Quantitative location criteria, shown in Table 22.2, can be directly measured or quantified. Of course, these quantitative factors include the costs of labor, materials, overhead, shipping, and any special packaging or insurance required for overseas operations. In addition to normal manufacturing costs, the firm must take into account taxes, duties, inventory carrying costs, and foreign currency rates. As a matter of fact, many location decisions hinge heavily on these additional costs or on incentives given by foreign governments to attract investments. The firm must also consider the ability to repatriate profits earned. For example, returns from investments in China today cannot be translated into hard currency and profits cannot be taken out of the country. This is true, to varying degrees, in other countries too.

There are also a large number of qualitative factors which need to be considered. These include political and economic stability, degree of government regulation, and specific laws. One of the most important factors in plant location is political and economic stability. Why invest in a country where the plant might be seized by the foreign government or the currency can change to the point where

TABLE 22.2
FACILITY LOCATION FACTORS

Quantitative Factors	Qualitative Factors
Cost of labor	Political stability
Cost of materials	Economic climate
Overhead costs	Government regulation
Shipping costs	Local laws
Special packaging	Domestic union reaction
Insurance	International coordination
Taxes	Cultural differences
Duties	Language
Inventory carrying costs	Investment restrictions
Foreign currency rates	Trade barriers
Government incentives	Unionization
Repatriation of profits	Size of market

the plant is worthless? Decision makers also should consider the regulatory policy of the government and the specific laws which affect the business. Firms cannot ignore the effect that offshore production might have on domestic union relations or the image of the company. Finally, the business must consider the need for international coordination of facilities. Coordination across borders presents a formidable cost and challenge to the novice firm. Some of the common problems are language difficulties, differences in operations philosophy, and cultural differences.

We complete this section by discussing movement of manufacturing offshore and back onshore. Since the 1970s, U.S. firms have been moving more and more production offshore, usually in search of cheap labor. For a while this situation reached epidemic proportions. Changes in exchange rates and a resurgence of manufacturing excellence in the United States have alleviated the situation to some extent but have not stopped it. Plants, particularly those which are labor-intensive, will continue to move offshore as the economy becomes more global in nature.

Despite the loss of domestic jobs, some offshore production is a good thing for the countries of the world, including the United States. To be competitive, U.S. firms must continue to locate labor-intensive activities offshore. But this should be viewed as an international strategy of diversification, rather than merely the chasing of cheap labor, as we have noted above.

One of the interesting offshore production alternatives is the Maquiladora zone in Mexico, just across the border from the United States. To date, about 1500 Maquiladora factories have been built by U.S. companies. These Mexican factories have a labor rate of about $1 per hour compared with $14 per hour for equivalent labor in the United States [see Flores (1987)]. In addition, overhead costs (staff and space costs) are much lower in Mexico. Because of the huge labor and overhead differential, firms have been moving labor-intensive activities across the border to Mexico.

In some cases, a U.S. factory is built near the border to team with a Maquiladora factory. The U.S. factory will send certain labor-intensive operations to Mexico, and then the Mexican factory will return the goods for more capital-intensive operations in the United States. The Mexican government does not charge duties in the Maquiladora zone, and the United States charges only a small duty on value added in Mexico. The Maquiladora factories illustrate a cooperative relationship where goods can be produced in more than one country. See Flores (1987) for more details.

Despite the use of offshore production, the United States is becoming a stronger manufacturing economy. There are very good reasons for keeping manufacturing onshore; differentiation is one reason and automated low-cost manufacturing is another. Note that Black & Decker is the worldwide low-cost producer of hand tools through its aggressive automation and product redesign efforts in the United States.

As U.S. manufacturing rebounds, the Japanese and Europeans are locating their plants in the United States in large numbers. For example, 450 foreign-owned plants were established in the United States by 1988. In the auto industry alone the Japanese will have 11 manufacturing plants in the United States by 1989 with a capacity to make 1.9 million vehicles per year. One factor contributing to this has been the declining dollar, but a more important reason is the desire of many firms to manufacture in their markets.

The Japanese typically follow their export sales worldwide with plants. This helps solidify the market gains and provides a defense against local content laws, trade barriers, and high tariffs. The Japanese have located plants in the United States as a long-run strategy even though costs in the United States were for sometime higher than Japan. When production is internationally distributed, the firm becomes more immune to short-term currency fluctuations and trade barriers. Market share is a more important goal for the Japanese than short-term profits. So the question of facility location ultimately comes back to the issues of corporate goals and corporate strategy.

YKK zipper provides a good example of a worldwide location strategy. YKK, a Japanese zipper company, initially imported zippers to the U.S. market in the early 1970s after gaining a 90 percent share of the zipper market in Japan. The company started importing zippers to the United States by selling standard zippers in long runs at lower prices. This could be accomplished because of their excellent low-cost production facilities in Japan. As the zipper business increased in the United States, YKK opened a plant in Macon, Georgia. This plant allowed the company to differentiate its product by providing faster service and more short runs of zippers. The plant has been expanded several times, and YKK now has 50 percent of the U.S. zipper market. In addition, it has substantial market shares in the Far East and in Europe. YKK has become an international firm with plants in 25 different countries around the world.

In summary, facility location should be based on strategy. Low cost is not the only objective; differentiation is also a powerful strategy. Various qualitative and quantitative criteria should be considered. Facilities can help the firm meet its marketing objectives by locating in the markets served. Offshore production can be a valuable strategy for highly labor-intensive products. International networks of plants and sources can be developed which provide a global operations strategy. This will be discussed in the next section.

22.7 OUTSOURCING

Outsourcing of materials and components is a common practice. Frequently, from 50 to 70 percent of the manufacturing cost of a product is spent for purchased materials. Many firms are reevaluating the value chain in terms of outsourcing. Some feel they are too vertically integrated and can achieve a higher return on capital by more outsourcing. Over the next few years, for example, General Motors plans to outsource $4 billion of parts and services [Callahan (1987)]. It is not only components which are being outsourced by GM, but engineering design services too. The outsourcing of engineering is aimed at reducing large internal staffs.

Recently, purchases of offshore components have been increasing. Outsourcing is moving production not only outside the company, but offshore too, as markets become more global. One estimate is that 13 percent of U.S. manufacturing purchasing is now obtained from offshore sources [Dowst (1987)].

In this section we will be discussing why and how international outsourcing should be done. In line with our previous discussions, outsourcing should be done for strategic reasons. Outsourcing gives a competitive advantage whenever a portion of the value chain can be located outside the host country to gain cost or differentiation advantages. This is in contrast to merely shopping for the lowest price of a component.

Therese Flaherty (1987) writes that much sourcing is done by catalog shopping or franchising. Catalog shopping is done primarily by purchasing managers on the basis of costs and specifications. Little consideration is given to the strategic benefits of finding foreign sources of supply. Franchising is duplicating the technology of the home plant in a foreign location. The foreign location works independently of the home unit and is managed on a local basis. There is little, or no, interaction among franchise locations.

In catalog shopping or franchising, little attempt is made to manage knowledge across international boundaries or to coordinate diverse sites of sourcing. A potential competitive advantage through sharing of knowledge is ignored by this type of sourcing. The typical situation without coordination is shown in Figure 22.4. In this case the factories and sources of supply in each country are operated pretty much independently. Note, each factory is assumed to be in a different country.

Figure 22.5 shows how an international network can be interconnected and coordinated. Information and materials are shared across international boundaries. The resulting coordination can result in a much stronger sourcing option. The objective of this type of integrative sourcing is to enhance the entire value chain.

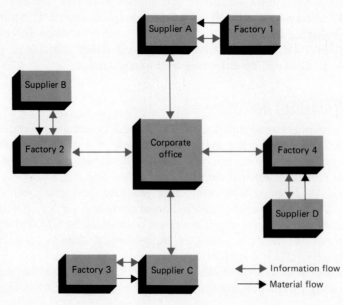

FIGURE 22.4
Minimum
coordination of
facilities
(multinational
firm).
*Source: Adapted from
Armistead (1987).*

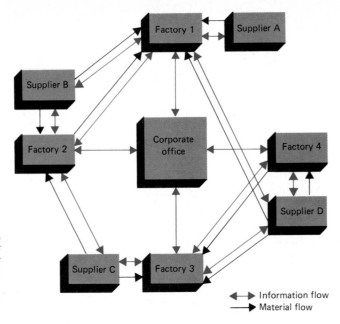

FIGURE 22.5
High degree of
coordination of
facilities (global
firm).
*Source: Adapted from
Armistead (1987).*

Flaherty illustrates this idea with the Applichem Company story. A worldwide business manager in the company was trying to stop losses in the specialty chemical business. He had six plants making essentially identical chemicals for local markets in the United States, Germany, Canada, Mexico, Venezuela, and Japan. The German plant made the least expensive product; Japan made the most expensive. The lowest-cost sourcing pattern, given the plants' current costs, required closing the Japanese and Canadian plants and supplying their markets with product from the United States and Germany. This would save roughly $1 million, which would go to profit.

But this is the traditional way of thinking about international sourcing. The decision would be made on the basis of current plant efficiencies and exchange rates. After commissioning an engineering study, the manager found that the Japanese plant was much better than the company's engineers thought was possible in their use of raw material. The people in the German plant could teach the Latin Americans and those in the United States quite a bit. Having all the plants make the most efficient use of materials would save the business about $7 million a year—much more than simply taking the efficiencies as given. This story illustrates that the international transfer of knowledge can be a powerful force in improving process technology and can result in better sourcing decisions than mere efficiency thinking.

International sourcing depends on a number of things. First, the product life cycle should be considered. Normally, a product is not outsourced in the early stages of the life cycle. During this period, the product design is being modified to improve market acceptance, and close contact is needed between manufacturing and engineering design. Later in the life cycle it is more appropriate to outsource the product in order to achieve additional capacity or to lower costs. By this time the product design will be stable and the process technology is more easily transferred to a supplier.

Another factor which affects outsourcing is the proprietary nature of technology. Normally, a product which is proprietary will be kept in-house in order to keep the technology secret. Some companies have a policy that all nonproprietary technology will be outsourced and the proprietary technology will be kept inside the company.

A third factor in outsourcing is the expertise of suppliers. A company usually cannot be competent at everything. Those areas where the company does not have a particular expertise can be outsourced to other companies that do. Suppliers should be viewed as a valuable source of knowledge and not only a source of cheap parts, as we have noted before. Depending on suppliers for knowledge requires a long-run relationship with suppliers.

Finally, outsourcing is done to reduce costs and to improve return on investment. As we have noted above, labor-intensive products could be outsourced to take advantage of cheaper sources of labor. Costs can also be saved in the overhead areas of staff salaries, cost of space, and managerial salaries. Often companies with unions will outsource to companies with nonunion work forces in lower-wage areas.

There are at least two drawbacks to outsourcing. One of these is the possible loss of technical expertise. There are important links between manufacturing and design. As a result, a loss of manufacturing ultimately leads to a loss of design expertise. Companies should therefore only outsource "noncritical" components which are not a part of the "character" of the product. Outsourcing of critical components can lead to ultimate loss of the product line itself. This has been referred to as a hollowing out of industry. As more and more functions are outsourced, the corporation becomes hollow in its ability to design and manufacture products. All that is left is a distribution organization, and even that can be lost if the supplier sets up its own distribution.

A second drawback of outsourcing is the hidden costs which are often present. The cost of outsourcing is much greater than the purchase price of the part. Sometimes the part must be redesigned for foreign manufacturing because the process technology is not identical at the foreign site. Usually a foreign office must be staffed to manage the external suppliers. This office is needed to communicate engineering change orders, to certify the suppliers for quality, and to solve technical problems when they occur. Normally a representative of the company, who speaks the foreign language, must be located in this office to properly represent the company. The costs of shipping, inventory carrying, insurance, duties, taxes, travel, and the like are also sometimes hidden from the purchase price.

When outsourcing is being considered, the following steps should be followed:

1. Decide on the strategic reasons for outsourcing. The operations strategy should state a policy on outsourcing. This will include how much outsourcing is desired, as a percentage of manufacturing costs; the type of outsourcing (e.g., nonproprie-

tary products only); the potential countries which will be considered; and the criteria to be applied in specific cases.

2. Establish a team to make outsourcing decisions. Frequently this team should include representatives from purchasing, manufacturing, engineering, marketing, and accounting. All the functional expertise of the company should be used on the team to generate and evaluate outsourcing options.

3. Set up a technical office overseas or consult with existing offices to gather information on potential sources of supply. Feed this information back to the outsourcing team for evaluation and decision.

4. Establish an ongoing relationship with the suppliers, not only a purchasing contract. This should include certification for quality and discussions regarding future business for other parts and components.

5. Consider strategic alliances with your suppliers. This could include joint ventures, acquisition of the supplier, or an equity position in the supplier.

From the above it should be clear that outsourcing is complex but can be a source of potential profit. The overriding reason for outsourcing should be to support the strategic objectives of the firm. Through establishment of international networks, it is possible to gain competitive advantage through knowledge and materials obtained from suppliers in additional to financial benefits.

INTERNATIONAL INFRASTRUCTURE

Up to this point we have been dealing with structural decisions: capacity, facilities, technology, and sourcing. These decisions require capital and affect the "bricks and mortar," or the tangible part of operations. The infrastructure is intangible and includes organization, people, information systems, materials management, and quality. These infrastructure decisions are just as important as structural decisions, but they are sometimes neglected in discussions of international operations.

We will deal with international infrastructure by comparing Japanese and German manufacturing firms with U.S. firms. The Japanese and Germans are particularly good at managing their infrastructure, and much can be learned from them. As business becomes more global, infrastructure becomes a powerful source of competitive advantage. Yet top management often pays the most attention to structural decisions, probably because these decisions are the most visible and require capital approval.

The German style of management will be discussed first, based on material from Hayes and Wheelwright (1984). A brief review is made of the German industrial record, followed by some observations about how the Germans manage their manufacturing infrastructure.

German Management

The German industrial economy has had good success in the 1970s and 1980s compared with the rest of the world. Productivity growth has averaged 5 percent a year during most of this period, and exports have increased over imports. The

Germans seem to know their economic strength is based on industrial power and have been emphasizing manufacturing. They have made these impressive improvements in the face of rising costs, some of the highest labor costs in the world, and very restrictive work rules. The German economy is composed of mostly smaller manufacturing companies, at least compared with U.S. and Japanese companies, and the German companies understand that export is critical to their survival. About 50 percent of all goods manufactured in Germany, and Japan, are exported.

Several characteristics seem to lead to the German success in manufacturing. First, the Germans emphasize *Gründlichkeit*, "getting everything right." The Germans are known to be neat and meticulous, and German products are recognized throughout the world for quality. The most widely known examples are their automobiles and machine tools.

The German managers have high regard for *Technik*. Roughly translated, this means an understanding of the art of manufacturing, including manufacturing techniques, equipment, and production management. Other managerial activities such as planning and control and strategy are relegated to secondary importance. Most German manufacturing managers have engineering degrees. It is a compliment to a German manager to say that he has knowledge of *Technik*.

The apprenticeship program in Germany is well known throughout the world. Half of all German students at age 16 enter an apprenticeship program for 3 years. The typical week includes 4 days of work and 1 day of classes. Over 350,000 German companies participate in this apprenticeship program, and as a result the Germans have very well trained workers in all the trades.

German firms have a strong customer orientation resting on finely engineered products. They believe that reputation earned by quality products, timely delivery, and excellent after-sales service is the best marketing tool. German firms are fussy about getting things right for the customer.

Managers in Germany tend to have a long-term orientation. Stockholders have a relatively minor influence, since more of the financing is obtained from banks. Bankers sit on the boards of directors and are more concerned with long-run survival than short-term profits. Managers and employees tend to stay with the same company for their careers and see their welfare as intimately tied to the company's performance over the long run.

The German's have consensus-seeking management. The German codetermination system legally requires managers to negotiate with worker-dominated councils at the plant level before implementing major changes. This makes it difficult to lay off workers or to move plants. As a result, German managers are consensus-seeking in their approach to management, not only due to the law, but because of their close identity with the workers.

An attitude of technological incrementalism prevails in the German firms. They seek to perfect state-of-the-art products by evolutionary means, rather than through dramatic leaps. German firms invest 8–12 percent of their annual sales in new plant and equipment. Most of this goes into enhancing manufacturing performance, not simply increasing capacity. Most of the U.S. capital expenditure, by contrast, goes into capacity expansion.

In a nutshell, the Germans have a technological orientation (for workers and managers), a slow consensus decision-making style, a commitment to enduring customer relations, a willingness to measure results over long periods of time, and technical incrementalism leading to high-quality products. Lest we think this is all good, there are also some drawbacks. The Germans are slow to change, and bound by strong work rules, all of which limits their flexibility. Nevertheless, the German style of management seems to be working quite well in the face of global competition, and the Germans are beginning to adapt to the new management styles, too.

Japanese Management

The Japanese have a drastically different approach to infrastructure than either the Germans or the Americans. The Japanese tend to stress cooperation among customers, workers, managers, and suppliers, and they relentlessly pursue the improvement of quality and productivity. Some of the key aspects of the Japanese environment and their management of infrastructure are noted below. See also Hayes and Wheelwright (1984) for more details.

Business within the Japanese borders is intensely competitive. As a result, those Japanese companies which survive the domestic competition are able international competitors. The postwar reconstruction of Japan emphasized new technology in steel, and other industries, and quality products. The limited space and limited resources in Japan also required Japanese companies to be extremely frugal with space and the use of natural resources. Any excess inventory or space beyond the absolute minimum needed to make the product was viewed as waste. Couple this with a homogeneous culture and the Japanese ability to work well in groups, and a formidable competitor emerged on the world scene.

Some of the aspects of infrastructure which have led to Japan's postwar industrial success are described below. First, the Japanese are devoted to cleanliness and orderliness. This is true not only in their factories, but in their homes, offices, and cities. Factory floors are very clean, machines are kept clean, and everything is put in its place. According to Hayes and Wheelwright (1984), "one American manager recounts with wonder being asked to put plastic covers on his shoes before being allowed to walk out on the floor of a plant that was at least 30 years old."

The Japanese are also very careful about caring for their equipment. Japanese machine operators have a much wider job description than their American counterparts, including being responsible for quality control, doing maintenance, and helping fellow workers. As a result, equipment is very well maintained and has excellent uptime. Machines can be run unattended, and the excellent maintenance supports JIT production concepts.

Through the use of JIT the Japanese are constantly reducing inventory. They think of inventory as the "root of all evil." As noted in Chapter 16, the Japanese pioneered JIT concepts, which are now also practiced in progressive U.S. and European companies. JIT principles are evident in low setup times, small batch sizes, pull systems, visual control, and good vendor relations. Use of JIT facilitates discovery and correction of quality problems.

The Japanese demonstrate a quality consciousness in all that they do. They not only build quality into the products; they "think it in." Quality in Japan is much more than the use of quality circles. Quality is assured by good product design, concurrent process design, attention to detail, and strong vendor relations. The Japanese have a saying that quality is "pursuing the last grain of rice in the box." They have quality which is measured in defects per million units produced, and they are striving for continuous improvement.

Lifelong employment in Japan is one of the most publicized practices. Yet only about two-thirds of employees in the large trading companies have lifelong employment (women were excluded until recently), and the small companies do not follow this practice. Nevertheless, lifelong employment creates a strong bond between employees and the company. Japanese managers treat human resources as largely a fixed expense and are willing to invest in continuous training and improvement of skills. Workers know that their interests are closely tied to company success, and managers are continually faced with making better use of existing employees.

The Japanese emphasize teamwork throughout the company. This occurs not only between management and workers, but between workers themselves, and between departments. Group goals are emphasized, and participation is a way of life. There is considerable pressure to meet group norms. By emphasizing the group, a spirit of cooperation and interdependence is stressed. Suggestion systems flourish in Japan.

Finally, the Japanese tend to make their own production equipment. About 50 percent of the equipment is made in-house, and the rest is purchased from outside but modified for internal use. This permits the development of proprietary processes and the tailoring of equipment to the company's needs. As a result, the Japanese company has a better chance to gain competitive advantage through technology than a company that buys all its equipment on the outside.

The onslaught of the Japanese, who have rapidly captured world markets, has led to many different explanations for their success. Too many have focused on structural differences such as quality circles, industrial policy (Japan, Inc.), or robots. Hayes and Wheelwright (1984) observe that the Japanese success is based on cooperative relations between customers, workers, managers, and suppliers and continuous improvement of quality and productivity. Unfortunately, these infrastructure traits are much harder to copy or neutralize than obvious structural differences.

22.9 WORLD-CLASS COMPETITORS

This section pulls together the observations of the last section regarding German and Japanese manufacturing management, particularly with regard to infrastructure. It also incorporates the principles followed by the excellent U.S. companies, as enunciated by Peters and Waterman (1982), and summarized in Chapter 17. Our basic thesis is that world-class competitors transcend national boundaries and follow most of the same principles of infrastructure management. Even if a company does not have an "international product," it can learn much from the companies that are world-class competitors.

The best companies in the world seem to implement the following seven principles for managing the infrastructure in their operations.

1. *Put the customer first.* This principle should be followed by the entire company, not just the sales force. Everyone talks about being close to the customers, but few truly are. The best companies are obsessive about serving their customers. They provide excellent quality and service because that is what the customers want the most. A customer orientation is not obtained by fixing complaints quickly, but by eliminating the need for customer complaints in the first place.

2. *Be quality-conscious.* A world-class competitor knows the value of quality in the customer's eyes and in reducing needless costs. The best companies do not just build quality in, they think it in, as the Japanese do. This is accomplished by superior product design and process design. Note that the Taguchi method of robust design was developed by the Japanese. Quality-conscious companies stress training of *workers, managers,* and *staff.* They involve the entire organization in quality, and they include outside suppliers. Continuous improvement of quality is the goal as described in detail in Chapters 20 and 21.

3. *Involve employees.* This means not only soliciting worker opinions, but seeking consensus and input from everyone. It includes the development of mutual respect and trust. Most companies say they are people-oriented, but they are not. The best American, German, and Japanese companies operate differently from the norm. They stress stable employment, and no layoffs, to build mutual goals and trust. They turn average people into superior performers by setting common goals and rewarding the achievement of these goals. The key is open communication, trust, and constant input from everyone. Managers act as coaches and team leaders, not controllers and commanders.

4. *Practice just-in-time production.* The world-class competitors use a JIT production philosophy. They strive to reduce waste of all forms, including inventory, space, overhead, wasted efforts, and errors. As the reader of Chapter 16 knows, this is done by using reduced setup times, small lot sizes, good quality, pull systems, and visual control systems. Companies which do not follow a JIT philosophy can no longer claim to have world-class status, especially in repetitive industries. Batch and job-shop industries with irregular master schedules can use all the JIT ideas except for the Kanban system.

5. *Emphasize technology.* There is no substitute for strong technical knowledge on the part of managers and workers. The Germans emphasize technology through the use of *Technik* and the apprenticeship program. The Japanese carry this one step further by use of proprietary equipment for competitive advantage. In addition to these steps, management should foster innovation and continuous improvement. Technological innovation through incrementalism, as well as the big breakthrough, is emphasized by all the world-class competitors.

6. *Emphasize long-term orientation.* Both Japanese and German firms emphasize long-term results more than the typical American company. This can be done

even with substantial stockholder interest, as the best U.S. companies have done. Top management should stress long-term results for survival and continuous growth in share price, rather than quick upturns and quarterly profits. A long-term orientation requires sufficient investment in the business to keep it healthy. Managing for the long run helps to maintain shareholder, customer, employee, and supplier confidence in the company.

7. *Be action-oriented.* The world-class competitor is lean and decentralized. The best companies have less overhead and smaller corporate staffs than their not-so-lean competitors. This principle also favors the smaller companies or very decentralized large companies. A flat organizational structure with few layers between the top and the bottom is needed. The organization should plan, but not to the extreme. Results are gained by taking action, even if it is sometimes the wrong action. The byword of the action-oriented company is ready-fire-aim.

Every company has to adapt to the circumstances that it finds in its industry. But the world-class companies seem to have some things in common. If these principles are applied with a grain of common sense and adaptation to the circumstances, management can develop a plan for achieving world-class status. That in the end is the essence of operations strategy, choosing that set of policies and principles that best seem to fit the situation and the objectives of the company.

22.10   KEY POINTS

This chapter examined the role of operations in international business and the impact of international business on operations. The chapter's key points include the following:

- There are three types of international companies: global, multinational, and export. The global firm operates in a worldwide market on the basis of global economies of scale and coordinated decision making. The multinational firm is decentralized by country, and each foreign subsidiary is treated as a separate business. The export firm exports products for sale or licenses its technology for use abroad.
- Operations decision making is affected by the environments of the countries in which the company operates. Understanding the effects of these different environments (social, political, economic, and legal) is the key to managing international operations.
- International business strategy can be based on low cost or differentiation. These strategies can be succinctly defined by the value chain for design, production, distribution, sales, and service of the product. Locating parts of the value chain in different countries is the essence of international strategy.
- Studies have shown that the best technology is not only the one with the lowest costs, but considers competition, product differentiation, and quality. Technology can be transferred by wholly owned subsidiaries, licenses, or joint venture. Knowledge must first be codified for orderly international transfer of technology.

- Facility location should be based on a low-cost or product differentiation strategy. Many other economic, social, legal, and political criteria should also be considered.
- Outsourcing should follow a strategy-driven approach. Much outsourcing is done by catalog shopping or franchising in order to minimize costs. Outsourcing depends on life cycle, proprietary nature of technology, expertise of suppliers, and return on investment. Drawbacks of outsourcing are the loss of technical expertise and hidden costs.
- World-class competitors seem to follow a common set of principles for infrastructure. These include a policy of putting the customer first, quality consciousness, employee involvement, JIT, an emphasis on technology, long-term orientation, and a bias for action. These principles are followed by the best Japanese, German, and American companies.

QUESTIONS

1. Identify one firm that is global, one that is multinational, and one that is export-oriented. Find an article in the library about each of these firms which describes its international operations.
2. A company has decided to reorganize its international business. Currently the general managers from each country report through an international chain of organization separate from U.S. product divisions. The proposal is to put worldwide responsibility under each product division manager and eliminate the international divisions.
   a. Will this make the company a global firm?
   b. What other steps might be needed to achieve global status?
3. A U.S. company is planning to license its technology from a German firm.
   a. How should the U.S. company evaluate whether this technology transfer is a good idea or not?
   b. What questions should the U.S. company ask the German company?
   c. What contract provisions should the U.S. company request to assure successful technology transfer?
4. Identify an international firm that competes on the basis of differentiation and another that competes on low cost. Find an article about each of the firms in the library. Contrast and compare their strategies.
5. From your experience select a company that has distributed its value chain across several different countries. What parts of the value chain are located in each country? Explain why the value chain is located this way.
6. A company which makes semiconductors is trying to decide whether to locate a plant in Japan. At the present time this company exports $20 million of semiconductors per year into the Japanese market. The minimum plant size is $15 million per year due to economies of scale. What factors should be considered in this decision?
7. A large multinational company which mines copper in Chile is considering closing its mines and smelters in that country. The reasons given by the company are high costs in Chile and overcapacity in the world copper market. What possible adverse effects could this have on the company and on Chile?
8. Under what circumstances should a company plan to locate a plant in a foreign country for lower labor costs? In other words, what conditions must prevail for this to be a good idea?
9. A U.S. company which sells batteries currently makes the battery cases out of hard

plastic. Sales are expected to double over the next 3 years, and the company is considering outsourcing the additional cases needed. What criteria should the company apply in making this decision. The alternative is to build another plant and acquire the equipment to make more battery cases internally instead of outsourcing.

10. It has been said that outsourcing requires considerable transfer of knowledge.
    a. What is meant by transfer of knowledge?
    b. How can knowledge be transferred?
11. Why is infrastructure an important part of international operations management?
12. Contrast and compare the Japanese and German approaches to infrastructure.
13. Develop a method of *diagnosis* for each of the infrastructure principles listed in Section 22.9 on world-class competitors. In other words, what questions would you ask in order to test the extent to which the company is following each of these principles?
14. How should a company decide whether to emphasize structure or infrastructure in its international operations?

SELECTED BIBLIOGRAPHY

ARMISTEAD, COLIN: "International Factory Networks," *Proceedings of Research Symposium: Issues in International Manufacturing*, INSEAD, Sept. 7–9, 1987.

CALLAHAN, JOSEPH: "GM Outsourcing $4 Billion More," *Automotive Industries*, April 1987.

DAVIDSON, WILLIAM H., and PHILIPPE HASPESLAGH: "Shaping a Global Product Organization," *Harvard Business Review*, July–August 1982.

DOWST, SOMERBY: "International Buying: The Fact and Foolishness," *Purchasing*, June 25, 1987.

DOZ, YVES, L., and C. K. PRAHALAD: "Headquarters Influence and Strategic Control in MNCs," *Sloan Management Review*, Fall 1981.

FERDOWS, KASRA, JEFFREY G. MILLER, JINICHIRO NAKANE, and THOMAS E. VOLLMANN: "Evolving Global Manufacturing Strategies: Projections into the 1990's," *International Journal of Operations and Production Management*, vol. 6, no. 4, 1986.

FLAHERTY, THERESE M.: "International Sourcing: Beyond Catalog Sourcing and Franchising," *Proceedings of Research Symposium: Issues in International Manufacturing*, INSEAD, Sept. 7–9, 1987.

FLORES, BENITO E.: "Mexico's Maquiladora Industries: An Overview and Perspectives," *Business Forum*, Texas A&M, vol. 4, no. 1, Fall 1987.

HAMEL, GARY, and C. K. PRAHALAD: "Do You Really Have a Global Strategy," *Harvard Business Review*, July–August 1985.

HAYES, ROBERT H., and STEVEN C. WHEELWRIGHT: *Restoring Our Competitive Edge: Competing through Manufacturing*, New York: Wiley, 1984.

KEDDIE, JAMES: "More on Production Techniques in Indonesia," in Robert Stobaugh and Louis T. Wells, Jr. (eds.), *Technology Crossing Borders*, Boston: Harvard Business School Press, 1984.

KOGUT, BRUCE: "Designing Global Strategies: Comparative and Competitive Value-Added Chains," *Sloan Management Review*, Summer 1985.

KOTKIN, JOEL: "The Case for Manufacturing in America," *INC*, March 1985.

LECRAW, DONALD, J.: "Choice of Technology in Thailand," in Robert Stobaugh and Louis T. Wells, Jr., (eds.), *Technology Crossing Borders*, Boston: Harvard Business School Press, 1984.

LEHNERD, ALVIN P.: "Revitalizing the Manufacture and Design of Mature Global Products," in Bruce R. Gile and Harvey Brooks (eds.), National Academy Press, 1987.

LEVITT, THEODORE: "The Globalization of Markets," *Harvard Business Review*, May–June 1983.

McGRATH, MICHAEL, and ROBERTO BEQUILLARD: "International Manufacturing Strategies and Infrastructural Considerations in the Electronics Industry," *Proceedings of Research Symposium: Issues in International Manufacturing*, INSEAD, Sept. 7–9, 1987.

O'REILLY, BRIAN: "Business Makes a Run for the Border," *Fortune*, Aug. 18, 1986.

PETERS, THOMAS J., and ROBERT WATERMAN, JR.: *In Search of Excellence: Lessons from America's Best-Run Companies*, New York: Harper & Row, 1982.

PORTER, MICHAEL E. (ed.): *Competitive Advantage*, New York: The Free Press, 1985.

———: *Competition in Global Industries*, Boston: Harvard Business School Press, 1986.

PRAHALAD, C. K., and YVES L. DOZ: "An Approach to Strategic Control in MNCs," *Sloan Management Review*, Summer 1981.

REICH, ROBERT, and ERIC MANKIN, "Joint Ventures with Japan Give Away Our Future," *Harvard Business Review*, March–April 1986.

STEERS, RICHARD M., and EDWIN MILLER: "Management in the 1990's: The International Challenge," *Academy of Management Executive*, February 1988.

STOBAUGH, ROBERT, and LOUIS T. WELLS, JR. (eds.): *Technology Crossing Borders*, Boston: Harvard Business School Press, 1984.

TEECE, DAVID, J.: "The Market for Know-How and the Efficient International Transfer of Technology," *ANNALS, The American Academy of Political and Social Science*, vol. 458, November 1981.

YEOMAN, WAYNE: "Selection of Production Processes by U.S.-Based Multinational Enterprises," in Robert Stobaugh and Louis T. Wells, Jr. (eds.), *Technology Crossing Borders*, Boston: Harvard Business School Press, 1984.

CHAPTER 23
Productivity

Productivity improvement is the engine behind economic progress and corporate profits. Productivity is also essential to wage increases and personal income. A country which does not improve its productivity will soon reduce its standard of living.

Productivity is defined as the relationship between inputs and outputs of a productive system. It is often convenient to measure this relationship as a ratio of output divided by input. If more output is produced with the same inputs, productivity is improved. Likewise, if fewer inputs are used for the same output, productivity is also improved. A full discussion of how productivity can be measured will be given later in the chapter.

Operations managers are the spearhead for improving productivity in the firm. Over the years, operations managers have improved productivity in the factory. A similar challenge is now being accepted by operations managers in service industries. But it is not enough simply to improve productivity in the operations function; some of the largest areas for productivity improvement are in sales,

662

finance, personnel, data processing, and other staff areas. In many organizations, the direct labor costs are already under good control, but high indirect costs are leading to low productivity. Productivity should, therefore, be thought of as an organization wide issue.

In operations, productivity is affected by all decisions, including process design, capacity, inventory, work force, and quality decisions. This chapter on productivity improvement will, therefore, draw on all the previous chapters in the text and will serve as an integrative chapter around the productivity theme. Since productivity is an overriding theme in operations, this chapter can just as well be used at the beginning of an operations management course as at the end.

Different individuals often address the productivity problem from different angles. The economists concentrate on the effect of investment and government regulation. The industrial engineers stress the effects of methods and work flow on productivity. The psychologists and management people concentrate on job design or other human relations approaches. This chapter will summarize, within a broad integrative framework, all the different approaches which have been suggested throughout the text for productivity improvement. A typical productivity decision problem is given in Box 23.1

NATIONAL PRODUCTIVITY

Although national productivity is often measured as a ratio of output divided by input, different ratios are possible, depending on the assumptions made. The total factor productivity ratio is obtained by dividing total output, measured by GNP, by the total of labor and capital inputs. Thus we have

$$\text{Total factor productivity} = \frac{\text{GNP}}{\text{labor} + \text{capital}}$$

There are also two partial productivity ratios—one for labor and the other for capital:

$$\text{Labor productivity} = \frac{\text{GNP}}{\text{labor hours}}$$

$$\text{Capital productivity} = \frac{\text{GNP}}{\text{capital}}$$

The total factor productivity ratio is the best one to use when describing national productivity, because it includes all the inputs used. The partial ratios consider only one input or the other. For example, the labor productivity ratio gives labor credit for the whole GNP output, even though changes in output may be due to increased utilization of capital. Labor productivity ratios are often used, however, because the data are readily available.

National productivity ratios are typically expressed as indexes over time. The ratio from one time period is compared with the base period to derive a percentage of increase or decrease in the productivity ratio. These indexes are typically calculated for annual and quarterly time periods.

BOX 23.1
HUGHES AIRCRAFT CO.

During the late 1970s and early 1980s, the aerospace industry underwent major changes. U.S. aerospace companies faced new demands and challenges as a result of major negative repercussions caused by fluctuating demand and growing competition from foreign producers. The achievement of productivity improvements was the strategy chosen by Hughes Aircraft Co. as the means of handling the changing environment. The productivity improvement program went beyond the traditional dependence on the use of advanced technologies to make productivity gains. The program incorporated human considerations such as employee morale level and organizational well-being.

One of the program components that emphasized the human element was the quality circle (QC) program. This QC program had over 500 circles, where more than 4000 employees participated in discussions on the work methods they used. The use of quality circles at Hughes made employees feel they were a part of the organization's creative and innovative processes. This feeling that they were a positive part of the organization led to employees' taking pride in the product they were producing. The QCs also resulted in the implementation of new techniques and systems.

Another area of emphasis in the productivity improvement program was the materials acquisition process. The portion of the overall plan that dealt with this area included methods for improved forecasting of commodities, better training of material purchasers, and a component standardization program. Since productivity gains at Hughes were tied, in part, to its suppliers' productivity, methods were chosen that improved not only Hughes's position but also its suppliers' ability to be competitive.

Mentioned above are just a few of the areas and associated methods considered in the overall productivity improvement plan at Hughes Aircraft Co. The plan went on to deal with additional areas where improvement was needed, such as interaction with governmental agencies.

Source: 1983 U.S. Industrial Outlook, U.S. Department of Commerce, Bureau of Industrial Economics, January 1983, pp. 31-3–31-10; John H. Richardson, "Manpower and Materials—Overlooked Elements of Productivity," Production Engineering, vol. 30, no. 8, August 1983, pp. 30–31.

Table 23.1 shows the United States total factor and partial productivity increases from the late 1800s, when productivity ratios were first calculated, until the present time. From 1889 to 1919, the total factor productivity in the United States increased at an annual rate of 1.7 percent. After World War I, from 1919 to 1948, the annual increase in total factor productivity grew to 2.2 percent despite the general depression of the 1930s. This growth in productivity is generally attributed to the adoption of scientific management methods, increased R&D expenditures, increasing automation, and a rapid increase in the average education of the work force. After World War II, from 1948 to 1966, the postwar economic expansion boosted increases in total factor productivity to an annual average of 2.8 percent. Since 1966, however, the growth of total factor productivi-

TABLE 23.1
CHANGE IN PRODUCTIVITY RATIOS

Real GNP per unit of:	Average percentage increase per year					
	1889–1919	1919–1948	1948–1966	1966–1973	1973–1978	Estimated 1980–1990
Labor (hours)	2.0	2.4	3.5	2.1	1.1	2.1
Capital	0.7	1.6	1.1	0.6	0.6	N/A
Total factor productivity	1.7	2.2	2.8	1.6	.8	1.6

Source: John W. Kendrick, *Improving Company Productivity*, Baltimore: Johns Hopkins Press, 1984.

ty has slowed considerably. This slowdown has led to great national interest in productivity improvement.

In comparing productivity ratios over time, one must be very cautious about year-to-year fluctuations. Figure 23.1, for example, shows the annual labor productivity changes for the period 1972 to 1987. Productivity is highly variable from year to year, and no conclusions can be drawn on the basis of 1 or 2 years of figures. For example, in 1974, productivity decreased by 3.4 percent, only to be followed by increases in 1975 of 2.1 percent and in 1976 of 4.5 percent. The media sometimes portray the latest productivity figures as significant, when in fact only 5- to 10-year trends are stable enough to support conclusions about real changes in productivity.

Recent labor productivity growth is dropping, as shown by the long-run trend

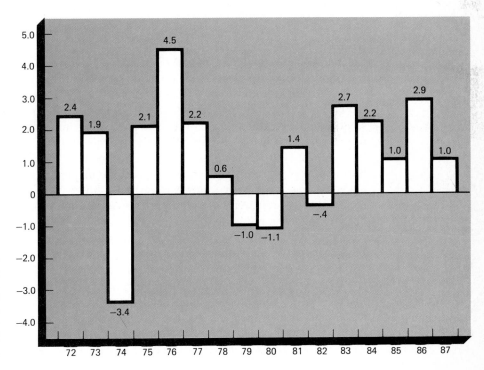

FIGURE 23.1
Real output per hour worked (annual percentage change).
Source: U.S. Department of Labor, Bureau of Labor Statistics.

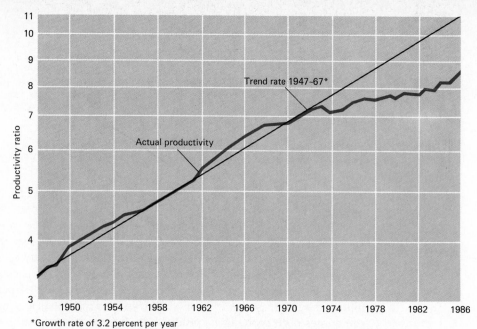

FIGURE 23.2
Productivity in
the private
business sector,
1947–1986 (1972
output dollars
per hour).
*Source: John W.
Kendrick, 1977 and
1984.*

*Growth rate of 3.2 percent per year

line in Figure 23.2. The productivity figures since 1973 are substantially below the 1947–1967 trend line of 3.2 percent per year. What the future holds is, however, very uncertain. Kendrick predicts that the total factor productivity in the 1980–1990 period will average about 1.6 percent increase per year.[1] This rate would be somewhat above the 0.8 percent rate of the 1973–1978 period but below the 2.8 percent rate of the 1948–1966 period. If Kendrick's projections are correct, the productivity growth rate will improve somewhat from its recent low point.

Productivity should not be viewed merely at the national level but also by industries. Projections for a representative sample of industries in Table 23.2 show some interesting differences. The basic processing industries such as petroleum refining have shown a drop in productivity over the 1979–1984 period. This has been attributed to lack of innovation, environmental concerns, and safety regulations. Some other industries with slow productivity growth are fabricated structural metals, gas and electric utilities, restaurants, hotels, and retail food stores. As a general rule, productivity growth in the service industries has lagged behind that in manufacturing industries.

Some might wonder why productivity should be improved. How serious is the recent slowdown in United States productivity growth?

There are many benefits from improved productivity. First, increasing productivity creates more real per capita income. Since World War I, the availability of all inputs—land, labor, and capital—has risen about as rapidly as population. Thus

---

[1] Kendrick's projection in output per hour for the same period is 2.1 percent per year.

TABLE 23.2

INDUSTRY PRODUCTIVITY RATIOS
(Output per Employee in Selected Industries)

Industry	Average annual change, percent	
	1970–1984	1979–1984
Manufacturing & mining		
Iron mining	1.5	5.3
Copper mining	3.6	10.5
Bakery products	1.0	3.3
Tobacco products	1.3	0.8
Hosiery	5.0	2.6
Saw mills	1.7	5.4
Household furniture	1.7	2.7
Soaps, detergents	1.3	−2.1
Petroleum refining	.5	−2.0
Fabricated structural metal	−0.6	−0.1
Major household appliances	3.2	2.5
Radio and T.V. sets	6.8	14.5
Service industries		
Railroads	4.0	8.2
Air transportation	4.0	3.8
Telephone communications	6.6	6.6
Gas and electric utilities	0.2	−1.9
Retail food stores	−1.1	−0.5
Eating and drinking places	−0.4	−1.0
Hotels and motels	1.3	−0.3
Beauty and barber shops	1.4	0.5

Source: Statistical Abstract of the United States, 107th ed., U.S. Dept of Commerce, 1987.

all growth in real income over this period can be attributed to productivity improvements. The average growth in total factor productivity has been about .2 percent a year since 1920, resulting in a doubling in the standard of living (real per capita income) every 30 years. Since World War I, the United States standard of living has quadrupled.

Another benefit from improved productivity is the favorable effect on the United States' world trade balance. Since our industries compete in world markets, trade balances are directly affected by productivity in other countries. The labor productivity increases for the United States, Japan, and some western European countries are shown in Figure 23.3. The low rate of improvement in United States productivity is one of the reasons for our increasingly adverse trade position.

Increased productivity will also tend to mitigate the effects of inflation. If productivity growth is 2 percent and wages are increased 8 percent, then 6 percent of the wage increase is inflationary and only 2 percent is real. Growth in productivity helps to maintain wage stability. Without offsetting increases in productivity, wage increases are purely inflationary.

From the standpoint of management, productivity growth is a way to increase profits. As a matter of fact, in some cases increased productivity may be a better

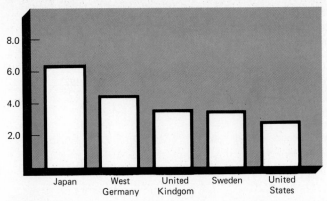

FIGURE 23.3
International productivity ratios (output per hour), annual percentage
change, 1970–1985.
Source: Statistical Abstract of the U.S., 1987, 107th ed., U.S. Department of Commerce.

way to improve profits than increased sales. For example, suppose a company has
sales of $100, $70 in variable costs, $20 in fixed costs, and a resulting profit of $10.
If sales are now increased by 10 percent, profits will increase by 30 percent. See
Table 23.3 for detailed calculations. On the other hand, if variable costs are
decreased by 10 percent due to improvements in productivity, profits will improve
by 70 percent. In this particular case, a 10 percent improvement in productivity
has a much greater effect on profits than a 10 percent increase in sales. The relative
strengths of these effects will, of course, depend on the numbers chosen. But
under certain conditions, productivity can have a greater effect on profits than
sales.

Finally, from the worker's viewpoint, improvement in productivity can lead to
increased wages. Nevertheless, the connection between wages and productivity
may seem very tenuous to workers, who may therefore restrict output. After all,
why should workers be willing to use better methods, suggest improved procedures, or put forward extra effort when the result is layoffs, more profits for the
owners, and nothing for themselves? When a direct connection between productivity improvements and wages is evident, however, the result may be much
different. How such a connection can be established will be discussed later in the
chapter.

No one is sure why United States productivity growth has slowed down,

TABLE 23.3
IMPROVEMENT IN PROFIT

	Before	After a 10% sales increase	After a 10% improvement in productivity
Sales	$100	$110	$100
Variable costs	70	77	63
Fixed costs	20	20	20
Profit	$10	$ 13 (+30%)	$ 17 (+70%)

although a number of theories have been advanced. For example, the National Center for Productivity and the Quality of Working Life has identified three reasons for the productivity slowdown of the 1970s and 1980s.

1. The lower rate of growth in capital stocks per worker
2. The increasing proportion of inexperienced employees in the work force
3. Adverse changes in the industrial composition of employment

With respect to the lower growth of capital stocks, the National Center observed three trends. First, as people have emphasized consumption rather than savings, capital formation has slowed in this country. This has resulted in a reduction in the investment capital available per worker. At the same time, the productivity of capital appears to have decreased since 1967. These two capital effects are believed to account for most of the slowdown in productivity observed. Burton Malkiel (1979), a noted economist, has called for a reversal in this trend and an increase in investment to improve productivity. Malkiel notes that the slowdown in productivity has also been aggravated by social forces, including a reduction in the shift from farm to nonfarm work and a change in the mix of the labor force from older, experienced workers to many more young and untried workers with less experience. Although we cannot control these latter factors, Malkiel emphasizes that we *can* do something about the recent low level of business investment, the apparent reduction in R&D expenditures, and the effects of escalating government regulation.

Other views have also been advanced to explain the slowdown in productivity growth. For example, Hayes and Abernathy (1980) have placed the blame directly on American managers for "managing our way to economic decline." They argue that European and Japanese managers have faced the same economic conditions as U.S. managers (and sometimes worse conditions), but our competitors have still managed larger productivity improvements. Hayes and Abernathy attribute this to the unwillingness of U.S. managers to aggressively pursue technological innovation in both products and processes. They believe this is caused, in turn, by a lack of risk taking, a short-range view, and inattention to the problems of designing, producing, and selling a product. Hayes and Abernathy conclude, "The key to long-term success—even survival—in business is what it has always been: to invest, to innovate, to create value where none existed before. Such determination, such striving to excel, requires leaders—not just controllers, market analysts, and portfolio managers. In our preoccupation with the braking systems and exterior trim, we may have neglected the drive trains of our corporations."

23.2 MEASUREMENT OF PRODUCTIVITY

It has been said, "If you can't measure it, you can't manage it." This is particularly true of productivity. In the last section, we concentrated on national productivity measurements and problems. In this section, we will concentrate on productivity measurements for the firm starting at the firmwide level and proceeding to various subunit measures.

Some examples of firmwide productivity measures are

$$\frac{\text{Sales}}{\text{Labor hours}}$$

$$\frac{\text{Sales}}{\text{Pay}}$$

$$\frac{\text{Shipments}}{\text{Direct labor + indirect labor + materials}}$$

$$\frac{\text{Production at standard price}}{\text{Labor + materials + overhead} + k(\text{capital invested})}$$

As at the national level, there are partial and total factor ratios at the level of the firm. The ratios of sales/labor hours and sales/pay are partial labor productivity ratios which ignore inputs of capital and material to the firm. These labor ratios should not be used unless they are the only measurements available. Furthermore, sales should not be used as a measure of output because sales figures are affected by inventory changes. Production is a far better measure of output than sales.

The best productivity ratio is the last one shown above, where production has been valued at standard price in the numerator and all inputs have been included in the denominator. In this case the capital input is represented by the unit cost of

BOX 23.2
PRODUCTIVITY RATIOS WITHIN FIRMS

1. *Sperry Flight Systems formula:*

$$\frac{\text{Revenue}}{\frac{\text{Direct}}{\text{labor}} + \frac{\text{indirect}}{\text{labor}} + \frac{\text{total direct}}{\text{procurement}} + \frac{\text{other}}{\text{expenses}} + \frac{\text{capital}}{\text{cost}} - \frac{\text{inventory}}{\text{change}}}$$

2. *General Electric formula:*

$$\frac{\text{Total goods and services billed (\$)}}{\frac{\text{Employee}}{\text{compensation}} + \frac{\text{facilities}}{\text{charge}} + \frac{\text{direct material}}{\text{cost}} + \frac{\text{business service}}{\text{cost}}}$$

3. *Western Electric formula:*

$$\frac{\text{Production} - \text{purchased material} - \text{depreciation} - \text{taxes}}{\text{Labor input (\$)} - \text{net investment (\$)} \times \text{rate of return}}$$

4. *Northrup Corporation formula:*

$$\frac{\text{Shipments (\$)}}{\text{Labor hours}}$$

5. *Honeywell formula:*

$$\frac{\text{Sales}}{\text{Pay}}$$

Source: Univac, mimeographed paper.

capital (k) times the amount of capital invested. The production should be valued at standard or constant prices (or costs) to weight the volumes of the various products. Since productivity is a measure of volume of output over input, changes in prices of outputs or inputs should not be allowed to affect the productivity ratio.

A variety of formulas used by industry are shown in Box 23.2. These formulas were chosen by each company to represent the availability of data and their particular needs for productivity measurement.

It is not enough simply to measure productivity at the firmwide level. Productivity ratios must also be developed at each level of the firm and for most if not all organizational units. Some examples of productivity measures for units or individual activities are

$$\frac{\text{Sales}}{\text{Salespeople}} \qquad \frac{\text{Accounts receivable}}{\text{Credit employees}}$$

$$\frac{\text{Engineering drawings}}{\text{Designer}} \qquad \frac{\text{Square feet of floor cleaned}}{\text{Janitor}}$$

$$\frac{\text{Total pay}}{\text{Personnel department pay}} \qquad \frac{\text{Yards of carpet laid}}{\text{Number of carpet layers}}$$

There are three principles which should be followed in measuring productivity at lower levels in the firm. First, department managers should be asked to develop their own measures, perhaps with the assistance of staff. Line department managers should set the measures, because managerial commitment is needed and the responsible line managers often know best how to measure outputs and inputs for their units. By having line managers determine the ratios, the firm will be able to develop a set of measurements unique to itself.

The second principle is that all productivity measurements should be linked in a hierarchical fashion, as shown in Figure 23.4. To ensure consistency of lower- and higher-level ratios, departmental managers should not establish their own ratios until the higher-level ratios have been determined. For example, it does little good to tell the janitor that his goal is to maximize profits. The janitor's goal

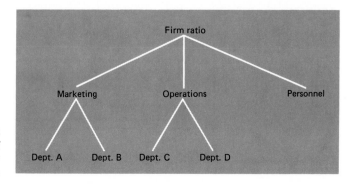

FIGURE 23.4
Hierarchy of productivity ratios.

should be stated in terms of floors cleaned, walls cleaned, and whatever else is related to the janitor's responsibility. Ultimately, all responsibilities should be linked to the firm's goals.

The third principle is that productivity ratios should incorporate all job responsibilities to the extent possible. In some cases, this may require construction of several productivity ratios or a weighted overall ratio. Whatever ratios are defined, they should represent a reasonable measure of the total job.

At this point, a few examples from industry may be useful to illustrate the principles involved. In the first case, a group of University of Minnesota students developed a productivity ratio for a factory in the Minneapolis area. After considering a variety of ratios, the student group suggested the following ratio:

$$\frac{\text{Production at fixed standard price}}{\text{Overhead} + \text{material} + \text{labor} + k(\text{controllable assets})}$$

In this case the output of various products was weighted by the standard prices previously developed by the company. The inputs consisted of all resources under the control of the plant manager.

Using actual company data, the students developed the graph shown in Figure 23.5. At first, the extreme fluctuation in the productivity ratio over time was disconcerting. How could standards or goals be established with such variability in productivity? Upon closer examination, however, it was determined that 79 percent of the variability in the productivity ratio could be explained by volume of output; see Figure 23.6. Since volume was outside the control of the plant manager, the productivity goals for the plant manager could be set as a function of

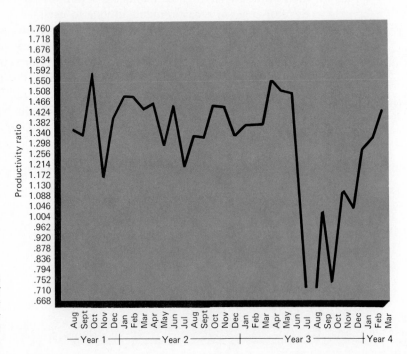

FIGURE 23.5
Example of factory productivity measurement: ratio overtime.

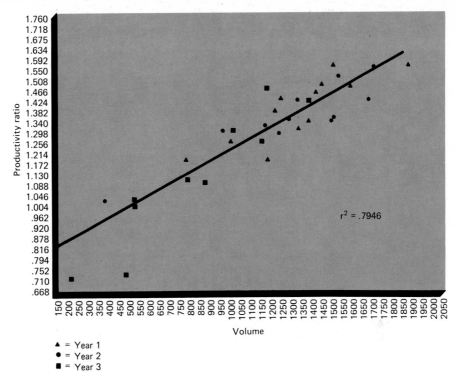

planned volume. As actual volume changed, the productivity goal would then be changed by use of the relationship in Figure 23.6. This case illustrates not only an actual measurement problem but also the important effect of volume on productivity.

The second case is the measurement of productivity for a data processing facility. Here the output is pure service, which further complicates the productivity measurement problem. To solve this problem, measures of effectiveness were developed along with measures of efficiency. Effectiveness of data processing was defined by timeliness in meeting output schedules and the degree of systems support provided. Efficiency was defined by the utilization of computer and peripheral support devices. Efficiency was measured by traditional output-input ratios, while effectiveness was related to the quality of output.

To combine the different effectiveness and efficiency measures, a point system was used. Each measure was allocated a number of points, and a total score was computed for each time period under measurement. The result was a total effectiveness score and a total efficiency score for each time period. Productivity was then defined as the product of effectiveness multiplied by efficiency. Since there was no constant measure of output, the effectiveness score was multiplied by the more familiar efficiency (output-input) ratio as follows:

$$\text{Productivity} = \text{effectiveness} \times \frac{\text{output}}{\text{input}}$$

This case illustrates an important assumption regarding simple productivity ratios: that quality or effectiveness of output is held constant. For a factory under constant quality control standards, this may be a realistic assumption. However, for many operations, both quality and productivity vary over time. In this case, the more complicated productivity measure should be used.

In a broad sense, productivity must be related to the objectives of operations. As first described in Chapter 2, operations objectives are stated in terms such as service, quality, and flexibility. If these objectives can be met at lower cost or with less investment, then productivity has been improved. Output refers to more than just "numbers of widgets." True output incorporates service levels, quality, and flexibility measures. Productivity is, therefore, a multiple dimensional quantity which is only imperfectly measured by simple ratios.

23.3 FACTORS AFFECTING PRODUCTIVITY

Measurement is only the first step in improving productivity. The second step is understanding the factors which affect productivity and selecting the appropriate improvement factors in any given situation.

In the literature on productivity, a partial list of factors is often given. This results from a behavioral, economic, or technical point of view which emphasizes one particular approach to productivity improvement. In this section, a comprehensive view of productivity will be given, including all the factors which might affect the productivity of operations: external, product, process, capacity, inventory, work force, and quality factors. These various factors, which we have been discussing throughout this textbook, are summarized by the productivity wheel in Figure 23.7.

External factors—including government regulation, competition from other firms, and customer demand—are outside the control of the firm. The external factors may affect both volume of output and the availability of scarce inputs. In some cases, external factors *may* be so strong as to offset steps which the firm may take to improve productivity. Generally speaking, this is not true; firms can do much to improve productivity within the external constraints.

The product is a factor which can greatly affect productivity. It is generally recognized that R&D leads to new product technologies which improve productivity. On the other hand, too much product innovation may slow down process innovation and lead to productivity decline. Product diversity may lead to greater productivity through increased sales and economies of scale. But product diversity may reduce productivity too, by unfocusing the process and spreading operations too thin.

In Part 2 of this book, we covered many ideas in process design which can be used to improve productivity. These improvement factors include process flow, automation, layout, and selection of process types. If the process type is not properly matched to the product and market, inefficiencies can result. Within a given process, there are many ways to organize the flow of information, material, and customers. These flows can be improved by better layouts or by process-flow analysis, with resulting increases in productivity.

FIGURE 23.7
Factors affecting
productivity (the
productivity
wheel).

One of the key methods used to improve productivity in the past has been automation, and it appears that the substitution of capital for labor can still be a powerful key to the improvement of productivity in the future. Many economists have identified investment slowdown as the primary reason for the decline in productivity growth in the United States during the last two decades.

Management of capacity and inventory is the fourth factor which can affect productivity. In the short run, excess capacity is often a factor which contributes to adverse productivity ratios. We have already seen, in the case of the University of Minnesota study, how volume affected a factory's productivity because of fixed capacity costs. Capacity can almost never be matched exactly to demand, but careful capacity planning can reduce both excess capacity and bottlenecks due to insufficient capacity.

Along the same lines, inventory can be either a hindrance or a help to a firm's productivity. Too little inventory will lead to lost sales, reduced volume, and eventually lower productivity. Too much inventory will lead to higher cost of capital and lower productivity. Recently, emphasis has been placed on inventory as the "root of all evil." The solution to this problem, for repetitive manufacturing firms, is said to be just-in-time inventory systems.

The fifth factor, the work force, is perhaps the most important of all, and it is receiving a great deal of attention today. The work force, in turn, is associated with a great number of subfactors: selection and placement, training, job design, supervision, organizational structure, rewards, goals, and unions.

The management of human resources in operations should be viewed as an integrated task beginning with the recruitment and selection of workers and proceeding through the motivation of workers, the measurement of results, and the giving of rewards for performance. The recruitment, selection, and placement of workers determines the "raw material" of human resources available to the firm. These resources can be made productive through training within a given organizational context. The organization context itself can be altered through job design, supervision, or authority relationships. Finally, rewards and goals can be used to motivate the work force within the given organizational context and the available level of training.

The sixth and last factor is quality. Only recently has it become clear that poor quality can also lead to poor productivity. In Chapter 20 we described how errors can be reduced which will then also increase productivity. Error prevention and doing the job right the first time are among the most powerful stimulants to both quality and productivity.

All the factors in the productivity wheel interact with each other. Thus management must carefully select a comprehensive approach to productivity improvement which may cut across many departmental lines and the entire range of variables. By using the productivity wheel in Figure 23.7, managers can view all the factors available and emphasize those which promise the greatest improvement in productivity.

23.4 PRODUCTIVITY IMPROVEMENT PROGRAMS

While many companies believe productivity should be improved, they often have trouble getting started. One company, Honeywell, Inc., started by asking the following questions as part of a companywide productivity improvement program:

What is our competitor's productivity?

How do our competitors achieve productivity?

Is there a universal productivity measure?

How labor-intensive should we be?

Can the productivity of creative work be quantified?

Who is in charge of productivity improvement?

Where can a manager get help when he or she has a productivity improvement problem?

What is the minimally acceptable productivity rate for a division? Department? Employee?

How should productivity improvement be woven into annual planning?

[Honeywell (n.d.)]

Every company will have its own particular set of questions, depending on its circumstances and situation. Answers to the questions in particular cases will lead to a wide variety of different productivity programs. But there are some things which all these programs have in common: measurement of productivity, organizational commitment, and feedback on results achieved. No productivity improvement program can succeed without these important features.

Some of the steps which should be followed to achieve measurement, commitment, and feedback in a productivity improvement program are as follows:

1. Develop productivity measures at all levels of the organization. These measures should be developed by the responsible line managers with staff assistance as needed. Some organizational units may have more than one measure or an aggregated overall measure.
2. Set goals for productivity improvement in terms of the measures stated. These productivity goals should be realistic and time-dependent. For example, a carpet-laying firm may set a productivity goal to improve yards of carpet laid per labor hour by 10 percent in the next year.
3. Develop plans to meet the goals. At this point the line management must decide exactly *how* the goals will be met. In the carpet-laying firm, for example, management might decide to purchase some new radio-dispatched trucks and to spend more money on training to reach the productivity improvement goals.
4. Implement the plan. This would normally be done through the line organization. Implementation is, of course, much easier if the line managers and work force have formulated the plan themselves, in the beginning.
5. Measure results. This step will require data collection and periodic assessment of progress in meeting goals set by step 2. If results are on track, no further action is required. If productivity improvement has fallen behind, corrective action will be needed or the goals should be revised in light of changing conditions.

The approach outlined above is nothing more than the standard method of management planning and control covered in most introductory business courses. The approach applies not only to productivity but also to quality, money, and other controllable factors. Furthermore, the planning and control process cannot be short-circuited, eliminated for the sake of convenience, or circumvented. Each step of the process is essential, even though the concept itself is quite simple.

A productivity improvement program which emphasizes measurement, feedback, and control requires the support and participation of top management. The improvement program must be given a high company priority and should be implemented from the top down. Since productivity improvement cuts across all organizational units, it should start with top management and focus on business goals and business strategy at the highest level.

For example, Honeywell's program started with the president and chairman of the board. Top management set productivity goals for the company, established staff support to plan and monitor the program, and insisted that line managers at every level measure and improve their productivity.

To improve productivity it may also be necessary to establish a formal program, perhaps giving it a catchy title such as Beech Aircraft's Employee Bonanza Plan. A person or committee might be appointed to establish the plan and monitor results. Incentives and prizes may be given to entice all employees to participate. The best productivity programs have found ways to stress productivity and to sell the plan to all managers and employees.

EXAMPLES OF PRODUCTIVITY IMPROVEMENT PROGRAMS

Two programs from industry illustrate the concepts described above. The first was initiated by Detroit Edison, a large utility supplying electricity to Detroit and southeastern Michigan. This program emphasized productivity measurement and involvement by all company employees. Detroit Edison has about 10,000 employees and annual revenues of $1 billion. Since the mid-1950s, the company has measured its productivity by megawatts of electric output per employee. Owing to rising costs and rate regulation, management decided to increase emphasis on productivity improvement by establishing a program called ACTION (All Committed to Improving Operations Now). This program was launched by the company president at a staff meeting attended by all members of management. He described ACTION as consisting of three phases:

• Phase I: Meeting with all employees and supervisors to clarify roles and responsibilities
• Phase II: Strengthening the company's MBO system to make the objectives more measureable and concrete
• Phase III: Establishing a productivity measurement and improvement program

As part of the ACTION program, a high-level productivity committee was established which interviewed managers in all 65 of the company's departments to determine what was currently being done to measure and improve productivity. One of the committee's principal findings was that only 50 percent of Detroit Edison's employees were currently under productivity measurement. A goal was then set to raise the figure to 75 percent of the employees within a year. The only employees exempted from measurement were those in functions that were extremely difficult to measure, such as the planning department and the public affairs office.

As a result of the measurement program, which led to the clarification of responsibilities and goals within the departments, productivity was improved. To keep the momentum going, an annual seminar on productivity was instituted; at that meeting, managers shared with each other the progress that had been achieved in their departments and discussed the methods they had used.

The Detroit Edison program shows how productivity can be improved through a formal, companywide measurement program initiated from the top down. The program involved all employees, and management insisted that a large portion of the departments in the company develop productivity measures.

The second productivity program, at Beech Aircraft, illustrates a different approach to productivity improvement. In this case, the company established specific programs aimed at product design, process design, and worker motivation, while measurement took a secondary role. This project was actually a series of programs initiated over a period of years.

Beech Aircraft is a manufacturer of small private and military aircraft; it has six plants in Kansas and Colorado. The first productivity improvement program to be established used work simplification. This program was based on the idea that each employee is the best judge of the work methods used on his or her job. Therefore each employee was asked to accept responsibility for improving productivity through self-initiated job changes. The industrial engineering staff was available to help, and each employee received some training in industrial engineering methods and work measurement. As a result of the program, many employees simplified their jobs and productivity was improved throughout the Beech Aircraft factories.

The second Beech aircraft program was called the Employees' Bonanza Plan, which provided group wage incentives for increased productivity. The plan was based on equivalent airframe pounds manufactured per payroll dollar, using the year before the plan was put into effect as the base year. Any improvement in productivity over the base year was shared 50 percent by management and 50 percent by the workers. During the first year, Bonanza Plan payments totaled $1.6 million; in the second year, the payments were $2.2 million. For an employee who made the average wage, the bonus payments totaled $575.

The third Beech Aircraft productivity improvement program was based on value engineering (VE). As described in Chapter 4, the idea of VE is to redesign existing products so they perform the equivalent function at less cost. This might be done by using different materials, taking off frills, or simplifying the product. The program was initiated by establishing a VE group with full-time engineers assigned within the engineering function. Their responsibility was to review all designs for VE changes, initiate changes, and monitor these changes into production. The criterion used to initiate a change was that the development and investment cost had to be paid back in 1 year.

Finally, Beech Aircraft initiated a commonality program to promote the use of common parts and assemblies throughout all products. By reducing the number of different parts used to make a given product line, economies of scale and simplification of field service were achieved. The program was initiated by forming a commonality group in the engineering department, which studied each assembly and subassembly for possible changes to increase commonality and reduce the variety of parts. The same cost criterion was used to select commonality changes as in the VE program.

The Beech Aircraft programs emphasized productivity improvement in both production and engineering. In production, productivity was improved through work simplification and wage incentives. In engineering, productivity was improved through value engineering and increased commonality of parts. Beech Aircraft utilized a variety of different approaches to improve productivity over a period of several years.

These examples and also the one in Box 23.1 illustrate that there is no one surefire approach to productivity improvement. The best approach in any particular company will be tailored to the company's problems and situation. In all cases, however, management must stress productivity and develop programs to constantly improve it.

 ## WAGE INCENTIVE PLANS

There has been a great deal of debate in the literature on the effect of pay on productivity. This debate was fueled by the human relations studies of the 1940s and later the work of Frederick Herzberg (1968). Herzberg's two-factor theory holds that factors intrinsic to the job itself (achievement, recognition, work, responsibility, and growth advancement) tend to satisfy workers, while extrinsic factors (pay, supervision, company policies, work conditions, etc.) are dissatisfiers. Some people have erroneously concluded from this research that pay is not a motivating factor. Herzberg's research, however, had nothing to do with performance or productivity; it simply addressed worker satisfaction.

There has been, however, a great deal of other research on the direct relationship between pay and productivity. This research generally supports the proposition that higher pay does lead to higher productivity. A careful study by Davison et al. (1958) examined the results of wage incentive plans on 15 operations in five different factories. Davison and his colleagues selected cases where all conditions were held constant except that a wage incentive plan was introduced; this plan paid higher wages for higher productivity. In all 15 cases, productivity improved from 7.5 to 291 percent, with half the cases falling between 43 and 76 percent improvement. These productivity increases were not temporary but were sustained over a period of time.

Another study of over 400 plants in the United States showed that work-measurement programs alone increased productivity by an average of 14.6 percent. When wage incentives were added to work measurement, productivity rose another 42.9 percent. The average increase from baseline to work measurement and incentives was 63.8 percent [Fein (1973).]

The evidence indicates that wage incentives should be considered seriously as one way to improve productivity. Yet only 26 percent of United States workers are on some type of wage incentive program. In some industries such as steel and sewn products, up to 80 percent of employees are on incentive plans. But other industries have not even considered the use of incentives.

Mitchell Fein gives three reasons why management is reluctant to install wage incentive plans.

1. Some managers are concerned that incentives will diminish their ability to control the operations and over a period of time the incentives will deteriorate, causing labor problems.
2. Some managers believe that productivity improvement is largely created by management efforts; there is no need to share productivity gains.
3. Management's rights advocates believe that improvement is best shared periodically as increases in wages and benefits.

Although all these arguments have merit, they must be balanced against the potential motivating effect of pay.

Productivity is a goal of management, not of the work force. The workers want tangible economic rewards (pay and benefits), job security, and a suitable working environment. There is a fundamental conflict between management's desire for productivity on the one hand and the workers' interests on the other. Wage incentive plans are one way to reconcile this conflict by automatically sharing the results of productivity increases between management and workers. Another way to reconcile this conflict is through collective bargaining. In this case the sharing of productivity improvements is considered part of the bargaining process. Whatever method is used to resolve the conflict, productivity is something a worker will not automatically seek.

In many companies, there are disincentives to increase productivity and the workers actively (but not openly) seek to restrict output. Disincentives occur when workers believe that increased productivity may lead to layoffs, job reassignment, and work speedups. Under these circumstances, management knowingly or unknowingly seeks to coerce the worker into higher productivity. Wage incentive plans are one way to make it clear that both parties will benefit from improved productivity.

There are two general types of incentive plans: individual and group. The individual plans include a variety of types: straight piece rate, piece rate with minimum pay, gain-sharing, and measured day work.

The straight-piece-rate plan is based on the concept that workers are paid directly for production, X dollars per unit. The piece rate (X) is usually set by the work-measurement techniques covered in Chapter 19 and represents the base rate at 100 percent effort. The worker is rewarded directly for any additional production and penalized for any lower production. Piece rates are widely used in industries where jobs are of a repetitive nature and the output is under the worker's direct control (e.g., sewing clothes). Piece rates do not work well where group interaction is important, where jobs are machine-paced, or where the work is not highly repetitive.

Another problem with piece rates is that earnings may vary widely from week to week, sometimes because of circumstances outside the control of the worker. To alleviate this problem, some piece-rate plans have a minimum or floor wage rate per hour (e.g., the Manchester plan). In this case, the worker is guaranteed at least the minimum wage regardless of the output level.

A gain-sharing or bonus plan (Rowan or Halsey plan) guarantees a base rate and divides any excess production between management and the worker. It is common to divide the extra production on a fifty-fifty basis, although other percentage splits are also used. Suppose, for example, that the base production rate is 10 units per hour, the base wage is $5 per hour, and 2500 units are actually produced in the course of a month (160 hours). In this case, the worker gets credit for 250 hours of work (2500/10). The first 160 hours are paid at $5 per hour and the additional 90 hours at $2.50 per hour (fifty-fifty sharing). The total wages are

$$160(5) + 90(2.50) = \$1025$$

Finally, the measured-day-work plan is similar to the others except that wages are adjusted every few weeks or months to provide more stability in take-home pay. Suppose, for example, wages are adjusted monthly. Each month, the hourly wage is computed on the basis of the number of units produced during the past month, the sharing percentage with management, and the minimum if applicable. This wage rate would then be paid for hours worked during the next month, after which the wage rate would again be recomputed.

The group plans are another form of wage incentive used to pay an entire department or entire plant at the same incentive bonus. These plans are used where jobs are highly interactive and one individual paces the work of another. Group plans are also used to bring indirect labor into the incentive plan, on the premise that they too should contribute to output. Three types of group incentive plans are in wide use: Scanlon, IMPROSHARE (Improving Productivity Through Sharing), and profit sharing.[2]

The Scanlon plan uses the idea of work groups and a plantwide incentive bonus. [See Geare (1976) for a review of Scanlon plans.] The work groups discuss work methods and procedures which may restrict output or decrease productivity. It has been found that many productivity bottlenecks can be eliminated through the sharing of common problems and concerns. The bonus in the Scanlon plan is usually based on past output divided by pay. If this ratio is improved, management and labor share the improvement on a fifty-fifty basis. The Scanlon plan or its variants are being used in about 500 plants in the United States.

There are three differences between the Scanlon plan and IMPROSHARE. First, with IMPROSHARE, the bonus is calculated on the basis of work standards adjusted for past actual output. Thus changes in product mix can be accurately reflected in the bonus paid. Second, changes in technology are reflected in IMPROSHARE. When productivity is improved by the addition of new machines, the workers get 10 percent of the improvement and management gets 90 percent. This gives management an incentive to continue to automate where it is economically justified. If machine productivity increases were shared with workers on a fifty-fifty basis, there would be a tendency to reduce automation and to create a competitive disadvantage for the company. Third, there is a ceiling on the incentive wages that can be paid and a buy-back provision to adjust the standards when the ceiling is reached. This limits management's risk to extraordinary productivity increases beyond the ceiling. Under the IMPROSHARE plan, group

[2]IMPROSHARE is a registered service mark of Mitchell Fein.

bonus payments are made weekly. Over 300 plants in the United States are using this plan.

Profit sharing is another form of group incentive plan. In some cases, profit sharing is an employee benefit because the amount received is small, and it is received infrequently, for example, once a year. If profit sharing is to be an incentive plan, it must be received frequently and in fairly large amounts. For example, some Japanese companies share profits semiannually, and the amount can be as large as 50 percent add-on to wages [Nanto (1982)]. Profit sharing tends to align the goals of the workers and managers, and it provides a broader basis for reward than incentive plans tied only to production output.

There are many types of incentive plans; only a few of these have been discussed here merely to indicate how wage incentives can affect productivity. Management should carefully consider such plans as one component of a total productivity improvement program. Of course, these plans are effective only when a reasonable measure of output can be devised and quality standards are held constant over time. If the plan is to be effective, the productivity measure must be considered to be fair by both management and the workers.

23.7   KEY POINTS

A variety of different measures and methods to improve productivity are available. It is management's responsibility to measure productivity constantly and to act in conjunction with the workers to improve it. Unfortunately, productivity is not adequately measured in many firms and management is sometimes reluctant to act.

The chapter's key points include the following:

- National productivity can be measured by either total factor productivity or partial ratios. The total factor productivity ratio is the best one because it considers all inputs used to produce output.
- United States productivity growth has decreased in the 1970s and 1980s. The decrease in growth is thought to be caused by lower investment in R&D, plant, and equipment; by increased government regulation; by poor management; and by the changing mix of the work force.
- Total firm productivity should be measured by the ratio of output at standard prices (or costs) to the sum of labor, material, overhead, and capital costs. When the productivity of a particular manager is being measured, only controllable inputs should be included in the ratio. These measures should be set by line management, and all measures should be linked in a hierarchical fashion. Measurements for individual managers should incorporate all job responsibilities, even if multiple ratios must be established. It is necessary to incorporate effectiveness in productivity measures when both effectiveness and efficiency vary over time.
- Many factors affect productivity in the firm, including external, product, process, capacity, inventory, work force, and quality factors. The proper mix of these factors must be selected for any particular productivity improvement program.

- Productivity improvement programs follow the standard planning and control process used in business. The steps required in these programs are: develop productivity measures, set productivity goals, develop plans to improve productivity, implement the plans, measure the results, and take corrective action. Regardless of the specific factors or approach selected to improve productivity, this planning and control process is essential.
- Productivity improvement is a goal of management. Workers cannot be expected to improve productivity unless there is a clear connection between productivity improvement and their welfare. One way to establish this connection is through wage incentive plans. Another way is through collective bargaining or through a consistent management track record of higher wages for improved productivity.
- Wage incentives have been shown to improve productivity in cases where an adequate productivity measure can be established and where management and workers support the wage incentive plan. Many types of individual and group incentive plans have been used, including straight-piece-rate, bonus, measured-day-work, Scanlon, IMPROSHARE, and profit-sharing plans.

QUESTIONS

1. The real GNP of a hypothetical country is shown below, along with the value of labor and capital inputs. Calculate the improvement in (a) total factor productivity and (b) partial productivity of labor and capital for years 2 and 3.

Years (billions of dollars)

	1	2	3
Real GNP	800	840	900
Labor	500	560	600
Capital	200	210	220

2. Why is it desirable to improve productivity? Discuss from a national, management, and labor perspective.
3. For the following data, calculate the effect on profit margins of improving labor productivity by 10 percent.
   Labor cost $75
   Other costs $10
   Profit $10
4. A firm has the following data:

	Year 1	Year 2
Sales	$100	$120
Direct labor	40	45
Materials	20	25
G & A expense	10	15
Depreciation	10	10
Other expenses	5	5
Total expenses	85	100
Profit	15	20
Inventory	90	60
Plant and equipment	50	60

    a. Using a cost of capital of 15 percent, calculate the change in total factor productivity using production/all inputs. Assume that prices were increased an average of 5 percent between year 1 and year 2.

    b. Using a ratio of sales/pay, calculate the change in productivity.

    c. Why do the measures calculated in *a* and *b* differ?

5. Devise a productivity measure for each of the following jobs:
   a. Plumber
   b. Civil engineer
   c. Nurse
   d. Doctor
   e. Professor

6. a. Evaluate the following hospital productivity measure:

$$\frac{\text{Beds filled}}{\text{Salaries of hospital personnel}}$$

    b. Devise a better productivity measure.

7. Classify the productivity changes made by Beech Aircraft according to the productivity factor wheel of Figure 23.7.

8. Amy Smith, who manages a bakery, says that productivity for her business cannot be measured. Suggest an approach that Amy could use. Amy also says that she has automated things to the maximum extent possible and that therefore no further improvements in productivity are possible. Discuss.

9. Discuss the pros and cons of using wage incentives to improve productivity.

10. When is it appropriate to use group incentives versus individual incentive plans?

11. There is a natural conflict between management and labor regarding productivity. Why does this conflict occur? What can be done about it?

12. A worker has produced 180 pieces of output in 6 hours. The hourly rate is $6 per hour and the standard production rate is 20 pieces per hour. Calculate the wages for the following incentive plans:
   a. Straight piece rate
   b. Fifty-fifty bonus-sharing plan

SELECTED BIBLIOGRAPHY

ADAM, N. R. and ALI DOGRAMACI (eds.): *Studies in Productivity Analysis,* vol. III, Boston: Martinus Nijhott, 1981.

COOK, RANDALL L., and ROGER W. SCHMENNER: "Explaining Productivity Differences in North Carolina Factories," Duke University, working paper, 1983.

DAVISON, J. P., et al.: *Productivity and Economic Incentives,* London: G. Allen, 1958.

EDOSOMWAN, JOHNSON, A., *Integrating Productivity and Quality,* New York: Marcel Dekker, 1987.

FEIN, MITCHELL: "Work Measurement and Wage Incentives," *Industrial Engineering,* September 1973.

————: "Designing and Operating an IMPROSHARE Plan," working paper, Hillsdale, N.J., 1976.

————: "An Alternative to Traditional Managing," working paper, Hillsdale, N.J., 1977.

GEARE, A. J.: "Productivity from Scanlon-Type Plans," *Academy of Management Review,* vol. 1, no. 3, July 1976, pp. 99–108.

HAYES, ROBERT H., and WILLIAM J. ABERNATHY: "Managing Our Way to Economic Decline," *Harvard Business Review,* July-August 1980, pp. 67–77.

HEATON, HERBERT: *Productivity in Service Organizations,* New York: McGraw-Hill, 1977.

HERZBERG, FREDERICK: "One More Time: How Do You Motivate Employees?" *Harvard Business Review,* January-February 1968.

HONEYWELL, INC.: *People, Productivity, Honeywell,* Minneapolis, n.d.

JOHNSON, TODD, et al.: "A Study of Plant Productivity Measurement," Plan B paper, Minneapolis: University of Minnesota, May 1977.

JUDSON, ARNOLD S.: "The Awkward Truth about Productivity," *Harvard Business Review,* September-October 1982, pp. 93–97.

KATZELL, RAYMOND A., PENNY BIENSTOCK, and PAUL FAERSTEIN: *A Guide to Worker Productivity Experiments in the United States, 1971–75,* New York: New York University Press, 1977.

KENDRICK, JOHN W.: *Understanding Productivity,* Baltimore: Johns Hopkins, 1977.

———: *Improving Company Productivity: Handbook with Cases,* Baltimore: Johns Hopkins University Press, 1984.

MALI, PAUL: *Improving Total Productivity,* New York: Wiley, 1978.

MALKIEL, BURTON G.: "Productivity—The Problem behind the Headlines," *Harvard Business Review,* May–June 1979.

NANTO, DICK K., "Management Japanese Style," in Sang M. Lee and Gary Schwendiman (eds.), *Management by Japanese Systems,* New York: Praeger, 1982.

NATIONAL CENTER FOR PRODUCTIVITY AND QUALITY OF WORKING LIFE: *Improving Productivity: A Description of Selected Company Programs,* series 1, Washington: U.S. Government Printing Office, December 1975.

———: *Productivity in the Changing World of the 1980's,* final report, Washington: U.S. Government Printing Office, 1978.

SELLIE, CLIFFORD: "Group and Individual Incentive Plans: A Comparison of Their Benefits and Drawbacks," *Industrial Engineering,* November 1982, pp. 62–66.

SHAW, JOHN C., and RAM CAPOOR: "Quality and Productivity: Mutually Exclusive or Interdependent in Service Organizations," *Management Review,* March 1979.

PART EIGHT

CASE STUDIES

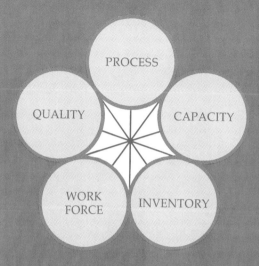

- **QUALITY PLANNING AND CONTROL**
  General Appliance Company
  Bayfield Mud Company
  Hank Kolb, Director, Quality Assurance
- **INTEGRATION OF OPERATIONS**
  Donaldson Company

The case studies in Part 8 are designed to provide practice in both the formulation and solution of problems. Not only do the cases require an understanding of the techniques and concepts covered in the text, they also require the application of common sense and the integration of material from the various chapters. None of the cases is simply a straightforward application of the techniques from the text. Creativity and the extension of concepts are needed.

All the cases are based on real business problems. In some instances the problems have been simplified or "pared down" to make them more manageable. The names of the companies and individuals have also been disguised in some of the cases. Nevertheless, the problems and situations are real.

The cases are organized according to the major divisions of the text. The appropriate chapters and material in each part should be covered prior to studying each particular case.

Sheldahl

In April 1984, James Wallace, general manager of the Advanced Products Division at Sheldahl, was considering a change in manufacturing strategy.[1] Recently, Mr. Wallace and his staff had revised the business strategy of the divisions. As a result, it became apparent that the marketing, engineering, and manufacturing strategies should also be revised.

The Sheldahl Company started in the aerospace business in the 1960s. In the early years, the company developed and produced the Echo weather satellites which were launched into space. More recently, the Sheldahl Company had diversified into three divisions located in Northfield, Minn.: the Electrical Products Division (EPD), the Materials Division (MD), and the Advanced Products Division (APD). EPD produced a variety of circuit boards and other electrical products for mass markets. MD produced laminated plastic materials which were sold to EPD, APD, and outside customers. APD manufactured specialty products to customer order. The sales growth and profitability of the company have been good for over the past 5 years, as shown in Exhibit 1.

[1]This case was prepared as a basis for class discussion, not to illustrate either effective or ineffective handling of an administrative situation.

Sales and profits of the APD division, however, have been somewhat erratic, also as shown in Exhibit 1.

The main product of the APD division is the aerostat, which is a large lighter-than-air blimp resembling the famous Goodyear blimp. These aerostats are sold to communications companies, the United States government, and foreign countries for communications uses. At the present time the APD division produces about 12 aerostats per year, and the aerostat accounts for about 50 percent of the APD division's sales.

The APD division also produces a variety of other specialty products made to customer order. These products include mine stoppers used to seal mining passages for ventilation control (see Exhibit 2) and blade liners used as inserts in helicopter blades to detect cracks. One unifying feature of these specialty products is that they are made from the laminated plastic materials supplied by the MD division of Sheldahl.

In formulating his business strategy, Mr. Wallace envisioned a gradual shift toward products which are sold to multiple customers and manufactured on a volume basis. The business strategy developed by Wallace and his staff is summarized as follows:

EXHIBIT 1
FINANCIAL DATA

	$ Thousands				
	1980	**1981**	**1982**	**1983**	**1984**
			Sheldahl Corp.		
Sales	34,884	41,029	46,824	41,914	37,857
Profits (after tax)	1,256	1,324	363	(1,035)	379
			APD Division		
Sales	5,977	6,508	4,080	7,600	5,179
Profits (after tax)	703	597	223	1,139	150

Sheldahl

Advanced Products Division
Northfield, Minnesota 55057
(507) 645-5633

**Reusable Ventilation
Control Stopping for
Underground Mines**
Part No. 10687

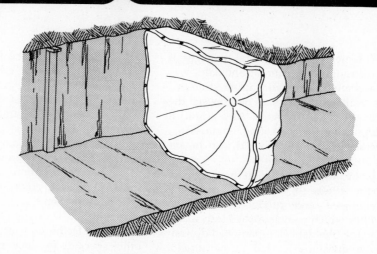

DESCRIPTION

• A **DIFFERENT BRATTICE** FOR EMERGENCY AND PRODUCTION
  VENTILATION CONTROL

• INSTALL IN MINUTES

• SELF SEALING

• REUSABLE

• RESISTANT TO BLAST FORCES

• FLAME RESISTANT (To NFPA 701-75 Spec. and ASTM E162 with Flame Spread
  Index of less than 25.)

• AN ACCESSORY HARNESS IS AVAILABLE TO CONVERT THIS UNIT INTO A
  "PARACHUTE" SINGLE POINT ATTACHMENT STOPPING

SIZING

For Airways smaller than 7'x8' order the **10687-012** Stopping.
For Airways between 7'x8' and 11'x12' order the **10687-016** Stopping.

EXHIBIT 2   Product description.

APD will continue to do what it has historically done best—respond to *individual customer* design requirements tailoring new products to unique customer applications. This business is characterized by low volume but sole-source products, by customer funding for product development, and by large year-to-year variations in sales and profits.

Concurrently and increasingly, APD will become more *market*-focused in its business and will apply resources toward market and product development programs. Our objective shall be to reduce but not eliminate APD dependence on short-run *customer*-specified products or projects and to bring on stream new products with higher-volume continuous production. APD will restrict its market development resources to certain market segments or "niches" of growth and to mature industries where there is a realistic opportunity and expectation of occupying a dominant or strong competitive position.

This heavy emphasis on marketing strategies will require enlargement of market research, market development, and sales distribution systems. Technologically, materials and systems engineering capabilities will have to be strengthened, as will the production engineering and production control disciplines. We will need to concentrate heavily on planning, and we must have the patience to focus on and stick to our strategies to see them through to fruition.

The business unit is growth-oriented with substantial resources directed to new-product/new-market strategies, making it a medium- to high-risk operation. Although investment in product development and capital equipment will be required, the business should retain its low-capital, high-labor-intensive character. Over the 5-year planning period, sales, profits, and asset levels should produce a return on net assets (RONA) in the 30 to 40 percent range. Additionally, the business will be a net cash user.

According to Mr. Wallace, the shift in business

strategy will require a corresponding change in manufacturing strategy. Manufacturing will need to develop facilities, people, and production control systems to support the gradual change from low-volume one-of-a-kind production to higher-volume standardized product lines. Among the results of this change in strategy could be changes in organization. The present organizational structure of the APD division is shown in Exhibit 3.

Mr. Wallace also felt that the shift in business strategy might affect the production and inventory control area. At the present time, production and inventory control is handled by two individuals who were transferred from the storeroom and the production floor. They have been trained on the job, and they have evolved a manual system of record keeping and production planning. The system appears to work quite well for the present situations, but constant expediting and stock chasing are necessary to keep production moving.

Inventory stock status is computerized by means of punched cards. Receipts and disbursements are sent to data processing and keypunched for entry into the computer. Because of time lags and problems of record accuracy, the production and inventory control people also keep manual records on the most important parts.

The Sheldahl Company recently signed a contract with Hewlett-Packard for a new computer which will arrive in the fall and replace the current Honeywell equipment. As part of the new computer conversion, the company has investigated software packages available from Hewlett-Packard. The production and inventory control (MRP) software package appears quite good, but conversion of existing computer software will have priority over new systems. The first priority, after the new computer is installed, will be the conversion of existing accounting and financial systems.

In viewing the situation, Mr. Wallace wondered what the manufacturing strategy over the next 5 years should be and how the strategy should be implemented. He knew that manufacturing should support the new divisional business strategy but was unsure about exactly what direction manufacturing should take.

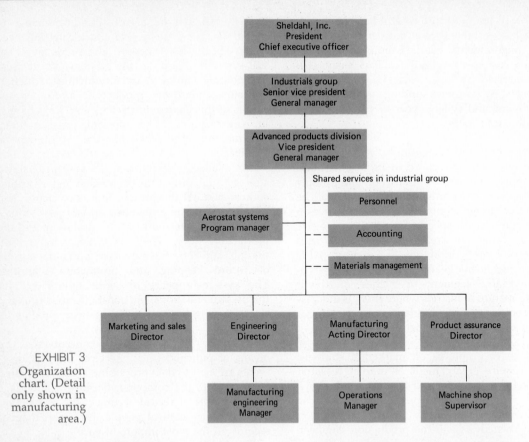

EXHIBIT 3 Organization chart. (Detail only shown in manufacturing area.)

DISCUSSION QUESTIONS

1. What objectives should be adopted in manufacturing with respect to cost, delivery, quality, and flexibility?

2. How should the objectives in manufacturing be achieved through process, organization, equipment, work force, and production and inventory control systems?

FHE, INC.

In April 1988, Lum Donaldson, product development engineering manager at FHE, Inc., was reviewing the process his company used to introduce new products.[1] Mr. Donaldson was responsible for the technical direction of all new-product development and revisions of existing products. He wondered whether the procedures, organization, and project control systems used at FHE might be improved to make new-product introductions go more smoothly.

FHE is a manufacturer of pumps and related fluid-handling equipment. The company supplies products used to transfer liquids of all types including paint, adhesives, and food products. The pumps supplied by the company are used by the automobile and appliance industries, in vehicle servicing, in home construction, and in other ways. In 1988, sales were $105,200,000 and profit after tax was $5,470,000. Over the last 5 years the company has been improving both sales and profits through aggressive new-product introductions.

ORGANIZATION

The organization of the engineering, marketing, and manufacturing departments at FHE is shown in Exhibit 1. Phil Thomas, the vice president of corporate development and marketing, has responsibility for both marketing and design engineering functions in the company. This arrangement is intended to facilitate cooperation between marketing and engineering, particularly on new-product introductions. Manufacturing is responsible for producing the product once it has been released to production.

On the engineering side of the organization,

three technical program managers (TPMs) report to Mr. Donaldson. These program managers are generally responsible for the technical direction of the projects assigned to them. Detailed responsibilities of the TPM are shown in Exhibit 2.

On the marketing side of the organization, three product managers report to Vince Kramer, the United States marketing manager. These product managers are responsible for developing new-product ideas and managing the business impact of new products. Detailed responsibilities of the product manager are shown in Exhibit 3.

Manufacturing managers are responsible for designing the production process, ordering materials, scheduling production, and processing materials and components into finished products. Product specifications are given to manufacturing by engineering. Manufacturing is expected to adhere to these specifications in making the product.

A great deal of coordination is required between the product managers in marketing, the TPMs in engineering, and manufacturing to successfully introduce a new product. When problems arise, it is not always clear who has the primary responsibility for resolving them. As a result, product managers, manufacturing managers, and TPMs must work closely together during the development process.

NEW-PRODUCT DEVELOPMENT PROCESS

The new-product development process begins with a formal marketing request which specifies in general terms the type of product needed and the market it will serve. As a result of the marketing request, a concept conference is conducted between marketing and engineering to determine whether to proceed, and if so, how. If the decision is made to proceed, a *Technical Specification Action*

[1]This case was prepared as a basis for class discussion, not to illustrate either effective or ineffective handling of an administrative situation.

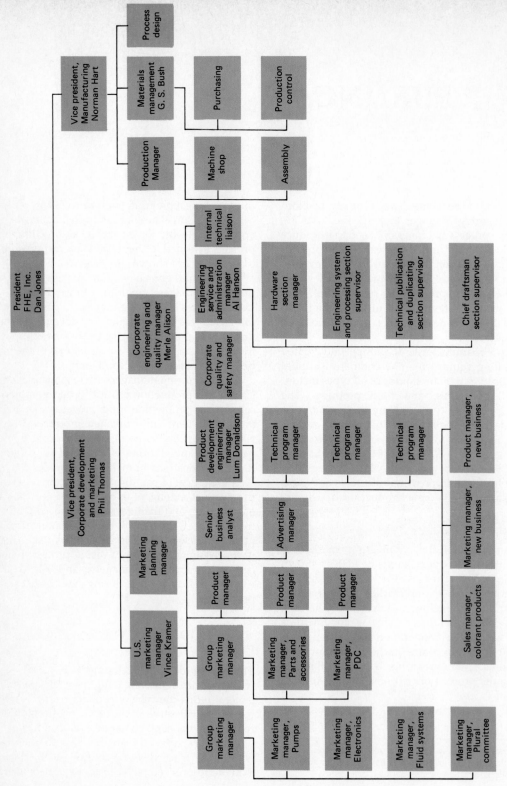

EXHIBIT 1   Organization chart.

TECHNICAL PROGRAM MANAGER—NEW PRODUCT DEVELOPMENT

General Summary Statement

The technical program manager—new product department reports to the manager
of product engineering and is responsible for planning, coordinating, and
directing the activities of projects in the program area(s) assigned to him or her.
(A "program area" is composed of one or more projects related to a particular
product application area, such as sanitary, plural components, and hydraulics.)
The technical program manager—new product department is responsible for personnel
assignments and the administration and control of all design personnel reporting to
him or her.

Typical Duties and Responsibilities

1. Assigns technical staff to maintain development schedules for all projects
   within his or her areas of program responsibility. Maintains the communication
   between development sections to ensure usage of critical skills and keep
   the state-of-the-art awareness with all personnel assigned.

2. Directs the design activities of a specific program area or areas to
   develop the design, select materials, prepare technical descriptions,
   conduct tests, meet performance, schedule, and cost objectives; is
   responsible for the program costs and status and presents timely reports
   and technical conclusions when directed; communicates with product managers,
   development engineers, and other design personnel, and maintains technical
   project files.

3. Coordinates with product management in defining technical customer
   specifications of currently planned product and product which is
   contemplated for future effort.

4. Reviews and directs the detail analysis prepared by development engineers,
   and is responsible for testing programs to ensure overall product design
   conformance to specifications. Reviews all cost inputs and directs
   completion of cost estimates.

5. Interfaces with all departments of company to coordinate product design
   completion; negotiates work schedules with hardware and software groups,
   purchasing, etc.

6. Identifies technical problem areas which will result in altered time, cost
   and/or performance schedules; defining alternative courses of action to
   meet same; and/or making visible to management these problems so that
   proper corrective management action can be taken.

7. Maintains continuing contact with product management, manufacturing, fluid
   systems, etc., where appropriate in obtaining the best technical solutions
   to the problems associated with his or her program area and in ensuring that
   product resulting from his team's efforts can be economically produced.

EXHIBIT 2
Position
description.

Report (TSAR) is prepared by engineering. The TSAR contains a great deal of detail on development costs, product costs, schedules, and product technical specifications. If the TSAR is approved, the project is formally authorized and engineering development begins. The project then proceeds through a series of steps, as summarized in Exhibit 4 for a typical project. These steps include actual design of the physical product, major design re-

views, testing, and finally release to production if the product is successfully developed.

Although the new-product development process is well defined at FHE, Mr. Donaldson has several reservations about its operation. First he continually encounters problems in coordinating the technical program managers and the product managers. Perhaps the division of responsibility is not as clear as it might be. He is also concerned

PRODUCT MANAGER RESPONSIBILITY PROFILE

A product manager's basic responsibility is to the development of
new products and to ensuring that the entire product line is properly servicing the needs of the marketplace. The product manager
would generally have a strong technical background and a working
knowledge of marketing concepts. He or she must possess leadership
qualities in that the tasks to be accomplished are through others
over whom the product manager has no direct control.

MAJOR DUTIES

I. New Product

    A. Develop product strategies that are in support of corporate
        objectives.

    B. Coordinate project definition.

        1. Evaluate the content of new product proposals (the product
            specification) and programs, responding to market opportuni-
            ties identified by U.S., Eurafrica, and regional international
            marketing groups.

        2. Evaluate the content of the technical specification and the
            project schedule assuring conformity with the product speci-
            fication and market timing requirements.

        3. Evaluate anticipated project costs.

        4. Analyze anticipated profitability of proposed programs (ROI).

        5. Generate the project authorization.

    C. Monitor project activity and take action where necessary to ensure
        integrity of project.

    D. Insure vendor quality.

    E. Ensure the coordination of all technical resources related to new
        product development and introduction; to include engineering,
        manufacturing, marketing and service.

EXHIBIT 3
Job description.

about the fluctuating work load in the engineering
services department.

ENGINEERING SERVICES

The engineering services department, managed by
Al Hanson, includes drafting services, the model
shop, testing facilities, and technical documentation services. Because all projects use these services, the work load for engineering services is
unpredictable and bottlenecks frequently occur in
this department. At any one time, as many as 20

new-product development projects may be in
progress, and they all seem to require the same
engineering services at the same time. Al Hanson
has continually asked the technical program managers to give him more advanced notice, but—due
to uncertainties in project schedules—requirements are often unknown until the last minute.

MANUFACTURING COORDINATION

Mr. Donaldson acknowledged that once a new
product is developed, it is often "thrown over the

II. Existing Product

    A. Monitor product line activity and take action where required.

        1. Sales volume.

        2. Competitive postures.

        3. Relationship to changing technology.

        4. Product quality.

    B. Control product line offering (no product proliferation).

    C. Monitor engineering change order activity and take action where required.

    D. Eliminate product from the offering as appropriate.

    E. Provide technical assessment on advertising and promotional aspects of the product line (catalogs, mailers, brochures, new product data sheets, etc.).

    F. Ensure that products comply to a variety of standards (corporate, governmental, industry, safety, etc.)

III. Competition

    A. Keep abreast of changes in product line.

    B. Maintain an in-depth knowledge of competitive product capabilities.

IV. Forecasting

    A. Unit forecast of specific product (category I).

    B. Forecast new product quantities for Lot I build.

    C. Forecast product to meet promotional activity.

    D. Monitor all significant deviations.

EXHIBIT 3
(Continued)

wall" to manufacturing. While manufacturing is consulted regarding technical feasibility and possible production constraints, little manufacturing input is received during product design. Lum Donaldson commented, "Manufacturing has enough problems to worry about with today's products without bringing new products into the picture too. We try to anticipate manufacturing problems for them before release to production. Of course, there is never enough time and inevitably some problems occur after the product is released."

FHE has been considering a new CAD-CAM system as a way of coordinating marketing, engineering, and manufacturing. According to the software supplier, the new-product configuration would be entered directly into the computer and then transmitted automatically to manufacturing. This approach promised to eliminate many of the errors which are encountered in translation from engineering to manufacturing. After the CAD system is installed, the CAM system will be designed to interface with it. FHE felt the computer would speed up the new-product introduction cycle and eliminate many of the production problems it was currently encountering.

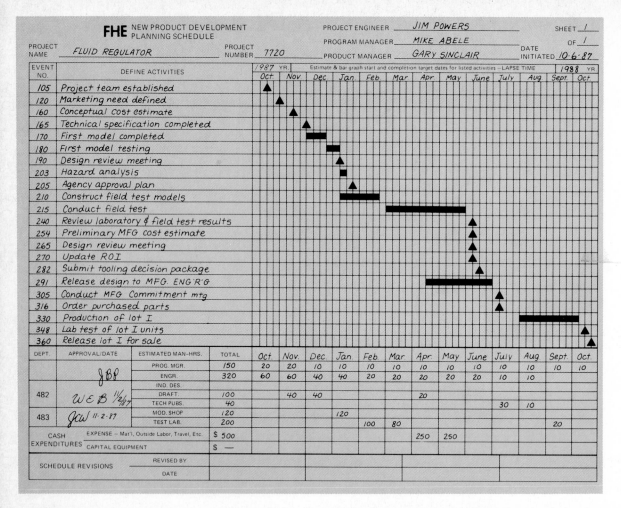

EXHIBIT 4   Gantt chart.

DISCUSSION QUESTIONS

1. What steps should Mr. Donaldson take to improve the new-product development process at FHE?
2. What could be done to clarify the organizational relationship between product managers, technical program managers, and manufacturing managers?
3. What can be done to better manage the work load of the engineering services department?
4. Evaluate the plans and the expected results from the new CAD-CAM system.

Merriwell Bag Company

Merriwell Bag Company is a small, family-owned corporation located in Seattle, Washington.[1] The stock of the company is equally divided among five members of the Merriwell family (husband, wife, and three sons), but the acknowledged leader is the founder and patriarch, Ed Merriwell. Ed Merriwell formed the company 20 years ago when he resigned as a mill supervisor for a large paper manufacturer. Ironically, the same manufacturer formed a container division five years ago and is presently one of Merriwell's competitors.

COMPANY STRATEGY

The family attributes the success of Merriwell Bag Company to the fact that it has found a market niche and has no "serious" competition. Merriwell supplies stock bags to many small chain stores scattered over a wide geographical area. It ships the bags directly to small regional warehouses or drop ships directly to the individual stores. The family reasons that the large bag manufacturers cannot profitably provide service to accounts on that small of a scale. In fact, Ed Merriwell formed the business with one secondhand bagging machine to provide bags for a small discount store chain and a regional chain of drug stores. These two organizations have grown tremendously over the years, and Ed Merriwell proudly points out that the bag company has grown with them. Today, these two original clients are Merriwell's largest customers.

The Merriwell family does not want its business to be too heavily reliant on any one customer. Hence, they have a policy that no single customer can account for over 15 percent of sales. In fact, Merriwell Bag Company encourages its major cus-

tomers to establish alternative sources of bag supply for insurance against stockouts because of paper shortages, freight line difficulties, local trucking/warehousing strikes, and production problems that may locally affect Merriwell's ability to supply bags.

Merriwell does not aggressively pursue new bag customers, yet it has over 500 customers. The smallest customers order five bales per year (smallest order processed and shipped), and the largest order 15,000 bales per year. The number of bags per bale varies according to the weight of paper used and the size of the bag. Merriwell manufactures only pinch-bottom general merchandise bags, ranging in size from small 2½" × 10" pencil bags to large 20" × 2" × 30" bags used for larger items sold in discount stores. They make no flat bottom (grocery) bags or bags that require sophisticated printing (specialty bags). Bag labels are restricted to 20 percent face coverage and one-ink color placed on one side only. Hence, Merriwell's central strategy is built around low unit cost production due to standardization which allows a selling price that is competitive with the large bag manufacturers. At the same time, Merriwell provides the shipping and inventory services that are on too small of a scale for most of the large manufacturers. The Merriwell family takes great pride in "taking care of" a customer who has an emergency need for additional bags or who would like Merriwell to warehouse a bag order for a given time because of storage problems at the customer's warehouse.

FORECASTING DEMAND

Providing this personal service requires tight inventory control and production scheduling at Merriwell's bag plant. A highly accurate demand forecast allows Merriwell to service the special

---

[1]Reprinted with permission of Charles E. Merrill Publishing Company.

Month	Sales (in no. of bales)				
	1983	1984	1985	1986	1987
January	2,000	3,000	2,000	5,000	5,000
February	3,000	4,000	5,000	4,000	2,000
March	3,000	3,000	5,000	4,000	3,000
April	3,000	5,000	3,000	2,000	2,000
May	4,000	5,000	4,000	5,000	7,000
June	6,000	8,000	6,000	7,000	6,000
July	7,000	3,000	7,000	10,000	8,000
August	6,000	8,000	10,000	14,000	10,000
September	10,000	12,000	15,000	16,000	20,000
October	12,000	12,000	15,000	16,000	20,000
November	14,000	16,000	18,000	20,000	22,000
December	8,000	10,000	8,000	12,000	8,000
	78,000	89,000	98,000	115,000	113,000

customer requests by use of Merriwell's own warehouse facilities and routing schedules of the company's truck line. Heretofore, Ed Merriwell could manage the demand forecasting and production scheduling by "feel." Because of the ever-growing number of accounts and changes in personnel in customer purchasing departments, the accuracy of Merriwell's forecasting has been rapidly declining. The percentage of short-shipped accounts for particular types of bags is increasing alarmingly. Conversely, the warehouse is becoming overstocked with other types of bags. As a result, a severe demurrage penalty on three boxcars of incoming rolls of paper was recently paid because the paper warehouse was partially used to store finished bags that spilled over from the finished-bag warehouse. This caused a delay in unloading the boxcars until space could be created in the raw-material warehouse.

Demand forecasting has historically been difficult due to the seasonal nature of the product. There is always a surge in demand for bags prior to a holiday season. The exact timing of the surge in demand for particular types of bags depends upon customer stocking policies and the dates that holiday promotional activities begin.

The Merriwell family needs a forecasting method that would take this seasonal factor into consideration. Moreover, they want a method that exhibits stability, because their market is relatively stable with a large number of repeat customers. Finally, they want a forecasting method that anticipates the growth patterns of their respective customers. A forecasting method with these specifications would greatly enhance the company's ability to service its market profitability. It is believed that if such a method could be applied to forecasting aggregate demand, the same method could be used to gain additional accuracy by forecasting demand of its larger customers. By having an accurate forecast of aggregate demand and demand of larger customers, the requirements of the smaller customers could be processed within the existing warehousing and shipping flexibility.

To develop such a method, the Merriwell family compiled the aggregate demand data shown above. This data shows the monthly sales of bags for the past 5 years.

DISCUSSION QUESTIONS

1. Develop and justify a forecasting method that fulfills the company's specifications.
2. Forecast aggregate demand by month for the year 1988.
3. In addition to forecasting demand of larger customers and aggregate demand, how might the accuracy of the forecast be improved?
4. What role should Ed Merriwell's "feel" of the market play in establishing new sales forecasts?

Benihana of Tokyo

"Some restauranteurs like myself have more fun than others," says Hiroaki (Rocky) Aoki, youthful president of Benihana of Tokyo.[1] Since 1964 he has gone from a deficit net worth to becoming president of a chain of 15 restaurants which grosses over $12 million per year. He sports a $4,000 sapphire ring, maintains a $250,000 home, keeps five cars including three Rolls-Royces. One wall of his office is completely covered with photographs of Rocky with famous personalities who have eaten at a Benihana. Rocky firmly believes: "In America money is always available if you work hard."

BACKGROUND

Benihana is basically a steakhouse with a difference—the food is cooked in front of the customer by native chefs and the decor is that of an authentically detailed Japanese country inn. From a humble 40-seat unit opened in midtown Manhattan in 1964, Benihana has grown to a chain of 15 units across the country. Nine are company-owned locations: New York (3), San Francisco, Chicago, Encino and Marina del Rey, Cal., Portland, Ore., and Honolulu. Five are franchised: Boston, Fort Lauderdale, Beverly Hills, Seattle and Harrisburg, Pa. The last unit, Las Vegas, is operated as a joint venture with Hilton Hotels Corporation. Rocky, who is a former Olympic wrestler, described his success as follows:

---

[1]This case was made possible by the cooperation of the Benihana Corporation and Mr. Russ Carpenter, Executive Editor of the magazine *Institutions/Volume Feeding*. It was prepared by Mr. John Klug, Research Assistant, under the direction of Assistant Professor W. Earl Sasser, as the basis for class discussion rather than to illustrate either effective or ineffective handling of an administrative situation.

In 1959, I came to the United States on a tour with my university wrestling team. I was twenty at the time. When I reached New York, it was love at first sight! I was convinced that there were more opportunities for me in America than Japan. In fact, the minute I was able to forget that I was Japanese, my success began. I decided to enroll in the School of Restaurant Management at City College basically because I knew that in the restaurant business I'd never go hungry. I earned money those early years by washing dishes, driving an ice cream truck and acting as a tour guide. Most importantly, I spent three years making a systematic analysis of the U.S. restaurant market. What I discovered is that Americans enjoy eating in exotic surroundings, but are deeply mistrustful of exotic foods. Also I learned that people very much enjoy watching their food being prepared. So I took $10,000 I had saved by 1963 and borrowed $20,000 more to open my first unit on the West side and tried to apply all that I had learned.

The origins of the Benihana of Tokyo actually date back to 1935. That was when Yunosuke Aoki (Rocky's father) opened the first of his chain of restaurants in Japan. He called it Benihana, after the small red flower that grew wild near the front door of the restaurant.

The elder Aoki ("Papasan"), like his son who was to follow in the family tradition, was a practical and resourceful restauranteur. In 1958, concerned about rising costs and increased competition, he first incorporated the hibachi table concept into his operations. Rocky borrowed this method of cooking from his father and commented as follows:

One of the things I learned in my analysis, for example, was that the number-one problem of

701

the restaurant industry in the U.S. is the shortage of skilled labor. By eliminating the need for a conventional kitchen with the hibachi table arrangement, the only "skilled" person I need is the chef. I can give an unusual amount of attentive service and still keep labor cost to 10%–12% of gross sales (food and beverage) depending whether a unit is at full volume. In addition, I was able to turn practically the entire restaurant into productive dining space. Only about 22% of the total space of a unit is a back-of-the-house including preparation areas, dry and refrigerated storage, employee dressing rooms and office space. Normally a restaurant requires 30% of its total space as back-of-the-house. (Operating statistics for a typical service restaurant are included in Exhibit 1.)

The other thing I discovered is that food storage and wastage contribute greatly to the overhead of the typical restaurant. By reducing my menu to only three simple "Middle American" entrees—steak, chicken, and shrimp, I have virtually no waste and can cut food costs to between 30% and 35% of food sales depending on the price of meat.

Finally, I insist on historical authenticity. The walls, ceilings, beams, artifacts, decorative lights of a Benihana are all from Japan. The building materials are gathered from old houses there, carefully disassembled, shipped in pieces to the U.S., where they are reassembled by one of my father's two crews of Japanese carpenters.

Rocky's first unit on the West side was such a success that it paid for itself in six months. He then built in 1966 a second unit 3 blocks away on the East side simply to cater to the overflow of the Benihana West. The Benihana East quickly developed a separate clientele and prospered. In 1967, Barron Hilton, who had eaten at Benihana, approached Rocky concerning the possibility of locating a unit in the Marina Towers in Chicago. Rocky flew to Chicago, rented a car and while driving to meet Mr. Hilton saw a vacant site. He immediately stopped, called the owner, and signed a lease the next day. Needless to say, a Benihana didn't go into the Marina Towers.

The #3 unit in Chicago has proved to be the company's largest money maker. It was an instant success and grosses approximately $1.3 million per year. The food and beverage split is 70/30 and management is able to keep food (30%), labor (10%), advertising (10%), and rent (5%) expense percentages at relatively low levels.

The fourth unit was in San Francisco and the fifth was a joint venture with International Hotel in Las Vegas in 1969. By this time literally hundreds of people were clamoring for franchises. Rocky sold a total of six until he decided in 1970 that it would be much more to his advantage to own rather than franchise. Following are the franchises that were granted:

- Puerto Rico (Not successful due to economic downturn)
- Harrisburg, Pa.
- Ft. Lauderdale
- Portland (Company bought unit back)
- Seattle
- Beverly Hills
- Boston

The decision to stop franchising was because of a number of problems. First, all the franchises were bought by investors, none of whom had any restaurant experience. Second, it was difficult for the American investor to relate to a predominantly native Japanese staff. Finally, control was considerably more difficult to maintain with a franchisee than a company employee manager. During the period to 1970 several groups attempted to imitate the Benihana success. One even included a group with intimate knowledge of the Benihana operation who set up in very close proximity to one Benihana unit. They, however, folded within the year. Bolstered by the confidence that the Benihana success could not be easily replicated, management felt that one of the classic pressures to franchise was eliminated—i.e., to expand extremely rapidly to preempt competitors.

The amount of space devoted to the bar/lounge/holding area accurately indicates when the unit was built. When Rocky opened his first unit, he saw the business as primarily food-service sales. The Benihana West has a tiny bar which seats about eight and has no lounge area. Rocky quickly learned that amount of bar space was insufficient and at the second unit, Benihana East, he doubled the size of the bar/lounge area. But since the whole

EXHIBIT 1

OPERATING STATISTICS FOR A TYPICAL AMERICAN SERVICE RESTAURANT

Sales	Ranges
Food	70.0 – 80.0
Beverage	20.0 – 30.0
Other income	
Total sales	100.0%
Cost of sales	
Food cost (raw food from suppliers)	38.0 – 48.0
Beverage cost	25.0 – 30.0
Other cost	
Total cost of sales	35.0 – 45.0
Gross profit	55.0 – 65.0
Operating expenses	
Controllable expenses	
Payroll	30.0 – 35.0
Employee benefits	3.0 – 5.0
Employee meals	1.0 – 5.0
Laundry, linen, uniforms	1.5 – 2.0
Replacements	0.5 – 1.0
Supplies (guest)	1.0 – 1.5
Menus & printing	0.25 – 0.5
Misc. contract expense (cleaning, garbage, extermination,	
equipment rental)	1.0 – 2.0
Music & entertainment (where applicable)	0.5 – 1.0
Advertising & promotion	0.75 – 2.0
Utilities	1.0 – 2.0
Management salary	2.0 – 6.0
Administration expense (including legal and accounting)	0.75 – 2.0
Repairs & maintenance	1.0 – 2.0
Occupation expense	
Rent	4.5 – 9.0
Taxes (real estate & personal property)	0.5 – 1.5
Insurance	0.75 – 1.0
Interest	0.3 – 1.0
Depreciation	2.0 – 4.0
Franchise royalties (where applicable)	3.0 – 6.0
Total operating expenses	55.0 – 65.0
Net profit before income tax	0.5 – 9.0%

Source: Bank of America *Small Business Reporter*, vol. 8, no. 2, 1968.

unit is larger, the ratio of space is not too different. A typical floor plan is included as Exhibit 2.

His third Manhattan operation, called Benihana Palace, opened about two years ago. Here, the bar/lounge area is enormous, even in ratio to size. Current figures bear out the wisdom of the growth.

At West, beverage sales represent about 18% of total sales. At East, they run 20%–22%. And at the Palace, they run a handsome 30%–33% of total sales. The beverage cost averages 20% of beverage sales.

The heart of the "show biz" lies in the dining

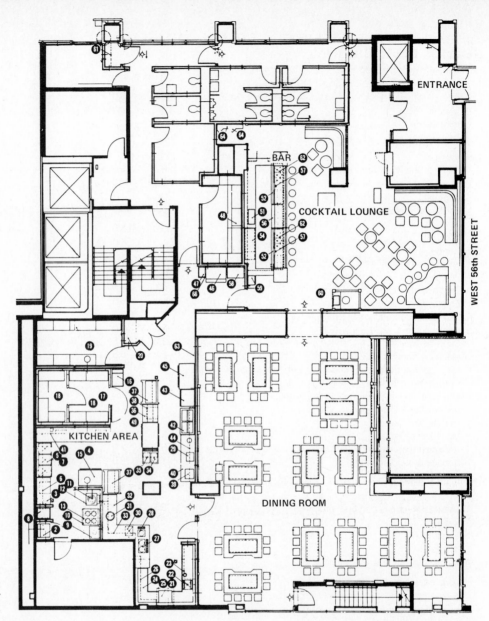

ENTRANCE

BAR

COCKTAIL LOUNGE

WEST 56th STREET

KITCHEN AREA

DINING ROOM

EXHIBIT 2
A typical
Benihana floor
plan.

area. The "teppanyaki" table is comprised of a steel griddle plate, with a 9½" wooden ledge bordering it to hold the ware. It is gas-fired. Above every table is an exhaust hood to remove cooking steam and odors and much of the heat from the griddle. Service is by a chef and waitress; each such team handles two regular tables.

The four food items—steak, filet mignon, chicken and shrimp—can either be had as single entree items or in combinations. A full dinner has three, with the shrimp as appetizer. The accompaniments are unvaried: beansprouts, zucchini, fresh mushrooms, onions, and rice.

Normally, a customer can come in, be seated,

have dinner and be on his way out in 45 minutes, if need be. The average turnover is an hour, up to an hour-and-a-half in slow periods.

The average check, including food and beverage, runs about $6 at lunch, about $10 at dinner. These figures include a drink (average price $1.50) at lunch, an average of one-plus at dinner.

The big purchase is meat. Only U.S.D.A. Prime Grade, tightly specified tenderloin and boneless strip loins are used. The steaks are further trimmed in-house. Only a bit of fat at the tail is left, and this is for effect. When the chef begins cooking the meat, he dramatically trims this part off and pushes it aside before cubing the remaining meat.

The hours of operation for the 15 units vary according to local requirements. All are open for lunch and dinner, though not necessarily every day for each. Lunch business is important; overall it accounts for about 30% to 40% of the total dollar volume despite a significantly lower check average. Essentially the same menu items are served for meals; the lower menu price average at lunch reflects smaller portions and fewer combinations.

SITE SELECTION

Because of the importance of lunch time business, Benihana has one basic criterion for site selection—high traffic. Management wants to be sure that a lot of people are nearby or going by both at lunch and at dinner. Rent normally runs 5–7% of sales for 5000–6000 square feet of floor space. Most units are located in a predominantly business district, though some have easy access to residential areas. Shopping center locations have been considered, but none accepted as yet.

TRAINING

Because the chef is considered by Benihana to be a key to its success, they are very highly trained. All are young and single native Japanese and all are "certified" which means that they have completed a two-year formal apprenticeship. They are then given a three- to six-month course in Japan in the English language and American manner as well as the Benihana form of cooking, which is mostly showmanship. The chefs are brought to the U.S. under a "trade treaty" agreement.

Training of the chefs within the U.S. is a contin-

uous process also. In addition to the competition among the chefs to perfect their art in hopes of becoming the chief chef, there is also a traveling chef who inspects each unit periodically as well as being involved in the grand opening of new units.

While Benihana finds it relatively difficult to attract chefs and other personnel from Japan due to the general level of prosperity there as well as competition from other restaurants bidding for their talents, once in the U.S. they are generally not anxious to leave. This is due to several factors. One is the rapidity with which they can rise in the U.S. Benihana operation versus the rather rigid hierarchy based on class, age, and education they would face in Japan. A second and major factor is the paternal attitude that Benihana takes toward all its employees. While personnel are well paid in a tangible sense, a large part of the compensation is intangible based on job security and a total commitment of Benihana to the well-being of its employees. As a result, turnover of personnel within the U.S. is very low, although most do eventually return to Japan. To fully appreciate the Benihana success, one must appreciate the unique combination of Japanese paternalism in an American setting. Or, as Rocky puts it: "At Benihana we combine Japanese workers with American management techniques."

ORGANIZATION AND CONTROL

Each restaurant carries a simple management structure. It has a manager ($15,000/year), and assistant manager ($12,000/year) and 2–3 "front men" ($9,000/year), who might be likened to maitre d's. These latter are really potential managers in training. All managers report to manager of operations Allen Saito who, in turn, reports to Bill Susha, vice president in charge of operations and business development. (See Exhibit 3.)

Susha came with Benihana in 1971, following food and beverage experience with Hilton, Loew's and the Flagship Hotel division of American Airlines. He described his job as follows:

> I see management growth as a priority objective. My first step was to establish some sort of control system by introducing sales goals and budgets. At the most recent manager workshop

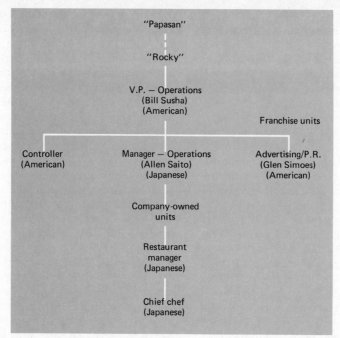

"Papasan"

"Rocky"

V.P. — Operations
(Bill Susha)
(American)

Franchise units

Controller
(American)

Manager — Operations
(Allen Saito)
(Japanese)

Advertising/P.R.
(Glen Simoes)
(American)

Company-owned
units

Restaurant
manager
(Japanese)

Chief chef
(Japanese)

EXHIBIT 3
Organization
chart.

meeting in New York, with managers attending from all over the country, I asked each to project his sales goal on an annual basis, then break it out by month, then by week, then by day. After I reached agreement with a manager on the individual quota figures, I instituted a bonus plan. Any unit that exceeds its quota on any basis—daily, weekly, monthly, yearly—will get a proportionate bonus, which will be prorated across the entire staff of the unit. I've also built up an accounting staff and controller to monitor our costs. It's been a slow but steady process. We have to be very careful to balance our needs for control with the amount of overhead we can stand. We can justify extra "front men" standing around in the units. At the corporate level, however, we have to be very careful. In fact, at the present the company is essentially being run by three people—Rocky, myself and Allen Saito.

ADVERTISING POLICY

Rocky considers that a vitally important factor in Benihana's success is a substantial investment in creative advertising and public relations. The com-

pany invests 8–10 percent of its gross sales on reaching the public.

Glen Simoes, the director of advertising and public relations summed it up:

We deliberately try to be different and original in our advertising approach. We never place advertisements on the entertainment pages of newspapers on the theory that they would be lost among the countless other restaurant advertisements.

We have a visual product to sell. Therefore, Benihana utilizes outstanding visuals in its ads. The accompanying copy is contemporary, sometimes offbeat. A recent full-page advertisement which appeared in the *New York Times, Women's Wear Daily* and *New York Magazine* did not contain the word "restaurant." We also conduct a considerable amount of market research to be sure we know who our customers really are.

Exhibit 4 shows the results of our market research survey. Exhibit 5 is a further discussion of

What the Customers Think

Every foodservice operator thinks he knows why customers come to his operation. Benihana, which has served two-and-a-quarter million customers in eight years, a high percentage of which were repeat business, thought it knew.

But when he joined as v-p of operations a year-and-a-half ago, Bill Susha wanted to be sure the hallowed presumptions were true. He devised a questionnaire, and arranged that it be handed to departing customers. A remarkable number took the time to fill out and return the form.

The percentage figures shown here are averages of six stores. While there were many variations from unit to unit, the general thrust was constant, so the six-store figures have been averaged to save space.

The six units included the three in New York City, plus Chicago, Encino, Cal., and Portland, Ore. The questions and averages are as follows:

Are you from out-of-town?
Yes	38.6%
No	61.4

Here on:
Business	38.7%
Pleasure	61.3

Do you live in the area?
Live	16.0%
Work	35.9
Both	45.1

Have you been to a Benihana in another city?
Yes	22.9%
No	77.3

How did you learn of us?
Newspaper	4.0%
Magazine	6.9
Radio	4.6
Recommended	67.0
TV show	1.0
Walk by	5.0
Other	11.5

Is this your first visit?
Yes	34.3%
No	65.7

What persuaded you to come?
Good food	46.7%
Service	8.2
Preparation	13.1
Atmosphere	13.3
Recommendation	5.7
Other	13.1

Food was:
Good	2.0%
Satisfactory	20.1
Excellent	77.9

Portions were:
Satisfactory	21.8%
Good	33.0
Excellent	45.4

Service was:
Satisfactory	9.8%
Good	21.6
Excellent	71.3

Atmosphere is:
Satisfactory	6.3%
Good	29.9
Excellent	63.2

Would you consider yourself a lunch or dinner customer?
Lunch	17.3%
Dinner	59.0
Both	23.7

Which aspect of our restaurant would you highlight?
Food	38.2%
Atmosphere	13.0
Preparation	24.6
Service	16.3
Different	2.2
Friendly	2.4
Other	3.3

How frequently do you come to Benihana?
Once a week or more	12.1%
Once a month or more	32.5
Once a year or more	55.6

Age:
10–20	4.2%
21–30	28.3
31–40	32.0
41–50	21.4
51–60	10.1
60 and over	4.0

Sex:
Male	71.4%
Female	28.6

Income:
$ 7,500–$10,000	16.8%
$10,000–$15,000	14.2
$15,000–$20,000	17.3
$20,000–$25,000	15.0
$25,000–$40,000	17.9
$40,000 and over	18.7

Occupation:
Managerial	23.0%
Professional	26.6
White Collar	36.9
Student	6.9
Housewife	5.0
Unskilled	1.1

EXHIBIT 4
Market survey.

Benihana advertising policy. Exhibits 6, 7, and 8 are examples of Benihana advertising copy.

FUTURE EXPANSION

Bill Susha summed up the problems of the future as he saw them:

I think the biggest problems facing us now are how to expand. We tried franchising and decided to discontinue the program for several rea-sons. Most of our franchisees were businessmen looking for investment opportunities and did not really know and understand the restaurant business—this was a problem. The Japanese staff we provided were our people and we have obligations to them that the franchisee could not or would not cope with which at the time made us unhappy. The uniqueness of our operation in the hands of novices to the business made control more difficult and finally, we found it more profitable to own and operate the restaurants ourselves.

No icky, sticky, slimy stuff

"Part of what makes Benihana successful," Rocky Aoki believes, *"is our advertising and promotion. It's different, and it makes us seem different to people."*

Indeed it is, and does. Much of the credit belongs to Glen Simoes, the hip director of advertising and public relations for Benihana of Tokyo. With a background mostly in financial public relations, Simoes joined the chain a little over two years ago to help open the flagship Benihana Palace. Since then, he's created a somewhat novel, all-embracing public relations program that succeeds on many levels.

"My basic job," he explains, *"is guardian of the image. The image is that of a dynamic chain of Japanese restaurants with phenomenal growth."* Keeping the image bright means exposure. Part of the exposure is a brilliant advertising campaign; part is publicity.

Each has its own function. Advertising is handled by Kracauer and Marvin, an outside agency, under Simoes' supervision and guidance. Its function is to bring in new customers.

"Our ads," Simoes points out, *"are characterized by a bold headline statement and an illustration that make you want to read on. The copy itself is fairly clever and cute. If it works properly, it will keep you reading until you get the message—which is to persuade a stranger to come into Benihana.*

"The ads are designed to still fears about icky, sticky, slimy stuff," he adds. *"We reassure folks that they will get wholesome, familiar food, with unusual, unique and delicious preparation, served in a fun atmosphere. We want to intrigue the people celebrating an anniversary or taking Aunt Sally out to dinner. A Japanese restaurant would normally never cross their minds. We're saying we're a fun place to try, and there's no slithery, fishy stuff.*

"We have an impact philosophy. We go for full pages in national publications on a now-and-then basis, rather than a regular schedule of small ads. We want that impact to bring the stranger into Benihana for the first time. After that, the restaurant will bring him back again and again, and he will bring his friends.

"We do a good media mix," Simoes concludes. *"We advertise in each of the cities in which we operate. Within each market we aim for two people: the resident, of course, but even more, the tourist-visitor. With them you know you're always talking to new people. We appear in city entertainment guides and work with convention and visitor bureaus to go after groups and conventions."*

The second factor is publicity. Here, the intent is not the quantity of mentions or exposure, but the type. As Simoes sees it, *"We are building. Each mention is a building block. Some are designed to bring customers into the store. Some are designed to bring us prospective financing, or suppliers, or friends, or whatever. We work many ways against the middle. And the middle is the company, the people, Rocky, the growth and all of it put together that makes the image."*

Publicity takes many forms, it's media stories, and TV demonstrations. Simoes cites clipping and viewing services to prove that every day of the year, something about Benihana appears either in print or on radio or TV, a record he believes is unique. Publicity is department store demonstrations, catering to celebrities, hosting youth groups, sending matchboxes to conventions and chopsticks to ladies clubs, scheduling Rocky for interviews and paying publicists to provide oneliners to columnists.

But no engine runs without fuel. And Rocky believes that advertising and promotion are a good investment. Believes so strongly, in fact, that he puts an almost unprecedented $1 million a year into advertising, and probably half that again into promotion, for a total expenditure of nearly 8% of gross sales in this area.

A few months back, Simoes, wholeheartedly pitching his company to a skeptical magazine writer, said heatedly there are "at least 25 reasons people come to Benihana." Challenged on the spot, he came back a few days later with a list of 31. They are:

1) the quality of the food; 2) the presentation of the food; 3) the preparation of the food; 4) the showmanship of the chef; 5) the taste of the food; 6) authenticity of construction; 7) authenticity of decor; 8) continuity of Japanese flavor throughout; 9) communal dining; 10) service—constant attention.

11) Youthfulness of staff; 12) frequent presence of celebrities; 13) excitement created by frequent promotions; 14) type of cuisine; 15) moderate price; 16) the uniqueness of appeal to the five senses; 17) the recent growth in popularity of things Japanese; 18) quick service; 19) unusual advertising concept; 20) publicity.

21) No stringent dress requirements; 22) recommendations from friends; 23) the basic meal is low-calorie; 24) banquet and party facilities; 25) the presence of Rocky Aoki, himself; 26) chance to meet people of the opposite sex; 27) the presence of many Japanese customers (about 20%); 28) locations in major cities giving a radiation effect; 29) acceptance of all major credit cards; 30) the informality of the dining experience; and 31) the use of the restaurant as a business tool.

EXHIBIT 5
Summary of
Benihana
marketing
philosophy.

Presently, we are limited to opening only 5 units a year because that is as fast as the two crews of Japanese carpenters we have can work. We are facing a decision and weighing the advantages and disadvantages of going into hotels with our type of restaurant. We are presently in two Hilton Hotels (Las Vegas and Honolulu) and have recently signed an agreement with Canadian Pacific Hotels. What we have done in these deals is to put "teeth" in the agreement so that we are not at the mercy of the hotel company's management.

Go forth now and cook amongst the Americans.

It's not easy earning the right to feed the people of America.

No, it's no picnic getting admitted to the league of Benihana chefs.

First, you must serve a 2 year apprenticeship in Japan. Then you must be accepted at the Benihana College of Chefs in Tokyo. There you have to spend fifteen gruelling weeks under Master Chef Shinji Fujisaku. You don't graduate unless the Master certifies that you've become an absolute whiz at Benihana's special style of Hibachi cooking (Japanese grill cuisine as opposed to classical Japanese cuisine.)

And what are some of the teachings of the Master?

Well, one of the first has to do with the cutting of the meat. "A Benihana chef is an artist, not a butcher," the Master says. So you must learn to wield a knife with dazzling grace, speed and precision. Your hands should move like Fred Astaire's feet.

You also learn that to a Benihana chef, Hibachi cooking is never solemn. As the Master says "It's an act of pure joy." So joy, really, is what you must bring to the Hibachi table. A joy that the people around you can see and feel. A joy they can catch as you sauté those jumbo shrimps. Or as you dust that chicken with sesame seeds. Or as you slam that pepper shaker against the grill and send the pepper swirling over those glorious chunks of steak.

Perhaps most important of all, is this saying of the Master's: "Benihana has no cooks. Only chefs." Which means that while you should be joyous, you must always strive for perfection. So you learn everything there is to learn about sauces and seasonings. You labor to make your shrimp the most succulent shrimp anyone's ever tasted. Your sirloin the most delicious and juicy. Your every mushroom and beansprout a song.

Over and over the Master drills you. Again and again you go through your paces. Fifteen exhausting, perfection-seeking weeks.

But the day comes when you're ready. Ready to bring what you've learned to the people of such faraway places as New York, Chicago and Los Angeles. It's a great moment.

"Sayonara, Honorable Teacher," you say.

"Knock 'em dead, Honorable Graduate," he replies.

BENIHANA of TOKYO

New York—Benihana Palace 15 W. 44 St., 682-7120   Benihana East 120 E. 56 St., 593-1627   Benihana West 61 W. 56 St., 581-0930
Boston, Harrisburg, Fort Lauderdale, Chicago, Seattle, Portland Ore., San Francisco, Las Vegas, Encino, Beverly Hills, Honolulu, Tokyo.

EXHIBIT 6
Advertisement.

Further, one of our biggest constraints is staff. Each unit requires approximately 30 people who are all Oriental. Six to eight of these are highly trained chefs.

Finally, there is the cost factor. Each new unit costs us a minimum of $300,000. My feeling is that we should confine ourselves to the major cities like Atlanta, Dallas, St. Louis, etc., in the near future. Then we can use all these units to expand into the suburbs.

We've been highly tempted to try to grow too fast without really considering the full implications of the move. One example was the franchise thing, but we found it unsatisfactory. Another example is that a large international banking organization offered to make a major

Two philosophies of the steak.

The basic philosophy of the American restaurant.

The chef throws a slab of raw steak into the kitchen broiler.

It sits there until it's rare, medium or well-done.

The waiter brings it to your table.

You eat it.

The Benihana philosophy.

The chef comes right up to your hibachi table. (Why shouldn't you see the man who's actually creating your meal?)

He bows. (There's no reason why a chef can't be a gentleman.)

He sets the raw steak in front of you. (Isn't it nice to see for yourself that you're getting the very freshest, prime cuts?)

He asks you how you want it. (There's no luxury like the luxury of dealing directly with your chef.)

He cuts your steak into bite-size morsels. (Why should _you_ have to perform any labor?)

His knife begins a snappy, rhythmic attack on the onions. (We believe there's as much drama in a dancing onion as in a dancing chorus girl.)

He slams the pepper shaker against the grill. (It's not good for a chef to suppress his excitement.)

As he cooks he adds all kinds of Japanese sauces and seasonings. (No, Worcester sauce is not part of our theory.)

At last he puts the sizzling steak directly on your plate. (The world's fastest waiter couldn't serve you better.)

You eat it. (Tell us. Has there ever been a more palatable philosophy?)

BENIHANA of TOKYO

New York — Benihana Palace 15 W. 44 St., 682-7120 • Benihana East 120 E. 56 St., 593-1627 • Benihana West 61 W. 56 St., 581-0930
Boston, Harrisburg, Fort Lauderdale, Chicago, Seattle, Portland Ore., San Francisco, Las Vegas, Encino, Marina Del Rey, Beverly Hills, Honolulu, Tokyo.

EXHIBIT 7
Advertisement.

investment in us which would have allowed us to grow at a terrific rate. But when we looked at the amount of control and autonomy we'd have to give up, it just wasn't worth it, at least in my mind.

Another thing I'm considering is whether it's worth it to import every item used in construction from Japan to make a Benihana 100% "authentic." Does an American really appreciate it and is it worth the cost? We could use material available here and achieve substantially the same effect. Also is it worth it to use Japanese carpenters and pay union carpenters to sit and watch? All these things could reduce our

costs tremendously and allow us to expand much faster.

Rocky described his perception of where the firm should go:

I see three principal areas for growth, the U.S., overseas, and Japan. In the U.S. we need to expand into the primary marketing areas Bill talked about that do not have a Benihana. But I think through our franchises we also learned that secondary markets such as Harrisburg, Pa. and Portland, Ore. also have potential. While their volume potential obviously will not match

The Mission of Rocky Aoki

When Rocky Aoki, owner of Benihana, came to America six years ago, this was how a great many Americans felt about Japanese food:

(1) It wasn't as good as Chinese food.
(2) It was mostly sukiyaki and soup that tasted like hot brown water.
(3) If you ordered anything besides sukiyaki, you'd wind up with raw, slithery fishy things.
(4) OK, the food was very prettily arranged. But youwalkedouttwiceashungryaswhenyouwalkedin.
(5) It wasn't as good as Chinese food.

"My task is clear," said Rocky. "I'm going to change the way Americans think about Japanese food. I'm going to introduce America to Hibachi cooking."

(Hibachi cooking or cooking on a grill, is nothing at all like the highly stylized classical Japanese cuisine.)

And so, in 1964, Rocky opened the first Benihana. It broke all the rules. You couldn't get sukiyaki there. Or raw fish. There wasn't even a conventional kitchen. You just sat around this big Hibachi table—a combination grill and dining table—and waited for your chef to appear.

When he did, he came bearing a feast. Basket upon basket of beautiful fresh meat, poultry and vegetables. Then, right in front of you, he sprang into action. Slicing, seasoning and cooking, he prepared your meal with a speed and skill bordering on wizardry.

It was hard to believe. No exquisitely carved carrot slices. No wispy vegetables arranged in perfect flower patterns. Instead, solid food in abundance. Jumbo shrimps sauteed with lemon. Succulent chunks of steak. Young chicken dusted with sesame seeds. Mushrooms, scallions, beansprouts—served not together in some kind of mish-mash, but individually. It was enough to bring joy to the most jaded gourmet, bliss to the most ravenous appetite.

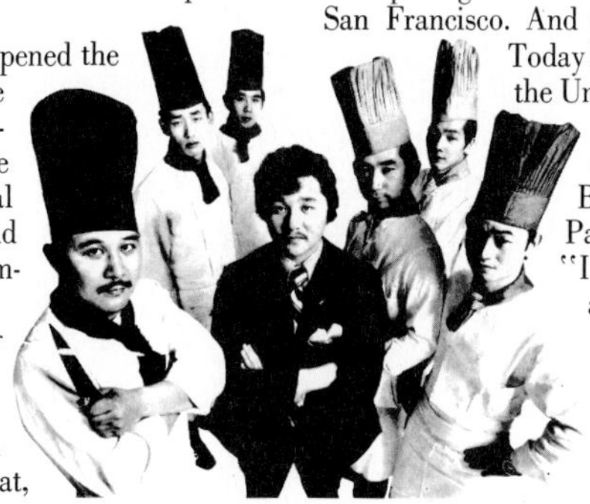

Well, the first New York Benihana was an enormous success. Within a year, Rocky had to open another one. That too became a smash. Soon Rocky was opening a Benihana in Chicago. And then one in San Francisco. And then another in Las Vegas. Today Rocky has Benihanas all over the United States.

Earlier this year, after opening his third New York Benihana—the Benihana Palace—Rocky Aoki declared: "I'll consider my mission accomplished when everyone in America has tried Hibachi cooking at least once."

Come in and give a nice Japanese boy a break.

BENIHANA of TOKYO

No slithery, fishy things.

New York—Benihana Palace 15 W. 44 St., 682-7120 Benihana East 120 E. 56 St., 593-1627 Benihana West 61 W. 56 St., 581-0930

Chicago, Los Angeles, Las Vegas, San Francisco, Harrisburg, Fort Lauderdale, Portland, Ore., Puerto Rico, Honolulu, Tokyo.

EXHIBIT 8
Advertisement.

that of a primary market, these smaller units offer fewer headaches and generate nice profits. Secondary markets being considered include Cincinnati and Indianapolis.

The third principal area I see for growth is in suburbia. No sites have yet been set, but I think it holds a great potential. A fourth growth area, not given the importance of the others, is further penetration into existing markets. Saturation is not a problem as illustrated by the fact that New York and greater Los Angeles have three units each, all doing well.

We are also considering someday going public. In the meantime, we are moving into joint ventures in Mexico and overseas. Each joint venture is unique in itself. We negotiate each on the basis that will be most advantageous to the parties concerned taking into account the contributions of each party in the form of services and cash. Once this is established, we agree on a formula for profits and away we go.

Four deals have now been consummated. Three are joint ventures out of the country. An agreement has already been reached to open a Benihana in the Royal York Hotel, Toronto, Canada. This will provide the vanguard for a march across Canada with units in or outside Canadian Pacific Hotels.

Second is a signed agreement for a new unit in Mexico City. From here, negotiations are under way on a new hotel to be built in Acapulco. Benihana stands ready to build and operate a unit in the hotel or, if possible, to take over management of the entire hotel. These units would form a base for expansion throughout Mexico.

The third extra-territorial arrangement was recently signed with David Paradine, Ltd., a British firm of investors headed by TV personality David Frost. Again, this is a joint venture, with the Paradine group to supply technical assistance, public relations, advertising and financing. Benihana the management and know-how. This venture hopes ultimately to have Benihana restaurants not only throughout Great Britain but across the Continent.

Rocky also has a number of diversification plans:

We have entered into an agreement with a firm that is researching and contacting large food processors in an effort to interest them into producing a line of Japanese food products under the Benihana label for retail sale. There has been a great deal of interest and we are close to concluding a deal.

I worry a lot. Right now we cater to a middle-income audience, not the younger generation. That makes a difference. We charge more, serve better quality, have a better atmosphere and more service. But we are in the planning stages for operations with appeal to the younger generation.

For instance, there is no Japanese quick service operation in this country. I think we should go into a combination Chinese-Japanese operation like this. The unit would also feature a dynamic cooking show exposed to the customers. Our initial projections show margins comparable to our present margins with Benihana of Tokyo. I see a check of about 99 cents. We are negotiating with an oil company to put small units in gas stations. They could be located anywhere—on turnpikes or in the Bronx. I think we should do this very soon. I think I will get a small store in Manhattan and try it out. This is the best kind of market research in the U.S. Market research works in other countries, but I don't believe in it here. We are also negotiating for a site on Guam and to take over a chain of beer halls in Japan.

The restaurant business is not my only business. I went into producing; I had two unsuccessful Broadway shows. The experience was very expensive, but I learned a great deal and learned it very fast. It's all up to the critics there. In the restaurant business, the critics don't write much about you if you're bad; but even if they do they can't kill you. On Broadway they can. They did.

I promoted a heavyweight boxing match in Japan. It was successful. I am going into promoting in the entertainment field in Japan. I am doing a Renoir exhibition in Japan with an auction over television. I am thinking about buying a Japanese movie series and bringing it here. I am also thinking of opening a model agency, probably specializing in Oriental models.

But everything always works back to Benihana. For instance, if I open a model agency, I will let the girls come to Benihana to eat. Twenty beautiful girls at the restaurant would mean 400 guys, which would mean 600 girls, and so on.

My philosophy of the restaurant business is simply to make people happy. We do it many ways in Benihana. As we start different types of operations, we will try to do it in other ways. I have no real worries about the future. The U.S. is the greatest country in the world to make money. Anybody can do it who wants to work hard and make people happy.

Russ Carpenter, a consultant and editor for *Institutions/Volume Feeding* magazine summed up his perceptions as follows:

I basically see two main problems.

What is Benihana really selling? Is it food, atmosphere, hospitality, a "watering hole" or what? Is having entertainment in the lounge, for example, consistent with the overall image? All the advertising emphasizes the chef and the food, but is that really what the public comes for? I don't know. I'm only raising the questions.

The other thing is how do you hedge your bets? Is Benihana really on the forefront of a trend of the future with their limited menu, cooking in front of you and Oriental atmosphere, or is it just a fad? This relates to whether it should emphasize restaurant operations only.

QUESTIONS

1. What are the keys to Rocky Aoki's success?
2. Analyze the process flows in a typical restaurant. Do this for a typical customer to identify flow times and bottlenecks.
3. What should Rocky do with respect to future expansion of capacity?

Eastern Gear, Inc.

Eastern Gear, Inc., in Philadelphia, Pa., is a manufacturer of custom-made gears ranging in weight from a few ounces to over 50 pounds.[1] The gears are made of different metals depending on the customer's requirements. Over the past year, 40 different types of steel and brass alloys have been used as raw materials. See Exhibit 1 for details.

Eastern Gear sells its products primarily to engineering research and development laboratories or very small manufacturers. As a result, the number of gears in most orders is small; rarely is exactly the same gear ordered more than once. The distribution of order sizes for March 1988 is shown in Exhibit 2.

Recently, the president of Eastern Gear decided to accept a few larger gear orders for 100 gears or more. Although lower prices were accepted on these orders, they helped pay the overhead. It was found that the large orders caused many of the small orders to wait for a long time before being processed. As a result, some deliveries of small orders were late.

ORDER ENTRY

When a customer wishes to order a gear, the order is taken by James Lord, sales manager and marketing vice president. The customer specifies the type of gear desired by submitting a blueprint or sketch. The quantity of gears required and the type of material are also specified by the customer. On occasion, the customer's engineer will call up after the order has been placed and request a change in the design. In these cases, it may be necessary to stop production and wait for new raw materials or

---

[1]This case was prepared as a basis for class discussion, not to illustrate either effective or ineffective handling of an administrative situation.

EXHIBIT 1
RAW MATERIALS

Type of material	1987 usage $(000)
A	$ 36
B	10
C	15
D	43
E	110
F	18
G	32
H	75
I	40
J	60
K	30
All others	53
Total	$522

EXHIBIT 2
SALES, MARCH 1988

Order size	Number of orders	Total $ value of orders
1	80	$ 3,200
2	53	4,250
3	69	8,163
4	32	4,800
5	82	16,392
8	47	15,987
10	64	26,871
15	22	13,172
20	42	31,555
25	27	23,682
30	18	21,600
40	22	32,000
50	10	18,693
100	4	12,500
200	2	14,068
400	1	9,652
700	2	35,600
1000	1	20,000
	578	$312,185

for the design to be clarified. The customer's prints submitted with the order do not always contain the tolerances or finishes required during machining. As a result, the customer is contacted directly when the information is needed.

After the order is received, one copy is sent to the production supervisor, Joe Irvine, and the second copy is sent to Sam Smith, the controller. Upon receipt of the customer's order, Mr. Smith places a purchase order for the raw materials required. These materials often take from 1 to 2 weeks to arrive, depending on the supplier and the type of material ordered.

After receiving the customer order, the supervisor reviews the order and places it on file until the raw material arrives. The customer order is then routed through the shop along with the materials. In the past, the production process for most gears has taken about 2 weeks after receipt of raw materials. Recently this production time has increased to 4 weeks.

Joe Irvine expressed concern about the bottlenecks which appear in the production process. One week the bottleneck may be in one machine center, and the next week it is in another. These bottlenecks make it difficult to get the orders out on time.

PHYSICAL LAYOUT AND MATERIALS FLOW

Eastern Gear utilizes a standard job-shop layout, as shown in Exhibit 3. Each work center has a common set of machines or processes. The materials flow from one work center to another, depending on the operations needed for a particular order.

A typical order will take the following path. First, the raw material, a gear blank, is sent to the milling work center. Here the teeth are cut into the edge of the gear according to the customer's specifications. Next, the gear blanks are sent to the drilling work center, where one or more holes may be drilled in the gear. The gear is then sent to a grinding center, where a finish is put on the gear teeth and the surface of the gear. Next, the gear may be sent to heat-treating if this operation is required by the customer. After the batch of gears is completed, they are inspected by the next available worker and shipped to the customer.

In Exhibit 3, note how the machines are grouped by similar type on the shop floor. For example, all drills are located together in one work center, and all milling machines are in another work center. While this layout facilitates develop-

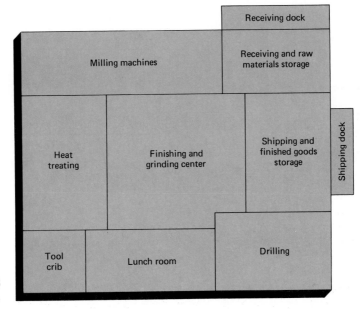

EXHIBIT 3
Layout.

ment of worker skills and training, it results in a jumbled flow of products through the shop.

There is constant interference of the orders being processed in the shop. The typical order spends 90 percent of its time waiting in line for a machine to become available. Only 10 percent of the time is actually spent processing the order on a machine. As a result, it takes a relatively long time (4 weeks) for an order to make its way through the shop.

Large and small orders are processed together. No special work flow is utilized for different order sizes. As a matter of fact, large orders are helping to keep the shop at full capacity.

COMPANY BACKGROUND

Business has been booming at Eastern Gear. For the first 2 years the company lost money, but over the last several months a small profit has been made. Sales are up by 100 percent in the last quarter. See Exhibit 4 for more details.

Although sales are rapidly increasing, a recent market survey has indicated that sales can be expanded even more in the next few years. According to the market survey, sales will be $5 million in calendar 1988 if the current delivery lead time of 5 to 6 weeks is maintained. If total delivery lead time can be reduced to the former 3 to 4 weeks, sales could be expanded to $5.5 million instead of $5 million.

Because of increased delivery lead times, the company has recently added an expediter, Matt Williams. Each morning Matt reviews the work in progress in the shop and selects those orders which appear to be behind schedule. Each order which is behind receives a red tag, indicating that it should be treated on a rush basis. At the present time about 20 percent of the orders have rush tags on them. Mr. Williams also spends his time looking for past-due raw materials and lost orders as well as explaining late orders to customers.

The organization chart for the company is shown in Exhibit 5. Roger Rhodes is the president and founder of Eastern Gear. Mr. Rhodes handles contacts with some of the large customers, arranges the financing needed by the company, and sits in on the weekly production meeting. During these meetings, scheduling problems, employee problems, and other production problems are discussed.

The company engineer is Sam Bartholomew. His responsibilities include design of the company's products, procurement and maintenance of equipment, and overseeing of the supervisor, Joe Irvine. Mr. Bartholomew also attends the weekly production meetings, and he spends about 10 hours a week on the factory floor talking with individual workers.

The company is currently experiencing about a 6 percent return rate on completed orders due to poor quality. In 75 percent of the cases, the re-

EXHIBIT 4
FINANCIAL DATA

	1985	1986	1987	First quarter, 1988
Sales	560*	1500	3100	1063
Manufacturing costs				
Materials	63	273	522	214
Labor	136	587	1063	327
Overhead	70	216	412	140
Depreciation	172	398	422	150
Total manufacturing costs	441	1474	2419	831
Sales expenses	70	130	263	80
G & A expense	75	110	297	93
Total costs	586	1714	2979	1004
Profit before tax	(26)	(214)	121	59

*All figures in thousands of dollars.

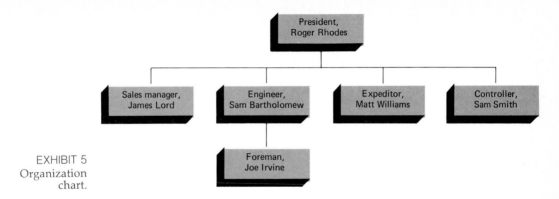

EXHIBIT 5
Organization
chart.

turned orders have failed to undergo one or more operations or the operations have been improperly done. For example, in one returned order, all the gears were missing a hole.

Occasionally, the company will receive rush orders from its customers. In this case the order is referred directly to Roger Rhodes for approval. If the order is accepted, the raw materials are rush-ordered and received the next day. After receipt of the raw materials, the order is rushed through production in 4 days. This is accomplished by Fred Dirkson, a trusted employee, who hand-carries the rush orders through all operations. About 10 percent of the orders are handled on a rush basis.

The work force consists of 50 employees who are highly skilled or semiskilled. The milling machine operators, for example, are highly skilled and require at least 2 years of vocational-technical training plus several months of on-the-job training. Within the last quarter, 10 new employees have been added to the work force. The employees are not unionized and good labor relations exist. The work force is managed using a family-type approach.

DISCUSSION QUESTIONS

1. What are the major problems being faced by Eastern Gear?
2. What action should Mr. Rhodes take to solve his problems?
3. How can this case be related to operations strategy and process design concepts?

First City National Bank

In March 1987, David Craig, vice president of operations for First City National Bank of Philadelphia, was considering a change in teller operations.[1] Currently, the bank's tellers were arranged in pods to handle customer transactions. There were four pods containing three teller stations each. One pod was used primarily for savings accounts, since some savings transactions took longer than other types of deposits or withdrawals. The major problem with the pod system was that one pod might be crowded while another was vacant. The distance between pods was such that customers were unwilling to move from one to another.

Mr. Craig was considering two alternatives to

the pod system. The first was a single-line teller arrangement as shown in Exhibit 1. Using this plan, all customers would wait in a single line until a teller became available. The person at the head of the line would then move to the open teller. Mr. Craig thought that about 10 tellers would be required to handle the bank's usual business. However, he could not be sure of the exact number without further study.

Exhibit 1 also shows the second alternative teller arrangement. Using this more conventional plan, the customers would form separate lines in front of each of the teller windows. Thus for 10 tellers, a total of 10 different lines could be formed.

In evaluating these alternatives, several issues were of utmost importance. First, Mr. Craig was concerned with both customer waiting time and teller efficiency. On the basis of past experience, Mr. Craig felt that more than 3 minutes of waiting

---

[1]This case was prepared as a basis for class discussion, not to illustrate either effective or ineffective handling of an administrative situation.

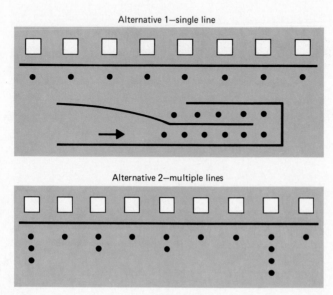

EXHIBIT 1
Teller arrangements.

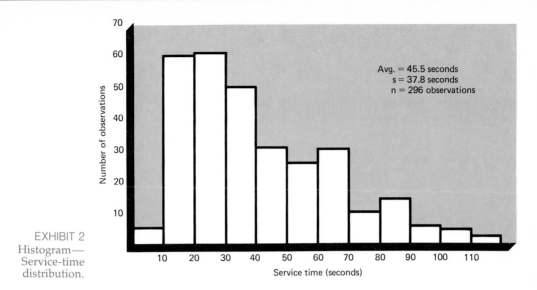

EXHIBIT 2
Histogram—
Service-time
distribution.

time would be unacceptable to most customers. He also felt that teller utilization should be as high as possible, perhaps in the 80 to 90 percent range. Since demand varied during the day, the number of tellers provided would have to vary to meet the customer-service and teller-utilization goals.

The statistical distribution of service time and arrival time is shown in Exhibits 2 and 3. The service time averages 45 seconds per customer and does not vary by time of day. On the other hand, the average time between arrivals does vary with the time of day. For example, between 11:45 and 12:45 on one particular day sampled, 431 customers arrived at the bank, with an average of 8.4 seconds between customers.

To estimate the average arrival rate during dif-

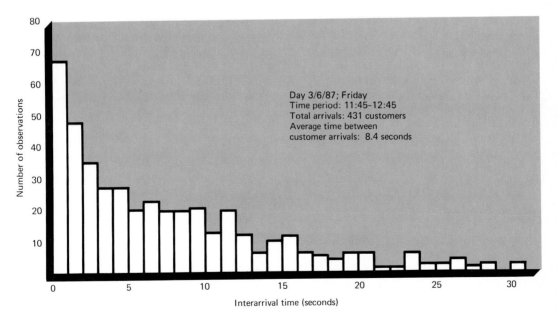

EXHIBIT 3   Histogram—Arrival-time distribution.

EXHIBIT 4

CHART OF AVERAGE CUSTOMER ARRIVAL RATES

	Normal days		Peak days		Super-peak days	
Time of day	Total number of arrivals	Average arrival rate*	Total number of arrivals	Average arrival rate*	Total number of arrivals	Average arrival rate*
8–8:30	803	19	625	22	331	25
8:30–9	919	22	758	27	418	32
9–9:30	1207	29	863	31	571	44
9:30–10	2580	63	2033	72	1228	94
10–10:30	2599	63	2237	80	1382	106
10:30–11	2870	70	2283	82	1337	103
11–11:30	3384	83	2625	94	1577	121
11:30–12	4548	111	4060	145	2325	179
12–12:30	5804	142	5329	190	2908	224
12:30–1	5351	131	4923	176	2724	210
1–1:30	4355	106	3983	142	2271	175
1:30–2	3632	89	3150	113	1991	153
2–2:30	2321	57	2012	72	1282	99
2:30–3	1935	47	1960	70	1206	93
3–3:30	2151	52	2064	74	1250	96
3:30–4	2115	52	2238	80	1328	102
4–4:30	2291	55	2340	84	1346	104
4:30–5	2054	50	2191	78	1216	93
5–5:30	1598	39	1763	63	924	71

Total normal days = 41, total peak days = 28, total super-peak days = 13.

*The total number of arrivals is divided by the number of days to arrive at the average arrival rate.

ferent times of the day, the data in Exhibit 4 were collected. Over the period between November 1, 1986, and February 28, 1987, arrivals were counted for each half-hour period. The days were then divided into normal days, peak days, and super-peak days, depending on the intensity of the flow. Although the average number of arrivals varied during each hour of the day, the statistical pattern of arrivals was stable during each particular hour.

In order to arrive at a decision, Mr. Craig requested an analysis of the single- and multiple-line teller arrangements. For a given number of tellers, Mr. Craig wanted to know which arrangement provided the best customer service. He also specified that the analysis should include a calculation of the number of tellers required at various times of the day, so that a teller staffing plan could be devised.

In addition to the statistical analysis, Mr. Craig wondered what the customer reaction to the single-line or double-line arrangement might be. Would the appearance of a long single line drive customers away, or would the customers perceive fast service from the rapidly moving line? Mr. Craig also wondered what the other advantages and disadvantages of a single line relative to the multiple lines might be.

DISCUSSION QUESTIONS

1. Which alternative arrangement of teller lines should Mr. Craig select? Support your recommendation with appropriate analysis and consideration of customer reaction.
2. For the alternative you recommend, develop appropriate staffing levels for each hour of the day.
3. Should other alternatives, not described in the case, be considered?

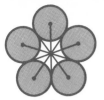

Commonwealth Ice Cream Company

The Commonwealth Ice Cream Company manufactures and distributes ice cream in the state of Virginia.[1] At the present time the company owns four ice cream plants located at Alexandria, Norfolk, Roanoke, and Richmond. These plants are used to manufacture and distribute ice cream throughout the state on a daily basis.

Due to the high rate of population growth in the Washington, D.C. area, the company is considering building a new plant at Arlington, Virginia. If the new plant were built, one or more of the existing plants might be phased out, depending on the economics of the situation and future demand levels.

The four plants distribute ice cream to six marketing areas, as shown in Exhibit 1. While each plant currently distributes to its own marketing area, this practice is not required. Any plant can distribute ice cream to any marketing area in the state.

The capacity of each plant and the costs of production are shown in Exhibit 2. As indicated, the costs of production vary from one location to another due to different labor costs, different costs of materials, and different plant efficiencies. If the new plant is built in Arlington, it will have a capacity of 1200 cwt (hundredweight, or 100 pounds) per day and a cost of production of $21 per cwt.

The current distribution plan is shown in Exhibit 3, along with the projected market demands for 5 years into the future. Demand in each market area with the exception of Danville and Alexandria is expected to increase by about 20 percent. Demand in the Danville area is expected to remain constant,

---

EXHIBIT 1 Marketing areas and plant locations.

while demand in the Alexandria area is expected to increase by 50 percent.

The shipping costs between each plant and each marketing area are shown in Exhibit 4. These costs vary because of the distances involved and the mode of transportation used. Projected shipping costs for the new plant at Arlington are also shown in Exhibit 4.

If the new plant is built at Arlington, it will cost $2 million to construct, and the plant will have approximately a 20-year lifetime. The company would utilize the new Arlington plant and existing plants, which would be kept open, for approximately 300 days each year.

EXHIBIT 2
PLANT DATA

Plant	Plant capacity cwt per day	Production cost per cwt
Alexandria	1000	$25
Richmond	800	23
Norfolk	800	21
Roanoke	500	22
Total	3100	

[1]This case was prepared as a basis for class discussion, not to illustrate either effective or ineffective handling of an administrative situation.

EXHIBIT 3
MARKET DATA

Market	Current demand cwt/day	5-year demand cwt/day	Currently served by plant at
Alexandria	500	750	Alexandria
Charlottesville	200	240	Alexandria
Roanoke	300	360	Roanoke
Danville	150	150	Roanoke
Richmond	600	720	Richmond
Norfolk	500	600	Norfolk
Total	2250	2820	

EXHIBIT 4
TRANSPORTATION COSTS ($ per cwt)

Market	Alexandria	Richmond	Norfolk	Roanoke	Arlington
Alexandria	$2.50	$3.80	$5.20	$4.60	$2.60
Charlottesville	3.40	3.20	4.10	3.10	3.50
Roanoke	4.60	3.10	3.80	2.90	4.70
Danville	5.20	2.90	3.10	3.30	5.10
Richmond	3.80	2.80	2.90	3.10	3.70
Norfolk	4.60	2.90	2.60	4.40	4.50

EXHIBIT 5
PLANT SALVAGE VALUES

Plant	Age in years	Salvage in $000
Alexandria	23	450
Richmond	15	600
Norfolk	9	800
Roanoke	4	400

The Arlington plant, if built, could be brought on-line in 1 year. In order to justify building the plant, Commonwealth Ice Cream expects to earn at least 10 percent real return on its investment after tax. Corporate taxes are 35 percent of pretax net income. The new plant can be depreciated over a 20-year period on a straight-line basis.

The ages of existing plants and their salvage values if they were shut down are shown in Exhibit 5. The salvage values assume the existing buildings and equipment can be sold off to the highest bidder.

The company would also like to know what the effect would be of expanding existing plants, rather than building the Arlington plant. You may assume that any plant can be expanded at its current

cost of production per hundred weight. The company would like to know how much expansion might be desirable at each location and the amount of investment that could be justified by expansion at each existing site.

DISCUSSION QUESTIONS

1. Should the new ice cream plant be built at Arlington, Virginia?
2. What other actions should the company take?
3. What assumptions are required in your answer to Question 1?
4. What risks are there in building the new plant now?

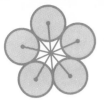

Lawn King, Inc.

John Conner, marketing manager for Lawn King, looked over the beautiful countryside as he drove to the corporate headquarters in Moline, Ill.[1] John had asked his boss, Kathy Wayne, the general manager of Lawn King, to call a meeting in order to review the latest forecast figures for fiscal year 1989.[2] When he arrived at the plant, the meeting was ready to begin. Others in attendance at the meeting were James Fairday, plant manager; Joan Peterson, controller; and Harold Pinter, personnel officer.

John started the meeting by reviewing the latest situation. "I've just returned from our annual sales meeting and I think we lost more sales last year than we thought, due to back-order conditions at the factory. We have also reviewed the forecast for next year and feel that sales will be 110,000 units in fiscal year 1989. The marketing department feels this forecast is realistic and could be exceeded if all goes well."

At this point, James Fairday interrupted by saying, "John, you've got to be kidding. Just three months ago we all sat in this same room and you predicted sales of 98,000 units for fiscal '89. Now you've raised the forecast by 12 percent. How can we do a reasonable job of production planning when we have a moving target to shoot at?"

Kathy interjected, "Jim, I appreciate your concern, but we have to be responsive to changing market conditions. Here we are in September and we still haven't got a firm plan for fiscal '89, which has just started. I want to use the new forecast and develop an aggregate plan for next year as soon as possible."

John added, "We've been talking to our best customers and they're complaining about back orders during the peak selling season. A few have threatened to drop our product line if they don't get better service next year. We have to produce not only enough product but also the right models to service the customer."

MANUFACTURING PROCESS

Lawn King is a medium-sized producer of lawn-mower equipment. Last year, sales were $14.5 million and pretax profits were $2 million, as shown in Exhibit 1. The company makes four lines of lawn mowers: an 18-inch push mower, a 20-inch push mower, a 20-inch self-propelled mower, and a 22-inch deluxe self-propelled mower. All these mowers are made on the same assembly line. During the year, the line is changed over from one mower to the next to meet the actual and projected demand.

The changeover cost of the production line depends on which type of mower is being pro-

---

[1]This case was prepared as a basis for class discussion, not to illustrate either effective or ineffective handling of an administrative situation.

[2]The Lawn King 1989 fiscal year runs from September 1, 1988 to August 31, 1989.

EXHIBIT 1
PROFIT AND LOSS STATEMENT ($000)

	FY87	FY88
Sales	$11,611	$14,462
Cost of goods sold		
Materials	6,340	8,005
Direct labor	2,100	2,595
Depreciation	743	962
Overhead	256	431
Total CGS	9,439	11,993
G & A expense	270	314
Selling expense	140	197
Total expenses	9,849	12,504
Pretax profit	1,762	1,958

EXHIBIT 2
LINE CHANGEOVER COST MATRIX

		Changed to			
		18"	20"	20" SP*	22" SP*
	18"	—	$2000	$2000	$2500
Changed from	20"	$2000	—	$500	$1500
	20" SP	$2000	$500	—	—
	22" SP	$2500	$1500	$1500	—

*SP denotes "self-propelled." Changeover cost includes the wages of the work force used to adjust the assembly line from one model configuration to another.

duced and the next production model planned. For example, it is relatively easy to change over from the 20-inch push mower to the 20-inch self-propelled mower, since the mower frame is the same. The self-propelled mower has a propulsion unit added and a slightly larger engine. The company estimated the changeover costs as shown in Exhibit 2.

Lawn King fabricates the metal frames and metal parts for their lawn mowers in their own machine shop. These fabricated parts are sent to the assembly line along with parts purchased directly from vendors. In the past year, approximately $8 million in parts and supplies were purchased, including engines, bolts, paint, wheels, and sheet steel. An inventory of $1 million in purchased parts is held to supply the machine shop and the assembly line. When a particular mower is running on the assembly line, only a few days of parts are kept at the plant, since supplies are constantly coming into the factory.

A total of 100 employees work at the main plant in Moline, Ill. These employees include 60 workers on the assembly line, 25 workers in the machine shop, 10 maintenance workers, and 5 office staff. A beginning assembly-line worker is paid $7.15 per hour plus $2.90 an hour in benefits. Senior maintenance and machine-shop employees earn as much as $14 per hour.

It generally takes about 2 weeks for a new employee to reach full productivity on the assembly line. After 3 months, an employee can request rotation to other jobs on the line if job variety is desired. At least some of the workers find the work quite repetitive and boring.

The plant is unionized, but relations between the union and the company have always been good. Nevertheless, employee turnover has been high. In the past year, approximately 50 percent of the employees left the company, representing a total training cost of $42,000 for the year. There is also considerable absenteeism, especially on Mondays and Fridays, causing production disruptions. To handle this situation, six "fillers" are kept on the work force to fill in for people who are absent on a given day. These fillers also help train the new employees when they are not needed for direct production work.

PRODUCTION PLANNING

The actual sales and forecasts are shown in Exhibit 3. Not only are the sales highly seasonal, but total

EXHIBIT 3
SALES DATA IN UNITS

	FY87 forecast	FY87 actual	FY88 forecast	FY88 actual	Latest FY89 forecast
18"	30,000	25,300	23,000	22,300	24,000
20"	11,900	15,680	20,300	23,500	35,500
20" SP	15,600	14,200	20,400	21,200	31,500
22" SP	10,500	14,320	21,300	17,600	19,000
Total	68,000	69,500	85,000	84,600	110,000

		18"	20"	20" SP	22" SP	Overtime hours
Beginning inventory		4,120	3,140	6,250	3,100	
Sept. 88	Production	3,000	3,100	–	–	–
	Sales	210	400	180	110	
Oct. 88	Production	–	–	3,400	3,500	–
	Sales	600	510	500	300	
Nov. 88	Production	3,000	3,800	–	–	–
	Sales	1,010	970	860	785	
Dec. 88	Production	–	–	4,400	3,750	1000
	Sales	1,200	1,420	1,030	930	
Jan. 88	Production	4,000	4,100			1500
	Sales	1,430	1,680	1,120	1,120	
Feb. 88	Production	–	–	4,400	3,500	1620
	Sales	2,140	2,210	2,180	1,850	
Mar. 88	Production	3,000	3,000	2,000	–	1240
	Sales	4,870	5,100	4,560	3,210	
Apr. 88	Production	–	–	2,000	4,500	–
	Sales	5,120	4,850	5,130	3,875	
May 88	Production	3,000	2,000	2,000	–	–
	Sales	-3,210	3,310	2,980	2,650	
June 88	Production	1,000		2,000	3,000	–
	Sales	1,400	1,500	1,320	800	
July 88	Production	2,000	3,000	2,000		–
	Sales	710	950	680	1,010	
Aug. 88	Production	2,000	2,000		2,000	–
	Sales	400	600	660	960	
Total FY 88	Production	21,000	21,000	22,200	20,250	
	Sales	22,300	23,500	21,200	17,600	
End inventory (8/31/88)		2,820	640	7,250	5,750	
Nominal production rate/day*		420	400	350	300	

EXHIBIT 4 Units of production and sales, fiscal year 1988. An asterisk (*) indicates the standard rate of production.

sales are dependent on the weather. If the weather is good in early spring, customers will be more inclined to buy a new mower. A good grass-growing season also encourages sales during the summer.

It appears that customers are more likely to buy the high-priced self-propelled mowers in good economic times. In recessionary periods, the bottom-of-the-line 18-inch mower does better.

The production strategy in current use might be described as a one-shift level-work-force strategy with overtime used as needed. The work force is not always exactly level due to turnover and short-run production requirements. Nevertheless, the policy is to keep the work force as level as possible. Overtime is used when the regular work force cannot meet production requirements.[3]

The actual monthly production output and sales for fiscal year 1988 are shown in Exhibit 4. Differences between sales and production were absorbed by the inventory. If stockouts occurred, the order was backlogged and filled from the next available

---

[3]Overtime work is paid at 150 percent of regular time.

production run. Lawn King utilized a 30 percent carrying cost per year for inventory.[4]

Each June, an aggregate production plan is prepared for the upcoming fiscal year. The plan shows the level of production for each model type and month of the year. The aggregate plan is used for personnel planning, inventory planning, and budget preparation. Each month during the year, the plan is revised on the basis of the latest conditions and data.

BACK TO THE MEETING

The meeting continued with Joan Peterson saying, "We must find a way to reduce our costs. Last year we carried too much inventory, which required a great deal of capital. At 30 percent carrying cost, we cannot afford to build up as much inventory again next year."

Harold Pinter added, "If we reduce our inventories by more nearly chasing demand, the labor force will fluctuate from month to month and our hiring and layoff costs will increase. It currently costs $800 to hire an employee, including the lower productivity on the line during the training period and the effort required to find new employees. I also believe it costs $1500 to layoff an

[4]This cost includes capital costs (20 percent), obsolescence (5 percent), and warehouse costs (5 percent).

employee, including the severance costs and supplemental unemployment benefits that we pay."

James Fairday expressed concern that a new shift might have to be added to accommodate the higher forecast. "We are already at plant capacity, and the additional units in the new forecast can't be made with one shift. I want to be sure these sales forecasts are realistic before we go through the trouble of hiring an entire second shift."

Lunchtime had arrived and the meeting was drawing to a close. Kathy Wayne emphasized that she wanted a new production plan developed soon. "Jim, I want you to develop an aggregate production plan that considers the costs of inventory, overtime, hiring, and layoff. If your plan results in back orders, we will have to incur greater costs later in the year to meet demand. I will not allow the same stockout situation that we experienced last year." The meeting adjourned for lunch.

DISCUSSION QUESTIONS

1. Develop a forecast to use as a basis for aggregate production planning.
2. Develop an aggregate production plan by month for fiscal '89. Consider the use of several different production strategies. Which strategy do you recommend?
3. (Optional Assignment) Use linear programming to solve for the lowest-cost strategy.

World Industrial Abrasives

The World Industrial Abrasives Company produces grit used in the manufacture of sandpaper and other products.[1] The production process starts with either aluminum oxide or silicon carbide as primary raw material, which is shipped to the company's crushing plant in railroad cars. The raw material passes through a series of crusher rollers, a furnace treatment, and screening operations to produce the finished grit in the desired sizes and shapes. The resulting grit can be glued to backing materials to form sandpaper and other abrasive products.

THE PRODUCTION PROCESS

A schematic representation of the grit production process is shown in Exhibit 1. Crude mineral is fed into a primary crush operation which produces a

---

[1]This case was prepared as a basis for class discussion, not to illustrate either effective or ineffective handling of an administrative situation.

pea-sized grit referred to as "5 and Finer." Three pairs of secondary crushing rolls are available for processing the 5-and-Finer grit size; one pair is dedicated to aluminum oxide, another to silicon carbide, and the third pair may be used for crushing either mineral. Several different operations or machine settings can be utilized for crushing the 5-and-Finer grit size. Each secondary crushing operation normally produces three ranges of grit sizes, called splits, and a miscellaneous grit output. Because crushing operations cannot produce single grits, overproduction of some grits is often unavoidable.

Output from secondary crushing operations is normally heat-treated, giving the mineral the proper characteristics required for adherence to the backing. The capacity of this furnace treatment operation is the primary constraint on system throughput time.

Eight screening machines, each having several setups, are available for separating the furnace-treated splits into individual grits. It is the combi-

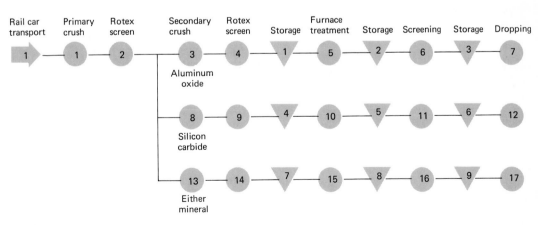

EXHIBIT 1   Grit-crushing system-flow-process diagram.

nation of secondary crushing and screening operations which determines the relative yield for each grit. A final sifting step, known as "dropping," purifies the individual grits. Approximately 10 percent of the input into the dropping operation is rejected because it is outside the quality tolerance range.

The buildup of both in-process and finished-grit inventories is an unavoidable consequence of the manufacturing process. The in-process inventory is necessary to decouple the various stages of production. The excessive finished-grit inventories are the result of the characteristics of the crushing operations, wherein single grits cannot be selectively produced. Storage of these excessive inventories represents another constraint on production. The limitations of on-site storage capacity require transportation of some mineral to a remote storage location at considerably greater cost.

A second unavoidable result of the production process is the recrushing of approximately 20 percent of the previously crushed mineral. Specific secondary crushing operations are dedicated to this function. The additional expense of these operations requires that original crushing and screening operations be chosen to minimize the need for recrushing.

Additionally, the difficulty of meeting the requirements exactly often results in the need to purchase finished, graded grit from outside suppliers at a premium price. This, combined with the problems of excess inventory and recrushing, requires the scheduler to make tradeoff decisions. Recognition of the costs associated with each tradeoff decision facilitates development of a production plan to minimize total costs.

PRODUCTION SCHEDULING

Each week a printout specifying the amounts of each grit size required is given to the production scheduler. These requirements are generated by an MRP program considering final demand, inventory available, and production lead time. The scheduler's job is to determine the amount of input (silicon dioxide and aluminum oxide) and the best crushing and screening operations to be used to produce the required amounts of each grit size.

In most cases, all requirements cannot be satisfied, but the scheduler attempts to come as close as possible to the required amounts of each grit size.

The development of a schedule for crushing and screening operations begins with the determination of net requirements by grit type. The scheduler analyzes the MRP requirements for an 8-week period, with primary emphasis placed on the next 4 weeks.

After reviewing the requirements, the scheduler selects a particular combination of crushes and screens and an input weight of silicon dioxide or aluminum oxide material. For these conditions the output of the production process is calculated. Performing the large number of calculations is a long and tedious process. The historical percentage outputs from each crushing and screening operation are obtained from a series of tables and used to predict the yields of the individual grits. Next, these yields must be compared with the requirements. If the yields do not compare favorably, the entire calculating process must be repeated using an alternative combination of crushes and screens. Because of the time involved in performing the calculations, only a limited number of alternatives can be considered. Therefore, experienced personnel are required to select the preferred combinations in a few trials. All together, there are 19 different crushing settings, 19 different primary screening operations, and 4 secondary screening operations which might be selected by the scheduler.

THE PROBLEM

In assessing the situation, Judy Samson, a systems analyst in the manufacturing department, felt that the situation could be improved by use of an interactive computer program. The proposed system would assist the scheduler in evaluating crushing and screening options. If an optimal solution could be identified, that would be desirable, but optimality was not required by the scheduling department. The objective of the scheduling department was to meet the requirements for crushed mineral at a reasonably low cost.

DISCUSSION QUESTIONS

1. Develop a detailed flowchart which replicates the manual method currently used by the scheduler.
2. Evaluate the advisability of using linear programming, simulation, heuristic rules, or the present scheduling method to solve this problem.
3. Develop a conceptual model to solve this problem. Specify the inputs, outputs, and computational algorithm you would use.

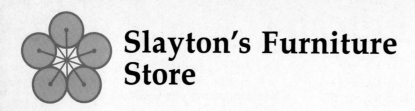

Slayton's Furniture Store

Slayton's Furniture Store is an upscale furniture store located near Lake Michigan in downtown Chicago.[1] The store generally carries medium- to high-price furniture in famous lines such as Drexel, Henredon, and Ethan Allen. In order to keep up with the latest trends, about 50 percent of the styles and fabrics change each year.

Joan Jeffery, furniture buyer for Slayton's, received a call from Eric Townsend, the Drexel Furniture sales representative. Eric began, "Joan, I can give you a better deal on our standard Dovetail bedroom furniture set if you buy a larger quantity. We have just received a new rate from our trucking firm which reduces the shipping cost from $10 per cwt (hundredweight, or 100 pounds) to $9 per cwt provided we ship a minimum of 100 cwt. This would require you to order at least 10 bedroom sets at a time instead of your current order size of 6 sets. If you order 10 at a time, we will pass along the freight savings to you: a saving of $10 a set just on freight alone. What do you think of the deal?"

Upon hearing the offer, Joan replied, "Eric, it sounds good, but I will have to do some checking and a little pencil pushing before I can decide what to do." Joan added, "Would there be a further economy if we ordered 15 sets at a time?" Excited by the prospects of more business, Eric responded, "The freight company would not reduce its price further, but we could give you a 2 percent price discount ($12 a set) if you order 15 sets or more. Why don't you think it over and I'll call you back next week to get your decision."

As Joan hung up the phone, she wondered what to do. There was room in the warehouse to store up to 15 bedroom sets, but there would be an opportunity cost, since the space would not be available

EXHIBIT 1
DOVETAIL BEDROOM SET

Selling price (each)	$1000.00
Unit cost (each)*	$600.00
Average annual sales	80 sets
Ordering cost†	$40 per order
Annual carrying cost‡	30%
Safety stock	2 sets
Weight per set	1000 lb
Lead time (average)	4 weeks

*Excludes freight cost.

†This cost includes receiving ($20 per order) and paperwork ($20 per order).

‡This cost includes the cost of capital (15%), insurance (3%), warehouse space (5%), and obsolescence (7%).

for other merchandise. Also, interest rates had been soaring in recent months, and the additional capital would be costly to obtain. Joan decided to work through the problem using available economic data for the product (see Exhibit 1).

Obsolescence was a significant factor in Joan's mind. While the annual carrying cost included 7 percent for obsolescence, she wondered if this were enough. Also, is the obsolescence factor included in the carrying cost the proper way to incorporate the risk of future markdowns required to sell slow-moving or out-of-style furniture?

DISCUSSION QUESTIONS

1. What should Joan do?
2. What assumptions are implicit in your analysis of the situation?

---

[1] This case was prepared as a basis for class discussion, not to illustrate either effective or ineffective handling of an administrative situation.

Consolidated Electric

Joe Henry, the sole owner and president of the Consolidated Electric Company, reflected on his inventory management problems.[1] He was a major wholesale supplier of equipment and supplies to electrical contractors, and his business hinged on the efficient management of inventories to meet his customers' needs. While Mr. Henry had built a very successful business, he was nearing retirement age and wanted to pass along a good inventory management system.

Mr. Henry's two sons-in-law were employed in the company. Carl Byerly, the older of the two, had a college degree in mathematics and was very interested in inventory formulas and computers. The other son-in-law, Edward Wright, had a degree in biology and was manager of one of the company's wholesale warehouses.

Joe Henry started the Consolidated Electric Company in the 1940s and built it into a highly profitable business. In 1987, the company had achieved $10 million dollars in sales and earned $1 million dollars in pretax profits. Consolidated Electric was currently the twelfth largest electrical wholesaler in the country.

Consolidated Electric operates through four warehouses in Iowa (Des Moines, Cedar Rapids, Sioux City, and Davenport). From these sites contractors in Iowa, Minnesota, Nebraska, Wisconsin, Illinois, and Missouri are supplied with a wide range of electrical equipment including wire, electrical boxes, connectors, lighting fixtures, and electrical controllers. The company stocks 20,000 separate line items in its inventory purchased from 200 different manufacturers. (A line item is defined as a particular item carried at a particular location.)

These items range from less than 1 cent each to several hundred dollars for the largest electrical controllers.

Of the 20,000 line items, a great many are carried to provide a full line of service. For example, the top 2000 items account for 50 percent of the sales and the bottom 10,000 items for only 20 percent. The remaining 8000 items account for 30 percent of the sales.

The company has continually purged its 20,000 inventory items to carry only those which are demanded at least once a year. As Mr. Henry says, "We live and die by good customer service at a reasonable selling price. If we do not meet this objective, the customer will go to another wholesaler or buy directly from the manufacturer."

Mr. Henry explained that he currently managed inventory by using an "earn and turn" concept. According to this concept, the earnings margin multiplied by the inventory turn ratio must equal a constant value of 2.0. For example, if a particular electrical item costs $6 to purchase wholesale and is sold for $10, then the earnings margin is $4 and the earn ratio for this item is $4/$10 = .40. If this item has a turn ratio of 5 times a year (sales is 5 times the average inventory carried), then the product of earn and turn is .4(5) = 2.0. If another item earns more, it can turn slower; if it earns less, it must turn faster.

Each year, Mr. Henry sets a target earn-turn ratio for the entire business and a value for each product line. These targets are based on the estimated costs of operations and the return-on-investment goal for the company. As stated above, the current target ratio for the business is 2.0. The purchasing agents and inventory managers at each location are measured by their ability to meet the target earn-turn ratios on their product lines. The actual ratios are reported monthly.

---

[1]This case was prepared as a basis for class discussion, not to illustrate either effective or ineffective handling of an administrative situation.

Although earn-turn ratios work quite well in controlling profitability of the business and entire product lines, they do not work very well for individual inventory items. Some line items tend to be in excess supply, while others are often out of stock.

The inventory is currently managed by use of a Cardex system. A card for each item is kept in a large file and a clerk posts transactions on the card as units are received or issued, thus keeping a running on-hand inventory balance. Periodically, a purchasing agent reviews the cards for a particular supplier. Then, using the order point and quantity printed on the card, the purchasing agent places an order for all items which are below their reorder point.

If the total quantities of all items required from a supplier do not meet the purchase discount minimums or a truckload lot, additional items near their reorder points are added to the order. This is not done when the total order size is too far from the minimums, since excessive inventories would build up.

The order quantity and reorder point printed on each card are based on judgment and past experience. Generally speaking, a 3-month supply is ordered for low-cost items and as little as a 1-month supply for expensive items. Most lines are reviewed on a weekly basis.

Over the past 2 years, Consolidated Electric had been converting its inventory records to the computer. At the present time, an on-hand balance is maintained on the computer and an accurate history of all orders placed, receipts, and issues is kept. A demand history for a typical item is shown in Appendix 1 on the next page.

Mr. Henry was anxious to automate the calculation of reorder points and order quantities, but he was unsure of the exact formulas to use. Using standard textbooks in the inventory field, Mr. Henry and Carl Byerly developed the formulas given in Exhibit 1. The EOQ formula utilizes a carrying cost of 28 percent and an ordering cost of $4.36 per order placed. These figures were based on past cost history at the company.

EXHIBIT 1

Delivery delay
$$= \frac{\text{maximum lead time} - \text{average lead time}}{\text{average lead time}}$$

Safety allowance
$$= \text{usage} \times \text{average lead time} \times .8 \times \text{delivery delay}$$

Order point
$$= \text{usage} \times \text{average lead time} + \text{safety allowance}$$

$$\text{EOQ} = \sqrt{\frac{2 \times 4.36 \times \text{daily usage} \times 365}{.28 \times \text{unit cost}}}$$

$$\text{Line point} = \text{daily usage} \times 7 + \text{order point}$$

Quantity to order = (order point) − (quantity on order)
− (quantity on hand)
+ quantity allocated + EOQ

Note: The line point is used to generate orders for all items in a line which are within 1 week of their order points. These orders may be used to meet truckload minimums or purchase discount minimums.

The formulas were programmed into the computer and tested on a pilot basis. For some items, the formulas seemed to work quite well, but for others they resulted in drastic departures from current practice and from common sense. For example, on one electrical box, the formulas would have ordered a 2-year supply. Mr. Henry wanted to get the new computerized system up as soon as possible, but he was not sure that the formulas would work properly. He wondered whether the formulas would meet the customer-service objectives of the business. Would they take advantage of truckload lots or purchase discounts whenever appropriate, and would the formulas result in reasonable inventory levels?

DISCUSSION QUESTIONS

1. Design an inventory control system for this business.

2. Describe how the system you have designed will help the company meet customer-service and cost objectives.

```
PRINT1                                    AUDIT TRAIL
     VENDOR- ABMU   CATALOG NO.- 700N200A1              BRANCH- Des Moines
 RECORD   CUSTOMER TICKET                      U
  TYPE     NUMBER  NUMBER   QUANTITY    DATE    N      COST      SELL
 SALES   12000-00 730606-0      1     8/10/87   E     16.32     21.60
 SALES   19461-00 729425-0     60     8/02/87   E     16.32     18.72
 SALES   22315-00 695421-0     65     7/31/87   E     16.32     18.72
 SALES   34515-00 728883-0      2     7/30/87   E     16.32     21.60
 SALES   02691-00 723670-0      1     7/24/87   E     16.32     21.60
 SALES   02145-00 723482-0      1     7/23/87   E     16.32     21.60
 SALES   81666-00 729920-0      8     7/23/87   E     16.32     18.72
 SALES   92535-00 722026-0      4     7/20/87   E     16.32     21.60
 SALES   81666-00 722637-0      6     7/16/87   E     16.32     18.72
 SALES   01209-00 722413-0      7     7/13/87   E     16.32     18.72
 SALES   81666-00 722409-0      8     7/13/87   E     16.32     18.72
 SALES   23556-00 722001-0      1     7/13/87   E     16.32     21.60
 SALES   51616-00 722418-0      3     7/11/87   E     16.32     21.60
 SALES   81666-00 722408-0      6     7/11/87   E     16.32     18.72
 SALES   26535-00 721861-0     20     7/11/87   E     16.32     18.72
PRINT1 S0015643                           AUDIT TRAIL
     VENDOR- ABMU   CATALOG NO.- 700N200A1              BRANCH- Des Moines
 RECORD   CUSTOMER TICKET                      U
  TYPE     NUMBER  NUMBER   QUANTITY    DATE    N      COST      SELL
 SALES   86190-00 721088-0      1     7/11/87   E     16.32     21.60
 SALES   18954-00 722080-0      4     7/10/87   E     16.32     18.72
 SALES   32550-00 698856-0      1     7/06/87   E     16.32     21.60
 SALES   53726-00 722205-0      4     7/05/87   E     16.32     18.72
 SALES   80925-02 721015-0      4     7/03/87   E     16.32     24.00
 SALES   39132-00 721235-0      6     7/02/87   E     16.32     21.60
 SALES   22315-00 695420-0     65     6/27/87   E     16.32     18.72
 SALES   15951-00 713019-0      5     6/26/87   E     16.32     18.72
 SALES   77137-00 712992-0      6     6/26/87   E     16.32     21.60
 SALES   14468-00 713269-0      2     6/25/87   E     16.32     21.60
 SALES   63180-00 701603-0     15     6/22/87   E     16.32     18.72
 SALES   12000-00 709765-0      2     6/15/87   E     16.32     21.60
 SALES   32550-00 709795-0      2     6/14/87   E     16.32     21.60
 SALES   29058-00 710405-0      1     6/13/87   E     16.32     21.60
 SALES   17862-00 710524-0      1     6/12/87   E     16.32     18.72
PRINT1 S0015626                           AUDIT TRAIL
     VENDOR- ABMU   CATALOG NO.- 700N200A1              BRANCH- Des Moines
 RECORD   CUSTOMER TICKET                      U
  TYPE     NUMBER  NUMBER   QUANTITY    DATE    N      COST      SELL
 SALES   81666-00 699732-0      6     6/12/87   E     16.32     18.72
 SALES   26535-00 710223-0     40     6/11/87   E     16.32     18.72
 SALES   34515-00 710679-0      1     6/04/87   E     16.32     21.60
 SALES   99940-00 710659-0      1     5/30/87   E     16.32     16.32
 SALES   15951-00 699254-0      5     5/29/87   E     16.32     18.72
 SALES   69576-00 710367-0      1     5/25/87   E     16.32     24.00
 SALES   15951-00 695114-0      1     5/25/87   E     16.32     18.72
 SALES   22315-00 695419-0     65     5/21/87   E     16.32     18.72
 SALES   12051-00 701595-0      2     5/18/87   E     16.32     21.60
 SALES   20631-00 701454-0      1     5/16/87   E     16.32     18.72
 SALES   40315-00 701018-0     20     5/14/87   E     16.32     18.72
 SALES   12051-00 700314-0     34     5/07/87   E     16.32     18.72
 SALES   39132-00 700208-0      2     5/04/87   E     16.32     21.60
 SALES   40315-00 691238-0     10     5/04/87   E     16.32     18.72
 SALES   74607-02 699132-0      2     4/30/87   E     16.32     18.72
PRINT1 S0015607                           AUDIT TRAIL
     VENDOR- ABMU   CATALOG NO.- 700N200A1              BRANCH- Des Moines
 RECORD   CUSTOMER TICKET                      U
  TYPE     NUMBER  NUMBER   QUANTITY    DATE    N      COST      SELL
 SALES   22315-00 689584-0     65     4/26/87   E     16.32     18.72
 SALES   99999-00 698384-0      1     4/20/87   E     16.32     21.60
 SALES   39132-00 695746-0      2     4/19/87   E     16.32     21.60
 SALES   34515-00 695597-0      1     4/17/87   E     16.32     21.60
 SALES   99999-00 695286-0      1     4/13/87   E     16.32     24.00
 SALES   39132-00 695198-0      3     4/13/87   E     16.32     21.60
 SALES   12000-00 694933-0      2     4/13/87   E     16.32     21.60
 SALES   36348-00 694138-0      2     4/11/87   E     16.32     18.72
 SALES   99940-00 694352-0     12     4/10/87   E     16.32     16.32
 SALES   40315-00 694047-0     25     4/06/87   E     15.36     17.52
 SALES   19760-00 691495-0      5     4/04/87   E     15.36     20.16
 SALES   17862-00 691365-0      5     4/04/87   E     15.36     17.52
 SALES   17862-00 691364-0     20     4/04/87   E     15.36     17.52
 SALES   34515-00 691409-0      1     4/03/87   E     15.36     20.16
 SALES   83226-00 691303-0      5     4/03/87   E     15.36     20.16
PRINT1 S0015588                           AUDIT TRAIL
     VENDOR- ABMU   CATALOG NO.- 700N200A1              BRANCH- Des Moines
 RECORD   CUSTOMER TICKET                      U
  TYPE     NUMBER  NUMBER   QUANTITY    DATE    N      COST      SELL
 SALES   14966-00 691504-0      2     4/02/87   E     15.36     20.16
 SALES   74607-02 689937-0      5     3/29/87   E     15.36     17.52
 SALES   34515-00 690284-0      4     3/28/87   E     15.36     20.16
 SALES   21333-00 690394-0      1     3/27/87   E     15.36     20.16
 SALES   01209-00 689985-0      1     3/23/87   E     15.36     17.52
 SALES   86190-00 690018-0      2     3/21/87   E     15.36     20.16
 SALES   02535-00 689959-0      2     3/20/87   E     15.36     20.16
 SALES   32550-00 670521-0      3     3/16/87   E     15.36     20.16
 SALES   17862-00 683189-0      1     3/14/87   E     15.36     17.52
 SALES   21333-00 683910-0      2     2/27/87   E     15.36     20.16
 SALES   48477-00 682354-0     10     2/26/87   E     15.36     17.52
 SALES   18954-00 682573-0      4     2/23/87   E     15.36     17.52
 SALES   19461-00 682104-0     50     2/22/87   E     15.36     17.52
 SALES   61842-00 681738-0      1     2/20/87   E     15.36     23.28
 SALES   74607-02 678243-0     12     2/20/87   E     15.36     17.52
PRINT1 S0015573                           AUDIT TRAIL
     VENDOR- ABMU   CATALOG NO.- 700N200A1              BRANCH- Des Moines
 RECORD   CUSTOMER TICKET                      U
  TYPE     NUMBER  NUMBER   QUANTITY    DATE    N      COST      SELL
 SALES   74607-02 678239-0      7     2/20/87   E     15.36     17.52
 SALES   74607-02 681673-0      5     2/19/87   E     15.36     17.52
 SALES   02535-00 681458-0      2     2/13/87   E     15.36     20.16
 SALES   63180-00 678329-0     12     2/12/87   E     15.36     17.52
 SALES   99899-00 678168-0      1     2/07/87   E     15.36     23.28
 SALES   99940-00 677897-0      1     2/02/87   E     15.36     15.36
 SALES   40315-00 677869-0      8     2/02/87   E     15.36     17.52
 SALES   79638-00 675976-0      4     2/01/87   E     15.36     17.52
 SALES   19461-00 668836-0     10     1/30/87   E     15.36     17.52
 SALES   39132-00 675497-0      1     1/26/87   E     15.36     20.16
 SALES   72650-00 679401-0     25     1/24/87   E     15.36     17.52
 SALES   39132-00 675474-0     10     1/23/87   E     15.36     20.16
 SALES   15951-00 656856-0      2     1/15/87   E     15.36     17.52
 SALES   22315-00 646309-0    100     1/15/87   E     15.36     17.52
 SALES   64974-00 669143-0      2     1/12/87   E     15.36     17.52
PRINT1 S                    ITEM INVENTORY FILE        Des Moines
  VEND CATALOG NO.     DESCRIPTION              INV/CLS   CARRIED IN
  ABMU 700N200A1    700N200A1 CONTROL RELAY        A          S
     QTY. ON     QTY. ON       QTY      ORDER                LEAD
     HAND        ORDER      ALLOCATED   POINT    E.O.Q.      TIME
     371         200           0         38       453     1   11
                                                          2   10
                                                          3   15
                                                         MAX  20

  QTY. SOLD     JUNE       MAY      APRIL     MARCH
  BY MONTH      121        154       76       293
  QTY. SOLD   JAN-MAR    OCT-DEC   JUL-SEP   APR-JUN
  BY QUARTER    356        292      505       201
```

APPENDIX 1
Demand history
for a typical item.

733

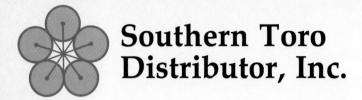

Southern Toro Distributor, Inc.

The following conversation was held between Joe Melaney, general manager and owner of the Toro distributorship in Galveston, Texas, and his son Joe Jr.:[1]

Joe: I called you in this morning to discuss the future of the company. I feel that you should be involved in more of the decision making around here because you will be taking over the company soon. Roger Kirk, the district sales manager from Toro, will be contacting us next week for our spring season order. We will need to order for the entire irrigation line at that time. (See Exhibit 1.)

As you know, we have been undergoing a number of changes around the office. One of our major changes was acquiring the IBM System 34. A computer run I received this morning combined with the upcoming order date started me thinking about the figures from the new computer. I was thinking back on the circumstances that led up to the purchase of the computer a year ago in October 1987. With the way costs were skyrocketing I had to cut down on my inventory without cutting service. The IBM representative said he could cut our inventory level by 30 percent, which sounded good enough for me. So I contracted with IBM for a System 34.

Max, our irrigation manager, swears by the numbers he gets out for order quantities. When this package was put into our computer, they (IBM reps) said it was designed for me, but I'm not sure that I can trust it. You remember the problems IBM had getting it running. If they have problems like that, why should I trust it to tell me how to spend millions of my dollars?

Joe Jr: You mentioned that IBM designed the software for us. How did they select the decision rule used in determining the order quantities?

Joe: I can't answer that. The consultants that came in told me the best way to determine the order quantities for my company was to use an economic order quantity (EOQ) and a reorder point for every item. (See Exhibit 2.) They said this was the best because we have three set order points during the year. I'm comfortable with the order point, but I'm not sure of the EOQ. I can tell you how the EOQ was made for us. They based it on the demand quantities from the past 4 years. (See Exhibit 3.) IBM said that they did not see the need for any additional measures. They also said it would work very smoothly since it wasn't necessary to change the EOQ once it was in.

As I said earlier, I'm not sure of the EOQ. You know how I've depended upon my gut feel for the market in the past. I've always ordered parts based on past usage. Then I adjust the numbers according to how many golf courses I expect to be built or modified, and on the contractors'/installers' comments on how they expect the spring to go in terms of the number of installations. I also meet with friends in the building industry to see what they expect in terms of housing starts for the spring. My only other adjustments come if I think a particular product isn't moving. I feel all goods should turn over at least three times a year. There are two items I am worried about at the present time because of that exact problem. One is the timing motor with gear service assembly (Part #1-7287), a low-volume service part carried for repair of monitor controllers, and the other is the Monitor Controller (Series 176) carried as an "insurance" end

---
[1]Prepared for use in class discussion by Roger G. Schroeder, E. R. Kunde, and Sue Flach.

EXHIBIT 1

IRRIGATION PRODUCTS, INC. CURRENT INVENTORIES
OCTOBER 15, 1988

Product description	Current inventory units	Current inventory $000	FY 1988 sales, $000
Free controllers series 150—4 + 8	283	12	15
Customer controllers series 123–8 +11	68	8	12
Monitor controllers series 176—11 + 23	51	15	26
¾" + 1" valve globe/angle in-line	4,430	46	78
1½" + 2" valve globe/angle in-line	281	6	62
Brass valves series 216	334	4	7
Pop-up bodies	50,841	20	77
570 series nozzles	90,056	14	68
Stream rotors series 300	2,043	13	144
Rain pros series 320	1,782	12	26
Gear driven rotary series 600	1,086	10	22
Gear driven rotary series 620	681	21	39
Gear driven rotary series 640	2,627	81	194
Gear driven rotary series 670	973	36	180
Totals		298	950

product for a few specialized customers. See Exhibits 4 and 5 for detailed descriptions of the Monitor Controller and the Series 230 valve.

Joe Jr: I haven't heard you mention the problem of running out of products. We have been having quite a problem with running out of the Series 230 1-inch valve, a high demand part which we use all the time. How would you handle this in ordering? I know that we tend to disagree on what level of inventory should be held. I don't think you are carrying a high enough inventory level on all parts to satisfy our customers. You have always said it is critical to the survival of the company that we have satisfied customers. I would tend to believe that this would require us to always have what our customers need on hand. The other problem I see resulting from stockouts is a loss of customers to our competitors. Any customer whose order we cannot fill will go to Rainbird, Weather Matic, or Nelson. Any of these competitors could supply the cus-

EXHIBIT 2
CURRENT COMPUTER SYSTEM RULES

For order quantity size*:

$$EOQ = \sqrt{\frac{2\,AD}{ic}}$$

- A = cost of placing an order, $
- D = annual demand in units
- i = "interest rate" for holding inventory for a year as a proportion of the unit cost
- c = unit cost of the item, $/unit
- EOQ = economic order quantity

For reorder point:

R = average demand over the lead time + safety stock

R is the reorder point where an order for more stock is placed

Currently, a 12-week lead time is used for all items in setting the reorder point.

*The current computer system uses a carrying cost i = 30% (20% cost of capital, 5% obsolescence, and 5% storage cost) and an ordering cost of $10 per order.

EXHIBIT 3
DEMAND FOR FISCAL YEARS 1985–1988

PART #1-7287 TIMING MOTOR WITH GEAR SERVICE ASSEMBLY (FOR MONITOR CONTROLLERS)

Distributor net $12.00

Selling price $26.00

	1985	1986	1987	1988
Unit sales	30	19	22	31

Current inventory = 9 units

Reorder point = 16 units, EOQ = 12 units

SERIES 230, 1″ VALVES

Distributor net $10.35

Selling price $13.75

	1985	1986	1987	1988
Unit sales	5210	3650	4441	5673

Current inventory = 4430 units

Reorder point = 2070 units, EOQ = 173 units

SERIES 176, MONITOR CONTROLLER

Distributor net $301.46

Selling price $400.00

	1985	1986	1987	1988
Unit sales	21	12	41	65

Current inventory = 51 units

Reorder point = 22 units, EOQ = 2 units

SERIES 230 & 240—
AUTOMATIC VALVES
¾" & 1" ELECTRIC AND HYDRAULIC VERSIONS
NORMALLY OPEN, PIN-TYPE, 24 V.A.C. ELECTRIC

Application

- Underground automatic systems with G.P.M. demand of 1 G.P.M. to 50 G.P.M.
- Residential or commercial
- Electric systems
- Normally open systems—dirty or clean water
- Pin-type systems—clean water

Features

All
- Globe valve for easy installation
- Economical/competitively priced
- High flow/low pressure loss
- Manual bleed
- Smooth opening and closing
- Opens and closes at low flow and pressure
- Bleed ports protected with built-in filter

¾"
- Corrosion resistant, glass filled nylon construction
- Small size, big performance

1"
- 230 series has manual flow control
- Corrosion resistant, Cycolac® and stainless steel construction
- Stainless steel reinforced solenoid
- Stainless steel collar over threaded 1" I.P.S. outlets

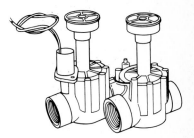

1"—230 SERIES
ELECTRIC or HYDRAULIC
with FLOW CONTROL

Specifications

¾"	1"
• 24 V.A.C. 　.36 amps inrush 　.18 amps holding	• Electric models 24 V.A.C. 　.400 amps inrush 　.200 amps holding
• Working pressure 　150 PSI maximum 　25 PSI maximum	• Working pressure 　150 PSI maximum 　10 PSI maximum
• ¾" I.P.S. male thread inlets	• Dimensions: 230—6"H, 4½"W
• Dimensions: 3"H, 4"W	240—4½"H, 4½"W

EXHIBIT 4
Series 230 and 240—Automatic valves. ¾" & 1" electric and hydraulic
versions normally open, pin-type, 24 V.A.C. electric.

SERIES 170—
MONITOR II AUTOMATIC CONTROLLERS
11 & 23 STATION, HYDRAULIC AND ELECTRIC

Application

- Heavy duty commercial
- Outdoor—wall or pedestal
- Parks—schools—cemeteries—condominiums—commercial buildings

Features

- 0–60 minute timing per station (infinite adjustment)
- 14 - day programming capability—easy to set
- Automatic, semi-automatic or manual operation
- Multi-cycling program—easily set
- Fused circuit protection—U.L. listed
- Dual programming on electric models (turf can be watered more frequently than shrubs)
- As many as four TORO electric valves can be operated on each station of electric models
- No time lag between stations
- Pump start circuit standard (Can also be used as a master valve control circuit)
- Locks are provided for timing mechanism cover and pedestal cabinet door
- Supply line filter included on hydraulic models
- Hydraulic models resist freeze-related damage
- Controller can be operated manually even if the timing mechanism has to be removed (use Model 995-24 accessory for electric models)
- Built in transformer on electric models
- Housing is heavy gauge steel, treated with rust inhibitor and painted forest green
- Mounting template for easy installation in concrete included

WALL MOUNT
CONTROLLER
SERIES 176

Specifications

- 45 V.A., 24 V.A.C. transformer (built in)
- Lightning protection devices available for lightning prone areas
- Dimensions—Wall Mount 8½'' x 10¾'' x 8½''
        Pedestal Mount 8¼'' x 12⅝'' x 31⅛''
- 115 V.A.C. input—24 V.A.C. output
- 2 separate ground wires required to utilize dual program
- Using normally open valves, tubing length from controller to valve should not exceed 1,000 feet
- Refer to page 30 for maximum number of valves allowable per station and other technical data

EXHIBIT 5   Series 170—Monitor II automatic controllers. 11 & 23 station, hydraulic and electric.

tomer with comparable equipment, and once the customers have made the change, how do we get them back?

Joe: I don't have the storage capacity to carry enough inventory to protect ourselves from ever having a stockout. My philosophy has been that you can't always satisfy the customer from on-hand inventory. But you better be able to satisfy them 90 percent of the time. When you don't have it on hand, you can usually get it from another distributor. It usually is a fairly fast process because we fly the parts in. Too bad we can't place rush orders with Toro, but they hold us to their standard ordering policy. (Exhibit 6.)

That reminds me, we have to face a possible stockout problem this year. When I was at the country club last week, George, the general manager at the club, was talking about the number of times their sprinkler system had failed. George mentioned that he had spoken to the board about replacing the system. While the board wouldn't commit themselves until the annual meeting in December, George felt that it was going to be approved. If they installed the system, they wanted it ready to go by their annual tournament in early April. George said his first choice would be us if we could supply the system within the time specified. This contract would be a highly profitable one. As you know, the course is 390 acres, and the entire system would have to be replaced. The replacement system would rely heavily on the use of the Series 230 valves.

Because of the size of the club's system, I checked with my banker on the cost of financing. Bank notes were quoted at 18 percent. I'm not sure whether I should risk financing, so I'm looking at cutting back in the spare parts area, where a lot of our cash is tied up. I figured that we have 25 percent of our inventory just sitting in the warehouse collecting dust. Many of these items are used by only a few of our customers. If I decide against the latter technique, we would have to rent storage space to handle the parts for the golf course installation. When I checked into this yesterday, I was quoted a price of $3.27 per square foot per year for rented warehouse storage space.

To assist in determining the appropriate quantities and to get a little insight into the chance of the club's installing the system, I called the National Weather Service this morning. They stated they expected the driest spring in 5 years. I'm not sure to what extent this would affect the sales of the irrigation products. To assist in determining the effect of weather on the sales, I have gone over the demand figures and the corresponding weather for the last 5 years. In 1984 and 1986 I greatly overstocked. During these years, the weather was extraordinarily wet and cloudy. During 1987 the reverse conditions existed. It was an abnormally dry season, and we stocked out of most of our goods. See Exhibit 7 for more market characteristics.

Joe Jr: With a business that is subject to the whims of nature, why do you stay in it? Is it really worth beating your head against the wall to get the kind of return on investment that we have been getting? Even though we get a 25 percent markup on all irrigation items, the results do not always appear on the bottom line. Maybe we

EXHIBIT 6

IRRIGATION DIVISION FY 1989 STOCKING PROGRAM, TERMS FOR SOUTHERN DISTRIBUTORS

Order placement	Shipping period	Dating terms
33% 1988 Forecast Oct. 15–Oct. 30	December and January	½ May 15—net ½ June 15—net
33% 1989 Forecast Feb. 15–Feb. 30	May and June	½ Sept. 15—net ½ Oct. 15—net
33% 1989 Forecast June 15–June 30	August and September	½ Nov. 15—net ½ Dec. 15—net

EXHIBIT 7

GALVESTON MARKET INFORMATION

SFDHH* $15–19M	SFDHH $20–24M	SFDHH $25–34M	SFDHH $35+	Total SFDHH	Total population
228,545	182,607	151,110	89,375	757,000	3,640,000

Number of golf courses: 158

Number of golf course holes: 2259

Irrigation potential market: (in purchases from Toro)†

Small turf‡	$403,830		Number of cemeteries: 71
Large turf‡	267,048		Number of parks: 14
Parts	175,160		Number of schools: 170
Total	$846,038		

*Number of persons living in single family dwelling households (SFDHH).

†This is an estimate of the market size for Toro in the area.

‡Small turf refers to residential installations while large turf refers to golf courses and other commercial installations.

could manage our inventories better and really make the business worthwhile. (See Exhibits 8, 9, and 10.)

EXHIBIT 8

INCOME STATEMENT
(Fiscal years ending June 30)

	1986	1987	1988
Net sales	$3,900,000	$3,500,000	$4,200,000
Cost of goods sold	2,800,000	2,700,000	$3,200,000
Gross profit	1,100,000	800,000	1,000,000
Expenses:			
Selling expense	440,000	272,000	350,000
Operating expense	455,000	318,000	400,000
Fixed expense	95,000	100,000	115,000
Total expenses	990,000	690,000	865,000
Net profit from operation	110,000	110,000	135,000
Other expenses	75,000	60,000	85,000
Income	15,000	10,000	25,000
Net profit before taxes	50,000	60,000	75,000
Taxes	12,000	27,000	36,000
Net profit	$ 38,000	$ 33,000	$ 39,000

Joe: In the past I stayed in this business because I started the business. It's my baby. I felt a great deal of achievement from it. I've always planned to pass the company on to you and let you operate it. Now is the time for you to decide how you would run this company if you were in charge and if the return on investment is good enough for you to be satisfied. We also have to decide what to order from Roger Kirk when he arrives next week and what to do about using the System 34. I have another meeting now, but I would like to get back to this discussion later.

DISCUSSION QUESTIONS

1. What would you recommend that Joe Jr. do, assuming he takes control of Southern Toro?

2. Evaluate the importance of inventory and inventory management of Southern Toro Distributorship, for both irrigation products and spare parts. Should the inventory be cut back?

3. Evaluate the current inventory management system at Southern Toro. What inventory management system would you recommend?

EXHIBIT 9
BALANCE SHEET
(Fiscal year-end June 30)

	1986	1987	1988
Assets			
Cash	$ 10,000	$ 35,000	$ 5,000
Accts. receivable	$492,000	$622,000	$647,000
Less doubtful accts.	17,000	22,000	22,000
Net accts. receivable	475,000	600,000	625,000
Inventory	620,000	600,000	1,000,000
Total current assets	1,105,000	1,235,000	1,630,000
Prepaid expenses	30,000	30,000	20,000
Equipment (net of department)	35,000	40,000	45,000
Total fixed assets	65,000	75,000	65,000
Total assets	1,170,000	1,305,000	1,695,000
Liabilities			
Notes payable (to banks)	207,000	329,000	700,000
Current position of long-term liabilities	20,000	20,000	20,000
Total current liabilities	227,000	349,000	720,000
Long-term liabilities	160,000	140,000	120,000
Total liabilities	387,000	489,000	840,000
Capital stock	200,000	200,000	200,000
Retained earnings	583,000	616,000	655,000
Net worth	783,000	816,000	855,000
Total liabilities and net worth	$1,170,000	$1,305,000	$1,695,000

EXHIBIT 10
FY 1988 DEPARTMENTAL ANALYSIS ($000)

	Total	Consumer products	Commercial products	Irrigation products	Parts	Service
Net sales	$4,500	$1,800	$850	$950	$550	$50
Cost of goods sold	3,200	1,435	650	750	350	15
Gross profit	1,000	365	200	200	200	35
Gross profit	23%	20%	23%	21%	36%	70%
Ending inventory	$1,000	$ 275	$250	$295	$180	—

ToysPlus, Inc.

Dale Long, vice president of manufacturing for ToysPlus, Inc., finished reading the weekly production report for the week ended September 23, 1988.[1] Inventories were up once again, and service levels were lower than expected. Dale wondered why these problems could not be solved once and for all. Last year he had installed a new IBM MAPICS production and inventory control system on the company's mainframe computer. While the system drastically reduced inventories and improved service levels at first, things had gotten worse over the last few months.

Dale took the report and walked to Andrea Meline's office next door. Andrea had received her M.B.A. a few years ago from a prestigious business school and was now in charge of production control for the company. After exchanging the usual greetings, Dale asked Andrea why the latest figures were not better. Andrea responded, "Dale, we continue to get poor forecasts from marketing, and we have to carry more inventory than we would like in order to protect ourselves from unreliable vendor deliveries. The sales promotion that we ran last week on surplus toy trucks did not work as well as we expected." Dale interrupted, "Andrea we can no longer afford to achieve these kinds of results. You have got to find a solution. I am counting on you to come up with something to improve the situation. Otherwise we may both be out of a job."

BACKGROUND

ToysPlus is a small, privately held company in the toy industry, with sales of about $20 million a year. The company was started in 1951, manufacturing

an innovative line of plastic toys and trucks that were very durable and low-priced. Over the years it has added several lines of toys and is now making 22 different toys consisting of games, dolls, toy vehicles, and novelty items. The company has a typical functional organization, as shown in Exhibit 1.

ToysPlus has had relatively poor financial results, as shown in Exhibit 2. Profits are only averaging 5 percent of sales, and return on assets is less than 10 percent. In order to improve the situation the company has decided to make a major effort to reduce inventories and to improve customer service. In an effort to reduce costs, the company has begun to redesign the toys for manufacturability and automation of the production process. The company feels that unit production costs could be reduced at least 5 percent per year by these efforts. The company also wants to achieve at least 15 inventory turns per year[1] and a service level of 95 percent. Service level is defined as the percentage of orders filled within 1 week of customer order. The current service level is 90 percent.

Manufacturing operations are organized around the different types of toys which are manufactured. Each type of toy has its own assembly line and its own dedicated workers. For example, three plastic toys: trucks, autos, and robots, are assembled on line 1. Only one toy can be assembled at a time on this line; then there is a changeover to the next toy. Currently, line 1 has 10 workers who engage in assembly, inspection, and packing of the toys. Some of the parts which are assembled into the finished toys are made on the company's plastic-molding machines. Other parts are purchased from outside suppliers.

Production control is based on the MAPICS

---

[1]This case was prepared as a basis for class discussion, not to illustrate either effective or ineffective handling of an administrative situation.

---

[1]Inventory turns are based on the ratio of COGS to inventory.

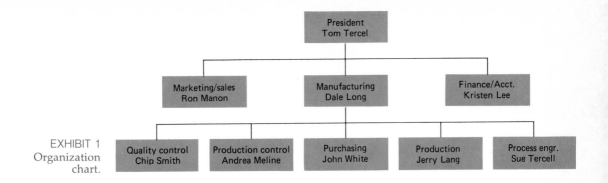

EXHIBIT 1
Organization
chart.

EXHIBIT 2
FINANCIAL STATEMENTS

Profit and Loss (in $000) Year Ending June 30, 1988		
Net sales	$20,100	
Cost of goods sold		
Direct labor	2,353	
Materials	6,794	
Overhead	2,608	
Total COGS	11,755	
Gross profit	8,345	
G&A expense	4,932	
Marketing costs	1,776	
Profit before Tax	1,637	
Income tax	650	
Net profit	987	

Balance Sheet (in $000) As of June 30, 1988		
Assets		
Current assets		
Cash	$1,050	
Accounts receivable	2,500	
Inventory	2,400	
Other	540	
Total curr. assets	6,490	
Fixed assets		
Net fixed assets	4,900	
Total assets	11,390	
Liabilities		
Current liabilities		
Notes payable	3,300	
Accounts payable	3,200	
Accruals	400	
Total curr. liab.	6,900	
Long-term debt	2,300	
Total liabilities	9,200	
Capital stock	1,500	
Retained earnings	690	
Total net worth	2,190	
Total liabilities and net worth	11,390	

EXHIBIT 3
MASTER SCHEDULE PREPARED SEPT. 19, 1988

	Week Beginning					
	Sept. 26	Oct. 3	Oct. 10	Oct. 17	Oct. 24	Oct. 31
Auto	3500	500				3500
Truck		1500	1750			
Robot				2333	2333	

WEEKLY FORECAST OF DEMAND

	Week Beginning					
	Sept. 26	Oct. 3	Oct. 10	Oct. 17	Oct. 24	Oct.31
Auto	1100	1150	1200	1300	1400	1500
Truck	500	450	400	350	300	300
Robot	700	650	650	625	625	600

Products

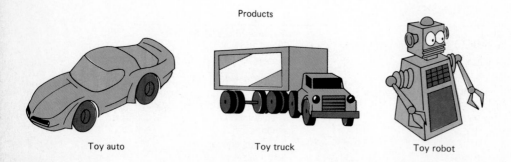

Toy auto   Toy truck   Toy robot

MRP system. Every week a master schedule is prepared for the next 6 weeks. This master schedule specifies for assembly line 1, for example, the number of trucks, autos, and robots which will be produced in each week, as shown in Exhibit 3. Forecasts of weekly demand are received each week from marketing. Based on past experience, these forecasts are adjusted by Andrea to reflect more realistic estimates of demand. She also utilizes the lot sizes which are shown in the Exhibit 3 master schedule for each of the three toys. These lot sizes are based on past practice in the company. A runout-time philosophy is used to schedule the toy first which has the lowest ratio of inventory to weekly demand. As a result, the master schedule is prepared and entered into the computer.

The computer then performs a parts explosion using the bill of materials and the on-hand inventories shown in Exhibit 4. Each toy requires several parts, as indicated in the bill of materials. For example, each auto requires 1 body, 4 wheels, 2 side windows and 1 windshield. These parts are assembled, the product is inspected, and the toy is packed, which requires a total of .1 labor hour per auto. With 10 people working on the assembly line, at present, there are 350 hours of productive time available per week (35 hours each times 10). If the entire week is used to make autos, a total of 3500 autos can be produced (350/.1). It takes .2 hour to make a truck and .15 hour to make a robot, thereby making it possible to produce a maximum of 1750 trucks or 2333 robots, if the entire line is devoted to either of these products. Production, however, is scheduled in lots, and the entire week is not necessarily devoted to only one toy.

In between products it takes all 10 people 1 hour to change the setup of the line. This changeover involves moving out the parts for the old toy,

EXHIBIT 4
BILL OF MATERIALS

Part Number	Description	Number Required per Unit	Cost Each	Weeks Lead Time	Current Inventory	On Order
1019	Toy auto		$3.90	1	4000	
523	Car body	1	1.45	3	2500	1000 due 10/3
525	Wheels	4	.30	2	9800	
529	Side windows	2	.15	1	4300	
531	Windshield	1	.25	2	2620	
1021	Toy truck		$6.50		2000	
615	Cab	1	1.70	3	1200	800 due 10/3
617	Wheels dual	8 sets	.25	2	9900	
619	Wheels single	2	.30	2	2500	
621	Trailer	1	2.20	4	4600	1200 due 10/10
1023	Toy robot		$5.40	1	1500	
730	Body	1	1.80	2	1600	
732	Arms	2	.35	2	3500	
734	Legs	2	.25	1	4020	
736	Head	1	1.10	2	2150	

moving in the parts for the new toy, arranging the jigs and fixtures for assembly, and making trial runs to make sure that quality is right. The shop labor rate is $6 per hour for wages, fringe benefits are 33 percent additional, and there is $6 per hour charged for overhead. It costs 25 percent to carry inventory for a year. For parts and components which are ordered, it costs $25 to place each order.

Purchasing does not always buy the exact number of parts which are ordered by the production control department. Adjustments are made to take advantage of price breaks from suppliers or to achieve full-truckload shipments. As a result, some additional parts might be purchased in order to reduce purchasing costs. Also, suppliers do not always ship the component parts when promised. As a result, ToysPlus carries safety stock inventory to protect the master production schedule and to keep the assembly lines running, no matter what. About 1 week of safety stock is carried to protect for late supplier deliveries. Management has mandated that the assembly lines will not shut down.

Dale Long has stated that the company will not lay off workers on a week-to-week basis. Thus, if demand should be less than capacity, for example

by 10 percent in a week, production will be scheduled to full capacity to keep the workers busy. If this condition should continue for several weeks, then workers will be laid off in order to adjust capacity. In a similar way, workers will be put on overtime in order to meet demand temporarily. But if demand exceeds normal capacity for several weeks, more workers will then be added.

A 6-week rolling production schedule, based on existing capacity and lead times, is used. Each week 1 more week is added to keep the total master schedule horizon at 6 weeks. Production is adjusted each week in line with available parts, capacity, and observed demand for toys.

Happy Hour

Andrea walked to the General Joe's, a favorite watering hole, for happy hour with her friend from purchasing, John White. Andrea began, "John, I don't know what I am going to do. Dale Long has laid the law down that I must reduce inventory and improve service levels. There is no alternative or excuses this time, I must do it! I'm not sure where to start. I would like better sales forecasts, but is that realistic to expect? Can I depend on marketing? I also could reduce inventory by achieving more reliable deliveries from our suppliers. Will they cooperate? Maybe, we will have to react faster in laying off and hiring workers in order to keep capacity closer to demand. What do you think of this situation? Is there a solution?"

John answered, "You must remember, Andrea, the world is filled with hustlers and liars. The salespeople lie to you about forecasts, so they can have more inventory, just in case they need it. We in purchasing lie to our suppliers about when we need the parts, so that we can be sure to get them when we really need them. You pad the production schedule a little bit, just to make sure you can meet the shipments. We all are trying to cover ourselves so that we don't run out of stock. There isn't a solution to this problem, because we are dealing with human nature. I hate to say it, but maybe top management's expectations are a bit unrealistic that inventory should be reduced and service improved. How can they expect anyone to accomplish these goals in an environment like this?"

DISCUSSION QUESTIONS

1. Calculate economic order quantities for each of the three types of toys.

2. Prepare a master production schedule for the next 6 weeks using the EOQs calculated in Question 1 and a work force of 10 employees. What inventory turnover ratio is achieved by this master schedule? How does this turnover compare with past levels and with management's goals?

3. Prepare a parts explosion to support the master schedule. What parts should be ordered each week?

4. What should Andrea Meline do in order to meet the inventory and service goals stated by management?

5. How should Andrea deal with the organization issues presented in this case?

U.S. Stroller

Clem Hawkins, director of manufacturing for U.S. Stroller, leaned back in his chair as he thought about the events of the past 2 weeks.[1] The president of the company, Judy Hawkins, Clem's sister, had just returned from a conference on JIT manufacturing at the University of North Carolina. After the conference, she commented to Clem, "We have got to do something about the high inventories, poor customer service, and high costs. I think that a JIT approach would work fine for our manufacturing plant. At the conference in North Carolina we heard of many companies that have used JIT as a way to reduce cycle time, improve quality, and ultimately reduce inventory and cost. In our industry, the Japanese are making a strong entry, and unless we do something now, we may lose our market share and margins. Clem, I want you to take a close look at the plant and get back to me on how we can go about implementing a JIT approach."

BACKGROUND

U.S. Stroller is a leader in the production and sales of baby strollers in the United States. It has historically made very high quality strollers which sell at a premium price. The company is known for its innovative designs and its good distribution system. U.S. Strollers are sold through major department stores, discount stores, and baby equipment stores. Altogether, 2000 different sites in the United States distribute the company's products.

U.S. Stroller has been a market leader for over 50 years. At the present time it has 40 percent of the U.S. market, a competitor Graco has 20 percent of the market, and Kolcraft has 10 percent of the

market. Various other companies, each with less than a 10 percent share, have the remainder of the market, including two Japanese companies which have just entered the U.S. market. The Japanese companies seem to be selling a low-price stroller which emphasizes quality and reliability of design.

U.S. Stroller started its business in 1934 with the introduction of the regular model which it still makes. While the regular model has been updated over the years for differences in fabric and style, the basic design is still the same. The regular model folds easily for storage or transportation and sells for $49 retail.

In 1955, the company introduced a deluxe model which sells for a premium price and is oriented to the upscale market. This model features a design which permits the stroller to be converted to a baby carriage, as well as folding for storage or transporting. It also has an adjustable footrest, a storage basket, and locking dual front-swivel wheels. This deluxe model sells for $99 retail (see Exhibit 1 for an illustration).

In 1974, the company introduced its shopping center stroller. This model is very heavy duty, it does not fold, and it stands up well to the abuse that strollers take in shopping centers. The shopping center model sells for $149 and has been extensively marketed in the United States.

Currently, the company is selling 106,000 units per year of the three types of strollers. The amount of each type sold is shown in Exhibit 2. These amounts are divided by 52 to arrive at an average weekly usage. Sales are, of course, irregular and can vary by 25 percent from the average weekly volumes shown in Exhibit 2. Production is leveled, to the extent possible, to attain a level work force.

The financial statements for U.S. Stroller are shown in Exhibit 3. Sales are approximately $4.5 million per year. The gross profit is 25 percent of sales, and the net profit, after tax, for the fiscal year

[1]This case was prepared as a basis for class discussion, not to illustrate either effective or ineffective handling of an administrative situation.

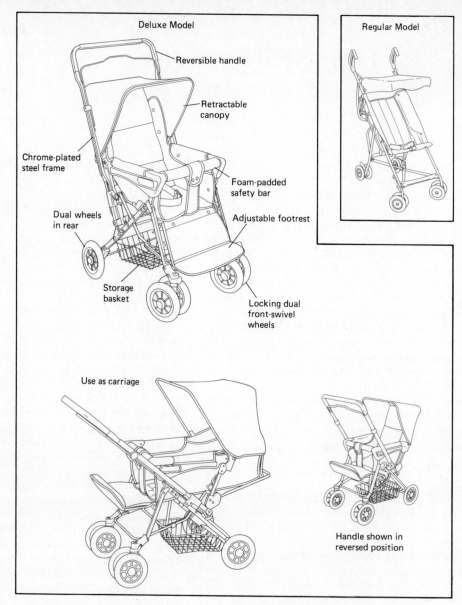

EXHIBIT 1
U.S. Stroller
products.

1988 was a disappointing 2 percent of sales. Profits have been dropping over the past 2 years because of price decreases and the inability to maintain margins. The balance sheet in Exhibit 3 shows that inventories are turning very slowly, at a rate of 2.4 times per year. The plant is fairly automated and includes up-to-date equipment. On an after-tax basis the company has earned 3 percent on net assets and 8 percent on owners equity. U.S. Stroller is a privately held company.

PLANT DESCRIPTION

Strollers made by the company consist of from 20 to 30 different parts. The frame is made out of

EXHIBIT 2
SALES VOLUMES

	Annual Sales	Average Weekly Sales
Regular	54,000	1040
Deluxe	24,960	480
Shopping center	27,040	520
Total	106,000	2040

chrome-plated tubing. The tubing is bought in standard lengths and then cut to size, bent to the proper shape, and drilled with holes for assembly. Each stroller has about 10 pieces of tubing which are assembled into the final frame. Wheels for the strollers are bought from an outside vendor and attached to the tube frames. The padded seats and backs are also purchased from outside. The strollers have a plywood insert inside the seat and in the back to give added strength. These plywood pieces are cut from large 4 × 8 foot sheets by the company and then inserted into the purchased fabric pieces. U.S. Stroller also buys other parts needed to make a stroller, including plastic parts, bolts, fasteners, wire baskets, etc. Altogether, about 50 percent of the cost of a stroller consists of materials which are purchased from outside.

The plant layout has several work centers,

EXHIBIT 3
FINANCIAL STATEMENTS ($000)
FY88 (YEAR ENDED JULY 1, 1988)

Income Statement		Balance Sheet	
Sales	$4558	Assets	
		Cash	106
Cost of goods		Accounts rec.	480
Materials	1682	Inventory	1424
Labor	894	Net plant	987
Overhead	842	Total assets	2997
Total	3418	Liabilities	
		Notes payable	1200
Gross profit	1140	Long-term debt	697
Sales expense	462	Owners equity	1100
G&A expenses	493	Total L&OE	2997
Subtotal	955		
Profit before tax	185		
Profit after tax	91		

shown in Exhibit 4. These work centers include a tube-cutting department with six nearly identical tube-cutting machines. After the tubes are cut, they are placed in tube inventory until they are needed by the tube-bending work center or the drilling work center. Tubes which need to be bent into special shapes are bent by the two presses in the bending department. Bent tubes and straight tubes are taken to the drilling department and drilled with the proper holes. Jigs are used to speed up the process and to ensure that the holes are located in the right places. The drilled tubes are then put back into inventory until they are needed by final assembly. There are a total of 10 different drilling machines in the drilling work center.

Final assembly consists of one assembly line which is used to assemble all three types of strollers. This assembly line is changed over from one model to the next according to the final assembly schedule. The woodworking department consists of one large saw which is used to cut seat and back inserts from large plywood sheets. These seats and backs are put into inventory until they are needed by final assembly. When final assembly is begun, all parts are in inventory or are expedited in order to make the required batch of finished product. Expediting is done both inside the plant, to get the missing parts, and with outside suppliers. This expediting is started 1 week ahead of when the material is needed in order to get all the material in-house to support the assembly schedule for the next week.

An MRP system is used to plan and control inventories. A master production schedule is prepared on a weekly basis for 8 weeks into the future. The master schedule is then frozen for 4 weeks in order to allow time to fabricate the parts required and to get the parts in from outside suppliers. Any parts which are not there when needed are expedited during the last week, as described above.

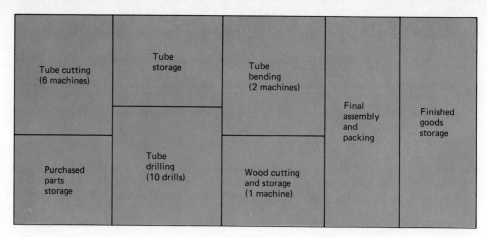

EXHIBIT 4
Plant layout.

New orders are only placed into week 5 or later in the master schedule.

The lot sizes for each of the strollers have been developed by use of the EOQ formula. This is done by considering the setup time of equipment and the carrying costs of inventory. The plant is scheduled on a lot-for-lot basis. For example, a lot in the master production schedule of 1000 regular strollers is translated directly into the parts needed to produce it. This would include 1000 stroller handles less any inventory on hand or on order. Due to lot-for-lot planning, a setup on the final assembly line also directly induces setups throughout the plant in tube cutting, drilling, bending, and seat cutting. The total cost of a changeover at final assembly is thus the cost of changing over the final assembly line itself, plus the cost of changing over all the other production equipment affected by the lot-for-lot calculations. As shown in Exhibit 5, for the regular model, the total setup time amounts to about 11 labor hours. The shop rate is currently $15 per hour, fully loaded. Therefore a setup for

EXHIBIT 5
SETUP TIME FOR REGULAR MODEL

Work Center	Setup Time, hours
Tube cutting	4.2
Drilling	2.4
Tube bending	1.6
Wood saw	0.5
Final assembly	2.3
Total	11.0

final assembly of the regular model costs $165. Similarly, the cost of changeover for the deluxe model is $185, and for the shopping center model it is $170.

Setup time includes not only changing the machine over, but also bringing in new materials and taking out the old, then making a pilot run to be sure the machine is making good parts. While there are minor setups when making different parts for the same stroller, the major setup is associated with changing over from one stroller model to another.

The EOQ calculations are shown in Exhibit 6. These calculations assume a holding charge of 25 percent per year. Note that the resulting EOQ for the regular model is 2400 units, which is approximately 1 week of production, since the line can produce 2500 regular units per week when the entire line is devoted to the regular model. Likewise, the deluxe model and the shopping center model will each require about .5 week of time to produce an EOQ.

Using the EOQs which have been calculated, a typical master production schedule is shown in Exhibit 7. This master schedule is constructed as follows. Suppose the regular model is put into production first. Then a batch of 2400 units of regular strollers is scheduled in week 1. But 2500 units can be produced in 1 week, and so with 5 days of production per week, the lot of 2400 units will take 4.8 days (2400/2500 × 5). It will then take an average of 2 hours per machine to change over the line to the next stroller, (time that results in lost capacity). As a result, the rest of the first week is devoted to changeover. Next, the deluxe

EXHIBIT 6
ECONOMIC ORDER QUANTITIES

Model	D Annual Sales	C Mfg. Cost	S Setup Cost	P Prod. Rate*	D Weekly Usage	1 − D/P	EOQ†
Regular	54,000	$21	$165	2500	1040	.584	2400
Deluxe	24,960	$37	$185	2000	480	.760	1150
Shopping	27,040	$56	$170	1800	520	.711	960

*This is the maximum weekly production rate for a single product being produced.

$$\dagger EOQ = \sqrt{\frac{2SD}{iC(1 - D/P)}}$$

model is scheduled in week 2, which requires 2.9 days of production (1150/2000 × 5 days) for the EOQ to be produced. Then 2 hours per machine are required to change over to the shopping center model. This process of scheduling is continued, resulting in the master schedule in Exhibit 7.

Inventory is maintained in finished goods ($765,000), work in process ($322,000), and raw materials ($337,000). The finished goods inventory is distributed through three warehouses located around the country. An average of 80 days of supply is carried at each warehouse. It takes 4 weeks to reorder from the factory and 1 week for transit. Some inventory is held in safety stock. Likewise, 4 weeks of in-process inventory is held to provide high machine utilization and to facilitate scheduling. The company also holds 12 weeks of purchased parts in order to facilitate scheduling with vendors and to prevent line stoppages.

OPTION 1: A PULL SYSTEM

In thinking about JIT, Clem Hawkins was considering two options. Option 1 involved going to a pull system of inventory control. Under this option, three separate final assembly lines would be set up, one for each finished product. This would elimi-

nate changeovers at final assembly. Clem was also considering mixed-model assembly, which would have a similar effect. But this could be more complicated and would require development of some tooling for instantaneous changeover of the line from one model to the next. Of course, setting up three assembly lines, instead of the present one line, would require additional investment (about $200,000) for jigs, fixtures, and assembly tables.

If three assembly lines were used, the master schedule would be drastically changed to the one shown in Exhibit 8. Each week the same amount is scheduled to meet the forecast, thereby putting a uniform load on the plant. This loading is, of course, required for a pull system to work. Clem thought he could also reduce the length of time that the master schedule is frozen to 2 weeks. This will make it possible to drastically reduce inventories at the field warehouses, to about a 15-to-30-day supply. He would like to achieve the guideline that what is ordered from the warehouses this week is scheduled to be produced next week.

Setting up permanent final assembly lines with a pull system makes it also possible to dedicate certain equipment in the plant to each of the product lines (see Exhibit 9). For example, there are six tube-cutting machines. Since about one-half of

EXHIBIT 7
MASTER SCHEDULE FOR JULY 1988

Model	Week 1	Week 2	Week 3	Week 4
Regular	2400		2000	400
Deluxe		1150		1150
Shopping		684	276	324

EXHIBIT 8
REVISED SCHEDULE (PULL SYSTEM)

Model	Week 1	Week 2	Week 3	Week 4
Regular	1040	1040	1040	1040
Deluxe	480	480	480	480
Shopping	520	520	520	520

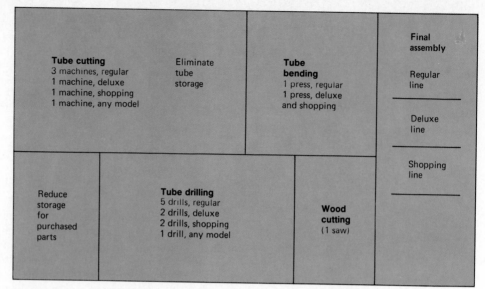

EXHIBIT 9
Pull system
layout, dedicated
equipment.

the capacity is devoted to regular strollers, three of the tube cutters could be set up permanently for regular strollers. Clem would also need 1.5 tube cutters for deluxe models and 1.5 cutters for shopping models. This presents a problem, either one machine could be dedicated to each model, or two machines could be. If one tube cutter were dedicated to each model, then one machine would be kept to change over as needed between the various models. If two machines were dedicated to each model, an additional machine would need to be purchased. Also, in this case there would be little flexibility with all dedicated machines. In a similar way, some drills and tube benders could be dedicated to each model. But the saw presents a problem since there is only one saw. Either smaller equipment must be purchased and dedicated to models, or the saw could continue to be changed over for each product.

Using the pull system, Kanban containers will be used to move inventory from one work center to the next. When the Kanban containers are full at a work center, all machines at the supplying work centers will be shut off, thereby limiting the maximum inventory to the number of full Kanban containers provided. The tube storage room will be eliminated, and all inventory will be held in Kanban containers on the shop floor.

A smaller storage room for purchased parts will be needed, but Clem did not think that he could supply all purchased parts directly to final assembly, at least not initially. But purchased inventories could be greatly reduced once the suppliers are also on the Kanban system. Purchased parts could be supplied on the basis of daily, or certainly weekly, deliveries for all "A" items and less frequently for "B" and "C" items.

OPTION 2: MANUFACTURING CELLS

In this option a manufacturing cell would be provided for each model. The layout would look roughly like Exhibit 10. Each product would be made in a U-shaped cell. In the regular model cell, there would be three tube cutting machines, one bending press, five drills, and the final assembly line. This arrangement would have dedicated equipment which would be located in close proximity to each other. Material would flow into one end of the cell and finished product out of the other end. Purchased parts would be delivered to the cell directly by the supplier or in kits from a central storage and kitting room. A kit would contain all the purchased parts needed to assemble one unit of the final product.

Two more cells could also be established: one for the deluxe model and one for the shopping center model. In this case we would need two tube

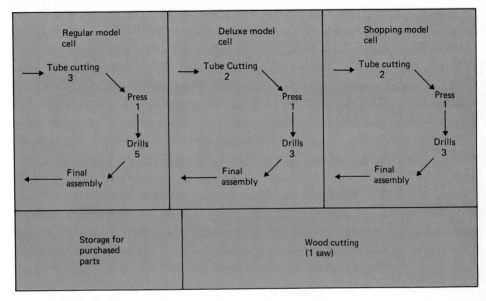

EXHIBIT 10
Cellular layout.

cutters, one press, and three drills in each of these cells in order to maintain the present capacity. This would require Clem to purchase additional equipment (one drill, one press, and one tube cutter) at a cost of about $150,000.

There are several advantages to the use of cells. As things are moved closer together, visual control of each cell can be maintained. When there is a quality or maintenance problem, it will be readily evident. Also, the people working in the cell will gain an identity with the particular product produced. The cell takes less space and provides the advantage of fast feedback, since everything is in close proximity. Of course, a Kanban system would also be used to pull parts through each of the cells.

Many of the inventory reduction advantages described above will also be gained by the use of cells. As a matter of fact, the throughput from a cell might even be faster than the Kanban system described in option 1. As a result, less inventory would be required by a cell. On the other hand, a cell gives less flexibility to demand changes, since all equipment is dedicated to that particular product line.

SUNDAY AFTERNOON

During halftime of the Vikings and Bears football game, Clem could not help thinking about the options available for JIT manufacturing. He wondered how much each of these options would save in production costs and inventories. Also, would these options have the same product quality, or would the cell produce a higher-quality product because of its close visual control? Clem decided that he would request a study of these options by his assistant, Joan Hankins. Joan had recently received her M.B.A. from UCLA and was a whiz at analyzing options such as these.

QUESTIONS

1. Evaluate the current situation facing U.S. Stroller.

2. Discuss the pros and cons of the options presented in the case.

3. What will be the impact of these options on the MRP system currently in use?

4. What option do you recommend and why?

Southwestern University

The mathematics department at Southwestern University employs 6 secretaries, 20 professors, and 40 graduate-student teaching assistants.[1] Since Robert Kirk took over the duties of department chairman a year ago, he has been wrestling with administrative problems. In particular, Professor Kirk has been trying to streamline the secretarial jobs, improve productivity, and raise morale among the secretaries.

Secretarial turnover in the department has been high. Of the six secretaries on the staff, one has worked in the office for 4 years, one for 2 years, and the other four have been in the office for a year or less (see Exhibit 1). Of the four secretaries who left the office in the past year, one moved to another city when her husband graduated from college, another took a job in the physics department, one returned to college to get a degree, and one went to work in a downtown office building. As a result of this turnover, a great deal of additional training has been required.

Absenteeism has also been a problem in the office. Over the past year, a total of 50 days of work have been missed by the six secretaries. A detailed list of days missed and longevity on the job is given in Exhibit 1. In most cases, the reason given for missing work was personal illness. Other reasons include car problems, dentist appointments, and illness in the family.[2]

Several secretaries have expressed dissatisfaction with the working conditions. One said, "All we get around here is a lot of work and not much thanks from the professors." Another said, "I see no future in this job. The work itself is mechanical and does not provide a challenge." There is a general feeling in the office among the secretaries that they are "used" and not really treated like professional clerical employees. While all the secretaries like some typing, the four new secretaries feel they do too much typing and not enough creative work.

Pay in the department is relatively low. A starting secretary makes $810 a month, as a typist I. A typist II makes $920 a month, a supervisor makes $1015 a month, and an administrative assistant makes $1160 a month. If a secretary is not promoted, a salary increase of about 5 percent a year can be expected provided performance is good. There is a merit pay system in effect at the

[1]This case was prepared as a basis for class discussion, not to illustrate either effective or ineffective handling of an administrative situation.

[2]The universitywide absenteeism rate averaged 5 days a year with a standard deviation of 2 days.

EXHIBIT 1
JOB DATA

	Title	Days absent last year	Months since hired
Betty Brier	Administrative assistant	3	48
Joan Erickson	Supervisor	2	24
Cheryl Peterson	Typist II	15	12
Cindy North	Typist I	6	8
Mary Short	Typist I	7	2
Sharon Homer	Typist I	17	6

university, but most employees receive the same increase. The civil service union has made it clear that longevity will receive more emphasis in pay increases than merit.

Recently women's liberation has been a factor in the office. One secretary complained to Professor Kirk about the sexist remarks made by a professor. Another secretary has refused to get coffee for professors, claiming this is not in her job description as a typist I.

Over the past year, the office has been experimenting with word processing equipment. The department purchased IBM computer equipment which can be used to store typewritten material on magnetic media. The record can be saved for later use and corrected when errors or changes occur. The IBM equipment can be used to insert paragraphs or words into the text, and it prints out the finished material at the rate of 10 pages per minute. The computer has been used primarily for form letters and for papers written by the professors. Some papers go through as many as four or five revisions before they are published. Occasionally the computer is used to type 10 to 20 copies of a form letter that is mailed to different addresses.

The department uses a secretarial pool concept. Secretaries do not work for individual professors; instead, they are given individual clerical jobs from the incoming work basket. All work is given to the office supervisor by the professors and teaching assistants. The supervisor then gives the work to the secretaries as they become available.

In addition to these typing assignments, the following duties are assigned to the secretarial staff:

- *Betty Brier* (administrative assistant). Betty is the administrative assistant to the department chairman. Her duties include assisting with budget preparation, faculty staffing, teaching-assistant appointments, new-student applications, course scheduling, and liaison with the university's central administration.

- *Joan Erickson* (supervisor). Joan is responsible for supervising the four typists in the office. She assigns the typing work to the other secretaries as it comes in. She is responsible for hiring new secretaries and evaluating their performance on the job. Joan also does typing when she is not busy running the office.

- *Cheryl Peterson* (typist II). Cheryl is responsible for typing papers and long reports. She is trained to operate the IBM equipment and is a very productive worker. Cheryl also handles all student grade reports for the department.

- *Cindy North* (typist I). Cindy does general typing work on class syllabi, letters, and reports. Cindy is not an extremely fast typist, but she is dependable and does high-quality work.

- *Mary Short* (typist I). As the newest member of the department, Mary is in charge of all copy work on the duplicating machine. It is the tradition in the department that the newest member does the copying. Mary spends an average of 4 hours a day on the duplicating machine. Some days she does copying work for the entire 8 hours. When she is not copying, Mary does general typing.

- *Sharon Homer* (typist I). Sharon acts as the receptionist and telephone operator for the department. When professors are not in, Sharon takes phone messages. She also answers student questions and provides information to outside callers. Sharon does typing when she is not busy on the phone. See Exhibit 2 for a detailed interview with Sharon Homer.

In reviewing the general situation, Professor Kirk was concerned about the recent friction between the secretaries and the professors, the uneven workload in the department, the high rate of secretarial turnover and absenteeism, and the need for improved productivity. Professor Kirk knew that something had to be done, but he was unsure of what to do next.

DISCUSSION QUESTIONS

1. What problems is Professor Kirk facing in dealing with the work force, and how should he handle these problems?

2. Design a method for measuring productivity in this office.

3. How can productivity be improved?

4. Describe a way to use job enrichment in this situation.

EXHIBIT 2
INTERVIEW WITH SHARON HOMER

Case writer: How do you like your job here?

Ms. Homer: There are certain parts of my job that I like very much and other parts that I do not like. I like a variety of activities. When I have to type for several hours straight, which happens occasionally, I go home very tired and depressed at night.

Case writer: Do you get a sense of accomplishment from your work?

Ms. Homer: I do take pride in a job well done. When the pressure is on to meet deadlines, however, I find it hard to maintain quality standards. All I ever hear from the professors is complaints about problems—never a word of thanks for good work.

Case writer: I notice you have been absent a number of times in the last six months. Is there some reason for this?

Ms. Homer: I have been ill twice since I came to work here. I also get migraine headaches from time to time and cannot come to work.

Case writer: How do you get along with the other secretaries?

Ms. Homer: That depends. Another woman and I are very good friends. I can work well with all of the others in the office, but I do not consider them personal friends. Occasionally, Joan gets on my nerves when she puts pressure on me.

Case writer: What do you like the least about your job?

Ms. Homer: The worst thing is the uneven workload. Some days, I sit around for several hours with nothing to do. The next day I will be swamped with work. Some of the deadlines seem arbitrary. Just last week one of the women started crying because she could not get all of her work out on time.

Case writier: What do you like best about your job?

Ms. Homer: I really like to work with other people, provided I am not under too much pressure to get the work out. I get a sense of pride from a neatly typed letter and a job well done. I do like some challenge in my work. I hope I will not be stuck in the same job forever.

Houston State Bank

The Houston State Bank is one of the two leading banks in Houston, Texas.[1] Its chief competitor and rival is Farmers and Mechanics Bank (F&M), also located in downtown Houston.

In 1989, the Houston State Bank (HSB) employed 1600 people and was ranked among the top 200 banks in the United States in terms of size. HSB provides a full range of bank services including retail banking, commercial banking, international accounts, credit cards, and branch banking at several sites in Texas and the southwest. HSB has been in business in the Houston area for 78 years, and its headquarters is in a modern 30-story building in downtown Houston. Many of the customers of the bank are leading corporations in the Houston area plus thousands of individuals who have checking and savings accounts.

Recently, Brent Woods took the position of senior vice president of operations. His predecessor was asked to retire after a series of problems were encountered. Some of these problems were personal in nature, and some resulted from the changing character of bank management. After stabilizing the situation, Mr. Woods wanted to make his own imprint on bank operations. In this connection he was given maximum support from his boss, Ivan Armstrong, president of Houston State Bank.

As Mr. Armstrong told him upon taking the job,

Brent, I want you to provide the services that our customers need at the lowest possible cost. This is your challenge. As you know, banking is moving rapidly into a deregulated environment. We are therefore coming under increased competition, not only from our traditional competi-

tor, F & M Bank, but from banks across the country. As such it will be necessary for banks to become more "operations oriented." We can no longer make our profits merely on the spread in interest between loans and deposits, because the rates are deregulated and the spread is becoming thinner and thinner. We must now look to noninterest expenses, which is where you come into the picture. As you know, most of the noninterest expenses are associated with wire transfer, check clearing, and other services we offer to our customers through your department.

Brent Woods realized there was a revolution in banking taking place. Banks, which had traditionally made their money in lending and borrowing, now had to pay more attention to the so-called back room. As a matter of fact, one of his challenges was to upgrade the morale and professionalism of people in operations at all levels. In banking, the dregs of the organization had traditionally ended up in operations—at least most people thought so, especially the operations people. As a result, employees and managers in operations had a low self-image. The place to get ahead in banking had always been in loans or in marketing, and a finance background was the assumed professional orientation needed. Now, with the changing times more and more people were being promoted from operations to key positions in the bank. As a matter of fact, Brent Woods himself represented one of the first of this new breed. He had a successful career in international and commercial banking prior to being asked to accept the position of senior vice president of operations. Ivan Armstrong told him at the time, "Brent, this represents an opportunity for you. In the next 10 years operations experience will be invaluable to your career, and I want you to

---

[1]The case was prepared as a basis for class discussion, not to illustrate either effective or ineffective handling of an administrative situation.

accept this challenge even though such a position has been viewed as a dead end in the past. All of our senior executives will come through operations in the future."

After getting his feet on the ground, Brent Woods tried to assess the status of his operations department. He had 850 employees in the department, over half of the people in the bank. He also used most of the data processing services, he had several million dollars worth of equipment, and, he had an annual budget of $12 million. The major departments within operations were: check clearing, wire transfer, cashiers, data processing, security, internal auditing, and accounting. An organization chart is shown in Exhibit 1.

Of the 850 employees in bank operations, about 150 were managers or professional people and 700 were hourly workers. The managerial titles were inflated, quite common in banking. Over 100 of his people were officers, and almost anyone of importance carried the title of director, assistant vice president, or manager, even though they were essentially supervisors. Title inflation led to some confusion in responsibilities, and some duplication of efforts and excessive pay for some people. For others, the pay was too low. For example, compe-

tent systems analysts and programmers were constantly being raided by other companies. They would have to be at least an assistant vice president to be paid enough to stay, but this was impractical for the responsibility and seniority they carried.

At the clerical level, low pay and high turnovers were problems. For example, employees who operated check clearing machines were paid the minimum wage, about $4 per hour, they were given little training, and the turnover was 50 percent a year in this job. While some of the employees, who were predominantly women, left to get married, many others found work at higher rates. As a result of this high turnover, Brent Woods wondered about the quality of work being done and the possible errors made. He was constantly hearing about mixups within operations which had affected key customers. In some cases, this cost the bank money because of interest lost or adjustments made to customers' accounts.

Woods also felt that the quality of supervision was a key factor for clerical people. To them, their supervisor was the "bank," yet the quality of supervision was variable. Some supervisors were excellent and had a very good education. Others

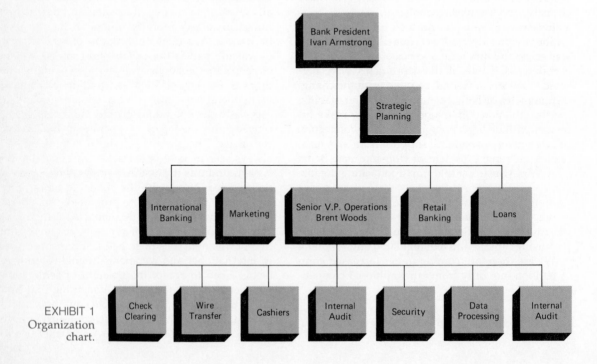

EXHIBIT 1
Organization chart.

had largely risen from the ranks, and one day they were asked to be a supervisor in order to fill a vacancy.

Bank operations were quite automated. The bank had 20 check clearing machines which cost about $100,000 each. It also operated over 100 automatic tellers at various locations, and it had several sophisticated sorting machines and computers. The sorting machines cost $500,000 each and were used to sort checks into outgoing mail. The bank's computers were the best in the industry and cost over $4 million. They were used for accounting services and other bank transactions. Over 30 programmers and systems analysts were employed to keep these computers operating. Obviously, with the advent of the personal computer and other technological changes, great changes in bank operations technology not only were possible but might be required to remain competitive.

The bank made a variety of quality and efficiency measurements. For example, it monitored the rate of daily production from each of the check clearing machines. It also kept records on errors made and the costs of correcting various types of errors. As a matter of fact, Woods sometimes felt he got too much detailed data and not enough management information. If only there were some way to monitor operations at various levels which would be consistent and reliable.

The bank also had a work planning system for managers and supervisors. Once a year each manager completed a detailed work plan which laid out objectives, key results measurement, and activities planned. This "MBO-type" system had been set up by the personnel department and was bankwide in nature. Since job responsibilities were unclear in some areas, the system did not work as well as it might have. Brent Woods also thought the system might have been a bit too rigid and too detailed.

In 1987, the bank had used the services of a well-known consultant to set up a work measurement system. The idea was to measure each clerical person's job and to set a time standard. The system would then be used to plan and control direct labor costs. The system had been a fiasco. Measurements were not accurate, many employees had been handled poorly, and jobs were not clearly defined. As a result, the system had been abandoned after over a year of work and the consultant permanently banished from the bank. Two years later there were still hard feelings among employees and managers over this "industrial engineering" system.

In viewing the situation it was clear that Woods had to take some action to "get a grip" on operations and to set a new direction for his years as senior vice president of operations. One of his staff had recently attended several seminars on quality circles (QC) and was pushing hard for the bank to start a QC program, but Woods wondered whether the bank was ready for quality circles.

He remembered the charge of his boss, "I want you to provide the services that our customers need at the lowest possible cost." How could he operationalize this charge? Should he do something to upgrade supervisors? Should he seek to reduce turnover? Should he tackle title inflation, the work planning system, the measurement and information system, technology? If he selected any one of these, how would he then deal with the others? Should a task force or an outside consultant be retained to help sort out the situation and set a direction? Brent Woods knew he needed to take charge as a leader, but he was unsure how to proceed.

DISCUSSION QUESTIONS

1. What are the problems that Brent Woods is facing?

2. What should be done about these problems?

3. What should Brent Woods do?

Minnesota Diversified Industries

Minnesota Diversified Industries (MDI) is a national model of an affirmative industry firm.[1] (An affirmative industry is a nonprofit organization whose primary goal is to provide employment to people who are handicapped.) Over 80 percent of the employees at MDI have social, physical, or mental handicaps. Although MDI is very similar to a business run for profit, there is one major distinction: where as the for-profit business is primarily concerned with earning profit for investors, the affirmative industry is concerned with providing meaningful employment opportunities to handicapped people who have traditionally been unable to work.

MDI engages in packaging operations, the recycling of returnable containers, the repair of wooden pallets, and other operations which can be performed by handicapped employees. Because MDI is a nonprofit organization, it must raise capital from donations by government and nongovernmental sources. Aside from the source of capital, the company is competitive in every respect with other business firms. On price, for example, MDI competes in the marketplace with other firms that do not employ handicapped workers. As a result, the employees of MDI must perform productive work in relation to the amount they are paid.

With respect to wages, MDI pays an hourly rate based on the level of production achieved. As a result, some of the severely handicapped employees earn as little as 10 or 25 percent of the minimum wage rate when they are first employed. As the employees are trained and become more productive, their wage rate is increased to reflect improved output. Many employees have equaled or exceeded the minimum wage rate after a period

of time with the company. Some employees were originally so severely handicapped they were released from sheltered workshop programs as "untrainable."

MDI also employs a number of "competitive" workers who do not have handicaps. These competitive workers serve as role models: they help train the handicapped workers and are used to define the 100 percent work pace. All together, 320 handicapped workers and 80 competitive workers are employees at MDI.

The MDI wage rate system is essential to the survival of the company. It allows MDI to control its costs on a competitive basis, and, more importantly, it provides the handicapped worker with a sense of progress and pride as the worker's productivity improves. One of the goals of the company is to monitor each employee carefully and help him or her to achieve wage improvement during each quarter of the year.

To implement the MDI wage policy, each employee who earns less than the minimum wage is subjected to a time study five times per quarter. Each time study lasts 10 minutes, during which the actual production rate is compared with the employee's current base rate for pay purposes. On the basis of the five quarterly time studies, the pay rate for the next quarter is set.

The pay rate for every employee is determined in relation to the pay for a competitive worker. Suppose, for example, that on a particular job the competitive worker earns $4 per hour and produces a standard output of 10 pieces per hour. The piece rate for this job is therefore 40¢ per piece produced. If a particular handicapped employee produces 5 pieces per hour, that employee's pay rate will then be 5 × 40¢ = $2 per hour.

For each employee, efficiency is also defined relative to the minimum wage. Suppose, for example, the minimum wage is $3.50 per hour. Then a

[1]This case was prepared as a basis for class discussion, not to illustrate either effective or ineffective handling of an administrative situation.

EXHIBIT 1
TIME STUDY SUMMARY (12/26/86 to 3/25/88)

Period covered	Status of those studied	# studied	# of individuals studied—times per quarter													Under 5 studies per individual		Of those studied less than 5 times— not studied in previous quarter	
			1	2	3	4	5	6	7	8	9	10	11	12	13	#	%	#	%
12/26/86 to 3/25/87	Main plant employees	87	9	12	14	13	9	9	8	2	3	6	1	1		48	55		
3/26/87 to 6/25/87	Main plant employees	92	23	9	11	12	9	12	5	6		5				55	60		
	Main plant trainees	30	5	5	5	1	4	1	6	1	2					16	53		
	Plant 1 employees	41	6	5	8	2	2	5	5	2	2	1	2		1	21	51		
6/26/87 to 9/25/87	Main plant employees	104	23	24	17	19	13		5	3						83	80	32	39
	Main plant trainees	37	7	10	3	4	6	4	1	2						24	65	12	50
	Plant 1 employees	45	19	13	11		2									43	96	12	28
9/26/87 to 12/25/87	Main plant employees	117	29	19	35	13	11	8	2							96	82	26	27
	Main plant trainees	46	9	8	13	5	8	2		1						35	76	19	54
	Plant 1 employees	51	9	7	15	7	9	2	1	1						38	75	9	24
12/26/87 to 3/25/88	Main plant employees	93	28	20	17	12	7	4	5							77	83	9	12
	Main plant trainees	37	9	8	5	1	4	3	3	2	2					23	62	9	39
	Plant 1 employees	28	16	9	3											28	100	0	0

worker earning the minimum wage should produce 3.50/.40 = 8.75 pieces per hour. The efficiency of the worker who produces 5 pieces per hour is therefore 5/8.75 = 57 percent. It is the goal of the company to improve the efficiency and therefore the pay rate of each worker.

Recently MDI has begun to review the method of time study used to set wage rates and efficiencies. Data in Exhibit 1, for example, indicate that substantial numbers of employees were not time-studied five times during each quarter due to overloading of the single time study employee available. It also was not possible to standardize the method and to rate each employee's pace in accordance with normal industrial engineering practice. As a result, the management of MDI felt that a better work measurement system could be devised. Perhaps the improved system could use

actual production records to determine the pay rate and efficiency figures. For certain purposes, properly conducted time studies might also be used. The company was eager to explore these options and to implement an improved work measurement system.

DISCUSSION QUESTIONS

1. What are the alternative approaches to work measurement that the company might use?

2. Describe a work measurement approach that you would recommend to the management of MDI.

3. How would you go about implementing the system that you recommend?

General Appliance Company

The Milwaukee Division of General Appliance Company manufactures freezers, vacuum cleaners, ice makers, and other consumer appliances.[1] For the General Appliance Company, quality has always been a source of pride and a competitive advantage. In view of the company's quality image, George Rodgers, director of quality assurance for the Milwaukee Division, was concerned about the quality of parts which were used on the freezer assembly line. While the quality of the finished product had, apparently, not suffered, "irregularities" had occurred in the quality control system, and Mr. Rodgers wanted to correct these. He therefore decided to conduct a complete review of the parts quality control system at the Milwaukee Division freezer plant.

Mr. Rodgers and Dick West, his quality control engineer, requested that a team of four M.B.A. students from Marquette University be assigned to conduct a quality audit. In briefing the M.B.A. team, Mr. West stated that he wanted the team to cover all aspects of parts through quality from receiving of incoming parts through sample parts inspection and management policies. In Mr. West's words, "No stones should be left unturned in reviewing the present quality control system and in recommending improvements."

The M.B.A. team set out to define the problems in more detail and to develop a methodology for the quality audit. As part of the problem definition, the team interviewed all managers and supervisors at the freezer plant about how the quality system functioned and about the problems they saw in its operation. In all, about 20 managers were interviewed. The team also collected information on the flow of parts from the time they were received until they reached the freezer line, and they collected copies of all written quality policies and procedures in effect. As a result of these initial efforts, several issues were identified for in-depth study.

A formal questionnaire was then designed to aid in detailed study of the issues and formulation of recommendations. The questionnaire was administered to 10 directors, 21 managers, 32 supervisors, and 32 engineers. A sample of some of the results of the questionnaire is shown in Exhibit 1.

The questionnaire seemed to indicate a certain lack of understanding of the "total" quality concept, where all departments are collectively responsible for producing a quality product. This problem was compounded by conflicting departmental goals, a lack of teamwork, and poor communications between the various departments. However, as may be noted in Exhibit 1, the agreement on these issues by the people interviewed was by no means unanimous.

In reviewing the results of the questionnaire, Mr. Rodgers felt that something should be done, but the proper action was not clear. He recognized that it was always easy to blame the quality control department when things went wrong. He wondered how this situation could be improved.

---

[1]This case was prepared as a basis for class discussion, not to illustrate either effective or ineffective handling of an administrative situation.

DISCUSSION QUESTIONS

1. What precisely are the problems in managing quality at General Appliance?

2. How should the management problems be resolved?

3. What steps should be taken in the short run and the long run?

EXHIBIT 1
QUALITY SURVEY

ITEM 3

What percentage of your time is devoted to quality assurance-related activities?

	Row pct.	Total count
1. None	7.4	7
2. 1–20% of the time	38.9	37
3. 21–30% of the time	11.6	11
4. 31–40% of the time	10.5	10
5. 41–50% of the time	7.4	7
6. 51–60% of the time	7.4	6
7. More than 61% of the time	17.9	17

Marginally significant (.0929) differences in time spent on quality-related activities occurred depending upon job title. Overall, foremen and the supervisor/engineer group spent more time with quality tasks than other groups. Sixty percent of the managers spent less than 20 percent of their time on quality-related activities.

ITEM 7

How often do you accept responsibility (blame) for a quality-related problem? Answer in terms of times you have accepted responsibility within the *last 6 months.*

	Row pct.	Total count
1. Never	31.2	29
2. Once	12.9	12
3. Twice	6.5	6
4. Three times	4.3	4
5. Four times	9.7	9
6. More than four times (specify)	35.5	33
(2 missing observations)		

This question revealed response differences depending on job title (.0018) as well as product line (.0613). Overall foremen represent the group which said they accepted blame most often, engineers were second. Responses for directors were at opposite ends of the response scale—60 percent indicated they accepted blame more than five times in the last 6 months while 40 percent responded "never."

ITEM 9

How would you rate the quality of the product(s) you are associated with?

	Row pct.	Total count
1. Excellent	15.4	14
2. Very good	49.5	45
3. Good	29.7	27
4. Fair	3.3	3
5. Poor	2.2	2
(4 missing observations)		

EXHIBIT 1 *(Continued)*

ITEM 10

How would you rate the job that the quality control department does?

	Row pct.	Total count
1. Outstanding	0	0
2. Very good	28.0	26
3. Good	51.6	48
4. Fair	18.3	17
5. Poor	2.2	2
(2 missing observations)		

ITEM 11

If your answer for question 10 was below "outstanding," what is the major factor preventing quality control from performing in an outstanding way?

	Row pct.	Total count
1. Lack of technical expertise in Q. C. department	7.9	7
2. Poor financial support	10.9	9
3. No commitment from other departments	14.6	13
4. Lack of direction	15.7	14
5. Low status of QC department compared with other departments	7.9	7
6. None of the above (specify)	31.5	28
7. I rated the QC department as outstanding	0.0	0
8. More than one reason	12.4	11

ITEM 21

Do you have quantifiable measures of performance in your management objectives which relate to quality?

	Row pct.	Total count
1. Yes	47.4	45
2. No	16.8	16
3. I have quality-related objectives, but they are not easily measured; in other words they are qualitative measures.	35.8	34

ITEM 24

Do you feel that quality goals from department to department are in conflict?

	Row pct.	Total count
1. Yes	62.2	56
2. No	37.8	34
(5 missing observations)		

Respondent comment: "Yes, budget control versus quality program implementation."

EXHIBIT 1   *(Continued)*

ITEM 26

Should the line be shut down more often for problems relating to quality?

	Row pct.	Total count
1. Yes	48.4	45
2. No	51.6	48
(2 missing observations)		

The majority within the managers, directors, and supervisor/engineers groups favored shutting down the line more often for quality-related problems. Foremen did not agree. This difference was significant at .0645.

ITEM 27

It has been said that too many decisions are attempted through *committees*. Do you feel that *individuals* should assume more responsibility for quality decisions?

	Row pct.	Total count
1. Yes	71.3	67
2. No	28.7	27
(1 missing observation)		

Respondent comments: "Let's get managers acting like managers." "When QC foremen make a decision too many times it is overridden by somebody higher up in quality control." "On some items it would be much better if individuals made the decisions."

ITEM 28

Would you be willing to accept such responsibility for quality decisions relating to your area of responsibility?

	Row pct.	Total count
1. Yes	89.4	84
2. No	10.6	10
(1 missing observation)		

ITEM 29

Do you feel that people will try to short-cut quality procedures because they take too much time?

	Row pct.	Total count
1. Yes	72.6	69
2. No	27.4	26

Bayfield Mud Company

In November, 1988, John Wells, a customer service representative of Bayfield Mud Company, was summoned to the Houston, Texas, warehouse of Wet-Land Drilling, Inc. to inspect three boxcars of mud treating agents which Bayfield Mud Company had shipped to the Houston firm.[1] (Bayfield's corporate offices and its largest plant are located in Orange, Texas, which is just west of the Louisiana-Texas border). Wet-Land Drilling had filed a complaint that the 50-pound bags of treating agents that it had just received from Bayfield were short-weight by approximately 5 percent.

The light-weight bags were initially detected by one of Wet-Land's receiving clerks who noticed that the railroad scale tickets indicated that the net weights were significantly less on all three of the boxcars than those of identical shipments received on October 25, 1988. Bayfield's traffic department was called to determine if lighter weight dunnage or pallets were used on the shipments. (This might explain the lighter net weights.) Bayfield indicated, however, that no changes had been made in the loading or palletizing procedures. Hence, Wet-Land randomly checked 50 of the bags and discovered that the average net weight was 47.51 pounds. They noted from past shipments that the bag net weights averaged exactly 50.0 pounds, with an acceptable standard deviation of 1.2 pounds. Consequently, they concluded that the sample indicated a significant short-weight. (The reader may wish to verify the above conclusion.) Bayfield was then contacted, and Wells was sent to investigate the complaint. Upon arrival, Wells verified the complaint and issued a 5 percent credit to Wet-Land.

Wet-Land's management, however, was not completely satisfied with only the issuance of

---

[1]Reprinted with permission of Charles E. Merrill Publishing Company.

credit for the short shipment. The charts followed by their mud engineers on the drilling platforms were based on 50-pound bags of treating agents. Lighter weight bags might result in poor chemical control during the drilling operation and might adversely affect drilling efficiency. (Mud-treating agents are used to control the pH and other chemical properties of the cone during drilling operation.) This could cause severe economic consequences because of the extremely high cost of oil and natural gas well-drilling operations. Consequently, special use instructions had to accompany the delivery of these shipments to the drilling platforms. Moreover, the light-weight shipments had to be isolated in Wet-Land's warehouse, causing extra handling and poor space utilization. Hence, Wells was informed that Wet-Land's Drilling might seek a new supplier of mud-treating agents if, in the future, it received bags that deviated significantly from 50 pounds.

The quality control department at Bayfield suspected that the light-weight bags may have resulted from "growing pains" at the Orange plant. Because of economic conditions, oil and natural gas exploration activity had greatly increased. This increased activity, in turn, created increased demand for products produced by related industries, including drilling muds. Consequently, Bayfield had to expand from a one-shift (6:00 A.M. to 2:00 P.M.) to a two-shift (6:00 A.M. to 10:00 P.M.) operation in mid-1986 and finally to a three-shift operation (24 hours per day) in the fall of 1988.

The additional night-shift bagging crew was staffed entirely by new employees. The most experienced foremen were temporarily assigned to supervise the night-shift employees. Most emphasis was placed on increasing the output of bags to meet the ever-increasing demand. It was suspected that only occasional reminders were made to double-check the bag weight-feeder. (A double-check is performed by systematically weighing a bag on a scale to determine if the proper weight is being loaded by the weight-feeder. If there is a significant deviation from 50 pounds, corrective adjustments are made to the weight-release mechanism.)

To verify this expectation, the quality control staff randomly sampled the bag output and prepared the following chart. Twenty-four bags were sampled and weighed each hour.

Time	Avg. weight (pounds)	Range Smallest	Largest
6:00 A.M.	49.6	48.7	50.7
7:00	50.2	49.1	51.2
8:00	50.6	49.6	51.4
9:00	50.8	50.2	51.8
10:00	49.9	49.2	52.3
11:00	50.3	48.6	51.7
12:00 Noon	48.6	46.2	50.4
1:00 P.M.	49.0	46.4	50.0
2:00	49.0	46.0	50.6
3:00	49.8	48.2	50.8
4:00	50.3	49.2	52.7
5:00	51.4	50.0	55.3
6:00	51.6	49.2	54.7
7:00	51.8	50.0	55.6
8:00	51.0	48.6	53.2
9:00	50.5	49.4	52.4
10:00	49.2	46.1	50.7
11:00	49.0	46.3	50.8
12:00 Midnight	48.4	45.4	50.2
1:00 A.M.	47.6	44.3	49.7
2:00	47.4	44.1	49.6
3:00	48.2	45.2	49.0
4:00	48.0	45.5	49.1
5:00	48.4	47.1	49.6
6:00	48.6	47.4	52.0
7:00	50.0	49.2	52.2
8:00	49.8	49.0	52.4
9:00	50.3	49.4	51.7
10:00	50.2	49.6	51.8
11:00	50.0	49.0	52.3
12:00 Noon	50.0	48.8	52.4
1:00 P.M.	50.1	49.4	53.6
2:00	49.7	48.6	51.0
3:00	48.4	47.2	51.7
4:00	47.2	45.3	50.9

Time	Avg. weight (pounds)	Range Smallest	Largest
5:00	46.8	44.1	49.0
6:00	46.8	41.0	51.2
7:00	50.0	46.2	51.7
8:00	47.4	44.0	48.7
9:00	47.0	44.2	48.9
10:00	47.2	46.6	50.2
11:00	48.6	47.0	50.0
12:00 Midnight	49.8	48.2	50.4
1:00 A.M.	49.6	48.4	51.7
2:00	50.0	49.0	52.2
3:00	50.0	49.2	50.0
4:00	47.2	46.3	50.5
5:00	47.0	44.1	49.7
6:00	48.4	45.0	49.0
7:00	48.8	44.8	49.7
8:00	49.6	48.0	51.8
9:00	50.0	48.1	52.7
10:00	51.0	48.1	55.2
11:00	50.4	49.5	54.1
12:00 Noon	50.0	48.7	50.9
1:00 P.M.	48.9	47.6	51.2
2:00	49.8	48.4	51.0
3:00	49.8	48.8	50.8
4:00	50.0	49.1	50.6
5:00	47.8	45.2	51.2
6:00	46.4	44.0	49.7
7:00	46.4	44.4	50.0
8:00	47.2	46.6	48.9
9:00	48.4	47.2	49.5
10:00	49.2	48.1	50.7
11:00	48.4	47.0	50.8
12:00 Midnight	47.2	46.4	49.2
1:00 A.M.	47.4	46.8	49.0
2:00	48.8	47.2	51.4
3:00	49.6	49.0	50.6
4:00	51.0	50.5	51.5
5:00	50.5	50.0	51.9

DISCUSSION QUESTIONS

1. What is your analysis of the bag weight problem?

2. What procedures would you recommend to maintain proper quality control?

Hank Kolb, Director, Quality Assurance

Hank Kolb was whistling as he walked toward his office, still feeling a bit like a stranger since he had been hired four weeks ago as director, quality assurance.[1] All last week he had been away from the plant at an interesting seminar entitled "Quality in the 90s" given for quality managers of manufacturing plants by the corporate training department. He was not looking forward to really digging into the quality problems at this industrial products plant employing 1,200 people.

Hank poked his head into Mark Hamler's office, his immediate subordinate, the quality control manager, and asked him how things had gone last week. Mark's muted smile and an "Oh, fine" stopped Hank in his tracks. He didn't know Mark very well and was unsure about pursuing this reply any further. Hank was still uncertain of how to start building his relationship with him since Mark had been passed over for the promotion to Hank's job—Mark's evaluation form had stated "superb technical knowledge; managerial skills lacking." Hank decided to inquire a little further and asked Mark what had happened. Mark replied:

Oh, just another typical quality snafu. We had a little problem on the Greasex line last week (a specialized degreasing solvent packed in a spray can for the high-technology sector). A little high pressure was found in some cans on the second shift, but a supervisor vented them so that we could ship them out. We met our delivery schedule!

Since Hank was still relatively unfamiliar with the plant and the products he asked Mark to elaborate. Painfully, Mark continued:

We've been having some trouble with the new filling equipment, and some of the cans were pressurized beyond our acceptable standard on a psi (pounds per square inch) rating scale. The production rate is still 50 percent of standard, about 14 cases per shift, and we caught it halfway into the shift. Mac Evans (the inspector for that line) picked it up, tagged the cases "Hold" and went on about his duties. When he returned at the end of the shift to write up the rejects, Wayne Simmons, first-line supervisor, was by a pallet of finished goods finishing sealing up a carton of the rejected Greasex: the reject "Hold" tags had been removed. He told Mac that he had heard about the high pressure from another inspector at coffee break, had come back, taken off the tags, individually turned the cans upside down and vented every one of them in the rejected eight cartons. He told Mac that production planning was really pushing for the stuff, and they couldn't delay by having it sent through the rework area. He told Mac that he would get on the operator to run the equipment right next time. Mac didn't write it up but came in about three days ago to tell me about it. Oh, it happens every once in a while, and I told him to make sure to check with maintenance to make sure the filling machine was adjusted; and I saw Wayne in the hall and told him that he ought to send the stuff through rework next time.

Hank was a bit dumbfounded at this and didn't say much—he didn't know if this was a "big deal" or not. When he got to his office he thought again what Mr. Morganthal, general manager, had said when he had hired Hank. He warned Hank about the "lack of quality attitude" in the plant and said that Hank "should try to do something about this."

[1]Reprinted with permission of the Harvard Business School.

He had further emphasized the quality problems in the plant. "We have to improve our quality, it's costing us a lot of money, I'm sure of it, but I can't prove it! Hank, you have my full support in this matter; you're in charge of these quality problems. This downward quality-productivity-turnover spiral has to end!"

The incident had happened a week ago; the goods were probably out in the customer's hands by now; everyone had forgotten about it (or wanted to!); and there seemed to be more pressing problems than this for Hank to spend his time on; but this continued to nag at him. He felt like the quality department was being treated as a joke, and it also felt to him like a personal slap from manufacturing. He didn't want to start a war with the production people but what could he do? He was troubled enough to cancel his appointments and spend the morning talking to a few people. After a long and very tactful morning, he learned the following:

A. From personnel—the operator for the filling equipment had just been transferred from shipping two weeks ago. He had had no formal training in this job but was being trained by Wayne, on the job, to run the equipment. When Mac had tested the high-pressure cans, the operator was nowhere to be found and had only learned of the rejected material from Wayne after the shift was over.

B. From plant maintenance—this particular piece of automated filling equipment had been purchased two years ago for use on another product. It had been switched to the Greasex line six months ago, and maintenance had had 12 work orders during the last month for repairs or adjustments on it. The equipment had been adapted by plant maintenance for handling the lower viscosity Greasex, which it had not originally been designed for. This included designing a special filling head. There was no scheduled preventive maintenance for this equipment, and the parts for the sensitive filling head, replaced three times in the last six months, had to be made at a nearby machine shop. Non-standard downtime was running at 15 percent of actual running times.

C. From purchasing—the plastic nozzle heads for the Greasex can, recently designed by a vendor

for this new product on a rush order, were often found with slight burrs on the inside rim, and this caused some trouble in fitting the top to the can. An increase in application pressure at the filling head by maintenance adjustment had solved the burr application problem or had at least "forced" the nozzle heads on despite burrs. Purchasing said that they were going to talk to the sales representative of the nozzle head supplier about this the next time he came in.

D. From product design and packaging—the can, designed especially for Greasex, had been contoured to allow better gripping by the user. This change, instigated by marketing research, set Greasex apart from the appearance of its competitors and was seen by the designers to be "significant." There had been no test of the effects of the contoured can on filling speed or filling hydrodynamics from a high-pressured filling head. Hank had a hunch that the new design was acting as a venturi when being filled, but the packaging designer thought that "unlikely."

E. From manufacturing manager—he had heard about the problem; in fact, Wayne had made a joke about it, bragging about how he beat his production quota to the other foremen and shift supervisors. Wayne was thought by the manufacturing manager to be one of the "best foremen we have . . . he always gets his production out." His promotion papers were actually on the manufacturing manager's desk when Hank dropped by. Wayne was being "strongly considered" for promotion to shift supervisor. The manufacturing manager, under pressure from Mr. Morganthal for cost improvements and reduced delivery times, sympathized with Hank but said that the rework area would have just vented with their pressure gauges that Wayne did by hand. "But, I'll speak with Wayne about the incident."

F. From marketing—the introduction of Greasex had been rushed to beat competitors to market and a major promotional/advertising campaign was now underway to increase consumer awareness. A deluge of orders was swamping the order-taking department right now and putting Greasex high on the back-order list. Production "had to turn the stuff out"; even a little off spec was tolerable because "it would be better to have it on the shelf than not there at all. Who cares if the label is a little crooked or the stuff comes out with a little too much pressure? We need market share now in that high-tech segment."

What bothered Hank the most was the safety issue of the high pressure in the cans. He had no way of knowing how much of a hazard the high pressure was or if Wayne had vented them enough to effectively reduce the hazard. The data from the can manufacturer which Mark had showed him indicated that the high pressure which the inspector had found was not in the danger area; but then again the inspector had only used a sample testing procedure to reject the eight cases. Even if he could morally accept that there was no product safety hazard, could he make sure that this never happened again?

Hank, skipping lunch, sat in his office and thought about the morning's events. Last week's seminar had talked about "the role of quality," "productivity and quality," "creating a new attitude," and the "quality challenge" but where had they told him what to do when this happens? He had left a very good job to come here because he thought the company was serious about the importance of quality, and he wanted a challenge. Hank had demanded and received a salary equal to the manufacturing, marketing, and R&D directors' and was one of the direct reports to the general manager. Yet he still didn't know exactly what he should or shouldn't do or even what he could or couldn't do.

DISCUSSION QUESTIONS

1. What is wrong with the way quality is managed in this company?

2. What should be done to improve quality management?

3. What should Hank Kolb do?

Donaldson Company

COMPANY BACKGROUND

The Donaldson Company is a Minneapolis-based firm engaged in the production and sale of air cleaners and filters, hydraulic filters, mufflers, and various dust collectors and control devices.[1] Donaldson products are distributed worldwide, principally to original equipment and manufacturers in the truck and bus, construction and mining, farm equipment, railroad, and manufacturing industries.

The Donaldson Company has several operating divisions: the Fluid Power Products Division produces hydraulic filters, Torit Division produces air pollution control equipment for industrial applications, and the Liquid Systems Division manufactures equipment designed to remove particles from liquids. The Donaldson Division, the largest of the divisions and subject of this case, manufactures heavy-duty air cleaners, replacement filter elements, mufflers, silencers, dust-control devices for mining operations, and various other specialized filters. The Donaldson Division produces approximately 70 percent of the Donaldson Company's total sales.

ORGANIZATION OF THE DONALDSON DIVISION

The Donaldson Division's manufacturing operations are conducted at eight plants located primarily in the Midwest. Production is geared to orders received, and plants typically carry only a small finished goods inventory. Individual products are set up and run approximately five to eight times per year.

Each plant produces a portion of the approxi-

mately 25,000 different line items that the division markets. Plant outputs vary considerably in terms of volume, product mix, market application, and manufacturing requirements. In addition, while some plants produce end-use products, others manufacture components that require further assembly at another plant.

Individual plants collect and maintain data on inventory levels and labor efficiency. However, most of the accounting for the individual plants is done at division headquarters in Bloomington, Minn. Individual plants are connected through a batch processing system with a computer in Bloomington for purposes of information processing.

Plant managers have substantial control over many aspects of a plant's operations and minimal control over a few areas. Certain functions—including marketing, purchasing, and accounting—are performed at the division level. Generally, a plant manager does not have significant control over production levels, sales prices, or raw materials prices.

The division staff in Bloomington performs the marketing function. Individual plant production forecasts are developed from the marketing forecasts, assigning production to a plant in line with the anticipated demand for the products made at that plant. Since the plant manager does not have effective control over the marketing effort and subsequent production requirements, the manager cannot control the plant utilization level as it relates to coverage of fixed expenses.

A second aspect of the centralized marketing function is that the plant managers have little impact on the prices at which the plant's production is sold. Pricing policies are determined at the division level, with prices based on market conditions as well as cost considerations. As will be explained later, these pricing policies have a signif-

---

[1]This case was prepared as a basis for class discussion, not to illustrate either effective or ineffective handling of an administrative situation.

icant impact on the measurement of current plant performance.

Finally, purchasing of significant materials is performed at the division level. Thus, the prices of raw materials at the plant level are largely beyond the control of the plant manager.

Apart from production volume, sales prices, and raw materials prices, the plant manager has substantial control over all other aspects of plant operations. Because of the impact on profits of the variables that the plant manager does not control, management feels it is more appropriate to view the individual plants as cost centers rather than profit centers.

EVALUATION OF A PLANT MANAGER'S PERFORMANCE

The Donaldson Division is oriented toward acceptable rates of profitability and return on assets. While profitability is easily measured at the division level, it is more difficult to measure the plant manager's contributions to profits. Since a plant manager controls only some of the variables that affect plant profits, plant net profit does not adequately reflect the plant manager's contribution.

The Donaldson Division currently utilizes a management by objectives (MBO) system. The MBO system defines nine measures for which the plant manager is held responsible. Three of these areas relate to division or corporate profitability; five are concerned with customer service, quality control, labor efficiency, inventory turnover, and return on assets employed. The other measure, called the profit improvement goal, attempts to measure the plant manager's contribution to profit by measuring the direct costs incurred at the plant level.

The nine measures have varying weights in the computation of the overall MBO performance appraisal. The weight of the profit improvement goal measure varies between 10 and 15 percent of a manager's total appraisal, depending on the plant involved. The vehicle for measuring a manager's accomplishment of the profit improvement goal is a monthly report titled the *Plant Goal Analysis* (PGA).

Recently, the Donaldson Division has questioned the use of the PGA report as an effective means of measuring a plant manager's achieve-

ment of the profit improvement goal. The stated objective of the profit improvement goal is to increase profit through reduction of direct plant costs. These costs are defined as material, direct labor, overhead, and direct plant general and administrative (G&A) expense. Performance is measured by a ratio of actual direct plant costs to target direct plant costs.

The PGA shows the actual and target direct plant costs on a monthly and year-to-date basis. Before looking at the PGA report itself, the budgeting process should be reviewed. An understanding of the flow of the budgeting process is essential to understanding the problems inherent in the PGA method.

BUDGETING PROCESS

The first step in the budgeting process is the division sales plan. Based on the division sales plan, production is assigned to the individual plants. Plant costs are then budgeted based on assigned production. Budgeted plant standard costs are computed as percentages of sales at the current selling price. If no price increases were planned, standard costs would be a constant percentage of sales throughout the year. However, because price increases are planned, standard costs decrease as a percentage of budgeted sales. No allowance is made in budgeted standard costs for cost increases because standards are fixed throughout the year. Expected cost increases are reflected in budgeted variances. An example of the profit and loss (P&L) budget for one plant is shown in Exhibit 1. The corresponding PGA for the plant is shown in Exhibit 2.

DESCRIPTION OF THE PLANT GOAL ANALYSIS

The plant manager is not responsible for purchasing or sales; therefore some of the budget variances of the PGA are beyond the manager's control. The PGA analyst identifies the variances which the plant manager controls in order to measure the manager's contribution to division profits. That is accomplished by converting the P&L budget, which is a fixed budget, into a variable budget. To do that, the items in the PGA are divided into three categories:

EXHIBIT 1

PROFIT & LOSS STATEMENT, DINKYTOWN PLANT
PERIOD OF 6 MONTHS ENDED JANUARY 31, 1989
(000's OMITTED)

	Current Month					Current year-to-date					Prior year-to-date		Incr./(decr.)	
	Actual	% of sales	Plan	% of sales	Over/(under) plan	Actual	% of sales	Plan	% of sales	Over/(under) plan	Actual	% of sales	Amount	%
Sales														
Customer	$1176	86.7	$1355	88.6	$(179)	$7293	88.4	$6955	88.4	$338	$4637	86.1	$2656	57.3
Interplant	180	13.3	175	11.4	5	960	11.6	910	11.6	50	748	13.9	212	28.3
Total	1356	100.0	1530	100.0	(174)	8253	100.0	7865	100.0	388	5385	100.0	2868	53.3
Cost of sales														
Material	584	43.1	699	45.7	(115)	3760	45.5	3584	45.6	176	2381	44.2	1379	57.9
Labor	99	7.3	119	7.8	(20)	641	7.8	609	7.7	32	422	7.8	219	51.9
Burden	354	26.1	314	20.5	40	1895	23.0	1742	22.2	153	1436	26.7	459	32.0
Tooling	21	1.5	21	1.4	—	125	1.5	125	1.6	—	109	2.0	16	14.7
Total	1058	78.0	1153	75.4	(95)	6421	77.8	6060	77.1	361	4348	80.7	2073	47.7
Gross margin	298	22.0	377	24.6	(79)	1832	22.2	1805	22.9	27	1037	19.3	795	76.7
Operating expenses														
Marketing	22	1.6	26	1.7	(4)	142	1.7	154	2.0	(12)	113	2.1	29	25.7
Physical distribution	20	1.5	16	1.0	4	110	1.3	94	1.2	16	70	1.3	40	57.1
Product engineering	57	4.2	57	3.7	—	323	3.9	348	4.4	(25)	305	5.7	18	5.9
Production development	—		—			—		—			—		—	
Plant G&A	22	1.6	21	1.4	1	130	1.6	125	1.6	5	100	1.9	30	20.0
Division G&A	32	2.4	35	2.3	(3)	190	2.3	212	2.7	(22)	151	2.8	39	25.8
Corporate services	5	.3	5	.3	—	31	.4	29	.3	2	44	.8	(13)	(29.5)
Subtotal	158	11.6	160	10.4	(2)	926	11.2	962	12.2	(36)	783	14.6	143	18.3
Other														
Other income	—		—			—		—			—		—	
Other expense	1	.1	—		1	1		1		1	—		1	
Total	159	11.7	160	10.4	(1)	927	11.2	962	12.2	(35)	783	14.6	144	18.4
Direct operating profit	$ 139	10.3	$ 217	14.2	$ (78)	$ 905	11.0	$ 843	10.7	$ 62	$ 254	4.7	$ 651	256.3

Manufacturing expense through 6 months has been increased by $51 due to adjustments of accruals. $39 of this total was adjusted in January.

EXHIBIT 2

DONALDSON COMPANY, INC.—PLANT GOAL ANALYSIS
PLANT: DINKYTOWN
MONTH: JANUARY 1989
(000'S OMITTED)

Description	Actual	%	Plan	%	Cum. actual	%	Cum. plan	%
Sales—customer	1176	86.7	1176	86.7	7303	88.5	7303	88.5
interplant	180	13.3	180	13.3	960	11.6	960	11.6
returns	—	—	—	—	(10)	(.1)	(10)	(.1)
Total net sales	1356	100.0	1356	100.0	8253	100.0	8253	100.0
COST OF SALES								
Direct material								
Std. mat'l.—reg.	387	32.9	425	36.1	2522	34.6	2627	36.0
Std. mat'l.—I.P.	80	44.4	76	42.2	411	42.8	405	42.2
Pur. var.—reg.	9	.7	9	.7	30	.4	30	.4
Pur. var.—I.P.	105	7.7	105	7.7	779	9.4	779	9.4
Res. for shrink	—	—	—	—	—	—	—	—
Methods variance	3	.2	3	.2	18	.2	18	.2
Total act. material	584	43.1	618	45.6	3760	45.5	3859	46.7
Direct labor								
Std. labor—regular	79	6.7	85	7.2	527	7.2	527	7.2
Std. labor— I.P.	10	5.6	11	6.1	61	6.4	60	6.3
Res. for shrink	1	.1	—	—	5	.1	4	—
Methods variance	9	.7	9	.7	48	.6	48	.6
Total act. labor	99	7.3	105	7.8	641	7.8	639	7.7
Manufacturing overhead								
Std. O.H.—reg.	195	16.6	200	17.0	1300	17.8	1255	17.2
Std. O.H.—I.P.	26	14.4	26	14.4	149	15.5	143	14.9
Mfg. expense*	339	25.0	291	21.4	1825	22.1	1745	21.1
Less: abs. overhead*	(228)	(16.8)	(228)	(16.8)	(1505)	(18.2)	(1505)	(18.2)
Unabsorbed overhead	111	8.2	63	4.6	320	3.9	240	2.9
Reserve for shrink	2	.1	2	.1	12	.1	12	.1
Methods variance	20	1.5	20	1.5	114	1.4	114	1.4
Total actual overhead	354	26.1	311	22.9	1895	23.0	1764	21.4
New model tooling	21	1.5	21	1.5	125	1.5	125	1.5
Total cost of sales	1058	78.0	1055	77.8	6421	77.8	6387	77.3
Less new model tooling	(21)	(1.5)	(21)	(1.5)	(125)	(1.5)	(125)	(1.5)
Plus direct G&A	22	1.6	21	1.5	130	1.6	125	1.5
Total direct plant costs	1059	78.1	1055	77.8	6426	77.9	6387	77.3

*Not included in totals

Manufacturing expense through 6 months has been increased by $51 due to adjustments of accruals. $39 of this total was adjusted in January.

Donaldson Division Accounting

Date ___February 10, 1989___

Goal measurement
  98.5% of plan = 100% accomplishment
100.0% of plan = 50% accomplishment
101.5% of plan =   0% accomplishment

Cumulative plant goal achievement: __30%__

1. Uncontrollable

2. Fixed

3. Variable

The uncontrollable items are sales, purchase variances, absorbed overhead, and new model tooling. For these items the plan is set equal to the actual, so that the variance is always zero. The fixed items are the reserves for shrink and direct G&A. For these items the plan is taken directly from the P&L budget.

The variable items are standard materials, standard labor, standard overhead, and the methods variances. The planned amounts for these items are computed as percentages of actual sales based on the corresponding percentages on the P&L budget. For example, if budgeted sales are $1 million and budgeted standard materials are $400,000 (on the P&L budget), and if actual sales are $1.1 million, then planned standard materials on the PGA would be $440,000. The result is that the manager is not penalized for costs over budget which are the result of sales over budget, nor is the manager rewarded for cost reductions which are the result of sales reductions.

Manufacturing expense is semivariable. The fixed and variable components are identified, and the plan amounts are computed separately. In addition, the variable component is broken down into two parts. Planned costs for direct departments are computed on the basis of direct hours, and planned costs for nondirect departments are based on product dollars produced. Exhibit 3 summarizes the calculation of the plan amounts for the various items.

The manager's performance on the profit improvement goal is computed by comparing total actual with total plan costs, as follows:

• Actual 98.5 percent of plan is 100 percent accomplishment.

• Actual 100 percent of plan is 50 percent accomplishment.

• Actual 101.5 percent of plan is 0 percent accomplishment.

Interpolation is used between the stated benchmarks. No allowance is made for accomplishment above 100 percent or below 0 percent. The percent accomplishment is included in each manager's MBO evaluation.

Donaldson management has identified three weaknesses in the formulation of the PGA which result in inadequacies in the measurement process:

1. The use of sales and cost of sales instead of production and cost of production.

2. The inclusion of uncontrollable items in the totals

3. The use of sales as a basis for computing variable costs

DONALDSON'S DILEMMA

Faced with these problems in measurement of plant performance, the management of the Donaldson Division recognized two alternatives. The first was to improve the PGA measurement system to more accurately reflect actual plant performance. The second alternative, representing an entirely different approach was to abandon the PGA form and develop a productivity measure for plant performance. The productivity measure could represent actual output divided by input, and it could be compared from one period to the next, independent of the plan. While a productivity measure might eliminate some of the problems with the PGA, it might create still other problems in the measurement of plant performance.

QUESTIONS

1. How should the current PGA measurement system be improved to more accurately reflect plant performance?

2. Devise a productivity measure for the Donaldson Company plants.

3. Discuss the pros and cons of using the PGA approach as opposed to the productivity measurement approach to evaluating plant performance.

EXHIBIT 3

DONALDSON COMPANY, INC.—PLANT GOAL ANALYSIS
PLANT _____
MONTH _____
(000'S OMITTED)

Description	Actual	%	Plan	%	Cum. actual	%	Cum. plan	%
Sales—customer	*							
interplant	*							
returns	*							
Total net sales								
COST OF SALES								
Direct material	*							
Std. mat'l.—reg.	***							
Std. mat'l.—I.P.	***							
Pur. var.—reg.	*							
Pur. var.—I.P.	*							
Res. for shrink	**							
Methods variance	***							
Total act. material								
Direct labor								
Std. labor—regular	***							
Std. labor—I.P.	***							
Res. for shrink	**							
Methods variance	***							
Total act. labor								
Manufacturing overhead								
Std. O.H.—reg.	***							
Std. O.H.—I.P.	***							
Mfg. expense	****							
Less: abs. overhead	*							
Unabsorbed overhead								
Reserve for shrink	**							
Methods variance	***							
Total actual overhead								
New model tooling	*							
Total cost of sales								
Less new model tooling	*							
Plus direct G&A	**							
Total direct plant costs								

KEY—
*Uncontrollable—Plan is set equal to actual.
**Fixed—Plan is taken directly from the P&L budget.
***Variable—Plan is computed as a percentage of sales.
****Semivariable—Fixed and variable components of the plan are computed separately.

Goal measurement
98.5% of plan = 100% accomplishment
100.0% of plan = 50% accomplishment
101.5% of plan = 0% accomplishment

Donaldson Division Accounting

Date _____

Cumulative plant goal achievement: _____

Inventory at month end = _____

APPENDIXES

APPENDIX A
AREAS UNDER THE STANDARD
NORMAL PROBABILITY DISTRIBUTION

Values in the table represent the proportion of area under the normal curve between the mean ($\mu = 0$) and a positive value of z.

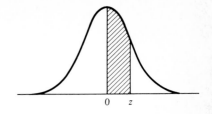

z	.00	.01	.02	.03	.04	.05	.06	.07	.08	.09
0.0	0.0000	0.0040	0.0080	0.0120	0.0160	0.0199	0.0239	0.0279	0.0319	0.0359
0.1	0.0398	0.0438	0.0478	0.0517	0.0557	0.0596	0.0636	0.0675	0.0714	0.0753
0.2	0.0793	0.0832	0.0871	0.0910	0.0948	0.0987	0.1026	0.1064	0.1103	0.1141
0.3	0.1179	0.1217	0.1255	0.1293	0.1331	0.1368	0.1406	0.1443	0.1480	0.1517
0.4	0.1554	0.1591	0.1628	0.1664	0.1700	0.1736	0.1772	0.1808	0.1844	0.1879
0.5	0.1915	0.1950	0.1985	0.2019	0.2054	0.2088	0.2123	0.2157	0.2190	0.2224
0.6	0.2257	0.2291	0.2324	0.2357	0.2389	0.2422	0.2454	0.2486	0.2517	0.2549
0.7	0.2580	0.2611	0.2642	0.2673	0.2703	0.2734	0.2764	0.2794	0.2823	0.2852
0.8	0.2881	0.2910	0.2939	0.2967	0.2995	0.3023	0.3051	0.3078	0.3106	0.3133
0.9	0.3159	0.3186	0.3212	0.3238	0.3264	0.3289	0.3315	0.3340	0.3365	0.3389
1.0	0.3413	0.3438	0.3461	0.3485	0.3508	0.3531	0.3554	0.3577	0.3599	0.3621
1.1	0.3643	0.3665	0.3686	0.3708	0.3729	0.3749	0.3770	0.3790	0.3810	0.3830
1.2	0.3849	0.3869	0.3888	0.3907	0.3925	0.3944	0.3962	0.3980	0.3997	0.4015
1.3	0.4032	0.4049	0.4066	0.4082	0.4099	0.4115	0.4131	0.4147	0.4162	0.4177
1.4	0.4192	0.4207	0.4222	0.4236	0.4251	0.4265	0.4279	0.4292	0.4306	0.4319
1.5	0.4332	0.4345	0.4357	0.4370	0.4382	0.4394	0.4406	0.4418	0.4429	0.4441
1.6	0.4452	0.4463	0.4474	0.4484	0.4495	0.4505	0.4515	0.4525	0.4535	0.4545
1.7	0.4554	0.4564	0.4573	0.4582	0.4591	0.4599	0.4608	0.4616	0.4625	0.4633
1.8	0.4641	0.4649	0.4656	0.4664	0.4671	0.4678	0.4686	0.4693	0.4699	0.4706
1.9	0.4713	0.4719	0.4726	0.4732	0.4738	0.4744	0.4750	0.4756	0.4761	0.4767
2.0	0.4772	0.4778	0.4783	0.4788	0.4793	0.4798	0.4803	0.4808	0.4812	0.4817
2.1	0.4821	0.4826	0.4830	0.4834	0.4838	0.4842	0.4846	0.4850	0.4854	0.4857
2.2	0.4861	0.4864	0.4868	0.4871	0.4875	0.4878	0.4881	0.4884	0.4887	0.4890
2.3	0.4893	0.4896	0.4898	0.4901	0.4904	0.4906	0.4909	0.4911	0.4913	0.4916
2.4	0.4918	0.4920	0.4922	0.4925	0.4927	0.4929	0.4931	0.4932	0.4934	0.4936
2.5	0.4938	0.4940	0.4941	0.4943	0.4945	0.4946	0.4948	0.4949	0.4951	0.4952
2.6	0.4953	0.4955	0.4956	0.4957	0.4959	0.4960	0.4961	0.4962	0.4963	0.4964
2.7	0.4965	0.4966	0.4967	0.4968	0.4969	0.4970	0.4971	0.4972	0.4973	0.4974
2.8	0.4974	0.4975	0.4976	0.4977	0.4977	0.4978	0.4979	0.4979	0.4980	0.4981
2.9	0.4981	0.4982	0.4982	0.4983	0.4984	0.4984	0.4985	0.4985	0.4986	0.4986
3.0	0.4987	0.4987	0.4987	0.4988	0.4988	0.4989	0.4989	0.4989	0.4990	0.4990

APPENDIX B
RANDOM NUMBER TABLE

27767	43584	85301	88977	29490	69714	94015	64874	32444	48277
13025	14338	54066	15243	47724	66733	74108	88222	88570	74015
80217	36292	98525	24335	24432	24896	62880	87873	95160	59221
10875	62004	90391	61105	57411	06368	11748	12102	80580	41867
54127	57326	26629	19087	24472	88779	17944	05600	60478	03343
60311	42824	37301	42678	45990	43242	66067	42792	95043	52680
49739	71484	92003	98086	76668	73209	54244	91030	45547	70818
78626	51594	16453	94614	39014	97066	30945	57589	31732	57260
66692	13986	99837	00582	81232	44987	69170	37403	86995	90307
44071	28091	07362	97703	76447	42537	08345	88975	35841	85771
59820	96163	78851	16499	87064	13075	73035	41207	74699	09310
25704	91035	26313	77463	55387	72681	47431	43905	31048	56699
22304	90314	78438	66276	18396	73538	43277	58874	11466	16082
17710	59621	15292	76139	59526	52113	53856	30743	08670	84741
25852	58905	55018	56374	35824	71708	30540	27886	61732	75454
46780	56487	75211	10271	36633	68424	17374	52003	70707	70214
59849	96169	87195	46092	26787	60939	59202	11973	02902	33250
47670	07654	30342	40277	11049	72049	83012	09832	25571	77628
94304	71803	73465	09819	58869	35220	09504	96412	90193	79568
08105	59987	21437	36786	49226	77837	98524	97831	65704	09514
64281	61826	18555	64937	64654	25843	41145	42820	14924	39650
66847	70495	32350	02985	01755	14750	48968	38603	70312	05682
72461	33230	21529	53424	72877	17334	39283	04149	90850	64618
21032	91050	13058	16218	06554	07850	73950	79552	24781	89683
95362	67011	06651	16136	57216	39618	49856	99326	40902	05069
49712	97380	10404	55452	09971	59481	37006	22186	72682	07385
58275	61764	97586	54716	61459	21647	87417	17198	21443	41808
89514	11788	68224	23417	46376	25366	94746	49580	01176	28838
15472	50669	48139	36732	26825	05511	12459	91314	80582	71944
12120	86124	51247	44302	87112	21476	14713	71181	13177	55292
95294	00556	70481	06905	21785	41101	49386	54480	23604	23554
66986	34099	74474	20740	47458	64809	06312	88940	15995	69321
80620	51790	11436	38072	40405	68032	60942	00307	11897	92674
55411	85667	77535	99892	71209	92061	92329	98932	78284	46347
95083	06783	28102	57816	85561	29671	77936	63574	31384	51924
90726	57166	98884	08583	95889	57067	38101	77756	11657	13897
68984	83620	89747	98882	92613	89719	39641	69457	91339	22502
36421	16489	18059	51061	67667	60631	84054	40455	99396	63680
92638	40333	67054	16067	24700	71594	47468	03577	57649	63266
21036	82808	77501	97427	76479	68562	43321	31370	28977	23896
13173	33365	41468	85149	49554	17994	91178	10174	29420	90438
86716	38746	94559	37559	49678	53119	98189	81851	29651	84215
92581	02262	41615	70360	64114	58660	96717	54244	10701	41393
12470	56500	50273	93113	41794	86861	39448	93136	25722	08564
01016	00857	41396	80504	90670	08289	58137	17820	22751	36518
34030	60726	25807	24260	71529	78920	47648	13885	70669	93406
50259	46345	06170	97965	88302	98041	11947	56203	19324	20504
73959	76145	60808	54444	74412	81105	69181	96845	38525	11600
46874	37088	80940	44893	10408	36222	14004	23153	69249	05747
60883	52109	19516	90120	46759	71643	62342	07589	08899	05985

APPENDIX C
PRESENT-VALUE FACTORS FOR FUTURE SINGLE PAYMENTS

Periods until payment	1%	2%	4%	6%	8%	10%	12%	14%	15%	16%	18%	20%	22%	24%	25%	26%	28%	30%
1	0.990	0.980	0.962	0.943	0.926	0.909	0.893	0.877	0.870	0.862	0.847	0.833	0.820	0.806	0.800	0.794	0.781	0.769
2	0.980	0.961	0.925	0.890	0.857	0.826	0.797	0.769	0.756	0.743	0.718	0.694	0.672	0.650	0.640	0.630	0.610	0.592
3	0.971	0.942	0.889	0.840	0.794	0.751	0.712	0.675	0.658	0.641	0.609	0.579	0.551	0.524	0.512	0.500	0.477	0.455
4	0.961	0.924	0.855	0.792	0.735	0.683	0.636	0.592	0.572	0.552	0.516	0.482	0.451	0.423	0.410	0.397	0.373	0.350
5	0.951	0.906	0.822	0.747	0.681	0.621	0.567	0.519	0.497	0.476	0.437	0.402	0.370	0.341	0.328	0.315	0.291	0.269
6	0.942	0.888	0.790	0.705	0.630	0.564	0.507	0.456	0.432	0.410	0.370	0.335	0.303	0.275	0.262	0.250	0.227	0.207
7	0.933	0.871	0.760	0.665	0.583	0.513	0.452	0.400	0.376	0.354	0.314	0.279	0.249	0.222	0.210	0.198	0.178	0.159
8	0.923	0.853	0.731	0.627	0.540	0.467	0.404	0.351	0.327	0.305	0.266	0.233	0.204	0.179	0.168	0.157	0.139	0.123
9	0.914	0.837	0.703	0.592	0.500	0.424	0.361	0.308	0.284	0.263	0.225	0.194	0.167	0.144	0.134	0.125	0.108	0.094
10	0.905	0.820	0.676	0.558	0.463	0.386	0.322	0.270	0.247	0.227	0.191	0.162	0.137	0.116	0.107	0.099	0.085	0.073
11	0.896	0.804	0.650	0.527	0.429	0.350	0.287	0.237	0.215	0.195	0.162	0.135	0.112	0.094	0.086	0.079	0.066	0.056
12	0.887	0.788	0.625	0.497	0.397	0.319	0.257	0.208	0.187	0.168	0.137	0.112	0.092	0.076	0.069	0.062	0.052	0.043
13	0.879	0.773	0.601	0.469	0.368	0.290	0.229	0.182	0.163	0.145	0.116	0.093	0.075	0.061	0.055	0.050	0.040	0.033
14	0.870	0.758	0.577	0.442	0.340	0.263	0.205	0.160	0.141	0.125	0.099	0.078	0.062	0.049	0.044	0.039	0.032	0.025
15	0.861	0.743	0.555	0.417	0.315	0.239	0.183	0.140	0.123	0.108	0.084	0.065	0.051	0.040	0.035	0.031	0.025	0.020
16	0.853	0.728	0.534	0.394	0.292	0.218	0.163	0.123	0.107	0.093	0.071	0.054	0.042	0.032	0.028	0.025	0.019	0.015
17	0.844	0.714	0.513	0.371	0.270	0.198	0.146	0.108	0.093	0.080	0.060	0.045	0.034	0.026	0.023	0.020	0.015	0.012
18	0.836	0.700	0.494	0.350	0.250	0.180	0.130	0.095	0.081	0.069	0.051	0.038	0.028	0.021	0.018	0.016	0.012	0.009
19	0.828	0.686	0.475	0.331	0.232	0.164	0.116	0.083	0.070	0.060	0.043	0.031	0.023	0.017	0.014	0.012	0.009	0.007
20	0.820	0.673	0.456	0.312	0.215	0.149	0.104	0.073	0.061	0.051	0.037	0.026	0.019	0.014	0.012	0.010	0.007	0.005
21	0.811	0.660	0.439	0.294	0.199	0.135	0.093	0.064	0.053	0.044	0.031	0.022	0.015	0.011	0.009	0.008	0.006	0.004
22	0.803	0.647	0.422	0.278	0.184	0.123	0.083	0.056	0.046	0.038	0.026	0.018	0.013	0.009	0.007	0.006	0.004	0.003
23	0.795	0.634	0.406	0.262	0.170	0.112	0.074	0.049	0.040	0.033	0.022	0.015	0.010	0.007	0.006	0.005	0.003	0.002
24	0.788	0.622	0.390	0.247	0.158	0.102	0.066	0.043	0.035	0.028	0.019	0.013	0.008	0.006	0.005	0.004	0.003	0.002
25	0.780	0.610	0.375	0.233	0.146	0.092	0.059	0.038	0.030	0.024	0.016	0.010	0.007	0.005	0.004	0.003	0.002	0.001
26	0.772	0.598	0.361	0.220	0.135	0.084	0.053	0.033	0.026	0.021	0.014	0.009	0.006	0.004	0.003	0.002	0.002	0.001
27	0.764	0.586	0.347	0.207	0.125	0.076	0.047	0.029	0.023	0.018	0.011	0.007	0.005	0.003	0.002	0.002	0.001	0.001
28	0.757	0.574	0.333	0.196	0.116	0.069	0.042	0.026	0.020	0.016	0.010	0.006	0.004	0.002	0.002	0.002	0.001	0.001
29	0.749	0.563	0.321	0.185	0.107	0.063	0.037	0.022	0.017	0.014	0.008	0.005	0.003	0.002	0.002	0.001	0.001	0.001
30	0.742	0.552	0.308	0.174	0.099	0.057	0.033	0.020	0.015	0.012	0.007	0.004	0.003	0.002	0.001	0.001	0.001	0.001

APPENDIX D
PRESENT-VALUE FACTORS FOR ANNUITIES

Years (N)	1%	2%	4%	6%	8%	10%	12%	14%	15%	16%	18%	20%	22%	24%	25%	26%	28%	30%
1	0.990	0.980	0.962	0.943	0.926	0.909	0.893	0.877	0.870	0.862	0.847	0.833	0.820	0.806	0.800	0.794	0.781	0.769
2	1.970	1.942	1.886	1.833	1.783	1.736	1.690	1.647	1.626	1.605	1.566	1.528	1.492	1.457	1.440	1.424	1.392	1.361
3	2.941	2.884	2.775	2.673	2.577	2.487	2.402	2.322	2.283	2.246	2.174	2.106	2.042	1.981	1.952	1.923	1.868	1.816
4	3.902	3.808	3.630	3.465	3.312	3.170	3.037	2.914	2.855	2.798	2.690	2.589	2.494	2.404	2.362	2.320	2.241	2.166
5	4.853	4.713	4.452	4.212	3.993	3.791	3.605	3.433	3.352	3.274	3.127	2.991	2.864	2.745	2.689	2.635	2.532	2.436
6	5.795	5.601	5.242	4.917	4.623	4.355	4.111	3.889	3.784	3.685	3.498	3.326	3.167	3.020	2.951	2.885	2.759	2.643
7	6.728	6.472	6.002	5.582	5.206	4.868	4.564	4.288	4.160	4.039	3.812	3.605	3.416	3.242	3.161	3.083	2.937	2.802
8	7.652	7.325	6.733	6.210	5.747	5.335	4.968	4.639	4.487	4.344	4.078	3.837	3.619	3.421	3.329	3.241	3.076	2.925
9	8.566	8.162	7.435	6.802	6.247	5.759	5.328	4.946	4.772	4.607	4.303	4.031	3.786	3.566	3.463	3.366	3.184	3.019
10	9.471	8.983	8.111	7.360	6.710	6.145	5.650	5.216	5.019	4.833	4.494	4.192	3.923	3.682	3.571	3.465	3.269	3.092
11	10.368	9.787	8.760	7.887	7.139	6.495	5.937	5.453	5.234	5.029	4.656	4.327	4.035	3.776	3.656	3.544	3.335	3.147
12	11.255	10.575	9.385	8.384	7.536	6.814	6.194	5.660	5.421	5.197	4.793	4.439	4.127	3.851	3.725	3.606	3.387	3.190
13	12.134	11.343	9.986	8.853	7.904	7.103	6.424	5.842	5.583	5.342	4.910	4.533	4.203	3.912	3.780	3.656	3.427	3.223
14	13.004	12.106	10.563	9.295	8.244	7.367	6.628	6.002	5.724	5.468	5.008	4.611	4.265	3.962	3.824	3.695	3.459	3.249
15	13.865	12.849	11.118	9.712	8.559	7.606	6.811	6.142	5.847	5.575	5.092	4.675	4.315	4.001	3.859	3.726	3.483	3.268
16	14.718	13.578	11.652	10.106	8.851	7.824	6.974	6.265	5.954	5.669	5.162	4.730	4.357	4.033	3.887	3.751	3.503	3.283
17	15.562	14.292	12.166	10.477	9.122	8.022	7.120	6.373	6.047	5.749	5.222	4.775	4.391	4.059	3.910	3.771	3.518	3.295
18	16.398	14.992	12.659	10.828	9.372	8.201	7.250	6.467	6.128	5.818	5.273	4.812	4.419	4.080	3.928	3.786	3.529	3.304
19	17.226	15.678	13.134	11.158	9.604	8.365	7.366	6.550	6.198	5.877	5.316	4.844	4.442	4.097	3.942	3.799	3.539	3.311
20	18.046	16.351	13.590	11.470	9.818	8.514	7.469	6.623	6.259	5.929	5.353	4.870	4.460	4.110	3.954	3.808	3.546	3.316
21	18.857	17.011	14.029	11.764	10.017	8.649	7.562	6.687	6.312	5.973	5.384	4.891	4.476	4.121	3.963	3.816	3.551	3.320
22	19.660	17.658	14.451	12.042	10.201	8.772	7.645	6.743	6.359	6.011	5.410	4.909	4.488	4.130	3.970	3.822	3.556	3.323
23	20.456	18.292	14.857	12.303	10.371	8.883	7.718	6.792	6.399	6.044	5.432	4.925	4.499	4.137	3.976	3.827	3.559	3.325
24	21.243	18.914	15.247	12.550	10.529	8.985	7.784	6.835	6.434	6.073	5.451	4.937	4.507	4.143	3.981	3.831	3.562	3.327
25	22.023	19.523	15.622	12.783	10.675	9.077	7.843	6.873	6.464	6.097	5.467	4.948	4.514	4.147	3.985	3.834	3.564	3.329
26	22.795	20.121	15.983	13.003	10.810	9.161	7.896	6.906	6.491	6.118	5.480	4.956	4.520	4.151	3.988	3.837	3.566	3.330
27	23.560	20.707	16.330	13.211	10.935	9.237	7.943	6.935	6.514	6.136	5.492	4.964	4.524	4.154	3.990	3.839	3.567	3.331
28	24.316	21.281	16.663	13.406	11.051	9.307	7.984	6.961	6.534	6.152	5.502	4.970	4.528	4.157	3.992	3.840	3.568	3.331
29	25.066	21.844	16.984	13.591	11.158	9.370	8.022	6.983	6.551	6.166	5.510	4.975	4.531	4.159	3.994	3.841	3.569	3.332
30	25.808	22.396	17.292	13.765	11.258	9.427	8.055	7.003	6.566	6.177	5.517	4.979	4.534	4.160	3.995	3.842	3.569	3.332

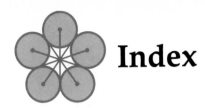

Index